# Streisand

OTHER BOOKS BY ANNE EDWARDS

BIOGRAPHY

Sonya: the Life of Countess Tolstoy

Vivien Leigh: a Biography

Judy Garland: a Biography

Road to Tara: the Life of Margaret Mitchell

Matriarch: Queen Mary and the House of Windsor

Katharine Hepburn: a Biography (US title A Remarkable
Woman: a Biography of Katharine Hepburn)

Early Reagan: the Rise to Power

Shirley Temple: American Princess

The De Milles: an American Family

Royal Sisters: Elizabeth and Margaret

The Grimaldis of Monaco: Centuries of Scandal/
Years of Grace

Throne of Gold: the Lives of the Aga Khans

NOVELS

La Divina

The Survivors

Shadow of a Lion

Haunted Summer

Miklos Alexandrovitch Is Missing

The Hesitant Heart

Child of Night

Wallis: the Novel

AUTOBIOGRAPHY

The Inn and Us (with Stephen Citron)

CHILDREN'S BOOKS

P. T. Barnum

The Great Houdini

A Child's Bible

# Streisand

## IT ONLY HAPPENS ONCE

Anne Edwards

Weidenfeld & Nicolson
LONDON

First published in Great Britain in 1996 by
Weidenfeld & Nicolson

The Orion Publishing Group Ltd
Orion House,
5 Upper Saint Martin's Lane,
London, WC2H 9EA.

A catalogue reference is available
from the British Library

ISBN 0 297 81712 4

Typeset by Selwood Systems
Midsomer Norton

Printed in Great Britain by
Butler & Tanner Co, Ltd.
Frome And London

# FOR STEVE

# Contents

# Illustrations

With Jon Peters[6]
With sometime lovers: Pierre Trudeau;[6] André Agassi[6] and Don Johnson[6]
Leaving London after her Wembley concert[6]
With AIDS activist/playwright Larry Kramer[14]
With Jason[15]
Four films: *Yentl, What's Up, Doc?, Funny Lady* and *The Owl and the Pussycat*[6]
After her 1994 Californian concert[6]


Credits. The author and publishers thank the following for permission to reproduce the above photographs:

1   Brooklyn Historical Society
2   Garson Kanin
3   Edward Carroll
4   Bob Schulenberg
5   Craig Simpson
6   AP/Wide World Photos
7   UPI/Bettmann
8   Henry Grossman, Life Magazine © Time Warner Inc
9   Howell Condit, Life Magazine © Time Warner Inc
10  B. Eppridge, Life Magazine © Time Warner Inc
11  Camera Press
12  CBS
13  Cecil Beaton, Camera Press
14  Anthony Savignano/Gallela Ltd
15  Albert Ortega/Gallela Ltd

# Acknowledgments

I HAVE THIS THEORY that the more we learn about the men and women we choose as our icons and heroes the more we learn about ourselves. Each biography I write is a self-journey in that discovery. Writing this book has taught me much about our admiration for people who are great survivors, perhaps because so few of us know their strength. It has brought me close to what it can cost to become rich and famous, but even more to be different from most other people, a one-off, unique.

I often think of myself not as a biographer but as a literary detective. But no one can make their way alone through the maze of truths and half-truths, the real and the imagined that constitute the days and years of someone's life. To be a good literary detective one needs the help of other attuned ears, expert witnesses, confidants, co-workers, contemporaries, family and friends – loving as well as injured and resentful – lovers, admirers, critics and fans. I have been most fortunate in having the help of representatives from each of these categories in writing this book. I wish I could thank every contributor personally. In the majority of my biographies I have been able to do so. Occasionally the subject of the biography creates a climate of fear that promises banishment from his or her good graces and perhaps loss of employment if an associate decides to tell the biographer a part of their own life that also happens to involve the subject. That has occurred in the writing of this book. None the less, well over a hundred people have chosen to discuss with me the part they played in the life of Barbra Streisand, many of them requesting that their names not be revealed. I have honoured their choice and here thank them publicly. I have already done so privately.

Not enough writers have been as fortunate as to have had Ion Trewin as an editor. Not only is he a man with tremendous grace, talent and sensitivity, he knows exactly when to stand tall and also bring the best of an author to the written page. I am eternally grateful for his major contribution to this book and to the many others that we have worked on together. My good fortune did not stop there for my two agents – Mitch Douglas in the United States and Gill Coleridge in Great Britain have been an enormous support. In the twenty years we have worked together, Mitch has always been there when I needed him, help offered without request, and friendship given freely. We have had a unique relationship and I am grateful for it. I want to add my thanks to Richard Aieli, Cassia Joll and Liz Cowen and to the ever cheerful Lilia Mejia, who brings so much special care to my working days.

My special appreciation to Garson Kanin, who not only gave freely of his time, but allowed me access to his extensive files on the stage production of *Funny Girl*, to Marian Seldes who added to this trove with files of her own, to Arthur Laurents, whose insights and recall added greatly to my understanding of many areas in which this story had to travel. And to Larry Kramer whose honesty and forthrightness was a gift that I shall treasure.

Of the many who gave so liberally of their time, allowing me to spend hours with them, interviewing them in depth, talking on the telephone, filling out questionnaires and tediously searching files for information and who made the writing of this book such a vital experience I would like to thank Peter Matz, Don Black, Lainie Kazan, Jack Kruschen, Ken Welch, Mitzie Welch, the late John Patrick, the late Jule Styne, Luther Henderson, Barry Dennen, Bob Schulenberg, David LeVine, Milton Mensch, Marcia Mae Jones, Madeline Lee Gilford, Walter Matthau, Anthony Newley, Ira Howard Levy, Ann Shanks, Bob Shanks, Herman Raucher, Rex Reed, Thomas Z. Shepard, Billy Barnes, Ed Holly, Blossom Kahn, Rose Tobias Shaw, Alan Shayne, Kathleen Brady, Martha Wilson, Harry Medved, Martha Weinman Lear, Louise Kerz, Al Hirschfeld, Jackie Sedeli, Sharon Palmer, Carl De Milia, Millard Vine Clark, Cindy Bouton, Ray Rominger, Maureen Stapleton, Eli Wallach, Judy Horgan, Michael Edwards, Michael Smith, Kristine Krueger, Michael Meltzer, Lila Burkeman, Alice Weiss, Richard LaGravenese, Amy Rosenfeld, Bella Linden, Jocelyn Clapp, Kelly Magio, Barbara Dunlap, Catherine Craco, Arthur Gelb, Graig Simpson, Tom Gates, Stanley Brassette, Angela Corio, Debra Cohen and Paul Arbor.

I would like to single out with special gratitude Sally Slaney Carr and Terence McCarthy, who were invaluable aids in my London research, Polly Brown in my Washington D.C. research and Jeffrey L. Carrier in Brooklyn; the staffs of the Academy of Motion Picture Arts and Sciences, the theatre library at Lincoln Center, the British Film Institute, Recording Industry Association of America, the Museum of Broadcasting and the Screen Actors Guild.

And last but always top – my love, admiration and gratitude to my husband Stephen Citron, whose musical expertise and knowledge as respected historian of the musical theatre added immeasurably to my work on this book.

I thank you all.


*Anne Edwards*
*Blandings Way, 1996*

'Any agent or mother or entrepreneur who believes he has another Barbra Streisand tucked away on a pedestal in the corner, waiting to be unveiled, had better change professions. There is just not going to be another Barbra Streisand, now or ever. What she is, happens once.'

ALAN JAY LERNER

# People

'It is fascinating to me that
she is so put down by the media.
People who know her love her.'

CIS CORMAN

# 1

'LISTEN, I CRIED, I was so moved,' Barbra Streisand bellowed over long-distance telephone to Larry Kramer. It was the spring of 1986. He was in New York; she was in Los Angeles. 'I gotta make the movie of your play,' she insisted. 'AIDS is killing all these beautiful young people and your story will wake up America to the crisis, to the fact that nothing *really important* is being done about it. I'm still shaken up from the images in the play. Yes! *Yes!* "We must love one another or die." ' She paused dramatically. 'We have to talk. Could you come out here?'

The play that had so aroused her emotions was Kramer's devastating drama *The Normal Heart* which had recently opened on the West Coast after a highly lauded run in New York. Kramer agreed to fly to Los Angeles to discuss the adaptation of his work for the screen. Streisand's enthusiasm, her strong feeling for the play, greatly energised him. He did not know what her background or orientation was to the subject of AIDS and he understood that she wanted to produce, direct and star in the film. The last was worrying because it was not as much Dr Emma Brookner's story (the only female member of the cast), as it was of the men whose lives were in mortal jeopardy with the advent of the plague.

Damaged lives and a government turned away from its people to its politics were themes that beat an insistent drum in Streisand's head at this time. She was going through a tremendous period of change in her lifestyle. The flamboyance, the passion of her intense seven-year love affair with film producer and studio head, Jon Peters, now behind her, her volatile life had mellowed with the relatively calm three-year relationship with Richard Baskin, her junior by eight years. Baskin was a lyricist and scion of the Baskin-Robbins ice-cream fortune.

Her ten-month odyssey in Europe directing herself in *Yentl*, shortly before Baskin entered her life, had strongly affected her attitudes and self-goals. She had a broader view of what she wanted to achieve: to make a statement with her talents; to break through the barriers for women in film. For sixteen years, *Yentl* had obsessed her. Making the film had been her rite of passage. She felt almost grown up now, although that vulnerable child she was always trying to subdue occasionally gained the upper hand. The wonder was that after twenty-two years of stardom, fame equalled by only a tiny few – Marilyn Monroe, Marlon Brando, Elizabeth Taylor – with a notoriety that never dwindled or showed signs of fading, she remained excited about life, people, ideas. Ambition had once possessed her, being someone, being rich. Now it was accomplishing things that mattered, contributing to a better understanding of a few of the world's problems.

The house on Carolwood Drive, high atop Holmby Hills a short distance from Sunset Boulevard, had become her home and work place in the last few years. Her meeting with Kramer was called for half-past one in her ground-floor study and she was nearly two hours late. Kramer and Cis Corman, her business partner and closest friend, would be waiting anxiously for her to join them. Barbra had first met Cis in an acting class when she was fifteen and Cis, almost a decade older, tall, slim, dark-haired and with a certain panache, was already married to a practising analyst, Dr Harvey Corman. Cis was the sanest thing that ever happened to Streisand. She greatly admired Cis's ability to ingratiate herself even in the most trying circumstances. A born mediator, a woman of classic understanding, Cis had early on become a substitute maternal figure to Barbra, a totally non-judgmental 'mommy' to whom she could reveal her worst feelings and fears, let everything hang out, so to speak, knowing that Cis would not castigate her for her honesty and would instead offer her some guidance.

Her friendship with Cis has remained the one constant in Streisand's close circle as lovers and business partners have moved in and out of her life with traumatic impact. The simple truth is that she trusts Cis as she does no one else. Cis was the first person to encourage her to sing. They have shared their dreams, gone through much together. Cis is probably the only person who can tell Streisand exactly what she thinks and have her opinion respected. Their relationship transcends ego and the usual built-in power structure endemic to a partnership where one member is a star of tremendous voltage and the other dependent upon that person for his or her career.

Streisand knew Cis would be discussing with Kramer the story problems that they had outlined together and that he would be well occupied. Still, she felt contrite about being so late. She was always suffering Jewish guilt for something or other. Just being late, as often happened and as she was now. Nobody understood. She had to give *everything* to a meeting like this. She could not talk to a writer about such a personal work as *The Normal Heart*, a play about AIDS, that she knew was, at least in part, autobiographical, without doing her homework. So she had remained in her upstairs bedroom suite, studying the text of the play, the screenplay that Kramer had adapted from his own work at an earlier time before her involvement in the project, and several scientific articles on the ravaging disease that was decimating the gay community.

The role she hoped to play in *The Normal Heart* was that of a wheelchair-bound doctor dedicated to help AIDS patients fight for their lives and, when all medical hope was gone, provide some dignity in dying. For her to succeed with the project she needed to understand as much as she could about AIDS. Like *Yentl*, this was a story with great personal meaning to her as so many men she had known and worked with had died of the disease, but as she started down the staircase in her home that dim, foggy afternoon in early March 1986, she had no idea that she had just taken her first steps to another ten years'-long odyssey.

Her time-consuming obsession with *Yentl* might well have cost her the great love of her life – Jon Peters. Having a man by her side and sharing her bed eased her insecurity. And so, three years after her break-up with the charismatic Peters, following a short, highly charged period of courting, Baskin moved in. Unlike Peters or her ex-husband Elliott Gould, or herself, Baskin had lived a privileged life. Good-looking, well built and towering over her by nearly a foot, he had a winning, boyish smile, a head of dark, curly hair and impeccable manners. Baskin brought a lightness to her life. They also shared an abiding passion for music and beautiful surroundings. Yet, when you looked around the rooms on the spacious ground floor of the Carolwood Drive house there was no sign of his three-year tenancy, so distinctly was her personality ingrained and so overwhelmingly did his seem to have been ignored.

She continued down the curved staircase and past the living room on the way to her study. With the exquisite pieces of art nouveau that she had been collecting through the years, the house had begun to look like a museum. Maybe it *was* a museum. Maybe all of her homes had become museums: this one, the five-house complex in Malibu, the West Side penthouse in New York. Bitten by the collector's bug early in her life, she had an eye for discovering rare and wonderful pieces. 'I didn't grow up with a sense of it around me,' she would tell people with a wide flourish of an elegant hand. 'My mother used to put newspapers on the floor and plastic covers on the furniture – plastic on the lampshades, plastic everywhere. But it always hurt my eyes in some way. For as long as I can remember I've had the desire to surround myself with beautiful objects.'

That was at the heart of her collecting mania, started when she was still in her teens. Ordinary surroundings depressed her. There had to be unique treasures wherever she looked to help block out the ugly images of her childhood environment, a childhood that haunted her, would not leave her in peace, that she hated for its pain and its commonness, whose spell, after years spent in therapy, she had been unable to break.

Her collecting had started with elegant old evening bags and empty antique picture frames that she filled with interesting, inexpensive prints – often bought for only a few dollars and hung on the walls of the small apartment, with its bathtub in the kitchen, that had been her earliest real home in New York City. With the money she had made from her first acting role on Broadway, when she was only nineteen years old, she had acquired the incredible German art nouveau desk that was in her bedroom. Unable to write a cheque for the full amount, $2,800, she paid it off over a six-month period and then let the antiques dealer, Lillian Nassau, keep it in her shop on 57th Street in Manhattan until she had a place to put it. Two years later, *Funny Girl* a big hit and her albums selling in the hundreds of thousands, she fell in love with a Tiffany lamp with a 'Peony' shade and a striking red turtleback base 'with the mosaics changing colors like the colors of the rainbow', and bought it for $45,000. It was now the centrepiece of the Carolwood Drive living room which she had designed around it. Even on a dull day like this one, the red glass in the base glowed as if lit by some magic inner fire.

Obsessed with collecting, whenever she saw an object that caught her eye and her imagination, she had to own it. Treasures small and large filled her homes, the overflow contained in giant packing cases with a Manhattan storage company: furniture, stained glass, bronze statues, paintings, china, glass, silver, fine antiques and twenties' kitsch – everything from a glamour-rating penny arcade game to a penny-a-pack cigarette dispenser. A 1926 Rolls-Royce Silver Ghost and a 1933 Dodge customised roadster were kept garaged at the Malibu ranch. Clothes of the twenties and thirties, bought in thrift shops and not worn in over twenty years, hung as artefacts on display in special closets that held nothing else. The sheer enormity of her possessions, however, had not vanquished the sense of deprivation that had pervaded her since childhood when her only doll had been a hot-water bottle 'dressed' in one of her outgrown sweaters. She often talked to friends about wanting to simplify her life, but her acquisitiveness defeated her.

Kramer, a kinetic, dark-haired man with a winsome smile who wore his fiftysome years with youthful panache, stood when she entered the all-white study decorated in what she called, 'Hollywood Forties Glamour'. Before her arrival, the room had been dominated by a white grand Steinway and two white overstuffed sofas. In her presence, everything diminished in size. Not that she is large. She is, in fact, a rather small woman, slim and around five feet four inches tall. That day she was dressed in a soft peach-pastel jogging suit, with immaculate white sneakers and clutched in her arms Kramer's play, a pad of notes and a tape-recorder. Her highlighted ash-blonde hair framed her angular, well-chiseled face in a mass of Medea-like curls. Her nose may be her best-known feature, but it is her startling blue eyes and the delicate translucence of her skin that hold one's attention and admiration. Not beautiful by accepted non-ethnic standards, she possesses a *presence* polished to an awesome glow by celebrity. By instinct, Streisand knows where to stand so that the light will be the kindest, how to position her head to lengthen her neck and shorten the image of her nose and when she held out her hand to Kramer it was as if an exotic flower with crimson-tipped petals had unfolded.

The day after she had seen the Los Angeles production of *The Normal Heart*, which had starred Richard Dreyfuss, who she was considering for the co-starring role in *Nuts*, her next film, she called Kramer's agent in New York. The playwright and his agent met for a drink later that afternoon. 'I have exciting news for you,' he told his client. 'Barbra Streisand is interested in *The Normal Heart*.' 'We were in a public place and I laid down on the floor like a nut and began hitting it and shaking my legs,' Kramer recalled. 'God knows what people thought. I was just so fucking thrilled. I wanted her to do it because I knew that if she did a lot of people would see it. The play meant a great deal to me. It was my life; at the same time it was a play that I knew could make a difference to the gay community if it were given wide, commercial exposure. Once I contained myself, my lawyer said, "Now, I want you to think what kind of deal you want."

'I made it clear that there had to be a proviso that I write the script,' Kramer continued. 'We agreed on the financial terms but the contract had not been finalised when I went out to California to discuss the play and its adaptation to the screen. She had a screenplay that I had done earlier, before her involvement, and we were going to talk about it and where we should go from there.'

Kramer was a screenwriter long before his success as a playwright. During Britain's film renaissance in the 1960s he had been transferred by Columbia Studios from their New York offices to the story department in their London branch. By the end of the decade he had formed his own company and wrote and produced the brilliant adaptation of D.H. Lawrence's *Women In Love*, with Glenda Jackson, for which he received an Academy Award nomination. 'The only reason I did *The Normal Heart* as a play was that I didn't think I could get a movie done of the subject and that a play was much faster. It was a story that had a message and had to get out fast. I believed it would change the world and Ronald Reagan would behave [regarding help to inaugurate government research into the AIDS virus].'

While contracts were being drawn, Streisand and Kramer set to work on a revised screenplay the morning after their first meeting. 'I was so impressed with the way she worked,' Kramer said, 'like a Trojan. We would start at 9 a.m. in the study and we would work until midnight. We never stopped to eat. She had food brought in, lots of it, well prepared. She could talk and eat at the same time without any problem. She never lost her train of thought, it was amazing. Kim Skalecki, her secretary/assistant would come in with important papers and things for her to sign, calls that had to be made. She handled it all in a thoroughly professional manner. She had converted a garage [at the

Carolwood Drive house] into separate quarters for offices for Kim and three other assistants.

'She had directed only one film, *Yentl*, at this time, and we were figuring out the sequence of the scenes mostly, the structure and what would happen within scenes and she would ask me a lot of questions about the characters and she would ask me a lot of questions about homosexuality. I would suspect that she knew about [her son] Jason's homosexuality, but it was not a subject that we talked about. Jason was still living at home then. He was about twenty. Only later did she try to educate herself about homosexuality. She would talk to various people in the industry who were out of the closet and ask them what made people gay. I gave her a pretty graphic book about gay sex and I'm sure it disturbed her, but I felt if she was going to direct *The Normal Heart* she had to understand something about the physical side of homosexual love.'

Her other project, *Nuts*, a compelling drama with a powerful woman's role, was based on Tom Topor's play about a prostitute, a victim of childhood abuse, fighting for her right to stand trial for the murder of one of her abusive clients, when both the state and her parents insist she is not mentally capable of doing so. What was of major importance to Streisand was that both *Nuts* and *The Normal Heart* had strong social themes, and had quite disparate roles for her to play that would, if she succeeded with them, prove once and for all to the critics who insisted on categorising her as a musical comedy star, that she was an actress first and foremost. People simply did not understand that since her voice was a natural talent, something she felt was God-given and not achieved through training, she derived little satisfaction from her acclaim as a singer. She most desperately wanted to be recognised as an actress and film-maker of merit and conscience.

'I'm at a place in my life where I'm almost realising my dreams,' she had told an interviewer a few years earlier. 'The other day, I was so anxious about it I started to cry when I said the words, "Oh, my God, I'm almost getting everything." It was a total emotional experience. Because I am so used to complaining, to being negative, that to be in a happy place is a whole new way of life for me.' She had been deeply, *deeply* in love with Peters, believing that she had found her life's partner. That dream had evaporated, but she was once again in a happy place. Baskin was a charming, intelligent man, supportive and loving, and he was undemanding of her. Still, he lacked Peters's charisma, the vital life force. There was no strong conflict of wills and egos, no speedway curves or roller-coaster emotions in their relationship. She was free to concentrate on her career and on developing projects in which she believed. Right now that project was *The Normal Heart*.

Day after day, for a period of two weeks, spring rain tapping at the windows, she sat with Larry Kramer in her dazzling white study and with him read all the parts in the script out loud and then voiced her comments on changes she thought should be made – a line of dialogue that was too raw, a speech that was over wordy, a point that required more emphasis.

'What I found difficult was – maybe because I had always loved her as a performer – getting beyond the fact that I was actually sitting with *her*, Barbra Streisand,' Kramer confessed. 'I was in awe of her – the talent, the fame. We all grew up with her. It's like a member of the older generation being in a one-to-one situation with Judy Garland. It took a while before I felt free to say what I actually thought. It's not that you edit what you think, but you do in a way. And if she would say something that I didn't agree with on the script, I would speak out and she would say, "Well, let's try it this way." Sometimes she would give in and sometimes she would say, "I want it this way." How much of a fight can you have? Not much.'

Kramer went back to New York believing he was to start work on the screenplay. He brought with him a sheaf of notes on changes to be made, scenes to be included, excluded, speeches cut, parts developed and enlarged (the doctor she was planning to play was to be more germane to the story). The contract was waiting for him to sign. There was no mention of his writing the final screenplay. 'I confronted my agent and told him he had not done what I wanted him to do. That I had to write the screenplay. I called Barbra on the phone and she got very angry with me and I said, "You don't under-stand. This is my life story. I have to write the final screenplay. No one else can be brought in."'

'Well, that is something I can never give up,' she told Kramer. 'I simply have to have my power and my control over the story.'

Kramer broke the deal. Streisand had lost *The Normal Heart*. Kramer could not have known how difficult this was for her. The play would haunt her for years, become an obsession in the same way that *Yentl* had. Still, he should have realised with his studio background how impossible it was for her to guarantee him the lone, final credit on a screenplay yet to be written. *Control* was the operative word. Streisand's need was to express *herself*, *her* views along with those of the author. In the end it would be Barbra Streisand not Larry Kramer who would be judged by the work presented on the screen. The media was always accusing her of being a control freak. The phrase rankled. She did not believe it was truthful, although she easily confessed that she was almost fetishistic about minutiae.

'My mother is a perfectionist in everything she does,' admitted Jason, who was just emerging from a belligerent and angry teen-age which had made communication difficult between them. 'She gets criticised for that. But it seems ridiculous that you can get criticised for caring too much about your work.'

Although Kramer's *The Normal Heart* now seemed lost to her, nagging thoughts on what *was* normal remained and were partially responsible for her decision to proceed immediately with *Nuts*, a film she would produce but not direct and in which she would play the idiosyncratic, high-priced call-girl who murders a client in self-defence.

Dim echoes of Streisand's own childhood permeated the story, how spoken truths can prove more life-threatening than defensive lies. Always striving for a deeper understanding of herself and of her many anxieties and resentments, Streisand had been in some form of therapy since fame came so suddenly to her in the early 1960s when she was just twenty years old. Since that time, she has moved from one therapist to another, ceaselessly engaged in attempts to come to terms with her past and the projects she chose reflected this theme.

With the approach of summer, Streisand, accompanied by Cis, who was to be the co-executive producer on *Nuts*, and Martin Ritt, the director with whom she would collaborate, began the strenuous task of researching neuro-psychiatric hospital facilities to help in her interpretation of the tormented, incarcerated, psychotic Claudia Draper. On these field trips, which took her to Bellevue Hospital in New York City and the Mental Health Court in the San Fernando Valley, she spoke to several dozen schizophrenic, seriously disturbed female patients, after which she confessed, 'I felt totally comfortable with them.'

'I don't believe any of the women Barbra met with knew who she was,' Cis observed. 'She could be herself. It must have been a refreshing feeling.'

*Being herself* was no easy matter. She was by now a cultural icon, presented by a good portion of the media as a controlling, vainglorious woman who at the same time just happened to be one of the greatest singers and personalities of the twentieth century. Very few people are able to be natural when confronted with such celebrity. It intimidates them. Streisand also has an abrasive manner and no patience with people whom she does not consider up to her standards in intelligence. She can even make very knowledgeable people feel inadequate. It is not an endearing character trait and it has kept her coterie of close friends rather limited. Most of them, like Cis Corman and lyricist Marilyn Bergman, have known her from the early days of her success. 'It is fascinating to me that she is so put down by the media,' Cis Corman criticises. 'People who know her love her.'

That was obviously not enough for Barbra Streisand who, after twenty years of therapy, was still trying to find good reason to love herself. Right now, she took a respite from therapy sessions to concentrate fully on the development and production of *Nuts*. Her top priority was to break through the 'old boy' monopoly in Hollywood with a picture that would be praised for its content and her performance as well as its production.

Martin Ritt, the director she had chosen, had sincere concern over social issues and a skill to elicit strong performances from his actors. From 1948 he had directed over 150 live dramas for the newly emerging television medium and acted in some 100 more until 1951 when he was blacklisted for his past 'suspected' Communist affiliations. He had taught at the Actors Studio for the next six years, coaching such future stars as Paul Newman, Joanne Woodward, Lee Remick and Rod Steiger. His foothold in films was gained in 1957 with *Edge of the City*, and since that time he had made many notable films[1] and had recently been named Distinguished Director in Residence at UCLA's College of Fine Arts. Streisand could not help but admire his work. At the same time there was a conflict because Ritt believed there could only be one director on a film and Streisand was not willing to relinquish her control.

'Marty and Barbra didn't always agree,' Maureen Stapleton, who gave a shattering performance as Streisand's mother in *Nuts*, said. 'But there weren't any big scenes between them – no flying off the handle or stomping off the set. I loved Barbra. We had good chemistry. She's such a professional. Sure, she's a perfectionist, but that's swell with me. I'm sure Marty respected her opinions. It's not a good thing for a director to lose control. I don't think he ever did. Everyone was very close while we made the picture. Of course Eli [Wallach, who played the court psychiatrist] is an old friend. Karl Malden, too [the fictional stepfather who has sexually abused Streisand's character]. When I think of it, except for Richard Dreyfuss [the beleaguered court-appointed defence attorney], everyone on the film was ages older than Barbra but somehow she seemed the most serious person around.'

The role of Claudia Draper was exhausting both emotionally and physically. The script went through numerous revisions with as many writers – six in all – and Streisand was deeply involved in the writing of each. The basic themes of the story – the lack of communication and understanding between a young girl and her mother and the abuse of a stepfather – stirred emotions that ran brutally deep. Her conversations with mental patients, visits to the women's wings of prisons and mental hospitals were disturbing. There was the realisation of how lucky she was that she had been both talented and ambitious, that she left home as early as she did and won fame so soon after. It was critical to her that the final screenplay by Alvin Sargent and Darryl Ponsican would not only make a statement that was meaningful, but would also explore the myth of accepted mores and what was deemed normal behaviour. She stressed to Martin Ritt the importance of making the film as real as possible, gritty and ugly when necessary. What she did not want was a glossy *Spellbound*.

The script, approved by Warner Brothers with a cost budget of $21,584,000, went before the cameras on 20 October 1986. Ritt was not too well and did

---

[1] A partial list of other memorable movies directed by Martin Ritt (1914–90) includes: *No Down Payment*, 1957; *The Long Hot Summer*, 1958; *The Sound and the Fury*, 1959; *Hud*, 1963; *The Spy Who Came in from the Cold*, 1965; *Hombre*, 1967; *Sounder*, 1972; *The Front*, 1976; and *Norma Rae*, 1979.

not have the patience with which Streisand's first film director, William Wyler (*Funny Girl*), had been endowed. A stocky, powerful-looking man with a massive and intelligent face that suggested an odd alliance between Charles Laughton and Mister Magoo, at seventy-two Ritt's knowledge was encyclopedic and unorthodox: he could casually quote Chaucer and Goethe alongside Al Capp and Charles Schultz. He told one intimate that he had 'learned my own judgment is the only one I can trust'.

'How old are you?' he asked Streisand at one of their early meetings.

She never blinked an eye. 'Forty-four,' she shot back.

'I think you're too old to play Claudia Draper. She's a much younger woman, still in her twenties. Tough from the vicissitudes of her career as a hooker, but young enough to pull in big bucks for her favours.' Later Ritt recalled the scene: 'I had to admire [Streisand]. She took it like a trooper. She could have thrown me off the picture. After all, she was the boss. Her body stiffened. I noticed that. There was fire in her eyes. "You're wrong," she said, "and I'm going to prove it to you!"'

The statement became a challenge and during the shooting a competitive atmosphere often existed between them. Ritt, like Streisand, was a scrupulous craftsman with an exact and exacting sense of place and period and although they were not destined to become friends, they both retained great respect of each other's ability.

Production ended on 3 February 1987. Ritt worked for ten weeks on the editing while Streisand hired herself to compose the picture's score ('Who else would hire me?' she has quipped.) As the film was a courtroom drama, it did not require much music and she had dreamed of scoring a movie (Charles Chaplin being perhaps the only other actor, producer, director who had accomplished this formidable task) for a number of years. 'The end title music,' she explained, 'was written to convey a sense of freedom and personal triumph [as Claudia is judged sane and competent to stand trial].' Later Alan and Marilyn Bergman added lyrics to it and the song became 'Two People' recorded for her *Till I Loved You* album released the following year.

Ritt, like other directors who had worked with Streisand since she formed her own company,[2] had not succeeded in winning approval on the final cut. His hope had been that she would like what she saw when she ran his version and it would stand. He felt confident that this would be the case. He had, in fact, confessed to her that he thought she had done a magnificent job of Claudia. He left believing the picture was finished. To others he confided that

---

[2] Streisand had signed a multi-faceted contract with Warner Brothers in June 1984 to develop a full range of motion-picture projects where she would work on all levels – as star, director or producer, or all three under the auspices of her own company, Barwood. *Nuts* was her initial venture. Cis Corman was named president.

he thought she would be nominated for an Academy Award.

As soon as she received Ritt's cut of the film Streisand went into virtual seclusion with it in her private editing room at her Malibu ranch estate with its separate editing cottage filled with half-a-million dollars' worth of the latest and finest editing equipment. For three weeks she worked night and day impressing on the film her own stamp and personality. She cut some of Stapleton's footage, the courtroom scenes, reworked the flashbacks that led to the murder sequence. Her role was always major. Now it almost overpowered the film and would have but for Dreyfuss's forceful performance. She worked, shut away, food brought to her, immersed, possessed by her need to achieve as near perfection as seemed possible.

With such dedication to her labour, there was little time or place in her life for Richard Baskin. He had accompanied her in February to the Grammy Awards where she was presented with an award for *The Broadway Album*, made early in 1986 and which had been a tremendous success. As she came off-stage, one of the show's producers touched her on the shoulder. She turned. Beside him was a handsome blond man whom she recognised. 'I'd like you to meet Don Johnson,' the producer introduced. Johnson smiled boyishly. 'Congratulations,' he offered, his china-blue eyes locked momentarily with hers. 'Yeah. Thanks,' she grinned and moved away.

'There's one damn sexy lady,' Johnson, currently the reigning American male sex symbol and star of the television series, *Miami Vice*, murmured as he watched her go.

Streisand glanced back over her shoulder, catching a fleeting glimpse of Johnson as Baskin and two security men led her to an exit door.

# 2

I N THE FALL of 1987, when she was mired in the final work before the release of *Nuts*, Richard Baskin moved out of the Carolwood Drive house. Streisand had harboured great hopes for this relationship, seemed desperately to need the stability it brought to her life. Just before the start of photography on *Nuts*, Baskin had proposed and she had seriously considered marrying him. But the relationship lacked that depth of feeling she had once felt for Elliott Gould, the father of her son Jason, and still nursed for Jon Peters. Let no one be misled. Barbra Streisand is a romantic, and one whose view of love was formed by her early passion for movies and the great cinematic love affairs that she avidly watched unfold on the screen as she, an awkward, unhappy youngster sat in a balcony seat in a darkened theatre in Brooklyn. Being in love still meant that special magnetic pull between two people, the sound of trumpets, the flash of fireworks.

Her separation from Baskin during the long weeks of discomfort as *Nuts* went before the cameras had been the breaking point. She had spent her days filming inside a women's prison, dressed in drab prison clothes, her hair a tangled Medea mass, taking on the terror of the real women dealing with madness and horrors she could only imagine who were trapped in that brutal life and she had not been easy to deal with. Although it was Baskin who made the final decision, the parting was not acrimonious. Still, it hurt all the same. She had failed once again in a relationship – and she was alone, a condition with which she never dealt well. Jason had gone back to New York to study at the NYU Film School to better prepare for his future as a movie maker. She was happy that he had found what it was he wanted to do, but his departure had come at a time when they had not worked through the problems in their relationship. She did not doubt Jason's love, it was their inability to communicate, to discuss the deeper issues that might be troubling him – his homosexuality, being the son of such famous parents and wanting to follow their careers in films.

Her impasse with Jason was all the more troubling because of her own struggle as a young woman to relate to *her* mother and how much pain her inability to do so had given her. She had meant things to be different for

Jason. She loved him dearly, wanted only the best for him and was exceptionally proud of the fine person he had become. She had not been a mother in the way a woman without a career of the magnitude of hers might have managed, but she had tried to compensate for these omissions in the quality of the time they spent together.

With Jason and Baskin gone she fought depression, went back into therapy and held on to the thought that *Nuts* would be a great success and that she would finally be recognised as a serious actress. The movie opened on 20 November to mixed reviews and strong criticism that she was miscast in the role of Claudia Draper, a prostitute with prodigious seductive powers. In retrospect it can only be assumed that the critics could not overcome their own strong image of Streisand. They viewed the film with a cliché'd idea of women in prostitution and Streisand's ethnic looks and intellectual approach to the character were not that. They were wrong, for Claudia Draper is one of Streisand's finest performances; chilling, moving, and especially *real*. It is shocking that she was overlooked in the Academy Awards for that year, a blow to Streisand, who considered her performance should have been acknowledged and she was not even mentioned. It did not ease her resentment that the film came in at $6 million over budget and did not do well at the box office, a situation she blamed, at least partly, on the press.

Streisand, the ultimate survivor, now threw all energies into acquiring a new project, *The Prince of Tides*, a best-selling book by Pat Conroy, author of *The Great Santini* and *The Lords of Discipline*. A big, sprawling novel about a dysfunctional Southern family with a dark secret of rape and murder at its centre, *The Prince of Tides* consumed Streisand's interest. Without doubt it was a filmic story, the characters were all well defined and interesting. Once again it was about a wounded family and those members who were fighting to keep their sanity and survive. And it had a role she wanted to play, Dr Lowenstein, a dedicated psychiatrist, unhappy in her own private life, who falls in love with her patient, Tom Wingo, whose suicidal twin sister, Savannah, was also her charge. Dr Lowenstein was not the main character in Conroy's novel but became the catalyst in the filmscript and the feminine half of the movie's love story.

As Christmas approached Streisand decided to spend a few weeks at the ski resort at Aspen, Colorado, which had in the past decade become the American Mecca for snow sports for the very rich and the glitterati of the entertainment world. Although not an expert skier, she liked the sport and the relaxed ambience of the resort. Aspen is also breathtakingly beautiful circled as it is by rugged, ice-sheathed peaks but with plenty of gentle, rolling slopes for the intermediate skier. The Bergmans, close friends since the mid-sixties, would be there and numerous other friends. Lyricist Marilyn Bergman, a blonde woman with a lovely face and the girthy look of an opera diva, was an active

Democrat and perhaps could be called Streisand's political guru, she and her soft-spoken, spare-built husband, Alan, had written lyrics to numerous songs that Streisand had recorded and into which she often had much input. Warmth, good music and engaging conversation abounded with the Bergmans, who also had a close circle in Aspen. It seemed like a good place for Streisand to spend the holidays rather than by herself in California. At a Boxing Day party at the Bergmans', the day after Christmas, she once again saw Don Johnson.

'That character he played in *Miami Vice* was an extension of things Don had done,' his longtime media consultant, Elliott Mintz, confided. 'He drove fancy cars when he was broke and wore fancy clothes when he couldn't afford them ... and he always had a strong effect on people. When he walked into a room, women – especially – reacted and sometimes in the most unabashed way ... and I'm talking long before *Miami Vice*.'

Johnson was a very sexy man who appealed to both men and women in the same way that movie idols like Tyrone Power and Tony Curtis had before him. The actor Sal Mineo once said of Don Johnson, 'I discovered him, put him in a play set in prison with a gay theme (*Fortune and Men's Eyes*). I lived with both Don and his sister, and people imagined all sorts of things ... I'll put it like this: Yes, I'm bisexual and blond guys are my favourite type, and I did enjoy seeing Don nude on the stage [in the play], and [bare-chested] on the silver screen, for that matter. Who wouldn't?'

Streisand and Johnson were immediately drawn to each other. Guests at the Aspen party say she was standing talking to someone and he came across the room, took her by the arm – without her objection – led her to a quiet corner and that they eventually left together. Johnson had an aura of invincibility, a vitality that was instantly appealing to her. He glowed with good health and his looks, the tousled gold hair streaked almost platinum in places by the sun and his strong, handsome well-proportioned features, were distinctive. Whatever the camera made of his appearance, in person there was something of the Fitzgerald anti-hero, a Gatsby of sorts, in his looks, the once-rough diamond polished to a shine but still showing small, giveaway imperfections.

Like Baskin, Johnson was eight years Streisand's junior, but his life had been anything but privileged. Born Don Wayne in Galena, Missouri, he was a rebellious youth from a working-class family who, as a teenager, landed in a detention school for car theft where he learned how to defend himself and work the system to his advantage. Shortly after his release, eighteen months later, he hustled his way into a drama course after being thrown out of his high school class for obstreperous behaviour. Bright and street-smart, he possessed incorrigible charm. Encouraged by a teacher, he went on to achieve a scholarship to the University of Kansas followed by a stint at the American Conservatory Theater in San Francisco. His theatre career was nearly throttled when he got hooked on drugs, alcohol and 'enough partying and casual sex to fuel the most hedonistic episode of *Miami Vice*'. Before he was thirty-two he had been married and divorced three times (actress Melanie Griffith, then only sixteen was his third wife), and in 1982 he fathered a son Jesse with his former mistress, Patti D'Arbanville, a tall, well-built comedic actress who had a small role with Streisand and Ryan O'Neal in *The Main Event* (1979) as O'Neal's gum-chewing, earthy girlfriend.

Fame had not come as suddenly or as early to Johnson as it had to Streisand, but his hard-knock years had not suppressed his natural exuberance. He talked easily, laughed heartily, exuded the same kind of appeal as Jon Peters, who had held Streisand in thrall for seven years. By New Year her new lover, blond, gorgeous, gentile, was standing by her side as co-host at a party she gave. They had more in common than first appearances might reveal. He was outspoken, tough, yet sensitive, and knowledgeable musically, in fact he had been singing all his life, and had recently cut a successful single 'Heartbeat' which had hit the charts. 'I have this persona as an actor and as a person of being this sort of street-smart tough guy. Tough guys don't sing or dance, do they?' he told *Playboy Magazine*. 'So here was a chance [to make a record] and say "Fuck you!"'

A perfectionist in his work, a workaholic by his own admission, a serious actor who wanted to direct, Johnson was not afraid to say what he felt or to go after what he wanted. He spoke with a candour that ranged 'from downright dangerous to outright playful', and he was going through a period in his life when he was trying to make some sense of his past.

'Nobody got higher than I did for longer than I did,' he admitted. 'I look back now and say, "What the fuck was I doing?" – waking up in a joint with a bunch of people lying around with needles in their arms.' Off drugs, in control of his addictions, Johnson was hell-bent for international success, but he had not lost his lust for life.

For Streisand, at that moment, Johnson was just the right man. He made her feel younger, more alive and self-confident as once Jon Peters had done.

'I don't think Barbra ever got over being a wallflower as a kid,' a member of her family confided. 'Until she left Brooklyn when she was seventeen or so, she didn't date much. I remember that she didn't go to her senior prom. It's always been important to her to be seen with a good-looking guy, a man other women also find attractive. Barbra always had to prove her own worth to herself, both in her work and the men she chose to love.' She looked like a woman in love. She and Johnson exchanged intimate glances in public, held hands, laughed at each other's jokes.

They were a good fit, able to mix sex, work and enthusiasms. Johnson wasted no time. He was in love with Streisand and believed he had 'run into the woman who could be *it*'. Three weeks later they were in New York together and it was apparent to Streisand's associates and the media alike, that she reciprocated his passion. In public they seemed unable to keep their hands off each other.

Johnson had gained twenty-five pounds to play a small-town building contractor who's depressed about the state of his marriage and growing old in *Sweet Hearts Dance*, the movie he had just completed, and was on a physical fitness regime to lose it and Streisand joined in. He played a competitive game of tennis. 'He has a killer instinct,' one of his opponents in a tournament in Aspen said. 'He can slam a ball with ferocious power.' He was less fierce when hitting the ball with Streisand, who was not anywhere in his league, but she worked hard to improve her game. She even responded to his enthusiasm for boating – he had won several major races – in fighting sea-sickness to ride the waves in a small craft with him.

No sooner had Johnson lost his excess weight than he was called in to reshoot the end of *Sweet Hearts Dance* and had to regain some of it. Streisand went on an eating spree with him, somehow managing to stay slim while he ballooned once again. They talked about his role, his interpretation, what he would do if he was directing the movie. Robert Greenhut was the director of the film but Johnson had directed several episodes of *Miami Vice* and hoped to do a feature as soon as possible. 'One day,' Greenhut remembers, 'Don said to me, "You know, Barbra may come out while we're shooting; is that OK?" And I said, "Sure, it's fine." But she never came.' When later he asked Streisand why she hadn't come. 'She looked at me, smiled and said, "Well, I decided there were enough directors on the set as it is!"' She viewed the rough cut of the film with Johnson and made 'some very, very good suggestions', Greenhut added.

They retained separate residences. Streisand was not yet ready to bring a man into her home again, although she spent all the time she could with Johnson, discussed her work with him and greatly respected his opinion. They were a couple but held on to their individual identities. She looked truly happy, laughed and clowned a lot, her eyes shone, her skin glowed. Wherever she went and there were photographers, Johnson was right there with her. He supported her dedication to getting *Prince of Tides* into production, not an easy task because she wanted to produce, direct and star in the film and the budget was high. 'Barbra not only makes me laugh, she makes me think,' he told an interviewer, adding, 'the possibilities are limitless!'

'Don makes me feel very feminine,' she told a member of her close circle. 'I have to be so strong for everyone – Mom, Jason, my staff – that it's nice to have someone be strong for me.' Her skin was bronzed from the sun and she wore clothes that showed her trim body off to its best advantage. Suddenly she seemed to have shed ten years. Dining out, going to the movies, shopping with Richard Baskin had been painful, for he had not been someone who was accustomed to the stares and attention that celebrity attracts. With Johnson it was entirely different. He was at the height of his fame, a raunchy sex symbol. Female fans went wild whenever they caught sight of him. Streisand, who had never been co-operative about signing autographs in public, now did. She was able to enjoy her fame, the attention of fans when she was in Johnson's company, because he received as much adulation as she did.

The ranch he owned in Colorado gave them time to be together out of the limelight. The house was on a large spread of land that looked out on a breathtaking vista of mountain and plain. Dawn was spectacular, night chillingly beautiful. There was something magical about the place. Johnson liked to mingle with his neighbours and fellow ranchers and so they spent considerable time in Colorado riding horseback, spending quiet evenings together at his ranch house before a roaring fire or relaxed in the company of his cronies. Johnson's six-year-old son, Jesse, sometimes rode with them and played golf at the local club alongside his father with a set of specially made small irons. Streisand could relive some of her happiest days when Jason was a small boy and she and Elliott took time out to be with him. Those times had not been often enough, she realised now.

For the first time in four presidential campaigns, she was not an active Democratic campaigner. Reagan had served his two terms. The battle for the White House would be fought by Massachusetts' Democratic Governor Michael Dukakis and George Bush. Despite the entreaties of the Bergmans, Streisand did not enter into the fray. She remained close to Johnson, sharing the sun sports he enjoyed. By the end of the golden summer of 1988 he looked like a Greek god and she was glowing with health and the kind of beauty that shines when a woman is in love. The intimacy between them was such that she was able to talk about her past, to explore her feelings. As she did, *The Prince of Tides* began to take on more meaning for her.

The character she wished to play, Dr Lowenstein, was described in Pat Conroy's book as 'one of those go-to-hell New York women with the incorruptible carriage of lionesses'. Conroy's Dr Lowenstein was a fictional blood cousin to Kramer's Dr Brookner in *The Normal Heart*. With childhood abuse and murder at its centre, *The Prince of Tides* contained overtones of *Nuts*. Streisand was searching through her work for answers to her own nagging psychological problems, carry-overs from childhood that neither success nor a loving relationship could obliterate. Several studios rejected the project, which only steeled her determination to make it. As the rejections mounted, she grew frantic and turned to Jon Peters, now a powerful studio head at Columbia, who took it under their auspices. 'It helps to have an influential ex-boyfriend,' she joked. But her ties to Peters were not really severed. It was one more relationship with which she had to make peace, not easy for despite her attachment to Johnson she felt tied to Peters emotionally and she would come away from a meeting with him feeling unnerved, perhaps just a little less sure of her commitment to Johnson.

'When I first read *The Prince of Tides* I knew I had to make it. [It] was about coming to terms with the people in our lives ... our parents ... our children ... our mates ... and even more important than that,' she said, 'as I am learning myself, it's about coming to terms with ourselves by accepting, loving and being in harmony with the child who still lives inside us.'

Barbra Streisand was ready, perhaps for the first time, to go back to the beginning, to try to make some sense of it all, to hold her life in her arms and learn to give it the love she thought she had never had. And yet, could she ever let go of the anger she felt for the bruises she bore? 'My mother could never make up for the part in my childhood that I never got,' she said bitterly at the time. The journey back would contain great emotional highs, unprecedented fame, and the love of several of the world's most desirable men. It would also be fraught with conflict as well as pain, but if she wanted to heal her wounds there was no other way to go. Once again, she returned to therapy.

# Roots

'It'd take a lifetime to know Brooklyn
t'roo and t'roo. An even den, yuh
wouldn't know it at all.'

THOMAS WOLFE Only the Dead Know
Brooklyn', 1935

'Terribly funny, yes, but Brooklyn is also a sad
brutal provincial lonesome human silent
sprawling innocent perverse tender
mysterious place, a place where Crane and
Whitman found poems, a mythical
dominion against whose shores the Coney
Island sea laps a wintry lament.'

TRUMAN CAPOTE, 1946

'I always wanted to get out of Brooklyn and be someone.'

BARBRA STREISAND, 1970

# 3

**B**ROOKLYN WAS HER universe for the first fifteen years of her life. She was born Barbara Joan Streisand on 24 April 1942, the second child of Emanuel and Diana Ida Rosen Streisand. America had entered the war only five months earlier and already one of Diana's two brothers had been inducted. Several young men in the modest apartment building at 457 Schnectady Avenue where the Streisands lived, had eagerly enlisted in the service. Boys in Emanuel's English classes at Brooklyn High School for Specialty Trades (later called George Westinghouse Vocational High School) where he taught, were already dropping out to join the forces. Aircraft carriers, battleships, cruisers, and destroyers were being built at the Brooklyn Navy Yard, with 75,000 workers the largest of its kind in the world. Fort Hamilton, Brooklyn's staging area for the army, was equipped to handle 8,000 men at a time. At night, a blackout was enforced over the entire borough, which was considered a strategic area. Security was diligent. No one was going to forget Pearl Harbor.

At the carefully guarded North River pier, silent lines of men in khaki waited to file aboard transport ships that would take them to Europe to meet the Nazi foe. The last view they would have of their country would be the murky dark waters that bordered the Brooklyn mainland. Wherever you were in Brooklyn, you had a sense of the sea, from the shorefront communities to the many bridges that linked Brooklyn to Manhattan, to the bustling ports, the names of the avenues and parkways – Atlantic, Ocean, Sea Gate, Pacific – to the 197-acre Brooklyn Navy Yard which skirted Wallabout Bay, a semi-circular elbow of the East River.

When it was first proposed in 1833 that the village of Brooklyn become incorporated into the city of New York, the idea was scoffed at. But geographically and hence commercially, Brooklyn was bound to the island of Manhattan and in 1898, fifteen years after the completion of the mighty Brooklyn Bridge, incorporation finally took place. Integration was another matter, slower to progress and perhaps never to be achieved. Brooklynites are a people unto themselves. Those raised there speak their own dialect and at the time of Barbara Joan Streisand's birth the tremendous number of foreign-born, over 900,000, and the majority of ethnic groups (over 1,000,000 of whom were Jewish) in the population of 2,800,000 made it quite different from any of New York City's boroughs and uniquely set it apart from other cities in America.

When war was declared, Brooklyn was one of the greatest maritime and industrial centres in the world. Forty per cent of the foreign commerce that moved out of the port of New York cleared through its thirty-three miles of developed waterfront. There were seventy steamship freight lines, fourteen trunk railways, and a series of huge shipping terminals. Brooklyn was the fifth largest manufacturing centre in the country. Industry, however, was largely concentrated within a few blocks of the waterfront. The rest of Brooklyn was one mammoth residential area, divided into sections by ethnic make-up more than boundaries. There were twenty distinct and separate Jewish communities. Several might have been classified as ghettos where many of the foreign-born Jews lived and where pushcarts still crowded the streets and there was a heady scent of sour rye bread fresh from the oven, fish – cooked and stuffed – and the sweet odour of honey cakes. Yiddish was the language between the older residents, while the youngsters mostly spoke English. Saturdays the streets were empty, sombre as the Sabbath was observed. But the majority of Jewish communities were middle class and upwardly mobile first- and second-generation Americans.

Barbara's parents were both raised in ghettos but, with time, their families had become just slightly removed from these more congested, unrelieved slum areas. Named Ida Rosen at her birth on 10 December 1908 (Diana was a teenage affectation), Barbara's mother was the third child of Louis Rosen, a tailor, and his wife Esther Etlin Rosen who emigrated to America during the pogroms in Russia shortly after the turn of the century. Louis was a religious Jew whose joy derived from his position as a part-time cantor in his *shul*.[1] Had his voice and interpretation been more inspired, his prospects might have been brighter for this was the era of cantorial glory, when great cantors would appear at different *shuls* as superstars in their field. A synagogue's ability to attract the most famous of these singers drew great respect from other *shuls*. Jews would walk miles to hear a celebrated cantor.

Louis lacked the vocal talent that was demanded for such a career. His failure embittered him, but it did not stop him from praying or singing. Four times a day he would walk around the Rosens' small, crowded apartment, his *tallis* draped around his sloping shoulders and *daven* in a sing-song voice. Sometimes he would sing Yiddish songs that came from *the old country*. The family spoke

---

[1] The word *shul* is derived from the Greek *schola*, via the German *Schule*. The Hebrew word for a house of prayer is *bet-haknesset*, a house of assembly. Similarly, the Greek word *synagogue* means 'assembly'. The two words are interchangeable, but often *shul* is used to describe a synagogue with a small congregation.

Yiddish, but among the younger members, English was preferred. 'Speak to me in English,' Diana was always telling her mother. And she and her sister Molly, who was next to her in age, seldom spoke Yiddish between themselves. There was the need to integrate, to become Americanised, and the sooner the better. Diana grew up to the sound of Yiddish music. She had a sweet, untrained soprano voice and liked to listen to operetta on the gramophone that was her father's great pride. At seventeen, pretty, petite, round-faced and with shining blue eyes, she tried out for the Metropolitan Opera chorus and was rejected. Three years later she went to work in an office filing and doing light book-keeping. She met Manny Streisand at a Purim celebration at the home of a friend whose father was the cantor for their *shul*.

Emanuel's father, Isaac Streisand, a tailor, emigrated from a small Jewish *shetl* in the village of Bryezany in Galicia, a section of Austria on the Hungarian border, in 1898. On marrying Anna Kessler Streisand, who also came from Bryezany, in 1907, Isaac sold the sewing machine he had carried on his back going from door to door to do small tailoring jobs, and used the money to set up a fish stand in the lower East Side ghetto where they lived. On 5 February 1908, Emanuel, their first child, was born. Three more sons, Murray, Hy and Phil, and a daughter, Molly, followed, and in 1920 Isaac opened a proper fish store on Summer Avenue in the Williamsburg section of Brooklyn. Emanuel, called Manny by friends and relatives, lived with his family in a crowded two-bedroom tenement apartment walking distance from his father's fish store. Manny, being the oldest son, helped his father more than his siblings.

Dealing in such perishable merchandise presented great difficulties for the family. The fish was bought in Manhattan from the Fulton Fish Market where Isaac had to drive at three in the morning in his erratic, worn-out truck bought from the former owner of his fish store. When not in school, Manny would help his father lift the fish in their large, heavy boxes layered in ice on and off the vehicle. When his mother was with his father in the store, he watched over his younger siblings at home and on Thursday evenings helped to chop and cut the fish to be sold the next day, the busiest they had, as Jewish households prepared for the Sabbath. After school Manny wrapped fish in newspapers and delivered it to houses in the neighbourhood. A work ethic was developed that would follow him through his life and in the long distant years be inherited by his future daughter.

As his business improved, Isaac moved his brood to more commodious accommodations in the Summer Avenue Housing Project a few streets down from his fish store where his oldest son, an exceptionally gifted student, had no intention of following in his father's footsteps. Yiddish was the first language in his home as well, but Manny was proud of his own mastery of English and had dreams of perhaps one day becoming a writer. With whatever extra money he received as tips, he bought books. When he finished his course of studies at the local *yeshiva*, which in the United States was a secondary Hebrew school, often with elementary classes as well, he knew that education was the only way he would one day be able to satisfy his ambition.

After graduating from Boys' High School in the summer of 1924, he entered City College of New York that autumn, supported by a small scholarship and part-time jobs as a lifeguard and a Good Humor Ice Cream truck driver. Learning, he believed, was the most saleable merchandise in the world. That lesson he learned from his mother, who went back to school after her children were in their teens to perfect her English and be able to read books that would open up the world to her. Her first-born resembled her in looks as well, inheriting her lively hazel eyes and wavy dark hair.

Manny received a Bachelor of Science degree from City College of New York in 1928. An all-round and well-liked young man, he was active in the Drama-tist, Math, Boxing, Fencing and Debating Clubs. 'Manny is one of those fortunate few who can graduate and say that college work has been easy,' it says beside his earnest photograph in the college year book. One is struck by the strength of his jaw bone and the exceptional intelligence in his eyes. His forehead is high, his cheekbones broad, his expression keen.

'There was something about Manny,' a fellow student recalled. 'It was not just that he was a genius, which everyone thought he was, he had a special quality. We all looked up to him, came to him for counsel.' With the help of night classes, he earned a Master's degree in Education in two years' time. He and Diana had just married and spent a weekend honeymoon in Manhattan. On their return they were in an automobile accident. Manny suffered a slight concussion. For a few weeks, he had severe headaches. They eased in intensity and he learned to cope with their frequent return. Manny was not a com-plainer. His attention was directed on positive action and his current goal to make something of his life.

After the Great Crash, jobs and money were scarce. Determined that he would not start a family until they could have a small place of their own in a more upwardly mobile neighbourhood, Manny accepted a position as an English teacher at Brooklyn High School for Specialty Trades. Diana, who had taken secretarial courses, managed to find office work. They were married by Rabbi Isaac Boomis on 24 December 1930, and moved into a three-room apartment in Flatbush, which was where many first- and second-generation European Jews aspired to live once they had achieved some measure of edu-cation and advancement. In 1930, 50 per cent of Flatbush's 85,000 residents were Jewish.

The newly married Streisands lived frugally, saving their money. In 1935, their son Sheldon Jay Streisand was born. His new responsibility inflamed Manny's ambition. He had a plan. One day soon he would go back to school and work for his doctoral. With a PhD he could teach at a university, which would be more lucrative and prestigious and he could eventually write – not novels, since he knew he didn't have the imagination that was necessary – but scholarly books. Diana never doubted that Manny had the intelligence and drive to do exactly that.

The students at Brooklyn High School for Specialty Trades tended to be truants, on the verge of dropping out, or general problem-makers. If they were over the age of sixteen, their required classes were strictly non-academic trades and skills, such as woodworking, or automotive work. But younger students had to take general classes – English, mathematics and social studies – as well for half a day. There were two sets of teachers, the technical staff and classroom instructors like Manny Streisand.

A fellow teacher, Nathan Clark, has retained warm memories of the time when he and Manny were associated. 'Many of his students,' said his former colleague, 'were rough, from bad homes and bad neighbourhoods, but they all respected Manny Streisand. He treated them with understanding and kindness, and they weren't used to that. He had no trouble from any student. They revered him, and if there was a student who caused a little trouble, Manny didn't march him down to see the principal; he handled it himself.'

Although the emphasis of the school was on vocational arts, Manny seemed determined that the young boys he taught would have an understanding of their language and be able to write it well enough to enhance their chances of a good life. He was a born educator, Clark recalled, a dedicated teacher, who was especially endowed with the ability to communicate his thirst for knowledge. He was a man who loved children and who was ambitious not only for himself, but to give his son and when Barbara was born, his baby daughter, a good life and a solid education. 'He was, I think,' Nathan Clark says, 'the finest man I ever worked with. Everyone loved him.'

When Sheldon Jay (Shelley) was a year old, Manny enrolled in the doctorate programme in education at Teacher's College, Columbia University, taking night classes while holding on to his job at the vocational high school. The commute was time-consuming. Columbia is all the way over on the west side of Manhattan on 116th Street, a long journey by IRT subway from Flatbush. The young couple did not have an easy time of it. Diana had to return to work to supplement their income. Shelley was left in the care of a close neighbour while she was employed as a file clerk. Manny would leave the house just about the time that Diana was coming home. When he returned Shelley was asleep. Weekends he graded his high-school class papers, prepared his lectures and then settled down to study for his doctorate which would take him years with the limited amount of credits he could manage each semester.

Diana's dreams were far more modest than Manny's. Not an intellectual, she did not understand what he was studying nor why he was unhappy with just being a high school teacher where the salary of $1,800 a year was low-paying but steady and the job genteel and respected. There were many things about Manny that she did not comprehend, but she loved him deeply and was awed by the wealth of his knowledge. She still liked to sing, although she had long ago put aside her faint aspirations to a vocal career. Times were hard. Her daily life went on as it had for years to rhythms set by a Depression whose grip remained unbroken. Manny and Diana were the lucky ones. They had weekly pay cheques, however small, while jobless men still haunted the streets, pleading for handouts. Neighbours did what they could to help each other by watching children and sharing a soup pot when they knew a relative, neighbour or friend might go hungry otherwise. The building the Streisands lived in was now half empty as families, unable to pay the rent, moved into already crowded rooms to live with relatives.

The war came as a feared surprise. For months the stage had been set for a distant but dangerous war. Yet, America was not prepared for Pearl Harbor. Manny was correcting papers on the kitchen table that Sunday afternoon, 7 December 1941 when it was announced over the radio that the Japanese had bombed Pearl Harbor. Doors were thrown open in neighbours' apartments as the occupants gathered in the hallways stunned, but united against 'those dirty yellow bastards'. Then everybody was screaming. It was bitterly cold that day, but people ran out into the already crowded street. Diana was four months' pregnant, grateful that her condition, Shelley, Manny's job as a teacher and a predisposition to migraines would most probably conspire to keep him out of uniform.

Over 300,000 men left their homes in Brooklyn to fight in the war. A day or two after Pearl Harbor there were air-raid scares that sent people scurrying to shelter areas. More than 400 sirens were installed at strategic stations throughout the New York area, nearly half of these in Brooklyn, and their wail was eerie and piercingly loud enough to place terror in any heart. None but the most necessary lights were kept burning behind blackout shades at night in order to eliminate the sky glow against which ships might be silhouetted and made easier prey for submarines. Manny's subway trips were conducted in near darkness. Windows of trains were painted black and even then only dim light was used inside the cars. It was all but impossible to read or do homework. Blackouts brought into action more than 150,000 air-raid wardens. Manny took a six-week training course based on the experience of wardens in Britain and was certified by the precinct warden commander before being assigned to a post. Two nights a week when he returned from Columbia he would put on a hard white helmet and an arm-band and patrol the dark streets of the neighbourhood with a protected flashlight before joining his small family.

The onset of Diana's labour came in the midst of an air-raid drill. Manny hailed an emergency taxi driver, one of the few vehicles allowed on the roads at such a time. Barbara Joan Streisand (after Anna Streisand's late sister, Berthe) was born at Israel Zion Hospital on 24 April 1942, healthy and strong-lunged. Family legend has it that her first cries were so loud they startled the delivery room staff. Until she was six months old she slept in a crib in her parents' room, then Shelley was moved to a cot in the living room and she occupied his former room. With a baby and a seven-year-old son, Diana could no longer work. Money was tight but she was against Manny abandoning his work on his doctorate to take a high-paying job at the shipyards, which were now going full steam. However difficult it was, the Streisands survived by living on a rigidly frugal budget. But the strain was hard on both of them.

As the summer of 1943 approached, Manny was offered a chance to help his friend, Nathan Spiro, an industrial arts teacher, as a counsellor at Camp Cascade in Highmount, New York, in the Catskills just east of the village of Fleischmanns adjoining New York State's richest farmlands. Camp Cascade was set in a protected glade in the foothills of the mountains and boasted a small waterfall and a natural swimming hole. The Streisands' Flatbush apartment, which was at the rear of the building, was stiflingly hot in the summer. In upper New York State there would be the mountains, cool fresh air, space and a chance for Manny to relax and be with his family.

A man gifted with entrepreneurial skills, Nate Spiro had rented the camp, which consisted of five large cabins, and a main building with a kitchen, dining room, lounge and staff quarters, for the season. There was no heat or hot water. Campers took cold showers, but Diana heated water for Barbara's bath on the huge wood cooking stove in the kitchen which also contained an old-fashioned, commodious ice box amply filled with vegetables and dairy products that came from a nearby farm.

Nate had made a good job of recruiting campers, mostly from Brooklyn's immigrant families. There would be room for both men and their wives (each of whom had a young baby) and space with the campers for Nate's four other children and for Shelley. Nate would teach the campers arts and crafts while Manny would organise a drama group. A camp cook qualified to cook kosher food was hired to join a staff which also included two cleaners and three more counsellors. Diana, Mrs Spiro and her teenage daughter, Helene, were to take care of the various other housekeeping chores while both men would supervise the sports with the help of the oldest of the 110 co-ed campers. Manny would be a great asset to the camp. An excellent swimmer, having once been a lifeguard, he was also proficient in squash and tennis.

Both families set off with great enthusiasm in three rather ancient, dilapidated, hired buses crowded with wide-eyed youngsters, most of whom had never before been in the country. Suitcases and equipment were tied on to the top of the vehicles. The small caravan moved sluggishly towards it destination, the children led in song by the adults while the older campers comforted the younger members who already were experiencing the first pangs of home-sickness.

Manny was in particularly high spirits, happy that he could spend the summer in the country with his family. A proud father, he wanted to see Shelley develop athletic skills. He doted on Barbara, and although she was not a beautiful child, being almost bald as an infant, she had a merry laugh and quick responses that made him certain she was intellectually gifted.

Manny lacked only one year's study for his doctorate in education at Columbia. During that summer he needed to think about his final thesis. The wooded camp setting, removed as it was from the heat and stress of summer in Brooklyn, would be a much better writing environment. The nearest town, Fleischmanns, normally a six-hour drive from Manhattan, but nearly a day's journey with the numerous stops along the way to accommodate weak bladders and the buses' leaky water pipes which caused them to hiss and overheat, had its heyday before World War One. The wealthy Fleischmann family, famous for their yeast product, had constructed a summer home there in the 1860s. A number of rich Austrian-Hungarian Jews followed, building grand estates with elegant verandas, magnificent gardens  and rooms large enough for lavish entertaining. By the end of the century, something like fifty hotels crowded Fleischmanns' borders. The town, however, lost its cachet between the wars as the affluent summer people, whose large homes were generally outside the village, moved to newer more popular communities closer to New York.

When Manny Streisand came to work at Camp Cascade, Fleischmanns was still suffering from the economic depression. The grand old Fleischmann house had burned to the ground years before and remained a charred ruin. Dotting the surrounding wooded areas were dozens of independent camps like the one that Nate had organised – all very primitive and catering for children of poor, foreign-born families.

The Streisands arrived at the end of June and were contracted for an eight-week stay. Within two weeks it began to look like their work would be more difficult than they had anticipated. After two of the counsellors quit, Manny doubled his duties and the number of campers in his care. The exercise was vigorous – hiking through the mountains, swimming in icy water, always having to be alert to danger from wild animals, brambles, insects or simply the rambunctiousness of his young group. Many campers did not speak English, having recently fled the Nazis. Nights were difficult as those scarred by what they had witnessed awoke with nightmares and had to be reassured that they were safe.

During his fifth week at Camp Cascade, Manny tripped over a rock while out hiking alone, hitting his head in the fall. Dazed, but noting there was no cut, he continued on his way back to camp. The following day he developed a paralysing migraine and went back to his cabin to lie down. Diana looked in on him a short time later and found him sleeping fitfully. When she returned in an hour, she could not rouse him. Alarmed, she ran to get Nate Spiro. Manny was unconscious, his pulse barely perceptible.

'It was terrible,' she recalled. 'We were so removed from everything. I suppose that made me ... frantic.'

The nearest hospital was in Margaretville, several miles further away than Fleischmanns. With the aid of some of the older campers, Nate got Manny into the one car they had at the camp. Diana accompanied them, leaving Barbara in the care of the Spiros' daughter Helene. The child cried loudly when the car drove off in a cloud of dust, down the dirt trail to Margaretville. Barbara was never to see her father again.

Twenty-four hours later, on 4 August, Emanuel Streisand was pronounced dead. He had never regained consciousness. Respiratory failure was cited on the death certificate as the cause of death. Theories were to circulate in the family for years: Manny had been the victim of hospital misdiagnosis, he had suffered an epileptic fit, he had died from concussion or a tumor on the brain, he had contracted an infectious disease which, because of his close association with so many young people, it was thought better not to disclose. The result of a concussion, complicated by his earlier injury and not treated fast enough or with the right drugs, is the more likely explanation. Diana remembered pacing the floor back in their room at the camp, trying as best she could to remain in control for the sake of the children. She had no idea what they were going to do.

She was in shock, unable to believe that she was now a widow and her two children fatherless. Nate Spiro took over immediate arrangements and through the local Jewish funeral home, contacted the Jewish Burial Organisation for assistance in paying for and transporting his friend's body back to Brooklyn. Carrying Barbara in her arms and holding on tightly to Shelley's hand, Diana left Fleischmanns the next morning on the same train as the coffin. Manny was buried almost immediately upon arrival at Mount Hebron Cemetery in Queens.

Barbara, just fifteen months old, could not understand why her mother was crying. But the child's grief for her lost father would very soon undermine her stability, form her character and breed within her such corrosive anger and sense of self-deprivation – *why me? why my father?* – that her future happiness would always be compromised.

# 4

WITH NO INSURANCE money and very little in savings, Diana was forced to leave the middle-class apartment in Flatbush and move into her parents' three-room apartment at 365 Pulaski Street, a four-storey building in the Bedford-Stuyvesant section of Brooklyn, named after New York State's first Governor – old peg-legged Peter Stuyvesant. The Bed-Stuy area, as it was called, embraced a mixture of religions reflected in the spires, campaniles and domes that rose above its skyline of converted brownstones and small apartment houses. A huge black ghetto burgeoned in the northern reaches where a direct train, which had inspired the Duke Ellington-Billy Strayhorn classic, 'Take the A Train', linked it to Harlem. The Polaski Street area was predominantly old-world Jewish and Irish Catholic, most of the first-generation offspring having left for more elite addresses in recent years.

To Barbara the area was fascinating. Pushcarts brimmed with a cornucopia of items – ripening fruits, enticing candies, bright fabrics, buttons, threads, mops and brooms and used clothing. Women in aprons and men in alpaca skull caps and silkoline coats bargained emotionally with the peddlers. Bed linen billowed out of windows and on warm days people sat on stoops and fire escapes or by the kerb in stiff, wooden chairs in the hot sunshine while children in minimal attire played on the sidewalks or on luckier days ran through the gushing cool water of an opened fire hydrant. These were impressions that would colour her life. Still, the move to Pulaski Street was not a happy one.

Bubbe and Zayde Rosen, as their grandchildren called them, occupied one room of the apartment, Diana and Barbara shared a bed in another and Sheldon slept on a folding cot in the third room which was furnished with a dark-wood dining table, chairs and a china cabinet. There was no living room: the 'family' room was the dining room with no space for a couch. ('Couches to me were like what rich people had,' Streisand would later say.)

The Rosens were decent, hardworking people, but there was scant love in the house. Zayde Rosen was a cold man, bitter at his failure to succeed in America and at his unfulfilled cantorial ambitions. Bubbe was asthmatic and the apartment was filled with the acrid smell of the camphor that she inhaled and the strong lye soap she used as she hunched bent over the deep white enamel sink in the kitchen and scrubbed the family's wash on a ridged metal board while her sprawling breasts shook beneath her cotton housedress and flowered apron.

Diana, a victim of depression, cried a lot. With two young children and a mother who was not well, she felt guilty to be living on the meagre army allotment cheques her bachelor brother had signed over to her, when it rightly should have gone to her parents. As a widow at thirty-four, with no money and two children, she feared she had no future marriage prospects, that her life was over. Her own trauma was so all-encompassing that she was unaware, or perhaps insensitive, to what Shelley and Barbara were suffering.

Shelley had lost his father at a crucial time in his childhood. Manny had always been able to communicate with young boys and help them with their problems. Shelley was artistic and Manny had encouraged his creativity. Never too busy to talk or listen to his son, a great bond had formed. Unable to relate to Diana in her state of depression and never at ease with his grandparents, Shelley felt the loss of his father keenly and during this time drew closer to his little sister, of whom he was protective.

Bubbe Rosen had not been prepared for young children to re-enter her household. The tumult they created jarred on her nerves and made her irritable. Shelley would run in and out of the apartment banging doors after himself. Barbara was all over the place, impossible to keep still, prone to knock things over as she played. Once she broke a piece of her grandmother's cut glass, Bubbe's most prized possessions carried with her so many years before on the boat from Russia. Shelley remembers that he and Barbara would scuttle under the dining-room table to avoid a beating whenever their mischievousness caused breakages or disruption. He was more fearful of his grandmother than Barbara, who treated both her grandparents with measured defiance. She seemed to know just how far to go before Zayde would get out his strap, and although he never hit either one of them with it, would crack the leather into a frightening sound that threatened he would.

Barbara simply could not relate to this elderly couple. Bubbe, a short, stout, full-breasted woman with wispy grey fly-away hair, would sit at the dining table and sip a glass of tea through a sugar lump she held between her teeth. She would sigh as she sat there, mumble things to herself. She seldom had a conversation with either of her grandchildren except to insist that they eat the food she always seemed to be preparing – cabbage soup, *gribinens* (the hard pieces that were left after chicken fat was rendered), *tsimmis* and honey cakes. She treated her frequent headaches by wrapping a vinegar-soaked cloth around her head. At those times Barbara knew she had to be especially quiet.

Of her two grandparents, Barbara was drawn more to Zayde. There was something mystical about his appearance, grey-blue eyes that seemed always to be seeing things in the distance that she could not, the movement of his oddly graceful stubby hands as he talked and the sing-song cadences of his chanting. Wearing a *yarmulkah* on his head, his *tallis* over his shoulders and his phylacteries (which were strips of parchment inscribed with words from the Torah) strapped to his forehead and left arm, Zayde would *daven* almost as soon as he awoke, facing east as he said his prayers for that is where *Eritz Yisroel* is. This intrigued Barbara and she would ask him questions about what he was doing and he would answer her unpatronisingly. It is doubtful that she understood what he was saying but she liked being spoken to as if he thought she could.

She and Shelley went to Zayde's small modest *shul* on special holidays like Succoth and Simcath Torah when children were given apples to eat. She was envious of the grand appearance of the nearby Catholic Church but could well have been proud of the sight of her Zayde as he stood on the *bima* before the Torah scrolls wrapped in crimson velvet embroidered with gold thread and containing the five books of Moses. A short, wiry man, Zayde suddenly took on stature as he held the holy scriptures in his arms.

Diana finally went back to work as a book-keeper, which aided her strained financial situation but created more responsibility for her ailing mother. Barbara was sent to the neighbourhood *yeshiva* pre-school when she was three. During that summer she was shipped off for several weeks to Diana's sister Anna and her husband who had a small house in western Connecticut. These experiences backfired. Parted from her mother, Barbara feared she would never see her again and clung to Diana even more when they were together.

Shelley was something of a surrogate parent during this period and when he was in school Barbara played on the stoop of the apartment building or in the hallways, cadging snacks from compassionate neighbours who believed her made-up stories that she had not been given lunch. When her brother came home, to his annoyance, she would follow him around until he went off to play stickball or other games with his friends. The building was not entirely occupied by Jewish families. There were Irish and Italian neighbours – non-kosher homes and had Diana or Bubbe Rosen known that she had eaten from these kitchens, they would have been furious. As it was, they never understood why she ate so little at mealtimes and worried that she would grow to be a sickly *skinny-marink*, considered a terrible fate for a Jewish girl, for what man would want to marry a scrawny woman? As a child, it took two years before her hair began to grow; later she said she looked like a martian. A slight cast in one eye made her eyes turn in at certain times, but their sheer blueness compensated for this distraction. Possessing extraordinary energy, she seemed to be a small Vesuvius about to erupt. As a child of three or four, Bubbe called her *farbrent*, which in Yiddish means 'on fire'. She refused to take no for an answer and always had an arsenal of arguments ready to win her point.

One stifling hot day in June when she was four and recovering from the chicken pox, she asked Bubbe if she could go out to play with some of the children from the building. 'What kind of *farchadat* idea is that?' Bubbe answered, and told her she was to remain exactly where she was. That happened to be on a cot near the fire escape. When Bubbe disappeared into the kitchen, Barbara dressed, climbed out of the window on to the fire escape and descended the treacherous iron staircase several steep flights to the courtyard below. She knew she would be disciplined when she returned. Her actions took a certain amount of bravery and audacity, not caring what the consequences were for herself or Bubbe, who was in a state of shock when she returned to find Barbara gone and the window by the fire escape wide open.

Everyone in these project buildings knew everyone else's business despite the ethnic clannishness of the residents. Pity was generated for the Rosens who now had their daughter and two grandchildren to take care of, one – the girl – impossible, her mother should be ashamed. Unsure of what she could do to change her situation, Diana found herself increasingly impatient with Barbara, for as soon as she came in from work, Bubbe would greet her with a list of her daughter's infractions that day. The beginning of the resentment that Barbara would always have toward her mother had its roots here. Thrilled to see her after being parted all day, she was greeted by a tearful, angry Diana. 'Why do you always make trouble?' Diana would cry, disappear into her room and shut the door between them.

Never feeling quite at home on Pulaski Street, Barbara liked to fantasise, often imagining her father was alive and that they lived in a grand house with a wide porch and a beautiful garden. She hated the ugliness, the smallness, the claustrophobic atmosphere of the Rosens' apartment. When the windows were open you could hear voices in anger strained to an ear-piercing pitch, doors slamming, toilets flushing, radios blasting. The daytime soap operas were popular with all nationalities – *Portia Faces Life*, *Myrt and Marge*, the kindly Papa David on *Life Can Be Beautiful* and the very popular *My Gal Sunday* that posed the question: 'Can a girl from a small mining town out West find happiness married to a rich and titled English Lord?' At night there were *The Goldbergs*, *One Man's Family* and the comedy programmes: *Duffy's Tavern*, Jack Benny, Bob Hope. Kids liked listening to the adventure and suspense stories like *The Shadow* and *The Green Hornet*, and with only one radio in most families, squabbles arose over who had priority. There was no question about the six o'clock evening news. Everyone gathered around their set to listen. It brought the war into their homes, their absent family members and friends closer. Many still had relatives in Europe whose fate remained uncertain.

Brooklyn lost over 3,000 men in the war, with many more suffering serious injury, but its end in 1945 heralded the safe return of Diana's brother Larry. Families were now reunited. Barbara could not understand why she did not have a daddy when the fathers of the other youngsters on Pulaski Street had returned from the services. She would ask Diana questions about her father and refused to accept the truth that she was never to see him again. In the intervening years since Manny's death, Diana had gained hope that she would meet a man who could provide for her two children and be a father to them. She felt inadequate to deal with her strong-willed daughter and never did understand what it was that made her so difficult to handle. She was certain that she was to blame for her daughter's unorthodox behaviour, her obstinacy and her lack of friends.

Very much of a loner, Barbara did have one comrade in the building, Irving Berakow. Irving's parents had a seven-and-a-half inch television set, one of the first in the Streisands' building. While Mrs Berakow, a generously built woman named Toby, cooked stuffed cabbage or knitted, the two youngsters would watch Laurel and Hardy through a magnifying window placed in front of the minuscule picture screen. This was Barbara's introduction to actors on film. She was entranced, quickly learned the comedians' routines and attempted imitations. She was able to make Irving and his mother laugh, but the same clowning had no effect on the members of her own family, who found such antics unfeminine and unbecoming.

At five, she entered kindergarten in her *yeshiva*. Never able to become part of a group, she tried to win the children over by acting crazy or doing something 'shocking'. When the rabbi would go out of the room, she would yell, 'Christmas! Christmas!' a word not spoken in a Hebrew school. But such actions only angered the rabbi and made her look foolish to her classmates.

Thoughts about religion and God aroused her curiosity. She remembers humid summer afternoons and evenings sitting on the iron-railed fire escape of her grandparents' apartment with two other children from the building, one a Catholic girl and one an atheist. 'It was so strange being so young, but we used to have debates about God,' she recalled. 'One night we were sitting there, with out blankets, and I said, "I'm going to show you there is a God. See that man walking down the street? I'm going to pray that he steps down off the kerb." I never prayed so hard in my life, yuh know what I mean? Just, "Please show me!" And the man stepped off the kerb. That experience was like . . . there must be a God. The guy stepped off the kerb!'

She claims she had no toys, only a hot-water bottle which she dressed as a doll. Diana insists this isn't true but that the toys she had were not to her liking. She had *dreydls* (a top engraved with Hebrew letters that spins) and picture books. 'The children on the street played hopscotch and jump rope. She had stuffed animals when she was little,' Diana maintained. The hot-water bottle was used once when she had a chill and she had refused to relinquish it, filling it every night thereafter with warm water to give it shape and 'life', wrapping it in one of her outgrown sweaters and sleeping with it hugged tightly against her body.

The possessor of a vivid imagination, she made up stories where she was someone else or fantasised that her father would come to rescue her and they would go off together. To Bubbe's irritation, she would smear Diana's make-up on her face with the edge of a towel or streak it with Shelley's school crayons in grotesque Indian signs which took a lot of scrubbing to remove. Shelley was artistic and loved stories and games about American Indians. He collected feathers from chickens, from pillows and bedcovers, from the street whenever pigeons were moulting, and turned them into Indian headdresses. These were sacrosanct, but Barbara would sneak them from his 'hiding' place when she knew he was going to be away for a while and wear them as she *whooped* through the apartment. She liked to play colourful characters, be someone other than who she was.

The summer she was five, painfully underweight and prone to bronchitis and ear infections, she was sent to a health camp in upper New York State sponsored by a Jewish organisation. 'I remember their taking off my clothes and dumping me into this bath like I was a piece of dirt,' she recalled. 'They scrubbed me and washed me and put this lice disinfectant in my hair, then they put me into their ugly uniform.' She found the idea of dressing like everyone else intolerable. After nearly drowning in the camp pool she refused to go into it. The camp session was six weeks. Parents were allowed to visit twice during this period. With no means of transportation, Diana was unable to get there. Although Barbara was not the only child who had no visitors, the sense of rejection was no less painful.

When she returned home she found Diana changed, 'dressing up' more, wearing new make-up, and having even less time for Shelley and Barbara than before. Diana had finally come out of her depression and was dating. 'I hated those men,' Streisand admits. 'Once I saw a man kissing my mother. I thought he was killing her. Except she was laughing.' Diana had met Louis Kind, attractive – well built, a distinguished profile, thick, dark hair flecked with grey and a certain dash in the way he dressed – fifteen years her senior.

Kind had emigrated from Russia with his family as a child of five and learned tailoring in the small pants' factory his father eventually established in Brooklyn. It was a career he detested and he ventured out on his own as a real-estate and used-car salesman. At one point, he took over the mortgages of several old rooming houses. A heavy gambler, he soon lost them and the rent money they had engendered. Recently separated from his wife Ida, with whom he had three grown children, he seemed genuinely taken with Diana. She was forewarned by friends of his instability and poor reputation. There were stories about the various loose women he had run around with and his gambling. Still, he was willing to take on the responsibility of another man's family and Diana found him to her liking.

Barbara was sent back to the detested health camp the following summer and hated it even more, although she was to remember with lingering fondness the sponge cake the children were served on Friday nights. When Diana drove up with Kind in his car to see how she was doing at the end of her second week, Barbara cried and carried on, insisting on going back to Brooklyn with them. Nothing would stop her. She put together her possessions and crawled into the back of the car and refused to be ejected. 'You are *not* leaving here without me!' she screamed. And they were forced to give in.

Diana became pregnant in the spring of 1951. Kind's divorce was not yet final and the atmosphere in the Rosen apartment was explosive. To have an unmarried daughter in such a condition was a *chanda*, a disgrace, a terrible thing. Kind was not allowed to come to the apartment. Diana was distraught, crying all the time. Finally, Kind came to her aid and rented a three-room apartment in a middle-class building, pretentiously named Vandemeer Estates, at 3102 Newkirk Street near the corner of Nostrand Street, a block away from the bustle of Flatbush Avenue and moved in with Diana and her two children. Diana quit her job and her neighbours were led to believe that she was married to Kind. He received his final divorce decree on 19 December 1951. Four days later, he and Diana were married in New Jersey by a Justice of the Peace and on 9 January 1952 their child, Rosalind, was born. Things appeared to be on the upturn for the little girl who had always wanted a father. The problem was that Barbara loathed Louis Kind from the very beginning.

Her stepfather was a man better able to communicate and charm outsiders than the members of his close family. 'He never talked to me except to order me around,' Streisand remembers bitterly. 'The only thing I can recall him saying to me was when I was riding in a car with my girlfriend. I was talking, and he said, "Why can't you be more like her? Quiet."' Kind was in deep financial problems almost from the start of his marriage to Diana. His gambling debts had mounted and he remained responsible for the support of his ex-wife. He was forced to take a job for the steady income it provided in a garment company as a cutter, work he had done in the past but felt was beneath him. The atmosphere in the Kind household grew very dark. Kind was moody, hostile. Diana's dream that he would be a father to her children was quickly crushed. Kind had no patience with either Shelley or Barbara. Uncomfortable around a teenage boy whom his wife expected him to counsel and befriend, he had even less tolerance for a difficult, resentful child who did not like him any better than he liked her. Diana expected him to take Barbara to the park or pony rides on his Sundays off. Kind had places of his own to go to when he had free time, women who did not care if a man was married.

In the beginning, Diana maintained, Kind tried to be nice to Barbara. He bought her gifts; colouring books and crayons, a jump rope, and on her eighth birthday a proper doll with eyes that opened and closed to replace the homemade water-bottle doll she slept with at nights. Barbara pushed the new doll aside. She had wanted roller skates she claimed. She found fault with every offering, it was never right or chosen just for her. Cold and antagonistic toward Kind from the outset, she never warmed to him or allowed herself to see any good in him. He had taken her father's place, scuttled her fantasy that he would one day return to his family. She would never forgive Kind for this, or her mother for marrying him. Yet, down deep, she desperately wanted and needed his approval but nothing she ever did pleased him.

The first night in their Flatbush apartment she had cried bitterly until, over Kind's strong verbal objections, she was allowed to sleep in her mother's bed as she had on Pulaski Street. Kind refused to share the bed with them and stormed from the apartment. The following morning Barbara awoke complaining of a clicking and buzzing in her ears. Diana, obviously under stress and suspicious that her daughter's complaint was a bid for attention, had her hold a hot-water bottle to her ear and as Barbara had neither fever nor pain, dismissed it. These distressing noises in her head continued without medical consultation throughout her pre-adolescence. She would wrap her head in a woollen scarf in the humid heat of the Brooklyn summer and press her fingers to her ears at other times. The sounds continued, never to disappear and many years later would be diagnosed as tinnitus aurium, a distressing chronic condition of the inner ear.

At turns she was all dreamer or all realist. She viewed her stepfather with a keen, cold eye surprising in one so young. 'Why do you take *his* side?' she quizzed Diana after a confrontation with Kind. 'He doesn't need you. *I* do. He doesn't even love you. If he did, he'd be nicer.' She could move her mother to injured tears, while she controlled her own emotions.

Her defence was to retreat further into a private world where Kind did not exist. Movies played a large role in her life. When she was very young, Diana or Shelley would take her to the neighbourhood movie house on a Saturday afternoon. Shelley liked Westerns and Buck Rogers and Flash Gordon serials; Diana comedies and romantic dramas. Barbara preferred going with her mother. Shelley was never too pleased to have his little sister tag along, but that was not entirely her reason. Barbara liked not having to share Diana and she was drawn to the images and the women she watched on the large screen in the darkened theatre when she was with her mother. The gamut of her imagination ran from being glamorous like Lana Turner to being glamorous like Rita Hayworth. She equated being loved with being beautiful and decided that one day she would be a movie star – and beautiful. That dream was her touchstone throughout childhood.

Around Kind, she remained sullen. It didn't help that Shelley kept telling her how wonderful their real father had been, or that her brother had known him where she had been denied any conscious memory of him. When not day-dreaming she was moody or unco-operative, always the rebel, refusing to do what was being asked of her. One time when Diana had lost her temper and slapped Barbara a glancing blow on the ear, she pretended for the rest of the day that she had been struck deaf and carried it off so well that her mother grew hysterical and was about to rush her to the hospital. Seeing Diana in honest turmoil Barbara finally confessed the truth.

'Barbara was a very complex child,' Diana has said. 'She bottled up every-thing inside her. Perhaps if she could have voiced to me how she was feeling things might have been easier, but she didn't. She had her own ideas, her own way of looking at life and that was the way she liked things to be. Barbara always saw everything depending on how it affected her, but it was not easy for her as a child.

'I knew that she resented not having a father, especially because Roslyn [Rosalind] had one, but she wouldn't talk about it to me,' Diana recalled. 'From the age of seven she wanted to be in films. I couldn't fathom why she wanted to be famous, but she did. I was worried that she wouldn't succeed and that she would be hurt, so I tried not to encourage her. But I couldn't break up her ideas and her thinking.'

The 'grand' apartment in Flatbush allowed little space for anyone. The new baby first slept in a crib in her parents' room. The dinette was turned into a small second bedroom for Shelley and Barbara slept on the couch in the front room. The fact that they now had a sofa did not make her feel 'rich' as she once thought it would. 'Ever sleep on a couch night after night?' she asked an interviewer. 'All you think about is, "How can I get a room of my own?" You get to the point where you *have* to make good!' There was at least one benefit. The couch was in the room with the new television set. Barbara quickly became addicted to it and all the early variety programmes: Arthur Godfrey, Sid Caesar, Milton Berle – the various daytime and weekly soap operas and dramas. She especially loved the commercials and committed many of them to memory and then would go into the bathroom and lock the door so that she could act them out in front of the medicine-chest mirror without interruption. She would pretend she was a sophisticated young woman smoking a cigarette, Betty Furness, the spokeswoman for Westinghouse, looking glamorous as she opened a refriger-ator door, the exotic South Sea Island girl who wore Tabu perfume and undulated seductively.

One day she would be beautiful and famous. She kept telling herself this over and over again and finally she came to believe it. Her attitude changed. She held her head up, her back straight. She seemed suddenly not just defiant, but a bit arrogant. It did not sit well with her stepfather, but Barbara had discovered that she had a fierce desire for survival, that she could make her dreams her reality, and that if she had to she could fight the world alone.

# 5

OXED IN BY his responsibilities, highly resentful at having to provide for a stepdaughter who was, in his opinion, ungrateful, Kind's hostile nature erupted frequently into a growing violence. Verbally abusive, bullying and threatening on occasion to Diana, his anger reached out to Barbara. There is no evidence that he ever beat her. He shouted a lot; Barbara would shout back and manage to get out of his way at the times when he seemed poised to take a swipe at her. Barbara's strident voice rose shrilly in defiance and Diana was mortified that the neighbours could hear what was going on in her home. She swore the older children to silence, never to discuss Kind's tyrannising abuse. Once he told Barbara that she could not have ice cream because she was so ugly. 'He was really mean to Barbara,' Shelley confirmed. 'He taunted her continually, telling her how plain she was compared to Rosalind.' With cruelty to Barbara, he referred to the half-sisters as 'beauty and the beast'.

'You're different, that's all, different and you're smarter than most kids your age,' Shelley would tell her to help build her ego. 'And being smart is what counts.' He defended her against Kind when he could. He felt protective of Barbara, but he was having his own difficulties in this unhappy home. His main objective was to leave there, go to college, make something of himself. He was a good artist (a talent his stepfather had very little regard for), and thought he might go into advertising. A winsome youngster, Shelley had grown into an attractive and popular young man of medium stature, but broad-shouldered and possessing an easy manner and a winning smile. Barbara was greatly possessive of him, jealous when girlfriends called and dreaded the day when he would no longer be her protector in the house.

At ten, after seeing the leggy, statuesque Cyd Charisse dance with Gene Kelly in *Singin' in the Rain*, Barbara made up her mind that she had to have ballet lessons and badgered her mother for weeks until finally Diana gave in, although it meant a sacrifice on her part. Money was scarce and she did not dare to ask Kind for help to finance what even she thought was a frivolous enterprise. Her hope was that the lessons would prove to Barbara how much she cared about her and would make her less difficult. To buy a pair of toe shoes and a leotard and to pay for ballet instruction at a small, local dancing school, she scraped together the money by economising on the table, using cheaper cuts of meat and fewer desserts, walking instead of taking public transport.

Barbara could not wait to attend her weekly class. Shorter and younger than most of the girls in her group, she applied herself with manic dedication to be just that much better prepared. She showed surprising ability for a youngster who was always considered to be awkward. 'When she came home [from dance class] she would practise and practise,' Diana recalled. 'She spent hours getting up on her toes and walking around the apartment. I was afraid it might hurt her feet – you never know what damage it could do to a child's toes.' Barbara pressed for private instruction, which was more costly. Kind was already complaining vociferously that Diana was wasting money on Barbara that should have been spent on the household. Diana found herself in the middle of a dysfunctional family, wanting to appease Kind and at the same time eager to make Barbara happier, less sulky and more outgoing. Her problem was solved when Miss Marsh, the ballet instructor, moved out of the neighbourhood. Barbara continued to bounce around the apartment, doing leaps and turns on her own, but her dream of becoming another Cyd Charisse was squashed. Not, however, her determination to be recognised, famous. In her mind, her vision of her future set her apart from her Flatbush peers.

There were children of all ages in Vandemeer Estates, in the backyards and on the streets it commanded. In good weather mothers would wheel baby carriages up and down the block, stop and talk with one another. Boys played stickball in the street and drivers would watch out for them and park their vehicles in places where they wouldn't block the game. Toddlers ran around on the small patches of lawn, an older family member watching from the viewpoint of a folding chair or stretched out on the grass beneath the warm fingers of the sun. Games of hide and seek were played where the kids would conceal themselves in the narrow crevices between the buildings, or in the labyrinth of alleys behind them. Girls played house with their dolls. Sometimes the neighbourhood youngsters put on talent shows. Believing these neighbourhood productions beneath her, Barbara preferred not to be included.

Newkirk Street had trees and in summer the pavements were dappled with shade. An ice-cream truck came by in the afternoon. A white uniformed driver sold dixie cups with pictures of movie stars on the inside cover. Kids collected and traded them and they would lick the ice cream off to see who they got – Betty Grable, Alice Faye, Tyrone Power, Judy Garland, Mickey Rooney, Clark Gable. Barbara bought pink, sweet-flavoured bubble gum for a penny at the corner market, chewed it and stored it nightly in a glass of cold water until its elasticity was gone. Chewing gum relaxed her, made her feel less tense.

Despite all the young people in the building and in the neighbourhood, she had trouble making friends. Louis Kind had told her she was ugly so often that she felt ugly deep inside. She had the habit of trying to outstare kids when they turned to look at her, or she would make faces. 'When I was nine years old, sometimes the girls would gang up on me in my neighbourhood, make a circle around me, make fun of me, and I'd start to cry,' she remembers. They called her 'Crazy Barbara' and 'Big Beak'. Barbara attributed these attacks to the shape and length of her nose. However in Flatbush with such a high percentage of Jewish, Italian, Polish and other ethnic groups who often inherited prominent noses, Barbara's was not that unique or oversized. The popular nose-bobbing operation that shortened, de-humped and remoulded an ethnic nose into the pert, snub, all-American profile of movie star Doris Day, was seldom performed before a girl was sixteen. In her pre-teens, Barbara's nose was in the ethnic majority and should not have incited the ugly epithets she claims, but she had a commanding, defiant look, too solemn an expression for a child and she was stand-offish. Because her astonishing blue eyes were set close together, her forehead high, and her mouth wide, greater attention was drawn to her nose, perhaps prompting the ridicule she received from the kids on her block.

The ridicule she suffered cut deeply and, added to Kind's cruel comments, would mark her for life. Kind – his very name a bitter reminder of his converse nature – became the enemy within her home, the children on the street and in school the enemy outside. She was constantly on guard and adapted an aloof attitude. Her peers at P.S. 89, where she attended grammar school, thought she was conceited and resented her natural intelligence which she could not refrain from displaying. She used words she had learned from the movies or television, corrected other children's grammar, stopped them if they had a fact wrong, gloated if they did not know an answer to a question. Much more daunting, she perceived herself as ugly, a *meeskite*, and transferred this impression to others.

Louis Kind had undermined her self-esteem and Diana had done very little to counter his effect on Barbara. 'She was critical of me and never believed in me,' Streisand says of her mother. 'She used to say, "I never want you to get a swelled head."' The youngster was riddled with self-doubt. It did not help that her straight hair was allowed to hang in an unflattering style. Being so thin, her head and hands looked too large for her small frame, a fact that was emphasised by the poor fit of her dresses, which Diana chose to buy large enough for her to grow into and then kept her in until she had outgrown them.

Barbara's fear became reality when, in the autumn of 1952, Shelley went off to City College of New York, lived with cousins in the East End and supported himself with the help of a scholarship and a part-time job. She envied his escape from Brooklyn and their unhappy home, but her anger at him grew for 'deserting' her. Rosalind, a chubby round-faced child with a happy disposition, commanded most of Diana's attention. Barbara bitterly resented her half-sister for having a father when she did not. The truth is, she would have welcomed Kind's paternal interest. A large part of her wanting to succeed had to do with proving to Kind how worthy she was of his admiration. In many families, where there is a frustrated and abusive parent, one child is singled out to be on the receiving end of this abuse. Barbara, with her airs and her trying disposition, was a ready victim for Kind.

Coinciding with Shelley's absence, the violent scenes between Louis Kind and Diana accelerated. He had a vicious temper, a cruel tongue and spoke demeaningly to Diana in front of the girls. She was stupid, a leech, unattractive, a nag. His face contorted, his voice threatened. Doors slammed. He would leave the house and not return until early the next morning or, sometimes, several days or a week later. Life at the Streisand-Kinds was painful, crushing. To break out, at the age of ten, Barbara would sneak a forbidden cigarette from Kind's bedside hoard and go up to the rooftop of their building to smoke. There, she slipped into fantasy and became the glamorous star of her dreams.

Vandemeer Estates was within walking distance of Loew's King Theater on Flatbush Avenue and on Saturday afternoons her world was brightened. Diana gave her twenty-five cents for a movie ticket and a Mello-Roll, a vanilla ice-cream confection of which she was fond. Entering Loew's King was like walking through a celluloid screen into an MGM spectacular. Built during the days of opulent movie palaces, it had a vaulted French Baroque grand lobby with brightly painted murals of exotic foreign vistas, mystical castles and lushly costumed men and women. There were mock gas lamps attached to the walls, a magnificent crystal chandelier and brightly polished brass railings on the sides of the massive, curved marble staircase, a deep red carpet down its centre.

At the back of the lobby was the refreshment stand with its tempting smell of buttered popcorn and spicy frankfurters impaled on a revolving grill and which, as they were *trayf* (non-kosher), she was forbidden to eat. The auditorium seated close to 3,800, within was a gigantic four-manual pipe organ referred to as the 'Wonder Morton' after its creator that filled the house with heavenly music when the lights were up. Barbara's refuge was the balcony nearest the starlit ceiling. She fell in love with Marlon Brando when at thirteen she saw him woo Jean Simmons in *Guys and Dolls*. As soon as *The End* flashed on the screen, she rushed to the bathroom so that she would not be told to leave. When she knew the film was being shown again, she left the rest room and made her way in the dark to an available empty seat to see her idol again, imagining herself in Jean Simmons's place as the recipient of his affection.

'I was a character in the movie,' she says. 'Not the actress, but the character. Not Vivien Leigh but Scarlett O'Hara. It was *me* up there and those attractive men were pursuing *me!*' She was greatly impressed by *Gone with the Wind* when in 1954 it was reissued in wide screen and stereophonic sound. Just turned twelve, she none the less identified with Scarlett – the determination, the fight for independence, the woman invading a man's world and being more exciting for it. The movies were more than a form of escapism, they had become a higher form of reality for her. She judged the humdrum experiences of her everyday life and the people she shared them with by what she saw in the movies. Those celluloid images were movers and shakers not observers and naysayers. She thought less of Diana for letting herself be a doormat for Louis Kind's bullying. The mother–daughter conflict was made all the more tense by Diana's inability to see Barbara as anything more than an unattractive girl with an aggressive and wildly imaginative nature. But in movies and her fast-growing dream of becoming a star and a part of that celluloid world, Barbara found what others sought in religion.

None of this could Diana comprehend. Mother and daughter were of vastly different temperament. Diana lacked Barbara's avid curiosity, her quick intelligence and ability to dream. Very much a pragmatist, when Barbara talked about becoming famous one day, Diana could not see that such a thing would ever occur. It was impossible, she would tell Barbara. 'You're not pretty enough.' She believed that to be true and felt she had to get her daughter to concentrate on a more reasonable goal. Barbara would come back with a cutting remark about Diana's lack of motivation, her allowing herself to be mistreated by Kind. The two women knew how to hurt each other most effectively.

Barbara entered Erasmus Hall High School in September 1955. Diana wanted her to take typing as an elective course her first term, to get all the nonsense about movies out of her head, to consider a sensible career, like being a secretary. Barbara would not hear of it and let her nails grow to ward off the dreaded prospect of typing lessons. She spent hours painting her lips a dark magenta and shadowing her eyes with blue make-up bought surreptitiously with her school-lunch money. 'Somehow,' she says, 'it made me think I was attractive.' She was hungry a lot of the time, and skinnier than ever, but it seemed important for her to prove to her mother and to Kind that she could be pretty. She remained a loner during her first year at Erasmus. It was not that she didn't want friends, *she did*, it was that she found it difficult to make the overtures. She had an unfortunate manner of putting potential friends off with what one schoolmate called, 'a smart-ass remark, just something that made you feel she thought she was smarter than you, like she was saying, "You dumb ox, don't you know *that*!" '

Erasmus Hall High School was one of the compensations for the many Jewish families living in Flatbush, for it held the highest scholastic rating of any public high school in Brooklyn or Manhattan. Founded in 1786 as a private academy by the venerable Dutch Reformed Church and on gifts from Aaron Burr, John Jay, Alexander Hamilton and other intellectuals, it became

ROOTS                                                                47

part of the public-school system two hundred years later. The original academy building with its hand-carved beams and clapboards was left standing in 1905 during the construction of a three-storey stone castellated building. The new edifice, a massive stone complex that took up a square city block, collegiate Gothic in design and separated by a grassy courtyard, was constructed around it. The school's enrolment exceeded 7,000 when Barbara, troubled and anti-social, entered aged thirteen, a year ahead of most of her peers.

The principal, Dr James McNeil, had been an air force colonel during the war and was an English teacher of some repute. Strait-laced and unap-proachable, he dressed in dark suits, conservative ties, vests, white shirts and pointed collars and operated the school like a flight squadron during wartime manoeuvres. His administrative assistant was Miss Grace L. Corey, who would dock teachers for being a minute late. One student recalled, 'That's the kind of school they ran. Nobody stepped out of line.'

It was the only high school in New York that taught classical Greek, and did not have girl cheerleaders. 'In every other high school, the kids went to study hall. In Erasmus, they went to "chapel" – which was the auditorium, but it had stained-glass windows. The Erasmus kids who were in government wore shirts and ties. They were college bound,' a classmate of Barbara's remembers.

Built like a medieval castle with an endless criss-crossing of corridors, the walk from one class room to another was exhausting and often difficult to make by the bell. 'I never knew how big Erasmus was,' another student recalled. 'I just walked in a door and stayed inside, going from classroom to classroom. I was a senior before I found out about the quad [the grassy square around the original structure] in the middle of the building.' Every day Barbara went from an apartment she loathed to a school that was a fortress, huge, intimidating. She almost always walked through the forbidding corridors by herself, posture haughty, diverting the glances of fellow students, always, *always* feeling the outsider.

Erasmus Hall serviced a large district with a variety of neighbourhoods and there was a dichotomy 'between the kids from the poor part of Flatbush ... and the ones from the rich'. Barbara lived in a lower-income but not an economically impoverished section of the area. It was true that a student's background often dictated the group with which he or she socialised. Yet, in a school the size of Erasmus with its highly diversified enrolment, taking in many ethnic roots and economic strata, there was certainly a niche for Barbara. But to find it she needed counselling and there was none to be had. Male students paid her little attention. Diana warned her never to hold hands with a boy, an idea that made her laugh.

'I was never asked out to any of the proms, and I never had a date for New Year's Eve,' she has said. 'I was pretty much of a loner. I was very independent. I never needed anybody, really.' This seems far from the truth. A classmate of hers recalled that Barbara often did do things to try to win friends and attention. 'Some of the kids wanted to set up a surprise for a teacher we liked who was celebrating his birthday. Barbara came up with a plan. She would "faint" in the hall adjoining the classroom. The teacher was called and ran to her side. A gift was then put on his desk. Barbara remained in a "faint" until all was clear. The teacher was completely fooled by her act. For a few days she seemed one of us. Then something happened. I don't know exactly what it was. But I think it had something to do with class elections. Her name was submitted for some office. But she wasn't elected, in fact she came in last.'

'She often appeared lonely,' a neighbour was later to claim. To counteract this she dug into her studies and was consistently in the top 10 per cent of her class. Knowledge excited her, was the only thing that made her feel exceptional. She liked knowing the answers, being the first one to raise her hand in class, to finish a test.

Still foregoing lunch in order to have an extra dime or quarter in her pocket, she would pose after school behind the curtains in photo booths, imitating her screen favourites. She had the voluptuous Mae West down pat – except for the swivelling hips which seemed to elude her, not surprisingly since she had so little flesh on her bones. She had seen a number of old Mae West movies and was fascinated by the ex-Brooklynite who had gone on to become a legend. To amuse her classmates she would do a takeoff of West spouting some of her most famous movie witticisms: to George Raft playing a gangster – 'Is that your gun in your pocket or are you *really* glad to see me?', or her oft-quoted philosophy – 'It's not the men in my life that count, it's the life in my men.' Yet Barbara never bothered to audition for school plays, 'Why go out for an amateurish high school production when you can do the real thing?' she later commented. Of course she was *not* doing 'the real thing' and it is much more likely that she was simply fearful of rejection.

One afternoon in 1956 when Barbara was fourteen, Louis Kind left the house on Newkirk Street ostensibly to buy a pack of cigarettes. He never returned. Once again Diana found office work and relied on neighbours to look after Rosalind. Although the apartment no longer had a tyrannising man at the helm, Kind's absence did not make Barbara's relationship with her mother any easier.

Without a man's presence, Diana lost interest in keeping the apartment attractive. Rather, she was concerned with minimising her work load. The couch and chairs in the living room were now covered in clear plastic and a girl's bare legs stuck to it on hot days. Lampshades were also covered, light switches wore protective shields and the kitchen floor was littered with newspaper after it had been washed. Barbara hated the pungent smell of the plastic, the absence of flowers, plants and bright toss pillows that she saw in other people's apartments. She seldom brought children home and Diana never entertained. They lived an insular life. Their occasional visits to Pulaski Street were never happy occurrences. They occasionally saw Manny's brother Phil and his wife Sylvia, but Aunt Anna, whom Barbara liked, lived in Connecticut and was too far away to visit often.

For many months after Kind's defection, Diana had only the small income she made from her office job. Finally, on 7 May 1957, she obtained a legal separation on the grounds of Kind's verbal abuse and was awarded $37 a week in support. Too often Kind fell far in arrears and never made up the deficit. This was the most difficult time in Barbara's childhood. There was not always enough to eat and Diana took on a second job, selling women's undergarments from a small valise she carried with her to the office or from apartment to apartment in her building.

In her freshman year Barbara took chorus and was a member of the Erasmus Choral Club, an interest she kept up throughout high school. She was aware that she possessed a good, clear voice, but had not given it much serious thought. Surrounded now by other singers of her age, she realised just how good her voice was and how fast she was able to grasp her part. Because her voice was stronger than other members of the chorus, Cosimo De Pietto, the choral director, placed her in the rear so that she would not overpower them. This disturbed her but she did not sing more softly to oblige. Solos, to Barbara's disappointment, usually went to Trudy Wallace, a pretty blonde with a pleasant soprano voice. Barbara had an unusual range, being able to sing both in chest and in head. She could reach and hold a high B flat. But she preferred the lower register that was used to advantage in popular and show music. She was therefore placed in the alto section of the Choral Club, where few female solos were required in the music that was performed.

She claims she had no thoughts of ever becoming a singer, although she had been singing for years to herself in the hallways of their apartment building, listening to the 'great echo sound ... thinking, "Oh, that's pleasant. It doesn't sound bad." ' She knew an enormous number of songs from Broadway shows, films and records. In winter she would often sit on the stairway with other kids in the building and lead them in the current popular songs. This won her new admiration. She was looked at for the first time in a different light and unlike her later experience at high school, it was because she *had* a strong voice, 'the loudest in the neighbourhood'. Conversely, she placed little importance upon this talent. Singing, she felt, was no big deal. 'It's only wind and noise. I open my mouth and the sound comes out,' she would later say. Much of this philosophy came from Diana, who thought popular music and the ability to sing it were of little worth.

Despite her own and Diana's dismissal of popular music and her singing talent, back in 1951, when she was only nine, Barbara had suddenly become consumed with the idea that she could be another Joni James, her favourite singer at the time and badgered Diana into taking her into New York and up to the studio of MGM Records, her idol's record label. As Diana had some errands to do in the city she had finally agreed to go with her to the recording studio. Barbara found out where the offices were and was the one who insisted on being heard once they got there. Mother and daughter had come in cold, without an introduction, agent, accompanist or musical arrangement. This took great *chutzpah* on Barbara's part and shows the tenacity of her will and her ability, even at this early age, to overpower her mother, who was certain her daughter's efforts would fail. When Barbara wanted something she jumped in, pushing aside all obstacles. In this instance, she also revealed a private need to prove she had talent as a singer that belies her future denials that she considered her singing voice was of no consequence.

For her audition, she sang Joni James's 'Have You Heard?' inside a glass booth, without accompaniment. Being caged in was a terrifying and claustrophobic experience that was to take years to overcome. Told to go home, study, and practise more, she did exactly that, but without benefit of professional help. Instead she spent more time in the hallways and lobby of their apartment house letting her voice bounce off the walls and echo back to her. When a neighbour complained, she would take herself to another part of the building or up to the roof to practise.

In the summer of 1955, the year she entered Erasmus Hall, Diana and the two girls had vacationed for a week in the Catskills, a gift paid for by Diana's family who were concerned about her health. They became friendly with a piano player from Brooklyn. Diana and Barbara sang some songs with him and he told them about Nola Studios in Steinway Hall on West 57th Street in Manhattan. The idea of recording her own singing voice appealed to Diana. The pianist agreed to go into New York with them. The Steinway showroom was on the ground floor, above it were studios occupied by theatrical teachers – dancing, piano, drama, voice – professional photographers and agents. Steinway Hall had several recording studios used mainly by fledgling singers and composers to make records to disperse to booking agents and producers. Anyone with four dollars to spend was welcome to cut two sides of a record. A sound engineer was supplied. You were given ten minutes to rehearse and then the needle cut into the acetate while the record was made. There were no retakes; what was recorded at that time was what you got.

In bird-like sound bites, Diana sang 'One Kiss', an operetta favourite. Barbara chose 'Zing Went the Strings of My Heart', a Judy Garland standard, and the 1930s ballad 'You'll Never Know', made popular by Alice Faye.

'My mother went first,' Streisand later recalled. 'She could hardly get a chorus in edgeways because the piano player kept launching into endless, elaborate refrains. As soon as he started that with me, I told him, "No, no we'll just do a *little* interlude and then I'll come back in." I had planned a simple

ending for "You'll Never Know", but got carried away. Those last few notes
". . . if you don't . . . *know-oh-oh* . . . now" took me by surprise. I guess it was
my first musical improvisation . . . [After I listened to the record] I wondered,
"Who was that? Where did that come from? It was like *The Exorcist.*" '

The making of this acetate record was one of the rare occasions where
mother and daughter shared a creative experience. Diana, in hopes of earning
some extra money, had renewed early aspirations to pursue a stage career. Any
such hope was shattered when she heard the playback. Her voice was ordinary
and she knew it. The amazing thing is that she did not recognise her daughter's
talent. The record, preserved lovingly by Barbara into her adult life, displays
not only a burgeoning talent but a rare individuality of style, but Diana told
Barbara to put aside any thoughts of a singing career. She believed she was
being protective, but was motivated by her own low esteem, fear of venturing
into unknown directions, her background that preached a woman was nothing
without a man, and that a *career* was something *he* had while *she worked*,
mainly to support herself until she married, and after, to supplement the
family income.

The following year, without Diana's knowledge, Barbara auditioned with a
group of other girls from her school for a radio show. She did a speech from
Shaw's *Saint Joan* – 'He who tells the truth shall surely be caught.' ('I always
felt that about myself,' she later said.) She was rejected, but one Saturday
afternoon in April 1956, she took the five dollars she had been given as a gift
from Diana for her fourteenth birthday (meant for her to purchase a blouse
or a sweater) and made her first solo trip out of Brooklyn by subway. The
local paper had printed a story that the Hollywood producer-director, Otto
Preminger, on a massive talent search for a young girl to play the title role of
Saint Joan in his next film, was having his staff conduct preliminary interviews
in New York on this day. It seemed fated. She went back to *Saint Joan*, studying
it at home and on the subway into New York. By the time she reached the
United Artists' offices where the interviews were being held, she could almost
feel the fire that had consumed Joan of Arc. When she filled out her application,
she was told she was too young. Mr Preminger was looking for a girl in her
late teens, nearer the age of Joan of Arc when she raised the siege at Orleans.
Barbara argued with the assistant to give her a chance and began to recite
some lines from Shaw's play.

'I'm sorry,' the assistant said, and turned away. 'Next!' he called.

She left the building feeling cheated, angry. She had not been given a fair
chance. The film company's offices were mid-town. She walked over to the
Cort Theater on 49th Street and bought a ticket for the matinée performance
of *The Diary of Anne Frank*, a poignant story about a sensitive young Jewish
girl who grows into womanhood while hiding from the Nazis in an attic in
Amsterdam with her family. She had chosen this particular play because it had

been discussed in her English class at school. 'At first, I was awfully disappointed, looking at the dreary setting,' she later commented. Then she became deeply and emotionally involved.[1] Seated at the rear of the second balcony, she recalled thinking that she could go up on the stage and play any role 'without any trouble at all'. Perhaps Saint Joan would have been a stretch, but Anne Frank and her family were people she could identify with – they were Jewish and had suffered. She had found a more accessible target for her unfocused ambitions – the stage.

'It was a thrilling experience,' she said of that time, 'sitting in the last seat of the balcony – I think the ticket was $2.85 in those days. There was something wonderful about not being able to afford to sit very close because when you sit far away you see the whole stage, you know. You don't see the reality of the actor's pores, you don't see the make-up. You get swept along with the illusion, with the make-believe truth.'

When she returned home late that day she told her mother about her disappointing interview with Preminger's assistant and her excitement when she saw *Anne Frank*. 'I've decided that no matter what, I'm going to be an actress,' she announced. Diana tried again to discourage her. 'I was so sure Barbara would be a fiasco,' she said later, adding that she wanted to 'save her from utter humiliation'.

Certain that Barbara would fail, that she was not pretty enough, talented enough to make a success of it, Diana did everything she could to discourage her. She was placing herself in her daughter's shoes. She had been too terrified, too insecure to compete in the world, to fight for anything. She thought it was love that guided her in discouraging what she saw as her daughter's futile dreams. Barbara was sure it was the opposite. She would always doubt the depth of Diana's love, resent her mother's stultifying attitude towards anything she set out to accomplish. It would form the basis of her life-long struggle to come to terms with her past.

Right now she had too much she wanted to accomplish in what she thought would be a very short time – her last high school years – to let her mother's negativism place obstacles in her path.

---

[1] Nearly thirty years later, Streisand visited Amsterdam and the tiny attic where Anne Frank had lived before being discovered by the Nazis and sent to a concentration camp where she later died. Streisand was overcome with emotion, shaking with sobs when she came back outside. It took several minutes for her to control herself.

# 6

**B**ARBARA WAS DETERMINED, possessed. No one had ever been able to stop her from doing what she wanted to do, but with Louis Kind's departure, when she was fourteen, she became a free spirit. At school she began to make friends, to laugh more easily and to wise-crack. She was outspoken in class, never shy about asking questions. She wanted reasons for everything.

In a high school noted for its allegiance to propriety, she stood out. 'I was this absolute misfit,' she confesses. Believed to have been the first girl in Erasmus Hall ever to wear mascara to class, she also accented her eyes with blue shadow, bleached blonde streaks into her hair, painted her dagger-long nails blood red, gold or black and remained razor thin. Yet, the overall effect was not cheap, it was theatrical. Many of the girls in her class admired her individuality and thought she was attractive. Classmates remember her beautiful eyes, expressive hands and the bravura way in which she carried herself. 'If only looks mattered, she could have been cast as Cleopatra,' one friend commented.

Cleverly, she played up these attributes. Her intense interest in offbeat fashion was not simply teenage rebellion. It was a means to personal expression, of setting herself apart from the rest of the girls at Erasmus. She liked the idea of being exotic, foreign, different, but it never gained her popularity with the boys in her school. She had a crush on Bobby Fischer, who was in the class below her and already an international chess champion. They would have lunch every day and 'he would sit there, laughing hysterically, reading *Mad* magazine. Right? And he wore these earflaps on his ears. He was always alone and very peculiar. But I found him sexy,' she recalled. However, this never flowered into a romance because Fischer seemed to regard her as little more than a lunchtime buddy.

Holidays and school dances threw her into a state of agitation. There were no invitations. Teenage boys found her too threatening. They were more comfortable with girls who fitted into neat categories; she was smarter than most of the boys and not afraid to let them know it. She fought disdain with disdain and developed what would one day become the famous Streisand shrug, left shoulder raised and angled forward, head turned sideways, chin up, eyebrow arched. Thought to be arrogant by her male peers, she was merely being defensive. If she encountered a boy in the hallways or rooms of Erasmus who seemed to be smirking at her, or whom she had heard pass a rude remark, she would slow down as she neared him, then give him an exaggerated shrug. She developed various expressions – boredom, happiness, sophistication – in front of the bathroom mirror or while aping cigarette commercials. One expression that she captured and used as a protective mask for her true feelings, was a cool, detached smile that she would adopt whenever she was in a public situation – at school gatherings or when she had to wait in line. She had the uncomfortable feeling at such times that everyone was looking at her critically.

Saturday afternoon movies remained a ritual. She would return home grumpy for the rest of the weekend because after the glamorous settings and sophisticated clothes she had seen in the films the Newkirk Street apartment and her limited wardrobe depressed her. She would read the *New York Times* apartment ads in the hopes of convincing Diana to move to Manhattan. 'Ma, look, one bedroom and it's only $105, why can't we afford that?' she would ask her mother, who was having trouble making ends meet at half that rent on the small income from the office job she held in a New York City public high school. Rosalind was now attending school and Barbara was expected to look after her when she got home from Erasmus, but there was always someone in the building who would help out. Louis Kind remained perpetually late with his support payments, often missing one. Diana had no money for extras. Barbara was only given what was essential. Small luxuries were supplied by her deftly performed shoplifting. 'I wouldn't take just stuff,' she once said, laughing in a high trill as she revealed her petty adventures in crime. 'I would walk around the store until I found a receipt on the floor and then go get that item – a compact, a lipstick, books, and candy – cinnamon hots, jujubes – they were my favourites, and even salt shakers. I love salt shakers, especially those fancy ones . . . whatever – and return most of what I took for the money.' She never got caught and Diana was unaware of her daughter's transgressions.

A small inheritance came her way in the late spring of 1957. Her grandfather Streisand had died and left her $150, a stroke of good fortune of which her mother did not immediately inform her. To Diana, her daughter's windfall was a *mitzvah*, a godsend. Two of Barbara's bicuspids became abscessed about the time of the funeral and the dentist insisted they must be pulled and replaced. Diana had not known how she was going to pay for the work. The two infected teeth were pulled before Barbara heard about her small legacy and she had quite a different idea on how she would have spent it.

An older girl who lived in the neighbourhood had spent the previous summer with a stock company in Malden Bridge, New York, a small town in the Adirondacks, twenty miles east of Albany, the state capital. Barbara questioned her endlessly about the experience. It sounded the most exciting place in the world to be if you were looking forward to a career in the theatre. Not only were stagecraft and acting taught, the students performed in well-known plays before a paying audience. Intrigued, she planned to do anything so that she could attend the following summer. She would wash dishes, wait on tables, anything to pay her tuition. A battle of wills between mother and daughter was fought. Barbara refused to part with what remained of her $150 to have the missing teeth replaced. 'You can't go around with gaps in your teeth!' Diana shouted. 'You'll look ridiculous!'

'I'll do something so that I won't have gaps!' Barbara hollered back. She bought some Aspergum (because the colour was close to that of tooth enamel), chewed it to make it pliable, moulded two teeth from it and pressed them into the empty spaces in her mouth. Diana finally gave in, as she usually did, and up Barbara went to the Malden Bridge Playhouse, with a supply of gum for false-teeth replacements.

Conditions were primitive. The playhouse was reached by a dirt road. Rough-hewn cabins offered bare essentials, nothing more. Water ran icy from the taps. Except for the main building, toilets were housed in outside structures. The scenery was, however, picturesque with a stream to one side of the heavily wooded property. The theatre was a converted farm building, but the enthusiasm of the group made up for what else might have been lacking. Barbara pitched in without complaint doing the most menial of tasks, sweeping the stage, helping to build and paint sets, even cleaning toilets.

Two of the plays staged that summer were John Patrick's *Teahouse of the August Moon* (based on a book by Vern J. Sneider) and William Marchant's *The Desk Set*. Streisand has been quoted as saying her first stage role was riding a goat in the John Patrick play, a tremendous Broadway success which had been recently transferred into a popular film. 'Incidentally,' John Patrick (whom everyone knows as 'Pat') confided to this author, 'the report that Streisand rode a goat in *Teahouse* must be wrong. You can't ride a goat. I know this as when I had a farm I had a hundred and fifty milk goats. In the play, however, I did have three goats riding in the back of a jeep and this is where the kids [the young characters in the play] rode. Perhaps this is where Streisand fitted in.'

The stage at Malden Bridge Playhouse was not large enough to accommodate a jeep. Patrick suggests that a cart loaded with two or three young performers and pulled by a defiant goat across the creaking boards of the stage marked the theatre debut of Barbara Streisand. Next she had a small role as a man-crazy receptionist in *The Desk Set*. 'Can't you just see me at fifteen coming on the stage, sitting down on a desk, swinging my legs and playing sexy?' she asked an interviewer once. The weekly local newspaper obviously had not found this difficult. 'The girl who plays the office vamp is very sexy, and her name is Barbara Streisand. *Down boys*,' its reviewer wrote.

The years of studying the walk and posture, the come-on looks and seductive smiles of sexy movie stars had contributed to a facile ability to project sexuality on stage. When she was acting she could be anyone she wanted to be. She liked the idea of being the vamp, of being desirable to men. Sex was a subject never discussed by Diana except in the form of a warning: a nice Jewish girl doesn't even think about such things. Barbara, and most of the girls she knew, thought constantly about it despite such admonishments. On stage she could live out her fantasy: she was beautiful and sexy enough to win Marlon Brando, her favourite actor. She had, in fact, developed a sensuality that she incorporated into her personality even at this young age, a flirtatious way of crossing her legs, holding her head, of pulling back her shoulders and thrusting her small but well-formed bosoms forward. She has said that a young man in the stock company took an interest in her. He was eighteen, Christian, with blond good looks and a glib tongue. They remained after rehearsals sitting in the empty theatre talking. He was off to university in the fall. But after college he claimed to be Hollywood bound. He told her he thought she had real talent, all she needed was the experience. They went for private walks along the wooded path of the narrow river that ran along one side of Malden Bridge. She claims Diana's warnings were heeded, but attraction to and for the young man was obvious to her colleagues.

The summer sped by. She had found what she was certain would be her life's work – acting. Determined to pay to get her teeth fixed – and to go back to Malden Bridge the following summer – on her return to Brooklyn she took a job evenings at the New China Restaurant, managed by her neighbours, Muriel and Jimmie Choy. Good at computing change, she became a cashier. Her nails were now Fu Manchu long and vividly lacquered, but she developed a way of punching the cash register keys without harming them. She also had acquired a working Chinese vocabulary and, she says, Muriel gave her a textbook explanation of the art of having sex along with her introduction to another culture. 'I loved the idea of belonging to a small minority group,' she professed. 'It was the world against us in the Chinese restaurant.' Diana was constantly lecturing her not to eat the *trayf* served at the New China. Barbara brought home shopping bags of day-old vegetables but at work she ate forbidden moo-shoo-pork.

Diana could not control her daughter's dietary habits once she had gained her first taste of independence, nor could she keep her at home. On the nights that she was not at school or working at the New China, she would take the IRT subway (which cost 15 cents) at the corner of Nostrand Avenue and go into Greenwich Village to hang out at the Cherry Lane Theater, where an acquaintance from Malden Bridge was working. Finally, the manager let her help backstage. One of the young performers, Anita Miller, who was married to Allan Miller, a drama teacher and member of the Lee Strasberg's Actors Studio where Marlon Brando had once studied, took an interest in her. Barbara went to the New York Public Library on 42nd Street and immersed herself in the plays of Ibsen, O'Neill, Williams and Inge. She would discuss a character with Anita and when the stage was not in use, try out a speech or two, always by memory, never with playscript in hand, and often – because she said it made things seem more real – with footlights or a spot. 'There's *something* about her,' Anita told her husband. 'You should talk to her. You should teach her.'

Anita Miller recognised that Barbara's was a charismatic personality that projected extremely well on stage. Rough and as untutored as she was, she seized one's attention with her inimitable speaking voice, natural, low and rushing, but not in any way stagy. She had a special way of suddenly stopping to stress key words that gave fresh insight into the lines she delivered, an eye-catching grace in the way she moved her exotic, elongated hands with their amazing fingernail extensions, and an uncanny instinct in how to stand in the stage lights to create the proper mood.

Allan Miller had her read for him. He agreed with his wife that she had potential but he did not like the idea of encouraging a fifteen-year-old offbeat-looking girl to go into the theatre where there were so few roles for anyone of her age and appearance. He told his wife to forget it. Anita persisted. One night, following a matinée performance, she brought Barbara back to their apartment for dinner. After they had eaten, Barbara did a scene for him. 'It was the single *worst* audition I think I've ever seen in my life,' he recalled, although unable to remember what scene she did. But he was struck by something raw and compelling in her. 'She didn't even try to imitate other actors. There was something striving in her to be really genuinely available to herself, but she didn't know how to put it together ... She was so full of this young, raw eagerness that I finally said, "OK, listen. I'll give you a scholarship to one of my classes. And she said, "I'll take them *all*." '

She managed as many classes with Miller as she could fit into her difficult schedule which included daily attendance at Erasmus, homework and cramming for mid-term finals. Battles ensued almost every time she left the house. Diana felt that she was going wild (Greenwich Village was filled with free-spirited youths and depraved elders in her mother's view), and would get a bad reputation. Neither her mother's pleas nor her tears could keep Barbara at home. She refused to be a babysitter for Rosalind. Her resentment of her little half-sister had not diminished with Louis Kind's departure. Rather it had grown as Rosalind occupied more and more of Diana's time and attention.

'I never meant to neglect Barbara,' Diana mused later in life. 'She was very independent and when she was in her teens Rosalind was a little girl, half her age. I thought I could do for her what I had failed to do with Barbara – be more involved in her life. The truth was, Barbara never let me be that. She never wanted advice, only approval. She frightened me a little. She was so smart, had an answer for most things. And what questions she did have I never knew how to answer.'

Like her father before her, Barbara was living a dual life, scuttling back and forth on the subway between Brooklyn and Manhattan as he had once done and, with his inherited energy, coping with everything. Always a top student, her grades were in the 90s. She excelled in Spanish. She had a natural talent for language and liked to experiment, speaking with a French, Spanish, German or Russian accent with much overkill. Her regard for the all-girl Choral Club held despite her inability to win the director's favour and her difficulty in singing Christian carols containing the word *Jesus*. The sound of female voices in harmony attracted her. She still preferred to sing popular to semi-classical music and she never asked to move from the alto to the soprano section. There was a good reason for this. Better clarity of diction could be achieved in the lower voice register and the words of a song meant almost more to her than the music. Unless she could convey the meaning of the words she sang, it seemed an empty exercise and one that did not interest her.

Occasionally she would see Erasmus Hall friends after classes but she wasn't like the other girls who hung out at Garfield's Cafeteria to meet their girlfriends and mingle with the neighbourhood boys. Her years at Erasmus Hall could not end too soon for her. She was to graduate the following year, June 1959, but she had accrued enough credits to allow her to do so six months earlier. Being an actress and going on the stage was all she could think about. She barraged Allan Miller with questions about what she was doing wrong or right and had he seen this actress or that and what did he remember most about their performance. She was working hard to get rid of her Brooklyn accent but was intent on keeping her own personality. Her years as a movie fan had taught her one thing: the actresses who became stars were unique and memorable characters. She told Miller she wanted to play all the great women's roles – Juliet, Desdemona, Ophelia – but she thought if she did she should come up with a new approach.

Working at the New China in the few spare hours she had each week, she earned enough money to have her two missing teeth replaced and, as well, to return to Malden Bridge in the summer of 1958. This time she immediately found her niche. Cast as the tomboy sister, Millie, in William Inge's *Picnic*, she split the skirt of her costume to the director's fury so that she could place her leg on a table in comedic imitation of Marlene Dietrich, a piece of stage business which was cheered by the audience and then was left in. Her next role was as the uneducated, over-sexed ingenue in Erskine Caldwell's lusty hit play *Tobacco Road*. She had the ability to uncover the humour in her lines and to speak them as if they were ad-libbed, fresh, giving the character greater humanity.

A small part as a French maid in Sandy Wilson's musical pastiche of the twenties, *The Boyfriend*, the first time she would sing on a stage, came next. 'She was extraordinary,' recalled actor Ron Rifkin, who also was performing at the theatre that summer. 'She made up this crazy accent – French from the moon – and during the rehearsal lunch breaks, she wouldn't eat but would stay in the empty theatre practising a song, "A Sleepin' Bee", [from the 1954 Broadway musical *House of Flowers*]. She was obsessed by it. There was a single-mindedness about her, a drive that I had never seen before.'

Rifkin appears to be the only co-worker to have recognised her singing ability. None the less, her brief appearance in *The Boyfriend* was a momentous step in her life. The short song she sang was a throwaway, of little importance in the score. She had tried out for the show with much trepidation, unsure that her voice was really any good and although she had no chance to display any true vocal ability, the idea that she *could* sing well enough to land a job in a musical, however small the part, began to brew. She knew if she was to attempt to try something along that line, she would have to have an audition piece and so she had chosen 'A Sleepin' Bee', an odd, non-commercial ballad – but very beautiful – that required as much acting as singing and which it seemed no other job aspirant would use.

Her work with Allan Miller continued. On her return from Malden Bridge, the first scene she did for him in his class was an earthy one of female seduction from Tennessee Williams's *The Rose Tattoo*. The character was a mature widow who finally puts aside the memory of her dead husband when she meets a robust truck driver. Barbara thought she couldn't do it but Miller convinced her she could if she kept the right image in her mind as she played it. 'A week or two later,' Miller recalled, 'she comes in with this scene. Within one minute, the boy doing it with her was beet red with embarrassment. It was the sexiest scene I think I have ever watched in my life.'

'It was a scene of sexual exploration,' Streisand herself explained. 'All I did was pick a technical task, which was just physically touching the actor I played with. At one point, he stood up and I stood on his feet; one time I jumped on his back; one time I pretended I was blind, and while I was talking I touched his face. It was this awkward sexuality. I didn't know what I would do next ... it's what they call inspiration.'

'The poor guy in the scene with her', Miller continued, 'couldn't deal with it. He could hardly put his hand on her without her turning it into a red-hot iron.'

Her talent for displaying an almost raw sexuality was the end result of all her self-practice in looking sexy. She now knew how to internalise the feeling by concentrating on something that could make her sexual temperature rise.

In the scene from *The Rose Tattoo*, it had been the need to touch and be touched. Once she mastered this technique, it seemed to free her as an actress, enabling her to begin to dredge up her own deeply felt emotions in performance, although off-stage she kept the same trained cool detachment caused by her fear of rejection. Among the Cherry Lane players, and in and out of the Millers' apartment and Allan Miller's teaching classes, were many attractive young actors, but Barbara was not ready for a relationship that might interfere with her dedication to her purpose of becoming a professional *and* famous actress. After all, Susan Strasberg was seventeen when she played Anne Frank on Broadway, the same age as Jean Seberg who had won the film role of Joan of Arc during Preminger's talent search.

The Millers had two small dogs and Barbara traded off lessons by dogsitting. By the end of a few weeks she was staying in Manhattan with them and commuting to Erasmus Hall to attend classes. Unable to get Barbara to return to Brooklyn, Diana called Miller and accused him of keeping her under-age daughter from her mother and her home. Miller left the decision to Barbara, who chose to remain with him and his wife. This was a wounding response which caused a deeper chasm between mother and daughter. Barbara was only sixteen at the time, and it would have been possible for Diana to seek a court order to make her return home. She did not, knowing that it would only make matters worse between them. Despite her anger and resentment, she was also confident that the Millers were good, respectable people.

Streisand has claimed that until this time the only books she had read other than those assigned in English classes were Nancy Drew mysteries, but her work with the Millers fired her with the need to read plays by great writers. The dramas she most liked were the ones that had once starred the likes of Bernhardt and Duse; those by Alexandre Dumas *fils*, Greek tragedies, Russian novels. Tolstoy's *Anna Karenina*, she says, changed her life.

'I had never been exposed to literature, to painting, to classical music. I remember hearing Respighi's *Pines of Rome* that summer; *The Rite of Spring* by Stravinsky. Can you imagine what that's like? To hear that music for the first time ... It was a very vivid experience, that first hearing of classical music when I was sixteen.'

A school paper written by her father at the same age had been the motivation for her cultural baptism. 'At sixteen, he wrote about all the things he loved, and I read it, and it was all the things I loved – I read Tolstoy for the first time, heard classical music for the first time. I went to the 42nd Street Library and read Victorien Sardou, Alexandre Dumas,' she said later, ticking off the similarities. 'Even though I never knew him, I am very much like my father.' She paused dramatically. 'That was the most exciting time of my life, I think.'

Her tendency was to dramatise her life, to reinvent certain periods of the past, to place an emphasis on events and non-events that altered their importance. Her English classes at Erasmus before she was sixteen certainly introduced her to literature – Hawthorne, Poe, Melville, Henry James, George Eliot. Diana liked to listen to light classical music and operetta on the radio. Shelley was an art major. Barbara, too, had been exposed to the arts, she simply had not pursued them further until the age of sixteen.

Her passion to consume new foods, culture, education was enormous. She was not satisfied to limit her acting lessons to Allan Miller. She wanted to work with the man *he* had learned from, Lee Strasberg, the master of theatre technique at that time. She wrote letters to him that she was yet too insecure to mail. In them she detailed her reactions to Miller's classes. The late 1950s in New York were an exciting time for young performers. Lee Strasberg's Actors Studio was the centre for *method* acting, a technique inspired by Stanislavsky's teaching which stressed the importance of the actor's inner identification with the character and the actor's natural use of body and voice. The Studio (as it was called) exerted considerable influence on the American theatre and cinema during that decade, having nurtured the talents of Marlon Brando, Montgomery Clift, James Dean, Eli Wallach, Paul Newman, Joanne Woodward and even Marilyn Monroe, who had fled Hollywood in 1955 to study what she termed 'serious acting' with Strasberg.

Suddenly, off-Broadway was burgeoning, bustling, electrifying – the place for serious theatre that found its home in vast, empty warehouses, small, raftered attics, vacant manufacturing lofts, the back rooms of bars and unused storage cellars, and the Village was the teeming heart of it all. Cabarets sprang up like wild flowers and a great army of struggling, unknown young performers lived on the edge of poverty and did so with willing enthusiasm while either auditioning or appearing in one of the dozens of Lilliputian venues. There was a sense of being in at the beginning of something terribly exciting. Unless you were in a Broadway show or you were a cabaret artist who could play the great clubs and hotel rooms, your pay as a performer was nominal, if at all. You acted because you loved the theatre and because you believed in the American dream that could breed hope for sudden stardom, a life where *you* were one of the specially anointed rich and famous.

Struggling neophytes like Streisand shared digs and mooched off friends. You learned to create a cup of free soup at the Automat by taking the tomato ketchup that was supplied for use with a paid-for meal and pouring some into a cup of boiling water provided for tea drinkers. 'Making it' meant eating in real restaurants where you were served and having your own apartment in a building with an elevator and a doorman out front. The lucky ones were few and Streisand's wish was to be among them as soon as possible.

Whereas she had hated being poor in Brooklyn she was energised by her early days of being nearly penniless in the Village, sleeping on someone's couch in a four-flight walk-up or a cold-water flat, gorging herself whenever she was invited out for a meal. The Village was young, experimental. There was the whiff of newness in the air – fresh, brash, biting. Barbara was drugged with the exhilaration of it and who could blame her? This was her time of self-discovery. She believed she could do anything. Nothing daunted her – empty purse, rejections, or her mother's harassment. She never sacrificed her work at Erasmus Hall. 'I learned a lot in Brooklyn,' she later acknowledged. 'Out there you couldn't be dumb and survive.'

Equally aware that you had to make your own luck, she never turned down a chance to audition for a good role however ill-suited it might seem to her looks, age and talent. At the same time she nurtured an unconcealed contempt for producers and casting directors. This perverse and imperious attitude did not endear her to the prospective hirer, but it did provide her with a ready excuse for failure to win a part. 'I would read magazines like *Show Business* in which they announced casting calls,' she recalled. 'I used to look like a real beatnik. I wore black stockings and had this trench coat and they wanted walk-ons for a breatnik. Now, you don't have to be Sarah Bernhardt to do a walk-on as a beatnik! I remember going to this audition and they said, "Well, we have to see your work." I said, "Why do you have to see my work? It's a walk-on. I don't even have to say anything." It was so nuts ... people in these powerful positions. That's when I got so angry and said, "Screw you, cause I ain't comin' back and asking you for no work." I was feeling this strange power of struggle. I felt that it was a very undignified position to ask anyone for a job. I decided I would design hats before I begged anyone for a job. That', she adds, 'was when I started to sing.'

The first person to whom she confided her decision to try her luck at singing was Carl Esser, a young acting hopeful and guitarist who had befriended her. He found her naturally musical and sometimes when the Cherry Lane was deserted, they would use a corner of the stage where Barbara would sing to his accompaniment. It was also about this time that she met Cis Corman. Married to a very nice young man who was just starting out in practice as an analyst, the older Cis, who was taking acting classes, became Barbara's confidante and adviser. Despite this, many months were to pass since their friendship began before Cis even became aware that Barbara had any vocal talent or thoughts along that line. One day Barbara asked her to stay a little later at the theatre. They were joined by Esser.

'I want to sing something for you,' Barbara told Cis, 'but you have to turn around so that I can't see you or I won't be able to do it.'

Cis did as she was asked. Barbara sang 'A Sleepin' Bee'. Cis was overwhelmed. What she heard was a voice and interpretation that was natural, yet highly professional, and lyrics that were phrased so meaningfully that the singer seemed to be inventing them. She encouraged her young friend and this new confidence bonded them further.

But aside from Cis and Esser she kept this side of her talent to herself for the time being, practising *a cappella* or with Esser whenever she had a private place to do so. Suddenly, she discovered something in herself when she sang. There was an involuntary connection between her throat and her heart. 'When I sing, something happens, and I can't even tell you what is in that process,' she later said, 'a certain musicality to the voice that is not even verbal. Speaking it's sometimes harder to connect the heart and the throat.' She chose ballads, show tunes, emotional songs. 'I don't know how to sing on the beat,' she explained, 'and I think you have to sing on the beat, in pop music.'

To her despair at this time she developed a serious case of acne. Her insecurities intensified. She took a part-time job as a theatre usher to help with her expenses and later claimed that she would turn her face away when people spoke to her, 'so that they wouldn't recognise me [when she became famous]'. The reality was more moving. She was self-conscious and embarrassed that she had acne. The skin eruptions could be partially masked with the use of thick make-up but the problem remained and caused her much angst. She took to wearing no make-up whenever possible, hoping it would help eliminate the condition. It became a daunting problem.

In October 1958, she was cast in a play called *Seawood* by the author-producer Armand de Beauchamp. Joan Rivers, then using her family name, Joan Molinsky, was also in the cast. ' "It's not the best production you'll ever be in and no money [I was told], but it can be a showcase." I said fine,' Rivers remembered. '*Showcase* is the talisman word which electrifies actors, enticing them into all kinds of absurdities in the hope that some agent will materialise and see gleams of talent.'

Armand de Beauchamp conducted his School for the Theater in an old sixth-floor brownstone walk-up. The attic above these quarters, named appropriately the Garret Theater, was where he staged his plays and it held – at full capacity – no more than twenty seats. De Beauchamp was a tall, pale, fleshy young man with flowing blond hair who was in the habit of wearing heavy, knee-high, storm-trooper boots. He would stare at his cast with faded, incurious blue eyes.

Readings and rehearsals were held in his living room. 'The place seemed furnished by an eccentric, impoverished maiden aunt with no taste and too much proximity to a Salvation Army,' Rivers recalled. There was a broken-down sofa. Tables held lamps with 'shades mottled black from burn spots'. A coffee table, once on someone's lawn, rusted and peeling, was littered with dog-eared *Theater Arts* magazines. On the blotched beige-papered walls 'were photographs of his grateful students, not one of them recognisable except for Tab Hunter,[1] prominently displayed and frequently mentioned by Armand', Rivers continues.

[1] Tab Hunter (born Arthur Gelien) had made his movie debut in 1950, at the age of

Rivers also remembered 'a skinny high school girl with a large nose and a pin that said GO ERASMUS' on her blouse. 'We had immediate rapport, maybe because she seemed a tough little hustler ... but obviously still vulnerable ... Despite being the youngest person by far, she was very outgoing and at the first rehearsal came right over to me and said, "Hi, what's your name? My name's Barbara Streisand."'

What impressed Rivers most was that Barbara was 'carrying at her age a full theatrical make-up kit with greasepaint in *tubes* and an Equity card earned in summer stock [Malden Bridge]'. Barbara did not befriend Rivers. She was always judgmental about the actors and directors with whom she worked. If she felt she had nothing to learn from them – a snap decision she often made – she did not encourage familiarity. Rivers was a complete novice at this time and Barbara felt more knowledgeable. She was not cold or indifferent, just self-involved. Cast in the play as lesbian lovers, they rehearsed their parts for two weeks. This was during a record January cold spell and de Beauchamp could not afford heat so during rehearsals the cast wore coats and gloves. The play was set in a cottage in the heat of summer and on opening night they almost froze in their skimpy beach-style costumes. To ward off frostbite, they waited for their entrances in front of the kitchen stove in the apartment while the small audience filed up the rickety stairs past them to the unheated attic theatre.

'The actual performance is a blur – the mind protects itself,' Rivers joked. 'I do remember I had a big love scene where I told Barbara I loved her very much and she rejected me and I had a knife in my hand and tried to kill her and then myself. I also remember a horrendous lot of coughing [from the audience] like a tubercular ward ...' A review in the next issue of *Show Business* proclaimed that the acting could not be evaluated because the material was so bad. De Beauchamp was undaunted and the play continued to run for six weeks to near-empty houses. One evening, about fifteen minutes before curtain, Rivers, descending the staircase of de Beauchamp's apartment, met Streisand on her way up. 'It's closed,' Rivers said. 'There's no play.'

Streisand shrugged. 'That's just as well. I got finals.'

She graduated from Erasmus two weeks later, at the end of January 1959, with a 93 per cent average and a medal for special achievement in Spanish. Trudy Wallace, who was in the Choral Club with her, was voted class singer. Streisand was so disturbed over this that years later resentment edged her words as she spoke of the still unknown opera hopeful: '*She* was going to be a big star they said.'

eighteen, in *The Lawless*. His all-American, blond, athletic good looks made him a teenage and homosexual idol during the 1950s. He appeared in many films, on television and in recent years on Broadway and in three campy movies pairing him with female impersonator Divine.

Shelley, now working in Manhattan, kept an eye on her and tried to steer her towards furthering her education, but to no avail. It does not seem that she made any college applications or cared about taking the final college boards. True, money was short, but her grades were high enough for her to have applied for a partial scholarship. The reality was that she was driven by one, and only one, aspiration – to become a rich and famous actress. To do so she would have to make enough money to tide her over until she found employment in the theatre. Her goal was $750. Shelley was an assistant art director at Ben Sackheim Advertising and he secured her a job as a receptionist for $90 a week. Reluctantly she agreed to a plan that her mother and brother devised. She would return to Newkirk Street, commute back and forth to Manhattan, and put away half of her salary until she had saved the money she required. The arrangement was not a happy one. She now had to contend with Rosalind, an overweight child of eight, who felt some resentment at the return of her older half-sister into a household that she had dominated in her absence. Nor was the arrangement an easy one for Diana. Her two daughters bickered constantly and Barbara would shout at her mother, 'Why do you keep pushing food in her mouth? She's fat and at this rate she's going to be obese.'

Actually, Barbara had a voracious appetite. She loved to eat and having often denied herself lunch as a young woman to buy make-up, food was the greatest reward she could give herself. She remained pencil-sharpened thin due to her tremendous nervous energy, chewed gum when she wasn't smoking a cigarette or eating, and kept up a steady flow of conversation if she felt so inclined. She hated her job and paid little attention to the way she dressed to go to work.

Ben Sackheim, her boss, had an eye for pretty girls and Barbara resembled none of the attractive women among his fifty or so female employees. 'She was waiflike, her hair pinned carelessly on top of her head. She wasn't attractive, well-dressed or even kempt,' Milton Mensch, an account supervisor with the same company recalled. 'Her dresses looked as if they needed to be pressed. And she had a terrible complexion – adolescence, I thought.

'Shelley and I used to have lunch together and two or three times Barbara joined us at a small restaurant near the office in mid-town Manhattan. Barbara spoke about her ambitions in the theatre and I thought, "How is this girl going to make it?" She had a mouth like a truck driver and used four-letter words comfortably. She quit after three or four months and shortly after she left Shelley asked me to see if my brother-in-law Ralph Mann, an agent, would represent her. She went to see him and Ralph as graciously as possible said *no*. He told me she didn't look like she could get an audience to rise to its feet.'

Again she left Diana and Brooklyn, this time for a short while she shared an apartment with Marilyn Fried, a friend from the Cherry Lane Theater. 'We lived in total poverty on Forty-Eighth Street,' Fried recounted. 'Each of us was getting thirty-two dollars a week in unemployment cheques. It barely covered the rent and our fees for acting classes. Once a week when it really got bad each of us had to go to see Mama, to get the bread and the margarine and the soup. Barbara would go to Brooklyn and I'd go to the Bronx to mine. We'd both come back with the groceries and we'd take everything out of the boxes in the kitchen and put it in the refrigerator. That is how we survived.

'Once Mrs Kind came down to Miller's workshop. She did not say a word after the performance. There was this terrible silence. Then, when we got upstairs to our apartment, it began. Her mother said that Barbara should get a job because she did not have the ability to be an actress. We spent half an hour in the bedroom listening to this nonsense. I was heartbroken because she was not encouraging Barbara ... One night Barbara and I sat together wondering what we would like most to do if ever we made it as actresses and she said, "First of all, I want to buy my mother a mink coat."'

This shocked Fried, who did not feel she should comment on how strange she found this wish in view of Diana's negative attitude toward Barbara's career. However, this was exactly what motivated Barbara's desire to give her mother such an extravagant gift. 'I'll show you!' she was saying. 'You thought I could never become rich and a star!'

Diana urged her to return to Newkirk Street. Shelley offered a small loan if she changed her mind about college, but she was consumed with the need to make her mark as quickly as she could. She had dreams – big dreams: stardom, nothing less would be acceptable. She intended to show Brooklyn, her family, her classmates that they were wrong about her. She was a winner. Not quite seventeen when she graduated from Erasmus Hall, she expected to be on her way to her goal in a year's time. Meanwhile, she continued to usher during Saturday matinée and evening performances in Broadway theatres. When there was no job, she would go back on unemployment.

Thinking perhaps that her own ethnic roots were a deterrent, she took the name Angelina Scarangella from the New York telephone book. Newly named, her hair dyed red, dressed in black tights, feather boas and 1925 hats, found for little money in Village secondhand stores, she went out unsuccessfully on auditions and finally dropped the *nom de plume*. Without telling Allan Miller, she started acting classes simultaneously with Eli Rill, also a disciple of Lee Strasberg. Her ability to make the other students laugh infuriated Rill. 'I kept telling her she had to develop what she had and not try to be somebody else,' Rill remembered. 'She would make it clear that my role was to make her into a tragic muse.'

She was still working on songs with Carl Esser and, except for Cis Corman, had not yet sung in front of anyone else. One evening Marilyn Fried was in the bedroom of their small apartment and Barbara was in the living room with Esser. 'He was strumming a guitar,' Fried recalled. 'I suddenly heard this remarkable voice coming out of the living room. My immediate reaction was to go to the radio and find out who was singing so marvellously. But the radio was not on. I realised there must be someone in this tiny apartment who had this magnitude, this power. [I went into the room] and asked Barbara, "Who was singing?" She said, "I was." ' Fried insisted that she must do something about it.

'Yeah? You really think so?' Barbara mused. Esser agreed with Fried that it was time she did. 'I don't know. What's it mean to be a singer?' she shrugged, appearing to Fried, at least, to think it was something demeaning.

None the less, the enthusiastic approval she had received did not go unnoticed nor had it been so innocently solicited. Privately, she had been honing her talent on the assumption that it might help pave the way to getting a role on Broadway. She had hoped that Marilyn Fried would react to her singing in the same way that Cis Corman had, needed that affirmation before she tested herself in a professional situation. Now she had it.

# 7

I N THE SUMMER of 1959, Barbara circulated a résumé to casting directors
stating that she was both an actress and a singer. Attached was a highly
idiosyncratic 8 × 10 glossy. Her features could hardly be discerned, and
certainly not her chronic skin condition, as she was 'swathed in cloaks and
veils and earrings and chatchkalas, looking like Ruth St Denis [the modern
dancer] in a moving moment'. Eddie Blum of the Rodgers and Hammerstein
casting office was so intrigued by the photograph that he called her and asked
her what she really looked like.

'What part are you asking me to audition for?' she shot back.

'It's for the Rodgers and Hammerstein musical *Sound of Music*,' he replied.

'Yeah?'

'Do you know the story?'

The show was about to go into rehearsal starring Mary Martin, as former
nun, Baroness Maria Von Trapp, who had escaped from the Nazis over the
Alps with a brood of singing stepchildren. Three years earlier a German film,
never released in the United States, had been made about the Von Trapp
family. Rodgers and Hammerstein had bought the rights to adapt it for the
stage. There had been various articles about the Von Trapps' adventure,
although Barbara had not read any of them.

'Sure!' she lied.

'Well, it's the oldest Von Trapp child, Lisl; the one who falls in love with the
boy in the Nazi youth movement. She's blonde, Christian and sixteen years
old,' he told her.

'I'd be perfect!' she exclaimed. She went right down to his office to read for
the part. Lisl was a singing role requiring a sweet soprano; her one solo was 'I
Am Sixteen Going on Seventeen' and was germane to the character who had
to convey girlish naïveté. Barbara went over the music a few times with the
rehearsal pianist and then gave it an admirable try. Blum knew from the
moment she had entered his office dressed in an outfit that could only be
described as '*Baby Doll* camp' (referring to the Tennessee Williams play about
a seductive child wife in the deep South), that she was entirely wrong for the
role and he warned her of this almost immediately. Her determination made

him curious enough to allow her to audition. After she sang Lisl's song, she sensed he was going to turn to her down.

'You should see me with blonde hair,' she pressed. 'I bleached it once and even my mother thought I was gentile.' Impressed with her voice, Blum suggested she apply her efforts more to singing.

With the few dollars she had, she began voice lessons. Her teacher, found through an advertisement in a theatre magazine, had once sung minor roles in a small opera company, and spent entire lessons on vocal exercises and voice production. 'I feel that singing is a natural thing,' Barbara said, recalling those lessons and how she was being taught to form sounds. 'It is an extension of speaking on a heightened level.' The singing lessons, which she had also found disturbing due to her chronic ear problem, came to an abrupt end.

The clicks and buzzing that she had once heard in her ears had evolved into a high-pitched noise, not a ringing that was spasmodic, but continuous. She never heard the silence. She had her ears examined and was told about her condition and that she had supersonic hearing. 'I hear high-range, high-pitch noises off the machine,' she explained. 'But I also hear this noise. There were periods in my life when I was very unhappy and it would drive me nuts ... I had this secret. I never told anybody. I didn't want to be different. I felt totally abnormal. It made me listen very carefully to life. I would listen like nobody listened. But it's not good, it's not fun. I'm like inside my body, I hear my body. I'm very aware of my body's functions. It's very frightening.'

This distressing affliction played a critical role in how she interpreted lines, lyrics and music. She could feel the cadences, the change in rhythm, the silence between beats. She could move effortlessly from the deeper chest sounds to the higher pitched head sounds, an ability that usually takes years of musical training to achieve. At the same time, since she heard things more clearly and sharply than most musicians, when she sang she was conscious of every small imperfection in her voice. She seldom listened to the radio because on the simple machines to which she had access the fidelity was poor and caused her to concentrate on the defects.

Shortly after the turn down by Eddie Blum, she cashed her last unemployment cheque and joined the Actors Co-op which consisted of a group of somewhat desperate out-of-work performers all hoping for an appearance in a legitimate theatre where they would be seen and reviewed. They leased the small off-Broadway Jan Hus Theater in Yorktown, Manhattan's German centre and, mysteriously, chose the brothers Karel and Josef Čapek's play, *The Insect Comedy*,[1] a satire on human society and totalitarianism. Written in 1920, all the actors in the play were citizens of an insect world. Streisand had three

---

[1] Called *The Insect Play* in Great Britain, it had John Gielgud in its original 1923 London cast as Felix, a small role. This was Gielgud's first West End appearance.

roles; as a butterfly, a moth and as Aparthera Clythia, a messenger.

Also in the company was Barry Dennen, a slim, dark-haired, charismatic young actor from Los Angeles, California, who was cast as a cricket and a snail. 'The whole production was slapped together,' Dennen remembers. 'It was unspeakable, tacky, awful, and Barbara was hysterically funny. She was young, endearing, and exceptionally serious about becoming an actress.'

The two were drawn to each other. Dennen, who had attended UCLA and was several years older than Barbara, came from a well-to-do West Coast Jewish family. Lean, lithe, bronzed by the sun which he loved, Dennen was most appealing. He was also well educated and possessed innate style. He was to be Streisand's first grand attraction and her mentor. Multi-talented, he could do mime, comedy or drama, had a unique singing style, was dedicated to theatre and dreamed eventually of becoming a director.[2]

They shared a sense of far-out humour and began to create short skits that had nothing to do with the Čapeks' play. In one, Barbara was Mae West and Dennen was an unscrupulous diamond smuggler who has forced a poodle to swallow the gems so that he can get them past customs. 'Whatsa matter with your animal?' Barbara would ask in her most seductive Mae West voice. This *double entendre* would be accompanied by a provocative sway of her shoulders and a raised eyebrow. They never got to Dennen's reply because they would be laughing so hard.

*The Insect World* closed on 11 May 1960, after three performances. 'No one [in this play] claimed to be anything like a pro ...' wrote the reviewer from the *World Telegram and Sun*. This was Barbara's first major press notice and it did nothing to get her career off to even a slow start. Her financial situation was desperate. She and Marilyn were about to be evicted from their apartment. She refused to go to Diana and Brooklyn. 'If I could sing like you, I'd know what to do,' Marilyn prodded. 'I'd try to get a singing job. All you need is a demo tape to give to an agent.' In view of their dire circumstances, Streisand agreed singing might be preferable to sleeping on a park bench. The problem was that making a tape would cost money that she did not have. Then she recalled that Dennen, suggesting they might record their comedy routine, had

---

[2] Barry Dennen would go on to create the show-stopping role of Pontius Pilate in the original Broadway production, film and the first double album of *Jesus Christ Superstar*. He was also the evil Emcee in the London company of *Cabaret*, for which he won the *Evening Standard Award* for Best Actor in 1968. He stayed in England and appeared in the BBC series *Oppenheimer*, *Beau Geste* and *Pictures*. On returning to the United States he had roles in numerous films and on television as a supporting player. More recently he has toured as Max Detweiler in *The Sound of Music*. In 1992, he won the Dramalogue Award for his performance as the Major-General in the Santa Barbara Light Opera Company's production of *The Pirates of Penzance*. He has also written for theatre, films and television.

told her he owned an excellent Ampex stereo tape recorder and two good mikes.

The next day she appeared at his apartment with Carl Esser in tow. 'We spent the afternoon taping [the song 'Day by Day'], and the moment I heard the first playback I went insane,' Dennen later related. 'I knew here was something special, a voice the microphone loved ... But I thought she had a better chance of getting an agent if she was performing somewhere. There was a club across the street from where I lived [on West Ninth Street in the Village], called The Lion. They had a talent contest on Thursdays. If she would actually walk in there and sign up, I would work with her on a set of songs, help her choose the material, and direct her act.' Her terms reversed the order. If she thought she had a chance *after* his coaching *then* she would sign up. Dennen agreed.

For the first time Barbara used a microphone. Transfixed by the experience, she spent hours experimenting with it, learning how to shade her voice, project it without strain. Under Dennen's fevered tutelage she mastered microphone technique in a matter of a few days, adding her own instinctive touches, never pausing to breathe in the middle of a lyric thought, bringing the instrument closer to her lips to enhance the intimacy of a phrase. Her phrasing – good to begin with – improved even more. Dennen pushed her as hard as he could and she responded with more questions, repeating a song dozens of times before she was satisfied with her interpretation.

At the end of a week, he accompanied her to The Lion, standing over her as she inscribed her name as *Barbra* Streisand on the audition sheet. It was not an accident, she told him later. There were too many *Barbaras* and she wanted to be different. She did, however, want to keep her last name so that everyone in Brooklyn would know it was her *when* she became famous. Dennen had recorded her practice sessions and played them back for her to study. The newly named Barbra Streisand was confident she was on the road to stardom, a belief that drove her to rehearse at fever pitch for the audition, not stopping until both of them were too exhausted to continue.

Dennen had made arrangements for her of 'A Sleepin' Bee' and 'Lover Come Back to Me', a 'switch', that is a song usually sung in slow tempo but given an up-tempo driving beat. He conceived 'A Sleepin' Bee' as a set theatre piece, evolving the character of the girl in the lyric story through various moods. It was a perfect choice, enabling Streisand to watch an imaginary bee who sleeps in the palm of her hand. Dennen told her the Jamaican legend of the insect which won't fly away, which won't sting you if you have found true love. Under his direction her graceful hands created a unique stage picture as she acted and sang to this tiny, fantasy creature which somehow seemed unbelievably real.

Demanding and tough, Dennen worked her hard, phrase by phrase, 'trying this, trying that, shaping gestures, timing, the kind of effect Barbra and I wanted'. She lent herself willingly to his strict instruction, picking up on everything he told her, adding her own improvements both musically and interpretatively; an unexpected change of key, a word given surprising stress. He warned her not to interact with the audience while she was performing as this would destroy the reality she was creating in her song. He taught her how to be still and yet commanding as she waited to begin her act, what to do with her hands, how to stand, how to sit, how to hold a microphone, how to look out at an audience without seeing them. He insisted she treat each song as if it was a short, crucial scene in a drama, to play a part with music and lyrics. She was a voracious student and by the end of the week had progressed from amateur to the threshold of professionalism. Clearly, they were a good creative team.

Dennen was falling in love with her but he also recognised her distinctiveness and her vast untapped talent. There was something almost obsessive about his need to develop her into a professional performer, which she had *not* been when they first began to work together. He later told this author, 'Barbra *was* my creation, at least I created her musical taste and gave her support, confidence and the direction she needed to be able to do anything.'

Although she recognised just how much Dennen could contribute to her future, she never appeared grateful. Dennen did not expect her to be. She had become enamoured with herself and he believed that quality was one that would have a positive effect on her performance. Whatever satisfaction he gained from helping her metamorphose into an exciting performer was her repayment. To Barbra, Dennen's considerable help and encouragement were deemed a small measure of compensation for all the years of being put down by Diana and that she considered was due from someone whom she loved.

Although Dennen had not yet found a theatre job that could pay his rent, he lived at a considerably higher standard than other struggling actors in a 'small, but modern, clean cockroachless apartment at 69 West Ninth Street' which he paid for with the help of his parents. In Barbra's eyes, the flat with its paisley fabric walls, black leather chairs and massive plants in containers made of bamboo, was the essence of sophistication. Dennen had flair and his two rooms, plus kitchen and bathroom, had been smartly turned out on a modest budget. He also had quality hi-fi equipment and an amazing collection of more than a thousand records of the great entertainers of the twentieth century which he had shipped from his family home on the West Coast.

Dennen's parents owned an estate in the fashionable stretch of Coldwater Canyon off Sunset Boulevard. His brother and he each had their own small house set a short distance from the main building with a swimming pool between them. Barbra never tired of hearing him describe the glamorous decor of that home, what the staff were like, and the parties the family hosted, movies shown in a private projection room, cocktail parties by the pool, huge barbecues, all attended by the rich and sometimes famous. She was impressed.

Dennen now proposed she move in with him. The decision was not difficult for they had developed an unusual closeness and she had been evicted from her former apartment. Not only was she dependent upon his emotional and financial support, she was in love. While preparing for her audition at The Lion, they entered into a physical relationship. Although she had been attracted to several young men during her early Village days, Dennen was her first real affair, and the only man she had lived with. She had not given up her prime ambition to be an actress, but she was now convinced that goal would be attainable if she could make a name for herself as a singer who *was* an actress. Phrasing, choice of material, putting together a class act was what was needed and her instincts told her that Dennen could expedite this.

Always together, in what free time they had he dragged her to thrift shops and costumiers to get together some outfits to wear in her act when she won the contest – he was so sure she would. He had an unerring eye for spotting the one elegant scarf, pair of gloves or shoes in a pile of junk, and Barbra was a fast learner who instinctively knew how to put together the bits and pieces of old-world elegance they found to make an intriguing and fashionable ensemble. The finished result, if somewhat bizarre, was a look that would be remembered.

This was at the time of the mid-calf hemline ushered in by Dior with skirts worn over several full petticoats, of wholesome vocalists such as Doris Day and Dinah Shore, of night-club singers gowned in glitzy gold and sequins. By contrast Barbra combined a short 1920s dress with coloured stockings and T-strapped twenties shoes with four-inch heels. For another costume, a boa in bright crimson was slung around the shoulders of an oyster-white Victorian negligée. Together Barbra and Dennen found extraordinary paste necklaces, dangly earrings and Venetian glass bracelets that she wore as she walked around the Village so that they became comfortable, old friends. She was costumed rather than dressed but she had gained a new persona. To some she looked kookie in her flea-market attire, but there was no doubt that she stood out from the crowd and that if she was viewed with a fashion-trained eye she was more *avant* than *derrière garde*.

At the end of this frantic week of transformation, she was ready. The talent contest, they both believed, would lead to her debut as a cabaret performer. The contest was held on 2 July 1960, a muggy, airless evening. Barbra had celebrated her eighteenth birthday the previous April. She looked older by a few years.

The Lion was a 'crummy' back room with tables where they served a limited menu. Summers, when their customers liked to go to Fire Island or various other beach areas, were slow. To stimulate business the owner had inaugurated a Thursday night talent contest, the winner to receive $50 a week for a two-week engagement and all the food and drink he or she could consume. The food offer was a great incentive to the hard-up young actress, who loved to eat. The Lion was not the hottest small club in town, but it was a good showcase for performers and was frequented by agents and scouts looking for new talent.

Among her six or seven competitors that evening were a comedian, a black blues singer and a duo who sang Broadway show songs. The room was dimly lit. There was no stage, just a dark area in front of the piano like a small dance floor. The comedian went first. Then came Barbra. Dennen handed her music to the accompanist and then held her back for a moment and asked for a spot. A few moments went by and a pink light came on. She stepped up to the piano looking like a bird of paradise, eyes outlined in blue, a silver and gold blouse with large Elizabethan sleeves worn over a shocking-pink fuchsia skirt a daring inch above the knee, chocolate brown stockings and her T-wrapped 1927 gold and silver vamp shoes with accents of red. A bang hid part of her forehead, the rest of her dyed auburn hair was piled up atop her head with an added hairpiece for extra height.

Glasses were lowered to study this apparition as she stood behind the microphone in the pink light. She should have looked simply weird. Instead she was startling, breathtakingly unique. She boosted herself on to the seat of a stool. She was chewing bubblegum and as she waited for silence (as Dennen had told her she must) she took the gum out of her mouth and stuck it under the seat – her own innovation. The audience laughed and immediately warmed to her.

Seated out front was a young, struggling actor named Dustin Hoffman who had been attending acting classes with her. 'I thought: "What a smart girl," ' he recalled, reflecting on that night. 'It was a seemingly natural act but it had method to its madness. It was quite provoking, and suddenly, out of this amiable ant-eater, came this *magic.*' She sang 'Sleepin' Bee' in a melting, completely original voice, nasal at times, that rose to the ceiling, circled the small, crowded, smoke-filled room and in the end brought the house to its feet (so much for agent Ralph Mann's dour prediction that this would never occur). The acts that followed had lost before they began.

Barbra Streisand had arrived.


Now that she had unleashed her voice, she realised its power and range. Despite her youth, it was none the less a mature woman's voice with a certain nasal urgency that was nothing like the youthful yearning, the throaty vulnerability that was so recognisably Judy Garland's at that same age. And when she sang, Brooklyn was lost – unless she chose to incorporate it for fun into a line. She became whoever she chose to be.

The amazing thing was how she learned so quickly to turn a song into a vignette, create an entire scene. To broaden her limited knowledge of vocal styling, Dennen played her countless records and tapes – Ruth Etting, Helen Morgan, Lee Wiley, Ethel Waters, Mabel Mercer, Shirley Temple, Fanny Brice and Fred Astaire – all performers who possessed strong individual styles. They would analyse and study the songs these artists sang. He recorded Astaire and Rogers dances from televised re-runs of their old films, and – a fine dancer – Dennen would whirl around the room with her, jumping on and off the bed and furniture in imitation of that great dance team.

A friend of Dennen's from California, Ira Levy, also lived in the Village and would join them with another friend, Stan Gurell. 'We would do an entire review in Barry's living room. All of us singing – but mainly Barbra – songs starting from the turn of the century and continuing on pretty much to the present. Barbra's voice was amazing. You could tell she had a future. And it was incredible how fast she got the period sounds – pre-World War One, the twenties, the thirties. She was terrific.'

Despite the comfort of his upbringing, Dennen's childhood and youth had been lonely as his parents had been preoccupied with their own lives. He longed for the sense of family that he felt he had missed. Marriage did not seem the answer for he was not yet prepared for such a step either emotionally or financially. But he welcomed with fond approval the fans, feathers, costume jewellery and vintage clothing that kept closet doors from closing; the Tiffany-style lamps that she had seized upon and that he had bought for her at a good price in their scavenging through the back rooms of thrift shops; the idiosyncratic collection of period bibelots, additional recording equipment, and the dozens of candles with which she lit their private dinners when she cooked. His modest-sized flat was crowded and overflowing with things that evoked her eclectic personality. 'Barbra had fully moved in and made the apartment her home,' he says. Still, it was not truly hers and the life she led with Dennen was filled with humiliations as well as with exciting highs. Believing his father would cut off his support if he knew he was living with Barbra, Dennen insisted she did not answer the telephone and introduced her to the doorman of the building as his cousin. This charade was kept up, although it is doubtful that the apartment staff were ever fooled.

Streisand was convinced she was deeply in love with Dennen. He possessed a prodigious memory and she was learning from him about music, history, politics. Ideas bounced back and forth between them. An eager pupil, she challenged him at every turn. She trusted and believed in his taste in clothes, decor and above all – music; consuming and squirrelling away everything he had to give her. She had found that she had learned more about acting from interpreting the lyrics of the songs than she had in most of her combined acting classes.

During her two-week run at The Lion, Dennen was there every evening taking notes on her performance and the reaction of the audience. And he would work with her on new numbers. 'I would pick material that was excellent musically,' Dennen explains, 'that would show off her voice and also songs that were unusual, forgotten, or outrageous. It was my idea to have her perform [later] "Who's Afraid of the Big Bad Wolf?" in front of New York's cleverest and sharpest [cabaret] audience.'[3]

Her affair with Dennen was something quite apart from first love. It was the beginning of learning to love herself. He was intelligent, possessed tremendous energy, talent, originality of thought and good taste and he had chosen her, believed she had the potential of becoming something special – *a star*. He also found her sexy, appealing. More unsure of himself at the time than his bravura indicated, Dennen benefited greatly from the knowledge that he had discovered someone original, bound for success and that her trust in him validated his own worth. His most important lesson to her as an artist was to show her that she could display her acting ability within the framework of a song; his greatest contributions to her as a woman were to help her feel beautiful, desired and confident.

Her two-week engagement at The Lion ended on 16 July. The best cabarets in New York would be closed for the month of August. Impatiently, she waited while the scorching late summer days stripped Manhattan of much of its glamour. Heat steamed up from the sidewalks, trapped between the tunnels of high-rises. Streets smelled pungently of burning rubber and baked-in waste matter. The fire department turned on the fire hydrants in the poor sections so that the kids could dart in and out of the water to cool off. Those who could packed their weekend bags for the country. Barbra remained in the city, hardly leaving Dennen's apartment.

He was preparing her for an audition at the Bon Soir, one of the most sophisticated and popular cabaret rooms in the Village. He was very strict with her, working on the act for hours on end. Dennen's good friend, Bob Schulenberg, arrived in the city from Los Angeles on the last day of The Lion engagement. Dennen met him at the airport and brought him down to the Village.

'The first time I saw her we were walking down Sixth Avenue,' Schulenberg remembered. 'Barbra approached us with two shopping bags in each hand and out of them were coming feathers, sequins, net, all sorts of accessory stuff,

---

[3] The original arrangement for 'Who's Afraid of the Big Bad Wolf?' was done by Peter Daniels.

lots of it ... She had little wisps of eyeliner and darkened eyelids under her brow. Her wide and generous mouth was accentuated with mahogany-purple lipstick ... Her earrings were glass balls that seemed to hang all the way down to her thorax and she had an assortment of necklace chains with glass interspersed and she had a dozen exquisite Venetian-glass bracelets on one arm, plus rings on practically all the fingers of her two hands. Outside of *The King and I* no one had looked that way ever, even on the streets of Greenwich Village.'

Schulenberg, a talented illustrator, make-up man and designer, was not so much taken aback as he was impressed. 'I found her extraordinary from the beginning. She was just so amazing. I never encountered someone with so many ideas and so many wishes, so many desires. We three became a kind of trio. We would terrorise the town, do numbers at the various clubs [to call attention to themselves], even tried to steal pottery from tables at restaurants.

'[She and Barry] talked about getting married and I was shocked. I was just really stunned,' Schulenberg says. 'They were very young. As I remember, Barbra was only eighteen and Barry twenty-one.' Dennen was rehearsing a role in *Measure for Measure* in a Shakespearean series being presented in Central Park. When she was on her own, Schulenberg would see that she was occupied. They became good friends. 'I think she was the most intelligent person I'd ever met. She had a great understanding of what she read and tremendous curiosity. If you were introducing a new topic to her she pelted you with questions. I don't recall her ever putting me off with a feminine tract. She was just her own person. There are certain woman who don't act like men but are people without any of the constrictions. Barbra was the first woman I had met that was like that. At the same time an intriguing aura of naïveté clung to her.

'I think I took her to the first [elegant] restaurant she'd ever been to ... a chic midtown smörgåsbord restaurant. She was fascinated by this huge table full of strange food. She would feel the texture of everything with her fingers. There was this marvellous orgiastic tactile experience of touching all the food ... "Look at this," she'd sigh. It was wonderful to watch. It was also poignant because you realised it was such a thrill for her. Doing things with Barbra in those days was like the first time it had ever been done.'

She auditioned for the Bon Soir on a humid Sunday evening in late July. 'This is the beginning of something,' she remembered thinking on the way to the club with Dennen, Schulenberg and Bark McHugh, an older off-Broadway producer Dennen knew who was also a scout for new cabaret talent and who had arranged the audition. When a cool breeze suddenly rose she felt a chill through her entire body. She has recalled that she felt different, surer of herself that evening. She walked so fast the men had a difficult time keeping up with her.

The Bon Soir was a Mafia-owned cellar club. The gay bar at the rear of the one large room it occupied existed through policy pay-offs. The club was known for its all-black company of regular performers, who included Mae Barnes, 'a five-by-five singer with dark saucer eyes, a grainy powerhouse voice, and the sassiest good-time spirit ever to haunt a night-club stage', as well as the Tiger Haynes Trio, each member a spectacular solo musician. It was also an important showcase for coming white performers – Kaye Ballard, Phyllis Diller and Dick Cavett among them.

With the club closed on Sundays, they entered through a rear door that led down a steep, dimly lit flight of stairs. The place was almost entirely in darkness. Only a few tables were occupied by the management and some employees. One overhead spot was illuminated. The respected guitarist Tiger Haynes watched her from across the room as she went over to the accompanist, the Englishman Peter Daniels, and discussed the music she had just handed him – 'A Sleepin' Bee' – and then went up on the narrow stage and positioned the microphone. A sense of command pervaded her attitude. The Bon Soir was several times larger than The Lion and although it was in the Village it had a reputation that brought New York's most sophisticated uptown cabaret-goers to its cellar doors on Eighth Street.

Her usual 'bizarre' attire was abandoned because of the intense heat for a simple, sleeveless brown cotton dress. Her hair was piled high on top her head. She insisted on a blue rather than a pink spotlight and the effect was startling. She looked like a Modigliani painting. A shock ran through the darkened, silent room the moment she started to sing, a spine-tingling urgency behind every note. The sound was pure, commanding, her phrasing remarkable. It was an astonishing performance. She played to that nearly empty room as though every chair was filled and the phantom occupants raptly listening to her. The magic in her voice was tangible. 'It looks good,' Bark McHugh told Dennen when she had finished. Tiger Haynes's girlfriend, a diminutive woman named Bea, came over to Streisand and said, 'Little girl, you got dollar signs written all over you!'

'Yeah? You really think so?' she grinned. 'Maybe you can tell the management.'

Her salary was $108 a week for a two-week engagement. She was only to be the featured artist. Comedian Phyllis Diller was the headliner. 'Hey!' Barbra told one friend. 'This is only the beginning. Next time the stakes will be higher and the place classier.'

'It's curious,' Bob Schulenberg confided, 'I always thought Barry would be the legend and Barbra the cabaret performer.' The two men had first met on the set of an amateur film that Dennen had written when they both were attending UCLA. 'He was a brilliant performer, very clever. He did performances of *Les Fourberies de Scapin* that I designed at UCLA and his French was so impeccable that everyone thought he was French. He's an amazing performer. A perfectionist, a visionary. He always brought something new to the character he played.'

Schulenberg had been an assistant art director for Berman Costumes in Hollywood, and had designed for the Ice Capades. He had arrived in New York to start a job as art director for the firm of West, Weir and Bartell, which was where – as coincidence would have it – Shelley was now employed. 'I liked him very much, but I had the sense that he was a little embarrassed by Barbra, at least at that point in time.' A great fan of both contemporary and legendary cabaret artists, Schulenberg had been overwhelmed with admiration for Barbra when he first heard her sing. He also felt that proper make-up would add much to her appearance.

'She was very young and she – well, she didn't look bad, but I think she thought that she did,' Schulenberg recalled. 'That was kind of heart-breaking because I knew how much she wanted to look beautiful and simply did not know how to bring it off. She really had a striking face, marvellous eyes and a profile that was pure Egyptian. I thought she could be really stunning and that I could help her, but it was a difficult, sensitive point. I thought about it a long time and in the end I made a simple drawing of her without any make-up so that I could study her face structure.'

During the month of August, while Dennen was rehearsing in the Central Park production of *Measure for Measure*, Schulenberg saw Barbra more frequently. During their wanderings about the Village, he gradually convinced her that she needed a make-up makeover. They were to attend Dennen's opening night together and this seemed to present itself as the perfect occasion. Schulenberg came early to the apartment, armed with a theatrical make-up kit. 'She had great eyes, a wonderful face. What I did was make cheekbones where there was still baby fat, and I contoured her eyes and feathered some false eyelashes shorter than her own, and I extended the line at the corner of her eyes. With each step I explained to her what I was doing and why. She didn't have deep-set eyes and so she had to enforce it. The double layer of eyelashes helped that effect. I used heavy grease paint to hide the scars of her skin condition.'

She kept staring at herself in the mirror, turning her face at different angles, mumbling excited comments. 'I see! I see! Hey! Not bad, huh?' She was very pleased, thrilled with the transformation.

Streisand and Schulenberg had been so involved with Barbra's makeover that they arrived too late at *Measure to Measure* to see Dennen perform. He was deeply hurt and although they continued to live together, there was now an edge to their relationship. Dennen helped her with the act she was soon to present at the Bon Soir, concentrating on the dramatic presentation. Streisand now had a clear concept of how she wanted to sound and what she wanted to sing – great Harold Arlen songs such as 'When the Sun Comes Out', Fats Waller's 'Keepin' Out of Mischief Now' (sung by her in a breathless, seductive voice), and the childlike 'Who's Afraid of the Big Bad Wolf?' which she turned into a campy, lively and raunchy interpretation. They were all included in her new act, which would work around the theme of a young girl's transition from tease to love awakening to lost love and maturity – every song performed under Dennen's direction as a mini-drama. Strong-willed, always striving to be at the top of her form, she was clever enough to accept outside ideas when she recognised their worth and she worked tirelessly to take in and adapt all he could contribute to her performance.

She practised her 'look' with Schulenberg with equal concentration. He did a portrait of Barbra with half her face made up as he designed it and the other side untouched. She would then take the drawing and all the make-up into the bathroom and patiently attempt to fill in the blank side of the picture on her face so that the two parts would match. When it did not she would scrub her face clean and start over again, sometimes four or five times, a process that often took several hours before she got it right.

Streisand was the centre of a curious trio, badgered and disciplined by two young men who were determined that she succeed – a Brooklyn Eliza Doolittle. But things are not always what they appear. Barbra Streisand's wish to succeed was even greater than her mentors' wish for her. Had they been less talented, had they not been able to help her advance her aims, she would have had little time for them. It was not that she was ungrateful. Streisand was in a desperate hurry to arrive at her planned destination and she accepted all that Dennen and Schulenberg could contribute to her growth as a performer.

She believed she loved Dennen, but she had no other experience with a close male-female relationship other than her mother's disastrous marriage to Kind. She was seeking love and approval, an alliance where she was the centre of attention and Dennen gave this to her. What more could she ask of a man or of an affair?

# 8

OPENING NIGHT AT the Bon Soir, Friday, 9 September 1960, she walked on stage to a packed house wearing a brown wool-jersey, thrift-shop dress, very tight fitting, a matching cloche hat from the twenties, and a pair of spike-heeled, ankle-strap shoes. Ice cubes clinked in glasses and people engaged in conversation as she tiptoed across the darkened stage to the microphone set up before a high stool. When the spotlight picked her up already seated, the audience took one look and mostly concluded that she was a comedienne.

A wave of terror washed over her. Unlike the audiences at The Lion, these were tough, up-town types who would judge her against the current top cabaret entertainers: Julie Wilson, Anita Ellis, Felicia Sanders, Portia Nelson and the sultry-voiced Julie London. She took a deep breath and began 'A Sleepin' Bee' in a hushed throb of a voice, the microphone no more than an inch from her mouth. It was a brave opening. Most cabaret acts started with a spirited number to catch the audience's attention. A few moments into the song, her voice grew in volume and she extended her arm and open-palmed her hand where the bee was supposed to lie sleeping. Heads turned towards her. People leaned forward in their chairs. She could feel the audience's attention. They exploded with applause when she ended the song and were entirely hers as she cut their response short and swept into 'When the Sun Comes Out' as if 'she were announcing the eclipse of Western civilisation'.

'When she got off the stage,' comedian and impressionist Larry Storch, who was also making his way in the cabaret world, remembered, 'Barbra was in a kind of a daze. I went to congratulate her. I think I said something like, "Kid, you are going to be a very great star!" Then they pushed her back on stage and, after singing those serious songs, she performed "Who's Afraid of the Big Bad Wolf?" How well planned that was! What a master stroke! It just killed everybody. They made her sing it three times. It was incredible. It was really like a scene from *A Star Is Born*.'[1]

---

[1] A future reviewer would write: '["Who's Afraid of the Big, Bad Wolf?" is] the song that children sing. But in her version, it seemed new, tripping perilously along the edge

Streisand was overwhelmed by the reception she received. There were tears in her eyes as she finished her set, she appeared feverish. More than her talent had been validated. Barbra Streisand had just discovered her power over an audience.

'I knew that this was a STAR! It was all there,' Phyllis Diller, who had the top billing that night, emphasises. 'On her third note, every hair stood up all over my body ... She was a disciplined, devoted worker, a brilliant genius – and she was a child!'

When Diana came to see her on the second night, Barbra had changed her first outfit for a white lace Victorian morning coat and pink satin shoes from the 1920s. Diana was horrified, certain that her daughter was singing in her nightgown. To Barbra, the outfit was beautiful. 'A few days later I realised people were talking about this girl who sings in these weird clothes. They thought it was a gimmick so I went back to the thrift shop ... I used to get lovely dresses at resale shops where rich ladies got rid of their stuff. What's to be ashamed of? Those ladies were clean ... Then Phyllis Diller said, "You can't wear that stuff," and took me shopping for a [contemporary] cocktail dress, and I actually put on one. I didn't want to make her feel bad, but I could never wear it again. It wasn't me.'

Diana admitted feeling a thrill with her daughter's auspicious reception. She recognised, perhaps for the first time, the enormity of Barbra's talent. She was proud and not hesitant in telling Shelley, who had accompanied her, that she didn't know Barbra could sing so well. Yet, when she greeted her later, she could only criticise what she had worn. 'Did you like the way I sang, Mama?' Streisand finally asked.

'Yeah, you did good,' Diana replied.

The two women were unable to break their pattern. Diana would always find one thing of which she disapproved, Streisand would continue to seek her approval and feel abused when she did not wholly receive it. Despite her ongoing conflict with her mother, with her twice-nightly engagement at the Bon Soir her confidence grew. She sang five songs in her set and when people would ask afterwards if they could buy her a drink, she would order a baked potato with 'hard crust and lots of butter'.

'At the Bon Soir I got special satisfaction out of performing,' Streisand says. 'Well, in life I felt, you know, people paid no attention to me. When I would talk it came out so enthusiastically that they would disregard it. All of a sudden, singing, I could say what I felt and I was listened to.'

She battled to overcome nightly sieges of stage fright before she performed. The cabaret's regulars were a boisterous group, a mix of gays who packed the

of probability, its innocence in doubt [in the dark room] which had suddenly become the dripping jaws of some unruly canine.' *Time*, 10 April 1964.

bar to 'shop' for a pick-up and high-tone, up-town night-club habitués who came to Village *boîtes* to listen to new talent with an arrogant 'show me' attitude. When a performer did, they could be fervent in their response. They could also be tough, daunting and clangorous.

'What do I do?' Streisand asked Dennen backstage one difficult night when a group in the audience seemed determined to continue laughing and talking during the act that preceded her. 'They're making a lot of noise.'

'Stare them down,' Dennen told her. 'Stand there and think, "Shut up! Listen to *me*! Look at *me*!" '

She went out front. The room was clouded with smoke and, except for one light over the cash register, in total blackness. Peter Daniels began the introduction to 'A Sleepin' Bee'. Conversation whirred, laughter trilled and cackled. Streisand stood there while Daniels repeated the introduction. This happened twice before someone could be heard saying, 'Shh! Shhh!' and she started to sing.

After a few performances, she grew easier and would talk to the audience between songs – not much, just to introduce her musicians. 'Weighing in at 183 pounds in black trunks ...' she would say in the seductive Mae West voice that Dennen had always thought was so funny. Before the end of her engagement a distinct group of devotees began to form. The word had got around. There was this odd-looking creature, clearly a misfit who sang 'songs of unrequited love or the sudden, surprise discovery of romance' in an inimitable voice. Her choice of material was unexpected, and there was simply no one else around who sounded or looked like her. Still, her first reviews were not all raves.

'At the Bon Soir, Barbra Streisand, singer – file and forget,' wrote Roger Whitaker in the *New Yorker*.

'That old fart! What does he know?' she snapped defiantly to Dennen, adding that the table section was booked to capacity and there was standing space only at the bar at the back of the room for her twice-nightly per-formances.

'She would just *do* things that you had never heard anybody ever do,' one regular remembers. 'She was a hurricane of a certain kind of unbridled passion. She would hold notes until she would turn blue. And she would just gasp at the end of words you know, like *uuuhhh!* There was always a sort of edge, the sense that she was giving you so much more than you deserved, as opposed to Liza Minnelli [or Judy Garland] who was just begging you to love her. Streisand never did that...'

The Bon Soir raised her salary to $125 a week and extended her engagement for eleven weeks. Streisand was determined that she would use that time to improve her performance. Her lifelong obsession with perfection in whatever she did had begun in earnest, along with the dedicated work ethic she had inherited from her father. During the first two weeks Dennen brought in his tape recorder and fastidiously taped her act. Later they would go over every number, change phrasing, the position of certain songs, the back-up sound. At the end of that time he delegated Bob Schulenberg to look after her and left to visit his family in California, issuing as a final instruction that she was never to call him there as he had not yet discussed their situation with his parents.

Streisand was injured by his dictatorial manner but agreed to his terms. 'He really cares about me,' she told Schulenberg. 'He'll tell his parents about us in his own time.'

'There was a certain date when Barry was coming back,' Schulenberg recalls. 'That night Barbra got all the things he loved to eat and we set up a beautiful table with a floral arrangement. We even had champagne in the refrigerator. We went to the Bon Soir and left him a note saying, "Eat up, we'll be back after the show." We ran back and he was not there. Barbra was really upset. She wondered if he'd missed the plane, but she couldn't call his family. We sat up until about three in the morning but Barry didn't call.'

The next night they went through the same procedure and when they returned to the apartment Dennen had still not returned. Days passed without any word from Dennen. She was at turns anxious, tearful and furious. 'After a week,' Schulenberg continues, 'I think Barbra ate up all her emotion for Barry. Finally he came back and she was very cool. She just said, "Hi, how was your trip? Is your family well? Great – [and by the way] I'm still singing at the Bon Soir."'

She remained at Dennen's apartment, controlling her anger and her growing hostility to him. The flame was gone and she blamed him for it. He had humiliated and rejected her. In a short time she would manage to obliterate all conscious awareness of his great contribution to her development as a performer and hang on to the injury she believed she had suffered at his hands. She could not let go completely because in truth she still needed Dennen's direction, but she began to rely more on Peter Daniels, her accompanist, who was now arranging her new material and with whom she had an empathetic alliance. This time, however, there was no sexual relationship and she was in control. She had growing respect for her own taste, perhaps shaped by Dennen but, none the less, now a reflection of herself.

Before her eleven-week engagement at the Bon Soir ended, she agreed to be represented by Ted Rozar, a talent agent who had gone backstage after hearing her sing and told her he wanted to be her manager. Curiously, this was the first inquiry she had received from an agent. The arrangement only lasted a few weeks.

'They never hit it off,' Schulenberg explained. 'I saw him sometime later when they had parted company and he told me that "my little friend" would never make it because she thought she was hot stuff but was too undisciplined for big-time show business.'

She then tried to find another agent, without much luck at first. 'They were very short-sighted,' said Irving Arthur, who booked acts at Associated Booking Corporation at the time. 'Her appearance kind of turned them off. But I had no doubt at all that she was going to be a star.' He had come down to hear her sing at the Bon Soir and then took her to a nearby coffee shop.

'I hired my first agent because he took me out for dinner. I could be bought for an avocado,' she later joked.

Every night near midnight she called to ask, 'Well? What have you got lined up for me tomorrow?' An intrusion into his home life that wasn't appreciated by Mrs Arthur.

'So who's this dame who's calling you every night?' she would ask him.

He would reply, 'Just a *star*.'

She finally moved out of Dennen's apartment after a serious argument over the tapes he had made of her voice, rehearsals and performances, dozens of them over the six months they had been together. She wanted the master tapes and Dennen refused. Streisand felt they belonged to her – they were of her voice. Dennen disagreed. He had initiated, directed and recorded the tapes. Neither would give in and there was a bitter, unpleasant parting. 'The tapes were like children in a divorce,' Dennen told this author. 'They represented a lot of things. We broke up as lovers who both felt hurt and misunderstood.'[2]

Streisand had nowhere to go and very little money. Packing what she had collected during her time with Dennen in boxes and shopping bags and with a folding cot she had acquired, she moved from one nightly 'safe haven' to another, refusing to go home to Diana and Brooklyn. She would spend a night or so with Schulenberg, at Peter Daniels's studio, Irving Arthur's office, the Millers – anywhere she could hang her hat. Her calls to Irving Arthur became more intense and he was relieved to inform her that he had arranged a tour from March to April 1961. The salary was $250 a week, out of which she had to pay her own living road expenses, which would eat up almost the entire amount. But she would be seen, accumulate reviews and perhaps interest a record company, so she agreed.

Before she left, Shelley took her to lunch. 'I made her walk three feet behind me because of her clothes [she was wearing one of her more colourful outfits],' he vividly remembers. 'People stared at her. She had these horrible rips in the back of her stockings. I offered to buy her a new pair. She said, "They're not

---

[2] Dennen never sent Streisand the controversial tapes. In 1994, Marty Erlichman approached Dennen about the possibility of including a number from the tapes in Streisand's *For the Record* album. 'He never followed up,' Dennen told me, 'consequently, I never played them for him.'

ripped in front and I don't see them in back, so they don't bother me," and refused to change them.' Shelley, who had recently married, remained as close to her as she would let him. He was in constant touch with Diana and Streisand did not want things she might say to Shelley to go back to their mother. But he was still her big brother, the only immediate male relative she had, and there was a genuine fondness between them.

The tour would take her by train to Detroit, Cleveland and St Louis among other cities. 'She was half exhilarated, half scared,' Schulenberg recalls. 'It was to be her first time out of New York. Finally [the day she was to leave] we packed her bags into a taxi and rode to the train station. Suddenly she asked if she could stop the taxi to get something at a drugstore ... She was late and I knew she would miss the train if we stopped, so I asked her point-blank what it was she *had* to get. She blurted out, "Do you think they have toothpaste in Detroit?"' exposing her fear of the unknown she faced, perhaps hoping to delay or postpone it.

Once in Detroit, and wanting to make herself seem more interesting, she developed an exotic story to tell the press: she was born in Turkey. The local newspaper hailed her as 'the Turkish-born, Brooklyn-raised songstress in a big hurry, with a totally untrained but remarkably true voice'.

An appearance on one of the popular television talk shows, she believed, would speed her ascent to heady stardom and she began to call and haunt the various programme bookers. 'I said no to Barbra Streisand,' bragged Bob Shanks, a talent co-ordinator for the *Tonight Show*, which was aired nationally every week night.[3] Streisand refused to accept his negative response and kept calling. 'Everybody in the business says you're so sensitive and understanding about talent that I've got to talk to you,' she told him. 'I need your advice.'

She then explained in a most dramatic fashion that her mother was gravely ill in Cleveland and anxious for her to return home to marry a childhood sweetheart, whom she did not love. 'If you could give me only one chance so that she could see me on the *Tonight Show*, it would keep me here and launch my career,' she begged in such a poignant manner that Shanks was taken in.

'Paar [who thought she was too overtly Jewish in looks and manner] didn't think she was right for his show,' Shanks says. But as fate would have it, Orson Bean – who had seen her at the Bon Soir and been overwhelmed by her talent – was to take over as guest host for Paar on 5 April and agreed with Shanks's suggestion to book her. She interrupted her engagement in Detroit and flew – half-terrified, she had never been on a plane before – to New York to appear on her first national television show. Phyllis Diller was also on the programme. Looking fresh and young in a short, slim black dress with spaghetti shoulder

---

[3] Successive hosts were Steve Allen, Johnny Carson and Jay Leno. The *Tonight Show*, which is still on the air, is the longest-running talk show in the United States.

straps – an outfit counselled by Schulenberg who told her that *simple* and *elegant* were also attention grabbers – she sang 'A Sleepin' Bee' and then somewhat nervously walked over to sit down between Diller and Bean.

'This is so exciting,' she beamed wide-eyed, her modish dress hiked several inches above the knees of her curvaceous crossed legs. 'All these people and cameras and lights and *people!*' She came off as this naïve, natural Brooklyn kook and the audience loved her.

Her television debut bolstered her self-confidence. She felt natural performing before the camera and not having to concern herself with a judgmental cabaret audience. This eased her tension and she talked glibly, sounding a bit oddball, but very likeable. She was, in effect, playing herself. This allowed her to capitalise only on the parts of her personality that she thought would create an interesting character, and she was right.

Immediately after the *Tonight Show* she flew back to Detroit and then went on to St Louis, from where she wrote Barry Dennen a businesslike letter asking him to send her the guitar chords he had arranged for 'A Taste of Honey'. She added that maybe he could come up with a substitute for 'Lover Come Back to Me' as the closing of her act.

He answered her request and suggested 'Cry Me a River', a plaintive song that Julie London had successfully recorded. She returned to New York with tapes of the local radio shows on which she had appeared during her tour. 'We went over them as we had at an earlier time,' Dennen says. 'I told her how to improve her performance, what songs to include in her repertoire: they were basically the ones she would later do in her first album. In May 1961, she came to my apartment one afternoon and we recorded "A Taste of Honey".' The reunion was not an easy one. 'We both felt bitter, misused, sad,' Dennen said. The love affair was over. They saw each other occasionally over the next few months, the meetings initiated by Streisand, who continued to seek his advice on musical arrangements. Then she simply stopped calling.

'Barbra loved Barry, but it was much more than that,' Schulenberg insists. 'She respected him as a teacher, a driving force. When it didn't work out between them, she was terribly hurt. She reacted by refusing to take advice from anyone.'

She appeared again at the Bon Soir shortly after her tour, including 'Cry Me a River' in her act, twisting the original concept of 'a repentant lover who had come back for a second chance' into a story about a once-scorned woman demanding tears of loss from the man who had involved her in a hurting relationship. 'When I sang that,' she admitted later, 'I was thinking of one particular person; I tried to recreate in my mind the details of his face.'[4] Barry Dennen.

[4] Eight years later she told a *Life* reporter: 'The song no longer works for me as well, mostly because I don't feel that way about that person any more.'

Unquestionably, Streisand owed a great deal to Dennen, but she was also driven to succeed. No doubt she would have landed on top without Dennen's coaching. None the less, he helped her speed up the progress. Once her transmogrification had occurred, she no longer needed him and she did not treat him kindly in the future when they happened to meet. 'When she's done with you, she's done with you,' another close associate observed. 'When her need for you is over, so is the relationship.'

Although she expected them to do so, neither the tour nor her one appearance on national television catapulted her to stardom. She was nervous, anxious, once more insecure. What had happened? What had she done wrong? Why hadn't she been offered a recording contract, a Broadway show, a screen test? 'Here I am! Look at me!' had been her attitude. Each day that passed without something spectacular happening in her career seemed a rejection. She suffered mood swings, ate compulsively and *still* lost weight. She did, however, undertake a three-week highly successful return engagement at the Bon Soir which counteracted some of her depression. But she was broke.

'Usually at the end of an engagement,' Tiger Haynes mused, 'the performers gave the musicians a gift. I got tons of cufflinks and cigarette lighters from [other acts]. Streisand was so poor that she gave each of us a package of cheese in little wedges. Stamped in purple on the back was the price – ninety-nine cents.' But to Streisand giving food was giving love and it would remain one of her favourite gifts for many years.

With no immediate work in sight and refusing to return to Brooklyn, she once again dragged her portable army cot around from a cousin's sublet for a night or two, to Peter Daniels's studio, to one acquaintance's pad to another. Frantic, Diana would call Shelley when she could not locate her. 'Do something, Shelley! Do something!' she would scream.

'I never questioned Barbra,' he says. 'I admired her spunk, I thought she should be left alone, she should be allowed to do what she wanted.'

Although she had no money, she did have a new manager, Marty Erlichman, a dark, husky man, about a decade her senior. Erlichman, raised in a predominantly Jewish section of the Bronx, was a determined, outspoken man who exuded sincerity and knew how to win over people's trust. Like Irving Arthur, he had come backstage to meet Streisand after her show at the Bon Soir. Did she have representation? he asked. Yeah, she replied, she did. He gave her a card with a telephone number where he could be reached and told her that if one day she thought she might like to make a change to call him. She liked the way he looked her straight in the eyes, direct. 'Yuh got many people you represent?' she asked.

'You'd make it two,' he replied honestly, his only other clients at the time being the Clancy Brothers, an Irish folksinging group.

Unhappy with the financial arrangements made by Arthur for the second tour, she telephoned Erlichman from Detroit. 'You still want to represent me?' she asked. He flew at his own expense to her side, renegotiated the last two weeks of her contract, getting her free meals along with a raise of $25 dollars a week. What Streisand did not know was that Erlichman paid the extra money out of his own pocket, sure that he would find her a high-paying club date or a role in a Broadway show on her return to New York, but even Erlichman's fired-up enthusiasm did not land her a job right away.

'I was pretty hard to reach in those days because I didn't have a phone,' Streisand later recalled. 'Neither did my manager, Marty Erlichman ... All he had was a roll of dimes and a phone booth on 53rd Street. He really believed in me because he sure went through a lot of change.'

She still was living a vagabond style without a key to her own apartment. 'I can't stand it when I read in [a book] that someone has said she was DIRTY, which is so much the opposite of the truth,' Schulenberg said angrily. 'She always had beautiful nail care, her hair was clean and so was she! I remember a whole evening with her when she was occupying [a friend] Don Goftness's office for the night and had to be out before the cleaning crew arrived in the morning – a whole evening she spent steaming and carefully wrapping her clothes in tissue paper – just like every teenager, right?'

She would put all the clothes she did not need in boxes and store them in the apartments of friends along with treasured items collected while living with Barry Dennen. 'When Barbra left an accommodation she had borrowed for a night or two,' a former host declares, 'it didn't even *need* a cleaning crew. She was immaculate and always left charming little thank-you notes. If this had not been the case people would not have been so willing to put her up.'

She never gave up auditioning for the theatre and was eventually offered a part in an off-Broadway revue *Another Evening with Harry Stoones*, with music and lyrics by Jeff Harris. The title was a take-off on the proliferation at that time of recent solo star Broadway appearances such as *An Evening with Marlene Dietrich*, but the revue had no character named Harry Stoones. The title was a gimmick, meant as a satirical comment. The show opened on 21 October 1961, at the Gramercy Arts Theater, a small house which did not even have a marquee. In the cast were two other newcomers, Dom de Luise and Diana Sands. Streisand contributed her own short and highly imaginative bio-graphical notes for the playbill.

'I wrote that I was born in Madagascar and reared in Rangoon, and attended the *yeshiva* in Brooklyn,' she later said. 'I didn't want people to read, "Streisand, Brooklyn, *yeshiva*," and say to themselves, "Oh yes, I see who she is."' She was required to do a great deal of ensemble work which she did not feel was right for her. By the end of rehearsals, she had two solos, 'Jersey' and 'Value', (also known as 'I'm in Love with Harold Mengert'). She bombarded the

director, G. Adam Jordan, with complaints: the lighting was wrong, the costumes cheesy, the orchestrations too thin. She turned to Peter Daniels for help,
with pleas of 'I'm trapped, I'm trapped', and he arranged the music on her
solos. She felt that it was important that New York audiences and critics see
her as more than a cabaret singer.

*Another Evening with Harry Stoones* closed after its opening night, but it gave
her a taste of appearing in the theatre, which she liked. Next time, she told
Erlichman, she wanted to move uptown to Broadway and do a full-scale, well-
financed musical. Meanwhile, as she was in between engagements at the
Bon Soir, she agreed with him that it was important for her to continue
to be visible. She made a series of television talk-show guest appearances on
the late-night theatrically oriented *Joe Franklin Show* and then was asked to
audition for the low-budget *P.M. East* hosted by Mike Wallace, which 'generally had to scrape pretty close to barrel bottom when it came to booking
talent'.

Pre-interviews were conducted with the show's lesser-known guests. 'I
remember [Barbra] was calling from a bar because she not only did not have
a phone, she had no apartment,' said Al Ramus, one of *P.M. East's* writer-
producers.

'When I find a place that's not being used or that has an extra room, I go
there,' she told him. 'I carry around a bunch of keys my friends gave me so I
can get in anywhere. I don't make much money singing in little places but I
have a typical Jewish mother. She waits outside wherever I'm singing till one
or two in the morning with frozen steaks' – an apocryphal story. Diana did
bring containers of chicken soup to the Bon Soir but came backstage to give
them to her. Streisand went on to tell him a fanciful story about her father:
he was a genius who had travelled around the country, a wanderer on a
bicycle. As a teenager Manny Streisand had hitchhiked through New Jersey
and Pennsylvania one summer and for a brief time had delivered telegrams
on a bicycle.

'The voice was pure Brooklyn . . . full of *chutzpah* . . . But there was something
about her, even over the phone, that was unique. She was like the *essence* of
every confused, not-very-attractive girl who wanted extravagantly more out
of life than birth or circumstances could possibly give her. Her voice, her
lifestyle, were almost fictional, they were also so right for the role that I told
her – by now it must've been past 1 a.m. – that whether she could sing or not
she was going to be a star.' He also arranged for her to audition the next day
for the show at the Dumont Studios in midtown Manhattan.

She arrived about twenty minutes late clutching her music and shedding
her coat on the floor as she hurried across the empty, unlighted stage. 'Hey,'
she yelled to the lighting man. 'Over here! Yeah!' She grabbed a stool and sat
on it, her back was broomstick straight, her legs gracefully posed, her head

raised to catch the spot when it flashed on. Her voice soared as she sang 'A Sleepin' Bee' to a piano accompaniment.

'[What happened] sounds like a bad Twentieth Century-Fox musical,' Ramus commented, 'but virtually everyone on the set, sound men, lighting men, secretaries ... they all stopped and listened. The night before I told her she'd be a star. Now I was sure of it.'

*P.M. East* had no studio audience (applause came from the technicians), and it was video-taped, both helpful in making a neophyte television performer feel relaxed. However, the show was built around a theme, which for this particular programme would be glamour. Two ravishing models who also happened to be sisters, Theodora and Suzy Parker, were to be guests along with model agent Candy Jones and photographer Milton Greene, famous for his pictures of Marilyn Monroe. 'Those models were dressed to kill,' Streisand later recalled, 'every hair in place as if they'd been carried on a stretcher from the beauty salon to the Dumont studios.'

Dressed in a sleeveless black dress, a large silver Indian thunderbird pinned to it, her hair piled up in a beehive topped by her 'Danish pastry' postiche she sang 'A Sleepin' Bee' seated on a stool and then climbed on to the top of the piano, legs crossed, skirt hiked so that her thigh was seductively visible and gave a scorching up-tempo rendition of 'Lover Come Back to Me'.

Then she sat down and talked in nasal Brooklynese to Wallace and his guests about her vagabond lifestyle. She was funny, far-out, unabashed – and an instant hit. Wallace, a charismatic personality who would go on to become American television's most outspoken and highest rated interviewer on *Sixty Minutes*, knew he had found a ratings' booster and booked Barbra over a dozen times during the next few months. And he was right. Ratings went up as 'this kook on TV with the knock-out voice' became more and more outrageous every week.

'The part I liked best [about appearing on the show],' Streisand says, 'was the talk segment. They never knew what I was going to say. Although sometimes I would suggest a topic – like nutrition, Zen Buddhism or the business about my keyring.'

One evening it would be the evils of drinking milk, which drew an angry response from the Dairy Association; another night she infuriated volatile television producer David Susskind, a guest on the show, by confronting him with a story about the time she had come into his office for an audition and he kept her waiting for hours and then didn't see her. 'People like you are ruining show business because you don't let new talent emerge, you think it's your duty to squelch them.' Susskind was stunned and seemed unable to reply to her. 'I scare you, don't I?' she smirked. 'I'm so far out, I'm in.'

The attack on Susskind, who was fairly powerful in the entertainment world, was bold and foolhardy at the same time. It was not likely that he would want to hire Streisand for a production of his after this assault, but she was getting to enjoy the power such confrontations on live television gave her. When host Mike Wallace told her his show could help her be seen by Broadway producers, she snapped, 'Now, let's be honest. Those people don't watch television, not the ones that do the hiring. A show like this gets the public interested in paying the minimum to see me at places like the Bon Soir.'

In January 1962, ending her appearances on *P.M. East*, she accepted a club tour to New Orleans, Miami and Chicago, this time with a considerable pay hike which enabled her to put some money aside. When she returned, she began yet another engagement at the Bon Soir. One night Michael Shurtleff, who worked as a casting director for the powerful Broadway producer, David Merrick, visited the club. Merrick, the producer of such stage hits as *Fanny*, *Gypsy*, *Do Re Me*, *Carnival* and *Irma La Douce*, was in pre-production of the show, *I Can Get It for You Wholesale*, based on the 1937 best-seller by Jerome Weidman about the New York garment district. A minor role in the script was that of a fifty-year-old Jewish secretary. The character was given one song about her psychosomatic abhorrence to the drab appellation with which she was continually addressed, 'Miss Marmelstein', but the character and the number had been recently cut. When Shurtleff heard Streisand sing at the Bon Soir he was determined to give her an audition with the hope that, hearing her, Merrick would reinstate the song which he greatly liked – with Streisand singing it.

There was one hitch. Merrick only liked beautiful women in his shows. Shurtleff took a hard look at Streisand and knew it might be difficult to convince 'the abominable showman', as Merrick was called by his many detractors, to make an exception this time. No less pushy than the lady he wanted to sell to his boss, the previous year Shurtleff had made up his mind that he would work for Merrick, wrote to him once a week for seven months discussing what was good and bad with each of Merrick's many former Broadway shows. Next, he had mutual friends write to the producer to plead his case. Finally, piqued by curiosity, Merrick agreed to see the offensive letter writer. Shurtleff kept the meeting going for four hours and ended up with a job as casting director.

Streisand's audition was scheduled by Shurtleff for late the next afternoon to follow several other singers trying out for minor roles, hoping that as the final auditionee of the day, her extraordinary voice would so outshine her predecessors, Merrick would not say – as he had so often before – 'Too ugly'.

That morning, she had moved into her first apartment, three rooms over Oscar's, a fish restaurant in the Sixties on the upper East Side, and in her words was 'excited and *furtumphed*'. She dashed out on the stage of the St James Theater on West 44th Street where the auditions were being held just as the final singer turned to leave. 'Hey, I'm sorry,' she said, staring at her unseen audience beyond the blinding footlights of the stage. 'On the way over, saw some things in a thrift shop window on Second Avenue near where I just rented my first apartment and I just had to go in and buy them – to celebrate, you know?' She did a model's turn to show off the forty-year-old amazingly stylish raccoon coat that she was wearing along with a commissar's hat in an unidentifiable fur which was perched precariously on top of her beehive hairdo.

'Do you like it?' she asked. When there was no reply, she stepped forward as far as she could without falling into the orchestra pit. The glare of the footlights made it difficult for her to see out into the otherwise vast, darkened 1,600-seat auditorium and she cupped her hands above her eyes attempting to see better. 'Is there anyone out there?' she asked in a thick Brooklyn twang.

'Is this girl sane?' Merrick asked Shurtleff, who was seated next to his boss about midway up the centre aisle of the orchestra section.

'No,' Shurtleff replied.

'Then, why are you putting us through this?' Merrick barked.

'Miss Streisand, would you sing?' Shurtleff called out.

She glanced uncomfortably around. Behind her was the backdrop, a New York skyline from Merrick's current musical offering, *Subways Are for Sleeping*.

'I had never seen her until she walked on to the stage for the audition,' *Wholesale*'s director, Arthur Laurents, told this author. 'She had on what I call her "calculated" look. Her thrift-shop look. She looked like an antique. And she did something right at the beginning that impressed me. I hadn't seen this done before – nor have I since. She had the pages of her music taped together. She put it on the piano stage-right, an upright piano. And then, with a flourish, flipped it like an accordion on to and across the stage. A great trick. And I thought, "She knows what she's doing."'

She glanced at the music spread out in front of her, unsure which of the three songs she had brought with her would be the most appropriate. Apart from Merrick, Shurtleff and Laurents, the small, select audience that she could not see included among others: Herbert Ross, the choreographer, Jerome Weidman, the author/playwright, and one of Hollywood and Broadway's most successful composer/lyricists, Harold Rome, who leaned forward and asked, 'Have you got an "up song" you can sing?'

'If I didn't have an "up song", would I be auditioning for a musical?' she replied.

Merrick bristled.

'I can't sing without a stool,' she complained. A stool was found and placed before the microphone. She removed her coat. 'Someone could maybe hold this while I sing?' she called out looking around her. A stagehand took it from her. Merrick was about to walk. Shurtleff placed a restraining hand on his arm.

She shuffled through her music, picked it up, and then conferred in a whispery voice with the rehearsal pianist.

'We're waiting, Miss Streisand,' Merrick yelled out.

'I'm coming! I'm coming,' she shouted back and lifted herself on to the stool.

She sang 'Value'. There was no response from the auditorium of the darkened theatre. She started across the stage to reclaim her coat. 'Could you sing a ballad for us?' Rome shouted.

'Sure, sure,' she said, and came back to the piano. A few moments later she was reseated on the stool and sang a lovely, lyrical story song, 'Too Long at the Fair' by Billy Barnes. Again there was no response other than some mumbling among her unseen audience. 'Well, did you like it or not?' she asked into the microphone.

'We liked it. But we need to be convinced,' Rome replied.

The third song she had brought with her was her favourite audition piece, 'A Sleepin' Bee'. 'When she sang that song,' Laurents says, 'I didn't care about anything else. I had never heard anyone sing like that. I just kept her singing. And it was extraordinary. Now there was no part for her at the time in the show. She was nineteen, unattractive and emphasised it, making herself look deliberately gawky. I think she sort of invented a character for that audition – this loose-limbed girl out of the woodwork. [I was so taken with her] I said to the authors, "Why does Miss Marmelstein have to be fifty? Why do we have to say her age?"'

'I sang,' Streisand later remembered, 'and then I sort of ran around the stage yelling my phone number and saying, "Wow! Will somebody call me, please! Even if I don't get the part, just call!" I yelled out the number and then repeated it. I'd gotten my first phone that day, and I was wild to get calls on it.' She was also admittedly excited and nervous over auditioning for a role in a major Broadway show.

She folded up her music and headed into the wings. Merrick turned sharply to Shurtleff and complained, 'How many times have I told you I don't want ugly girls in my shows?'

'You can get her for scale,' Harold Rome intervened, thinking much as Laurents had and hoping that he could reintroduce 'Miss Marmelstein' into the score.

'You're the most anti-Semitic guy I know,' Merrick countered. 'You've hired every ugly Jew in town for this show, and now you want me to hire this *meeskite*.'

Finally, in view of the zeal of the show's creators, Merrick agreed to give her a chance *if* Miss Marmelstein was reinstated. She was asked to come back on to the stage where Shurtleff introduced her to Merrick, Laurents, Ross, Rome and Weidman. She was given the music to 'Miss Marmelstein' and told to return for a second audition in a few hours. She immediately called Peter Daniels, dashed over to his studio and ran through the number several times. Although she did not read music, she had the ability of hearing a song once and recording the music in her head. She also possessed the gift of perfect pitch.

'When I returned to the theatre that afternoon,' she recalled, 'I wanted to sing the number sitting down for two reasons. One – because I was nervous, and two – because I thought it would be funny to have a secretary moving her chair around the stage with her legs, like a wallflower on wheels. So I sat down, took my gum out of my mouth, stuck it under the chair and sang.'

Arthur Laurents claims that there was never a secretary's chair on the stage for the audition, that Streisand sang Miss Marmelstein' perched on the stool, although she did store her gum under the seat. 'The moving chair came later, during rehearsals,' Laurents insists. Whatever the prop was that she used, her interpretation of the song impressed both its composer and Laurents. That night, Laurents went down to the Bon Soir and after her performance told her that she was hired. The next day she signed a contract for $165 a week on conditional terms which gave Merrick the right to fire her on a week's notice.

Slouched in the back of the darkened theatre on the cold November day in 1961 of Streisand's audition, Elliott Gould, the young man just cast as the romantic lead, was fascinated by 'this strange-looking, skinny creature with long, spiky hair, spidery hands, two-inch nails and purple lipstick'.

'A freak – a fantastic freak!' Gould thought at the time. That evening before she left for her stint at the Bon Soir he telephoned her. 'You said you wanted to get calls, so I called,' he said. 'You were brilliant.' Then he hung up.

# Broadway Baby

'She was the most innocent thing I'd
ever seen, like a beautiful flower that
hadn't blossomed yet. But she was so
strange that I was afraid.'

ELLIOTT GOULD

# 9

BARBRA STREISAND HAD made it to Broadway at the age of nineteen. Her initiation was not going to be easy. Almost the entire company of *I Can Get It for You Wholesale* were seasoned performers. In this story of the brash, opportunistic young Jew, Harry Bogen (Elliott), he uses a strike in the firm of Maurice Pulverman (Jack Kruschen) to his own advantage. Miss Marmelstein was Pulverman's secretary. Except for Kruschen, who had been the Oscar nominee for supporting player the previous year for his role in Billy Wilder's *The Apartment*, most of the other cast members were counting on this show to mark either their rise to stardom or their comeback.[1] It was an intense, make-or-break situation not ameliorated by the tough treatment Streisand met at the hands of her producer and director.

Kruschen, a bear of a man always younger than the roles he played, felt 'bad for Barbra. She had poise. But she didn't have the wordliness to know how to handle some of David Merrick's or Arthur Laurents's brusque, hard knocks. One morning during rehearsals she arrived a little late. She liked to shop at places like the Goodwill, and she was wearing this 1920s diaphanous kind of day dress – foamy, filmy – kind of odd. Arthur, who wasn't the nicest guy to her, told her to go change her clothes. He was directing, and he was fresh out of his big success as the librettist of *West Side Story* and *Gypsy* and he was feeling exceptionally macho.

'I thought she was going to cry. He had chosen to tell her this in front of the entire company. There was nothing she could have done but go home and change her clothes. And he said, "I don't care what you put on, but don't put on stuff like this and don't come to work like this again." I felt – how dare he. His rough treatment of her endeared her to me. She knew very little about the stage. Sometimes she'd hit a mark [where she was supposed to stand on stage] and sometimes she wouldn't. That caused problems for the rest of the cast. As

---

[1] In the other main roles were Sheree North (*femme fatale* in the show), old-timer Lillian Roth (as Bogen's mother), Harold Lang (star of the 1952 revival of *Pal Joey* about another 24-carat heel), Bambi Linn (who had made her debut sixteen years earlier in Rodgers' and Hammerstein's *Carousel*), and Marilyn Cooper as the ingenue lead.

Spencer Tracy once told some young performers, "Learn your lines and for God's sake, don't bump into each other." '

Arthur Laurents replies, 'I was tough on Barbra because she wanted to do what she wanted to do and as director I couldn't have that. I can remember one time, I staged a scene so that when a character entered, everyone had to turn their back on him, he was ostracised, but she didn't. She said she didn't feel like it. She didn't realise that unless you're [a monologuist], you cannot play alone. You have an obligation. You have to be there for your fellow actors. A musical has to be carefully blocked. You can't decide suddenly to go here or there.'

Laurents was firm with her, but he also recognised her potential and was one of her staunchest enthusiasts. 'Shortly after her audition for the show, I sent her to Goddard Lieberson, then head of Columbia Records. She thanked me,' he smiled with an appreciative look on his intelligent face. 'Then I got a note from him: "Thank you for sending me Barbra Streisand. Indeed, she has a spectacular voice, but she is too special for records." I also dragged Stephen Sondheim down to the Bon Soir before the show opened. He didn't like the way she sang.[2] Then, at the time of *Anyone Can Whistle*, I sent her some of the songs and she didn't like his songs. [Much later she would have a change of heart.]

'I thought she had an extraordinary voice and was very talented as an actress, but she was really so inexperienced and more concerned with what she was doing with her *nails* than with the other players. I told her, "When you cut your nails I'll know you really want to be an actress." '

Laurents is, and was at that time, one of the American theatre's finest playwrights as well as a director and Streisand quickly recognised that she had much she could learn from him. 'I began fattening her part because it was obvious that she was a phenomenal talent, which she knew and told us she was. She had no doubt she was going to be a star. It was not shared [by Merrick and others] I think because of what she looked like.'

Elliott, on the other hand, thought she looked just dandy and was intrigued by her eclecticism. They did not actually meet until the first day of rehearsals which she attended in a man's tattered black coat, circa 1930, that reached her ankles, the sleeves turned back so that her hands could show, a turn-of-the-century, black medical satchel bag serving as a purse. Outside, February winds blasted through the tunnel-like streets of New York, wintry blue-grey skyscrapers rising like steel traps on either side. Her face was red with cold. 'She looked like a young Fagin,' Elliott remembers. 'She scared me, but I really dug her. I think I was the first person who ever did.'

[2] Laurents wrote the book and Sondheim the score for *Anyone Can Whistle*. They had also worked together on *West Side Story* (1957) and *Gypsy* (1959) for which Sondheim wrote only lyrics. Laurents's non-musical plays include *Home of the Brave, The Time of the Cuckoo, A Clearing in the Woods* and *Invitation to a March*. He also wrote the screenplays for *The Way We Were, The Snake Pit, Rope* and *Anastasia* among many others.

This, of course, was not true, but Elliott saw her with new romantic eyes. She was not a woman he wanted to change or a performer he wished to mould. He loved her kookiness, her naturalness, her hunger to devour food, people, new experiences. She was drawn to him almost immediately. He was distinctive but he did not look like her idea of a leading man. Tall (six feet, three inches), chunky, with dark bushy hair and ethnic features, his clothes, whether custom-tailored or ready-made – never quite fitted. He managed to execute a dance when required with surprising expertise, but was constantly stumbling on and off stage.

Born in 1938 and four years older than Streisand, he was the product of a frustrated, confused childhood with an overbearing mother, an overshadowed father and all the tensions that go with being an only male child in a middle-class Jewish household. Until the age of eleven he had shared a small bedroom in a cramped $2\frac{1}{2}$ room flat in the Bensonhurst section of Brooklyn with his parents, Lucille and Bernard Goldstein. Bernard was a book-keeper in New York's garment district. From an early age, Elliott recognised that his intrusion into Bernard's otherwise ordered life was resented.

Bensonhurst was Jewish and Italian and only a short distance from the slightly more affluent Flatbush area where Streisand lived after her mother's marriage to Louis Kind. It was said that the slain bodies of infamous members of Murder Inc. were buried near the school he attended, but neighbours looked after each other's kids and the streets were kept reasonably safe for them to gather.

'We'd play things like Ring-o-leevio, Three Feet to Germany, Johnny on the Pony,' Gould recalled, 'but I excelled at flipping trading cards bought by the fistful down at Irving's Candy Store. There were Smilin' Jack cards, baseball cards, World War Two cards with General MacArthur and the bombing of Tokyo on them,' he added fondly. He was, he insists, 'terribly conscious of a degree of vulnerability, of not wanting to make a fool of myself. I didn't feel abnormal, but I certainly didn't feel normal.'

Lucille's memories are sharper. 'This child was too good to be true. He was too well behaved. He wanted to please so desperately. I was too strict with him.' She shakes her head. 'Yes, Mama watched over him perhaps too closely. But it was done out of love. I wouldn't leave any stone unturned as far as this child went. I'd cut off my arm for this child.' Alone with her somewhat bumbling son, when Bernard went off to fight during World War Two, Lucille decided he must have drama, singing and dancing lessons to help him gain self-confidence. She took him to Charlie Lowe's Broadway Show Business School for Children.

'He'll never dance,' she told Charlie firmly. 'Just fix up his diction and the way he walks.' Instead Charlie Lowe put Elliott through the regular routine that he taught.

'That meant everything,' Elliott claimed. 'Blow-your-nose lessons, dance lessons, wipe yourself lessons, masturbation lessons, bunko. Compulsions for a dissatisfied mother. Why did I go? Because I loved my mother a lot. That's why I did it.' Within a year Charlie Lowe placed Elliott on local TV shows to sing and dance. As he was about to go on camera for the first time, Lowe asked him if he would like to be announced as Gold, instead of Goldstein. Elliott said, 'No, Gould,' bearing in mind the well-known composer and orchestra leader Morton Gould.

He went on to Professional Children's School in Manhattan and, when his father returned from the war, the family would vacation each year in the Catskill borscht belt[3] where Elliott won dance contests doing the mambo with his mother.

'When an entertainer needed a stooge,' his father remembered, 'Elliott would be the one they'd choose. [At the age of fifteen] he could do a dozen dialects – German, Italian, Jewish, all of them.' After he graduated from high school, he spent three weeks in summer stock. This was followed by a second lead in a pre-Broadway show at Woodstock, *Some Little Honor* (1955), which never made it into Manhattan.

'He was always doing bits,' one friend added. 'He would go into a diner, sit next to a little old lady and calmly make a meal out of his paper napkin – complete with salt, pepper and ketchup. He also liked to knock on strangers' doors and inquire politely, "Is this the party?" Or walk into one door of a Checker cab stopped in traffic and out the other, apologising to the passenger as he made his exit.'

He won a job in his first Broadway show when he was eighteen by telephoning one of the producers, impersonating a well-known agent and selling the talents of 'a kid named Elliott Gould'. Hired in 1957 for the chorus line, the show, *Rumple*, closed after forty-five performances which was fortunate because he was plagued with bursitis from lifting the rather hefty chorines in the dance numbers. Despite this experience, he went on to dance in the chorus of the Jule Styne show, *Say, Darling* (1958) and a revival of *Hit the Deck* at Jones Beach. Then came odd jobs such as a speed punching-bag demonstrator at Bloomingdale's Department Store and as a toy salesman and elevator operator at both Gimbel's and Macy's.

A loner, not terribly popular with the girls, he began to place bets on the horses. By the time he was eighteen, he had run up debts he could not pay, 'borrowed' his father's jewellery to pawn and used the money he received to pay off the bookies. He also had the Goldstein's home telephone disconnected when hoods started calling to demand the rest of their payment. His parents

---

[3] The Catskill Mountains, 150 miles north of New York City, were dotted with resort hotels featuring kosher food and catering to a Jewish clientèle.

were furious but, fearful he might end up in the East River with a cement block attached to his feet, helped him out of his predicament. Elliott was screaming out for attention, however bad it was and he gambled as many habitual betters do – ultimately to lose because their failure validates their theory that fate does not look well upon them, that they hold no responsibility for what has happened in their lives.

A job in the chorus of the David Merrick musical, *Irma La Douce* in 1960, led to his being hired first as the understudy to the lead in *I Can Get It for You Wholesale*, which originally was to have featured British actor Laurence Harvey. When Harvey backed out of his contract, the role went to the surprised Elliott. Open, friendly, funny, he was well liked by the members of the company, but it was Streisand to whom he paid the most attention. Once rehearsals began, he thought she was even more brilliant than he had first believed her to be. He treated her deferentially and often spent the little free time he had, for he was in a large percentage of the show's scenes, listening to her practise.

'I used to hear her warm up,' Jack Kruschen remembered. 'She had the most beautiful vocal acrobatics ... perfect pitch. She just blew my socks away the first time I heard her sing. *Wholesale* was one of the earliest Broadway shows where dialogue blended with music, where there was a great deal of recitative. Barbra had the only solo in one [in front of the curtain], 'Miss Marmelstein'. She had her own ideas about how she wanted to sing it and Arthur did not always agree with her. It was a running battle.'

Streisand later confided to journalist Joe Morgenstern, 'I spent weeks trying to convince Arthur to let me use my secretary's chair which had a movable seat that you could twist and tilt. I was told, "You've got no discipline, you can't do anything twice the same way." They yelled at me because I didn't do the song with the same gestures each time I sang it. I kept asking for my chair. Finally, Arthur said, "All right, use your chair if you want to," and when we opened in Philadelphia I stopped the show. I can't tell you how I felt stopping that show. I felt *guilty*.'

Laurents counters, 'Nobody remembers the same thing. There are stories that start out an anecdote then become columnists' grist and then they become fact. It is curious to me how they creep and spread. A recent book on Barbra has several lies in it about *Wholesale*. In fact the author told one lie three times. The basic lie is I never staged "Miss Marmelstein", Herb Ross did.'

This would imply that Streisand's fight for the moving chair was with Ross, not Laurents, but whoever her adversary, the struggle had not been in vain. She had managed to convert the one number she had into a star turn calling attention to herself and away from the rest of the cast. And she had approximately four minutes of her own on stage in which to wheel and twirl her secretary's chair contorting her legs and arms and never allowing any of this action to disrupt the flow and clarity of the comedic song-story she sang in thick Brooklynese. She gambled in a different way from Elliott – with her talent, her creative ability, her driven ambition that pushed aside all other considerations. She played for higher stakes – her career, which was to say *her life*. And she only knew how to gamble one way – to win.

In November, shortly before her audition for *Wholesale*, Streisand had made an unexpected one-night appearance at the Blue Angel, an elite cabaret at 152 East 55th Street. The front-room lounge wrapped you in a cloak of sophistication as soon as you walked into its gleaming black and white cocktail lounge with its black bar, booths and patent-leather walls. The back room held the small stage, a plaster angel suspended over it. The stage was lit by a fixed spotlight, the room decorated in a deep lush pink, leather on the banquettes, fabric on the walls. The long, narrow room was difficult to play and yet, it was a launching pad for top artists (Dorothy Louden, Carol Burnett and Henry Belafonte had all sung there), a place where one came expressly to hear the entertainer. On the night that Streisand first appeared, Felicia Saunders was the star performer, but there was also a comic and he got violently ill just before the show. Desperate for someone to fill in and recalling things he had heard about Streisand being a funny lady, Herbert Jacoby, the co-owner, called her to come in for the single performance.

'Two singers were never billed on one show,' Arthur Gelb, of the *New York Times* said. 'Jacoby must have thought Barbra was a comic. I was there to review Saunders and was overwhelmed when this strange-looking girl in a beaded dress took to the stage. Everyone was spellbound. I went back to the paper and wrote about this great new talent. I think it was the first review she ever got in a major paper and brought her to the attention of a lot of people.'

While *Wholesale* was in rehearsal, she went back to the Blue Angel as the headliner. The club's audience was far more conservative than the habitués of the Bon Soir. Frightening though it might have been to play to such an urbane group, Streisand liked being able to sing songs differently, to experiment. She sang an exquisite arrangement by Peter Daniels of the Harry Schmidt/Tom Jones song from *The Fantastics* 'Soon It's Going to Rain' and an upbeat rendition of Leonard Bernstein's seldom performed 'I Hate Music'.

Her reviews were glowing but a generally laudatory one in the show business bible, *Variety*, included an indelicate suggestion that she get a 'schnoz bob'. Erlichman was furious. 'I couldn't believe that a guy like Abel Greene, the respected publisher of *Variety*, who's entire life had been devoted to the business, would use an expression like "schnoz bob" for a nineteen-year-old girl,' he said. 'Against the advice of the press agent for the Blue Angel, who was worried about a possible backlash, I called Abel Greene and really yelled at him. "Would you do that to your own daughter? You can say nose job or have the nose fixed, but where do you come off saying, "schnoz bob"? It's vulgar and tasteless." And he apologised to me.' The remark, however phrased, was inappropriate in a review of a singer.

To compound this painful jibe, Radie Harris, a columnist for the *Hollywood Reporter*, described her as having, 'mousy-colored hair which hung straight and looked unwashed, a nose that a plastic surgeon would have loved to use his scalpel on, and she wore a black blouse and skirt that looked as though they'd been bought in Klein's bargain basement.' Unwittingly she validated Diana's concern when she wrote near the conclusion of her review: '"Why would anyone who looks like that think she has a future in show business?" I thought as she sat nervous and uneasy beside me.' But she added, 'And then she got up to sing, and I knew why. Barbra Streisand was suddenly beautiful.'

For weeks Streisand talked about nothing else except whether she should or should not have a nose job. 'Can you become a new person with a new nose?' Elliott asked her. They were seeing quite a lot of each other. One night he took her to a horror movie about giant caterpillars that ate cars. Later they went to a Chinese restaurant. About 2 a.m. it began to snow.

'We were walking around the skating rink at Rockefeller Center when Elly chased me and we had a snow fight,' she remembered. 'He never held me around or anything, but he put snow on my face and kissed me, very lightly. It sounds *ookhy*, but it was great. Like out of a movie!'

A few weeks after the snow fight, she thought he was paying too much attention to Marilyn Cooper, the ingenue in the show, and refused to talk to him. That night he wandered the city and used up a pocketful of change calling her telephone number. Each time she hung up. Finally he went home to his small apartment on Morton Street in the Village. 'About 4 a.m. my bell rings, and Barbra's standing there like a little orphan child, in her nightgown, some kind of crocheted thing over her shoulders, tears streaming her face. I wrapped her up in a warm coat and took her home but when we reached her building, which housed a fish restaurant on the ground floor, the hallway stunk so that I refused to go upstairs.'

'I didn't care about the smell,' Streisand once said. 'For the first time in my life I had my own apartment.' A connection might well be made with the fact that Manny Streisand had spent his early years in a flat over a fish market. Her father figured frequently in her conversations with Elliott and with Shelley. Her reverence for his reported intelligence, his ambition to make something of his life that might have taken him and his family out of Brooklyn, had grown to mythic proportions. Living over a fish restaurant perhaps gave her a sense of familiarity with something he had experienced. The $62 monthly rent was also cheaper than for most other apartments of its size and location and one she could afford. Money was always a consideration. She did not mind sacrificing something others might think a necessity for what was important to her. As a youngster she had forfeited lunch to buy cosmetics.

Now she endured the odour of fish so that she could have some extra money for the purchase of clothes, furniture or items that caught her eye, and a telephone so that she did not have to hang around someone's office or a telephone booth to receive a call.

Although he kept the Morton Street apartment, Elliott managed to overcome his olfactory objections and was soon sharing the flat a good part of the time with her. 'The only window looked out on a black brick wall,' he recollected. 'A big rat named Oscar [in dubious honour of the restaurant below] lived in the kitchen.' They were very private about their relationship. At this point no one in the cast even knew they were living together. Their combined incomes after taxes was modest (his salary in *Wholesale* was not much larger than hers.) They entertained themselves on the cheap. Besides seeing horror movies, they played pokerino in penny arcades, saving up coupons from his winnings to supply their flat with dishes and glassware. She filled the apartment with scented candles and perfumed Chinese incense to overcome the odour of fish, but there was still the hallway to conquer. Elliott took the steps three at a time without breathing.

Diana did not know that her daughter and Elliott were co-habiting. She would come by the theatre during rehearsals bringing large containers of chicken soup. 'All those stories she tells about her mother,' Laurents says, 'it's odd because her mother was very much there. When she introduced me to Mrs Kind, very fleetingly, it reminded me of Sandra Church when she was [starring] in *Gypsy*, introducing me to her mother, whose name was Rose. It seemed to me that they had a similar attitude, "Well, here's Rose [Gypsy's mother in the play and real life]." Meaning – pushy, and the daughter wanted to dismiss the mother. It may be that what Barbra has said about her mother is true. But she did bring chicken soup and it was very good and we all had it!'

She continued to experiment with ways to play Miss Marmelstein, attempting to get a deeper understanding of the character. She was all over the place, making a mess of Laurents's careful blocking. Then there was the matter of her chewing gum while on stage.

'Get rid of it,' he demanded one day in rehearsal.

'Why?' she argued. 'If you ask me Yetta Marmelstein would've chewed gum in the office.'

Before singing her big solo at the top of Act Two, she defiantly told him that she had pressed the wad of gum against her upper palate but she wouldn't get rid of it.

'I knew no one could sing like she did with a wad of chewing gum in her mouth,' Laurents said later. 'One day she pretended to take it out and press it on the bottom of her chair. After she finished her number, I asked my assistant to upturn the chair. There was nothing there. I then asked her to spit it out and she was silent for a moment. Then she said she'd swallowed it . . . I'm sure there never had been any chewing gum in the first place . . . In Boston,' he continued, 'Merrick wanted her fired. He felt she wasn't funny enough. And she wasn't. Audiences really didn't get her until we got to New York. She wasn't that successful on the road and she was madly in love with Elliott, who Merrick also wanted to fire. He wasn't happy with Elliott. He wasn't attractive and he had an unfortunate problem. Elliott is a sweater. He sweated so much that when he did a dance scene, the sweat blew over the first three rows of the audience. Merrick had him call Dr Miracle, Max Jacobson [who was known to push drugs on many Hollywood-New York celebrities] to get something to stop it. Whatever he gave Elliott worked – but it closed his vocal chords and he had to stop taking it.

'I never saw anything quite like it. She wanted Elliott and she got him. But they were sweet together, really sweet. Romeo and Juliet. Besides Elliott, her close friend in the show was Sheree North. She was ten years older, had been around [a bride at fifteen, mother at sixteen], married four times and she had been having a rough time [after being dropped by Twentieth Century-Fox in 1958]. But Barbra recognised that there was a real purity in Sheree North. Sheree was going through a very, very bad patch and Barbra was good to her.'

Sheree North was also the first movie star – albeit one on her uppers – with whom Streisand had ever had close contact. North had starred opposite Dan Dailey, Gordon MacCrae and Robert Cummings and once had been considered Betty Grable's replacement at her studio. Streisand bombarded her with questions about Hollywood, what it was like to be under contract to a studio, how pictures were made and North, pleased to be asked, answered in detail. But Ellie Stone, who was Streisand's understudy, and several of the other female members of the cast, say Streisand was cold and sometimes cruel to them. 'She knew how to cut you down,' one of them said, 'make a stabbing remark about something you missed in your performance. She could use Sheree but she was a regular Eve [a reference to the overly ambitious character in the film *All About Eve*] with the other young women in the cast. You just knew she would go on half-dead before she would let an understudy go on for her. I had the feeling she considered Marilyn Cooper her arch enemy – maybe because of Elliott, but more likely because she had a larger role and was on stage more often.'

In Philadelphia, Merrick's threats to fire her began to look serious. With amazing *chutzpah* she went to Laurents and asked him to recast her in Marilyn Cooper's role. 'I told her – "It's better to steal the show than play that part." It just shows you that Barbra's eye was on the brass ring all the time.' The creative team were finding her abrasiveness and strong mindset difficult to take. 'I have dealt with revolting people all my life,' Jerome Weidman, the author, was quoted as saying. 'I began my career working in the Garment

Center after all. As far as I'm concerned she has not earned the right to act that way.' He was referring to her continued lateness to rehearsals and her insistence on overruling Laurents's direction. Even her champion, Harold Rome, found her cold and overbearingly self-absorbed.

But Elliott was smitten. They were always together. Both of them loved to shop. In Boston, where the reviews were lukewarm, they discovered Filene's Basement which was stocked with marked-down merchandise. In Philadelphia, where the reviews were not much better, they combed the city's thrift shops. She was redoing the walk-up apartment better to accommodate the two of them and she sent parcels back on a daily basis containing anything from bits of fabric and lace to an old sewing-machine table with wrought-iron legs which she could make pillows and curtains with and also use as a table when it was closed. They could not be apart for more than half an hour. When she couldn't be found during rehearsals, a chorus of voices would shout out, 'Try Elliott's dressing room!'

The show opened in New York on the blustery night of 22 March 1962 at the Shubert Theater. An air of nostalgia pervaded the audience, many of whom had come to see old-timer Lillian Roth, who played Elliott's mother, or had personal ties to the garment industry. 'This could have meant they would be user-friendly or coldly critical,' one cast member said. 'We were all exceptionally nervous backstage, especially after the rather cool reception we received in Boston and then in Philadelphia.'

Streisand, who occupied a small dressing room of her own, arrived early at the theatre and remained cloistered behind its closed door until curtain time although Elliott was seen to enter, remain about fifteen minutes and then leave. She was shaking as she stood in the wings preparing to make her entrance. 'Once she was on stage,' a co-worker recalled, 'she was in total control. I never saw anything like it.'

'She really hit her stride with "Miss Marmelstein",' an investor who had seen the out-of-town performances said. 'This was *her* kind of audience – New Yorkers, predominantly Jewish or of some ethnic culture. Not Boston Brahmins or Philadelphia socialites. It was thrilling to watch as she twisted and twirled in her secretary's chair, her voice startling in its uniqueness. She had the audience in the palm of her hand and you had the feeling that she knew it. When she finished her number, they went wild.'

As she came off the stage into the wings, Elliott gave her a bear hug. She was flushed with excitement.

'The evening's find is Barbra Streisand, a girl with an oafish expression, a loud irascible voice and an arpeggiated laugh,' wrote Harold Taubman, the theatre critic for the *New York Times*.

'Miss Streisand possesses nothing short of a Chekhovian brand of heart-breaking merriment,' John Simon enthused in *Theater Arts*. 'Gifted with a face

that shuttles between those of a tremulous young borzoi and a fatigued
Talmudic scholar ... she can also sing the lament of the unreconstructed
drudge with the clarion peal of an Unliberty Bell.'

Most of the reviews had very little to say in favour of the show's attributes,
although Elliott, Kruschen, Roth, Lang, Cooper, North and Linn received good
personal notices. But it was Streisand who was lauded as a star discovery. Photo
articles in *Life* and *Look*, the two picture magazines with the largest national
circulation, and a two-page profile in *Time* appeared shortly after the opening
of the show. She was portrayed as a startling, new discovery, but her first
name was occasionally spelled with three *a's* and interviewers mispronounced
Streisand.

Merrick still had her on a week-to-week contract. He was now forced to
renegotiate with Marty Erlichman to make certain she remained with the
show for six months. Merrick offered her much the same terms. She refused,
which left him with a new star who could leave on a week's notice. Furious at
her 'attempted blackmail', he had all her out-front theatre photographs taken
down and killed her publicity. 'So she came to me crying, puzzled,' Laurents
recalled, 'and I said to her, "Why should he build you up if you're going
to leave?" She said, "Oh ..." and signed an extended contract, but it was
renegotiated with better terms for her.' She was to receive a $50 weekly raise,
a sum which hardly made her rich.

During the rest of their time in the show,[4] she and Elliott holed up in the
cluttered, 'remodelled' flat over Oscar's, the small rooms littered with her
thrift-shop scavenges including a battered dentist's cabinet filled with old shoe
buckles and an apothecary's jar of faded beauty marks. They would still go
down to Elliott's apartment in the Village to keep up the façade.

They loved to play games – Monopoly, chess, checkers, cards – and made
wild plans. 'Barbra decided we should speak a secret language nobody else
could understand,' Elliott explained. 'We swore never to be apart on our
birthdays, and we shopped for special presents.' He gave her a blue marble egg
that she cherished. She presented him with a gold cup inscribed 'First Annual
Alexander the Great Award', since he was a great admirer of the indomitable
Greek conqueror.

Barbra Streisand had not only made it on to Broadway, she had a lover for
whom she cared deeply. This should have made her ecstatically happy, but it
was not enough. Perhaps nothing ever would be.

[4] *I Can Get It for You Wholesale* closed after eight-and-a-half months and 300 performances on 8 December 1962. In the last ten weeks of the run, Barbra Streisand was
replaced by Louise Lasser. Elliott Gould was replaced by Larry Kert at about the same
time.

# 10

THEY EXISTED IN a romantic aura. Hurtful memories of Barry Dennen were assuaged by Elliott's honest love and affection. There was something childlike in their relationship, artless, natural. They did not have to put on airs with each other. Both were Jewish and from Brooklyn. She never had to prove herself to Elliott as she had felt obliged to with Dennen. They shared the same far-out humour; they were conspirators; it was them against the world. She thought he was an intuitively gifted actor, that all he had to be was himself – a funny, crazy person – and he would succeed. She felt safe with him, protected, small, feminine. She liked watching him pull his big mitt-like hands through his thick, dark, curly hair; was touched when he gazed endearingly at her with his enormous velvet brown eyes, found the deep cleft in his chin sexy. He had a cuddly teddy bear quality about him and yet he was this enormous *fella* 6'3" tall, weighing 206 pounds. She believed she loved Elliott.

Elliott never doubted the depth of his feelings for her. 'It was my love that powered the relationship,' he confesses. 'I don't think Barbra knew how to love me back. She was incapable of real love because she never had it from her father, and I don't think she ever came to terms with that. So I gave her something she had never had before: a true, normal, natural love. But I never was able to accept that she didn't know how to love me back. I felt it was my fault ... I told her once, "Your mother thinks affection is something people use to get something." Barbra replied, "That's why I am the way I am."'

She played the seductress but sex was given as a reward. She was, he admitted, self-involved, happiest when *he* was concentrating on *her* problems. He was convinced he could change all that. He had never had a strong man–woman relationship before. He loved her unreservedly and thought she was beautiful when she awoke all rumpled in the morning. He considered her the smartest person he ever knew and the most talented. He found it difficult to keep his hands off her – she was incredibly sexy to him. He wanted to get married and move into an apartment that did not stink of fish. She wanted to wait.

'I don't think she even wanted to marry me,' Elliott says in retrospect. 'I dwelled on it and insisted. I sublimated my own personality in my quest to please Barbra ... I so needed attention that I overcompensated by being good to Barbra, believing I would get it that way, overly trying to please. I *really* loved her. My love for her was pure and never exploitative nor opportunistic. She once said she thought I loved her more than anyone else could. Maybe that's right.'

He was understanding and supportive of the long hours she worked during the show's run, as she was 'doubling out' after the show, appearing late at night – first at the Bon Soir and then the Blue Angel and then back again at the Bon Soir. Her stamina was tremendous. She would go straight from final curtain to a waiting taxi and on to the cabaret where she was performing. During the days when there wasn't a matinée she would often tape guest spots on TV. On 29 May, not long after *Wholesale* opened, she created a sensation on the *Garry Moore Show*. Every week Moore celebrated a particular year in music. The chosen date for the show with Streisand's segment was 1929, remembered always as the year the stock market crashed. For Streisand's appearance, the Emmy-winning writer and musical director of the show, Ken Welch, chose to use 'Happy Days Are Here Again', a Depression song usually sung up-beat and associated with political conventions.

When she expressed her discomfort with singing the number as written, Ken Welch and his talented writer-wife, Mitzie Welch, wrote a verse for it and created a scene where a woman had lost all her money and most of her jewels in the crash. Adding to the irony of the song, they had Streisand seated alone in a plush night club. She splurges and orders champagne. A smartly turned-out waiter presents her with the check, she slowly removes her diamond earrings and places them on his tray. A haunting vamp by Ken Welch, that telegraphs the rhythm to come, sets the tone for what has – perhaps more than any one of her numbers – become Streisand's musical signature. The Welches slowed down the tempo of the song and added some lush, moving chords. The difference was startling. They had given an old standard a fresh and moving new life.

Her rendition of 'Happy Days Are Here Again' was memorable. The lyrics no longer connoted the past, nor did they seem to have anything to do with a political party as they once had. The familiar words and tune took on a poignant irony. Streisand had personalised them, become a woman who had lost in love and security, a model with whom everyone could identify. Immediate interest in her as a recording artist was generated. She cut an audition demo for RCA Records, ten songs from her cabaret repertoire, with Marty Gold, their staff accompanist. Included was an arrangement by Barry Dennen of 'At the Codfish Ball', an old Shirley Temple number. RCA were convinced she was uncommercial and to her great disappointment did not sign her.

Then the cast recording of *Wholesale* was released and sold well and a record she made along with several other artists as a twenty-fifth anniversary edition of Harold Rome's 1937 revue *Pins and Needles*, in which she gave a 'gorgeously funny performance' of 'Nobody Makes a Pass at Me', a precursor to 'Miss Marmelstein', netted her good reviews. Both records were produced by Columbia. Erlichman tried to convince them to sign her. The executives there thought she was too removed in style from the commercial scene of pop records.

Her hopes soared once again when record and cabaret revue producer Bill Bagley approached her to join Carol Channing and Jerry Orbach on an album he was compiling to feature rare songs of the late lyricist John Latouche, who with composer Vernon Duke had written the score to *Cabin in the Sky* and with Jerome Moross *The Golden Apple*, both shows critical standouts. Streisand, a tremendous fan of Latouche, was to sing 'Takin' a Chance on Love' from the first and 'It's the Going Home Together' and 'Lazy Afternoon' from the latter.[1] The rights to the songs, however, were withdrawn shortly before the recording session was to be conducted and the album was abandoned.

A jazz label, Atlantic Records, which issued mostly singles, now offered her a contract but Erlichman decided they should hold out for an album-producing company. 'It was a difficult thing to do,' he confessed, 'turning down an offer after we had waited so long. And neither of us had much money. But we both thought it would be better not to jump at the first offer just because we were hungry.'

Early in the run of *Wholesale* Streisand and Sandy Dennis, for *Who's Afraid of Virginia Woolf?*, tied in the New York Critics Award for Best Supporting Actress of 1962. Streisand's hopes were high that she would win the coveted Tony for the same category in a musical, but she was severely disappointed when it went to Phyllis Newman from David Merrick's *Subway's Are for Sleeping*. She found it difficult to be a good loser. It wasn't that she doubted the other person's right to win, rather it made her worry about *why* she had not won, what was wrong with her performance. On the taxi ride home, up the stairs to their apartment and in the kitchen as they shared a late-night snack (assorted deli meats, pickles and ice cream), she kept up a running inquisition with Elliott on why she had lost the award, finally deciding that she had not had a strong enough speaking role. In the next show – and there would be a next show, she insisted – her part would have to be considerably larger and more central to the story.

Towards the end of the New York run, Arthur Laurents often drove Elliott

---

[1] John Latouche (1917–56) was a brilliant lyricist, considered by current musicologists to be the precursor of Stephen Sondheim. He was noted for his original rhyming talents and the depth of feeling his lyrics expressed. Streisand would later record both 'Lazy Afternoon' and 'Takin' a Chance on Love'.

and Barbra in his convertible into the country on antique outings. She was a compulsive collector, loved the texture and feel of objects and fabrics, could indulge in an orgy of touching – the curves of a vase, the soft pile of velvet, the cool, hard feel of marble. Elliott shared her enthusiasm, although not with the same consuming passion.

'I never had much as a girl,' she told him. 'I like to own beautiful things. It makes me feel rich, even if I'm not.' She made a habit of keeping a record of what she paid for each item. 'Well, I might want to sell something one day,' she said, 'and it would be dumb if I didn't remember how much it cost.'

*Wholesale* closed on 8 December 1962. 'I was very friendly with Lena Horne and with Anita Ellis, the jazz singer,' Arthur Laurents recalls, 'and I gave a small party and invited these two ladies and Barbra. I remember Christmas tree trimmings. It was at my house in the Village. Well, Barbra was afraid to even walk into the room. She was odd that way. Obsessed by her own fame at the time, timid of the fame of others. She was in awe of Lena and, if you listen, you will hear some of Lena in her voice – and why not? We take the best we can from the artists we most admire whatever our field of art. You have to have the taste and good sense to pick up the right things from the right people and she certainly did.'

Erlichman did not want her to lose the momentum she had gained from her Broadway debut. She appeared on three segments of the new *Johnny Carson Tonight Show* which was filmed in New York. She then flew out to California to tape an appearance on the popular weekly *Dinah Shore Show*. It was the first time she and Elliott were separated. 'It was hell,' Streisand admitted. 'I had to be out there for seven days and I cried every day.'

Within a short time, she grew more accustomed to their separations as Erlichman secured an engagement for her at Mr Kelly's in Chicago and the Hungry i in San Francisco. Erlichman was commanding $5,000 a week for her by the time she returned to New York for an engagement at the extremely popular upscale cabaret, Basin Street East. Her new wealth gave her a sense of independence. With her ability to demand this kind of money had come power and she liked the feeling.

Then the moment that she and Marty Erlichman had been waiting for suddenly happened. Goddard Lieberson had been following her career ever since Laurents had first sent her to him. One of the problems, he claimed, was that in listening to an in-performance cabaret tape she had made at the Hungry i,[2] he could not tell if she was black or white. Erlichman persuaded him to come to the Blue Angel and hear her live. Lieberson liked what he heard and agreed to sign her to a five-year contract with Columbia Records.

[2] A bootleg album of this cabaret tape entitled *Barbra Streisand – Life, 1963* surfaced in 1985. Streisand sued the company and the album was withdrawn.

By forfeiting an even larger up-front payment – she received $20,000 which seemed a fortune to her – Erlichman gained her complete artistic control, most unusual for all but well-proven and top-selling recording artists. But Lieberson believed she was going to be a big asset to his company. Hers would be the final say, from the quality of studio recording to the design of the album cover, a precedent that would influence all her future business contracts. Power was the operative word, and with artistic control she had it.

Before recording her first album, she cut a single 45 rpm record in the Columbia studio on 30th Street: 'Happy Days Are Here Again' on the A side, 'When the Sun Comes Out', the Harold Arlen classic, on the back. The record went nowhere. This was followed by a second release, John Kander and Fred Ebb's 'My Coloring Book' on one side, 'Lover, Come Back to Me' on the flip side; it did not sell either. Erlichman and Columbia executives met to discuss the album Streisand was to make. She did not feel comfortable recording in a studio, he explained. She needed a live audience and familiar surroundings. Columbia agreed to have her record in performance at the Bon Soir with Peter Daniels on the piano and the Tiger Haynes Trio as back-up.

The record company transported its engineering crew to the Bon Soir on Monday evening, 5 November. 'They brought in a paid audience,' Tiger Haynes remembered, 'and recorded her first show for the rest of the week, through Saturday. Same musicians, same songs, every night, so that they had six tracks of every number.' After listening to the playback of the edited tape, she insisted that they record another live performance. This one had flaws in the musical accompaniment and in her performance. She had sung the wrong lyrics at one point, not gone for an obligatory high note at another. 'I can do better,' she kept urging. 'Let's try again.'

'Columbia scrapped the whole bunch of tapes,' Haynes continued, 'but Streisand made sure we got paid.' This setback only fired her drive to make a commercial record. She needed a musical director, a professional who like Dennen could put together a solid, cohesive set of songs. Through composer Harold Arlen, many of whose songs she sang and whose advice she sought after he had seen her and come backstage following a cabaret performance, she met musical director and arranger Peter Matz. Matz would create the musical back-up that would help Streisand transform herself from a cabaret performer with a limited audience into a wildly successful commercial recording artist.

Matz brought a rhythmic vitality to her recording performance that she did not have in the early singles and the aborted Bon Soir album.[3] At that time,

---

[3] Eight songs from this aborted album were included in Streisand's 1989 four-disc collection *Just for the Record*. 'Codfish Ball' was excluded and another recording of 'A Sleepin' Bee' included.

many singers, including Sinatra, were backed up on recordings by a sweeping string section. For Streisand, Matz brought the brass and the winds into play and when he needed the music to weep, he swept in the strings. This gave her records a fresh, new sound and brought out an urgency to her voice. The intimacy she had as a live cabaret performer was replaced by a startling record voice, full-bodied, soaring, able to move an audience even though disembodied, the acting conveyed solely through the voice of the singer. Matz had given her the commercial sound that would make her a recording success.

An innovative musician in his early thirties, Matz was raised in Los Angeles where, like Barry Dennen, he had attended UCLA, but it had taken a year in France and several more in New York for him to develop his talent. Of medium stature, wiry, with penetrating eyes and an enthusiastic manner of speaking, it was his keen intelligence and immense energy that captured Streisand's attention. She liked him immediately, respected his opinions and advice and the way he matched her industry in preparing the material for what would be her first released album.

'You could smell the air of desperation about her,' one associate observed. She was determined to become a star and so far she had been a supporting player and a cabaret performer, however highly praised or well paid. Matz understood what it was beside her amazing voice that set her apart from other singers. The very thing that Barry Dennen had known instinctively. At heart she was more actress than singer. Each song became a solid, complete scene – a musical soliloquy. What had to be done was to put all these segments together to form a whole. That could be achieved by placing the songs correctly and then using daring and fresh orchestrations to unite them. Streisand recognised what Matz could contribute to her growth as a major artist.

With Matz conducting, Streisand began to record on 23 January 1963. She was in the hands of ultimate professionals and she knew it. She came dressed in an old, loose sweater and a pair of khaki pants, no eccentric clothes. There was no audience, no one to play to. It didn't matter that her hair needed washing and hung limply. Except for a smudge of lipstick and the pencil lines that extended the width of her eyelids and had become habit, she wore no make-up. The acne had greatly subsided since *Wholesale* and her relationship with Elliott, but in the photographs taken during these sessions the marks from it are plainly visible on her chin and right cheek. She usually masked this evidence of her adolescence with make-up. She was, however, here to work, not to impress, and present only were Matz, the recording producer Mike Berniker, the engineers and the musicians. She badgered all of them into excessive overtime to try 'just one more' take.

Obsessed with the need to get it right, as perfect as she could, she approached the making of this album as she would every subsequent endeavour of her career. She would listen to a replay over and over, hearing things others often did not, a breathiness in her voice that she did not like, a word in a lyric not emphasised to its best advantage. She refused to settle, to compromise, to consider the time and effort this was costing other people. This was *her* record. She would be the one to be judged.

In three days, she recorded eleven songs for *The Barbra Streisand Album*, most of them numbers she performed in cabaret but with new arrangements: 'Cry Me a River', 'My Honey's Loving Arms', 'I'll Tell the Man on the Street', 'A Taste of Honey', 'Who's Afraid of the Big Bad Wolf?' and 'Soon It's Gonna Rain' on one side, 'Happy Days Are Here Again', 'Keepin' Out of Mischief Now', 'Much More', 'Come to the Supermarket in Old Peking' and 'A Sleepin' Bee' on the other. 'Come to the Supermarket in Old Peking', a comic number, was written by Cole Porter for a television production of *Aladdin*. It presented her with her most difficult problem. She seemed unable to get a proper handle on the lyrics, which were not Porter's best (it was his last show and his usually trenchant wit had failed him). But 'Soon It's Gonna Rain' and 'Cry Me a River', sung with a full, rich vocal quality, were so moving that even the experienced technicians who worked on the final cut (with Streisand standing over their shoulders) claimed they got goosebumps each time they heard them.

Columbia executives, however, were mixed in their opinions, uncertain about the marketability of a concept album with no new songs on it that might take off and help it hit the charts. To make the album even more chancy, she had insisted on using on the cover a photograph of herself singing at the Bon Soir, her face half-concealed in darkness (even her bright china-blue eyes look brown in this picture), and wearing a white blouse with a Peter Pan collar, a bow at the neck and a loose-fitting herring-bone vest. Where was the sex?

Ten years later she was to say, 'I hear that first album of mine, where I'm *geshreying* and getting so emotional, I think, "Oh my God, how did they ever like me?" I'm embarrassed by it. The ending was totally wrong. It was the end of the world, "Happy Days". It went Oooooo, aaaaaay, my voice cracked. It was crazy. I guess in a sense that was the purest me. I was yearning for just so much that you hear it in my voice. It's very young, very high, very thin, like a bird. I think my voice has actually gotten better, warmer, mellower. But I probably lost some of my high notes. I don't think I can sing as high.'

On the record's release, 25 February 1963, Streisand was sent on a promotion tour which began that week with a return engagement at the Blue Angel and was to end with an appearance at the Eden Roc Hotel in Miami Beach on 27 March. 'Her nose is more evocative of moose than muse, and her eyes at best could be called Nilotic only by way of mascara, but about 2 a.m., when she sings "Any Place I Hang My Hat Is Home", she's beautiful, if home is only Brooklyn,' wrote Robert Rourk, a respected critic, reviewing her Blue Angel opening. 'She has a three-octave promiscuity of range, she packs more personal dynamic power than anybody I can recall since Libby Hollman or Helen

Morgan. She can sing as loud as Ethel Merman and as persuasively as Lena or Ella.' And he continued, 'She is the hottest thing to hit the entertainment field since Lena Horne erupted, and she will be around 50 years from now if good songs are still written to be sung by good singers.'

By the second week in March *The Barbra Streisand Album* had made the charts. She was a recording star with huge revenues from royalties almost within her grasp. On the other hand, Elliott was having a tough time getting cast in another Broadway show. 'My mate was making it and was very happy about it. I had to deal with it and I did,' he says. They were both offered roles in the first London production of the Leonard Bernstein, Betty Comden and Adolph Green musical *On the Town*, Streisand in the part created on Broadway by Nancy Walker and Elliott to play the clownish sailor Ozzie, one of the three male leads in this ensemble piece. Erlichman advised her against leaving the country at such a critical time in her career. She was singing at the Eden Roc Hotel in Miami Beach at the time and a jobless Elliott was with her.

Insecure at leaving her behind with the buzzards of success encircling her, he kept up a running argument on why they should get married right away. She wouldn't have to deal with Broadway wolves, and – more importantly – it would give them both a purpose in what they were doing. He had signed to appear in the production of *On the Town* only for the first three months of the show – and hey – she could come over to be with him during that time if only for a few days or a week.

'How would it look in a piss-elegant place like London for us to stay together and *not* be married?' he asserted.

Elliott was actually proposing in a back-handed manner. Streisand, not yet ready to make such a commitment, agreed only that it might be a problem and with her usual flair for fictionalising her past life to the press, issued a story that they had just been married in Florida by a justice of the peace. The news hit all the columns. Friends and associates sent congratulations. Even Diana, who had met and liked Elliott, believed her daughter was now Mrs Gould. Two days after the fraudulent wedding announcement, Elliott left for London.

Streisand was to follow shortly thereafter. She had been invited to sing at the Kennedy White House on 17 May, at a gala in honour of the Foreign Press Correspondents and at which she wore her first-ever, genuine ball gown, a glamorous white satin affair with miles of material in the skirt and a provocative neckline that exposed her well-divided cleavage. The gown was a great change from her flea-market wardrobe, but this was a special occasion. She was in genuine awe of President Kennedy – whom she had been too young to vote for – of being a guest at the White House, of the First Lady whose style and class she greatly admired.

'You're a doll,' she told the President when they were introduced.

He laughed and she instantly liked the crinkles on his face. 'How long have you been singing?' he asked.

'About as long as you've been president,' she replied.

She had just celebrated her twenty-first birthday (24 April 1963), and she had made it big enough to meet the President and the First Lady of the United States. Pretty good for a girl from Brooklyn whom everyone thought was too homely to go on the stage.

*On the Town* was to open in London in a week's time. Streisand and Elliott had spoken for an hour or more daily since their parting. Whether it was neediness or longing, motivated by a fear of losing him or a love that she neither knew how to express nor to control, she could not bear to be away from Elliott. It made her crazy and terrified at the same time. More and more she was asserting her independence in her career, gaining a sense of power, the feeling of exhilaration that came from her success. And yet she longed to be with Elliott, missed him dreadfully. She needed to be loved and to love, but she was driven even harder by her need to concentrate all her efforts on her career. She was torn, but two days after her appearance at the White House, she flew to London to join him. London was swinging. A spirit of rebellion had swept over this once conservative society. Skirts were up, restrictions down. She trusted Elliott but not her ability to hold him with a vast distance between them.

# 11

ON THE TOWN opened to cool reviews on 26 May 1963, just a few days after Streisand joined Elliott in London. Elliott received almost no personal notices: 'long, lean and galvanically fit' was all the *Daily Telegraph* said about his performance. Elliott, his hopes unrealised, fell into frequent gloomy moods. Streisand's antidote was to keep him busy when he wasn't appearing on stage. On Saturdays before his matinée, she dragged him down the many side streets off Portobello Road to weave in and out of the myriad displays of antiques, oddities, plain junk and souvenirs.

One Sunday she hired a car and they drove out into the country, sampled bangers swilled down with beer at a pub and stopped at every antique shop on the way. She had discovered that the best values were Victoriana and 1920–30 art deco and as these periods had always appealed to her, she sent copious packages back to New York. She could afford almost anything she wanted. 'A new apartment,' she promised Elliott, ready for them when he came home. With the poor ticket sales of *On the Town*, it looked as if this might be sooner than they had anticipated.

They were inseparable during her stay. 'Elliott even looked happy despite the half-empty houses we played to at the Prince of Wales Theatre,' one member of the cast recalled. 'I think he wanted the show to be over so that he could go back to the States and be with Barbra. They were always touching and camping around. No one in Britain knew much about her yet. I remember some small mention of her in the London papers. Her first record was not yet released in Britain. They said they were married and no one had any reason *not* to believe it. Nor do I believe that anyone truly cared. She seemed to be gone almost as soon as she had arrived.'

In fact, she had been booked on 9 June to appear on the *Ed Sullivan Show*, the most popular television variety programme in America. 'I liked Ed,' she later carped, 'but one thing that makes me crazy is how many people mispronounce my name. He was no exception. All during dress rehearsals I kept hearing him say, "And now let's hear it from the Columbia recording star Barbra Streis-*land*!" It made me so nervous that during the actual broadcast, when it was my turn, I stepped behind the curtain whispering, "Streis-*sand*!

Streis-*sand*! Like sand on the beach!" He ended up doing it right.'

Three weeks later she was on her way to Las Vegas for an appearance as the opening act for Liberace in the massive show room at the Riviera Hotel. Streisand knew it was a mistake from the moment she stepped into the flashy lobby filled with slot machines and the jangling sound of the coins they take and dispense. Las Vegas is a gaudy Disneyland for middle-aged and retired people. It is not so much a place as an upside-down world where reality is checked at the front desks of garish hotels. People came to enjoy the desert heat, the gambling tables, and a chance to see in person the sophisticated old pros such as Liberace, Frank Sinatra, Dean Martin, Tony Bennett, Sammy Davis Jr, Noël Coward and the great stand-up comedians – Milton Berle, Sid Caesar, Joey Bishop and Jerry Lewis – who had won early fame in the Catskills and went on to radio, films and television. Vegas audiences liked ostentation, the beautiful, long-legged showgirls in glitzy, sexy costumes, and the great female entertainers like Lena Horne who knew how to razzle-dazzle her fans.

Mid-June temperatures were in the 90s when Streisand arrived, her suitcase packed with the simple muted brown and tawny grey gowns she had chosen especially for the engagement. She had decided to dress 'down' for Vegas – elegantly, she believed, to create a stark contrast with the surroundings, to focus attention on herself. She chose slow ballads to sing to an audience to whom she was little known and who had paid a high price to see Liberace's outrageous costumes and hear his flamboyant piano arrangements. Her act backfired, the audience tepid in their response. The hotel threatened to fire her. Liberace, who thought her voice and phrasing brilliant, prevailed.

A meeting was called with the management. He would open the show, dressed in a red sequin tuxedo, with a big, up-beat number. Then he would introduce her as his discovery, make a big thing about it, play on his fans' great love for him and promise to be back to play and sing all their favourites. Her act was cut from six to four songs and she was coerced into wearing a gold dress and some showy earrings that came from the hotel's expensive boutique. She did not receive a standing ovation but the crowd, responding to the new theatricality of her appearance, were far more accepting and she won a host of fans. Still, her first night experience had been jolting. She had never previously appeared before a hostile audience. Liberace's support had helped her through but her life-long struggle with stage-fright was born.

She went on to the Coconut Grove, situated in the luxurious Ambassador Hotel and perhaps the most glamorous dinner-nightclub room in Los Angeles, able to accommodate over a thousand people and frequented by Hollywood's famous and elite who kept up with who was new and hot in show business. This time she was the solo attraction, her material to include numbers from her first hit album, and 'Miss Marmelstein' as an encore. This was her dream, to come to Hollywood and to be so sensational that she would be signed to a movie contract on the spot, an event that would show Diana that she *was* attractive enough to be in pictures. Once again she gave great thought to what she would wear.

Clothes had become an important disguise for her. What she wore helped to define the person she wanted to be at a particular time. After her mis-calculation in Vegas, for this engagement she had designed a red and white checked gingham jumper worn over a white cotton top with voluminous long sleeves – meant to be a parody of the kind of Swiss peasant dresses worn on Broadway by Mary Martin in *The Sound of Music*, which had been bought by Twentieth Century-Fox and would soon star Julie Andrews in the screen version. She thought it made a statement, showed how 'with it' she was, and that it would catch the audience's attention in a positive way.

Both she and Marty Erlichman had been given accommodation at the Ambassador. Although she had a successful rehearsal on the afternoon before her opening, by the time she was due to appear stage-fright had enveloped her. It was nearly an hour before Erlichman managed to persuade her to leave her room on the fifth floor, step into the elevator and ride down to the Grove.

A rumble of unrest and disapproval at being kept waiting had spread between the giant palm trees that grew incongruously in huge pots rimming the vast interior of the legendary room, three storeys high with a ceiling painted to look like a sky with sparkling stars. Her entrance was made from the back, a spotlight lighting her way. She was wide-eyed at seeing so many famous stars – Kirk Douglas, Henry Fonda, Ray Milland and Edward G. Robinson were in the audience. As she went past a well-known producer and his heavily jewelled companion, she overheard the woman say as she stared at her gingham dress, 'And I've had to wait all this time to hear some *farchadat* [dopey] country singer?' Never able to forget a detractor, she would comment sharply years later, '*I'm* still here! I wonder where *she* is!'

'At first I guess they thought I was some kind of kook. I thought, "Gee, they're going to hate me for being so late." I made some cockamamie reason for it and they laughed. Henry Fonda even stood up and applauded after one song. Henry Fonda!'

Her reviews were sensational. The critics all commented wryly on her outfit. Hollywood enjoyed jokes on itself. But no one was interested in her for movies. Producers and agents in Hollywood spoke another language – 'bankable' (a star who could get financing for a film), 'big at the box office', and 'a power to deal with'. Still, she liked the place, declared that one day soon she would be all three, that she and Elliott would set the town on its ass. Via long distance, Elliott cheered her on, soothed her nerves, told her how much he loved and missed her. The overseas calls were the highlight of his day. Every evening he expected to walk into the Prince of Wales and see a closing notice posted to the stage door, disappointed that it wasn't there. He wanted to go home, to see Barbra, to make sure she was all right, that *they* still had a future together.

He seldom went back to his digs after a performance. London was at the height of its gambling club popularity where members (or guests of members) could dine sumptuously and then go upstairs to the gaming rooms. Each club had select memberships. Theatre and film people were mostly concentrated at the White Elephant, the Curzon and the River Club, all three boasting elegant interiors. There was an excitement, an edge that permeated such establishments. Hit once again by the gambling bug, Elliott managed to run up several hundred pounds in debts, a significant sum considering the state of his finances at the time.

'I didn't have it to pay,' he admitted later. 'Five hundred dollars, and I think this was a larger sum, was enormous to me then. I went through some of the best acting I've ever done to escape; made up great inventive tales of why I was temporarily without funds.' Fortunately, the show's closing notice in early August spared him further humiliation. In Los Angeles Streisand was ending her Coconut Grove engagement, having just finished recording sessions with Peter Matz on her second album which included several Harold Arlen songs and some newer material like Billy Barnes's dramatic piece, 'I Stayed Too Long at the Fair', already a favourite of hers, and Matz's own 'Gotta Move'. After all, she had just been named Entertainer of the Year by *Cue* magazine and the Top-Selling Female Vocalist by the National Association of Record Manufacturers. It pleased but did not satisfy her. She wanted to be recognised by her peers for a Grammy. Her contract terms settled, she accepted Liberace's proposal to appear with him in Lake Tahoe, a three-hour drive from Los Angeles. After that engagement she would return to New York to start work on her third album for Columbia, who wanted to cash in as quickly as possible on her success.

Elliott could not wait that long. He flew directly from London to Los Angeles where she was still appearing. The day after he arrived was his birthday. They were eating in the coffee shop of her hotel. The waitress set down a piece of cake with a flickering candle on it. 'Make a wish!' Streisand demanded.

'I hope the Dodgers win the pennant!' he replied, and blew out the flame.

She laughed, that inimitable sound she made half-way between a snortle and a yelp.

He leaned across the table. 'Let's get married,' he amended.

'Too late. Candle's out,' she snapped back. Elliott was disappointed but not despairing, certain that eventually she would say 'yes'.

A few days later they left in a leased car for Lake Tahoe, a picturesque year-round vacation and gambling town high in the Sierra Nevada mountains on the California/Nevada state lines. The hotels and casinos almost all overlooked the unbelievably deep, clear lake that is fed by many mountain streams. At every performance she received a standing ovation, always graciously acknowledged by a smiling Liberace, who enjoyed telling the crowd that he was proud of their enthusiastic reception because he had discovered her. Elliott almost never left her side. Neither did he gamble, which he took as a good omen. Streisand counted on his being there when she came off-stage, to talk to her about her performance, to hold her in his bear arms when she was tired and needed comforting. He never gave up his entreaties that they get married. After all, he would reason when passion had not won his cause, most people already thought they were married.

Finally, she accepted his proposal and on 13 September 1963, they drove to nearby Carson City, Nevada, the state capital where the Comstock lode was found in the bluish desert sand in 1859 and scores of men became fabulously rich in silver mined there. Vestiges of the Old West had been preserved, but Carson City was now firmly entrenched in the twentieth century. With Marty Erlichman as best man, they were married by a justice of the peace who had never heard of her and appeared shocked at the passionate kiss they exchanged at the end of his short, no-frills ceremony. Elliott let out a *whoop* when they were outside again, picked her up and carried her to the car. She was now Barbra Joan Streisand Gould.

*The Second Barbra Streisand Album* hit Number 1 on the *Variety* charts, sold over 300,000 copies and had earned well up into six figures. She was richer than she could ever have imagined, enough for her to get the New York apartment she had dreamed of one day renting. It turned out to be a spectacular seven-room duplex penthouse once the home of the urbane lyricist Lorenz Hart, in the Ardsley, on the twenty-first and twenty-second floors with a view from Central Park West clear across the park to the East side. Anyone who had been anyone on Broadway in the twenty years before World War Two had been in this apartment. Streisand claimed she could still feel the vibes of the former occupant. When she and Elliott returned from the West Coast a few days after their wedding, they drove directly from the airport to their new home.

Packing cases were everywhere as she had been collecting items from England and on her tour. She had encamped like a gypsy. The kitchen was in a shambles, deep-red patent leather (her original idea) only half applied to the scraped-down walls, scraps of old paper and pots of glue were underfoot. A glorious Aubusson rug that was to adorn the living-room floor was rolled up in brown paper across the foyer, the walls of which were being decorated with flocked red velvet paper. One upstairs bedroom had been made into a sewing room and all her antique hats, shoes and oddments were stacked in boxes as the wardrobe, where they were to be stored, had not yet arrived. The only room that appeared to be complete was her small dressing area with its built-in vanity, mirrors and professional hair dryer set off by a tasseled drape that hung on the one narrow wall with a window.

The first new acquisition she showed Elliott was the fully stocked freezer-refrigerator bulging with TV dinners (Swanson's frozen fried-chicken dinners were her favourite), coffee ice-cream, green dill pickles and delicatessen meats – salami, tongue, pastrami. Then she grabbed his hand and marched him through the dining room with its French gilt chairs, to the den where an ebony Steinway grand piano almost filled the room, and then up to the master bedroom dominated by a huge Jacobean four-poster canopy bed that sat on a raised dais of two steps. The interior of the wood canopy was magnificently carved. She jumped on to the quilted mattress and squealed, 'It doesn't get any better than this, does it?'

But it did.

Not only was she rich, she was in love and happy in her work, although she liked it much better when she was off the road and performing at the Bon Soir, which had become her 'room'. Clubs with featured singers were at their zenith. Top performers drew loyal fans and glittering audiences. Streisand's two best-selling albums had made her a national, much talked-about celebrity. The Bon Soir was packed whenever she appeared. Mention of her name evoked immediate interest, 'I saw her at The Lion Club,' an apocryphal claim, for The Lion Club was too small and her engagement too short to encompass the many people  who were said to have seen her there. At twenty-one this was pretty heady business. Her time in Hollywood had further fuelled her dream of becoming a movie star. She needed a leading role in a big-budget Broadway musical, a showcase for Hollywood to see that she could act as well as sing.

Marty Erlichman kept up with all the shows that were currently in development, but the 1962–3 musical comedy season had been dismal. Even Irving Berlin's *Mr President* had closed after a disappointing eight-month run. Only one musical, *Oliver!*, Lionel Bart's adaptation of Dickens's *Oliver Twist*, had been a hit. Erlichman, despite his enthusiasm for his client's talents, could not have foreseen a lead in a Broadway musical in her immediate future. He was, after all, well aware of her ethnic image, of the lack of roles that might suit her. Dutifully, he put out word that Streisand would welcome a Broadway role again, in a part more fulfilling than Miss Marmelstein.

For a year, a musical on the life of the Ziegfold Follies star, Fanny Brice, had been a work in progress. A few years before her death in 1951 at the age of fifty-nine, Fanny Brice had made several unprofessional tapes recording memories, impressions of people, the highs and lows of her private life. The tapes were to be used in the writing of her autobiography titled *The Fabulous Fanny* for which she had been paid a $50,000 advance (substantial at the time) by Random House, who expected her to reveal the more scandalous episodes in her life and in those of other celebrities she knew. Brice found herself unable to do this and she never completed the book. Eventually, Ray Stark, Brice's

ambitious son-in-law, a former agent turned producer and a man of tremendous tenacity and indomitable moxie, bought back the rights for the original
advance.[1] He hired Ben Hecht and several other top film writers to adapt the
book for the screen, with no success.

Stark turned to Isobel Lennart whose 1945 original musical, *Anchors Aweigh*,
with Gene Kelly and Frank Sinatra, had been a huge moneymaker for MGM.
Her screenplay was also rejected. Studios were not only concerned with the
weak script but with how audiences would accept another actress portraying
Brice, who remained well remembered and well loved. The original concept
was to use Fanny Brice's old recordings on the soundtrack as had been done
with *The Jolsen Story*. None of these efforts came to fruition and Stark then
decided to have Lennart's screenplay adapted for the theatre.

When playwright John Patrick, who had been the scriptwriter on Stark's
first film venture, *The World of Suzie Wong*, turned him down, Lennart was
recalled. She was a capable and often inspired writer, but she lacked theatrical
experience. However, Brice's story was a good one, a tale that was filled with
laughter and tears, a winning theatre combination as Brice, herself, had noted.
Fanny Brice made her mark at the age of nineteen when the exceptional
showman, Florenz Ziegfeld, signed her as a headliner in his *Follies*. A natural
comedienne, she also had a strong contralto singing voice that could be filled
with humour or pathos at a turn. She understood a lyric, every song she sang
became a self-contained scene, and she could move with a sudden grace that
made her audiences wonder why she was considered homely. Brice had fallen
in love with Nicky Arnstein, an inveterate gambler and a stylish ladies' man.
He quickly became 'Mr Brice' as her star rose ever brighter and his luck ran
out. When he was accused of fraud and forgery in a bond scandal, she refused
to believe the charges.

'Are you sure your memory is as bad as that, Miss Brice?' the district attorney
asked her during an investigation into Arnstein's whereabouts.

'Yes, it is very bad,' she replied. 'I can only remember songs and telephone
numbers.'

The day Arnstein went to jail, Brice appeared in the *Follies*, dressed – not in
her usual comedienne's costumes but in a clinging, black satin gown, standing
in the light of one bright spot and singing English lyrics by Channing Pollock
for the French torch song 'Mon Homme'.

> 'It cost me a lot but there's one thing that I've got
> It's my man...'

With her poignant rendition of that song, sung in a husky alto voice and
which became her signature piece, audiences worldwide fell under Brice's spell,

---

[1] *The Fabulous Fanny* was later finished and published posthumously.

regarding her suddenly as much more than a comedienne. She was now a woman who had overcome personal tragedy with great dignity. Her comedy matched Charlie Chaplin's poor, little tramp or Buster Keaton's sad-faced loser. Lennart wrote numerous versions of Brice's life. There were almost as many titles: *Fanny Brice*, *My Man*, *The Funny Girl*, and finally simply *Funny Girl*.

Fran Stark, Ray Stark's wife, watched over the story development with vigilance. Her father, Nicky Arnstein, was still alive and she wanted him presented in a sympathetic fashion, his culpability in the securities swindle that sent him to prison underplayed. The timing of certain events had to be altered: in no way was Lennart to indicate that her parents had lived together unmarried until after her birth. Nor did the restrictions end there: since Fanny Brice's second husband, the composer-showman Billy Rose, was alive and litigious, the story was only to encompass Brice's great love for Nicky Arnstein.[2] Ray Stark felt he needed an experienced theatre man to help transfer the story to the stage and joined forces with Streisand's former nemesis, David Merrick, the theatrical producer of *The World of Suzi Wong*. For the score he turned to Jule Styne (composer) and Stephen Sondheim (lyricist) who had collaborated on *Gypsy*. After *West Side Story* and *Gypsy*, where he had been limited to writing only the lyrics, Sondheim wanted a show where he could write the entire score. Nor could he imagine Mary Martin, Stark's choice for the lead, as Fanny Brice. When Sondheim refused Stark's offer, Merrick paired composer Styne with lyricist Robert Merrill. After they had written four songs,[3] Mary Martin decided she did not want to do the role.

Casting around for an alternative, Fran Stark settled on Anne Bancroft, whom she had loved in the original stage version of William Gibson's *Two for the Seesaw* and had her heart set on this fine dramatic actress to play her mother. Jule Styne once said, 'Merrick was never in favor of Anne Bancroft. He asked me to go down to the Bon Soir and see Barbra Streisand ... It was the first time I had seen Streisand perform in a café and I saw a tremendous star dimension ... I returned to the Bon Soir twenty-seven nights out of twenty-eight in a row. I took several of my friends to see her and got opinions from all sides.' One of his friends was Jerry Robbins, at that time thought of as the future director for the show. Both agreed that Streisand would be right in the role but Stark, with his wife pressuring him, remained adamant in his choice of Bancroft. No one was sure if she could sing well enough, and Stark asked her to audition for Styne and Merrill. She sang numerous songs – ballads and up-tempo numbers – with surprising panache. Everyone thought that she was a good enough performer to carry it off and the Starks went away certain

---

[2] Fanny Brice once said, 'I loved the man [Arnstein] I didn't like and liked the man [Rose] I didn't love.'

[3] 'I'm the Greatest Star', 'Don't Rain on My Parade', 'Who Are You Now?' and 'People'.

that she would agree to play the role and that their casting problems were over.

In early summer of 1963, John Patrick and Stark met in his New York apartment. 'I pointed out that Bancroft would be miscast and would probably realise that. I remember him saying to me, "She wouldn't dare turn down a role like this." The phone rang and I answered it for Ray. It was Bancroft on the line – declining the part.'

Patrick was committed to Stark to write two scripts, a contract that guaranteed him $1,300,000. He told Stark how sorry he felt, but he could not adapt Lennart's screenplay-cum-playscript because he was not a fan of Fanny Brice. 'I thought she was often vulgar and her material sometimes in bad taste.' Stark turned the script back to Lennart but asked Patrick to become part of the production team as his assistant or so-called editor.

'A classmate of Ray's from Rutgers' came to me and suggested I recommend Streisand to Ray as he had seen her at the Bon Soir,' Patrick recalled. 'I went down to see her for myself. She seemed right for the part and I knew she would do justice to Jule and Bob's score. When I suggested Streisand, I remember his reaction. He thought she was unattractive and showed no enthusiasm. I pointed out to him that Fanny Brice, his mother-in-law, had never been a beauty, but sang "My Man" like an angel.'

Stark would not be convinced. He turned to Eydie Gormé and then to Carol Burnett, who told him honestly, 'You need a Jewish girl to play this. It's a whole different quality.' John Patrick called Marty Erlichman to inform him that he was going to bring Fran and Ray Stark down to the Bon Soir but not to let anyone except Barbra know this. Streisand was extremely nervous on the appointed night. This was the opportunity she had been hoping for. The room was packed, a very receptive audience, and she responded with a performance that was one of her best.

'Ray thought she sang well but Fran hated her, and told me, "I'll never let that girl play my mother."' Brice's private and public persona differed drastically. On stage she was the raucous ethnic comedienne; socially she was an elegant, Americanised, well-spoken woman with exquisite taste,[4] a talented

---

[4] Born Fanny Borach in New York City, 29 October 1891, Fanny Brice had neither a Brooklyn nor a Jewish accent. Her parents were saloon keepers in a predominantly Irish neighbourhood. In a tape made for her proposed autobiography Brice said, 'In 1910 I needed a song to sing to audition for a job in "College Girls". I raced up to where Irving Berlin had an office and asked him if he had a song for me. Irving sang in a Jewish accent "Sadie Salome, Come Home" a song about a girl from the Bronx who became a hula-hula dancer, that he had written the lyrics but not the music for. I had never had any idea of doing a song with a Jewish accent, didn't even understand Yiddish. But I thought, if that's the way Irving sings it, that's the way I'll sing it. If he had sung it with an Irish brogue, I probably would have become an Irish comedienne. So Irving is really responsible for the whole thing.' Florenz Ziegfeld later hired her for $75 a week to appear

interior decorator whose home was a sophisticated showplace and who dressed with great style. Fran Stark only saw Streisand's Jewishness and was vehement that her mother not be portrayed in that light.

Disregarding the Starks' objections to Streisand, Erlichman and Robbins arranged for Streisand to read a few scenes from the play with Merrick, Styne, Merrill, Isobel Lennart, the Starks and Patrick present. 'I can't tell you how horrible she looked,' Patrick alleged. 'She wore a Cossack uniform kind of thing. She read the scene where Fanny's husband Nicky Arnstein has just left her. Tears were called for and she could not manage it.' Ray Stark was now as adamant as his wife that Streisand would not play Fanny Brice.

Robbins and Styne insisted she be given another chance. The group gathered for the second time. Again Streisand could not cry. This time she whipped around to Robbins at the end of the scene. 'Mr Robbins,' she said sharply, 'I can't cry with those words!'

Shortly thereafter, Robbins left the project and *Funny Girl* looked as though it would be cancelled. Then Bob Fosse was hired to replace Robbins and the show was once again on. A few weeks later, Fosse quit. The producers turned to Sidney Lumet. After telling them that the book needed drastic revision, he was gone. All this time Streisand was in anguish, believing in her heart that here was her chance to prove that she could be a star.

Fortunately, the show's producers refused to let *Funny Girl* slide into oblivion. They knew the book was the problem and called Garson Kanin, who had been a close friend of Brice's, and asked him if he would consider collaborating with Isobel Lennart on a rewrite. Kanin, who had successfully written four filmscripts with his wife, actress-writer Ruth Gordon, declined. 'Isobel was an excellent screenwriter, but she had no experience in the lyric theatre,' Kanin explained. 'When I met with Stark and Merrick, I told them their difficulty was not that they had a bad book but that they had no book at all.' The story was the all-too-familiar backstage drama of the ugly-duckling-novice who becomes a star at the sacrifice of the man she loves. Kanin had previously worked with Jule Styne on *Do Re Me*, but they had not got on well and he was hesitant to go through a similar experience again. Despite this, when offered the job as director, he accepted. Stark was pleased because he felt that with John Patrick and Ruth Gordon (who always was at her husband's side) unofficially overseeing the script along with Kanin, Lennart would be able to pull it off.

Streisand now found her mentor to be none other than David Merrick. His instinct, he told Kanin, was that she should play Fanny. Streisand was currently appearing at Basin Street East. The Kanins found that her act was beautifully

in his *1910 Follies* after hearing her sing in dialect. Berlin wrote music and lyrics for 'Goodbye, Becky Cohen', also a dialect song, for her. It became a hit. Thereafter, she used the dialect in her comedy skits although not when she sang ballads.

conceived, paced well – strong ballads balanced by humorous set-pieces and, like Brice, she had the ability to move her audience to both laughter and tears. She was that strange anomaly: a woman who could be called homely by some and stunningly beautiful by others.

The Kanins were convinced that Streisand was the ideal choice and that with Garson's close knowledge of Fanny Brice and his ability to work with strong women (Katherine Hepburn, Carole Lombard and Ginger Rogers had been the leading ladies of films that he had either written or directed) he could get a terrific performance from her. A lunch was arranged for them to get acquainted and to see if he could work with her.

Nothing was going to stop Streisand from getting this role. Determined to charm the Kanins, she read as much as she could about them. Ruth Gordon had been one of the great leading ladies of the American stage, as well as a successful playwright and screenwriter. By now in her early sixties, a petite, vital woman, with an expressive rather than beautiful face and a shiny dark cap of hair to frame it, she was quick-witted, merry, and a walking encyclopedia of theatre knowledge. She was the first woman of Streisand's acquaintance who was so multi-talented, which greatly impressed her. Garson Kanin, a decade younger than his wife, was equally sharp, a short, feisty, spry man with intelligent brown eyes and a smile that slid saucily across his face when he was amused – which was often – and who appreciated the turn of a woman's ankle as well as her intelligence and talent.

'I liked Barbra immediately,' Kanin recalled. 'She was funny, relentlessly ambitious, nothing was going to keep her down. I felt those qualities were very important because they were principal aspects of the Fanny Brice I knew.' He went home from their lunch, which had lasted several hours, and reread Lennart's libretto. He now could hear Streisand's voice as he read certain lines and had begun to visualise her, *not* Fanny, in the role. He was excited and passed on his enthusiasm to Stark, who still was not certain Streisand could carry a show or that she was attractive enough to please an audience or his wife. He was talking to Shirley MacLaine about the role, he told Kanin.

While Streisand fretted nervously about what was happening and kept nudging Marty Erlichman to do something about getting a decision on whether she had the part, a meeting was called with all the principal players, Merrick, the Starks, the Kanins, Patrick, Lennart, Styne and Merrill. The Kanins made a lively plea in Streisand's defence. A mesmerising performer, she had the quirkiness, the Jewish *shtick*, the stage charisma also possessed by Brice. Styne and Merrill insisted she was the only one to sing the score. The Starks were difficult to convince but finally yielded to the overwhelming majority.

Streisand was asked to meet Stark at his office. Erlichman had already told her she had won the role. Merrick was also there. For Streisand it was an important moment. Fanny Brice was not only the lead of *Funny Girl*, she was the main focus of the story. Streisand had gone from supporting player to star. In playing the role she could be funny, romantic, tragic, joyous, sexy. She could prove that she could act. Stark remained cool throughout most of the meeting. Merrill thought maybe he had changed his mind. Midway through, Streisand began talking a lot out of sheer irrepressible nervousness. 'It wasn't what she said, it was the way she rattled it off,' Merrick recalled. 'She somehow got under your skin. She was naturally funny. Ray loosened up and by the time she left it was agreed. She would play Fanny Brice.'

Starry-eyed, she signed a contract with Merrick's company as Stark, whose first play this was to be, did not yet have an Actors Equity agreement. She was flying high. Despite all the problems she had encountered in *I Can Get It for You Wholesale*, she was confident that she and the play would succeed. Stardom was within her grasp.

She left for Los Angeles on 3 October in an euphoric mood to appear on *The Judy Garland Show*, where she planned to announce that she was to play Fanny Brice. Garland's show had been moulded into an imitation of other prosaic television variety shows, although the one-woman concert format was where she felt most comfortable. CBS forced her to make chitchat with her guests and to take a back seat while they performed. It was to prove disastrous for Garland but for Streisand it was a grandstand opportunity to display her talent on a television programme watched by millions and she ran with it. Originally scheduled to sing one solo and one duet with Garland, she doubled her spots with Garland's approval once they were in rehearsal.

A generous performer, Garland was much taken by Streisand's talent. Mel Tormé, musical director of the show, recalled being asked during rehearsals to see Garland in her dressing room. 'She was playing Streisand's record of "Happy Days Are Here Again". As Streisand's voice came through the speaker, Judy began to sing "Get Happy" in counterpoint to "Happy Days". The result was electrifying.'

Tormé went directly to his office and called Streisand. He was sitting at the piano waiting for her when she came. 'Since you sing in any key, try "Happy Days" in this one,' he said. Then beginning the introduction in a key suitable to his own range, he motioned her to start, whereupon he joined in, as Garland had, with 'Get Happy'. 'Barbra kept singing as she half-turned to me, a wide smile on her face. When we finished she exclaimed, "That's terrific! I mean it! Your idea?"'

'No, Judy's,' he replied honestly.

Ethel Merman was taping *The Red Skelton Show* in the adjoining studio and agreed to appear in one segment when she would 'accidentally' be discovered in the audience and brought up on stage where the three women would try to outbelt each other in a rousing rendition of 'There's No Business Like Show Business'. Merman was the indisputable decibel winner, but the show placed

Streisand on a new plateau, equal with the two icons with whom she appeared.

Her high spirits prevailed upon her return to New York as she looked forward to the next step up in her career – the lead in a Broadway show. At this point Stark and Merrick suffered a hard falling out over who would have final word on production matters. It was a power struggle and Stark would not give in. 'Life is too short to deal with Ray Stark,' Merrick said and backed out of the agreement. For a week Streisand was left in limbo. She was near hysteria, on the telephone constantly to Erlichman, wolfing ice-cream and walking the floors half the night as she worried out loud to a groggy Elliott, refusing to talk to Diana who kept calling to find out if she did or did not have the role. One day the show was being abandoned, the next it was back on. Finally Erlichman called her to tell her the good news. Stark was ready to go into production and he, and Bella Linden, who had become Streisand's lawyer, were renegotiating better terms for her.

Seduced by the lure of her name in lights on Broadway, she hurtled forward, self-absorbed. Elliott had not had an offer for a show since his return from London. She knew he was depressed about this, that she should spend more time and effort with him in working out his problems, but she could not stop or slow down on her momentum to do so. Up ahead was the realisation of all her dreams.

That is, if she played it right.

# 12

FROM THE OUTSET she knew that *Funny Girl* was her one-way ticket to fame. Everything in her was now geared for becoming a star. That brought added responsibility, but it also meant that if she succeeded – and she refused to think otherwise – she would not just be on her way, she would already have arrived.

Fanny Brice was not the usual light-hearted, simple-minded, Broadway musical comedy heroine. Brice was a woman of strong character, outrageously funny as a performer, a real woman with whom audiences could identify. Brice had once said, 'People like to feel miserable. You make them laugh they will forget you, but if you make them cry they will never forget you.' The marvellous thing about Fanny Brice was that she could make you do both – laugh and cry. Brice also contended that it was her good fortune to have been born homely – it had given her the desperate ambition to become a great star and she had not settled for less.

'It was scary,' Streisand admitted, 'I read certain conversations that had never been published [from the transcript of Brice's tapes] and it was very peculiar. We were very much alike in a very deep area, in spirit. I knew that I would do her justice by being true to myself. It didn't interest me to have copied her walk. I was interested in the essence of her. Her essence and my essence were very similar. That is a little spooky, you know?'

One of the greatest problems she would have with audiences and critics was being compared to Brice who had died only twelve years earlier and who had been much loved by the American public during the last twenty years of her life as radio's Baby Snooks. Every interview that Streisand gave at this time included a denial that she had ever heard or seen Fanny Brice perform, which is likely as Brice's last movie was released in 1946.[1] However, according to Barry Dennen, this was not true. He had played numerous Brice recordings

---

[1] Fanny Brice made only sporadic film appearances. But she had played a cameo as herself in *The Great Ziegfeld* (1936), was part of the all-star cast in *Everybody Sing* (1938), in which she sang a duet with Judy Garland and in *Ziegfeld Follies* (1946) did a sketch with Hume Cronyn. Brice also appeared in the part-talkie film *My Man* and headlined in *By Yourself* shortly after.

when they were living together. Streisand apparently wished to give the impression that she was creating the character from her own perception of the playscript.

On the first day of rehearsal, 6 December 1963, her hair piled high in a huge beehive, bangs falling over her forehead, Streisand arrived an hour late at the Winter Garden (ironically the same theatre where Brice had last appeared in the *Follies*), wearing high brown snow boots and a chic chocolate-brown wool suit under a 1920s coccoon-shaped brown caracul coat. She now shopped at Bergdorf Goodman, one of New York City's most fashionable department stores. Although she had not discarded her eclectic thrift-shop wardrobe, she liked to mix new with old. And so with boots that cost over $100 and a suit for which she had paid three times that amount, she wore a $20 second-hand fur coat. She was particularly fond of furs, especially striking ones like leopard and pony and was having several of her own designs for suits and coats made up. She realised that, like Fanny Brice, she had a natural flair for design and decoration. Of greater significance were their similar ethnic backgrounds, their drive and their early success – Brice had her big chance at nineteen as a star of the *Ziegfeld Follies*.

The cast was gathered on the large stage where Garson Kanin was discussing procedures with them. He stopped when he saw Streisand and went over to where she was standing by an upright piano. She talked quietly with him for a few moments about some of her scenes, but remained fairly aloof from the rest of the company as introductions were made. Ruth Gordon then took her backstage to her dressing room. 'She wasn't sure how the star of a show should behave,' Gordon said later. 'How could she? I thought she was shy and that her coolness was a cover for her nervousness.' But her attitude had not been well received by most of the cast members.

Streisand's situation differed greatly from her last experience where she had been a supporting player with no major credits, a small salary and only one song to sing. Now she was the star of the show and the score was being written expressly with her voice and character in mind. Since 10 November, two weeks before rehearsals, she had worked on the songs with Jule Styne and Robert Merrill at Peter Daniels's studio, where she had slept in less affluent days. (Daniels was the show's associate musical director.) She was more comfortable with Styne and Merrill than she was with the cast. Styne was an energetic man with a buoyant personality and an incredibly facile ability to compose good, singable melodies. Normally a bright mood prevailed at these rehearsals, but on 22 November President Kennedy had been assassinated in Dallas. The country was in despair. Streisand wept openly as they went over her songs and smoothed out some of the rough spots. She had been awed by Kennedy when they had met at the White House. Her sense of loss translated into the emotion with which she sang.

Styne and Merrill recognised that they had a singing star of the first magnitude and the power and meaning that she gave their songs encouraged them
to write more numbers for her. Styne would claim that he composed fifty-five
pieces of music for *Funny Girl*. In the end there were fifteen songs, some
instrumental interludes and dance music (the latter arranged by Luther
Henderson). Her rendition of 'People' so overwhelmed the song's writers that
a decision was made for her to record it as a single and release it as soon as
possible, with the hope that its success would give the show momentum.
Columbia, Streisand's regular label, recorded 'People' with 'I Am Woman' on
the flip side[2] with Peter Daniels on piano, the orchestra under the direction of
Peter Matz. When they listened to the playback after the session, composer
and lyricist were certain that the release would be a big hit.

Styne and Merrill were a cohesive team although they appeared to have
little else in common. Of small, neatly compressed stature, Styne seemed to
be in perpetual movement, hands gesticulating as he spoke a rapid verbal
shorthand of phrases that was often difficult to follow, his short legs carrying
him in double time when he walked. Born in the East End of London in 1907,
at the age three he emigrated with his family to Chicago. Five years later his
parents were sure he would be a concert pianist, but his hands were deemed
too small by his piano teacher. Instead, he played dance music and the popular
songs of the day, ending up as a teenager playing on an upright in a burlesque
house and making his first bet on the ponies. Unfortunately he won, and he
was to be compulsive, self-destructive gambler for the better part of his life.
He started composing for films in the late 1930s and for the musical theatre
in 1947, careening from one success to another – *Gentlemen Prefer Blondes*,
*Bells Are Ringing* and *Gypsy*.

Styne should have been a rich man. Instead he was on the brink of financial
disaster and heavily in debt to the IRS (who eventually appropriated most of
his earnings from *Funny Girl*.) For a time he worked tirelessly on *Funny Girl*
and *Fade Out, Fade In* with Carol Burnett, in tandem. That did not stop him
from betting, but it did set an exhausting pace for his lyricist, who was more
easy-going.

At 6'2", Merrill towered over Styne. A man of even disposition and of a more
conservative nature, he had been a popular songwriter until 1957 when he
wrote music and lyrics for *New Girl in Town* and followed this with Jackie
Gleason's hit show, *Take Me Along*, and his finest score, *Carnival* in 1961, which
was still running on Broadway. Styne and Merrill were both brilliant at what
they did and Stark trusted their first decision on *Funny Girl* not to include any
of the numbers that Fanny Brice had made famous such as 'My Man', 'Rose of

---

[2] 'I am Woman' is the same song as 'You Are Woman'. In this case it was sung as a
solo and with feminine lyrics.

Washington Square', or 'I'm an Indian'. Instead they created new songs –
'Private Schwartz', 'The Music that Makes Me Dance' – numbers that were
original, contemporary and evocative at the same time.

*Funny Girl* was to rehearse in New York for three weeks, then play out of
town in two cities – Boston and Philadelphia – before coming to Broadway at
the Winter Garden on 27 February, the planned opening date. Nine days into
the cast rehearsals on the stage of the Winter Garden, the schedule looked
unrealistic. Things were definitely not going well. Sydney Chaplin, son of the
great Charles, had been cast as Nicky Arnstein and although a 'gorgeous' hunk
of a man, as required for the role, he was as charmless in his readings as he
had been winning in his performance opposite Judy Holiday in the Styne,
Comden and Green Broadway hit, *Bells Are Ringing*.

'If we could give him an image to imitate it might help,' Ray Stark told
Garson Kanin, 'William Powell or Errol Flynn rather than his trying to be Cary
Grant.' Then, going down a list of other problems in the cast, he added,
'Strangely, Barbra doesn't have a sense of humour about herself from her
reading. She does things that are funny but they don't come out of inner
humour.'

Throughout rehearsals during the frigid weeks in December, the air in the
cavernous Winter Garden was raw with cold, the heat miserly low to save
costs. One sub-zero, blustery day, Ray and Fran Stark – his dark red hair
meticulously barbered, her make-up impeccably applied – were seated in the
auditorium along with Lennart, Merrill (Styne was up on stage), Gordon,
Erlichman and Patrick ('I don't think anyone in the company knew why I was
there,' Patrick later said). On the otherwise bare stage, members of the cast sat
on straight-backed wooden chairs arranged in a circle around Garson Kanin,
wearing a dapper brown pin-striped suit, a small brimmed black hat that was
his talisman (a gift from Spencer Tracy), cocked on his head. Streisand stood
somewhat aloof on the edge of the circle wrapped in her caracul coat, which
she had been wearing almost every day. Kanin was giving a pep talk to his cast
and Streisand seemed impatient for it to end.

'I need your imagination,' Kanin told his company. 'The best of our show is
the unexplored areas. Do not be inhibited. If something tends to come up,
then let go. And as you go along you will begin to anticipate problems. Please
bring those problems to me. We're all terribly, terribly kind here.'

In an apparent attempt to ease the tension between Streisand and the cast,
Kay Medford, who was playing Mama Brice, leaned back in her chair and
stage-whispered in a Yiddish accent to Streisand, who was standing behind
her, 'Did you get the coat honestly?'

Streisand glanced down at her unamused.

Styne was bouncing around the stage, talking to the technicians, hands
flying. Kanin's assistant gave the order to please clear the stage for the first run

through. The director moved with Styne out into the orchestra and sat down behind a wooden table with a microphone atop it. The order was given for the run through to start. Streisand entered from the wings still bundled up in her fur coat. She crossed slowly to the stage piano and began to finger the keys. At the rear of the stage was a brick wall with painted grey steam pipes running along the bottom half.

The show opened backstage. Fanny was already a star, with many memories and a broken marriage; Arnstein after being released from jail has just walked out on her. She sings a song, later cut, and then the story moves back to her youth. A piano in the orchestra pit starts the song. The musician cannot be seen. It is an eager, eighteen-year-old bespectacled Marvin Hamlisch (who ten years later would compose the score for *Chorus Line*) hired for his first big job as rehearsal pianist. Everyone is edgy. Streisand has moved too slowly. She's not standing where she has been told to stand. Then she begins to sing.

'Her voice came off this bare stage and it started to reach around the empty theatre,' reported Jimmy Breslin who was seated in the auditorium to write one of Streisand's first profiles as a coming star. 'She was doing some sort of a dance while she sang and when her voice came on stronger Jule Styne, slumped in his seat, began to nod with the tune. Then there was this sort of growl in Barbra Streisand's voice and now you didn't notice the bare stage or the chairs or the guy carrying the ladder. It didn't matter where you were. She is that kind of a singer.'

Kanin's head rocked back and forth with the song. 'Yeah,' he said out loud and smiled as she sang.

Fran Stark, always smartly turned out and quick with her opinion, was still not convinced that Streisand could or should play her mother, but it was now too late to do anything about it. Marty Erlichman and Streisand's lawyer, Bella Linden, had seen to it that their client was well paid at $5,000 a week, plus a percentage of the gross, and safeguarded: if fired she would have to be paid off handsomely. The already escalating costs of the show – now upwards of $500,000 – seemed to prohibit such a move. Memos flew back and forth between Ray Stark (often dictated by Fran) and Kanin. Putting it simply, Fran thought Streisand lacked class – the element that had always been evident in Fanny Brice's on and off-stage demeanour, even her comedic roles – and how did one teach a performer class? Kanin was sure he could. He called it elegance.

He took Streisand aside. 'Elegance is making an art of life,' he told her. He went on to explain that an artist's function was to achieve a modicum of order out of chaos. From order came refinement, which in art, meant rhythm, tempo, style, form and – 'best of all – elegance. Fanny Brice had elegance,' he stressed, adding, 'there has never been a great comedian who did not have elegance.'

For the next three weeks while they were still rehearsing in New York, Kanin took her aside whenever he could and worked with her on the matter of elegance. He told her about Chaplin, Brice, Keaton – legendary comedians who had brought dignity to their art. 'I want you to stand tall, lift your head, listen to your fellow actors when they are talking to you on stage. Don't make the mistake of believing that the public loves you for yourself when in truth they only love you for your talent.

'Finally, it penetrated,' he recalled. 'She had more dignity, human nobility, self-respect and respect for the audience. She left all the common and cheap effect and was on the road.'

Streisand was learning things from Kanin that she knew would benefit her immensely – how to move on stage, project her voice, react to what other performers were saying. She lapped up this kind of teaching, pulled more and more from him, wanted to know more about the stars he had worked with like Katherine Hepburn and Judy Holiday. Kanin kept her as sheltered as possible from the confusion that raged around her. The script was in a constant state of flux, which did not seem to trouble Streisand, who would learn a new scene in a matter of minutes.

The most pressing problems were, and would continue to be, the weak portrait of Nicky Arnstein, the downhill slide of the second act and the unhappy ending which was totally contrary to what was then expected in musical comedies even eighteen years after Rodgers' and Hammerstein's *Carousel*, which had endowed the genre with a new seriousness of purpose. Lennart would write a new scene according to suggestions given to her by the Starks and Kanin. Ruth Gordon privately sent memos of her ideas. John Patrick, meanwhile, confided his comments to Ray Stark, who passed many of them on to Lennart, who wrote and rewrote and rewrote again. Streisand took all these changes with seasoned equanimity. In fact, as she has said, she loved the process of reworking scenes in rehearsals – 'week after week being able to experiment, to modify, to change, to discover what worked and what didn't, and why'.

No one knew the extent to which Lennart's private life was in upheaval and the strain, the pressures of the show, exacted on her. She had been an informer during the early 1950s for Senator Joseph McCarthy and the hearings of the House UnAmerican Activities Committee when so many of her former co-workers' lives were ruined and many more painfully affected and blacklisted.[3]

---

[3] People brought up before HUAC were asked to name friends and co-workers whose liberal views made them suspect as fellow travellers or communists. Many frightened witnesses implicated others innocent of nothing more than a belief in something they considered to be an American right – freedom of speech. It was one of the darkest periods in American history.

Wounds ran deep and there were bitter feelings towards those who had informed on friends and colleagues. Some members of the executive staff of *Funny Girl* and the cast looked upon her as a pariah and she felt their scorn. Her son was being treated for drug addiction, her husband drinking heavily and, as they were both 3,000 miles away in California, her telephone bills were astronomic. She was on edge and quickly dissolved into tears under stress. To bridge this problem, Stark now had Patrick work with Lennart in her hotel suite so that she would not be exposed to his criticism at meetings or allow any rumours to spread that he was acting as a play doctor.

Streisand remained detached from the members of the company. 'Once in a while I would sit on the floor next to her during rehearsals,' John Patrick said, 'but we never became close. She was not, in my opinion, a lovable human being, as most actors are. There was a great hostility in the company. [At the beginning] Barbra and Sydney Chaplin, her leading man, hated each other. In the scene where she sat on the doorsteps and sang "People", he would look up at her adoringly, and whisper out of the side of his mouth, "You're off key, you bitch!" Ray tried to fire him but he had a run-of-the-play contract. Ray used me to talk to him and order him not to invent dialogue of his own. Sydney would reply, "Well, I don't like the dialogue I'm given, so I'm inventing my own." Ray devised several funny schemes to make him quit, but Sydney paid no attention to them.'

On the few days that Streisand had off from rehearsals she indulged in her most consuming passion – shopping for antiques. She and Elliott were still in the throes of decorating their duplex penthouse. No longer limited to thrift-shop purchasing, she dragged Elliott to Manhattan's high-priced wholesale antique district with the same avidity. She plunged into vast warehouses, trailed by Elliott and their decorator, dashing from item to item, shouting 'How much?', the decorator, hired on a friend's recommendation, busily making notes. They would thread from one warehouse to another.

During one such buying orgy, when they were accompanied by *Life*'s Shana Alexander, the hefty owners of a shop specialising in mirrors and glass refused to haggle over the price. Suddenly the Goulds fancied that the proprietors of *this* shop didn't like them. 'It's a front, Barbra. It's a bookie joint. They're gangsters,' Alexander quoted Elliott as saying to soothe his wife's ego and then wandered off to investigate on his own. A while later on their way back up the street Streisand rapped on the window of the supposed 'bookie joint' and, waving a sales check from another establishment, shouted: 'Yah! You thought I wasn't gonna buy, huh? Well, I spent $3,000 next door.'

She had bought five glorious crystal chandeliers and an ornate early nine-teenth-century piano, its interior no longer operative. Once again reunited with Elliott, she excitedly told him about the piano. 'How could you buy a piano without consulting me?' he demanded, seriously offended.

'Don't you care about our home?' she countered. 'It's the most beautiful piano I've ever seen!'

'It's hideous!' he yelled.

'Elly, it has *painted scenes* on it,' she shot back stubbornly.

There followed 'a screaming, four-letter fight in the street, hopping in and out of taxis, over curbs, past startled pedestrians, oblivious of decorator [reporter] and passersby,' Alexander wrote of her eye-witness involvement.

In the weeks since Streisand had started rehearsals, she and Elliott had engaged in a great many verbal battles in less than private situations – stores, restaurants, the lobby of their building – which would end in a cold silence between them and could last from one day to the next. 'Elliott was fighting for what he considered to be his masculine identity. Barbra could not and would not understand that,' one friend said. They disagreed about almost every item Streisand bought for the penthouse. Beyond that, they fought about what was to go where, notably her decision – which she won – to hang one of the ornate chandeliers in the master bedroom. Their bed was the one exception. Both of them wanted it to approximate a stage setting. 'It should be like the place Desdemona got strangled in,' Elliott told a bewildered upholsterer commissioned to make the quilted spread and hangings in green brocade for it. On the bedside table was a gilt-edged photo of Streisand licking a large lollipop and inscribed: 'Too Eleot i wuv you Barbrra'.

Streisand was undergoing a major upheaval in her career and in her private life. Celebrity and riches had come to her in a span of only three years and she had not been prepared for the drastic changes they would bring with them. The newly wedded Goulds seldom had time alone together. Now she was too involved in what was happening at the Winter Garden and in her career to share much else and she moved in a crowd of people: Erlichman, record producers and representatives, her musical director and arranger, staff from the show, reporters, decorators, drivers and dedicated fans who were happy to be gofers, running errands, fetching the containers of Chinese food that she greedily devoured.

In rehearsals she was proving to be difficult. Nothing escaped her critical attention. A costume or wig that did not fit exactly right was rejected. She did not like a song 'I Tried' that Styne and Merrill had written for the finale and refused to sing it. It was cut from the show. Unsure of her dancing ability she was constantly at dagger's end with Carol Haney, the choreographer. A roller-skate number had been written and choreographed for her and despite the fact that the logo for the show had been drawn from this number (Fanny upside down with skates in the air) she insisted that it be cut.

Her behaviour did not endear her to her co-workers, but by now there was a general consensus that the success of *Funny Girl* was greatly dependent upon her performance and the power of her voice. Kanin sincerely believed no other actress/singer could carry the show and he did his best to appease her detractors. 'Barbra's just tense,' he would say. 'She's new at this and she's carrying a heavy weight on her shoulders.'

One day during rehearsal Kanin noticed a man – unknown to him – seated in the balcony apparently taking notes. Outsiders were not permitted into rehearsals and so he went up to confront him. Streisand, nervous about the slow progress she was making in bringing her character to life, had called Allan Miller to come in secretly to observe everything she was doing and work with her on her interpretation. Miller claims she also called on him when she was in rehearsals for *I Can Get It for You Wholesale*.

'Who are you?' Kanin asked. 'And why are you sitting up here taking notes?'

'I'm Barbra's cousin,' Miller said.

Kanin was not taken in. He had heard a rumour that his star was working with a coach in private, a situation intolerable for a director staging a show. 'There is only one director here,' Kanin insisted. Miller departed but Streisand made certain that Kanin knew she was displeased. During another rehearsal, Kanin had her repeat a line numerous times. There were words. It was the star's will against the director's and it looked for an hour or so that one of them might quit. It ended in a draw.

Her faith had been lost in Kanin, believing that he did not understand the character as deeply as she did or that he could help her bring more strength and pathos to interpretation. Frustrated, fearful that her great opportunity might slip her grasp, she became tense and short-tempered.

The day following her stand-off with Kanin, Milton Rosenstock, the musical director, arrived early for rehearsal. Streisand – who was usually late – was sitting on a stool, waiting under a single work light. Rosenstock felt 'a dread, as if a dynamite fuse had been lighted in the theatre. She hardly spoke to him and remained where she was without moving. The cast wandered in. She glared at them with defiance, as if to say, 'Goddamit, you didn't expect me today, did you?' Rosenstock noted.

'OK let's take it from the top,' Kanin ordered when he arrived on the scene.

Rosenstock remembered 'an absolute hush in the theatre for a few minutes. Then, as the music [to 'People'] started, what Streisand did went purposefully against every instruction Kanin had given her. If she was supposed to stand still, she moved; if she was supposed to move, she stood still. She was running all over the stage, doing crazy things. She was like a maniac, improvising. As I looked back toward the seats, I saw Garson sitting with his mouth open. Then Jule was on me in a minute, squeezing my shoulder until it hurt. His face was white. He literally snarled, "Leave her alone, Milt, she's on fire. Just follow, follow..."'

Finally, when the rehearsal moved on to 'Don't Rain on My Parade', she collapsed into sobs. 'I'm sorry,' she cried, 'I'm so sorry.' No one came forward to comfort her. Rosenstock stopped the orchestra and she walked off the stage. Kanin cancelled rehearsals for the rest of the day.

Rosenstock said she came to him a few days later and said, 'I got it now. It's a duet.'

'What do you mean, a duet?' he asked.

'I'm not alone up there. I've got you. I've got the whole orchestra. I'm not up there alone.'

'Jesus Christ, no, you're not alone,' Rosenstock replied with strong irritation.

None the less, she never overcame the sense of 'being out there alone', of having only herself to rely upon. A manifestation of her insecurity, her fear that she would fail because of *other* people, it made her seem aloof, utterly self-centred. She did not have the close companionship of Elliott or Sheree North as she had in *Wholesale*, or the empathy of a Jack Kruschen. One cast member recalls. 'It was strange. Although she was the star, Barbra always seemed to be the outsider.'

The libretto was in deeper trouble than ever. Streisand and the rest of the company would have to memorise new scenes and complicated song and dance numbers on a daily basis. Now even the survival of the song 'People', which she had already recorded as a single, was questioned. Kanin believed that it was a great number but that it set the wrong mood and did not belong in the show.

'At that moment ... [Fanny's] just met the fellow [Nick]. Why should she become philosophical?' Kanin asked the song's writers. Kanin had not been the first or only one to think 'People' was wrong for the show. Stark agreed, and Styne and Merrill might well have given in, but they were certain that Streisand's recording of it would be a big hit. They promised to write a back-up to 'People' if Kanin would leave the number in during the Boston try-out and after the record's release.

'I promise you, Gar, when you put the right light on her opening night and she sings this song she'll bring the house down,' Merrill vowed. 'People' stayed in.

A few days before the *Funny Girl* company was to leave for Boston, Elliott was cast as the court jester in a television version of Mary Rodgers' *Once Upon a Mattress*, a musical based on the fairy tale *The Princess and the Pea*, which starred Carol Burnett as the zany princess, a role she had played in the original Broadway production five years earlier. Since that time, Burnett had become a huge television star. Though only two weeks' work, it was the first job Elliott had had since *On the Town*. Streisand left for the Boston and Philadelphia try-outs without him. In Boston, she was given a suite in the Ritz Carlton Hotel.

Sydney Chaplin was down the hall.

# 13

S WADDLED IN A new mink coat, a matching hat pulled down over her ears, Streisand stepped off the train in Boston and into the shivery cold. It was late afternoon on 7 January 1964, and in six days *Funny Girl* would open there at the Shubert Theater. A state of frenzy existed as Carol Haney instituted new dance routines, Irene Sharaff redesigned costumes, Isobel Lennart persistently reworked the second act, and Styne and Merrill put the finishing touches to five new songs that in the end would be cut before they left Boston. Despite the large company, Streisand at first appeared very much alone. She missed Elliott, the carefree times they had shared during the out-of-town try-out of *I Can Get It for You Wholesale*, shopping for cheap treasures for their walk-up railroad flat. There had been no intermediate stage in her life. One day she lived over a fish restaurant, the next her home was a lavish Central Park West penthouse.

As she was in almost every scene in the show and had to learn new lines with each rehearsal, she had little outside time. Allan Miller came up from New York at her request and without Kanin's knowledge and again worked privately with her on her performance, trying to get her to relate what was happening in certain scenes with events in her own life. To infuse more emotional depth into her interpretation he told her to think about her father and how she would feel if he were in the audience. To bring the role closer to her, he would have done better to introduce the similarities to Brice, the maturing process of a girl deemed homely, the unerring taste, the penchant for both comedy and tragedy and even a marriage to an unrepentant gambler. Miller claims a great measure of responsibility for Streisand's effectiveness in the role, but his presence was also detrimental to her relationship with Kanin and her ability to take direction from him. In the end it added to her confusion.

Well aware that she was carrying the show, that if she failed it would ultimately fail, too, her responsibility was awesome. 'She had a killer instinct,' one member of the company said, 'very sophisticated for someone so new to the theatre. Whenever a new scene or song was introduced that could in any way take the spotlight from her we knew it would either get cut or twisted around to her advantage. And it always did. Syd had a solo, I think the only one he had left at that point, and she began improvising dialogue that she interjected as he sang ['You Are Woman']. Well, her lines were great and it did help the number when Styne and Merrill turned the solo into a duet with Barbra filling in counter-harmony with comic patter. But since she now had all the gag lines it quickly became her scene. There was a good supporting character, a beautiful Ziegfeld girl, Georgia, who was the great producer's mistress. The part got whittled down until it just disappeared.' Except for Kay Medford's role as Mama Brice, that left no other woman in a major part.

Allyn Ann McLerie, a bright, talented dancer and singer whom Kanin particularly liked and who had received excellent reviews in the co-starring part of Amy in a recent Ray Bolger revival of *Where's Charley?*, had been cast as Georgia. McLerie originally had a song and dance called 'Baltimore', but by the time *Funny Girl* began rehearsals in Boston, the number first had been shifted to Streisand and then cut. When they left for Philadelphia, McLerie's role was excised from the show. Kanin was not happy about this for he felt that Georgia gave Streisand someone to play off in the second act. Streisand did not agree. For Fanny to have a beautiful showgirl as a confidante was not in character. The show was considerably overlong and McLerie's role was not germane to the plot. Georgia could be cut without additional rewriting. Kanin finally gave in and the character was sacrificed.[1]

Kanin was under fire. He and Jule Styne were at loggerheads. Ray Stark was sending memos, numerous pages in length. Fran had her say through her husband in equally lengthy dictated letters. Chaplin was disgruntled, Lennart near collapse, Irene Sharaff and Carol Haney fighting over the dance costumes, and the whole cast having problems with the amplification system in the Shubert. Despite these tensions, cast members insist Kanin was at all times a gentleman, handling cast and crew with strength, but also with tact and with respect for their feelings.

Styne was one of the few composers at the time who liked heavy microphone amplification and had even installed hidden mikes in the footlights when Ethel Merman, known for her ability to project, had starred in *Gypsy*. Streisand found the body mike offensive. When she realised that some lyrics and dialogue might be lost without them, she complied, but the mechanical device slowed her costume changes and was uncomfortable to wear. The microphone was most frequently attached under the front section of her wigs beneath

---

[1] Garson Kanin's *Funny Girl* files contain an exchange of letters between Kanin and Allyn Ann McLerie regarding this episode. On 28 February 1964, as the show got set for its New York previews, Kanin wrote McLerie, 'I would have had it otherwise, Allyn Ann. I believed, then and now, that you brought a note to the show which it needed and needs now. You are wildly attractive and brilliantly talented. You are original and one hell of an actress.' McLerie answered that she did not blame him in any way, it was just 'the hazards of the trade!'

either forehead curls or bangs. The wires ran under the wig, down the back of her neck and were connected to batteries in a mike pack strapped to the inside of her thigh.[2]

'I don't know what happened at this point to change Chaplin's attitude toward Barbra, but about the second week in Boston they suddenly became chummy,' Kay Medford said. With Elliott in New York, Streisand was no doubt lonely and in desperate need of someone to turn to for support. She had alienated many members of the cast and crew. Being the 'star' was a new experience for her and perhaps she didn't handle her position well. She distanced herself from those who did attempt to befriend her and was thought to be aloof, cool, always guarded.

Despite Chaplin's good looks and apparent charm, Fanny and Nicky were not setting off sparks when together on stage, a chemistry that was needed for the story to work. Streisand had much to gain by encouraging Chaplin's attention. She would have a close confidant in the company and her scenes with him would play better. There was a steady parade back and forth between their rooms. Chaplin arranged some quiet dinners for the two of them and Streisand was extremely flattered by his attention. In rehearsals he softened his attitude towards her. On stage, new excitement generated between them. It turned 'You Are Woman' into a sensual, sexy number and made the final dénouement when the two parted more poignant. Unhappily rumours began to appear in some Broadway columns. 'What new musical comedy star and her leading man are a romantic duet off stage to the fury of the actor's beautiful wife?'[3] Earl Wilson wrote. Nothing was said about Elliott, but he was no fool and there were accusatory, emotional telephone calls in which he displayed his jealousy toward Chaplin and she blamed him for upsetting her at a time when she had to be as collected as possible.

Possessing a striking, distinguished manner and good looks which he came by naturally as the son of Charles Chaplin and his second wife, the enchanting silent-screen actress Lita Grey, Chaplin was a formidable suitor. He told Streisand stories about his father and Hollywood and the stars and she learned from him about the shocking effect of the McCarthy years on the film industry when Chaplin and so many other brilliant film-makers had been persecuted. She devoured Chaplin's narratives as hungrily as she did their private dinners, often served in her hotel suite. They were both married and as public figures in danger of being exposed as lovers at a time when moral standards were

[2] According to the sound designers T. Richard Fitzgerald and Otis Munderloh, *Funny Girl* was the first Broadway show to use body mikes. *Golden Boy*, which opened six months later, was the second.

[3] Sydney Chaplin was married to dancer Noelle Adams.

rigid. Streisand was also taking a chance of jeopardising her marriage.

*Funny Girl* opened in Boston on 13 January. After the performance the company all waited in a restaurant next door to the theatre for the morning reviews. 'For some reason,' John Patrick says, 'I was given the critics' reviews to read aloud at the table where we all sat. When I read aloud one critic who said, "Miss Streisand can sing, but she certainly can't act," Streisand put her head down on the table and burst into tears. I remember saying to her, "That's nonsense – you can act!" But I don't think she paid much attention. She left the table almost immediately after.'

A few days later, *Variety* reported: '*Funny Girl* is a gem of a show which took off at the Shubert [in Boston] and shows considerable box office strength. Barbra Streisand provides brilliance in every scene – singing, dancing, clowning, mugging. She has a wonderful voice and the right fizz to carry the Fanny Brice role in high musical comedy style.' This should have cheered Streisand, but the critic had added: 'Show however, needs polishing and work in its second act ... With some thirty minutes already cut from [a benefit performance the previous night], *Funny Girl* can gain by more editing – especially in the second act.'

The length of the show remained a problem. 'Our curtain went down at 11:09 Saturday night,' Ray Stark advised Kanin, adding that with all the new material Lennart was writing the curtain would not come down until 11:31. 'Do you feel this estimate is reasonably accurate?' he asked. 'And is there anything you would like me to do in reference to the situation?' Kanin responded by speeding up the movement and cutting a large production number, 'Sleep Now Baby Bunting', as well as 'Baltimore Sun', and three other numbers.[4]

After a week of performances in Boston the company left for Philadelphia. It did not take a genius to know that the show was in for a bumpy ride. Playwright/screenwriter and well-known play doctor, Norman Krasna, flew in from Klosters, Switzerland where he had a home, to work with Lennart on the libretto, which still had John Patrick as consultant and the Kanins, the Starks and Styne and Merrill adding their ideas. 'Isobel felt ignored,' Patrick recalled, 'and once burst into tears at being shunned. Thereafter, I always stood behind

[4] From the time of its first performance in Boston until it moved on to Philadelphia at least six songs were cut: 'Baltimore Sun', 'A Helluva Group', 'It's Home', 'Took a Little Time', 'Sleep Now Baby Bunting' and 'Absent-Minded Me', which Streisand later recorded on a single. Other numbers that were cut either before Boston or after Philadelphia were: 'I Tried', 'I Did It on Roller Skates', 'A Temporary Arrangement', 'My Daughter, Fanny the Star', 'He's Got Larceny in His Heart', 'He' and 'Do Puppies Go to Heaven?' Although the majority of these songs were never mounted in the production, the sheer number written for the show is unusual.

her chair [during story discussions] so it would look as if questions being directed to me to take notes on were directed at her.'

Stark remained adamant in wanting to fire Sydney Chaplin and both Hal Linden and Darren McGavin (at different times) were brought secretly to Philadelphia to audition privately, but neither had the right chemistry and Stark dropped the idea. Streisand was comfortable with Chaplin, who she knew would not diminish or compete with her star turn. He was charming and adequate in the role, no more. Her concern was that Kanin would not bring the show together in time for its Broadway opening. Gripped by fear that her great chance for stardom might get sidetracked, or even derailed, she went to Ray Stark and complained, 'I think I'm not being directed enough. I need a lot more direction.'

Stark was in a quandary. Jule Styne, who had the hotel suite below his in Philadelphia, claimed that one morning Stark lowered a bedspread outside his window, a note attached to the end of it printed with the word *HELP!* Stark finally turned to Jerome Robbins, whom – as he was both a choreographer and a director and had previously been involved in the project – he felt would be able to pull things together. Robbins was not sure he wanted to take on the task and for the moment remained in New York. *Funny Girl* opened on 4 February 1964, at the Forrest Theater in Philadelphia to glowing notices for Streisand. 'All in all, the evening is a Streisand triumph,' reported the critic on the *Philadelphia Inquirer*.

'But in dealing with the unhappy marriage between Fanny Brice and gambler Nick Arnstein, who is stiffly played by Sydney Chaplin, *Funny Girl* is unfortunately weighted down by a dull and unimaginative treatment,' the critic for the *Evening Bulletin* added. 'There are long arid stretches that will have to be eliminated and, no doubt, director Garson Kanin knows exactly where they are.'

Apparently Ray Stark did not think that was the case because the day before the show closed in Philadelphia, the Kanins received an expensive present of antique china from the Starks, and the next day Jerome Robbins arrived on the scene. He was not to replace him, Kanin was told, but to act as Production Supervisor. From the moment of his arrival, Streisand turned to Robbins for the direction she had asked for. But his appearance at this late date caused a great deal of upheaval in the company.

'Whatever Ray Stark wanted to call Jerry's involvement I considered that I had been fired,' Kanin said. 'I did not desert the company entirely, but I withdrew and Jerry took over. The final credit, "Directed by Garson Kanin – Production Supervised by Jerome Robbins", was as confusing to me as it was to everyone else.' The Kanins remained in Philadelphia for the show's run and silently attended the pre-Broadway New York rehearsals.

John Patrick left the company as soon as Robbins (like Lennart, an informer

Emanuel (Manny) Streisand whose death when Barbara was still an infant created a life-long void never filled.

# WHERE IS THE WONDER ?

Recorded by
BARBRA STREISAND

LYRIC by DION McGREGOR
MUSIC by MICHAEL BARR

Barbara Joan Streisand – age seven. She yearned for love and struggled to meet the hurtful insults of her peers and her step-father with dignity.

June 2 Custom

EMANUEL MUSIC CORP.

on COLUMBIA RECORDS

75¢

Bob Schulenberg (above left), Barry Dennen (below right) with two shots of Barbra (circa 1960). Dennen was her first love, coach and advisor. With designer Schulenberg's assistance, he transformed the awkward Brooklyn girl into a clothes-conscious maverick who stunned New York City's elite cabaret audiences. But it was her decision to change her first name to Barbra.

In performance at the Bon Soir, the cabaret she considered 'her room'.

Singing 'Miss Marmelstein' in *I Can Get It For You Wholesale*, her first Broadway show. She kept a wad of bubble gum under the seat of the infamous chair on wheels, and overnight became a sensation.

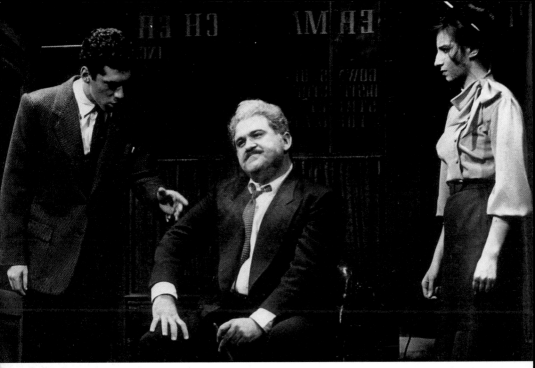

Elliott, Jack Kruschen and Streisand in *I Can Get It For You Wholesale*. All the cast knew she and Elliott were lovers. Whenever she could not be found, a cry went up, 'Check out Elliott's dressing-room!'

Her obsession with antiques and shopping began during her relationship with Barry Dennen. It became full-blown with her marriage to Elliott and the lease on a penthouse that once had belonged to the legendary Lorenz Hart. (Right) Posing on the staircase of her Manhattan eyrie.

Fran Stark, wife of the producer and daughter of Fanny Brice, did not think she was elegant enough to play her mother. With director Garson Kanin's support she won the role anyway. Here in rehearsal for *Funny Girl*, Kanin is wearing his favourite hat, which had once belonged to Spencer Tracy. (Right) Barbra singing the song from the show, 'I'm the Greatest Star', which would prove prophetic.

There were over 40 last scenes written for the show by Isobel Lennart (seated next to Kanin). Streisand's co-star, Sydney Chaplin, started out disliking her. They ended up as a romantic item.

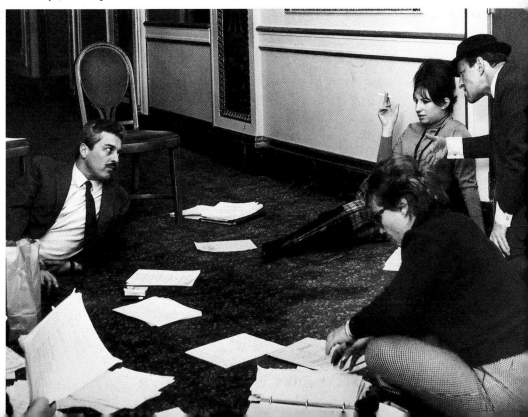

(Right) Recording her second album under the direction of Peter Matz. Like the first one, it shot right up into the top 20.

(Above) with Ray Stark, producer of *Funny Girl*, for which Jule Styne (right) wrote the music. Stark had signed her to a film contract when she played Fanny Brice on Broadway. They had a hate-love business relationship for years.

At the London première of the film (left), with co-star and former lover Omar Sharif, she meets Princess Margaret who admitted she had seen the play twice. Streisand did not think as an American she should curtsy. 'Well, she's not my royal highness', she told Tommy Steele.

After her half-sister Roslyn's opening at the Persian Room in New York. Roslyn found she could not follow in her famous sibling's footsteps. Her mother Diana (inset), whose approval she has always desperately wanted.

Her older brother Shelley tried to protect her as a child. He was seven years her senior. Roslyn, whom she resented in youth, is seven years younger than her.

With Jason (1½ years), soon to be a child of divorce, something Streisand had never wanted to happen.

Elliott would have a short reign as a top box-office star. A drug problem and his bizarre behaviour while filming in London nearly ended his career.

After starring opposite her in *Hello, Dolly!* Walter Matthau said, 'I'd like to work with her again in something appropriate. Perhaps Macbeth.' (Below) As the beautiful Melinda in *On a Clear Day You Can See Forever*, costumes (and photograph) by Cecil Beaton. He thought she was 'very clever – and meticulous'.

Marty Erlichman (seen here in costume with Streisand at a party to celebrate the opening of *On a Clear Day You Can See Forever*) was her manager and agent when she was beginning. He was still on her team as part of her production company. (Right) 'Hullo, Gorgeous!' she cried when handed her Oscar for *Funny Girl* by Ingrid Bergman who was stunned by Streisand's shocking see-through trouser suit with its rather ungraceful rear design.

Signing the contract with Paul
Newman and Sidney Poitier
for their new company First
Artists. The partners did not
get on well.

Politics now took her interest.
She opened the garden of the
New York house she bought
(and quickly sold) to raise
funds for Democratic
Congressional candidate,
Bella Abzug.

With Prince Charles in Hollywood. He came to hear her record for her film *Funny Lady*. 'I could have been the first Jewish princess', she later joked.

Waving 'goodbye' to London, where her London concerts had been a huge success. But she was criticised by the British press for some of the commercial aspects.

*A Star is Born*. She wears a new curly, youthful look to please her new love, Jon Peters. 'You have a great ass', he told her the first time they met.

In a wistful mood celebrating her 45th birthday with Peters. Tulips are her favourite flowers.

There were other lovers in her life – (above) Canadian Prime Minister Pierre Trudeau, tennis great André Agassi (here seen below with Michael Bolton) and macho television star Don Johnson (left) – but none of them were as intense or lasting as her relationship with Peters.

Jason was now writing and hoping to direct. They attended the 1992 Academy Awards together. She was bitter over the industry's lack of recognition of her directorial work on *The Prince of Tides*.

AIDS activist/playwright Larry Kramer's *The Normal Heart* was a project she was determined to film. After ten years she lost the rights and she and Kramer (seen here at a reading of the play to raise funds for AIDS) had a public dispute.

Scenes from a stellar career: (clockwise from top left) *Yentl* (here seen with Robert Evans), *The Owl and the Pussycat*, *What's Up, Doc?*, *Funny Lady*.

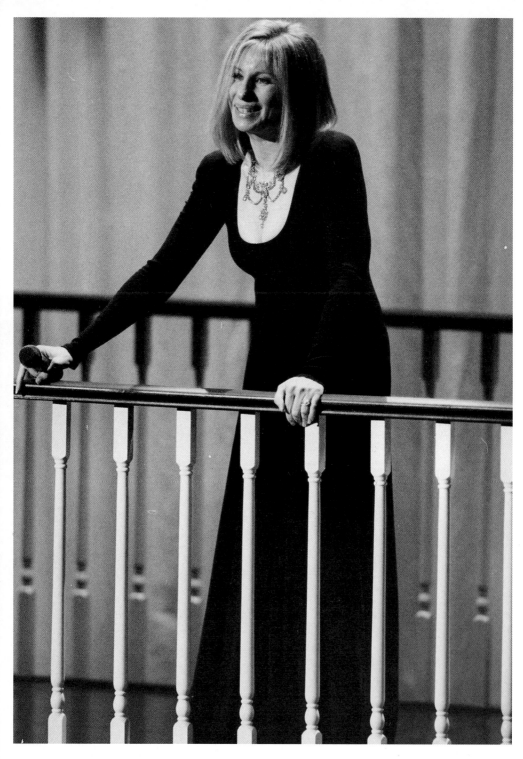

Looking great after her concert at Anaheim, California, 1994. Her tour had been one of the largest money-makers in music history.

before the House UnAmerican Activities Committee) was hired. 'My own impression [of the show in New York] was that he took out a lot of good things that Gar had put in, and added a few absurd ones of his own,' Patrick commented. The company returned to New York to prepare for a series of previews before the planned opening, which would eventually be postponed four times. Meanwhile, Lennart holed up once again in her hotel room and with Krasna's help began to rewrite part of the second act and the ending once again. The final scene eventually had forty-one revisions, almost certainly a Broadway record, before the show opened.

Streisand went home to her Manhattan penthouse and to Elliott, her affair with Chaplin apparently over. With no job offers in view, a good portion of Elliott's time was spent in bolstering his wife and making sure she took care of herself. ('Sometimes, I think Barbra is twenty-two, going on eight,' he was heard to comment.) The day began with him shouting to her on the intercom from the floor below their bedroom where she was still resting, 'Come and get your chicken soup!' He made sure that the kitchen was stocked with the foods she liked. Streisand ate like a woman three times her weight, which miraculously remained at 125 pounds. They had installed a small refrigerator in an antique chest beside their bed so that she could dig into a pint of coffee ice-cream while watching late-night television. On top of the chest was a copy of J.D. Salinger's *Franny and Zooey* and *How to Achieve and Maintain Complete Sexual Happiness in Marriage*. She was, however, more of a romantic than her reading material would suggest.

She ordered two dozen gardenias to be delivered to the apartment each week. They floated in an urn in the kitchen, a cut crystal bowl in the dining room, a Baccarat champagne glass in the master bathroom, and a shallow Victorian dish beside her bed. 'A gardenia is like a free spirit,' she told one reporter. 'Its fragrance cannot be captured. It's like it doesn't want to be tied down and destroyed by all the sterility of the modern times.' After a short pause, she added, 'I think sensory. I always tell Elliott to speak to me sensory.'

Ray Stark viewed her in a different light. 'She is like a barracuda. She devours every piece of intelligence to the bone,' he asserted. One of the actors in the company told a *Time* interviewer, 'She is like a filter that filters out everything except what relates to herself. If I said, "There's been an earthquake in Brazil," she would answer, "Well, there aren't any Brazilians in the audience tonight, so it doesn't matter." '

Streisand *was* self-absorbed when she worked. Everything was geared to succeeding in *Funny Girl*, to becoming a Broadway star. She had added to her performance a dazzling spray of gestures, inflections and small takes that had made the role distinctively hers. She felt ready to carry the show on her own, and there were many who believed that this had been her intent from the very start. In the fifteen weeks in which the show had made its precarious way to the Winter Garden, she had submitted herself to an intensive education in the art of stagecraft, how to project her speaking voice, move, walk, exit. Miss Marmelstein had been mainly a singing role. Now she had to age, to show many different emotions, love, anger, joy, bitterness. She was seldom off-stage and during those times she had many costume and mood changes to master. If she had not been self-absorbed, she probably would not have been able to rise above the additional and multitudinous problems in the out-of-town try-outs.

Once back in New York from Philadelphia, her relationship with Chaplin moved on to a more professional level. Whatever free time she had was spent with Elliott. They still fought but they appeared, like a Tracy-Hepburn movie, to be fiercely in love. 'He looked at her adoringly,' one friend said, 'and she always lighted up when he was near. There was a lot of touching – his arm around her waist, her hand on his arm or chest, her fingers going through his hair. They shared quantities of food, always with mutual gusto, whispered to each other – secret jokes apparently. Barbra would not be able to control her squeals of giggle-laughter. Elliott was protective, caring and amazingly understanding. She could run hot and cold about people. And she had a quick temper. Very combative. But he knew exactly how to handle her. She could not be diverted or cajoled. You had to stand up to her. She respected that and I never saw Elliott back down.'

Her long hours of rehearsals and then as the previews began, the performances and daily changes in the script and music that had to be memorised at short notice, left him extended time alone. His part in the television production of *Once Upon a Mattress* had not generated any potential jobs. Calls to his agent were disappointing. He had worked for only twelve weeks that year and had earned very little money. He found it difficult to be supported by his wife, not to have cash in his pocket. Before her *Funny Girl* involvement he had collected unemployment. He later said, 'I felt like such a failure collecting that fifty dollars. I couldn't justify taking it and I hated waiting in line to collect it.' He drifted back to gambling, small bets with a bookie on horses or sports events. If Streisand was aware of his problems she was able to block them out as she ploughed straight ahead in her consuming passion to make the critics recognise her acting acumen and *Funny Girl* a smash hit.

Like many other recording artists who had risen to the top of the charts with shocking suddenness, Streisand did not know how rich she was. Accountants took care of her financial affairs and paid her bills. She claims she took a weekly allowance of twenty-five dollars. However, she seldom paid for anything out of pocket. She was living high but certainly not loose. Never would she divest herself of that love of bargaining, an art at which she had already become expert. Whether she was dealing with the butcher or an antique dealer, a discount was anticipated. 'Let's see, with twenty per cent off that makes –', she would begin. 'Whaddaya mean that's your price?' she would ask with dismay if the answer was negative, 'I deserve *something*.'

Before going on the road she had recorded *Barbra Streisand/The Third Album* which was released in February while *Funny Girl* was in New York previews. A few weeks later she cut the cast album, with a *Life* reporter and photographer chronicling the session. She wore 'smudged white Capri pants, knee-high crocodile boots, a flowing, fur-collared cape and a hat like a bishop's miter', *Life* reported. 'She was an hour late, but she entered the roomful of irritable musicians with the confidence of Clyde Beatty. You could almost see the cane chair and the whip in her hand. She took no warm-up, and when she sang she was the complete pro.'

The *Funny Girl* cast album was Number Two on *Variety*'s list of best-selling albums within three weeks of its release – before the show opened. *The Third Album* surfaced at Number Twenty-One and began to make its way up the list where *The Second Album* was still in the top ten. Simultaneously 'People' was in the top ten on the singles chart. Streisand was making more money from her records than she could ever accrue from the show. Marty Erlichman felt she was actually losing money, as he could have booked her for high fees in the best night clubs in the country. She would think about that at another time. Now her concentration was on her role in a show that was moving inexorably – despite all its postponements – to zero hour, opening night.

To add to her pressures *Hello, Dolly!*, starring Carol Channing, had just opened and was being hailed as the biggest musical hit since *My Fair Lady* debuted eight years earlier. Streisand feared her own success would be over-shadowed by Channing, who was the toast of Broadway, the darling of the reviewers. Both *Hello, Dolly!* and *Funny Girl* would be compared as period musicals with strikingly similar numbers – Streisand's 'Don't Rain on My Parade' and Channing's 'Before the Parade Passes Me By'. Both shows were about strong, controlling women, although Dolly gets her man in the end.

The day before opening night, the first and final scenes still were not set. Jerry Robbins now had Fanny entering with two Russian wolfhounds on a leash. Handling the dogs while crossing the stage, pausing midway to shrug her shoulders and then continuing, proved – thanks to the misbehaviour of the animals – to be more daunting than any of her splashy musical numbers. The scene remained until the last preview, after which – Streisand in a frazzle – the dogs were fired. The next morning the scene was rehearsed with Fanny sweeping on and across the stage as before but sans animals. The last scene was rewritten and rehearsed just three hours before the curtain rose on opening night, 26 March 1964.

A state of anxiety enveloped Streisand. Elliott remained in her dressing room with her until her last call. She crushed out the umpteenth cigarette she had puffed on sporadically while she waited. Her dresser gave her costume and hair a final check. The assistant stage manager escorted her across the vast backstage area to the wing from where she would make her entrance.

Milton Rosenstock led the orchestra into the final chords of the overture. The curtain began to rise and she started forward on stage to her entrance. There was wild applause the moment she reached mid-stage, a surprise as she had not realised so many of her record fans would be in the audience. The applause remained thunderous after each one of her solos. Her ability to match Fanny Brice's gifts for hilarity and pathos overrode any objections to the weak book, or the skimpiness of the Ziegfeld Follies numbers that the rising cost of the production had exacted. Her regal descent down a Ziegfeld staircase, dressed as a pregnant bride as a tenor sang 'His Love Makes Me Beautiful' was as memorable as Channing's descent down the famous red-carpeted stairway at the Harmonia Gardens. There were no dancing waiters to sweep her off her feet at the bottom of the staircase, but her 'Oy vey, am I beautiful!' as she openly advertised her condition by placing her arms around the swollen stomach beneath her lavish wedding gown, brought the audience to its feet just the same. It was also clear that the number that was almost scrapped, 'People', which she sang standing alone on a stage lit by a summer moon, was the hit of the show and that whatever fate was in store for *Funny Girl*, Barbra Streisand was now a bonafide star.

The standing ovation she received when she took her curtain bows brought this smack home to her. She was in a state of high exhilaration when Elliott came backstage directly afterwards. He understood, better than anyone, what her personal success meant to her. Although she had always said she wanted to be an actress, her ambition was to become a *star*. Never would she have been satisfied to act without stardom as so many fine professionals do and as Elliott thought would probably be true in his case. Barbra needed stardom as a way to validate her worth and he was glad for her yet frightened at the same time that her fame might adversely affect their relationship.

A lavish party at the Rainbow Room following the opening had been arranged by Ray Stark. Wearing borrowed diamonds as her own had been stolen the week before from the Starks' palatial East Side apartment, Fran presided elegantly over the party. The cavernous Rainbow Room, sixty-five storeys above the streets of New York, its window wall looking out on a brilliantly lit Manhattan night view, was filled with illustrious guests, who for some reason were greeted on arrival by the band with several resounding choruses of 'Hello, Dolly!' Former New York State Governor Thomas Dewey and Dr Ralph Bunche, who had won the Nobel Peace Prize for mediating the 1948 Arab-Israeli truce, were chatting warmly. New York Senator Jacob Javits was talking to an ebullient Sophie Tucker, the last of the red-hot mamas. Greek shipping tycoon Aristotle Onassis was hosting a large table of high-society guests. Bette Davis, Gary Cooper and his stunning, socialite wife, Rocky, and something like 300 others had gathered and were waiting at their tables, along with those in the company who had already arrived, for the star to appear.

At the stage door of the Winter Garden, with Elliott clearing a path, Streisand forced her way through the throng of fans, reporters and well-wishers. Microphones were pushed in front of her, cameras flashed in her face, blinding her. She clung to Elliott. 'I can't believe this,' she muttered, terrified. People were pawing her even as Elliott and a chauffeur helped her into the rear seat of her newly purchased Bentley. She had just experienced perhaps the single, greatest, personal triumph Broadway had seen in many years. There had been too many curtain calls for her to count. Channing was marvellous in *Hello, Dolly!* but it was a role that many others could and would play, eventually including Streisand herself. *Funny Girl* would be a hit only because Streisand's performance was memorable. And because she had made the role so very much her own – as with Yul Brynner in *The King and I* – it would impede the success of any other performer doing it.[5]

She looked elegant as she entered the Rainbow Room on Elliott's arm, he in a handsome tuxedo and she in a dramatic, form-fitting black gown. Her hair, cut short for the wigs she had to wear in the show, was coiffed in a gleaming copper helmet around her face. A tremendous ovation greeted her arrival. Everyone stood up, even Bette Davis who was notorious for her lack of enthusiasm in matters of theatrical protocol. Ray Stark rushed up to his star and guided her through the groups of cheering people while the band played 'I'm the Greatest Star' and then segued into 'Coronet Man'. She finally sat down with Elliott at a reserved table overlooking the dance floor where the seventy-five-year-old Sophie Tucker plunged into a frenzied dance with a young man one-third her age. Champagne was poured, food was served in great abundance while everyone, including Diana in a designer gown bought for her by Streisand, waited for the morning papers with the reviews to arrive.

'This is a talent, total, complete, utter and practicing. Vast talent, the kind that comes once in many years. That talent in *Funny Girl* flares and shimmers,' wrote Whitney Bolton in the *Morning Telegraph*. 'When she is a clown, she is an all-out clown, and when she is young Fanny fetched by handsome, dapper Nicky, confronted by a romance that could lead to more intimate association she manages first to josh the whole idea, then to hurl herself at their relationship and take it whole to her heart. Miss Streisand, also like Fanny, is no pretty girl, no merely pretty girl. She does not need to be and never will. That talent will flame for a long time. Much longer than the vapid accident of beauty.'

That about said it all, but the rest of her notices were nearly as glowing. When

<hr>

[5] Although Carol Channing would make a career of playing Dolly Levi in various touring companies and revivals, the black version with Pearl Bailey was a huge success, as were productions starring Ginger Rogers, Dorothy Lamour and Betty Grable.

the reviews were read there was much cheering and applauding. Champagne glasses were raised and raised again. A crush of people moved towards Streisand. Elliott held on to her elbow. He knew that crowds petrified her and he was giving her tangible support. Guests and the press brushed by him trying to get her attention. She was too caught up in the moment to be aware that her husband was being socially acknowledged but otherwise ignored. There was too much else to think about.

She had made it as a Broadway star. The accomplishment was exhilarating. She more than gloried in her fame, she revelled in it, reading everything that was printed about her. She confided to the few old friends like Cis Corman (who was now a casting director) that she was glad she had never changed her last name, as all her early detractors now knew she was famous and there was great satisfaction to be gained from that. And yet, already that was not enough. Broadway stars seldom attained the kind of fame she dreamed about. The great fantasy of her childhood and youth remained out of reach – although closer. Her contract with Ray Stark stipulated that if *Funny Girl* was made into a movie she would repeat her role as Fanny Brice. Only then would she be truly famous, recognised all over the world – perhaps even immortal. All her considerable energy would now be pressed into service to make that dream a reality.

# Making It

'I always knew I wanted to be famous.
I knew it; I wanted it; I was never contented.
I was always trying to be something I wasn't.
I wanted to prove to the world that they
shouldn't make fun of me.'

BARBRA STREISAND, 1966

# 14

A DAY SELDOM passed without Streisand's name appearing in the press – what she said, what she wore, where she went. The spotlight had caught her in a blaze of stardom. She was *'the Face'*, she was everywhere – on the cover of five major magazines, on the pages of *Vogue*, the jackets of three best-selling albums, the theatre pages of the nation's leading newspapers. She could, as well, have been called *'the Voice'* as her records were played so frequently on radio and over Musak, piped into elevators and through restaurant sound systems. She had made it from the enormous, grim society of Nobodies into the small, enchanted circle of Somebodies.

*Vogue* described her as having an 'odd, compelling beauty ... the length of her neck, the slant of eyes, the round mouth. The way she moves her arms, her hands, with rare grace – but not too much'. A few months earlier she had been called a *kook* for the way she dressed, now she was a controversial fashion leader who by the end of the year appeared on the lists of both the ten best-dressed *and* the ten worst-dressed women.

'Some stories make it sound like I used to be an outrageous ragamuffin and now only wear designer fashions,' she said shortly after *Funny Girl* opened. 'To keep warm I used to wear layers and layers of clothing – boots, leotards, wool dresses, big heavy coats, scarves, the works. As soon as the first leaf falls from a tree, I'm chilled to the bone. Now I can afford fur, and it's like discovering a whole new world.' A pony-skin peacoat was lined in bleached raccoon with a matching sailor cap and boots also made out of pony skins. Jaguar skins were used for a severely tailored, double-breasted man's-style suit. The old caracul coccoon-shaped coat, purchased two years earlier for twenty dollars at a thrift shop, had been copied in white fur. She shopped with Elliott for men's shirts and ties to wear with the men's wear suits she currently favoured and that looked especially good with her new, boyish bob, adapted for a better fit of her costume wigs. She refused to wear the then obligatory girdle because she believed in 'a minimum of underwear so that the body is unconfined'.

'What about formal gowns?' a fashion reporter asked her.

'I can always take down the drapes and make a dress!' she said, eyeing the deep red velvet ones near where she was sitting. Then with a good imitation of Scarlett O'Hara, rose from her chair, sidled over to the plush fabric and drew a corner of it under her chin. 'Fiddle-de-de,' she trilled in a Southern accent, 'who cares!'

There was a Streisand *look*, far out but fashionable, and a Streisand *sound*, the nasal Brooklyn-Jewish tone. After her performances in *Funny Girl* the rich and famous who were in the audience came to her dressing room to meet and congratulate this new phenomenon. She was invited to, and enjoyed attending, celebrity parties, revelling in the knowledge that she was now one of *them*. The master pianist Vladimir Horowitz confided, 'I like listening to Streisand. I don't know why but I do. I have her records although I don't listen much to popular music ... A recording should have a balanced programme – like she does it.'

She gave copies of her albums to all the members of her family. 'Would you believe my Aunt Muriel and Uncle Larry didn't know it was me when I played my first record for them,' she commented. That her Aunt Anna had died the day she made her debut on television with Orson Bean, nagged at her. Family recognition meant a great deal.

Much of the credit for the selection of the songs in her albums belonged to Streisand, but Peter Matz's arrangements and the quality of the orchestra under his baton gave them their shining excellence. Matz had begun his musical career by creating the orchestrations, vocal arrangements and dance music for Harold Arlen's *House of Flowers* (the score containing Streisand's favourite song, 'A Sleepin' Bee'), and the composer's next show, *Jamaica*, which starred Lena Horne. These had been followed with the arrangements for Noël Coward's celebrated Las Vegas engagement and his Broadway show *Sail Away*. Matz was expert at working with unique singers and unusual material. His skills were perfectly suited to Streisand's talents.

In his artful arrangements, Matz avoided gimmicks or other crutches. He backed her as a master jeweller positioned a precious diamond in a setting to display all the gem's facets and call no attention to itself. Like Streisand he was a perfectionist. She would insist on many more takes than the record producer asked for and was severely critical of her performance. She recorded her fourth album, *People*, in August 1964. Released the first week in September it quickly rose to the top of the charts. Most of the collection was devoted to good songs that were seldom heard or had just come into their own. But it also included a sophisticated version of Cy Coleman and Carolyn Leigh's 'When in Rome', a masterful arrangement of Rodgers' and Hammerstein's 'My Lord and Master' (from *The King and I*) which recast a pentatonic song into a pop song, and offered a new (and perhaps the best) arrangement of 'People' – this time with a quiet, touching ending, her voice soft but steady with emotion.

The same quest for perfection that she pursued in her recordings was evident in her attention to every detail of the production of *Funny Girl* once it had opened. Chronically late to rehearsals, she was never late once the show opened. Due to an impacted wisdom tooth, she agreed to let her standby, Lainie Kazan, play Fanny for that evening's performance. Kazan, who would later become well known in cabaret, films, and television, alerted the press. When word of this got back to Streisand she appeared, minutes before curtain, and went on heavily dosed on painkillers. The critics thus saw the star of the show in one of her poorer vocal performances, although she gave her spoken scenes an added urgency.

The next day, in agony, the tooth was extracted and she was forced to remain home that evening for fear of haemorrhage. Once again Kazan notified the press that she would play Fanny Brice that night. Mention of her ability to carry off the role exceptionally well appeared in the press the next day. Fuel for Streisand's wrath towards Kazan was added as Kazan was seriously involved in a romance with Peter Daniels, whom she subsequently married, and sang arrangements he had made for Streisand in her cabaret act. A schism between Daniels and Streisand over this took years to heal. She expected absolute loyalty from her friends. Infractions were not to be tolerated.

Although she gloried in being the star, she did not enjoy the monotony of repeating the same performance eight times a week. 'Truthfully, I couldn't wait for the show to close,' she later said. 'Once the show was frozen, I felt frozen too. Suddenly I felt I was expected to do the same things in the same way, night after night. But that's not the way I work ... When I'm on stage I'm living the moment; no two performances are ever exactly the same. That's the challenge – to make every night as fresh as opening night.' These changes in performance – a pause taken before a line, a new hand gesture or voice intonation – were microscopic to an audience, but to an artist like Streisand they were enormous.

One evening she became incensed because the wax flowers used in a scene had not been dusted; another that a spotlight had not been well directed. Her habit was to write notes immediately upon her last curtain listing what was amiss in the performance and hand them to the stage manager to attend to the next day, when she would check out that they had been. She had learned quickly the meaning of star power and how to exert it.

Less than a month into the show's run, Elliott left for Jamaica to play a deaf mute, a small supporting role, in his first film, *Quick Let's Get Married*, starring Ginger Rogers and Ray Milland. It would prove to be thankless for a movie debut. None the less, it was work *and* it was the movies. 'Look what playing a deaf mute did for Jane Wyman,' he joked, a reference to Wyman's Academy Award performance in *Johnny Belinda*. He was in Jamaica on 24 April, Streisand's twenty-second birthday. As she took her curtain, a member of the audience shouted out his greetings and the rest of the theatre took up the cry. Milton Rosenstock led the orchestra in an enthusiastic chorus of 'Happy Birthday'. An armful of roses was presented to her and she tossed them one by one over the footlights. Backstage, Ray Stark had arranged a cast party with champagne and a two-tier chocolate cake. Her co-workers gave her an irresistible fluffy, white, miniature poodle with melting brown eyes, the first dog she had ever owned. She named her Sadie and fell in love with her immediately.

After the cast party Marty Erlichman hosted a festive late supper for about twenty guests including Diana, Shelley and his wife and the Starks. Streisand seemed *wistful*. It had become more and more difficult for her to appear in public. People rushed over to her for autographs in restaurants, stores, on the street. She could not even go to the ladies' room in a public place without being approached for an autograph and several times an over-enthusiastic fan had thrust a piece of paper and a pen under the closed door of the cubicle she occupied. She had lost any semblance of privacy and she claimed she *still* saw herself as a victim. 'Ya know, why me? Even my success makes me a victim. I think, "Oh, God, don't envy me. I have my own pains. Money doesn't wipe that out." ' And she told Shana Alexander, 'The only happiness I *know* is real is the happiness I get from eating coffee ice cream.' Stardom had been her dream and there was no way she was going to let it slip from her grasp, but she had discovered early that everything has a price – in many ways one she hugely resented paying.

She was feeling the pressure and having difficulty getting through her performances every night. A large wall calendar hung in her dressing room and she would cross off each day at the end of a performance and jot down how many more were left. All the publicity, the massive press coverage had made her crazy. How was she going to maintain this fame? What was going to happen next? She didn't want to hurt Elliott and she thought her celebrity would do this. She suffered severe stomach pains and a doctor put her on large doses of Donnatal, a prescription drug.

Her relationship with her mother had not improved much. Diana, who still worked in a Manhattan high school, viewed her daughter's extravagant new style with a critical eye and a dire warning that fame and money could disappear as fast as it came. Diana was unable to say the things that Streisand wanted to hear – that she was proud of her, that she was terrific, that she had turned from an ugly duckling into a silken swan. When Streisand appeared on a magazine cover it was either, 'Why were you wearing your bangs down over your eyes?' Or 'You can see the turn in your eye,' or 'The neckline of your dress is cut too low.'

'I wish I could give you the terrible problem I have with my ears!' Streisand once roared at a fan who told her she wished she could be her. And unless

Elliott's career took off soon, she was aware that there would be serious trouble ahead in their marriage. At Cis Corman's husband's suggestion, she started therapy sessions three times a week with a psychoanalyst. She would continue therapy on and off, but mostly on, for the next thirty years, but these were the sessions where her childhood and youth, so painful to her, were still fresh, smarting wounds, where her resentments toward Diana were constantly dissected and discussed. Unable to shed the past she carried it around with her like an injured child.

These problems were pushed aside when Erlichman negotiated an astronomical contract for her to receive in excess of $5 million for ten television specials for CBS. An even higher fee could have been commanded, but Erlichman had insisted on her retaining complete artistic control and choice of material. She formed Ellbar, a production company which included Elliott as an executive partner. As no acting offers were forthcoming they decided that it might be best if he kept an eye on her business interests and helped to scout suitable projects, not necessarily requiring her appearance, for their company. At the Tony Awards dinner in May 1964 she lost to Carol Channing but soon afterwards received a Grammy – Best Vocal Performance–Female – for the *People* album, for which Peter Matz also won a Grammy for Best Arranger. Competitive by nature, being passed by a second time for a Tony ate away at her. Was she *really* not as good as Carol Channing? Did the theatre community have something against her? She fretted about such things, turned them over and over in her mind.

In October, Elliott was cast opposite Lesley Anne Warren in *Drat the Cat!*, a musical with a score that Streisand admired. Two songs, 'He Touched Me' and 'I Like Him', would become part of her repertory. In *Drat the Cat!*, a throwback to the mock-melodramas of the 1930s, Elliott played an inept policeman in love with a kooky, criminally minded heiress. It opened to negative reviews, survived a single week and closed leaving him back where he was before – without a job.

'I thought a lot about what I should do,' he recalled. He told Streisand that he wanted to strike out on his own, maybe try Hollywood. 'I need you,' she cried. 'You've got to be there to protect me.' It was the affirmation he wanted to hear and he remained in New York. They were most happy late at night when her entourage had finally departed and they could have a few quiet hours to themselves. She could be like a child at those times, clinging to him. She harboured many fears. A naked wire hanger in a closet terrified her and had to be removed. Half-lowered window shades resembled lidded eyes and seemed evil to her. These were phobias she was unable to admit to anyone. Elliott was different. He was her one true friend; the only person with whom she felt completely safe and with whom she could be herself, artifice shed, fame of no consequence. The problem was, she did not like the person their absence revealed and sometimes that made her angry with Elliott for exposing the *nothing* she feared she really was.

Her contract with Ray Stark to appear in *Funny Girl* had also included the stipulation that she make four films for his company, Rastar. She had only wanted to do *Funny Girl*, but Stark refused to make a deal with her unless she acceded to his terms. 'I remember Marty Erlichman saying to me, "Look if you're prepared to lose it, then we can say, sorry, we'll sign only one picture at a time," ' Streisand has said, adding: 'I was not prepared to lose it.' This agreement would cause many future problems in her relationship with Ray Stark, which vacillated alarmingly between hate and love, regard for a mentor and resentment because of his hold over her. She called him 'a character, an original'. He was a smart promoter, a tough businessman and he had, in her view, taken more than he had given. Her contract with him had guaranteed her star status but it had cost her high – her freedom.

Work began on her first television special when *Funny Girl* was midway through its New York run. She dashed between the television studio, the Winter Garden and back to the studio late at night to listen to playbacks and view the results of the day's filming with Dwight Hemion, her director. She started the enterprise knowing very little about the medium; a week later she was acting like an expert. Her contract with CBS gave her complete artistic control and she exercised it fully. CBS executives had fought her with all their corporate muscle to get her to have guest stars on her show as other television specials did. In the end, her resolve was so strong that they backed down. The show would be a one-woman production with a full orchestra and an occasional chorus to support her.

The title, *My Name is Barbra*, was taken from Leonard Bernstein's song cycle, 'I Hate Music'.[1] Peter Matz arranged and conducted the music. The production numbers were conceived, staged and choreographed by Joe Layton, Elliott's director on both *On the Town* and *Once Upon a Mattress*, and recent Tony Award winner for his work on Richard Rodgers' *No Strings*. Streisand was in good hands but she never let the control slip from her own. Her involvement in every phase in the making of the show was intense.

She was quick to respond to the reputation she was gaining in the industry as a 'ball breaker', a 'control freak'. 'Well, control means artistic responsibility, being completely dedicated to a project, having a total vision, being interested in all aspects down to the copy on the radio commercials,' she countered. 'I want to be responsible for everything I do in my life, whether it's good or bad. I have visions in my head. I hear music; I dream. It's very rewarding to have

[1] Leonard Bernstein's 'My Name is Barbara' was previously introduced by mezzo-soprano Jennie Teurel, a noted concert artist of the 1950s and 1960s.

them materialise.' She thought for a moment. 'If a man did what I did he would be called thorough, while a woman's called a ball-breaker. I resent that.'

Playing to the camera was a thrilling and satisfying experience for her. She fell instantly in love with the medium of film, the process of editing, the ability to refine and correct what she did not like in the way she moved or looked or sang. She learned quickly what angles showed her to her best advantage, that her left profile photographed better than her right, and that if she lifted her chin it made her nose appear shorter.

*My Name Is Barbra* was filmed in black and white and aired on 28 April 1965. 'There's a play on Broadway,' she told her unseen audience, *'Funny Girl*. I kind of like it. In fact I go there every evening,' and instantly established a rapport with the millions of people who were seeing her for the first time. 'I can't believe this is my own show!' she told them. Divided into four musical segments, *My Name Is Barbra* was cleverly set so that commercials would not be obtrusive. One was a view of childhood involving a chorus of off-camera children screaming, 'Crazy Barbra! Crazy Barbra!' that recalled Brooklyn and being called 'Big Beak'. In this personal reminiscence, she used giant-size props which dwarfed her and wore children's clothes. In the second segment she moved seductively among the tuxedo-clad members of the orchestra as she segued smoothly from number to number: 'Lover Come Back to Me', 'How Does the Wine Taste?', 'Don't Rain on My Parade', and 'People'. Next, she took a whirlwind tour of her favourite Manhattan department store, Bergdorf Goodman, modelling outlandish furs and singing a medley of Depression era songs: 'Second Hand Rose', 'Brother Can You Spare a Dime?', 'Nobody Wants You When You're Down and Out'. She saved a stylish concert for last, singing on a dark stage in a single spotlight to spectacular effect: 'When the Sun Comes Out', 'Why Did I Choose You?', 'I Am Woman, You Are Man', 'My Man', and closing with 'Happy Days Are Here Again'.

'The result was a pinnacle moment in American show business, in any form, in any period,' wrote the reviewer for *United Press International*. 'She is so great it is shocking, something like being in love ... She may well be the most supremely talented and complete popular entertainer that this country has ever produced. She simply dwarfs such contemporary stars as Julie Andrews, Elizabeth Taylor, Judy Garland and Carol Burnett. Anything they can do, she can do light years better. She is alternately gamin-like, sexy, mischievous, innocent, confident, insouciant, girlish, and radiating warmth. So she touches you, to your toes and then she knocks you out.'

The show won two Grammys – Outstanding Program Achievement in Entertainment and Outstanding Individual Achievement by an Actor or Performer. Ratings were higher than any other variety show released that year. CBS's network's executives wanted her to start almost immediately on a second special that could be released at the beginning of 1966. Streisand could not help but be elated at her instant success in television. Her confidence was bolstered with the knowledge that she could project well on camera and sustain an hour programme that would be seen by several million people. Her goal – to star in a movie – was closer to her grasp.

Her run in the New York production of *Funny Girl* was about to end. 'Truthfully, I couldn't wait for it to end,' she later confessed. 'When it did end, though, on 26 December 1965 [Mimi Hines was to take over from her] I was overwhelmed by the intensity of my emotions; I broke down on stage, and was completely unprepared for the cast and audience singing "Auld Lang Syne" back to me.' The last performance was also the only time she ever sang Fanny Brice's famous number, 'My Man', at the Winter Garden. 'I did it for Ray [Stark],' she explained, 'because he always loved it. And I did it for Fanny Brice. After all was said and done, it was still her song.'

CBS agreed that her next special be filmed in colour, which was now employed for most variety programmes. Called *Color Me Barbra*, it was again produced by Ellbar, her company. Her schedule was fierce: not only the television contract to fulfil, but her record commitments, a concert tour, the London production and, she hoped, the film of *Funny Girl*. As her income rose dramatically, Elliott was finding it increasingly difficult to adjust himself to their fast-paced lifestyle and his wife's fame. He was not happy at, in essence, working for her and not at all sure that his job, to look for new projects, was essential. The London production of *Funny Girl* was to open on 13 April 1966, and Elliott would accompany her and stay throughout the run, but for the moment they celebrated New Year's Eve, 1965, quietly, Elliott more in love with her than ever, obsessed with her, he would later admit.

'She was so vulnerable, I thought. But I think that was a real trap, and of course, I was taken by it. She used her vulnerability and insecurities as a seduction, like a laser beam. It was very attractive, and that's part of her art ... her vulnerability is like one of those snowstorms in a globe that you shake; it's behind glass. She plays vulnerability and has always played it really masterfully.

'She is very cold, smart and acutely business oriented. She was that way from the time of *Funny Girl*. Maybe before, but I didn't notice it then. She keeps herself isolated to maintain the status quo of her situation. I told her once, "Everyone is afraid of you, they tell you only what you really want to hear." She was so afraid of being hurt that she made herself inaccessible. She lacked trust and faith, and being so successful so young, she could make herself untouchable and unapproachable. Poor baby was miserable. She must be the most miserable person I've ever known. She keeps herself occupied with so many things because she's so afraid to fail, so afraid of the truth.'

Sadie, her cherished poodle, went everywhere with her. She cuddled and coddled the small pet. She considered the idea that she and Elliott needed a child. She had no doubt that he would be a good father, but was unsure about her own role as a future mother. These thoughts were not far from her mind as she began the New York rehearsals on *Color Me Barbra* the same day that Shelley's daughter, Erica, was born. 'Hey, whaddaya know? I'm an aunt!' she announced as she entered the dank studio in the east Seventies, wearing a floppy hat, her mink cape, aquamarine slacks and matching suede shoes 'with a strip of maroon across the instep', an observer noted. 'She was not pretty. It is not, however, the nose. The nose is beautiful. Rather it is her eyes, set too close together and somehow chilly.'

On board were all the men she had come to count on – Marty Erlichman, Joe Layton, Dwight Hemion, Peter Matz and, of course, Elliott. She felt secure. Her mood was phlegmatic. Mid-afternoon, Sadie arrived fresh from the poodle-parlour. She scooped the small white fluff of a dog, smelling of scented soap, into her arms, kissed her and carried her over her shoulder as she walked through the next phase of the rehearsal.

A short while later she was asked to sign for a registered package. It contained a jewelled brooch which she immediately pinned to the sweater she was wearing. 'I'm crazy about brooches,' she declared. 'I pass these things in store windows and I say to an assistant, "Go call that guy!" ' Besides an assistant, she now had a secretary, her agent, business manager, accountant, lawyer, dress designer, hairdresser, and press agent, all of whom were at the rehearsal along with Elliott, two CBS executives, the sponsor's advertising representative, photographers and reporters from three newspapers and two magazines. In the middle of the rehearsal hall was a trampoline that she had to use during one of her production numbers. An instructor, who was giving a demonstration on an intricate leap she was to negotiate, lost her balance and fell through the springs before finally being able to rise to her feet, stunned but unharmed. This did not daunt Streisand, who tried the flip for herself, sprawling awkwardly, crashing to the canvas and almost bouncing out of control. Sadie, sitting haunched on the sidelines, barked and ran around in circles. The brooch came undone and flew across the floor. Streisand got up and tried the flip again.

*Color Me Barbra* was to be filmed inside the Philadelphia Museum of Art. After six days of rehearsals in New York, Streisand, Elliott, the entire crew, her entourage, Sadie and the members of the press – about thirty-five people – arrived in Philadelphia on one of the coldest days of the season. With Sadie clutched tightly under one arm, she inspected the hotel suite she was to occupy, pulling up the shades, flicking on the lights, shouting for someone to call room service for a pot of tea and whatever else looked good on the menu. 'How about I go get some Chinese?' Elliott offered. She liked the idea but insisted a staff member be sent.

Food gave her instant gratification. 'I'm not comfortable sitting down to a formal dinner,' she told one reporter. 'I like standing up and eating out of three pots on a stove. I love Cokes, and cones and French fries that taste of bacon, like you get in greasy spoons. I love greasy spoons. Recently, after a late party for Princess Margaret – it was a bore – I had the urge for rice pudding without raisins. Some people like it with raisins, I like it without raisins. Well, I had this urge, and every place was closed, but Elliott found a waterfront diner that was open. We could have gone to the Automat, I suppose. I like the Automat. You put in the nickels and get what you want – pies, cakes, sandwiches. But you know, nowadays, it's hard for me to go to the Automat. I mean, people *know* me and inhibit my eating.'

In a suite on a lower floor Rex Reed, the darkly handsome actor/columnist (soon to co-star in the transvestite role of Myron in the film adaptation of Gore Vidal's book *Myra Breckinridge*) was waiting with six or eight of Streisand's publicity staff for her to come down for his scheduled interview. He waited three-and-a-half hours. 'OK, you have twenty minutes,' she told him when she arrived, sat in a chair and began to wolf down some fruit in a large basket on a table near her.

She bristled at Reed's first question – what had fame cost her?

'Listen, all my life I wanted to be famous,' she replied, a note of hostility in her voice. 'I knew nothing about music. I never had a victrola 'til I was eighteen. I used to buy clothes in thrift shops. Now I don't go there any more 'cause people bother me. Besides, they've gone up. I always dreamed of a penthouse, right? So now I'm a big star I got one and it's not much fun. I used to dream about terraces, now I gotta spend $500 just to convert mine from summer to winter. Let me tell you, it's just as dirty with soot up there on the 22nd floor as it is down there on the bottom.' Reed was surprised by her defensive attitude, but with the suddenness of fame had also come some disenchantment. Nothing was ever as perfect as she had fantasised it would be.

Shooting began at 5 p.m. when the museum closed. The doors were locked and manned by security guards. Outside the local branch of her fast-growing fan club, some forty members, peered through the beaded glass windows carrying a sign that read, 'Welcome Barb'. 'Barbra even has a fan club in a prison,' a woman press agent told Reed. Streisand was ready for the cameras at 7.30. Elliott arrived at about 11.30 p.m. carrying a large brown paper bag and stood on the sidelines as she ran past twelve pillars and up thirty-five stone stairs in the massive front room of the museum singing 'Yesterday'. She sighted him and they both went over to some chairs and sat down as she hungrily dug into the bag and pulled out a hot pastrami sandwich and a container of sour green tomatoes while Sadie danced around her feet and was fed the meat from half a sandwich. At 2 a.m., after a dozen costume changes and scenes played up and down the stone stairs, past walls filled with Cézannes, Picassos and Matisses, the session ended, to be continued the next day.

Her energy was intimidating to even the hardest workers in the crew. She arrived in the morning for the second part of the shooting fresh and with a sheaf of notes for everyone from Peter Matz to the property man. 'She's not dumb,' a CBS official told Reed. 'She heads two corporations – one packages her specials, pays her everything, then the profit she makes is the difference between her expenses and what CBS pays her. This includes her salary. It's a one-woman show, so it would be very weird if she was not the boss.' She was, of course, but she never permitted herself any liberties. She worked harder than anyone else and never showed exhaustion. 'If the star gives up, everybody gives up,' she told Reed. 'I gotta keep smiling.'[2]

That evening, at 7 p.m., she began an eight-hour recording siege with Matz and a 33-piece orchestra. An exhausted Elliott, who had not left her side, warned her against fatigue hoarseness.

'Hoarse?' she growled, and waved her hands. 'Hoarse! I don't get hoarse! What's hoarse?' Elliott rubbed her back and held her hands as she listened to the playbacks and selected the ones she wanted to use. She complained only once. Her feet hurt.

She slept until noon the next day when Diana arrived from New York at her invitation to watch as sequences of the show were being filmed before a live audience. Streisand was singing a camped-up version of 'One Kiss'. 'I made a record of "One Kiss" once,' Diana wistfully told a reporter (who noted that she was 'a round-faced, round woman who wears her hair piled youthfully high on her head'). 'Of course I sang it my own way,' she added and proceeded to sing a few bars in a thin, trilly soprano.

It was midnight when the audience sections were finished. Streisand then called for a meeting with a press agent and looked over colour slides of publicity photographs with a professional magnifying flashlight while she dictated marking for each picture according to its merits as a reflection of herself.

'Somebody else could do this,' she told one of the last lingering reporters, 'if only I didn't care so much.'

In *Color Me Barbra* she was the only human figure on view. She did acrobatic jumps on the trampoline, sang 'Animal Crackers' to an anteater (and had the camera superimpose her profile at one point over his), appeared as the Egyptian Queen Nefertiti whose bust was one of the treasures of the museum, as Marie Antoinette on her way to the guillotine, as a Modigliani lady singing at a café

---

[2] Streisand was furious with Reed after the publication of his article because of his stress on her cryptic comments and on her eating habits. 'She never spoke to me again,' he said in 1977. Several years later, Streisand's anger subsided and they double-dated – Streisand and Jon Peters, Reed and Streisand's then current agent Sue Mengers – to the première of Streisand's production of *A Star Is Born*.

table, 'Non C'est Rien', serenaded Sadie (in her television debut) with 'C'est Si Bon', swung from a trapeze and danced with a chorus line of penguins.

'For Barbra Streisand's second spec of the season,' the *Variety* critic wrote, 'CBS delivered a true one-woman turn – not another biped in sight the whole hour distance. As it turned out, the exercise in conceit was justified.'

Directly after *Color Me Barbra* was shot, Streisand prepared to leave for the London West End production of *Funny Girl*. Elliott preceded her to find somewhere suitable to live. He had been offered the role of Nicky Arnstein and they had lengthy discussions about it before he turned it down. 'I'm more talented than all the guys who played Nicky put together,' he later said. 'I'm not being immodest. Nicky Arnstein was not played. He was never written.' However, he rejected the chance, which would have given a great boost to his career at the time, because he did not want to put further strain on their marriage. Jule Styne believed that a husband and wife playing opposite each other did not generate sexual excitement as everyone knew they shared a bed. In the end, English actor Michael Craig was signed to play Nicky Arnstein.

In Hollywood, Columbia Studios remained reluctant to approve her in the film version of *Funny Girl*. They were demanding tests be shot in London to see how she looked on a film screen. Television was one thing, they said, but film close-ups would magnify every fault she had. It mattered not that her skin was now near to flawless, all the old signs of acne miraculously gone, that her hair was groomed and shiny, that the costume department could take care of her figure if help was needed, that her talent was never in question. The bone of contention was her nose. The studio thought she should have it reconstructed. Streisand would not hear of it.

# 15

S TREISAND'S PLANE LANDED at Heathrow Airport in the early morning, the sky still too dark to see more than a flickering of lights as London awakened from the night. Under a mink coat she wore pants and a big sweater. A travel representative met her at passport control. She had not had much sleep but the activity in the customs hall energised her and she insisted on helping the agent locate her thirty-five suitcases monogrammed BSG. Sighting Elliott, who had arrived ten days earlier, behind the barrier in the waiting area outside the customs hall, she waved frantically and ran towards him. Suddenly, she became aware of the crush of press photographers as flash cameras exploded. She slowed her gait, put on her big sunglasses and pulled down the wide brim of her fur hat to conceal the disappointment on her face. She and Elliott were not going to be allowed a private reunion. They hugged tentatively and then Elliott, his arm protectively about her, bustled her through the pressing crowds led by an airport official and the agent, past a door marked 'private' that led to a guarded exit. Not having expected such a large turnout so early in the morning, she was stunned and her face reflected her fear as she clung to Elliott's arm.

He had rented an elegant townhouse at 48 Ennismore Gardens behind the Brompton Oratory and facing a lovely private green oasis with patches of bright, early spring flowers. The weather was mild for February, winter greyness dispelled by short bursts of sun. But with three records in the British charts and the publicity accompanying her arrival, she was unable to go anywhere without being gaped at and besieged for autographs. As she and Elliott were to have two weeks together before rehearsals began and Chemstrand, her television sponsor, was paying the bills, they flew first to Paris, where *Vogue* was to do a photo article on her. She had just been placed eighth in the list of America's Best Dressed Women (topped by Jacqueline Kennedy), an honour that thrilled her.

In one year she had managed to turn her image around, to prove that her taste for the outlandish was *avant garde* and not bizarre. 'Now I hope people will stop calling me "kooky," ' she said, and admitted that she still bought some of her shoes and other accessories second-hand at thrift shops and occasionally drove her Bentley up to Loman's in the Bronx to buy cut-rate originals minus the designer's label. This did not turn off Parisian *haute couture*. She had been invited to all the major collections. Designer Marc Bohan gave a luncheon for her with some of the most prestigious fashion figures present – Dior, Grés, Cardin, Balmain. She was seated at Bohan's right and never stopped talking. 'My husband and I went to Grand Vefour [a four-star restaurant] for dinner,' she told him. 'I always judge the cooking by the chocolate soufflé. The cream was sour.' She had apparently never had *crème fraîche*, that classic staple of fine French cuisine.

'I hope you will approve the one my chef has prepared,' Bohan smiled drily.

As Bohan's butler went to fill her glass with wine, she asked for a Coca-Cola with a perfect French accent. 'I have a good ear,' she leaned over to tell Bohan when he complimented her. Actually, she had been studying French with a tutor and had recently recorded a French album *Je M'appelle Barbra* with Michel Legrand which included 'Ma Première Chanson', a striking song of her own composition. Although a lamentably pretentious album, many of the songs were sung in excellent French and it sold well if not *as well* as her previous records, her fans not quite sure what to make of a Streisand *à la* Piaf.

She had something provocative to say about each designer. After the Cardin show in which the clothes all had a look of the twenty-first century, short and angular, she commented, 'Those girls didn't have a thing on under their dresses. I could see right through. I was embarrassed.' At Grés, watching a large tent dress sway past, she stage-whispered, 'You'd never be able to tell *what* was going on under there!' Her only purchases were made at Dior, where she bought day dresses, suits, evening gowns, sports clothes, hats, shoes and coats at a cost of $20,000. Dior was a very *today* designer, she said. And, indeed, he was.

She posed for the *Vogue* fashion layout in her ocelot coat and a glamorous, body-clinging evening dress and visited the Louvre and several antique shops before Elliott whisked her off to Rome, Florence and Venice where, as her records were not yet well known, she could travel with anonymity. The short tour gave the couple a chance to share things without too much outside interference. It was a highly romantic time and Streisand arrived at the Prince of Wales Theatre (where Elliott had appeared in *On the Town*) on the first day of rehearsals of *Funny Girl* in an exhilarated mood. By day's end her spirits were low. The production would not be up to the standards she had expected.

Kay Medford was the only other member of the original American cast in the London production. The director, Lawrence Kasha, was also American, only thirty-three – and considered to be a bright, new theatre talent. Having played over 800 performances out of town and on Broadway, Streisand felt she was the only one who knew how the show should go and what worked for her. The auditorium at the Prince of Wales had dead spots, which meant that however well-miked, unless the orchestra could be masked, voices from the stage would be difficult to hear from certain seats. There was also the problem of the British members of the cast who were playing New York and Broadway types with forced accents. Michael Craig, then best known as a British light-romantic film actor – good-looking and capable though he was – seemed fatally miscast as Nicky Arnstein. This was going to be an up-hill struggle and at the end, whatever the outcome, she would bear the consequence.

She remained, as in New York, stand-offish with members of the company. She became increasingly testy with the British press, whom she found even more forward and invasive in their questions than their counterparts in the States. Ray Stark, battened down for the duration of the rehearsals in a regal suite at the Dorchester, soothed as many of the targets of her verbal assaults as he could by telling everyone what a wonderful performer she was. 'The only thing she has not learned is tact,' he was quoted as saying.

To a reporter's question as to why she thought she was so successful, she replied: 'The only way I can account for it is that whatever ability other performers have, I must have it plus. On stage I am a cross between a washerwoman and a princess. I am a bit coarse, a bit low, a bit vulgar and a bit ignorant. But I am also part princess – sophisticated, elegant and controlled. I can appeal to everybody.' With this hard-eyed self-perception came her ever-present self-doubt. 'When I am not performing, however,' she added, 'I don't think I have that definite a personality. I think maybe I have nothing.'

In the first week of April, she learned that she was pregnant. The news was both exciting and frightening. Neither Elliott nor Barbra knew if they were ready to become parents, but soon got used to the idea. Streisand shopped at Harrods, which was not far from her house, for skeins of fine wool, all in different shades of pink. She knitted like mad for a week on a baby blanket and then realised the child might be a boy and stopped because she wasn't too fond of the colour blue. She bought a book by the Englishman who pioneered the natural-childbirth movement, Dr Grantly Dick-Read, and became a dedicated follower. Elliott, wanting to share the experience of their baby's birth, agreed to go to natural childbirth classes with her as soon as they returned to New York.

'To say I love Barbra,' he told a reporter, 'that's obvious. Otherwise I couldn't have stood it. I know the traps. I know the wounds, and I've decided it's worth it in the end to wage the battle. People say theatrical marriages don't work. Our battle is especially difficult because we're real people, not just two profiles on a magazine cover. We really love one another.'

They did not anticipate that her condition would interfere with her fourteen-week commitment to the London production of *Funny Girl*. But with the baby due on 15 December, it was generally assumed that she would cancel her upcoming million-dollar concert tour of the States from August through October. Following the announcement the press soon referred to the unborn child as the 'Million Dollar Baby'.

'I can't suddenly get poor,' Streisand told the American feminist writer Gloria Steinem. 'But I don't want a kid who has nothing but toys from F.A.O. Schwartz. Kids like simple things to play with: a piece of paper, a walnut shell, I had a hot-water bottle for a doll,' a surprising comment in view of her painful public recall of her own toyless childhood and how she felt at not having a selection of toys. She went on to say, 'The most important thing is that she feels loved and has *both* parents,' obviously still leaning towards the idea that she would have a girl. Filming of *Funny Girl* was almost a year away, time enough for her to get her figure back. Still of concern, however, were these constant demands that she seriously consider having cosmetic nose surgery prior to making her movie debut.

The subject of her nose had come up frequently during the year. Fanny Brice, she was told, had bobbed her nose before going to Hollywood. A list of other famous stars who had 'constructive' surgery or cosmetic assistance was rattled off to her. It was said that Marilyn Monroe had breast implants. Rita Hayworth had extreme electrolysis to raise her hairline. Clark Gable had all his teeth pulled and wore a false set to give him a better smile. She consulted noted eye, ear and nose specialists whose opinions were that nose surgery either might or might not affect her voice. She would be taking a chance. The nasality that so identified her singing voice could be lost. Pictures were drawn to show her what she would look like with the alterations that would be made – the bump removed, the nose narrowed and slightly clipped. She hated it. It simply wasn't her. If anything was done, she wanted only the bump smoothed. She was afraid she would regret the results and she was terrified of pain. And certainly she could not have surgery done while she was pregnant.

Under tremendous pressure, none the less she pushed on energetically. The English production of *Funny Girl* was beginning to shape up as it went into dress rehearsals. The week before opening night she was frantic. Her nerves frayed, she and Elliott began to fight and the rows grew in intensity. She was, he claims, afraid to trust his love or his judgment.

'She loves from the point of view of a materialist,' he has said. 'If she doesn't commit to true love she won't lose anything. She doesn't really give. I told her: "You destroy what you don't understand and can't control."' He was determined she would not destroy him. He was trying to gain leverage, to get her to turn to him for certain decisions, to lean on his strength and save hers. Streisand was that contradictory woman who wanted a strong man whom she could control, itself a paradox. Things had to be *her* way, her word final. Able only to respect a man who could stand up to her, she was compelled to test her power against his. It became a kind of emotional hand-wrestling that could spill over into violence if not controlled, a situation both were aware of as fists had flown from time to time, stopped by sheer force of will before any serious damage was done.

One night, neither could govern their anger. An argument had started over Streisand's need to control the people around her, Elliott included. The fact that she could not stop him from gambling infuriated her. Her attacks on his habit only angered him more, making him feel that she was castrating and robbing him of his independence. They were screaming at each other. Streisand said some harsh things framed in expletives, and slammed and locked the bedroom door after herself.

'Open that door!' he shouted. He received no response. 'I'm kicking it down if you don't open it up this minute!' he yelled louder. When he saw that she was not going to do as he asked, he stepped back, then ran forward and rammed the door with his shoulder, breaking the lock – and nearly his arm.

'I don't want your child!' she sobbed when she saw him hulking in the open doorway, holding his injured arm close to his body.

'It was the worst thing she could have said to me,' he grimaced, recalling the incident. 'Barbra's infantile in some ways, immature in others, no matter how brilliant she may be. But it was wrong of me at that point in her pregnancy to kick the door down.'

Arthur Laurents was in London around this time and with Herb Ross and his wife, Nora Kaye, they had dinner with Barbra and Elliott. 'The conversation all revolved around Barbra and at one point Elliott got up and excused himself and went across the street to a gambling casino, I think it was Crockford's. He returned about forty-five minutes later and said, "Well, I just lost $25,000." It was more than compulsive gambling. It was getting at her. When she did *Wholesale* Elliott was the star. Then came *Funny Girl*. She didn't need him. And in the lives of those people that is very important.'

*Funny Girl* opened in London on 13 April to mixed reviews for the show. She was unprepared for British audiences, who were not as enthusiastic in their response to a performer. The laughs came in different places and were not as hearty, the applause thin. 'One of the most nonsensical plots in the history of American musicals,' *The Times* reported. 'The only reason for seeing this thunderously publicized show is the redeeming presence of Barbra Streisand.' Her personal notices were extraordinary. The *Daily Sketch* called her 'the most phenomenal creature of strange chemistry ever to set foot on a stage. She sings, and there are saxophones and trumpets and violins in her throat. Her voice takes off on smooth gravel, and soars about in some previously unchartered musical magic land of sweetness.'

'She is the heart, the soul, the sound and the music,' the *Daily Mail* rhapsodised. 'If those magical cords and that insolently sexy frame should temporarily be indisposed, my heart would bleed for the palpitating understudy.'[1]

London was *en fête* with Streisand's success. Princess Margaret came backstage to congratulate her and the rest of the cast on their performance. Streisand joined the receiving line a few minutes late. 'Well she isn't *my* royal highness,' she had commented to Tommy Steele in New York at a party in honour of the Queen's sister and was accused of being rude, arriving late and refusing to curtsy. 'I just could not say, "Hello your Royal Highness" to anyone. It doesn't suit me. So I just sort of said, "Hello". Princess Margaret looked at me almost like a fan, and told me she had all my records. I didn't know what to say so I just stood there and replied, "Yeah?" Then May Britt [the Swedish actress then married to Sammy Davis Jr] asked me how come I was so late. I said, "I got screwed up!" The Princess looked bewildered. It was like a scene from a bad movie. I quickly said, "I mean I got fouled up." [Another guest claims that what she said was *fucked up*.]

'Tommy Steele [who was in New York starring in *Half a Sixpence*] looked white and shocked. I didn't know what to do so I turned to him and asked: "You two know each other from London, huh?" Tommy was speechless. The Princess turned her head away. Nobody said anything. "I mean," I said, "You have worked for her sister?" Tommy answered stiffly, "I have performed for Her Majesty and Princess Margaret, too." I said, "Yeah, that's what I mean."'

The incident had been widely covered by the press, and now here she was once again confronted by the Princess, this time in England where any infraction of manners would be considered not only rude but insulting. 'Oh, cripes!' she said out of the side of her mouth to co-star Michael Craig, who stood next to her in the receiving line. 'You don't suppose she didn't notice I was late?' Margaret glanced her way. She had been talking to the theatre manager. She gave him a cordial nod of dismissal and walked directly over to Streisand, smiled regally and congratulated her on her performance. 'Thanks,' Streisand replied feebly.

'This is the second time I've seen *Funny Girl*,' Margaret admitted. 'And I enjoyed it both times – here and New York.'

'Yeah? Twice?' Streisand replied uneasily. 'Really?' She heaved a sigh of exasperation and touched her hand to her forehead as if to say, 'Oy vey! Am I dumb or something?'

Margaret eased her smile and moved on down the line to shake hands with Michael Craig.

---

[1] Streisand's London understudy, Lisa Shane, did take over the role of Fanny Brice for one performance when Streisand was suffering severe nausea due to her pregnancy. Enraged when Michael Craig announced the cast change before curtain, a good section of the audience left for a refund. Shane received good notices the next morning, but the incident convinced the producers that the show would not survive long once Streisand left the cast.

On another night, Prince Charles came backstage after a performance. He, too, was an obvious fan and, like his Aunt Margaret, an avid collector of her records. Noticeably taken with her, he spoke to Streisand at unusual length about several of her records and the songs on them. She was more relaxed, able to be herself, joke a bit. 'How are things at the palace?' she was reported as asking. At the United States embassy, Noël Coward toasted her when she was presented with the Anglo-American Award as the best American performer of the 1966 London season, which had also included a badly miscast Mary Martin in *Hello, Dolly!*

Although the British lived in a culture (at that time, at least) not quite as transfixed by celebrity as the States, the public and the press had warmed to Streisand. There had been some earlier clashes where she was lambasted for her American brassiness. But once *Funny Girl* opened, any transgressions were most often overlooked. She was even forgiven her 'American vulgarity' in discussing how much money she made from her records. 'The Beatles have to divide *their* royalties four ways, so I make four times as much as each one of them!' she declared to columnist Sheilah Graham.

When she wasn't at the theatre, she roamed through antique shops and art galleries. She bought fourteen paintings from artist Jason Monet, several of them with the artist's pregnant wife as a recurring subject. Streisand was glowing, proud of her own condition which had been widely reported in the press. She suffered some morning sickness in the early weeks and cancelled her two weekly matinées, but her energy level never seemed to drop nor was the excellence of her performances affected.

Ray Stark, meanwhile, was continuing negotiations with Columbia Pictures for *Funny Girl*. Along with other Hollywood studios, Columbia was struggling to compete with television. Unable to sustain a large production staff, top directors, and a contract list of stars and supporting players as they had in the past, the studios were becoming used to making deals with independents.

Stark never wavered in his belief that no one *but* Streisand should play Fanny Brice. The question of the photogenic problems that might be caused by her nose had ended, as she had adamantly refused to undergo cosmetic surgery. Ray Stark stood behind her in this decision. He showed *Color Me Barbra* on a full-sized movie screen to studio executives in Columbia's London office to convince them of her photogenic appeal. It was evident that Streisand had one of those faces that loved the camera and came fully alive through its lens. None the less, her looks were so far out of the spectrum of the pert cheerleader or chocolate-box beauty movie audiences expected of leading ladies that Columbia was still not yet fully convinced she should play the part.

Stark kept all negative reactions to himself, positive that in the end Columbia would see that Streisand *was Funny Girl*. He engaged a European-based script-writer to adapt the show for the screen. This was not as strange a choice as it might appear. In the 1950s, the House Un-American Activities Committee under the heel of Senator McCarthy, had purged Hollywood of many of its top writing, directing, production and acting talents. Several hundred 'names' were placed on a blacklist composed of people whose associations and liberal leanings made them suspect of having communist affiliations. Unable to ply their craft in Hollywood, many writers crossed the Atlantic to work, albeit most often uncredited and for far less money than was paid to those men and women unscathed and still employed in Hollywood.

Stark approached Sidney Buchman, former vice-president of Columbia, who, either alone or in collaboration had been responsible for some of Hollywood's most sophisticated comedies and musicals – *The Awful Truth, Holiday, Mr Smith Goes to Washington, Here Comes Mr Jordan, A Song to Remember, The Jolson Story.* Sidney had refused to name names before the Committee and was thus found in contempt of Congress and given a year's suspended sentence. Fired from the studio, blacklisted and unable to work in Hollywood, he had gone to London first and then established residence in Cannes. Handsome enough in his youth to have starred in his own films, in his sixties he remained a good-looking man of regal bearing with startling china-blue eyes, glistening silver hair and the nonchalant air of a worldly man who has intimately known prominence, fortune and numerous beautiful women.

After more than a decade of struggle, Sidney had just made a breakthrough with a successful movie version of Mary McCarthy's best-selling novel, *The Group*, which he had adapted and produced. When Ray Stark rang him in Cannes and asked if he would be interested in writing the adaptation of *Funny Girl*, Sidney said he'd let him know. He then called me. I had also come to London in the 1950s from Hollywood and was a member of the clubby group of expatriate writers caught in this treacherous political maelstrom. In order to keep myself and my two children afloat I had happily worked on numerous screenplays without credit.

Sidney did not like to work alone and we had found in the past that we were compatible as a team. He flew to London and took me to see *Funny Girl*. Would I work with him on the screenplay? The story was the weakest element of the show, but I was drawn to the classic theme – a woman caught between two great passions – the man she loved and the career that had given her independence and gratification. I agreed. Sidney promised that he would see what he could do about getting me credit. I believed then, and still believe, that he meant it at the time. Financially I knew he was being scrupulously fair – but then Sidney had a cavalier attitude towards money. He liked to spend it.

The material we had to work with consisted of the playscript, Isobel Lennart's original screenplay, *My Man* (written before the play), and the lengthy reel-to-reel tapes recorded by Fanny Brice that she had used for her aborted autobiography. The main problems as we saw them were to open the story up for film, and give Nicky Arnstein greater dimension while keeping Fanny Brice front and centre as much as possible. There was also the challenge of creating bridges for the songs so that they would flow smoothly from the spoken dialogue that preceded and followed them. We were still working on the script when Streisand played her last performance of the London production of *Funny Girl*[2] on 15 July, the show closing the same night.

Streisand and Elliott returned to New York. Booked into twenty cities for her contracted tour, she had to cancel all but four of them – the Newport Jazz Festival, the John F. Kennedy Stadium in Philadelphia, the Atlanta Stadium and Soldiers Field in Chicago, which were completely sold out months in advance. In Newport she greeted 117,000 fans, nearly 40,000 more than had attended a recent Frank Sinatra concert there. Because Streisand was a half-hour late, John Dupont gave a short organ recital to keep the crowds happy. About nine o'clock the 35-piece orchestra, directed by Peter Matz, and concealed behind a scrim on which lighted effects were used for visual interest, played a lengthy overture of Streisand's numbers. She was given a standing ovation when she finally appeared in a glowing orange and gold chiffon gown with one shoe and one earring of each colour and a tiny coronet of orange rosebuds twined in her hair. She made use of an orange stool as a prop and occasionally came forward on to a special runway built out from the stage for closer rapport with the audience.

Her programme would be much the same in each city of the tour: after belting out 'Where Am I Going?' and 'I Got No Strings', the latter from the Walt Disney film *Pinocchio*, she gave a charmingly whimsical interpretation of Leonard Bernstein's 'I Hate Music'.

At the end of 'Cry Me a River', she stood perfectly still centre stage, a brilliant butterfly trapped in the light, her colourful skirt billowing out on both sides of her as a soft breeze blew across the open arena. The audience cheered wildly. Streisand did not react to these mass outpourings of love and admiration as Judy Garland might have. There were no tears, no convulsive hand gestures to indicate emotion, no moves to the edge of the proscenium to touch and be touched by her audience. She remained imperturbably where she had ended the song, looking pleased, patient, accepting – and controlled as she waited for the shouts and cheers to subside. 'Thank you,' she acknowledged, 'thank

---

[2] *Funny Girl* was still playing at the Winter Garden in New York with Mimi Hines in the role of Fanny Brice. It closed on 1 July 1967, after a total of 1,348 performances. Hines then went on the road with the show, which travelled across the United States for the next six months. Two summer stock presentations, one starring Edie Adams, the other Carol Lawrence, were presented in 1968. In 1982 the show was optioned for a London revival, which never materialised. 1997 New York revival is scheduled.

you,' and then sang 'Down with Love' to a thumping string bass accompaniment.

Her voice was exquisite in Lionel Bart's 'Who Will Buy?' from *Oliver!*, the pure and plaintive tone almost unbearably moving. She ended the first half with a stirring arrangement of Harold Arlen's classic 'When the Sun Comes Out'. After the intermission she reappeared in a shimmering, black sequined Empire-line evening gown and startled everyone as she launched into a thoroughly unorthodox rendition of 'Silent Night' – part carol, part Broadway show tune – that brought wolf whistles unexpectedly from the audience. Included in this section were several songs from her French album, a poignant version of 'He Touched Me' and a rousing 'Second Hand Rose'. She closed with 'People' and 'Happy Days Are Here Again', which brought the audience to their feet vainly screaming 'More!'

Since the night when Elliott had knocked down the door to their bedroom there had been a harder edge to their relationship. Streisand had felt fiercely violated by his action, Elliott repentant while at the same time struggling with the emasculation of her terrible oath that she did not want his child, but it was obvious now that both of them did, indeed, look forward to parenthood. As Streisand moved into the last months of her pregnancy, Elliott doted on her, waiting backstage at every performance until she returned to her dressing room, usually a makeshift affair, rubbing her back and her hands. There was always a local doctor on hand, but she seemed in good health and spirits.

In Atlanta, rain drenched the outdoor arena the day of the performance, washing out rehearsal plans. That night the field was so muddy that people had difficulty getting to their seats. Many of those with front-row tickets had to be satisfied to sit in the less muddy rear rows. Streisand sang only a few notes of her opening number and then stopped, complaining of an echo split. Ticket holders had heard it too and began to crawl over seats to move back in the grandstand where the acoustics were much better. No one left. Streisand mania had swept the country. It was not the same kind of overwhelming public adoration that the Beatles or Elvis evoked. Her fans were somewhat older, more sophisticated. She gave them the best she had to give – which was a great deal – and she did so on every song she sang. Perfect weather the following day hiked ticket sales to over 18,000, and the concert did equally well in Philadelphia.

They reached Chicago for the last week of concerts at the end of September. The stage was erected on the ten-yard line of Soldiers Field. The crowd of 14,220 people sprawled into the end-zone stands. A whistle whined from the neighbourhood railway yard. 'My God!' Streisand cried into the microphone, 'it's got poifect pitch!' She was six months' pregnant and showing noticeably. She patted her tummy when she sang 'Happy Days Are Here Again', to thunderous cheers. After more than a dozen bows she retreated to the house-trailer that had been supplied to her as a dressing room and ordered her hairdresser to cut her hair into a gamine Mia Farrow style. She squealed with delight as she looked at herself in the mirror and then headed back to New York with Elliott in a chartered Aero Commander jet. They were to vacation for a few weeks in a rented beach house at Sands Point on Long Island Sound. 'I've got to have time to catch up with the world,' she said. 'I've had no time to read about Vietnam and Black power.' She had not been able to relax since Paris and their trip to the Continent. She walked barefoot in the sand with Elliott, and planned for the baby's imminent arrival.

They returned to New York in October, the baby due in two months' time. Deciding that the penthouse, which lacked a separate wing for a nursery, would hardly be the right environment in which to raise a child, she set out with Elliott in search of a new home. They found what they thought was the ideal apartment for $200,000 in a prestigious Westside building, but were turned down by the co-op board. The rejection shocked and infuriated her. 'I'm not sure it was because I was an actress or because I was Jewish – or both ... I am deeply Jewish, but in a place where I don't even know where it is ... and I thought, "I don't want to live in a city where I can't get a place to live ... where there is this kind of prejudice."' For the time being they would remain in the penthouse and redo her sewing room into a nursery.

There were two false alarms before labour began two weeks late at 6 a.m. on 29 December 1966. Streisand, escorted by Elliott, his arm protectively around her, arrived at New York City's Mount Sinai Hospital at 9 a.m. He remained in a labour room with her until shortly before the birth and then went with her into delivery. 'It was very traumatic, but Barbra was very brave,' he said. 'We held hands and talked about a son or daughter. If it was a girl, she was to be called Samantha.' At 3 p.m. Jason Emanuel Gould, weighing seven pounds, twelve ounces was born. His father stood close enough to catch a glimpse of him as he entered this life.

'My God, I'm a mother. I'm a little girl myself, and now I'm a mother,' were Streisand's first words to Elliott when the nurse handed her the child in her private room, number 507. 'He's so delicate,' the new mother whispered, tears rolling down her face.

'You know my baby didn't cry,' Elliott bragged when Jason was returned to the hospital nursery. 'All the other babies were crying, and had their eyes closed, and this woman next to me said, "Look at that brand new baby with its eyes wide open," and it was my baby. He looks like Barbra, only he has a cleft in his chin and dark hair, like me,' he added laughing proudly. 'He's got the brightest, bluest, flashingest eyes. Just like her. Exactly. Beautiful.' Jason's blue eyes changed to brown a few weeks later.

Their son's birth seemed to have brought his young parents closer together. Although she claimed she was not the maternal type, Streisand was caught up in the excitement and the thrill of having brought a child into the world. There were a nurse and a nanny. The small nursery was decorated in purple and lavender. Three months after Jason's arrival she was to leave for rehearsals and costume fittings in Hollywood. Jason would go with her. Elliott had been cast in Jules Feiffer's *Little Murders* which was to have a limited New York run, and would join them on the coast when the play, a brilliant but non-commercial vehicle, ended. This had been her dream, to be a Hollywood star. Yet where would Elliott be once she had established herself as she knew she would do?

Their marriage was almost a retelling of the Fanny Brice story. Like Nicky Arnstein Elliott was a gambler. Intense therapy had not cured him of his habit, and he was unable to earn anywhere near what she did. The library walls of the penthouse were crowded with her gold records – seven of them – that had made over $1,000,000 each. She had earned several hundred thousand dollars on the tour, and she would receive $200,000 for her role in *Funny Girl*, which was scheduled to go before the cameras in May.

'I remember two things about this time,' Arthur Laurents recalled. 'She was giving a party in the penthouse apartment and she called and said, "The party's just for friends. Why don't you bring Lena?" Which I thought was odd because she didn't know Lena Horne very well and I said, "Well, she really doesn't like to go to parties." I went up there without Lena thinking it was just going to be friends and there was Ava Gardner and George C. Scott, who at that time [in their affair] were busy beating each other up and Ava was all black and blue and he was bruised. I remember we all fell on the floor playing "Spoons" – it's a game like musical chairs except you do it with spoons. Everyone grabs for a spoon when the music stops. And she had a set of new silverware and she screamed, "Oy! You're bending my silver!"

'Another time, not long before she filmed *Funny Girl*, I went up there and the living room was swarming with men in blue suits – her business manager, her accountant, her attorney, her agent – and I knew it was over'; the young woman he had known had become a superstar and more a product than a person. 'I said, "Barbra, I'll see you," and I left.'

In February 1967, before departing for California and pre-production duties, she recorded an album of standards, *Simply Streisand*, singing straight, no characteristic vocal embellishments. An interesting recording that would eventually form part of the Streisand legacy with songs such as 'When Sunny Gets Blue', 'Lover Man', 'More than You Know', it also contained a new suggestive interpretation of the Rudolf Friml/Oscar Hammerstein II song, 'Stout Hearted Men', from the operetta *Rose Marie*. Streisand sang the number openly imitating Mae West's insinuating, breathy phrasing as she camped her way through it. When released as a single, it became a huge hit in gay bars across the country.

Mae West, the bosomy blonde icon of camp, had influenced Streisand since her youth in Brooklyn and would continue to do so for years to come. This star of a bygone age of Hollywood glamour evoked empathy and admiration in her. Mae West was an original, and although Streisand parodied her well, it was a great mistake to do so as it took away from her own distinct individuality.

In early March she returned to New York just to film her third CBS special, eventually titled *The Belle of 14th Street*. The show was a misguided journey back to the turn of the century. This time Streisand had two guests: the actor Jason Robards and old-time black vaudevillian John Bubbles appearing in a distasteful, blatantly racist song and dance dressed as a chicken. The special misfired, but the concert section, which constituted the last third of the show – especially a definitive rendition of 'My Buddy' – was classic Streisand, at her very best. Physically she was in amazingly good shape considering Jason's recent arrival. She danced, 'flew' *à la* Peter Pan across the stage in one number and in another did a partial striptease wearing a breakaway costume. She also brought out her Mae West parody again with a provocative rendition of 'A Good Man Is Hard to Find'.

*The Belle of 14th Street* proved that Streisand had been right in her original determination to appear solo on her earlier television specials. At last she had yielded to CBS's request for a variety theme. Never an ensemble player, she was unable to enter into the team spirit evident with other vocalists on television, stalwarts such as Frank Sinatra, Judy Garland, Dinah Shore, Perry Como, Nat King Cole or Andy Williams. She was not good at making small talk or cracking jokes that tried to sound unrehearsed. Every word she spoke had to be scripted. And she drew the line when it came to having another singer as a guest, for she recalled all too well how she had been able to appropriate the limelight for herself during her early guest appearances on television with Garland and Shore.

Ray Stark meanwhile met Gene Kelly in Hollywood about directing *Funny Girl*, but Kelly's schedule would have delayed the production. Gower Champion, a superb dancer and choreographer, was considered. Although he had directed such Broadway hits as *Bye Bye, Birdie, Carnival, I Do! I Do!* and *Hello, Dolly!*, Champion's only directional film effort had been *My Six Loves*, a syrupy theatrical story starring Debbie Reynolds. Streisand insisted that she needed someone more experienced in film who could help her with her acting performance and film technique. Stark turned to Sidney Lumet, the son of a veteran Yiddish theatre actor who was known as a sensitive director with a serious approach to story. Lumet had directed *The Group* and Sidney Buchman enthusiastically sang his praises to Stark.

The story of *Funny Girl* was not any easier to adapt to the screen than it had been to the stage. Fran Stark's restrictions still prevailed, Nicky Arnstein would remain one-dimensional. Sidney and I tried to give him more depth of character within these limitations, to make the scenes between Fanny and Nick more confrontational. *Funny Girl* was to be a familiar backstage drama that had been told and retold many times before. It would succeed or fail on Streisand's performance.

Buchman and I had reinstated the role of Georgia, the showgirl and mistress to the great Ziegfeld. The character, who becomes an alcoholic in the course of the film, provided an opportunity for Fanny to show her compassion while at the same time giving her someone understanding to play off and advance the story line. Sidney predicted, 'Georgia's scenes will end up on the cutting room floor. Streisand will shoot down any female competition as quickly as she can.' He was right. She would have dead-eye aim with the male members of the cast as well.

The first draft screenplay was completed in August 1966. Sidney flew to New York for script discussions with Ray Stark. Letters (in Sidney's minuscule handwriting), telegrams and telephone calls went back and forth between us. Everything was all right, Sidney assured me. Not to worry. Then he called, a little less confident, and asked me to fly over. Nicky Arnstein's role was to be drastically pared. A scene that we were particularly attached to was the first to go. In it Fanny visits Nicky in jail, finds him dressed not in prison clothes but as stylishly as ever and playing a high-stakes game of poker with other inmates. Although reminiscent of a Rhett Butler episode in *Gone with the Wind*, the story was based on one Brice had recorded in her autobiographical tapes. Our first draft of the screenplay had started with this scene, played entirely from Fanny's point of view. Realising that Nicky is never to change, Fanny leaves the prison in her chauffeured car, and studying her image in the rear view mirror utters those famous word, 'Hello, gorgeous,' and then the story flashes back to her youth.

We also reinstated the roller-skating number and, using the original 'Baltimore' number as a basis, a new scene had been created in the Baltimore railroad station, introducing the great black performer Bert Williams as a character (he was in the *Follies* with Fanny). Williams, though a Ziegfeld star, is not allowed to sit in the same car as Fanny and Georgia and the other players with whom he is on tour, which was the unvarnished and ugly truth. Nicky shows up, tells Fanny he is going to Europe to recoup his gambling losses and wants her to go with him. She says no. As she stands in the vast, Victorian-style station waiting to board her train, she changes her mind, leaves the show, goes to New York, takes a tug boat to reach the ship he has boarded and is helped on to it as it moves out to sea. Most of this sequence survived.

In January 1967, because of a strong personality clash between star and director, Lumet left the project. Within a few weeks, William Wyler was brought on board. Wyler had received three Academy Awards for Direction and Best Picture: *Mrs Miniver*, *The Best Years of Our Lives* and *Ben Hur*. Four actresses, Bette Davis (*Jezebel*), Olivia de Havilland (*The Heiress*), Audrey Hepburn (*Roman Holiday*) and Greer Garson (*Mrs Miniver*), had each won the Academy Award for Best Actress under his direction. Wyler was a Hollywood legend, his work known and admired around the world. A meticulous crafts-man, he revolutionised the look of films in the 1940s by using a deep-focus shot perfected by cameraman Greg Toland which allowed him to film long takes in which characters appear in the same frame for the duration of entire scenes. Called '90 take Wyler', he was a hard taskmaster, and one of the most innovative of Hollywood's directors. He had never before made a musical but it was certain that he would be able to turn Streisand into a major film performer if she co-operated with him.

Wyler made it a condition of his contract that a choreographer be placed in charge of all musical sequences. Herbert Ross, who had worked with Streisand as the choreographer on *I Can Get It for You Wholesale*, was signed. Production on *Funny Girl* was now scheduled to start in July, but there would be musical rehearsals preceding this date. Elliott remained in New York ostensibly on business for one of their companies while Streisand, Jason in her arms, Sadie on a lead, arrived in California on 2 May to settle into a house that had once belonged to Greta Garbo.

# 16

DUSK WAS SETTLING as the limousine that had met Streisand at the airport cut through Beverly Hills in the direction of Sunset Boulevard. The studio representative sat in the front seat with the driver, the nanny, Jason and Sadie with her in the rear. Most of her baggage was to follow in another car. The day had been one of unusual warmth for early May and sprinklers whirled and cascaded water over the rich green front lawns of houses that they passed. The car turned on to Sunset, drove past the sprawling, gaudy pink stucco Beverly Hills Hotel, its grounds rimmed in palm trees, took an immediate right to the entrance of Benedict Canyon and then into the driveway of 904 North Bedford Drive, one house removed from the corner of Sunset. They paused before the garage gates where a code was pressed to allow them to pass inside.

The house was set in a pretty white-walled garden, with masses of deep burgundy bougainvillaea streaming down one side. Garbo had once cut down most of it with her bare hands, but that was nearly two decades before. None the less, her celebrity had given the property an aura and star maps sold by vendors on the boulevard still listed it as her residence, a curious inclusion as her address had been kept secret during the years she had lived there; even her mail was sent elsewhere.

The inside of the house, built in the Spanish style, was larger than Streisand expected. There would be plenty of room for herself, Jason, Elliott and a nanny, although as it had been rented fully furnished, the decoration was not entirely to her taste – a combination of California casual and Hollywood decorator chic. As soon as Jason was settled she began to rearrange things more to her liking. It was almost impossible to believe. She was here in Hollywood, preparing to star in a movie and living in a house once occupied by Garbo.

Four days later the Starks gave her a welcoming party at their Holmby Hills estate. For the girl from Brooklyn, meeting Hollywood celebrities was a heady experience. The next day she was shocked when the studio demanded she make a screen test. New trepidation had arisen as to how she was going to photograph. She was furious, first refused, then, fearful she might lose the role after all, agreed.

'We were all very unsure that Barbra would succeed with a film audience ... because, at the time the movie was made, her very special qualities were still relatively unfamiliar and certainly nobody in the history of film had ever had that particular combination of – what Barbra did,' Herb Ross recalled. 'So, we did a very, very careful screen test of her. And once we saw her on the screen – and I was the one who did that test – we knew that she was able to project on film as well as she projected on stage. In fact, the medium was even more flattering to her than the stage.' The studio's enthusiasm was greater than Ross indicates.

On 16 June, a Friday, she flew to New York, where she gave a one-woman concert in Central Park the following evening. The event was free to the public and was televised in a condensed hour-long version by CBS in September. The Six Day Arab-Israeli War had ended on 10 June after Israel launched a massive air assault. They now controlled the Sinai peninsula, Jerusalem's Old City and had gained a hold on the strategic Golan Heights. Not surprisingly Streisand had received several threats and was thus justifiably terrified to appear before 135,000 people in an open area where she could not be fully protected. The possibility of cancelling was discussed, but the Central Park concert had been announced long in advance of the Arab-Israeli hostilities and there was a recording and television contract to be considered. CBS promised Streisand she would receive the best protection they could obtain. CIA and private security personnel were stationed close to the stage and throughout the audience.

She looked especially lovely, a summer breeze causing the voluminous chiffon gowns, designed by Irene Sharaff, that she wore in the two segments to billow gracefully as she glided across the stage and up and down a ramp during the two-and-a-half hour concert. Her fear never subsided although the audience was unaware of her anxiety, which gave an edge to her spectacular performance. When she walked off the stage after her final bow she collapsed in sobs in Elliott's arms. This frightening experience would affect her decision not to do concerts again for many years.

Once more Elliott remained in New York to handle business matters as Streisand returned to California the following Monday to resume music rehearsals. The movie would have sixteen songs (approximately one hour of music, 40 per cent of the picture). When Fanny was in performance in the Ziegfeld Follies, there would be band and period music. In anything apart from the theatre sequences Walter Scharf, the musical director, was using full, contemporary orchestrations and up to eighty musicians. The pre-recording sessions were to end on 3 August; studio photography was scheduled to start on 7 August, a Monday.[1]

---

[1] Songs cut from the movie of *Funny Girl* were: 'The Music that Makes Me Dance' and

Wyler was demanding more and more revisions. Streisand had her say, Fran and Ray Stark theirs. Sidney and I were off the assignment. We returned to Europe. Ben Hecht and John Patrick were consulted and, finally, Isobel Lennart was called back into service.[2] It was, according to a letter Lennart wrote to Garson Kanin, 'the worst time of my life'. She now looked back on the months on the road with the show as 'strangely happy'.

The casting of Nicky Arnstein remained unsettled. The role had never been allowed to develop. Attracting a star for what was essentially a supporting part had proved difficult, almost insurmountable. However, Wyler was noted for his ability to turn a secondary role into a noteworthy performance as he had done with Montgomery Cliff in *The Heiress*. *Funny Girl* was already well into pre-production and music rehearsals begun before Wyler cast Omar Sharif, who had starred as *Doctor Zhivago* and a most unlikely choice, in the part.

Sharif was making a Western in Hollywood – *Mackenna's Gold*, and he was seated at lunch in the studio commissary every day at the next table to Ray Stark and William Wyler. 'They were getting ready to do *Funny Girl* and were looking for a co-star,' he later related. 'That wasn't an easy assignment. The screenplay was built around Barbra. What actor would agree to play her straight man? Fanny Brice sang, cracked jokes, fascinated the audiences; Nick Arnstein had to content himself with looking good in a tuxedo. Apparently it was no cinch to find an actor who could look relaxed in a tuxedo. I just happened to be one of those rare individuals, something that started people in the studio canteen joking: "Why not Omar Sharif?"'

Sharif, an Egyptian, playing the Jewish Arnstein?

'Well, *why not* Omar Sharif?' countered a desperate Wyler. 'Think about it,' he said, turning to Sharif. 'It's not such a bad idea at that.'

Sharif was available and keen to remain in Hollywood. With its $8,800,000 budget, and the great William Wyler directing, *Funny Girl* would be a major film. Sharif would receive co-starring credit equal to Streisand's. 'A few days after I signed my contract Arabs and Israelis were locked in the Six-Day War,' he recounted. 'All the investors in the production were Jewish. The atmosphere at [Columbia] was pro-Israel and my co-star was Jewish. And I was an Egyptian. An Egyptian from Nasser's regime. There was fear of a pro-Israel backlash against me, and subsequently, *Funny Girl*.

'A wave of panic swept over the set. Ray Stark spoke of breaking my contract. Fortunately William Wyler, who was also Jewish, reacted strenuously. "We're

'Coronet Man', 'I Want to Be Seen With You', 'Rat-a-tat-tat' (Private Schwartz from Rockaway), 'Who Taught Her Everything She Knows', and the chorus number 'Henry Street'. Four songs were added: 'Roller Skate Rag' (which had its roots in an earlier, similar song) and 'Funny Girl' by Styne and Merrill, and 'I'd Rather Be Blue over You' (written in the 1920s by Fred Fisher) and 'My Man'.

    [2] Isobel Lennart would receive the final screenplay credit.

in America, the land of freedom," he said. "Not hiring an actor because he's
Egyptian is outrageous. If Omar doesn't make the film I don't make it either!" '

Streisand reserved judgment. The dreamy-eyed Sharif possessed a suavely
charming manner and his dark good looks allowed him to pass for Jewish, but
as an Egyptian he might feel antagonistic toward Jews and that would impede
their working together. A lunch meeting was arranged. Not only was Sharif
an anti-nationalist who disapproved of religious fanaticism and bore only
contempt for racism, he had potent seductive powers to which she was not
immune.

'You don't become *really* famous until you're a movie star,' she once had said.
Well, here she was in Hollywood, starring in her first film. The fantasy was
now reality. She felt a shivery thrill each time she drove her large Chrysler
Imperial through the front gates of Columbia Studios and heard the guard say,
'Good morning, Miss Streisand,' and parked in her private space near her
specially decorated dressing-room trailer. She was fascinated with every aspect
of the studio and claimed she suddenly felt at home. Then there were times,
like when she met Marlon Brando at lunch one day, that she became insecure.
'How can I be a star when he's a star?' she questioned later. She acknowledged
their introduction with a mumbled greeting as she found herself almost unable
to speak.

On 7 August, when the film first went before the cameras, Streisand treated
Wyler not unkindly but with a certain hauteur. 'At that point, I think I knew
more about *Funny Girl* than Mr Wyler,' she later said. 'I had played it a
thousand times and had read all the revisions of all the scripts – for the movies
and the play.' To a reporter during the first week of shooting she explained,
'He [Wyler] does things one way, I do them another.'

'My principal concern', Wyler confided, was to present her under the best
possible conditions as a new star and a new personality. She was terribly eager,
like Bette Davis used to be, to do different and new things. She wanted
everything to be the very best. The same as I do.' Wyler was a man of infinite
patience. He celebrated his sixty-fifth birthday on the first day of shooting,
but had made his debut as a director at the age of twenty-three, shortly after
arriving from his native Alsace. He had directed a plethora of difficult female
stars and been married to one – Margaret Sullavan. Streisand's *mishegoss*, her
compulsive behaviour, lateness on the set, her need to be involved in every
aspect of the film, barely fazed him; he had been through it all before. Short
and feisty with grey-speckled hair, Wyler had a charismatic smile and a merry
glint in his blue eyes. Clouds of smoke curled upward from the cigarettes he
chain-smoked as he sat in his director's chair watching a scene in progress.
When he spoke he never wasted words. He had lost the hearing of one ear
during World War Two, as the result of high-altitude flying, a disability he had

learned to use to his advantage; he turned his hearing aid off when Streisand, or any performer, was being troublesome.

'I don't just expect obedience. I don't like an actor or actress who says, "OK, boss, what do you want me to do?"' he said of himself. 'I say to them, "What do *you* want to do? You've read the script and you know what's in it so *you* show *me*." The actor has to put himself in another person's skin and think like somebody he isn't. I can help and guide but he has to do it finally. Barbra responded to direction very well.'

Streisand took another view. 'I feel we had a great sort of chemical relationship. Willy can't, um, dissect a scene for you. I mean, he would go, "Oomph, a little more oomph," and I'd say, "OK, I know what you mean." And I would give it a little more oomph. He let me see the rushes with him and I'm supposedly the first actress who's seen them. He knows I'm not destructive. I'm very objective about my work.'

She spoke the truth. Able to view herself with cold objectivity, she would often ask to reshoot a scene the next day if she did not like her performance or the technical work in a scene. But she saw things in relation to herself. At such times, Wyler stood firm. They had battles, more in the first few weeks of shooting than as the production was well underway. He insisted that a Henry Street waif (Fanny) in 1910 would not have two-inch Mandarin fingernails. 'Why? Why not?' she kept screaming. 'The Chinese have worn them for centuries!' Wyler gave in, which was a mistake as her feline claws present a jarring image on screen with the period costumes.

Wyler admired Streisand, thought she was a true artist and encouraged her passion to learn all she could about making films as fast as she could. He also knew exactly when to display his sharp edge, but he gave her suggestions serious consideration and often reshot a scene if she showed good cause to do so. A studio worker on the set was heard saying to another, 'Willy shouldn't be so hard on her. After all, this is the first picture she's ever directed.'

One time, after Wyler had her repeat a scene in rehearsal for the ninth or tenth time she came over to him, her voice ear-piercing, her hands 'going everywhere, like an Italian woman explaining a traffic accident to a cop'. Wyler held up an open palm. 'Just tone it down,' he ordered sternly. 'They looked at one another,' an observer on the set noted. 'Everyone waited for her to explode and say the hell with you! Streisand nodded and walked back out on to the cold cement rehearsal floor.' This time she gave Wyler what he wanted and he flashed a broad smile of approval.

*Funny Girl* took four months to shoot. Streisand loved making the picture, being the star. She never wanted to leave the studio. She brought Wyler 'eleven versions of each scene. Things that we had tried out in Philadelphia and Boston or that had been left out of the show.'

This was the living enactment of her dream. 'See, Ma, you were wrong. The homely kid from Brooklyn made it to Hollywood and is a movie star.' Of course, she loved to see those nightly rushes. There she was in the darkness, watching herself up on the big screen, her image filling it, looking like she always dreamed she would look – different but beautiful.

Elliott joined her in Hollywood a few weeks into the shooting schedule. Streisand was having terrible clashes with Ray Stark, who wanted her to commit her next film to his company and go straight from *Funny Girl* into a second film for him, although she had the contractual option of making an outside film first. She did not like the project. Elliott took on the position of mediator. Wyler was privy to some of these rather ugly confrontations and saw how Elliott had dealt with her after she emerged from them, fuming, near hysteria. It reminded him of his marriage to Margaret Sullavan, 'But Elliott handled these things a lot better than I did. He came in and sort of straightened things out. He was very good at that.' Still it was obvious that things were not harmonious in the Gould household.

Elliott was trying to develop projects for Streisand's television production company other than those that would star his wife. 'I had good ideas that would have worked if they could have been executed,' he remembered. 'But the television companies were impossible to deal with. I failed completely. I had no track record. I used to deal with all the no men at the networks – a bunch of fucking pigs. I hated them and I hated myself and I hated going someplace with an idea two notches above things that had been done again and again and being strung along and then rejected . . . I never sold any[thing]. Meanwhile my wife was starring in *Funny Girl* and was the biggest thing in the business and I had all this spare time on my hands . . . I had more self-respect when I was a teenager, operating the night elevator in the Park Royal Hotel on 73rd Street [in New York].'

His life took an upward turn when, just two weeks after he had arrived in California he was cast in *The Night They Raided Minsky's* which would feature Jason Robards, Norman Wisdom, Bert Lahr, Harry Andrews, Denholm Elliott and Britt Ekland. His role was not large, but it was showy. However, the movie was to go immediately into production in New York. Alone in California with Jason, Streisand felt deserted and turned – as she had once before – to her leading man. Sharif was married to an Egyptian actress who had not accompanied him to the United States. He had a reputation for having affairs with his co-stars. He said he worshipped 'a certain type of woman. The kind who can use both her intelligence and her femininity.' Streisand seemed ideal casting. 'As for carnal love,' he added, 'they've never found a substitute for it.' And she was ready for an amorous adventure.

'Barbra struck me as being ugly at first,' Sharif ungallantly recalled. 'Gradually she cast her spell over me. I fell madly in love with her talent and her personality. The feeling was mutual for four months – the time it took to shoot the picture. We spent our evenings, our weekends at her place. We led the very simple life of people in love. We used to cook. When I'd used up all my Italian recipes [learned from Sophia Loren] – Barbra would heat TV dinners. We would enjoy simple food, relax in armchairs, watch television and make love.'

Eventually they ventured out to the home of friends like Gregory Peck and his French wife, Veronique. 'Like everyone else [in the beginning], Greg knew nothing about the affair Barbra and I were having, and he had invited me over,' Sharif remembered. 'So I asked him if I could bring somebody with me. I knew he wouldn't let the news out.' Sharif was a man who played at life as he would at cards or dice, without counting the cost. He lived in an eternal present. 'They say I'm pathologically unfaithful. No. I'm never unfaithful,' he argued. 'I simply fall in love a lot, often and fast.'

'Did I love my wife?' Sharif questioned and then answered. 'Yes, in the Middle Eastern way. My marriage wasn't a marriage of love, in the sense of passionate love. It was a marriage of compatibility, affection, friendship.' Faten Hamama was ten years older than he, one of Egypt's most famous and beloved stars, the Shirley Temple of the Near East in her youth who had grown into a beautiful leading lady. Eclipsed by his wife's fame in their native country, Sharif sought work abroad, finally succeeding with his role as Ali, the Arabian friend of Peter O'Toole in *Lawrence of Arabia*. He had gone on to play the title role in *Dr Zhivago*.

When Elliott was in New York, Streisand and Sharif were together most evenings. 'He made himself quite comfortably at home,' one of Streisand's personal staff said. Members of the *Funny Girl* company were aware that Streisand and Sharif were lovers, although Elliott later claimed he did not know what was going on. He spoke to Streisand every night. She regaled him with her problems at the studio, on the set, with Ray Stark. Despite these complaints she claimed she loved Hollywood, the weather, the space, the studio; Elliott hated it, the artificiality, false values and 'what really got me down was the loss of my second name. As Barbra's husband, I was either Mr Streisand or Elliott who?'

Not taken in by Hollywood's glamour, Elliott understood, where Streisand did not, the Eldorado lifestyle in which careers and fortunes could shoot up or plummet down on no more than rumours, the hint of scandal, the news that a film was about to bomb. Hollywood was a closed and inbred society which existed and thrived entirely on its own myths. A killer instinct prevailed, like the tennis pro who specialised in smashing his opponent's serve. No one believed in playing the game. Winning was all that mattered. Frankly, Hollywood scared the hell out of Elliott and he tried, to no avail, to convince his wife not to make it their permanent home.

Although he flew back and forth to the Coast, Elliott spent most of the time in New York, giving Streisand the opportunity to pursue her affair with Sharif, who became progressively more possessive. On the set, his hands rested comfortably on her waist, her shoulder. 'I make women happy with the tenderness, love and thrills I give them,' he proclaimed. 'I get any woman I want because I give all of myself. And who can refuse so much human warmth? Giving, consoling, protecting, guiding – these are a man's privileges. Take them away and you take away his male prerogatives. The woman, on her part, must give the impression that she needs the man, even if she's perfectly capable of running her own life. A woman mustn't contradict me openly. I can contradict a woman because I'm a man and because arrogance is in the nature of men.'

Streisand appeared to find Sharif's macho attitude amusing. She smiled a lot at him, complimented him on a scene or how it looked. Meanwhile his role was shrinking on a daily basis. On the set, she would take him aside and they would talk in hushed voices and she would giggle like a naïve adolescent when he whispered something into her ear.

Sharif portrayed Nicky Arnstein as part saint and part Dr Zhivago, a seductive gaze in his huge dark eyes as he played to Fanny/Streisand, the camera and any woman who had business to be on the set. Nicky Arnstein was buried beneath a starched shirt front and a bow tie. What was left was a one-dimensional character. After the first rushes there was talk of replacing him. Streisand would not hear of it. She liked the way she played off him, could feel the sparks, the sexual vibes as Fanny fell in love with him on screen. Wyler agreed that this was true – no dialogue was needed to understand why Fanny was so in love with Arnstein. It was pure carnal desire. More of Sharif's scenes were cut. 'If it was Barbra's plan to keep *Funny Girl* a one star picture, she was being devilishly clever,' a member of the cast said. 'She got what she wanted and Omar as well.'

Sharif was fascinated by American women. 'The self-confidence, superiority and independence of American women! These very beautiful women whom I wanted to seduce and perhaps dominate. These women so different from the ones I'd known. These women who dared to breathe without the artificial lung of the male!' He called himself a Europeanised Middle Eastern man. 'For me,' he confessed, 'the bed is the holy table. One love drives away another and the woman who's inspiring that love at the time fills my entire world.' Stories circulated among Sharif's many former mistresses of how he could hold an erection for hours using the mind-control ancient Arabic art of *imsák*, also practised by the well-known playboy, Aly Khan.

Caught up in her passion for her lover, the contradiction in Streisand's character was startling. A woman with a fierce streak of independence, she was besotted with a man who demeaned her sex by reducing them to love objects. Yet, at no time during the making of *Funny Girl* did Sharif gain the upper hand. His lust for her gave Streisand a heightened sense of her desirability. It also increased her ability to manipulate and control scenes in which they played together. He was, in fact, the one being used.

Her affair with Sharif stimulated her appetite for European culture. She became a dedicated collector of information, details, facts. 'TolsteiGorgolTurgenevetheGreeksChekhovMolièreRacine,' she rattled off at breakneck speed to an interviewer, 'I'm reading them *all*. My attention span is very short, I get involved with one book and then I move to another, then I go back to the first. Ya know what I mean?' She shifted from one area of filmmaking to another with this same configuration, able to retain bits and pieces first, and then a working understanding of each field with amazing grasp. She was a college student body of one, hand-selecting the top studio expert in lighting, sound, cinematography and editing as her professors.

The more knowledgeable she became, the more she tested her power. Wyler was amused by her at first, then he realised she was a genuine force to be dealt with. She had come to Hollywood where people did things like robots, she told Elliott in one of their daily coast-to-coast telephone conversations, but then added with pride, 'I have the courage to talk back.'

'Every day, Barbra would see the rushes,' Anne Francis, who had been cast as Georgia, recalled, 'and the next day my part was cut or something else was cut. Barbra ran the whole show – Ray Stark, Willie Wyler, Herb Ross. She had the Ziegfeld Girls scenes changed – one day she told Wyler to move a girl standing next to her because she was too pretty, and the girl wound up in the background. Eventually, the Ziegfeld girls' scenes were eliminated altogether.

'She told Harry Stradling how to [photograph] her and Wyler how to direct ... It was all like an experience out of *Gaslight*. There was an unreality about it. Only the crew was terrific. They were so kind and friendly ... I had only one unpleasant meeting with Barbra the entire five months of rehearsals and production. But the way I was treated, it was a nightmare. And my scenes were whittled from three very good ones and a lot of other ones, to two minutes of voice-over in a New Jersey railroad station.'

Although Streisand and Elliott still shared their New York apartment, they appeared troubled and he did not accompany her on location in New Jersey when the company moved to an East River pier near the Manhattan Bridge to photograph the ferryboat scene for 'Don't Rain on My Parade'.

For that sequence Streisand had to run down the length of the pier several times in her high-heeled shoes holding two suitcases and a bunch of roses. 'Boy, am I going to sue you,' she ribbed Ray Stark who was watching the progress of the scene. 'My back hurts. My feet hurt. This is the hardest work I've ever done. I'll probably get sick on the tugboat and I got thorns in my fingers from all these damned roses!'

She returned to Hollywood without Elliott and was reunited with Jason, who had remained there in the care of a nurse and a nanny. It seemed not to disturb her that she was disliked by the majority of the cast. A member of the chorus was heard to say after one difficult day when she was particularly hard to please, 'Who does she think she is, Joan Crawford?' Newspaper columnists railed her about being a 'girl monster'. It was not easy for her to take. But Streisand was fearful that this was her one and only chance. If she did not make it as a big movie star with *Funny Girl*, if it bombed and she went down with it, it would be almost impossible to regain the kind of momentum she now had. The smallest detail mattered: a wisp of her hair creating a shadow, an item on a table distracting the eye. She had to be lit perfectly and having learned which spots flattered her, she kept after the cinematographer, Harry Stradling, to make sure they were used in all her scenes. No person or object could upstage her in a scene. Her costumes had to be spotless, seamless. She insisted on still another take even when Wyler or Ross were satisfied. She worked with the sound men and mastered the technique of dubbing. She brought her own make-up kit on to the stage and touched up her face when the make-up men were done.

'I feel like a boxer in the ring,' she said. 'In Hollywood they have people for everything. If there is a stain on my dress, I'm not supposed to clean it. Then I'm criticised if I stand up and shout, "Stain person!" until someone from the wardrobe department finally comes. If I didn't shout, a whole half-hour could go by before the stain person got there!'

'People were saying she was paranoid,' a dancer in the film said, 'but I want to be fair. That's a lie. She is, in her own way, the sanest person in the world. A paranoid person is someone who imagines he has enemies. She did not have to invent them. She *had* enemies.'

She also had strong supporters. As with the play, *Funny Girl* the movie was fast becoming Streisand's vehicle, the rushes revealing a new, totally original movie personality was blazing into incandescent existence and she so lit up the film that its success seemed as assured as had her own. The studio was pleased, Wyler was satisfied and Ray Stark, to whom she was contracted to do three more pictures, was ecstatic. 'Sure, she's tough,' Stradling commented, 'but she has an unerring eye.'

'You have to understand,' Sharif told the *Los Angeles Times*, 'she's a kid from Brooklyn. She had a terrible background. She didn't just think she was plain – she thought she was ugly. So no wonder that insecurity. No wonder, when people suddenly start to make a fuss over you, you don't know whether it's for you, or who you are. Those weren't rumors that she caused trouble during the filming of *Funny Girl*. There *was* trouble – in wardrobe, in make-up and so on. But when the whole film sinks or swims on you, you're in trouble.'

What Sharif did not understand was that Streisand thrived on trouble and often was its instigator. Trouble fed her churning mind, gave impetus to her determination, and reason for some of her otherwise unconscionable actions.

# 17

WITH ELLIOTT IN New York, Streisand's affair with Sharif intensified. She had become the woman she was portraying, madly in love with the gorgeous Nicky Arnstein. From the days that she saw movies from a balcony seat she had fantasised herself as the woman *in* the story, not the movie star playing her. 'I never wanted to be Vivien Leigh,' she had said. 'I desperately wanted to be Scarlett O'Hara.' She had believed that Scarlett and Rhett were real people and the love scenes in the film had an aura of *cinéma vérité*, real people in moments of true passion. Wyler saw what was happening and said nothing as the rushes were incendiary and just what he wanted. She glowed on screen and off. The set buzzed with gossip – *Would she leave Elliott? Would Sharif leave his wife?* The lovers remained discreet off the set until near the end of filming when they appeared at various social gatherings together and these 'sightings' were reported in the press. After they were photographed together at an exclusive charity fashion show at the Factory Discothèque in Hollywood, Elliott telephoned her hurt and angry from New York.

'Why in hell did you go to the fashion show with Omar?' he screamed across the telephone lines.

'Because the ticket would have cost me $250,' he said she replied. Elliott apparently embraced that response at face value, unable to accept the role of the cuckolded husband. Also, it did not sound that unreasonable as Streisand had hung on to many of her old money-pinching habits and was always pleased when someone picked up the tab for her. Then, the following Sunday night she dined alone with Sharif at Matteo's, one of Hollywood's 'in' restaurants.

Wanting to avoid a scandal, Elliott told columnist Irv Kupcinet, 'Barbra's always been a cheapskate. She accepted those dates with Sharif because she doesn't like buying her own dinners.' Cornered by Sheilah Graham, he told her, 'I'm furious with Barbra and told her that. She should have known that she is in a very difficult position out there, where the press doesn't like her because she has been uncooperative. I'm just furious with her for putting herself in this kind of position. I'm a very secure person but as a man I have certain reactions.'

By down-playing the relationship, he was telegraphing to the public the message that Streisand had done nothing overtly wrong, that she was simply terribly naïve. The situation darkened when Sharif told a reporter with the *Los Angeles Times*, 'It's true, I lusted after Barbra.'

Such a passionate declaration from a lover, who was a handsome leading man known to have had affairs with some of the world's most beautiful women, fed Streisand's ego. Critical remarks about her nose, her looks, were always appearing in print and despite her ability to laugh at them in public, they hurt – deeply. She wanted desperately to be seen as being a desirable, attractive woman, but perhaps, even more, she longed to feel that way about herself. She saw herself as the great love of two men – her husband and her lover. In such a scenario Elliott would be expected to fly to her side and fight for her.

His reaction to the affair was far different from what she anticipated. Elliott treated it as if it was an invention of the press and not true, and remained in New York. Streisand, incensed at his cool attitude, was more outspoken about the significance of her relationship with Sharif. 'I know Elliott thinks it's just another Hollywood fantasy,' she told a reporter, 'but it's not – Omar has told me many times that he loves me.'

She learned quickly that Sharif had his own interpretation of love. To him, it was something that could be collected and then left on a shelf. His scenes completed before Streisand's, he departed Hollywood for Europe a few days later to star with Catherine Deneuve, James Mason and Ava Gardner in *Mayerling*. Within a few weeks, rumours came back that he was having a torrid affair with Ava. Both Streisand and Elliott looked the naïve fools in this typically tawdry Hollywood love triangle. When Elliott returned to California they acted – at least in public – as if nothing had happened between them. Elliott, who was already having difficulty with being the less successful husband of a star, was acutely injured by Streisand's actions. Streisand, for her part, no longer was sure of her feelings for Elliott.

They were still living together, but seeing separate lawyers in an attempt to work out an amicable trial separation. An announcement was prepared for the press, then yanked back, brought out again, then yanked back again. Their mutual business interests, since Elliott was a partner in both her companies, were complicated, and Jason's custody presented problems. Elliott wanted to have the child with him for a fair amount of time, Streisand was not willing to compromise. She planned to stay in Hollywood while Elliott was in New York, which would have made joint custody difficult with a child so young.

This was not simply the classic story of the price of stardom. Streisand and Elliott both had deep-seated emotional difficulties that pre-dated her rise to fame. Elliott's love and devotion had apparently not been enough to build her self-confidence as a woman. No matter how successful she was, self-doubt remained. Winning the love of her handsome leading man had helped – but just for a time. She needed more freedom to find herself, to experience more in her personal life. Still, she was not sure she wanted to let go of Elliott, or that she should. She began therapy sessions anew. Her long investigation into her past and the reasons for her actions, fears, and insecurities began again. She would spend years speaking about the loss of her father and her painful childhood.

'I don't believe in psychoanalysis per se,' she was to say, 'but that's what makes up our personality. Only when you get older can you look at things [that happened in childhood] with some distance, and if you have the courage you can feel the pain.' She laid much of the guilt for that pain on Diana and Louis Kind. 'Even though you – complain – about your parents,' she added in a tone of gingerly forgiveness, 'you find you're like them in many ways.' Fascinated with tales of herself and her past, she would talk to interviewers freely about them, dogmatically certain she was telling the truth. She was binding her own life into a book of her invention, no doubt based on honest remembrance, but it was *her* truth, a story told from only one point of view – her own. She portrayed herself as a victim of any unhappy childhood, a sexist world. To an extent, this was true. Life, however, is seldom so black and white. A case can be put forward that she made herself a victim by believing it was so, and that despite the many injustices worldwide towards women, she had suffered fewer than most.

Nothing was done at this time to start proceedings for divorce. Elliott still occupied a place in her life. He was a true friend, the father of her child. The one thing of which she was sure was her deep commitment to making movies. She loved the medium, felt 'at home' in it, was endlessly intrigued by the camera and the possibilities that film presented. On the last day of production on *Funny Girl*, she gave Wyler an eighteenth-century gold watch inscribed: 'To make up for lost time'. Wyler presented her with a megaphone engraved *Barbra Streisand – Director*. It meant a lot to her. She now dreamed of one day producing and directing her own film, one that had a theme that *she* wanted to present, something so good she could feel that it came from her *kiskhes*, her gut. In whatever free time she had, she would read – books, manuscripts, playscripts, articles – always looking for the story that she could believe in and embrace.

News travels fast in the powerful front offices of studio executives and long before filming of *Funny Girl* ended, Hollywood knew Barbra Streisand was on her way to superstardom. Academy Award producer/writer Ernest Lehman wanted her to star in the movie version of *Hello, Dolly!* scheduled to go before the cameras almost immediately upon the completion of *Funny Girl*. She had great trepidation about accepting the offer even though the money, $750,000, was enticing and as an outside picture, not involving Ray Stark, she would be the sole financial beneficiary of the fee. She thought, quite rightly, that she was too young for the role of Dolly Levi, the widowed marriage broker who tricks the ageing, crotchety Horace Vandergelder into marriage. The press agreed with her. When Streisand finally announced she had accepted the part, the press called her a 'role stealer'. A divided camp was rooting for either Lucille Ball or Carol Channing to be cast as Dolly.

Stark filed suit and asked for an injunction to prevent her from appearing in a movie for another company as she was contractually tied to his. He submitted two scripts to her, *Wait Till the Sun Shines, Nellie* and a musical version of William Gibson's stage hit, *Two for the Seesaw*.[1] Streisand hated both projects and threatened to go to court to avoid making them. After several fiery meetings between their representatives, their differences were settled. She would do three more films for his company, but they were to follow two pictures for Twentieth – *Hello, Dolly!* and *On a Clear Day You Can See Forever*, the adaptation of the Alan Jay Lerner-Burton Lane Broadway musical. She claimed she signed for *Hello, Dolly!* partly out of pique and partly because it presented a challenge to take a familiar character and make it her own. It was to be a greater test than she anticipated.

In the few weeks between the end of production on *Funny Girl* and the recording sessions on *Hello, Dolly!*, which were to be done first then dubbed into the film after the numbers were shot, she returned to New York to appear at a charity concert at Carnegie Hall. She came on stage in a black dress made memorable by the yards of black lace she had wound into a ruff around her neck, and peered at Leonard Bernstein, the conductor, through a diamond lorgnette 'like a diva soprano looking for her pianist'. She seemed gentler, less acerbic. She did a small parody of herself, twitching her long gown into place with an exaggerated simper and rolling the whites of her eyes like a turn-of-the-century tragedienne. She sang two songs, Bernstein's 'Lucky to Be Me' from *On the Town*, and 'People'.

While in New York, she engaged a researcher to ferret out information on Yonkers and Manhattan in the 1890s, the two major locations of the film, and information about well-known people of that era, what they wore, ate and where they went. She bought antique dresses of the period and wore them during the day to get the feel and look of the period and with the help of her hairdresser, Ara Gallant, and a pair of curling tongs she recreated a nineteenth-century hairstyle, with tight curls framing her face, that was most becoming.

Elliott had moved into a small apartment in the Village and she occupied

---

[1] *Wait Till the Sun Shines, Nellie* was to be a musical remake of a film of that title made in 1952. *Two for the Seesaw* was adapted as a stage musical retitled *Seesaw* (1973), with a score by Cy Coleman and Dorothy Fields. Neither of these projects reached the screen.

the penthouse. He had withdrawn from his involvement in Streisand's career and business interests and was concentrating on his own career and was fast slipping away from her. But she still did not know what she wanted to do about their marriage. She returned to Jason and California alone.

The talk in Hollywood was that Elliott had exhibited star potential in the yet-to-be-released *The Night They Raided Minsky's*. Elliott was being viewed in a different light. He was funny, irreverent and almost acceptably anti-social. *Minsky's* was a period film and yet due to the burlesque background it scored a wickedly comic punch. Elliott had somehow upstaged the rest of the older, highly professional cast. He was offered a leading role in the profane contemporary comedy, *Bob & Carol & Ted & Alice*, about sexual freedom and open relationships, in which he was to play Ted, a young man with a confused identity in a neurotic urban world. The prospects for such a film seemed limited and his pay cheque reflected this, but he liked his role of the less sophisticated of the two men, and felt a great kinship to the character. More important, he was pleased to be carving out a career for himself and harboured hopes that it would help to resurrect his failing marriage.

Streisand had always seen Elliott as a very funny, special person, a nonconformist who had not found his niche. But had she held him back because she demanded so much attention herself? Did he gamble because he was screaming for her help? And was he now heavily into smoking marijuana to avoid the nowhere reality of their relationship? All these questions pointed to a yes answer, triggering emotions of guilt. And there was Jason to consider. She knew how terribly painful it could be to grow up without your father in the house, and she decided to give their marriage another try. Since Elliott so disliked Hollywood, she agreed to compromise and work out a schedule where they could live a comfortable bi-coastal life.

On 13 February 1968, with *Funny Girl* not ready for release for another six or seven months, she reported to Twentieth Century-Fox for her first costume fittings for *Hello, Dolly!* Her role was that of a woman old enough to be '*Funny Girl*'s Yiddisher Mama. Not only was she too young for the part, this time she would not be playing a character created in large part for her specific talents and personality. Carol Channing, who appeared as Dolly on Broadway for eighteen months,[2] had been Ernest Lehman's first choice. But Channing did not photograph well. Lehman had also considered Elizabeth Taylor.

---

[2] After five years, *Hello, Dolly!* was still on Broadway, now restaged by Gower Champion (the original director) with an all-black cast headed by Pearl Bailey and Cab Calloway. Before the glorious Miss Bailey, Dolly had been played by Ginger Rogers. Other Broadway Dollys were: Martha Raye, Phyllis Diller, Betty Grable, Eve Arden, Dorothy Lamour, Ethel Merman and in London, Mary Martin. The title song was adapted as 'Hello, Lyndon!' to become President Johnson's campaign theme music in 1964.

'I talked to Elizabeth and asked her whether she'd ever thought of doing a musical. She got quite excited at the prospect,' Lehman said. 'When I came to cast the picture, her agent rang me up and told me Elizabeth really wanted to play Dolly. And I must admit I felt very guilty at having mentioned it to her, because it was a thoroughly rotten notion of mine. At least I *think* it was. In this business you can never, ever, tell until after the event.'

A slender man in his early fifties with long, greying sideburns and thinning hair arranged artfully across the top of his balding head, Lehman was one of Hollywood's top screen writers, responsible for three of the highest-grossing movie musicals ever produced: *The Sound of Music*, *West Side Story* and *The King and I*, the last considered by critics to be a landmark film musical. These three, with two of his straight dramas: the original screenplay for the great Hitchcock film *North by Northwest* and the Academy Award-winning *Who's Afraid of Virginia Woolf?*, had brought him five Academy nominations. Lehman wore a persistent look of pain on his narrow face and on his wrist a thin gold watch with the letters of his name replacing the numbers. 'You've got to have twelve letters in your name or it won't work,' he'd tell anyone who asked about it, 'and it helps if there are six in the first and the last.'

Lehman had been working on the filmscript of *Hello, Dolly!* over a period of three years, having seen Jerry Herman's Broadway musical adaptation of the 1938 Thornton Wilder's *The Merchant of Yonkers*,[3] when Carol Channing was still in the cast, and had found himself, 'strangely moved, suddenly filled with nostalgia for a New York I never knew – a kind of gay and charming world in which even the wicked were innocent'. He saw Dolly Levi as a countrified cousin to the materialistic Lorelei (also played on Broadway by Channing) in *Gentlemen Prefer Blondes*.

Streisand's struggle would be to make Dolly believable. Dolly Levi was a dreadnought, triumphantly sailing the perilous seas of widowhood, using wits, guts and a surface of supreme confidence. In an age of anti-heroes, she was the ultimate heroine. Her victory – over the past, over loneliness, over despondency – radiated hope and much good cheer. And whatever else she was, she could never be dull. Bringing Dolly to full-blooded life on screen was not going to be Streisand's only problem. Three stars had already recorded cast

[3] Thornton Wilder had himself adapted *The Merchant of Yonkers* from *A Day Well Spent*, written in 1835 by John Oxenford and produced in London. A German adaptation of the same play by John Nestroy appeared in Vienna in 1842 under the title *Einen Jux Will es Nochen*. First produced on Broadway in 1938, Wilder's version, which starred Jane Cowl, was not a success. Fifteen years later he rewrote the play, which he now called *The Matchmaker*. It opened in London in 1954 starring Ruth Gordon and was a great success. The following year David Merrick optioned the rights and Ruth Gordon repeated her performance on Broadway for 486 performances. The play was made into a film by Paramount in 1958 starring Shirley Booth as Dolly Levi.

albums, Carol Channing, Mary Martin, and Pearl Bailey. Louis Armstrong had made an outstanding hit record of the title song. Not only would she be on screen for less than two-thirds of the film, there would be another character, the beautiful, young Irene Molloy (Marianne McAndrew) integral to the plot, who had two lovely ballads. She had to move the spotlight directly on herself and tailor Dolly's character to her own concept.

She began this metamorphosis by influencing the design, by Irene Sharaff, of Dolly's famous Harmonia Gardens costume. The film's key scene is when Dolly struts down the grand, red-carpeted staircase of that establishment and sings the title song with the waiters who are welcoming her back after fourteen years' absence (which means she could not very well have been much younger than thirty-five). Sharaff had designed a startling red gown. Michael Stewart, the librettist of the Broadway show, asserted that Dolly's scarlet gown was symbolic of life returning to her. Photographs of Channing in the plush, vivid, figure-moulding crimson gown she had worn in that descent had proliferated in the media and she had appeared several times as a television variety special guest in the costume singing the title song. Streisand refused to wear a gown of that colour and fought onerous battles with Sharaff and Lehman over the design. One day she refused to leave her dressing room unless it was agreed that a new design in gold would be forthcoming. Sharaff compromised and designed a richly beaded topaz dress which pleased Streisand. The stand-off was to be a harbinger of bitter conflicts to come.

Gene Kelly, one of Hollywood's most beloved and admired musical stars, fresh from his success as a director with *A Guide for the Married Man*,[4] was signed as the director. 'Like Barbra, Gene was a hot property and it seemed a smart move. *Was* a smart move,' Lehman recalled. 'There was no one else around whose knowledge of musicals was as wide and varied as his. He had exactly the qualities we needed on the picture. Tremendous energy, vitality, and a maddening cheerfulness. But Barbra and Gene – they were just not meant to communicate on this earth.'

'I'd heard that she was a difficult lady,' Kelly said, 'so as soon as I agreed to do the picture, I flew to New York [where she had gone to look for a new apartment] and met her for lunch at the Oak Room in the Plaza Hotel, and I came straight out with it and said, "Barbra, is there any truth to all these stories that you don't want to rehearse and that you're difficult?"

'Me?' she replied. 'I'm a nervous *chalaria* maybe, but I'm not difficult.' All she needed, she told him, was a director to guide her.

'She also said she was dying to do the role, and that I could count on her,'

---

[4] Gene Kelly made his directorial debut as co-director with Stanley Donen for *On the Town* (1948). The two men also took co-directorial credit for *Singin' in the Rain* (1952). His solo directorial effort was *Invitation to the Dance* (1956).

Kelly added. She had actually agreed conditionally, wanting first to be assured that Jerry Herman would write more songs for her, as the original score gave Dolly Levi only three solos.[5]

By the time she returned to California, she had changed her mind. She had read and reread the screenplay and was convinced she was far too young to play Dolly and, equally serious, the story was not all that much about the title character. 'It devotes as much time to Cornelius and Barnaby and their two young women – all of whom are naïve and childish,' Lehman explained, 'and there was nothing I could do about it . . . It was the nature of the beast. *Hello, Dolly!* is a pretty infantile story. Barbra would telephone me in the middle of the night. "What the hell am I doing in this picture?" she demanded to know. "There is no way I can play Dolly Levi in a way that makes sense of the woman!" She wanted out. I assured her that Gene would be able to mould Dolly's excesses into a workable characterisation.'

'If only there'd been more time,' Kelly defended, 'I'd have tried to help her work out a clear-cut characterisation, but we had a tight schedule and I left it up to her. With the result that she was being Mae West one minute, Fanny Brice the other, and Barbra Streisand the next. Her accent varied as much as her mannerisms. She kept experimenting with new things out of sheer desperation, none of which really worked to her satisfaction. And as she's such a perfectionist, she became terribly neurotic and insecure.'

The major interior set constructed for *Hello, Dolly!* on the Twentieth lot was the Harmonia Gardens, a combination bar, restaurant and night club popular in the 1890s. Its decor was suggested by combining elements of Tony Pastor's in New York, Maxime's in Paris and London's Crystal Palace. Built on four levels, it was filled with fountains, candelabra, chandeliers, statues and greenery; marble, gold and crystal appointments and furnishings in mutations of red from scarlet to salmon. 'I'd say you've built one hell of a saloon,' Lehman told production designer John DeCuir, who had created much of Rome and Alexandria for Elizabeth Taylor's *Cleopatra*.

Streisand made an electrifying entrance in her topaz gown, shimmering beneath the blinding lights and then descending the wide red carpeted staircase. 'What I needed was Rhett Butler to sweep me back up again,' she told her stand-in Marie Rhodes. 'What I got was Walter Matthau.' Rhodes had been Marlon Brando's stand-in for years – the only woman of her profession known to have doubled for both a great male and female star. ('I rather like the

[5] Herman negotiated a new contract for the additional material and quickly supplied 'Just Leave Everything to Me' and a ballad, 'Love Is Only Love'. When Lehman learned the latter song was originally written, although not used, for Herman's *Mame* he was furious but helpless to do anything about it. The lyrics, however, were new and Streisand approved the songs.

change,' she said. 'At least I don't have to wear pants every day.') Streisand never tired of hearing from Rhodes about her idol.

The topaz gown weighed over twenty pounds and the length of the skirt presented the danger of tripping. The scene had to be reshot several times and took two days to complete. The gown did not have the dramatic impact it might have had in red, but it gave Streisand a marvellously voluptuous figure and the colour was a strong contrast against all the red used in the decor. She wore the gown for nearly two weeks as other scenes in the Harmonia Gardens were shot, the most memorable being the sequence in which Dolly, wolfing turkey, dumplings and beets, rejects, as a ploy, a proposal of marriage from Horace Vandergelder, the widower she has been pursuing. At the same time as she ate heartily, Streisand had to maintain delicacy and attractiveness. By the third take, the dumplings, which were made of egg whites, were hard for her to swallow, and by the fifth she almost choked while downing a piece of turkey.

She also wore the unwieldy gown as she made a 360 degree tour of the Gardens accompanied by the elaborately capering, acrobatic, singing waiters and sang a duet with Louis Armstrong, making a cameo appearance in the film. Never satisfied with a take, she insisted that scenes be shot over and over, with everyone else seeming to tire but herself. She was grateful that Harry Stradling was manning the camera as he had for *Funny Girl*. He was her one ally.

Her chemistry with Kelly was explosive. He expected a certain respect for his position as her director and because of his many years' experience in films. She thought he had an attitude problem. Politeness was not her strong suit. She said what she felt, when she felt it. Kelly was not the only one who had trouble dealing with her. Her leading man, Walter Matthau, found it 'painful to adjust to her personality, particularly as she made no attempt to adjust to mine'.

Matthau was the complete professional. At the age of forty-eight, he had been in show business for thirty-seven years, having made his debut at eleven in the Yiddish theatre. As a respected supporting player, he had shuttled between Broadway and Hollywood for years when in 1965 he soared to sudden Broadway stardom in *The Odd Couple* in a role that Neil Simon had written especially for him. He had just co-starred with Jack Lemmon in the film adaptation and had won the Academy Award for Supporting Actor in 1966 for his role in *The Fortune Cookie*, also with Lemmon. The same slouching posture, the craggy face and growling voice that had kept him for years from becoming a leading man, now proved to be his best assets. He was, and would remain for two decades, Hollywood's favourite lead comedian.

'The trouble with Barbra,' he contended, 'is she became a star long before she became an actress. Which is a pity, because if she learned her trade properly she might become a competent actress instead of a freak attraction – like a boa constrictor – I was appalled at every move she made ... The thing about working with her was that you never knew what she was going to do next and were afraid she'd do it. I found it a most unpleasant picture to work on and, as most of my scenes were with her, extremely distasteful. I developed all kinds of symptoms. Pains in the lower abdomen, severe headaches, palpitations: I was in agony most of the time, every move she made.

'Once I heard her tell Lennie Hayton, our musical director, that the flutes were coming in too soon, and that the violins were too fast. Then she started telling Gene how she thought I should feed her lines. He should have told her to mind her own business and do as she was told and not pay so much attention to other people as she had a lot to learn herself. And when she had twenty years' more experience, then she should still shut up because she wasn't the director. The poor girl was corrupted by power in her second movie!'

Streisand and Matthau nearly came to blows the day after Senator Robert Kennedy was assassinated. The company was sweltering in 98-degree heat on location in Garrison, a small town near West Point in upstate New York, fighting mosquitos, and suffering beneath the weight of heavy costumes. Emotions ran high. Another assassination, another Kennedy dead. Streisand was distressed, as everyone was. Kelly considered ending the day early but for the cost in money and time. The co-stars were shooting an exterior for 'Before the Parade passes By' which involved 2,500 extras and the entire cast, the chorus and dancers. Streisand was determined to 'get it right'. When she had recorded the song, her final note had been a C-sharp at the top of her range and she held it for ten bars and a beat, longer than she had ever previously done. There was no way she was going to let the scene be less than the song. Streisand wanted to do the scene over. Reshooting such a complicated musical number with all those people was an enormous task, and everyone was tense. Kelly, after a sharp exchange with Streisand, made the decision to reshoot.

She upstaged her own rousing rendition of 'Hello, Dolly!' with 'Before the Parade passes By' which starts quietly with Dolly seated alone on a park bench, reminiscing about her late husband Ephraim, and proceeds into an extravagant street parade with several full marching bands, floats, and cavalry troops carrying large flags. In the midst of all this, Dolly struts and weaves through the lines of brightly costumed people and high-stepping horses as she sings her final note, said to be the longest note held by a singer in any movie musical including Judy Garland's legendary rendition of 'Johnny One-note', in *Words and Music*.

'As if contending with [all these problems] were not enough,' Matthau said, 'Barbra kept asking Gene whether he didn't think it would be better if I did this on this line, and that on the other, etc., etc. – and I told her to stop directing the fucking picture, which she took exception to, and there was a blow-up in which I also told her she was a pip-squeak who didn't have the talent of a butterfly's fart. To which she replied that I was jealous because I wasn't as good as she was. We began a slanging match like a couple of kids from the ghetto. I think Gene thought one of us was going to die of apoplexy or something [in fact, Matthau had recently recovered from a serious heart attack and Kelly was right to be concerned], or that I'd belt her, or that maybe she'd scratch my eyes out – or worse, that we'd just walk off leaving twenty million dollars' worth of movie go down the drain.'

Things did not get better. 'It was not, in retrospect,' Lehman recalled, 'a happy film. There were things going on that were terrible. The intrigues, the bitterness, the backbiting, the deceits, the misery, the gloom. Most unpleasant. It's quite amazing what people go through to make something entertaining for others.'

Matthau's outburst had hurt Streisand more than she wanted anyone in the film to suspect. He had since shouted at her that 'Everyone in the cast hates you!' She was fearful that it was the truth. No one appeared friendly. Michael Crawford, who would gain fame years later – first as *Barnum* in the original British stage production, then in the title role in both Britain and the United States of Andrew Lloyd Webber's musical, *Phantom of the Opera* – who played Cornelius Hackl, the juvenile lead, hardly spoke to her off-camera. The same was true of the other young players, who were in some cases actually older than Streisand. Lehman walked around with a dour face. Kelly was cool in his attitude, although he appeared to try harder to appease her than the others and did listen to what she had to say, even if in the end he ignored her advice. This was not the experience she had on *Funny Girl* with Wyler. Suddenly she had been thrown into a hostile world where she felt like the outsider.

Never able to get Dolly Levi's character in one piece, she none the less brought a tremendous vitality to the role and fresh insight into Herman's score (which was not as tailored for her voice as the songs from *Funny Girl*). Her key changes in the 'Sunday Clothes' number are remarkable and she added a delightful comic note to 'So Long Dearie' – despite Kelly's arguments with her over a few lines in the bridge of the song where she imitates Mae West. 'It's anachronistic!' he insisted rightly. 'Mae West wasn't even born in 1890.'

'I can't help it,' she retorted, shifting into her Westian voice, 'I saw *My Little Chickadee* [one of West's most famous movies] last night and it stuck.'

Two multi-million dollar musicals had been constructed around her. Yet, since neither had been released, she did not know if they would succeed and if she would become a bonafide movie star. Her marriage was in eggshell-thin condition and her mother was pressing her from New York to do something to help Rosalind, recently graduated from high school. The young woman had changed her first name from Rosalind to *Roslyn* and decided she, *too*, wanted to become a singer. Diana would fault her again and Roslyn would hate her for telling the truth – that first she had to prove to herself that she had the talent before anyone, even a famous sister, could help her.

Despite her fame, Streisand was insecure, frightened and there was no way she could let anyone but her therapist know it. She took Jason and the nanny to the studio with her as often as she could once the *Hello, Dolly!* unit had returned from location. And when she wasn't needed on the set she would lock the door of her enormous dressing-room trailer and she would read to Jason and hold him in her arms. At such moments, her loneliness seemed less acute. Once she was back on the set she was as feisty as ever, the restless champ fighting all comers and bravely defending her title. 'I'm the star of this damned picture,' she shouted at Matthau during one of their skirmishes.

'Betty Hutton once said the same thing,' he shot back, 'and she's just filed for bankruptcy.'

# 18

KLEIG LIGHTS SCRAPED the sky, eerily turning night into day as an unwelcome October chill nipped the air. Streisand, arriving late as usual, stepped out of a limousine and on to a red carpet that extended from the kerb to the entrance of the Egyptian Theater, for the West Coast première of *Funny Girl*. She looked startled as she walked the narrow gauntlet between the cordons of curious, shrieking fans, many of whom had gathered early that morning with their camp stools and lunch bags to ensure themselves a position where they could see the stars up close. Elliott held her arm securely, the two of them flanked by some twenty bodyguards while press cameramen jumped into their path several times to get their picture. Streisand appeared unnerved and Elliott increasingly agitated as they fended off these interruptions with their accompanying flashes of blinding light.

Wearing eye-catching, shocking pink evening pants, a floor-length lamb's wool embroidered evening coat lined in pink, and a matching pillbox hat, all rather Russian-Cossack in appearance, Streisand covered her face protectively, a gesture immediately hostile to Ray Stark's planned media blitz. The photographers complained loudly as she and Elliott pressed forward, the security men having to quicken their step to keep up with them as they crossed the cement forecourt.

On entering the grand foyer, she was greeted by Fran and Ray Stark, who were hosting a benefit post-film supper party for over 1,000 guests under a giant tent in the parking lot adjacent to the theatre. Everyone connected with the film already knew that Barbra Streisand was to be a megastar, even Streisand herself, for the movie had been premièred in New York at the Criterion Theater on 19 September 1968, some two weeks earlier, and her personal reviews had been spectacular. Streisand first saw the final cut of *Funny Girl* in a private screening room, then at the New York première. Tonight would be her third viewing of the finished product. Always the perfectionist, she still wished she could reshoot some sequences. Despite her optimism for the film's and her own success, she could not calm her nerves. New York had somehow lost its excitement for her. Hollywood had replaced it and it was here that she felt she must be recognised.

She gave new meaning to the words – 'chronic worrier'. When asked by a business manager if she would like to hear the good or bad news first, she said, 'Tell me the bad news first. Then when I hear the good news I'll know what else I should worry about.' She had a team of well-paid business advisers. Marty Erlichman diligently worked on behalf of her career. All sights pointed to success, but everything still came back to her ability to become more than just a one-movie, one-role star. She was well aware of the vagaries of the picture business and the men who ran it, whose motto was 'You're as only as good as the box office returns from your last movie.' *Funny Girl* looked as if it would be a hit. She was not that sure about *Hello, Dolly!*

Ray Stark led as Streisand and Elliott made their way with him into the auditorium. Above their heads was the cathedral-like dome ceiling from which hung an enormous chandelier of Egyptian design, all wrought in shades of gold with golden iridescent rays emanating from an ingenious system of concealed lights, giving the effect of a colossal sunburst. She shielded her eyes as she glanced up at it and then laughing, whispered something to Elliott, who smiled broadly. Possibly she was making a comparison to the chandeliers in their New York apartment. They remained talking with the Starks until almost everyone else had taken their seats, and then were ushered down the aisle to a roped-in section towards the front of the theatre. Once she was seated, the lights dimmed and then went out. There was silence. The film began. Barbra Streisand was alone in the dark with a giant image of herself as once she had shared a similar darkness with her movie idols from the balcony of a Brooklyn theatre.

The experience of seeing oneself on a screen in a darkened movie palace with 1,500 pairs of eyes watching with you is surreal. Many film actors find the event so painful they refuse to subject themselves to it. Streisand's reaction was contrary. Guests seated in the row behind her say she leaned forward, watching intently, whispering comments to Elliott, on the aisle to her left and Stark, on her right. And she had not removed her hat. The person seated directly behind her, too embarrassed to ask her to do so, angled himself to one side.

When the lights came on again there was enthusiastic applause as there always was at the end of a Hollywood première – good or bad. People rushed down the aisle shouting their congratulations. A small smile tugged at the corners of her mouth. Otherwise her face was almost sphinx-like, her pleasure entombed behind steely glances as she slowly made her way towards an exit and, bodyguards and Elliott once again forming a phalanx, went out of a side door across to the tented parking lot. Inside the circus-sized tent, the lower East Side New York in the early 1920s, where Fanny Brice had lived, had been recreated. The bar from the Brice family saloon, used in the movie, had been set up on one side. Each corner of the enormous tent had a New York street sign – Henry Street, Washington Square, Second Avenue, Delancey Street – serving as guideposts so people could locate their tables. These were centred with potted ferns, each supporting a dozen bagels on a stick, a jarring sight, misguidedly meant to create a New York deli atmosphere.

As Streisand entered the band played a chorus of 'Funny Girl', the obligatory new song (with the same title, but not the same melody as one cut from the stage production) that was added to the score of the film. Omar Sharif had flown back from location for the première and posed with Streisand for the press, Elliott glowering in the background. Sharif, holding hands with his newest lady friend, actress Anjanette Comer, had also attended with the Goulds the New York première at the Criterion Theater two weeks earlier and the post-movie fund-raiser held in a similar tent constructed on the parking-lot site where the old Astor Hotel had recently stood. That sumptuous affair had been utter chaos as about 1,300 people, including scores of famous people from both social and entertainment circles, had been invited, over 100 more than could be seated. Irate guests, having paid $100 for the privilege of being there, shouted insults at the staff, demanded other people who were not on the grand list be removed and their seats given to them. Men came close to throwing punches. The Starks gave up their seats and wandered from table to crowded table. Some people shared chairs, others remained standing. Streisand, elegantly garbed in a flesh-coloured gown set with sprays of rhinestones, her hair hidden beneath a striking wig that added several inches to her height and escorted by a wary Elliott, was seated with him at the table marked 1 along with Marty Erlichman and Diana, but she appeared ill at ease.

There was no such mayhem at the Hollywood post-movie festivities. As the New York critics had already endorsed her performance as a knockout, there was little suspense. For Streisand, the one thing she enjoyed more than being at a party with the movie legends she had so long ago adored, was being the toast of it.

'I always wanted to meet Marlon Brando,' she recalled. 'I wanted to say to him, "Let us speak to one another, because I understand you. You are just like me. So ... somebody comes up behind me and starts caressing my shoulder and nuzzling my neck. And I turn around and there he is! It's Brando! And he says – you know kidding – "I'm letting you off easy," and I laughed and said, "Whaddaya mean easy? This is the best part!" I don't know – what the hell was there to say? It was kind of sad, because he *wasn't* just like me at all. He was a real movie star, a legend and somehow I didn't want him to be real.'

When the evening was over, there was no doubt that her performance had scored bi-coastally, but she still did not feel like she belonged in that Valhalla of movie idols.

'Bravo!' Pauline Kael, *The New Yorker* critic wrote. 'Streisand has the gift of making old written dialogue sound like inspired improvisation; almost every line she says seems to have just sprung to mind and out. Her inflections are witty and surprising, and, more surprisingly, delicate; she can probably do more for a line than any screen comedienne since Jean Arthur, in the thirties ... It is Streisand's peculiar triumph that in the second half, when the routine heartbreak comes, as it apparently must in all musical biographies, she shows an aptitude for suffering that those clever actresses didn't. Where they became sanctimonious and noble, thereby violating everything we had loved them for, she simply drips as unself-consciously and impersonally as a true tragic muse.'

Streisand had evolved into a thoroughly original self-invention, resembling no one else. She was a heroine with 'a particular desperation all her own'. Much as she decried her Brooklyn roots, she had made them her special territory. To the public she had become 'a regular person with a genuine past from a real place. She had this Jewish problem, and this homely problem ... she was pure oddball', Joe Morgenstern reported in *Newsweek*.

The energy she displayed in her performance was limitless. Yes, some co-workers, like the disgruntled Anne Francis, faulted her for being ruthless, but she had also been courageous and taken artistic gambles without hedging her bets. Although the score of *Funny Girl* had been pre-recorded,[1] she decided to take the risk of having 'My Man' recorded live which gave the number tremendous presence. After dreadful arguments with Irene Sharaff over a striking wine velvet dress she had designed for the scene, Streisand wore a black gown and stood against a black background so that only her face and two hands were visible as she sang in a soft, poignant voice. At the end of the first chorus she stepped into an arc of light as her voice gained strength and soared defiantly. She had lost Nicky Arnstein but she had sung herself back into being. To hear her sing this song is to believe that she is the character she is playing and it is that amazing ability that makes *Funny Girl*, with its feeble story, implausibly credible.

'The audience', she ventured, 'cannot be lied to. I mean ... the slightest tinge of falseness, they go back from you, they retreat. The truth brings them

---

[1] The original soundtrack recording of *Funny Girl* was released a month in advance of the film but was pre-empted by Diana Ross's *Funny Girl* album, *Diana Ross and the Supremes Sing and Perform* Funny Girl. To Streisand and Stark's amazement, Jule Styne had assisted Ross with the recording and had written the liner notes and Peter Matz had helped with the arrangements. 'I just don't like the idea of her singing my songs and with my musical arranger,' Streisand is reported as saying. 'Who the hell does she think she is? The world doesn't need another Streisand!' Ross had a keen sense of competition with Streisand, believing that if she had been white, like Streisand, 'it would have been a hundred times easier for her'. Ross's album was one of her few commercial failures. Streisand's original soundtrack recording, on the other hand, did extremely well, although not as well as the original Broadway cast recording.

closer. They don't know why, they can't intellectualise it, but they know the moment is right or wrong ... I guess my best attribute is my instinct. Elliott's grandmother, who is about eighty-five, said she liked me because I was so natural – so *natchel*.' She thought about it for a moment. 'Acting is like music,' she continued. 'I believe in rhythm, you know? Everything is so dominated by our heartbeats, by our pulses, when one goes against certain rhythms it's jarring ... I mean I *hear* it! I read a script and just *hear* and I *see* what the people are doing, and I'll have an idea right off the bat, and it's always my first instinct that I trust.'

Perhaps that was true, but *Funny Girl* had occupied four years of her life. She had been able to fashion the character into a clone of herself, very much the same young woman millions of viewers had come to know through her television specials and guest appearances. And she had already familiarised her audience with the album of the show and numerous other recordings where she had included 'My Man' along with some of *Funny Girl's* score. Few in the audience came into the movie theatre cold, having to be won over by an actress playing an unknown role. She had the advantage that seasoned and well-loved film stars held over audiences – that of simply being who they were, the character and the performer fusing into one person in their mind. Cary Grant was one such example, but it had taken him years to ingrain his personality so deeply upon movie audiences. The same could be said about Cagney, Bogart, Lemmon and Matthau among a score of others. Streisand's experience was unique in that *Funny Girl* was her first picture.

The studio's estimates were that *Funny Girl* would gross $65 million in the United States alone.[2] If it did it would make Ray Stark a huge fortune as he received 10 per cent of the gross plus 50 per cent of the net, an almost unprecedented profit margin. 'Barbra also stands to make a million dollars from her salary and subsidiary rights [the record and future television and video rights] and she's worth one-half of every cent of it!' he quipped to *Variety*, adding: 'I'm only kidding.' Streisand did not find Stark's comment amusing. She believed, rightly, that she was as responsible for the success of the film version of *Funny Girl* as she was for the stage production. And although $1 million was not to be minimised, it no where compared with the $20 million or more that Ray Stark eventually stood to make.

Yet had it not been for Stark and *Funny Girl*, Streisand's climb to fame might well have taken considerably longer. When Stark first signed her for the stage

---

[2] In its first domestic release *Funny Girl* grossed $25 million. It eventually did reach the revenues projected by Columbia Studio and Ray Stark in foreign and further releases, television and video sales. At the figures quoted in the text, Stark received $2.5 million from the gross at the end of the first year of its release. Barbra Streisand received her $200,000 contracted fee, her royalties from the original soundtrack recording and the later income generated by her royalties on the film's television and video release.

version, he gambled on a young woman who had not yet proved that she could carry a show. A prototype of the new style of movie producer: a man who puts together star, story and director as a package to make a picture, a friend remembers him as 'a little guy who would run up and down Sunset Boulevard, waving a contract and shouting: "I got a deal! I got a deal!"' Before he returned to California for the West Coast première of *Funny Girl*, he told Vincent Canby of the *New York Times*: 'I'm making this deal [for another movie] and we have this far-out script ... I mean, I read it and frankly I didn't understand it, but it could be fantastic!' He did not reveal the name of the property, but his next picture would be *The Owl and the Pussycat*.

Streisand could be angry at Stark on one level, but the sheer *chutzpah* of the man appealed to her. He was, she claimed, 'the great Oz of Hollywood', and she forgave him many things because this quality of his so fascinated her. Having settled his lawsuit against her enabling her to make movies independently of his company, they had reached a detente, and she would soon start production without him on her third film (this time for Paramount Pictures), *On a Clear Day You Can See Forever*.

A good portion of the picture was to be shot in England. This meant being separated for eight weeks from Jason, but she could not see taking him with her as they would have so little time together. She had recently bought and moved into a house on Carolwood Drive in Holmby Hills near the Gregory Pecks. Jason had settled in and was attached to his nanny. It seemed wrong to uproot him. She called Elliott and he promised to fly out to California and spend as much time as possible with his son.

The bi-coastal lifestyle they had carved out for themselves had failed. Neither of them seemed able to handle the tremendous pressures on their marriage. They were living separate lives, gathering private memories. Elliott was treading water as he waited for *Bob & Carol & Ted & Alice* to be released. He was finely tuned, frazzled, expectant, fearful, doubtful, on edge, living in an extravagant style paid for by his wife and gambling again with heavy losses (over $50,000 that year, he was later to admit). He saw other women and felt instantly guilty. Streisand managed to blind herself to her marital problems, to lose herself in her work, in the swift ascent of her career, her business enterprises, and in Jason. Yet, she remained strongly bound to Elliott. In some way he represented her past and she was not ready or able to let him go.

Paramount had paid $750,000 for the rights of *On A Clear Day You Can See Forever*, and were now contracted to pay Streisand $1 million, astronomical figures for Hollywood in the 1960s. Despite her current popularity, the studio was fearful that they had acted hastily. With period costumes and foreign locations involved, the budget had soared to an unrealistic $20 million and the story, about a naïve Brooklyn girl, Daisy Gamble, who under hypnosis relives an earlier existence as an English seductress, Melinda Tentrees, was anything but mainstream. The Broadway show had been placed in the eighteenth century. The film was pushed forward to the early nineteenth century in Regency England to avoid the use of powdered wigs and more cumbersome costumes. Alan Jay Lerner, the author and lyricist of the show, was currently taken with the idea of reincarnation. Lerner, who had recently ended his long association with composer Frederick Loewe,[3] worked this time with Burton Lane, composer of the very successful *Finian's Rainbow*.

'When Alan came to me with *On a Clear Day* I thought the premise simply wonderful,' Lane said. 'The story in the past was too heavy-handed and not joyful, but it did have such wit and imagination that I finally got excited about it. How that score ever turned out as good as it did is a mystery to me. [It was] the worst two years of my life. Alan was on drugs and I don't know how to deal with people who are on liquor or anything else.'

The show lasted only 280 performances on Broadway, starring Barbara Harris in the dual role of Daisy and Melinda, but Streisand greatly admired the score and viewed the double role as a rare opportunity to display her acting ability. In October 1968, just days after the East and West Coast premières of *Funny Girl*, Streisand began rehearsals, working closely with Lerner on her role.

Lerner was a tortured man, Stef Sheahan, his secretary, told his biographer, Stephen Citron. 'If he was really working hard on a lyric, he could lose about six pounds in a day. You could feel him burning it off in the room. He'd just be there with his white gloves on, which he always wore to keep himself from biting his nails.' Highly strung, heavily addicted to drugs that kept him in a state of agitation, his marriage to his fifth wife shaky, he was in a perpetual state of nerves. None the less, Streisand was able to get the most from their collaboration. Her voice stirred Lerner, her phrasing of his lyrics gave him new ideas. He held her in a kind of awe, believed she was the greatest entertainer of the twentieth century. He tailored the filmscript to her special talents, her dialogue as Daisy containing more of the sound of her own manner of speaking although he was careful to omit any Jewish overtones. He left Melinda as originally created, trusting his instinct that Streisand could, if well directed, project – as Garson Kanin had also believed – the necessary elegance the role demanded.

Vincente Minnelli, former husband of Judy Garland, father of Liza, who had directed the film versions of Lerner and Loewe's *Brigadoon* and *Gigi*, was to direct. Arnold Scaasi was hired to do the modern costumes; Cecil Beaton, the period costumes. Scaasi flew out to Los Angeles from New York to consult with Streisand. 'We spent a whole day going over the styles she was to wear as Daisy,' Scaasi remembered. 'By eight o'clock I was ready to quit. I had been

---

[3] Lerner and Loewe had written the scores for *Brigadoon*, *Paint Your Wagon*, *My Fair Lady*, *Gigi* and *Camelot*.

invited to the Minnellis' for dinner, so I stood up and said, "Barbra, I must leave, I have a previous engagement." She lifted her eyes from the sketches and very quietly said, "Arnold, why did you come out to Los Angeles?" I immediately realised what she meant and agreed that she was right. I was there on business, not on a social call. I phoned Vincente Minnelli and excused myself from dinner.' And he added thoughtfully, 'She has this uncanny eye for detail. Once when I sent her an embossed invitation to the opening of my collection, she wrote me a note explaining that she would be out of town on that date and she added a postscript to call my attention to a misprint in the invitation.'

Ten days before production was to start, Streisand stopped off in New York on her way across the Atlantic for the London and Paris premières of *Funny Girl*. To her shock, she learned that Elliott was living with Jenny Bogart, the waif-like eighteen-year-old daughter of director Paul Bogart. Despite her own transgressions with Chaplin and Sharif, knowledge of his affair deeply cut Streisand. She asked Elliott to break off the relationship, to come with her to Europe. Elliott could not see his way to do that. Jenny needed him, he told her, she was so young, so helpless; he thought he had something to give her, a feeling that someone cared. Angry, sad, in pain, Streisand insisted they draw up a separation agreement and threatened to file for divorce. She left New York for *Funny Girl*'s London première deeply distressed. Omar Sharif stood by his leading lady's side, the ashes long cooled on their relationship, and Marty Erlichman was her escort at a gala post-première dinner party, also attended by Princess Margaret.

As she prepared to fly to Paris before returning to California to start shooting the studio scenes for *On A Clear Day*, she learned she was one of the five nominees for Best Actress at the upcoming Academy Awards. She had also signed a $5 million contract with the new Las Vegas International Hotel, the highest sum ever paid for a night-club engagement, and she had just met a fascinating man to whom she was instantly drawn and who appeared to be similarly attracted to her. Pierre Elliott Trudeau, Prime Minister of Canada, a brilliant, utterly charming, 48-year-old bachelor who had won his election the previous year largely on the youth vote. They met at a small dinner party at the home of a mutual acquaintance the night before her departure. 'Sparks flew,' a guest recalled.

Sexually drawn to this intense, wiry man with summer-sky blue eyes, Streisand found out all she could about him. In Canada Trudeau-mania was at its height. After only one year as Prime Minister, the polls showed that he had the highest percentage rate of endorsement of any Prime Minister in Canada's history. By nature Trudeau was a questioner and a listener, but she got him to talk about himself. His mother was Scots by origin, his father French Canadian. He was bilingual, educated at Montreal University, the London School of

Economics and Harvard. Contrary to this conservative beginning, in his youth he had crossed five continents and twenty countries with a knapsack on his back. His smile was boyish, his charm difficult to resist and Streisand saw no reason to do so. Since the impressionable time she had met John Kennedy, power and politics had intrigued her. She promised that somehow she would manage to see him again – very soon.

Her life was programmed from the moment of her return to Hollywood, as she plunged into work on *A Clear Day* in which she co-starred with Yves Montand, cast as the professor/hypnotist who, while attempting to cure Daisy's smoking habit, sends her back – in her mind – to her previous life as the temptress, Melinda Tentrees. He then falls in love with Melinda during Daisy's hypnotic sessions. Also appearing were Larry Blyden as Daisy's stuffy fiancé and Jack Nicholson in a small but amusing role as her half-brother. She got along well with Nicholson, but her working relationship with Montand was strained, although certainly not as difficult as it had been when she played opposite Walter Matthau. This time she had a leading man who was well known as a singer (in his native country, France, at least), the first time this had occurred. A ruggedly attractive man in his late forties, Montand was urbane and a lively individualist. Married to the French actress Simone Signoret, he had weathered stormy affairs with Edith Piaf (who had guided him to stardom as one of France's leading chansoniers), and with Marilyn Monroe, his co-star in *Let's Make Love* (1960). Primarily known as a singing star, his role in Clouzot's classic thriller, *The Wages of Fear* (1953) had catapulted him to international fame as a dramatic actor. As a result he sustained two careers – dramatic roles in Europe and more romantic parts in Hollywood, where he could exude his Gallic charm. Seductive though he was, Streisand was not attracted to him.

Wary of Europeans after her affair with Omar Sharif, she concentrated on the film. Vincente Minnelli, the director of *On a Clear Day*, allowed her great independence and as with *Funny Girl* and *Hello, Dolly!* she involved herself in everything to do with her character from costumes, lighting, hair, make-up, to interpretation. Caught up in the art of film-making, she was preparing herself for the future although she was not yet fully aware of it. After *Dolly* and her problems with Matthau, she worked hard to protect her performance, making sure that she was the prime character in the film, that she had the majority of the songs and the full attention of the camera.

'When we commenced *On a Clear Day*,' Montand said later, 'I had the mistaken impression that I was the co-star. I was Miss Streisand's first leading man who can sing, even though this was her third musical. I thought she was my leading lady, a partner. I doubt I shall ever choose to work again in Hollywood [which he never did].'

She flew to New York for location work as the Daisy character and then, a week later, to England for Melinda's Dickensian poor-house sequence and the elaborate scenes in the Royal Pavilion in Brighton, the latter to be shot first. Cecil Beaton's costumes for her were spectacular. Beaton was an accomplished author, photographer and theatrical set and costume designer, known equally well for his portraiture of Britain's royal family, his persistent pursuit of Greta Garbo and his wit. He had won two Academy Awards for his sets and costume designs for *My Fair Lady*, for which he had also created the original stage decor. Beaton claimed that the memorable white satin Regency gown which revealed a voluptuous bosom with imposing cleavage that Streisand wore in the banquet scene of *On a Clear Day* was a shared creation. 'It was inspired – and both our ideas, really – to wrap the Streisand features in a glorious white turban, to further accent her strong profile. At the same time, she was totally feminine, beguiling, shamelessly sexual. I tried to stress ... the physical if not spiritual splendour of the period. On a less gifted actress and model, on almost any American actress I can think of, this would have been wasted and somewhat ludicrous. Barbra has a less monotonously American-type [look] than most actresses of her nationality.'

The banquet scene at the Royal Pavilion was the most ornate in the film. Minnelli, who had started his career as a set designer, insisted that every detail be true to the lavish display of the period. Over 100 extras magnificently costumed in regal Regency clothes sat at an enormous banquet table before mounds of food – all real and prepared by leading English chefs. Streisand sat across the table from languid-eyed John Richardson, playing Robert Tentrees, Melinda's future husband. Close shots would be filmed later of their sexual wooing as they ate and drank in a powerfully seductive manner. For now, they were simply guests at the royal banquet. 'Eat up!' Minnelli shouted, as the cameras began turning, 'Devour everything in sight! Shove it all in! You're all gourmets.' Streisand did as requested, along with the extras.

That night she had a date with George Lazenby, an Australian actor who had just made his film debut as James Bond in *On Her Majesty's Secret Service*. They had dinner at a kosher restaurant. Unable to resist some of her Jewish favourites – knishes, dill pickles, latkes – Streisand gorged herself and fell ill by the end of the evening. Early the following morning (Easter Sunday and double-time for the crew, but Minnelli wanted to limit his days of foreign production), she had to report to the studio to shoot the scene as Melinda in the royal kitchens. The set was decorated with great sides of beef, game and geese, baskets of fish, trays of game and sweet pies, rounds of pungent Stilton cheese and a suckling pig on the fire. 'The most uncongenial atmosphere for someone with a weak stomach,' Cecil Beaton commented. 'The smell of food was so high that it had to be sweetened by atomiser sprays.' Streisand persisted though obviously ill. Beaton marvelled at her stamina after what must have been 'a night of much vomiting'.

'Barbra is one of two kinds of superstars: the coolly detached and the fanatically involved,' he professed. 'Barbra is the latter. Barbra and I talked our way into everything, and I trusted her judgment, something I seldom do with any actor, especially a relative neophyte. I had never met anyone so young who had such an awareness and knowledge of herself. Both Audrey Hepburn's wardrobe for *My Fair Lady* and Barbra's for *A Clear Day* contained before-and-after outfits. Both women are very different, yet they're both regal, and that came through in the clothes I designed for them. Melinda [in early scenes] came from lower-class origins and was dressed in a rather grubby, unflattering manner, much as Eliza Doolittle during her Covent Garden days. Both women were marvellous at conveying this earthiness, and seemed to relish the chance to wear rags and carry on like craven guttersnipes. But as grand ladies, dressed to the hilt, they were truly in their element, aware that everything had been building up to that moment – neither had a lack of confidence in their ability to act regal and look monumental, despite their widely varying types and images.'

Beaton claimed, as did Minnelli, that there were no great contests of will between them during production, although he was somewhat perturbed that Streisand would only approve his still photographs 'when lines, marks and a spot on the chin had been brushed out'. When she returned to the States, he wrote in his diary: 'I like B.S. very much: she is a good, fine girl. If we do not speak the same language, at least we are in sympathy with one another. She is very clever – and meticulous.'

Her romance with Lazenby was short lived. She left London without ties, but not without romantic thoughts. The good-looking Prime Minister of Canada had unsettled her. Not only had she found him sexually exciting and intellectually challenging, she was confident that he felt the same way about her.

# 19

THREE DATES WITH Warren Beatty – a 'fling' she called it – proved disappointing. She demanded more than good sex from a man. She expected commitment. She romanticised Trudeau – the intellectual father figure – respected the power he wielded, the world stage he occupied. Their affair was moving slowly. They spoke on the telephone. She read up on Canadian history and current political leaders. They met briefly in New York, he was there on official business and she once more was looking for a new Manhattan residence.

The world did not know yet that she and Elliott were going their separate ways and for the moment they both preferred to keep the press guessing. He came out to California to discuss the divorce and, to keep up appearances, escorted her to the 41st Academy Award Oscar presentations on 14 April 1969, held in the Dorothy Chandler Pavilion in the new Los Angeles Music Center. The long drive down to the auditorium in a chauffeured limousine was rife with tension. A concerted effort was made by both of them to avoid personal issues. Seeing him again, watching his tenderness with Jason, had touched her. Elliott was a good father and Jason adored him and she could not dismiss her own confused feelings about him that made her question her decision to obtain a divorce.

She had been nominated for the Best Actress Award with four other exceptional performers: Katharine Hepburn, for *The Lion in Winter*; Patricia Neal for *The Subject Was Roses*; Vanessa Redgrave for *Isadora* and Joanne Woodward for *Rachel, Rachel*. Her competition was formidable, all four women were known for their roles in dramatic films. *Funny Girl* was a musical and she had played Fanny Brice in such a spontaneously natural manner that the critics had not viewed her performance as 'acting'. For many, it was hard to distinguish between the actress who played the role and the woman in real life.

The Academy Awards Ceremony was to start at exactly 6 p.m. and all the participants had been notified that the doors to the Pavilion would be locked at that hour as the show was being televised. At 5.45, Streisand and Elliott were tied up in grid-locked traffic. She became agitated, her voice, as she railed against the traffic jam, high-pitched, strained. Elliott attempted to calm her.

The driver assured them both that they would make it in time. Other guests were jumping out of nearby limousines, stalled in the pile-up of cars, and were making swift tracks towards the front doors of the Pavilion.

Streisand refused to make a running entrance, and eventually, with about two minutes to spare, walked gracefully towards the auditorium, Elliott close by her side, and smiled at several of the press photographers.

Beneath a tent-shaped, black taffeta evening coat, she wore a see-through, black chiffon pyjama outfit with starched white puritan cuffs and collar and traces of black jet. Designed by Scaasi for Daisy in *On a Clear Day*, the outfit had been rejected as too revealing for the character to wear. There were shocked faces turned to her as she entered the packed wood-panelled auditorium with its gleaming crystal chandeliers. One row of the audience applauded as she walked down the aisle past them. For all the costume's seductive design and shocking sheerness, it did not lack style and she looked especially lovely, her skin glowing, her hair coiffed beautifully in a loose, casual manner, blonde streaks highlighting it, eyes bright, smile radiant, bravely masking her inner anxiety.

The Oscars are an especially long ceremony and the awards for Best Actress, Actor and Film are at the end of an often tedious evening. Streisand sat stiffly as all the nominated members of the *Funny Girl* company were passed over; *Oliver!* winning the larger share of the evening's Oscars for best picture, musical score, best art direction and best direction. Ruth Gordon won Best Supporting Actress for *Rosemary's Baby* over Kay Medford's performance as Mama Brice.

Ingrid Bergman, looking luminously beautiful, opened the envelope containing the winner for Best Actress of 1968. For a moment a look of astonishment came over her lovely face. In a stunned voice, she cried out, 'It's a tie!' and then read off the names, 'Katharine Hepburn for *Lion in Winter*,' and then had to wait until the applause abated before she added in a strong and pleased voice, 'and Barbra Streisand for *Funny Girl*!'

Streisand rose briskly from her seat, ran up the aisle and the steps to the wide stage, gargantuan golden Oscars standing sentinel at the rear of it, and stood beaming beside Bergman. Hepburn was in New York and her director, Anthony Harvey, accepted the award in her name and then stepped away from the podium. 'Congratulations!' Bergman said to Streisand, who grasped the gold Oscar in her hands and in strident Brooklynese exclaimed, 'Hullo, gorgeous!' There was a wave of laughter, wild applause. When the audience quieted, she graciously declared, 'I am honoured to be in such magnificent company as Katharine Hepburn.'[1]

---

[1] Hepburn and Streisand were the first co-winners of an Academy Award since 1932 when Fredric March (*Dr Jekyll and Mr Hyde*) shared the honour with Wallace Beery (*The Champ*.)

The next day Streisand called Diana. 'Well, Ma, what do you think about the award?' she asked.

'What kind of a dress was that to wear in public?' was her mother's reply.

Despite Streisand's intense therapy, she remained unable to deal rationally with her mother's negativism. The rejected child she harboured inside her refused to let go. As with so many areas in her life – her career, her male-female relationships, Streisand wanted things on her terms and these were often founded on unrealistic demands. In her late fifties by now, Diana was not going to change. Plumpish, resigned to life without a partner, she remained much the same as she had always been, harbouring old-world Jewish fears and superstitions that to speak well of things, to be too optimistic was to court disaster. She was no less pessimistic with Shelley, but he was better able to cope with his mother. Content in his career, very much the family man, he did not have the need to seek Diana's approval. Nor did his sister's success and fame threaten or overwhelm him. He and Barbra remained close in spirit. Streisand knew Shelley would be there for her if she needed him, and the reverse was true. But their lifestyles, their friends and interests were far apart. She would see him and his family when she was in New York, a family visit, welcomed but disconnected from her everyday life. With Diana, it was quite a different matter. Open wounds still festered.

At present, Diana was caught up in Roslyn's career, which was not moving along at any great speed. She was defensive when the press claimed the half-sisters did not get along. 'Barbra loves Rozie very much,' she told a reporter. 'But Roz was a little shy and didn't know how to approach a big sister who had gotten so famous. When Barbra was in *Funny Girl* on Broadway, Roz went to forty matinées and stood through them all. At home she would play the *Funny Girl* album day and night, lip-syncing and imitating Barbra. She was really her best imitator.' Which was Roslyn's immense failing, for she was not as gifted.

Asked for her advice on child-rearing, Diana replied candidly, 'Never give your kids too much praise. In fact, I try to tone them down if I see they have an exaggerated opinion of themselves. I just kind of make a remark that calms them down.'

Roslyn entered the room at this point. 'She says something like, "Don't forget you got it from me; you didn't fall out of a tree."'

'Yeah. My voice comes from my mother,' Streisand says. 'How else can I explain it?' Yet even this acknowledgment of Diana's talent was spoken with an air of disaffection.

Neither woman understood the other. Diana's life had been one of compromise which she both accepted and resented. Pragmatic, lacking drive, the desperation to learn, absorb, improve, Diana's character was completely at odds with that of her famous daughter and of the image Streisand nurtured of her father, the intellectual scholar, the man who refused to compromise his ambitions, who was so supportive of the young people he taught.

Her father, she was told, had spoken several languages – English, German, Yiddish. She was now studying French and Italian and had started private instruction in music theory. 'That was fascinating: to create sound and tone from a mathematical concept, to be able to say that something I hear in my head is an F-sharp minor chord with a flatted fifth,' she mused. 'I studied piano till my teacher said I had to cut my nails. I said, "I'm not going to be a concert pianist – so what if I do make some clicking noises on the keys?" ' Yet, she realised that a flat-fingered position was no way to play the piano and the lessons soon ended.

Valiantly she tried to keep up with the stacks of political journals to which she subscribed. 'There is so much more to learn, so much more to do,' she said excitedly. 'I love the movies – life is so tentative and short that I want something to remain as proof that I existed. I think that's why I like antiques – because they have proven their immortality. They know something I don't.' Antiques were survivors like herself.

The insistent buzzing in her ears that made her so sensitive to sound remained a constant source of distraction. Maybe sometimes, she said, it made her walk around 'like a *farbissiner* – which means kind of depressed [more literally – soured]. I get these letters from kids telling me that I am "different" just like them. I write back. "Do you have a buzzing in *your* ears?" '

Her success did not ease her acute insecurity. She suffered immense fear that she could – if not protective – lose her status. She wanted, and sought, greater control in the movies she would make in the future. There was a strong indication that the musical as a popular art form was in crisis. The common Hollywood practice of adapting a hit musical for the screen might soon be obsolete and her hold could loosen with it if she did not make the transition, which she had always yearned for anyway, into a straight dramatic actress. This was easier said than done since studio executives were doubtful that the movie-going public would accept her in a new image. To her, this left only one alternative. She must form her own film production company, a costly and perilous adventure for the possibility had to be considered that she might fall flat on her face.

At that time the greater part of her income came from records and concerts not from movies. Her last five albums, the soundtrack of *Funny Girl*, *A Happening in Central Park*, *Simply Streisand*, *A Christmas Album* and *Je M'Appelle Barbra*, may not have reached the top of the charts, but her immense earnings on all her records, which included her previous album hits, were estimated as being over $3 million annually. Her albums, released twice a year, kept her constantly before the public, the records played consistently over radio. She more than realised how important it was for her to keep in step with the changes in the music world. The music she sang in movies, the Broadway sound, was fast losing its hold on young people and she did not want to become set in the concrete past.

Just after the Academy Awards, she recorded a new album, her sixteenth, *What About Today?*, her first pop album. The songs on it – from Jim Webb's anti-war elegy 'Little Tin Soldier' to other compositions by Paul Simon, Paul McCartney/John Lennon, and Buffy Saint-Marie – were mostly protest songs. She had accomplished an amazing feat and made the cross-over on record to a contemporary sound without losing the dramatic, distinctive quality for which she was famous. It would be this remarkable ability she had to move vocally with the times while still maintaining her skill with a show tune or classic, that would sustain her recording career and win her throngs of new, young fans with each release.

Flower children and student violence were the mark of the two last years of the 1960s. In the summer of 1968, American students had fought a pitched battle with 11,900 of the Chicago police force, 7,500 of the National Guard, and 1,000 FBI and Secret Service Men. There had been over 200 university demonstrations since then. American participation in the Vietnam War was dividing a nation. Draft-card burning, flag-burning, bra-burning and the woman's movement all gripped the nation. Student radicals had been a powerful force in Eugene McCarthy's bid for the presidency, which Streisand supported. They won the media contest but they could not get McCarthy the nomination, nor could they prevent the man Streisand hated most, Richard Nixon, from becoming President.

She was in a time warp, trying desperately to break loose. She celebrated her twenty-seventh birthday on 24 April 1969. For nearly a decade she had lived and worked in a world comprised of much older people. She had few young friends and now thought she was in love with a man, Pierre Trudeau, over twenty years her senior, an affair that must, because of the seriousness of his purpose and her marital status, be kept hidden from the public. It meant catching a day or a weekend together in a secret liaison. Trudeau was fascinated by her. Her fame was a potent attraction, but she also brought something fresh into his life. He confided to friends that he thought she was one of the most beautiful women he had ever known, that she possessed innate majesty. He was amazed at the sharpness of her mind. They were a curious match – a Jewess and a devout Catholic, a movie star and the Canadian Prime Minister. Yet a strong sexual attraction was fuelled by these very differences. Always paradoxical, she fantasised about marrying the older and more conservative Trudeau at the same time as she explored youth-oriented music, smoked marijuana and contracted to appear at the new International Hotel in Las Vegas, an establishment whose primary objective was to attract customers to the hotel's gambling tables. Returning to Las Vegas, where she had been so unhappy, had more to do with money than morals. Despite the high sums she earned, she always feared that one day she might not have enough.

The International Hotel was two and a half times the size of the splashy reigning favourite, Caesar's Palace. Every feature of the hotel was elephantine; its height of thirty storeys ('the tallest building in the state of Nevada'); its pool ('second only to Lake Mead'); its casino (the largest in the world with over a thousand slot machines); and its three enormous entertainment facilities – a lounge, a legitimate theatre and the Showroom – each starring a well-known personality in productions to rival, in glitz at least, whatever Paris or New York could offer. Streisand's engagement began on 2 July, and in the summer the desert heat could reach over 120 degrees. But there was no need for a hotel guest ever to leave the air-conditioned gilded palace, where there were no clocks in the gambling rooms to remind players of the lateness of the hour.

However, the International was still under final construction when Streisand arrived and it appeared, from its unfinished state, that it would not be complete in time to open the Showroom. While she was rehearsing, curtains were being draped, light fixtures installed, and plaster fell like snow over a stage large enough to accommodate both the Ziegfeld and Goldwyn Girls as well as the Rockerfeller Rockettes. In addition to her fee, her contract included 20,000 shares of stock in the hotel, each worth $50 by opening night. Expectations of her twice-nightly, four-week stint were high. She had just won the Academy Award and *Funny Girl* was now breaking movie-house records across the country.

For her much-heralded Vegas opening she wore a gauzy, gold creation of Scaasi's, her hair coiffed into a chic upswept, and sang into a hand-held jewelled microphone. Backed by a sixteen-piece band conducted by Peter Matz, sometimes she stood centre stage, sometimes near the piano, or perched on a high, shocking-pink stool. Unlike other Vegas cabaret shows, there was no opening act, no beautiful, pony-legged showgirls in scanty, colourful costumes, no back-up singers, no lavish sets – none of the things Las Vegas audiences expected. At the top of her form, her programme was almost identical to her Central Park appearance the previous year, with two new numbers: 'In the Wee Small Hours of the Morning' and 'When You Gotta Go' in a 'stunning exhibition of stylistic and vocal virtuosity'. Yet, as word of the lack of production values in her act spread, reservations dwindled. Her instincts – that audiences would want to see and hear her not showgirls in a flashy show – had betrayed her.

She became restive. Fear plagued her. She would forget her lyrics. When columnist Joyce Haber visited her dressing room during her engagement, she showed her a calendar with each day she had already appeared crossed out. 'Only thirty-nine performances to go,' she sighed. She hated the repetitive nature of the show, any show – having to do the same thing twice a night.

Accustomed now to the business of making films, a staff to cater to her every need, the absence of a live audience who could boo as well as cheer her, and the ability to perfect her performance in a cutting room, she felt trapped. On screen she could sell her image; on stage she had to sell herself.

Elvis Presley was to follow her into the Showroom. He slipped into the back of the balcony to watch her work during the first week of her engagement. 'He pointed mutely to all the empty seats around him,' one of his biographers, Albert Goldman, wrote. 'Then, he settled down to listen to the program. He gave no signs of pleasure. When it was all over, he turned to [an assistant] and said two words: "She sucks!" Then, he went downstairs to her dressing room to tell Barbra how much he had enjoyed her performance. When he was admitted ... he was astonished to find the great star alone. Elvis had never been alone for one moment in his entire life. Two or three men always accompanied him even to the bathroom. Streisand made no bones about her disgust with the audience and the hotel. "This place isn't even built yet!" she fumed. "I wouldn't be surprised if some night while I'm out there working some schmuck doesn't walk by with a ladder on his shoulder!"'

She vowed to him that she would never work Vegas again. (Later she admitted, 'I really didn't enjoy performing live any more.') The two shook hands, she wished him more luck than she'd had, and they parted.[2]

In order to ease her nerves at other times in Las Vegas, she took several drags of marijuana just before she stepped out on stage and stowed several joints in the pocket of the black jewelled jacket of one of her gowns. At one point she took out a joint to light it. 'First, just faking it,' she later told *Rolling Stone* magazine. 'Then I started lighting live joints, passing them around to the band – you know. It was *great*. It relieved all my tensions. I ended up with the greatest supply of grass ever. Other acts started sending me the best dope in the world. I never ran out.' However true or exaggerated that claim was, drugs were not a part of her life. She smoked a joint to relax, a habit she had shared with Elliott.

Many of the Vegas performers who were paid huge salaries lost most at the gaming tables. Gambling never intrigued her, it brought Elliott to her mind and she desperately wanted not to think about him. Elliott had suddenly become a huge star in his own right. The bang-up acting job he had done as the square, bumbling lawyer who succumbs to an affair in *Bob & Carol & Ted & Alice*, a satire of southern California sex, sensitivity and spouse-swapping, was

---

[2] Elsewhere it has been written that Elvis made a sexual overture to Streisand at the time and, picking up a bottle of nail varnish from her dressing-room table, knelt before her to paint her famous finger talons. Streisand has told friends, 'When have you ever heard of a man painting a woman's finger nails as an ode to seduction? It would stick to *everything*!'

talked about as the best of the year, a shoe-in for an Oscar. He was natural, unmanicured, good-looking, but nothing like a movie star, all of which made him a new kind of sensation, 'a hero for an uptight generation', *Time* said. By October 1969, he had made three more movies in which he played a lead: *M\*A\*S\*H* (as Trapper John), *Getting Straight* and *Move*. And he was contracted to star in three more films the following year – *I Love My Wife*, *The Touch* and *Little Murders*. He had been steam-rolled into stardom. 'I always knew there were things going on in me, that I had something to express,' he told Judy Klemsrud of the *New York Times*. 'However, I don't take success seriously. But I'm pleased for my friends. There are a lot of people I want to be able to help – actors, writers, and directors. And now I'm in a position to do so.'

Streisand was happy for his success, to validate her early belief in Elliott and for what it would mean to Jason. It also set her to wonder if she had done the right thing in splitting up. Then reality would set in. Fame, she knew, did not change the basic person. She was still carrying around her bag of insecurities and Elliott his. What had brought them together had also driven them apart. Streisand had believed that with success in her career and Elliott's love and support she would overcome her insecurities. When that had not occurred, she turned away from him, searching elsewhere for an elusive panacea to happiness.

Elliott, for his part, wanted success and was uncomfortable with his own as well as Streisand's, at the same time. Success meant responsibilities that he feared he could not carry through. He felt that he had failed in his marriage, that they both had let Jason down, and he was unsure of what he wanted from life. He was 'something of a paradox', one interviewer wrote. 'At times you detect flashes of shyness and vulnerability. But mostly, he comes across as just plain tense ... When he's not pacing the floor, he sits on a couch cracking his knuckles, gulping water and chain-smoking cigarettes.' He was also using large amounts of uppers and downers, had lost almost all he had earned in the past year gambling and was seeing a psychiatrist five days a week. He was willing to admit in print that he still cared earnestly for Barbra. 'We have a very deep personal relationship. I chose Barbra and Barbra chose me because we fell in love ... we have a great son. He's like a little tiger – beautiful. He looks like both of us. He is the best thing that either of us could ever hope to do. I want Jason to have the kind of mother Barbra wants to be, and she wants for him what I want for him.

'Maybe we'll get back together again, maybe we won't. I know that I'll never take her out in public again, like I did to the Academy Awards last spring [where he had felt ignored]. When I see her now, we go to little out-of-the-way places where no one sees us.'

They were dating from time to time, private dinners to talk about Jason or discuss their current problems, things they found they could not talk about with others – their families, their fears, their self-doubts. One subject, however, not discussed was her attraction for Trudeau.

She was living a dual life, dating Trudeau secretly and being seen at grand openings and galas amidst a crush of the curious and admiring. *Hello, Dolly!* premièred at the Rivoli in New York on 16 December before a black-tie socialite audience. Marty Erlichman accompanied her, Streisand exotically dressed in a fox-fur-trimmed embroidered coat, high boots and a pillbox hat, her hair drawn back smoothly from her face, 'looking like an elegant Nefertiti'. Two blocks from the theatre they were trapped inside their black Rolls-Royce limousine by about fifty over-enthusiastic fans who ran alongside the vehicle, slowed it to a crawl and then started rocking it. Streisand, terrified, let out an ear-splitting scream. The zealots drew back, allowing the driver to reach the theatre. Frightened to get out, fearing she might be attacked, Streisand remained inside the vehicle for several minutes. When she finally emerged, Erlichman, the driver and several security and police officers (the première was ironically for the benefit of the Police Athletic League), formed a semi-circle around her, but the fans broke through and she was swept up in a shoving, elbowing crowd that converged from all directions. She was in a panic when she reached the lobby. Erlichman had been hit in the head by a camera, punched and knocked to the ground in the mêlée.

'Oh my God, what's happening?' Streisand cried as he was helped inside, spurting blood. A doctor among the invited guests took Erlichman, Streisand refusing to leave his side, into a private office to clean the wound which looked more serious than it was. The showing of the film was delayed for half an hour until both of them finally took their seats, Streisand next to Louis Armstrong. After the showing, she was whisked away in a different car, parked at a side entrance. Fans caught sight of her and ran after the vehicle for a few feet, and then fell back.

The after-theatre supper dance was held at the Pierre Hotel and Armstrong sang a lusty chorus of 'Hello, Dolly!' with the band and then did some smart hoofing with a dance group to entertain the guests. Streisand looked pale through the entire evening and fretted over Erlichman's injuries, even though he was well enough to join her.

'I will never go to another première,' she vowed afterwards. 'It's inhumane.'

'She is one of the few, mysteriously natural, unique performing talents of our time,' Vincent Canby wrote in the *New York Times*. 'She has become a National Treasure. Casting her as Dolly Levi, is rather like trying to display Yellowstone National Park in a one-geyser forest preserve.'

But the film did not work and no one knew that better than Streisand. All the problems she had first seen remained. She was too young for Dolly Levi and both she and Matthau were too often off-camera, at which time the movie featured young members of the cast in some truly silly plot devices. The sets were certainly spectacular. Lehman and Kelly had been reverential to history and architecture to the point of idiocy. By preserving a slim and often witless musical on a large movie screen, they had inflated its faults to elephantine proportions. She was criticised in most of the major reviews for her 'Mae West' inclusions, although it did work well for her in what was probably her best number in the picture, 'Goodbye, Dearie'. But the movie looked good and so did she. Matthau was droll and crusty as required and there were moments of great joy, Louis Armstrong's appearance being one of them, as was her arrival scene at the Harmonia Gardens.

Despite protestations to the contrary, Streisand, swathed in white mink, did attend the glittering Hollywood première of the film and the post-movie supper dance in the huge adjoining tent. Matthau gave her a wild greeting when he caught sight of her, grabbing her up in his arms and kissing her – much to her surprise and that of others who knew how volatile their relationship had been on the set of the film. Later, asked by a reporter how it was to work with her, he replied diplomatically, 'Barbra had moments of likability.'[3] She came down the aisle of the theatre with Erlichman, flanked on all sides by security guards, who took their post outside the ladies' room during the intermission, allowing no one in until she reappeared.

Her romance with Pierre Trudeau was still very much alive. He had flown to New York shortly after the première there and they had ventured out to a restaurant where he was photographed smiling intimately at her across the table. She appeared shy in his company, quieter – but glowing. Once she returned to California they spoke frequently on the telephone. At his invitation, on 25 January she flew to Ottawa where, over the next three days, they spent as much time together as he could spare. It was the first time that she played a supporting role in a relationship.

She sat in the visitors' gallery of the imposing Canadian House of Commons and listened intently as he brilliantly parried questions from his colleagues while stealing glances up at her. At one point he appeared not to have heard a question. 'If the Prime Minister can take his eyes and his mind off the visitors' gallery . . .' the MP who had the floor remonstrated. Trudeau smiled sheepishly as the Members laughed. After the session he was detained, and then ran to her car as she was leaving, helped her inside and held her hand for a long moment before pulling away and returning to his job.

She believed she was in love. At least, she confided to others that this was the case. There was a strong physical attraction, a great excitement when they were together. She was proud that so prominent and intelligent a man found her attractive, and she was in awe of his mind, his grasp of world situations.

---

[3] Asked the same question by this author, Matthau replied, 'I take the Fifth [Amendment]!'

Still, she was unsure how they would ever make it as a couple. There were so many things she had still to prove to herself. She now wanted to produce her own movies, to establish her place as a dramatic actress, and Hollywood was the best place for those ambitions. Then, too, she would have trouble taking a back seat to such a powerful husband. And there was Jason. How would such a marriage affect him? Would Elliott remain a strong presence in their son's life as she wanted him to be? There were their religious differences. Then, too, Trudeau had not proposed marriage; she had no guarantee that he would, that he wanted any more from her than a brief affair might offer.

On Manitoba Night, a yearly Canadian celebration, he escorted her to a gala celebration at the National Arts Center. She looked especially lovely, very dramatic with a tallish white mink hat, her hair again parted in the centre and drawn back from her face, her ensemble trimmed in white mink on the collar, cuff and hem, her long, angular hands with their polished extensions plunged deep in a muff of the same fur, in a kind of 'Greta Garbo as Anna Karenina' look. All through the evening Trudeau gazed lovingly at her while she remained restrained, cool, somewhat diffident. Doubts had continued to assail her during the day and Trudeau's public recognition of them as a couple made her situation difficult.

The following evening they dined alone at the Prime Minister's residence. She was ushered into an austere reception room, 'heavy Victorian ornaments, dour, unsmiling family portraits, gray everywhere', and told, 'The Prime Minister will be down shortly.' This sober introduction into his private lifestyle was in direct contrast to the man she thought she knew and whose informal approach to politics, which included wearing sandals in Parliament on humid summer days, was debated with lively enthusiasm in the press.

For two years before becoming Prime Minister, Trudeau had been Minister of Justice in the Lester Pearson government and had brought sweeping reforms to Canada's judicial system. As a champion for human rights, he became 'the beloved black sheep of the Liberal Party', but there was also the private man with a reputation as a heart-breaker. In the words of Margaret Sinclair, with whom he was soon to be romantically involved, Trudeau 'had a silky, warm, charming manner that eased any initial awkwardness a woman might be feeling'. It has been said that 'Charm is the power to please by force of personality and intellect, an instinct for the persuasiveness of sympathy, the indefinable effect of an enchantment.' Trudeau possessed these things and Streisand was moved and captivated by him at turns.

He joined her almost immediately upon her arrival. According to a servant's report, they dined by candlelight at a table set up before a roaring fire. The food was bland but the conversation was spirited. Trudeau possessed a gentle, teasing way of speaking, 'a sort of old-fashioned gallantry'. After dinner they took a walk in the garden. The air was cutting cold as they wandered briskly by the river that bordered the property, the lights of the city reflected on its surface. Then they returned to the residence. Backstairs' reporting went no further. The servant left the two alone in the house to retire to her own quarters.

For all his phenomenal success, Trudeau was a solitary man who had never lived with any woman very long, but he had reached an age when he wanted children, a family. Exactly how Streisand fitted in with his scheme for his future is cloudy. Known to be attracted to women in the public eye, his affairs were invariably short-lived. Reason overcame passion and he would move on rather than become inextricably entangled in a relationship that was not to his liking or that might be injurious to his political career.

She left the next day for New York, where she was to begin shooting *The Owl and the Pussycat*, her first non-musical movie, confused, not sure what she should do, break it off before she was too deeply involved or continue to see him.

'Yeah, sure, I thought about being first lady of Canada,' she later acknowledged. 'I thought it would be fantastic. I'd have to learn how to speak French. I would do only movies made in Canada. I had it all figured out. I would campaign for him and become totally politically involved in all the causes, abortion and whatever,' obviously forgetting in her enthusiasm that as a Catholic, Trudeau could not covenant abortion and that her status as a divorced woman, if marriage was ever proposed, would become an almost insurmountable obstacle.

Still, the old self-doubts prevailed. 'I was concerned with being looked down upon as an actress,' she admitted. 'I felt that certain people thought, oh, you're an actress, ah. Cheap. Vulgar. Loose. Immoral. Amoral ... People want to be friendly with actresses, they're so *charming, so amusing*. It's all so condescending, like having a clown, having this toy.'

'Is it love?' a reporter asked Diana Kind, a most unlikely person to know her daughter's heart as Streisand discussed nothing of a personal nature with her mother. 'Who knows?' Diana replied, offering her customary platitudes. 'Barbra has a lot of interesting friends.'

In late February her relationship with Trudeau came to a sudden end. He had fallen in love with Margaret Sinclair, a nineteen-year-old Canadian whom, Streisand learned, he was seeing when she was visiting him in Ottawa.[4] She

---

[4] In her memoirs, Margaret Sinclair Trudeau wrote: 'He flew Barbra Streisand up to Ottawa to accompany him to a gala at the Arts Center ... It was a romance. Every paper carried it. For the next few days my pique and jealousy was such that each time Pierre rang I slammed down the phone: "Go back to your American actress!" I yelled at him.' The future Mrs Trudeau converted to Catholicism and married the Prime Minister eighteen months later. Despite her religious conversion, she eventually divorced Trudeau.

was hurt and confused. For years she had turned to Elliott in troubled times. He was in Sweden making *The Touch* with one of the world's greatest directors, Ingmar Bergman, and had been nominated for an Oscar for Best Actor in *Bob & Carol & Ted & Alice*. Maybe the time when they had first met and married had just been too premature. Now, with both of them enjoying fame, they could do fantastic things together. She had always believed in him as he had believed in her. She had a short break in her shooting schedule. Taking a wild chance, she flew to Stockholm to talk with him.

'Barbra wanted us to get back together immediately,' Elliott recalled. She brought up Jason, their history together, her continuing feeling for him, her sense of loss without him. 'I didn't know that was my last opportunity, and I don't know if it would have made a difference if I had,' he said. 'I told her, "If that's what you want, then that's what I want, but I can't just disregard Jenny."' He suggested that they wait before moving back together so that he could have a chance to see that Jenny did not feel deserted, that she had someone to help her make the transition to being on her own again. 'But Barbra needed immediate validation,' and he could not give it to her. Nursing her injured feelings, she returned to New York.

Although unable to surrender all her ties to Elliott, she knew now that their marriage was really over. She suspected she would never want to remarry. 'Jason already *has* a father,' she told a close friend, 'I have a special destiny to fulfil.' She had felt that way since childhood. Then, she believed it meant she would one day be a great Hollywood star. Having achieved that wish she set her goal higher.

'After she *schlepped* through *Hello, Dolly!*,' Barry Dennen said, 'I wrote her a telegram with just three words, "What a pity." But I never did send it.'

He did not have to. Streisand agreed. She had caught her second wind and was ready for the onset of a different phase in her career – to succeed as a dramatic actress, to direct and produce her own movies – and then? Her life was like an ocean, wave lapping against wave – and always there was deeper water to tread beyond.

# 20

S TREISAND ENTERED FILMS at a time when strong women with powerful screen personalities were an endangered species. The industry was male dominated, with a profusion of macho stars and adventure films. Good female roles were almost non-existent and women in executive positions unwelcome. Welcomed or not, she intended to break through the male bastion that controlled Hollywood. *Look out world, here I come!* was her attitude. *That* world was making movies, now her world, her life and she intended to make of it what she wanted.

The days of gutsy actresses such as Joan Crawford, Bette Davis, Katharine Hepburn, Susan Hayward, Carole Lombard and Rosalind Russell were over. Marilyn Monroe was dead and with her had died the Hollywood sex queen. In 1970 there were only two major female American film stars – Barbra Streisand and Jane Fonda. Streisand was offered, and refused, two roles – that of the marathon dancer in *They Shoot Horses, Don't They?* (1969), and the brittle New York call-girl in *Klute* (1971) – both went to Fonda, the latter winning her an Academy Award. Neither role appealed to Streisand. Too downbeat.

Shortly after *Klute*, Fonda plunged into a plethora of anti-Establishment causes, championing the Black Panthers and a campaign to end the war in southeast Asia – activities unacceptable to Hollywood film backers. This put an end, temporarily, to her film career and left Streisand virtually alone in the field without contenders. She had the power, now she must decide how to use it.

Possessing a strong screen presence even when miscast, as she had been in *Hello, Dolly!*, finding a role to fulfil her potential was a rough and tumble struggle. If she wanted good roles in interesting films, Streisand would have to become her own producer. In Hollywood, however, the more a woman used her energy, her brains, and her talent, the more she was resented. A woman like Streisand, who fought for every inch she gained, was a threat.

Although called a castrating, hard-driving bitch by some of the men she worked with, a man in the same circumstances would have been respected for his drive and ambition. All around her she saw male stars – Kirk Douglas, Burt Lancaster, John Wayne, Jack Lemmon – organising their own production companies, receiving the profits that had hitherto gone to their employers. She decided that was what she must do and was also smart enough to know that she could not go it alone.

Marty Erlichman still functioned as her personal manager, overseeing her career, but her agent at this time was the high-powered, super-salesman Freddie Fields who in 1961, with his ex-partner David Begelman, had started a talent agency, then called Creative Management Associates (later to become International Creative Management). Streisand had signed with CMA during her 1963 engagement at the Coconut Grove, realising that to make it in movies she had to have a knowledgeable and established Hollywood agency behind her. Fields, a man with a ready smile, sharp wit and a penchant for grand gestures – extravagant gifts, chauffeured Rolls-Royces to take his stars to their public engagements – had renegotiated, with attorney Bella Linden's considerable help, Streisand's original *Funny Girl* contract.

Freddie Fields was a genius at putting together package deals – star, property, director – but Streisand was the agency's only bankable star. Determined to overtake William Morris, then the top Hollywood talent agency, Fields came up with an idea that he felt certain would attract other talents of her calibre (necessarily men – there were no female stars in her orbit) to his agency list. Sue Mengers was his prime talent-acquisition agent. Fields put together the idea of a company that would be owned partially by the stars who would be partners in the company and partially by the public. He needed Streisand as bait to bring in performers in her strata and promised her the world – artistic freedom, here's your chance to do your own projects, whatever you want to do, virtually no strings attached. She would get 10 per cent of the gross and would agree to deliver three pictures to this company. Streisand, feeling this was just the opportunity she was looking for to have control over her films, agreed. Mengers then went all out to woo other candidates away from their current agents. It did not take long before she had convinced Paul Newman and Sidney Poitier of the viability and advantage of such a company. On the surface the three stars seemed a good match as they were serious performers each with a strong social conscience.

Her agents, Fields and Mengers, a formidable duo, set up a press conference on 11 June 1969, in New York at the Plaza Hotel where, at a table in one of the ballrooms, the three stars signed incorporation papers for The First Artists Production Company, Ltd in front of over 300 press photographers, reporters and television news cameramen. Each of the three stars had made an initial commitment to produce and appear in three films. Additionally, the company planned to engage in television production, music publishing, recording and other ancillary activities.[1]

---

[1] Forty years earlier film stars Mary Pickford, Charles Chaplin, Douglas Fairbanks and

Speaking first, Streisand said in a clear, authoritative voice she saw the new company as 'a natural development, a logical progression. I have always had to be free to play the roles and sing the songs I felt strongly and instinctively were right for me. We'll be making many diverse films and we're determined that every one of them – drama or comedy or musical – will reach the very high standards we demand of ourselves.'

Newman added that the purpose of their company was 'not necessarily to economise, but to put film production on a more efficient basis'. Poitier spoke more about the new era of the motion picture industry. 'You either lead it, or move with it, or follow it. We have opted for leadership.'

After the announcement the stellar triumvirate adjourned to a private suite where they drank champagne and talked glibly among themselves and their representatives, but there was a curious lack of chemistry between them. On Streisand's part, 'a cool suspicion of the others', a staff member who was present at the gathering recalled. She was the lone woman in a company with two powerful men who were both as valuable at the box office as she was. Although they parted amiably, a competitive spirit was unleashed. Plans for the company moved forward, guided in these early months by Fields and by Mengers who managed not long after to snag Steve McQueen from William Morris as a fourth member of First Artists. Warner Brothers was to supply the financing along with a British merchant bank, Arbuthnot Latham & Co Ltd.

One of Streisand's prime reasons for becoming a partner in First Artists was to choose her own projects. The one closest to her heart was an Isaac Bashevis Singer story, 'Yentl, the Yeshiva Boy', which had been sent to her by producer Valentine Sherry in 1968 just after she had completed *Funny Girl*. Having read it, she called Fields to tell him that she wanted to do it as her next movie. Fields tried to convince her that she should not do another ethnic role so soon after playing Fanny Brice. Streisand was persistent and took an option on the property.

Set in nineteenth-century Poland, the story centred on Yentl, only child of a widowed Talmudic scholar who had instilled in his daughter a love of learning. After his death, and as girls were denied an education in Talmudic law at that time, the teenaged Yentl disguises herself as a boy, cuts off her hair, straps down her breasts, adopts male clothing, renames herself Anshel, and runs away to another town. There, accepted as a boy, she attends a *yeshivah* and falls in love with an older male student, Avigdor, to whom she does not dare to confide the truth. Finally she is pressured into a marriage to the

William Hart formed United Artists to distribute their own independent productions. Hart dropped out two weeks later but United Artists became a major film distributor in Hollywood and earned sizeable profits from the release of its movies for its founders. The precedent, therefore, had been set for Streisand, her star partners, and First Artists.

beautiful young woman, Hadass, whom Avigdor loves but cannot marry. Yentl eventually reveals her true identity and embarks for America, where to continue her education she will no longer have to pretend to be male.

The story appealed to Streisand on several levels. It was about a girl who had lost her father, a man of learning; it dealt with equal opportunity and education for women, and it was rooted in the history of the Jewish people. She approached the Czechoslovakian director, Ivan Passer, the son of wealthy Jewish parents who had survived the Holocaust. He seemed exactly the right choice to develop *Yentl*. He struggled with the story for a while and then backed out, telling Streisand that she was too old and too famous to play the part. Also, women masquerading as men had never been accepted on the screen. He reminded her of Katharine Hepburn's disastrous film, *Christopher Strong* (1933) in which she donned masculine attire, a movie that was a failure at the box office and earned Hepburn the wrath of critics. Apart from that, he could see no way to overcome the climatic wedding night scene between two women – Hadass and Yentl. Nor, for that matter, had Paramount when she approached them originally seeking financing.

'I would think, "I can never make this movie. Maybe Ivan was right; I'm too old. Maybe I'm too famous." I was so scared that I would talk to everyone about it and after a while I began to really hear myself, and hear this person talking about this dream they had, but being too frightened to go after the dream.' She continued to talk about it but she went on with her commitment to star in the film adaptation of Bill Manhoff's *The Owl and the Pussycat*, a whimsical version of the Pygmalion myth that had been more successful as a play on Broadway than the West End. She played Doris, a luckless prostitute, brassy, fast-talking, an overbearing character who was, none the less, vulnerable and likeable – a sort of ethnic, apolitical Billie Dawn from *Born Yesterday*. Doris was Streisand's first straight comedy role and she began shooting on location in New York with great enthusiasm.

Originally conceived for two characters, a black woman and a white man, the Broadway production of *The Owl and the Pussycat* had starred Alan Alda and Diana Sands, with whom Streisand had appeared in *Another Evening with Harry Stoones*. Streisand's co-star was George Segal. They worked magically as a team. In a farcical inversion of the movie cliché, Segal played the reticent maiden to Streisand's incorrigible seducer. As one writer astutely noted, they illustrated 'Schopenhauer's theory that the ideal couple is the one in which the man's feminine components equally match the woman's masculine traits'.

In the story Segal's character, Felix, a bookstore clerk with pretensions to becoming a writer, is distressed by the late-night sexual activity of his neighbour, Doris, a hooker who calls herself a model and actress. Felix reports her behaviour to their landlord. Doris is evicted and, with no place to go, brazens her way into Felix's apartment, refusing to leave. Verbal battles lead to sexual seduction. The dialogue is fast and witty; the romantic ending as Doris abandons prostitution and Felix accepts his future as nothing more than a bookstore clerk, is thoroughly satisfying.

Except for the sudden death of her much-relied-upon cinematographer, Harry Stradling,[2] during the making of *The Owl and the Pussycat*, Streisand's first film for Ray Stark since *Funny Girl*, was a happy working experience. She was thrilled to be cast in a straight romantic comedy, to prove that she could succeed without singing a note. And she liked and understood the character she played. This time she and Stark got on well. Her old friend Herbert Ross directed the film. Robert Greenhut, who would go on to produce most of Woody Allen's movies, was production manager and always helpful. And she had an exceptional rapport with George Segal whose offbeat personality appealed to her. Segal was not only an actor who could move deftly from drama to comedy and from stage to film, he was a dedicated jazz musician, singer and conductor (under his baton, his Beverly Hills Unlisted Jazz Band would perform in 1981 at Carnegie Hall).

The movie, which began shooting on 6 October 1969, was filmed entirely in New York using the city streets, Doubleday Bookstore on Fifth Avenue, Riker's Restaurant, Club 45 and Central Park for locations, and a small studio on West Fifty-Sixth Street for all other scenes. Fearing Streisand might create problems if she did not have a luxurious dressing room, Stark had the film's production designer John Robert Lloyd create a suitable one for her. Lloyd completely mirrored the walls, 'put in thick white carpeting, and all kinds of funny things – beanbag chairs, things that were faddish. And I made her a special dressing-room table with those three-fold dressing-room mirrors with lights around them like the old-fashioned dressing rooms used to have. And I put a star on the door.' Streisand was pleased with the result and except for one scene, where she was to be filmed topless, she was never difficult.

'She only calls me "Herbie" when she's uptight,' Herbert Ross explained. 'Otherwise I'm Herbert. For that scene, as soon as I heard "Herbie, I gotta talk to you," I knew she had big reservations even though I thought we'd worked them all out. She got me into a corner and said, "Herbie, I can't. I've got goose bumps and they'll show. Herbie, I just can't. What would my mother think?"'

Arguments went back and forth for nearly an hour. 'Oh, what the hell. I'll do it once!' she finally exclaimed, disrobed and crossed the set bare-breasted to where Segal waited on the bed.

'Cut! Print! Beautiful!' Ross shouted.

When she saw the rushes, although her nudity revealed a splendid, sensual

---

[2] Harry Stradling died on 14 February 1970, shortly after completion of photography on *The Owl and the Pussycat*; cinematographer Andrew Laszlo took over to supervise all retakes and second unit work.

body, she insisted the scene be cut, claiming it destroyed the impact of the scene that followed. Reluctantly Ross acquiesced and turned over, at Streisand's request, the negative frames in which she had been topless.[3]

This was during her romance with Pierre Trudeau, which more than possibly had influenced her decision. Her association with the Prime Minister deepened her interest in politics and provided her with another stage on which to exercise – not just her ego – but her enormous intelligence. None of her films had allowed her to express her concern for social ills, or dissatisfaction with the status quo. In her first two years in Hollywood her main efforts were to establish herself as a superstar. Having accomplished this, she was now feeling intellectually dissatisfied. She detested the loss of privacy that fame had extracted. She was followed by *paparazzi* wherever she went. Fans seemed to feel they had the right to intrude on her private time – attending a children's movie with five-year-old Jason, dining with friends. Becoming more actively involved in politics afforded her the opportunity to use her celebrity to validate her beliefs.

So much had happened to her and the country since she had first gone to Hollywood in 1967 that it hardly seemed possible that only three years had intervened. An American space ship had landed on the moon. Richard M. Nixon, a man she loathed, was President. Unrest spread on college campuses as the Vietnam War dragged disastrously on. There were over 44,000 American casualties, another 300,000 men had been wounded, bombing had been intensified, Cambodia invaded and a unit of the US army in Vietnam had massacred 347 civilians, women and children included, in the tiny village of My Lai.

Vigorously anti-war, while she was in New York making *The Owl and the Pussycat*, she became involved in the Congressional campaign of Bella Selitsky Abzug, a stocky, middle-aged lawyer, with a forthright style, belting voice, and a taste for large, slouchy hats who was not only staunchly anti-war but a dedicated proponent of women's rights. Abzug was a true original, employing a New York confrontational style with a talent for outsized theatrics. As a young woman she had been in the Stalinist wing of the Democratic Party. Although her views had mellowed, she was a fighting liberal as, in fact, was the Democratic Congressman from New York City, Leonard Farbstein, whose thirty-year tenure as the representative for the 19th Congressional District she was challenging in the 23 June (1970) Primary.

The Abzug–Farbstein contest grew ugly. Farbstein accused his opponent of

[3] Ten years later the magazine *High Society* somehow got hold of either the original negative frames or pirated copies of Streisand's discarded topless scene and published several stills. Streisand attempted to block publication and sued for $5 million in damages. The judge ruled against her, although he ordered the publisher to notify wholesalers to tear the offending pages from the magazine before putting them on news stands. There is no way of knowing how many wholesalers obliged.

being, among other things, a Communist and anti-Israel (neither accusation correct) and Abzug charged him with being against the women's movement and more hawk than dove (also not exactly the truth). Streisand met Abzug through Cis Corman. The two women hit it off straight away. 'They shared a kind of mirror image,' one near observer said. 'Bella nursed fantasies of being a great performer and Barbra of political power.'

Streisand's views were to the far left, but certainly not radical in a time when Leonard Bernstein hosted fund-raisers for the Black Panthers and there was a nationwide protest when four students were killed by Ohio National Guardsmen during an anti-war rally at Kent State University. Streisand, seldom neutral, was a sometime antagonist, meaning that she believed in the liberal issues, lent her celebrity, donated money and helped to fund raise, but her career and her personal life took precedence. She was also not against the publicity value and the means to attract new fans that her association with such meaningful, newsworthy causes generated. The ideal of female equality was, however, deep-rooted in her consciousness. And as new role models such as Bella Abzug, Gloria Steinem and Betty Friedan (who asserted, 'This is not a bedroom war. This is a political movement'), came on the scene, she joined with them in a spirit of community.

Reacting to the excitement of the city during political campaigns, Streisand decided she wanted to return to New York but not to her old apartment. On 31 March she bought a town house for $375,000 (the asking price had been $420,000) at 49 East 80th, circumventing board approval on co-op apartments. But she was quickly disenchanted with the house. 'I would much rather have the seventeen rooms horizontally than vertically – or on two instead of five levels,' she admitted only weeks later, adding that she would sell 'if a buyer could be found and I could purchase a suitable co-op in an apartment building where I am welcome'.

The house on East 80th Street was built in 1929 when the art deco movement was at its height. The residence was an impressive stone structure entered through an iron-and-glass front door from a walled courtyard. Streisand had the front windows replaced with leaded glass panels from a Victorian gazebo that she had bought from a set of *On a Clear Day*. She took the Russian-born well-known art deco artist Erté on a tour of the house and incorporated some of his ideas – a 1920s period mural in the dining room and indirect lighting which had been popular at that time. The décor, however, was to incorporate Regency, Victorian, art nouveau, deco *and* contemporary influences, to include the furnishings from the penthouse and to showcase the many stored pieces of antique furniture, paintings, and *objets d'art* she had been collecting over the years.

Working with an architect and a decorator she redesigned the new house to her needs and liking. Jason would have a suite of rooms. His bedroom was to be fashioned around a colourful, contemporary Frank Stella painting and filled with white furniture. The adjoining playroom would contain the Victorian shop furnishings she had bought when she was filming *On a Clear Day* in England, and included an ice-cream parlour bar, a gum machine, and penny candy and toy cabinets. The library was to be a repository for her art nouveau furniture, turn-of-the-century art glass, German Expressionist art works by Gustav Klimt and Egon Schiele and Czech artist Alphonse Mucha's celebrated art nouveau posters. She was having structural work done in the kitchen – 'everything in stainless steel, white and red – I love red,' she said, adding: 'I hate the kitchen being in the basement. Well, I'll have to leave a supply of cup cakes on every floor.' Her own suite was to be in shades of rose. The bed that she and Elliott had once shared was to be replaced by a 1920s satin-tufted model.

While all this was being prepared, she remained with Jason at the Ardsley. By the middle of May it became evident that the renovations would take longer than she had hoped and as the house would have to remain empty for the workers she agreed to open it to the public on Tuesday evening, 9 June, for a fund-raising party at which paying guests would meet Democratic Congressional hopeful Bella Abzug.

Three thousand invitations were sent out, urging all who wished to contribute $25 to the cause of 'sending to Washington next January that very special lady running for Congress who is dedicated to peace' to drop in between 5 and 8 p.m. 'There will be stars of stage, screen and radio! – drinks, canapés but *no* furniture!!' Bella-Boosters, as campaign helpers called themselves, worked for a week to clean up the house, scrubbing and waxing floors, washing windows. 'Hey! Now I can see the sycamore out front!' Streisand exclaimed as she came by to see how things were going.

Wearing a bright yellow pants suit, her hair loose and soft about her face and very little make-up, Streisand appeared in high spirits the evening of the open house although she remained fortified in a corner of the walled garden. Numerous staff members and Bella-Boosters were at hand so that very few of the guests could make their way through to greet her, and there was tight security at the doors. About 2,000 people came to support Abzug and to see Streisand and her house and as the premises were not large enough to accommodate such numbers, lines formed at the front door and queued down the street. Waiting supporters complained loudly, especially when well-known personalities were seen to circumvent the lines and enter through a side door. None the less, the publicity given the event was tremendous and there could be no doubt that Streisand's endorsement of Abzug was strategically successful. Photographs of the two of them together appeared in all the New York City newspapers.

For almost as long as Hollywood has existed, politicians have been aware that movie personalities create deeper and more immediate bonds with the public than they can, that seeing that the stars whom they admire respect a candidate is a great vote-getter and the more famous the celebrity or cultural icon – as Streisand was now – the better the politician's chances of claiming a large block of votes. Abzug garnered a comfortable lead at this stage over Farbstein. The election in November would present Abzug's next challenge and Streisand agreed to lend her name and to appear at a pre-election concert to be held on Sunday evening, 1 November, at the Felt Forum at Madison Square Gardens.

The same week that Abzug won the Democratic nomination, *On a Clear Day* premièred. Initially envisioned as a three-hour-road-show presentation, the film had been cut mercilessly. Any narrative flow Vincente Minnelli's direction had given it was lost in the elimination of fifty minutes of footage. Jack Nicholson's character was so abbreviated that it was hard to know what he was doing in the picture. Yves Montand was charming but strangely unpersuasive as the psychiatrist who falls in love with Daisy's former incarnation and he sometimes spoke lines and sang lyrics as if he was doing so phonetically. And yet Streisand was delightful as Daisy and mesmerising as Melinda, and I have to agree with Vincent Canby of the *New York Times* that the high point of the picture and one of the most graceful Streisand moments ever put on film, is the royal dinner 'at which Minnelli's camera explores her in loving, circling close-up while her voice is heard on the soundtrack singing "Love With All the Trimmings".'

'She looks grand as Melinda, stroking her breast with a cool crystal goblet of white wine to arouse a man ogling her at dinner (the gambit would work equally well with red wine),' the critic at *Newsweek* wrote. 'She's a thoroughbred clothes horse for Cecil Beaton's costumes. She flashes lightning-like between Melinda's airs and Daisy's earthiness and when her Daisy admits to possession of various psychic powers she does so ruefully, as if it were a curse and she were Mrs Job.'

The picture, one of the last of big-budget Hollywood musicals, is beautifully filmed. Streisand is hypnotic at times, pure joy at others, and she looks spectacularly beautiful as Melinda. Despite the butchery that took place once it was in the cutting rooms, *On a Clear Day* is a visual delight. The score is not up to the standard of either Alan Jay Lerner's or Burton Lane's best shows, but it has some fine songs, tailor-made for Streisand's voice. However, the public was simply not interested in a movie about hypnotism, psychics and reincarnation even if it starred Barbra Streisand. Her fans were content to buy the original soundtrack album where they could listen to her sing in her distinctive voice in more intimate surroundings, and the film had a poor return at the box office.[4]

[4] *On a Clear Day* would later recoup its losses when it was released to television and sold as a video cassette.

Elliott had met Streisand in New York shortly before the open house for Bella Abzug and taken Jason to his first circus. Elliott's film M*A*S*H had taken the top prize at the Cannes Film Festival. His career at this moment lapped Streisand's. Elliott was, in fact, number five and Streisand rated in ninth position – the only woman – in the Top Ten Box Office Stars for 1970. She was having renewed thoughts about a reconciliation and asked him the status of his relationship with Jenny Bogart. He told her that Jenny was pregnant with his child.

The news of his mistress's impending motherhood shook Streisand and, much distressed, she asked Elliott to file suit for divorce as soon as possible.

He flew to the Dominican Republic, which had recently passed a law permitting foreigners to obtain a divorce in seven days. Jenny, now five months' pregnant, accompanied him. On 6 July the deed was done. Streisand was a divorced woman. 'I remember the various court officials in their donnish robes and hats,' Elliott later recalled. 'They said in Spanish, "Are you sure you want to go through with it?" My better self thought no, I don't. But I had to follow through. I did it for Barbra's sake, it was what she wanted,' a cold and cavalier attitude towards Jenny considering her condition.

Streisand – and even Elliott, himself – did not realise how serious his drug addiction had become. 'I didn't know how dangerous acid was,' he says. 'I never tried to kill myself but I think I came close. Acid opened up a lot of things. Maybe it opened my mind up too much.' Almost immediately following his trip to the Dominican Republic to obtain their divorce, he started a film under the aegis of Warner Brothers, A Glimpse of Tiger, an original screenplay by Herman Raucher, on which he was both producer (with Jack Brodsky) and star. The story was about a big bear of a man, on drugs, who is growing progressively mad, but funnily so. He works the subways pretending to be blind and meets a prim young woman who is taken with his far-out humour and his daring. The two are drawn into a bizarre affair and in the end the man murders the woman. Despite its dark subject, the script was crisp and funny, and even the dénouement more black comedy than horror.

As shooting progressed, the times Elliott was on acid increased. He became impossibly aggressive and Anthony Harvey, the director, quit. To ease the tension and believing he was being funny, Elliott came on to the set the next morning 'wearing his M*A*S*H helmet, a stocking over his face and sucking on a baby's [pacifier]'. When Harvey returned, lured back by the film company executives, Elliott became enraged and had to be restrained from attacking the director.

Kim Darby, his co-star, was terrified that he had gone mad and demanded security guards be hired by the movie company to protect her in case he became violent. A week later the film was cancelled. Worse was to follow. The company, to collect their insurance, had amassed a file on Elliott's bizarre behaviour during the weeks of production. He was examined by two psychiatrists who certified him mentally unbalanced, permitting the company to collect $1,500,000 in insurance.

Although *M*A*S*H* and *Getting Straight* were in general release and *Move* and *I Love My Wife* being readied for production, Elliott's meteoric rise to fame, a matter of two years and six major award-winning box-office successes, would come to a numbing and almost sudden end. He was no longer financeable. Two years later he was able to return to work and would star as Raymond Chandler's fictional detective Philip Marlowe in *The Long Goodbye* and in 1976 with James Caan in the farcical *Harry and Walter Go to New York*, but his short reign as a cult hero and box-office star was over. He was, he says, 'skirting insanity, skating through it'.

Streisand was devastated over Elliott's condition and his fall from grace. 'Oh, my God,' she sobbed to a friend, 'not Elly.'

Adding to the strangeness of the situation, Streisand had a financial interest in *A Glimpse of Tiger*. John Calley, President of Warner Brothers, called Raucher (whose adaptation of his own novel *The Summer of '42* was also a Warner Brothers film) to tell him that Streisand liked the story and that he thought the project could be salvaged if he could reverse the roles and write an upbeat ending. Raucher went to see her. 'She made chicken soup and was extremely helpful,' he recalls. 'But after two meetings and several dry starts on the new approach I decided it wouldn't work.' Warner, whose investment had been considerable in the failed project, did not agree and turned to other writers.

Meanwhile, Streisand had been taken by Anne Richardson Roiphe's novel, *Up the Sandbox*, and optioned it for development. But there was no film in her immediate future. She was at odds with herself, having to cope with the impact Elliott's breakdown and illness might have on her son's life and her own. Elliott had been more than her lover and mate, he had been her friend and protector.

In October 1970, much saddened and concerned, she moved into her New York town house. The tree-lined street glowed autumnal red. Light glimmered brilliantly through the deep red stain-glassed window panes she had put in some of the ground-floor windows. Sliding glass doors led from the kitchen to the walled-in garden where Jason did tumblesaults on the grass and learned how to catch a ball. Yet the house depressed her. New York brought back too many memories. She decided to sell the East Side townhouse and return to the Ardsley, having not yet given up her lease.

She was scheduled in late November and December to undertake two concurrent engagements at the Riviera and International Hilton Hotels in Las Vegas. First, however, she was committed to the fund-raising, vote-rallying evening concert for Bella Abzug being held just two days before the November election. A lot of mud had stuck to Abzug from the bitter campaign she had fought with Farbstein and she was not a shoo-in by any means. About four or five weeks before the concert, Streisand announced that she could not take on an entire evening. 'It seemed as though she really wanted to back out,' Madeline Lee, the producer of the concert recalled. 'Marty Erlichman met with me, the director, Stanley Prager, Hal Prince who was guiding the event and the rest of the executive staff, all of us doing our jobs without compensation. He said Barbra now wanted to do the second half of the programme and only then if for the first act we could get three performers – specifically Zero Mostel, Godfrey Cambridge and Woody Allen. (They had to be of that calibre and not singers.) I think that Marty was hoping that the whole thing would go away and that these conditions would let Barbra off the hook. Tickets had already been sold for a concert of Barbra Streisand for Bella Abzug. This was a terrible set-back. I tried but none of the three men were available on that night. When I reported this back to Marty he seemed very happy because it would free Streisand of her obligation.

'We just couldn't afford to lose Streisand's name value. Bella had been under vitriolic attack. Rocks were thrown through the windows of her campaign headquarters by militant supporters of Israel who thought she was anti-Israel. We were rather desperate. I came up with an idea called *Broadway for Bella*, where in the first half top Broadway stars would sing and perform numbers from current hit shows. Most theatres were dark on Sunday night and I thought I had a good chance of getting the stars. Marty was not too enthusiastic, but he agreed to have Barbra wait for a week to see if it could be accomplished.'

At week's end, Lee had signed up Joel Grey, Jack Gilford [Lee's husband], Lauren Bacall, James Coca, Rita Moreno, Phyllis Newman, Donna McKechnie, Alan Alda, George Segal, Tammy Grimes and the entire cast of *Hair*. Erlichman agreed to go forward, but all advertisements and the programme itself had to read *Broadway for Bella* starring BARBRA STREISAND. An unflattering caricature of her as Fanny Brice by Al Hirshfield was chosen for the programme. She hated it, but in the end allowed it to be used.

'The place was jammed – I don't know – maybe 20,000 people,' Lee continued. 'Lauren Bacall was one of the guest hosts. She was starring in *Applause* at the time. She came out and in a husky, cigarette voice (about two notes deeper than Bella's), said, "I guess you don't know why I'm here tonight. Well, I'm Bella Abzug's vocal coach!"' The first half was sensational. Then Barbra appeared in a slim-lined, black evening gown with spaghetti shoulder straps. Her hair was simple and back in a plain little chignon and she had a red chiffon scarf. She looked stunning. This was during a period when they were dressing her up in films and in Las Vegas with wigs and costumes and *ongepotchket* [overly decorated] evening outfits. We had a twenty-three piece orchestra and she sang seven songs and an encore, I believe. A beautiful Russian lullaby that had been cut out of *Funny Girl* (she tied the scarf under her chin like a babushka for that one), 'People' and numbers that she was planning to use in Las Vegas. She was so good she was chilling. She never sang better, she never looked better. Much to our horror people ran up the aisles wanting to touch her. She looked terrified. I think it was Alan Alda who came out on stage and helped her off.' The coverage was enormous and Abzug was duly elected to Congress two days later.

*The Owl and the Pussycat* opened the following week. 'Barbra Streisand's delicate snarl is the voice of New York tuned to a parodist's sensibility,' Pauline Kael wrote in the *New Yorker*. 'It's the sound of urban character armor; she rattles it for a finely modulated raucousness ... She is a living, talking cliff-hanger ... Though she doesn't sing in this picture, she's still a singing actress; she makes her lines funny musically, and she can ring more changes on a line than anybody since W.C. Fields, who was also a master of inflection.' The film was a huge success at the box office and was in the black within a few weeks of its release. Streisand had proved that she did not have to sing in a movie for it to be profitable. She pressed forward on the non-singing stories she was developing – *Up the Sandbox*, *Yentl* and *What's Up, Doc?*

She no longer enjoyed performing live and her return to Las Vegas was fraught with dissatisfaction. Stage fright plagued her. The late hours, gaudy ambiance of the hotels and of Las Vegas annoyed her. She could not wait to honour her contracts and return to California. Her impatience and irritation did not affect her performance. The rooms she played were packed and there were standing ovations after each show which ended with 'In the Wee Small Hours of the Morning' and 'When You Gotta Go'. 'The lyrics,' she claimed, 'with their "Auld Lang Syne" sentiment, seemed like a fitting way to bid farewell to a decade full of dreams, challenges and adventures.'

Her last performance was on New Year's Eve. It was 1971, a year into a new decade, destined to be the most tempestuous time in her life.

# Making Movies, Making Love

'One of the reasons I care about being a movie
actress is to be remembered, to be slightly
immortal; because I think life is so short that
by the time we get to see things with some sense
of reality and truth, it's all over. I'm sure
that's why I care so much about making movies: It
prolongs your life.'

BARBRA STREISAND, 1977

'People say I got this strange hold over Barbra.
I do. It's called love.'

JON PETERS, 1977

# 21

**B**EING A MOVIE star was no longer enough. Life was incomplete without a man by her side. Her closest friends – Cis Corman and lyricist Marilyn Bergman, whom she had met since coming to California – seemed to be happily married. Streisand was sensitive to their supportive, loving relationships. Every man she dated was viewed by her as a prospective life-partner. They all failed her standard. She wanted *poifect*, nothing less.

'Actually, I believe women are superior to men, I don't even think we're equal,' she professed. 'Among other things, women are stronger than men. They have more heart attacks, ulcers, nervous breakdowns and suicides. Their façade is killing them.' Thoughtfully, she added, 'I have enormous compassion for men, which really came into focus with the birth of my own son. This little boy who wanted to be held and comforted and soothed has to grow up in a world where he cannot cry because it is "unmanly".'

Tender sentiments, yet it is doubtful that she would have welcomed a man in her life who would not be able to control such emotions. She had only recently confided to friends that she was tired of being 'the man around the house, of making the money and all the decisions'. Ambiguity, thy name is Barbra.

The house in New York was put up for sale and sold swiftly. After all these years of renting, she bought the Central Park West penthouse and set about redecorating it, removing all the former Louis XVI influences, the red flocked wallpaper and large mirrors in highly decorated gold frames. 'Look, this was my first real home,' she told an interviewer for *Architectural Digest*. 'Let me tell you. I wanted Louis, Louis, Louis – as much as I could lay my hands on. And I got it: chandeliers, bronzes, porcelains, satin. Now I've become far more sophisticated.'

She was in what she called, 'my burgundy era ... Art Nouveau, Art Déco – all those rusts, mauves and greens, and those swooning fin-de-siècle colors and sinuous shapes!' She had become so knowledgeable about these two early twentieth-century design periods that she could have given a concise lecture on their roots and differences. Her tastes had changed but not her penchant for setting fashion trends. Hot pants, platform shoes, polyester and Day-Glo colours were the current vogue. The young seemed determined to express themselves in what they wore. Their clothes had a certain tackiness to them that Streisand disliked. She led the way with designer blue jeans and tie-dyed shirts for relaxation, long slinky gowns in black, grey or white for evening. The elaborate coiffures she had endorsed after *On a Clear Day* were replaced by long, straightened, flaxen-bleached hair. Motivated by a desire for youth and some of the fun she might have missed earlier in her life, she strove to keep fit. Her ice-cream binges occurred less often, her passion for delicatessen food was disciplined. She jogged on the beach in the mornings and played tennis with Burt Bacharach, who was working with her on a proposed album. On 14 March 1971, she made her first television appearance in three years (when the much delayed concert in Central Park taped just after she had made *Funny Girl*, was shown) on Bacharach's CBS special, joining him at the piano to sing 'Close to Me' and several other Bacharach/David songs.

Her old albums continued to sell at a steady rate. American record sales had tripled in the last decade. To the shock of their millions of horrified fans, the Beatles, rock music's reigning superstars, went their separate ways. But the Rolling Stones, Temptations, Fifth Dimension, Blood, Sweat and Tears and the Doors were all in the Top Forty and Streisand was one of the few solo singers with them. The Turtles and the Temptations played the Nixon White House. ('Me? Never!' she had commented.) In England, an LP called *Empty Sky* introduced a young Elton John. Elvis Presley, Joan Baez and Bob Dylan were a force, but new sounds were emerging – Marvin Gaye, James Taylor, Carole King. At the height of their fame Janis Joplin and Jimi Hendrix died tragic deaths – victims of living in the fast lane. The music world was going through a transitional time with great contrasts. Streisand was determined to keep up with the changing market and explore material she had not sung before with the same deep scrutiny she had given to Arlen, Styne, Merrill, Lerner and Lane.

Afraid the public might not want a 'different' Barbra Streisand, she recorded eight songs for an album titled *The Singer*,[1] which was to combine old and new music. When Clive Davis, the president of Columbia Records, heard these tracks he was concerned that she was walking the line too cautiously and asked her to consider putting work on *The Singer* aside to collaborate with a new producer (she had been working with Wally Gold), Richard Perry, on a more contemporary album. When she and Perry met he played her some of the songs he wanted her to sing if she agreed to do the replacement album with him. One of them was Laura Nyro's 'Stoney End'; others were Randy

[1] The title song of the abandoned album, *The Singer*, written by Walter Marks and arranged by Peter Matz, had its inspiration in French singer Edith Piaf. The music is very Gallic, the lyrics suited to cabaret. Streisand later released it in *Just for the Record*.

Newman's 'I'll Be Home', Harry Nilssen's 'Maybe' and Joni Mitchell's 'I Don't Know Where I Stand'. She agreed to go ahead with the album which would become *Stoney End*.

The venture was to be one of the few times she would not have Peter Matz as her musical arranger and/or conductor, the first time that she would have a back-up group (three female singers) and the first time, as well, that the musicians and technicians were either her age or younger. 'Richard was always trying to get me to sing on the beat,' she recalls, 'which I found very hard to do.' She was sceptical about the album's acceptance. Although not yet thirty, she considered herself part of the old guard of singers, her sound more Broadway than rock. Now she proved that she was a singer for any day. Each number is sung beautifully, with tremendous energy and with lyric attitudes that brought the songs to a brilliant polish. She happily lost a bet to Perry that the record would not be a hit. Released only a week before her *Broadway for Bella* concert, it was Number One on several national charts by the time she returned to Los Angeles after her Las Vegas engagements.

Suddenly she felt younger, gayer, more energised. She made a second album with Perry, *Barbra Joan Streisand*, designed to appeal to a wider audience with the inclusion of some rock and roll numbers. At best the album is a mixed bag. She tried hard to pump drama and give some stature to the lyrics of 'Space Captain' and belted out a grating primal shriek in John Lennon's 'Mother', failing in both cases to add anything to the original material. Yet, a Burt Bacharach–Hal David medley, and a fugue-like duet with herself, both vintage Streisand, vindicate the less successful numbers. The album wavered at the bottom of the charts, but it did reveal that she was not afraid of new music trends.

Making movies, her *own* movies, remained her top priority. *Yentl* was at a complete halt, *Up the Sandbox* was taking time to develop. Her contract with Ray Stark for two more movies would bring her a tenth of what she would have been paid elsewhere. She had a genuine fear of doing concerts. Records were her greatest source of income.

In Hollywood, where money is more highly valued than anything else, it is earnestly believed that the larger the budget of a picture the more successful it will be. How the money is consumed – on the highest paid stars, expensive writers, super-lavish settings – does not much matter. Streisand did not subscribe to that philosophy. She had been overwhelmed with the amounts of money lavished on the sets and costumes for *On a Clear Day*. She saw nothing inherently bad or wrong about artists making millions of dollars. She was, however, wary of sacrificing creativity for money – they were not interchangeable.

By nature frugal, a tough bargainer, during the early days of her success she had been extravagant, spending quantities of money on furs and furnishings.

Still, she was never wasteful. 'I can't throw away a half a yard of material or four inches of satin ribbon or a button or ... or a left-over slice of roast beef or a spoonful of peas!' she once said. She still had the clothes she had bought when she was appearing at The Lion and the Bon Soir. The most exotic hung on padded hangers decorating her dressing room. Others, she had remade or used the fabric elsewhere for throw pillows or to decorate container boxes for her dressing room. Left-over food was recycled or frozen. She still delighted in getting something free, being taken out to dinner or given special perks such as a chauffeured car paid for by the studio. Yet, her funds were, as they had been for years, handled by others. Although doing well, she was not making the great sums of money from films that were reported in the press. She insisted that 'the things you read in the paper about million-dollar this and million-dollar that, that's all bullshit. That's not true. I have never made as big a salary as many secondary male stars do today.' She was referring to the pictures she had made under her Raystar contract. She had, of course, drawn a high salary for her two Fox pictures.

Managers, agents and financial advisers took a considerable percentage of her earnings (at least 25 per cent) and the investments on her behalf in the stock market had not proved successful. She claims she 'never knew what was really going on ... never really read the contracts – understood the deals. I didn't care!' What she wanted now was to feel responsible for her own actions.

Divorced from Elliott, a free woman, able to date openly, she met through friends blond, boyishly handsome Ryan O'Neal who had just separated from his second wife, Leigh Taylor-Hunt, with whom he had co-starred for five years on the popular *Peyton Place* television series. Streisand's affair with O'Neal was a light-hearted, Californian-oriented relationship – days at the beach where O'Neal had once been a lifeguard, casual parties with friends and, on chill, damp evenings, romantic *tête-à-têtes* before a roaring fire in the comfortable den in his beach house. O'Neal had two children, Tatum, eight, and Griffin, six, with his first wife and on weekends when he had custody, Jason, who was now five, had companions,[2] which pleased her. Her inability to spend much time with her son in these formative years distressed her. With the pressures of her career and her active social life, it was often difficult. And although Jason was now in private day school in Santa Monica, he was an only child surrounded by a large female staff. Elliott objected to this, but his life was in too much turmoil to offer an alternative. Weekends spent with his mother, O'Neal and his two offspring seemed a viable and thoroughly pleasant arrangement.

---

[2] Ryan O'Neal's first wife was actress Joanna Moore. Both their children, Griffin and Tatum became actors. Tatum starred in her first movie at the age of ten with her father in *Paper Moon* (1973), and became the youngest person ever to win an Academy Award.

Ryan was Hollywood's newest and most promising leading man, having just been nominated for an Academy Award for his first major role in the highly successful film adaptation of Erich Segal's best-selling novel, *Love Story*. The idea brewed: why shouldn't Streisand and O'Neal make a movie together? They met with Sue Mengers, who represented them both. John Calley was still hopeful that Streisand would do *A Glimpse of Tiger*, Mengers told them. Maybe that was the way to go.

About this time the young writer/director Peter Bogdanovich, who had just made the critically acclaimed *The Last Picture Show*, entered the scene. Bogdanovich read the script of *Glimpse of Tiger* and did not think it could work even with a reversal of roles. A movie buff since childhood when, he said, he 'used to live inside films and act out all the parts all week long', one of his favourite genres was the 'screwball comedy' which had starred the likes of Carole Lombard, Katharine Hepburn and Jean Arthur. Although *Glimpse of Tiger* had gone awry, it did have its roots in those madcap movies of the 1930s. Using this as a springboard, borrowing quite blatantly from the classic Hepburn–Cary Grant 1938 picture, *Bringing Up Baby*, and 'stealing from everything you could imagine including Feydeau farce, vaudeville, and silent film comedy', Bogdanovich helped to transform Elliott's *boîte noire* into a spirited romp with the help of writers Buck Henry, who had done a superb job of adapting *The Owl and the Pussycat*, Robert Benton, and David Newman. *A Glimpse of Tiger* went into production on 16 August 1971, and was immediately renamed *What's Up, Doc?*

The story was set in San Francisco, where an absent-minded young musicologist (O'Neal) has come in pursuit of a grant accompanied by his dominating fiancée (hilariously played by Madeline Kahn). In the hotel drugstore he meets an anarchic and disaster-prone polymath (Streisand). All three are caught up in a wildly complicated sub-plot involving mixed-up suitcases, missing jewels, spies and gangsters, moving far away from the original concept. The verbal and visual gags are fast and funny. There is an inventive chase up and down the switchback streets of San Francisco, ending with a cavalcade of vehicles hurtling like lemmings into the Bay.

With Ryan, Jason and his nanny, Streisand settled into the exclusive Huntington Hotel while they were on location in San Francisco. She was in high spirits, glowing from Ryan's attention, when an unidentified telephone caller threatened to kidnap Jason. All her old fears returned. Under stress and justifiably concerned, she insisted on tighter security and took the youngster with her to the set every day. Her relationship with Ryan suffered with her nervous agitation and she threw all her energy into the making of the comedy, a genre she was expert at and her co-star a novice, relying on her to set the timing.

She was in her element and the pace of the picture zinged along. Although not a musical, she sang a sizzling version of Cole Porter's 'You're the Top' behind the titles. She also sang Herbert Hupfield's classic 'As Time Goes By' in the body of the movie in a scene where she seduces Ryan as he accompanies her on the piano upon which she first sits, then slithers across. Warner were confident that they had a hit, and this proved to be the case, but during the filming the relationship between the two stars cooled. Ryan turned out not to be quick enough or bright enough to sustain her interest. By the end of the production he had been reconciled with his wife, although they later divorced.

The break-up of her affair with Ryan did not disrupt her life. She returned to Las Vegas in December for the last of her contracted appearances and swore all over again that she would not do concerts or night-club work ever again. Fear and anxiety were her excuse, but there was more to it. Film and recordings, where she performed in a professional atmosphere, were her chosen arena of expression. They were immeasurably safer. A song could be recorded over and over and then edited until it was exactly the way she wanted it to sound and there were no outsiders, no one but herself to please. When making a movie, lighting, make-up and the work of some of the industry's top cameramen assured that not only would she look her best, she could be made to be beautiful or sexy or sophisticated. She had grown up living within the fantasy of the screen, imagining herself as any of the great beauties she had admired. Now that she could be one herself she was mature enough to understand that much of what a movie-goer thinks is real is illusion. Still, she was in love with herself on film, and insecure about her looks in true life, fearful – *yes* – that a terrorist or a crazy person could bring her harm, or that exuberant fans could injure her or crush her to death as they tore at her clothes or pulled her hair. Just recently, Diana Ross had had a wig painfully yanked from her head in an emotional attack by fans who appeared to have just wanted to touch or take away something that belonged to her. Unfortunately, the wig had been attached for security with a copious amount of hairpins. Streisand, the perfectionist, was equally terrified at the thought of forgetting lyrics, of mild applause or worse, jeers or hecklers.

As soon as she returned from Las Vegas she enthusiastically set to work on *Up the Sandbox*. The film's strongest appeal to her was its theme of women's equality with men. She played Margaret, a woman torn between her needs to strike a blow for female independence and her need to be a good wife and a loving mother to her two small children. She escapes into fantasy – daydreams in which she is the heroine of garish adventures. She has a bizarre affair with Fidel Castro (who turns out to be a lesbian in male attire), attacks her obnoxious mother with a baked meringue, joins a group of black revolutionaries in a plot to blow up the Statue of Liberty and goes on an African expedition to learn the secret of painless childbirth.

The shooting schedule was to start in Los Angeles in early March then move six weeks later to New York for a month of location work before continuing on to Uganda in East Africa, where – after a recent *coup d'état* the previous year – the country was in the hands of Major-General Idi Amin and the Ugandan army. Border clashes with Tanzania were being reported, diplomatic arguments with the United States and Israel were heated, and Amin was engaged on a reign of terror that would within a few years take the lives of 250,000 Ugandans. It hardly seemed like an intelligent location for a Hollywood movie, despite the promised savings in location costs in a place where labour was cheap and there were no unions to set a minimum wage.

*Up the Sandbox* was nominally Streisand's film, and as her initial venture for First Artists Productions she could have been expected to take full control. Instead, she stepped cautiously into the baptismal waters and let her producers, Irwin Winkler and Robert Chartoff hold the reins, although she retained artistic authority and supported herself with close associates and friends – Marty Erlichman as Associate Producer, Cis Corman, casting director. She worked on the screenplay with playwright/screenwriter Paul Zindel. *Up the Sandbox* put her in touch with herself, her feelings, her viewpoints on the difficulty of being a woman in a male-dominated world, and she was able to include these ideas in the script.

Despite her vows never again to appear before the public in a large concert, she was convinced by Warren Beatty and his sister, Shirley MacLaine, that she should do so one more time to help get the Democratic presidential nominee US Senator from South Dakota, George McGovern, elected, and in so doing remove Sneaky Dick Nixon from the White House. Every move that Nixon made seemed to pull the United States deeper into the Vietnamese War. In 1970, less than a week after Streisand's twenty-eighth birthday, Nixon had announced that he was sending American soldiers into Cambodia. The Vietcong sanctuaries had to be cleared, Nixon declared, 'the world's most powerful nation cannot afford to act like a pitiful, helpless giant'. Something had to be done to stop the madness of supposedly shortening the war by escalating it. Nixon had to be routed from office and Beatty was enlisting all the power stars he could to help.

In the two years since their brief affair, Beatty had emerged as a high-profile political advocate. For all his renown as Hollywood's Don Juan, Beatty was' and is an intelligent man with strong political views. In 1968, following his huge success in *Bonnie and Clyde*, he campaigned for Robert Kennedy in the presidential race. After Kennedy's assassination, he stopped filming for two years and devoted his energies to gun control legislation. He had enlisted early in McGovern's 1972 dark-horse candidacy, as had Shirley MacLaine, who in 1969 gathered Hollywood's liberal elite at her Encino home to meet Senator McGovern, a spokesman for anti-war and environmental sentiments, women's activities and civil rights.

McGovern had one fatal flaw for a politician. As a speaker he was so boring 'he made your skull feel like it was imploding', and he spoke in a tired whine. MacLaine, 'who could talk to anybody about anything', and Beatty, who was a compelling speaker, travelled with the candidate, introduced him, knocked on doors and spoke in living rooms, union halls, and college campuses in attempts to mitigate this shortcoming.

Nixon's celebrity entourage, made up of ageing luminaries such as Jack Benny, John Wayne, Lawrence Welk, Art Linkletter and Jack Warner, was wryly called 'The Hollywood Wax Museum'. Beatty helped to surround McGovern with predominantly young, hip, irreverent stars. After the Florida primary, with the campaign low on funds, Beatty proposed to raise money with a series of coast-to-coast rock concerts beginning in Los Angeles in April and concluding two months later in New York. He talked Streisand into appearing in the opening fund-raising concert on 15 April at the Los Angeles Forum, promising her that the security would be tighter than Fort Knox and that she could record the concert for commercial sale.

Although the show was also to feature James Taylor, Carole King and Quincy Jones (though not mentioned nor included on the subsequent album, giving the false impression that it had been a solo Streisand concert), she was to receive star billing. Eighteen thousand people bought tickets that cost up to $100 a seat, raising $300,000 for McGovern's campaign. As with the concert two years earlier for Bella Abzug, Streisand occupied the entire last half of the programme.

'If I would have known there would be so many people on the two sides of me I would have had my nose fixed,' she quipped when the applause finally quieted at her entrance. There were shouts of, 'Don't do it, Barbra!' and she said huskily into the microphone, 'Never!'

She appeared more relaxed than ever before in concert. She opened with Joe Raposo's 'Sing', one of Jason's favourite songs from *Sesame Street*. She was in top form and her renditions of 'Starting Here, Starting Now' and Jimmy Webb's 'Didn't We' displayed her great control in the use of voice dynamics. What distinguished this concert from earlier ones was her tremendous rapport with her audience. In the middle of the first act she took time out to engage in a five-minute monologue. Holding a glass of iced tea (supposedly booze) she took a loud slurp.

'Ya know – to conquer their fears some performers drink,' she said, taking another noisy swallow. 'I really hate the taste of liquor. Some take pills. I can't even swallow an aspirin. I believe performers should be strong. We should face our problems head on.' She withdrew from the skirt pocket of a black evening dress what looked like a joint and took a long drag. 'Is it still illegal?' she asked, and was answered by a loud 'Yes!'

'The way to conquer fear is to talk about it freely, get it out in the open and discuss it,' she went on conversationally, inhaled deeply and turned to David Shire, the conductor, and in a mock stoned voice added, 'Ya know that wonderful chord you just played? What was it? An F Minor seventh with a demented pinky on the fifth? It was really – high.' The audience roared their approval. Then, having milked the moment for what it was worth she became sober, although not yet entirely serious. 'As I spend a lot of time in L.A. I thought I'd dedicate the next song to [smoggy] L.A.' And she launched into a masterful arrangement of 'On a Clear Day (You Can See Forever)'. Marijuana, although she did smoke it occasionally, was not really part of her lifestyle. Bringing it into her performance in such an open manner was a calculated move to create an immediate rapport with the younger and freer members of the audience. The concert ended in a contemporary rendition of 'Happy Days Are Here Again', arranged by Don Hannah, complete with a female back-up group, that brought the audience to its feet and raised vociferous cheers.

Nixon placed her on his list of 'political enemies' following the concert and doom-sayers claimed that 'this enforced hollering' was destroying her voice and that she was relying too much on *cannabis* and would probably go 'the Judy Garland way' in a couple of years. None of this greatly disturbed her. With Jason and his nanny, she flew to New York two days after the concert, happy to be back in the newly refurbished penthouse.

With filming in Manhattan completed on 19 May, she had her staff pack over forty suitcases (supplies, clothes, gifts for the natives) and made the long flight that would take her with shocking swiftness to Africa and a completely alien culture. At first the women of the Samburu tribe in the section where the film company for *Up the Sandbox* set up their cameras refused to be photographed and had to be cajoled to play bit parts in the movie. They were suspicious, slow and sometimes unknowingly destructive, moving things about, interrupting shooting.

Irvin Kershner, the director, was an urbane, witty man, balding, tall and lean, a student of Zen and a man with some mystery about his early background. His most recent films, *The Luck of Ginger Coffey* (1964), *A Fine Madness* (1966), *The Flim Flam Man* (UK *One Born Every Minute* – 1967), and *Loving* (1970) had established his reputation as a director of great originality and sensitivity, but he was not bankable and although the members of the cast were all competent actors, Streisand was the only star in the movie. Once again, she was carrying a project on her back. This weakened any power Kershner might have had over her performance and the script. *Up the Sandbox* did not succeed as a film, either critically or commercially, but there is something in her performance – 'a deeper and warmer presence', *New Yorker* critic, Pauline Kael, called it – that for the first time on film revealed a great undeveloped actress. 'She hasn't the training to play the classical roles that still define how an actress's greatness is expressed,' Kael added. 'But in movies new ways may be found.'

Streisand was determined that would be the case. She was happier, far more comfortable, making movies than she ever had been appearing on the stage or in concert. Even bad reviews did not sting as sorely as they came so long after the completion of a movie, usually when she was already engaged in another production, hopes soaring – *This will be the one* – *the movie that will say all I want to convey without sacrificing commerciality.* She could not imagine herself ever giving up acting to sing in concert. 'I'm very fragile emotionally,' she said at the time. 'I'm not strong; I take it all so seriously, so hard, it becomes painful to me. I get palpitations, I get ill, I get sick to my stomach, I get terrible headaches. I just become a mess. I say, What do I need this aggravation for? It's much easier just to act.' By that she meant in movies where there was no audience except herself and a director to please, and an atmosphere that was calculated to help her perform her task to its best advantage in every possible way.

Acting met a deep personality need for her. It was a way of living, and not just a means of earning a living. Having reached the top, she maintained a fierce drive to become better, to improve. That meant never repeating herself. Her great problem was finding suitable roles in a script that excited her interest and in which she saw social overtones, something meaningful. She also needed a gifted director who was not too arrogant to accept her input but who at the same time was strong enough to provide the necessary perspective, experience and professionalism and who fully understood what it was she was after even though she often felt that she held the tail of a tiger who was swinging her into uncharted country.

She also possessed an equal need for a man who could bring to her personal life these same qualities. Streisand could grandstand as often as she liked about women's independence, sexual freedom and equality with men, but that was not what she really longed for. What she wanted – *what she had always wanted* – was a man who could stand up to her, who did not feel intimidated by her fame and her strength, who would love her unconditionally with raw sexual passion and not feel threatened by her intelligence and ambition, a man who would be the masculine to her feminine, the feminine to her masculine – a perfect match. But what man in her circle *was* such a person? So far she had not met one.

She was ready for a relationship, was desperately seeking one. This was a time of sexual freedom, pre-Aids and after the pill liberated woman's libido. There were flings, short affairs that bored her and fizzled out after only a few meetings. She feared that they went to bed with her just *because* she was Barbra Streisand, that they might never have been attracted to her otherwise. On 24 April 1972, she celebrated her thirtieth birthday. Diana retired from her job in New York and moved out to California with Roslyn. They were living in a two-bedroom apartment in Beverly Hills. Although Streisand had provided the funds and encouraged it, she suddenly had misgivings. Her mother's near proximity brought back painful childhood memories.

Believing *Up the Sandbox* was a well-made, major movie, she was shocked when it was badly received during its first sneak preview in San Francisco. After re-editing it, the film was released a week before Christmas 1972, to audience apathy and bad reviews.

'Barbra was baffled by the failure of *Up the Sandbox*,' Arthur Laurents recalled. 'She had been told that she was star insurance and she believed it. She could blame the financial fiascos of *On a Clear Day* and *Hello, Dolly!* on the mistakes of overproduction combined with a shrinking market for big musicals. But *Sandbox* was her own little picture. She had thought it would be a fine film and a valuable statement on the theme of women's liberation. Now her pride and joy was rejected. She was as depressed and belligerent as the mother of a whiz kid who had flunked the spelling bee over p-s-y-c-h-o-l-o-g-y.'

Arthur Laurents had written a film treatment for Ray Stark that would later evolve into *The Way We Were*, encompassing all the facets of the Streisand he had seen evolve from feisty Brooklyn girl to somewhat disillusioned Hollywood movie star in her prime and encapsulated them into Katie Morosky, the story's protagonist. After reading the fifty-page treatment, she called Laurents and shouted into the telephone: 'That's me! You've got it!'

# 22

AUNTED BY THE past, unable to shed it, the therapy sessions in
California continued. She could not let go of her father's death,
still felt deserted and cheated by it. She always imagined that her
childhood would have been much different had he lived, dwelled on it,
fantasised about what it would have been like. She viewed her early years in a
negative light, the cause of great unhappiness and pain. In one session when
her early past was under discussion, the analyst touched her hand and she
broke down and sobbed, leaning against the woman's shoulder. But the ache
did not go away, she held it close to her like an injured child. We are often
formed from what was missing in our childhood, not what we had, and Manny
Streisand's tragic early death could well have been responsible for her desperate
need to achieve, to be someone, to make the name *Streisand* one to be remembered and respected. Her extraordinary success was a tribute to her father's too
brief life, but it never seemed to satisfy her own needs.

Things might well have been different had Manny Streisand lived. She might
have been content to be daddy's girl, another man's wife, a mother to their
children, or she might have felt deprived of her independence, of the right to
fulfil her own ambitions. She was wise enough, in touch with herself enough,
to know that, and still she could not let go. It was not as though Manny
Streisand's death and her personal loss were all that was on her mind. She
was caught up in the snares of stardom, surrounded – as Arthur Laurents
commented – 'by those blue-suited men'.

'Ray was looking for a property for Barbra,' Laurents recalls of this time
frame. 'She wasn't mad about him and she wanted to get out of their contract
and he was getting desperate. He came to see me in New York. He had an idea,
a sort of combination of *Sound of Music* and another movie – you know the
way Hollywood producers do. It was impossible but I told him I'd think about
a story. I'm very good at whipping up something and I did get a story fixed in
my mind. On my way up to see Barbra [at the Ardsley] I thought, "This is
terrible." When I got there I said, "I'm not going to tell it to you. It's awful."

' "Well, what are you going to do?" she asked.

' "Oh, I don't know, if I think of something, I'll write it." She then asked me to give her a list of books to read and I wrote out a list which included Solzhenitsyn's *The First Circle* and *Cancer Ward* [1968]. Later, he got the Nobel Prize [1970] and she called me and said, "Hey! Your guy won!"

' "Did you read any of them?" I asked.

' "No. Too big a mountain to climb," she replied.

'Anyway, the story that finally came to me was *The Way We Were*. I knew a girl at Cornell, whose name was – believe it or not – Fanny Price, who was rather like Barbra and she was in the YCL [Young Communist League]. I dabbled in that and I knew a lot about the Hollywood witch-hunts.[1] Then I was very attached to Jigee Viertel[2] and I combined the two women. I wrote a treatment and gave it to Ray, who was still in New York. He got on a plane and called me when he arrived in Los Angeles. "It's wonderful. I want to do it!" he said.

'Ray sent it to Barbra to read – she was well under the influence of Cis Corman by then. They were close friends – knew each other from the early sixties. Barbra trusted her judgment, and now Cis was her right hand, reading scripts, helping to develop properties. I think Cis had a great influence in what Barbra chose to do. Anyway, Barbra made a curious remark. There's something in that treatment that Katie never used four-letter words until she went to Hollywood, and Barbra said, "That's me!" She can be surprisingly prudish, but that hardly seemed the case. I've always thought she sort of invented herself.

'She loved it. I suggested Sydney Pollack as a director, although I didn't know him at the time, because I had just seen *They Shoot Horses, Don't They?*, which I liked. Pollack was very close to Robert Redford [whom he had directed in the adaptation of Tennessee Williams's *This Property Is Condemned* (1966)], and so that was the way they eventually got Redford, but not without a struggle.

'Barbra had changed, become very Hollywood. When I was working on the first draft of the script, instead of discussing the part, she wanted to know how many changes of hairdos and clothes she would go through in the years the script covered. She asked if she could wear jeans at any point in the story. I realised she was indeed the idealistic Katie put through the Hollywood grind, but the early curiosity was no longer there. There was a time when you could talk to Barbra for hours on any subject and be constantly stimulated intellectually. Now she was beginning to bore me.'

Laurents's relationship to Streisand was on an entirely new level here – star and screenwriter, the latter a replaceable commodity in Hollywood, whereas

---

[1] Arthur Laurents had been blacklisted during the early years of the hearings of the Hollywood Un-American Activity Committee.

[2] Virginia Jigee Viertel, Peter Viertel's wife, previously married to Budd Schulberg, who was active in Hollywood political life during the 1940s.

a performer of Barbra Streisand's bankability was not. 'They were insecure about the first draft and they fired me,' Laurents recalled. 'Sydney called me and said that he had bad news, that Ray was firing me. "But, you're the director," I replied. Sydney said he could do nothing. A half-hour later Ray called and said Sydney was firing me, and he, the producer, could do nothing.' They brought in eleven writers in all, including well-known Hollywood scribes Dalton Trumbo, Francis Coppola, Judith Rasco, Alvin Sargent and one of Streisand's former brief *flings* from earlier times, David Rayfiel. Paddy Chayefsky and Herb Gardner, both from New York, were consulted. 'They told Ray they wouldn't touch it, it was wonderful, to leave it alone,' Laurents added. 'But Ray and Sydney started to muck around with it. It was really painful because I cared a great deal about that story. Much of it was from my own life and was about the witch-hunt which they knew nothing about. A lot of the rewriting was to make Redford's part bigger.

'Sydney would never let me meet Redford. It was very odd. He gave me a tape of a conversation they had about the script. Why he gave it to me, I don't know. People do self-destruct. At one point on the tape, Redford shouted, "But her part's bigger!" I told Sydney, "I know how you feel about Redford, but the story is hers. No matter what you do you can't change that, but you can hurt it."

'They started shooting and got into trouble and Ray called me. By then I was over the pain, but I was also over the Walter Mitty dream. It wasn't pleasurable. It was uncomfortable and, of course, I *really* wasn't over it. I still cared about it. I asked for a lot of money. I also said, "I'll come out there and tell you what I think and if you don't like it, I'll come right back." It was an armed truce.' Laurents returned to the project and received full credit.

'The person who was terrific was Barbra,' he asserts. 'She's like a pack-rat, you know? She saves every line of every script. She kept saying, "What about this? What about that?' She fought to keep meaningful things in the script – [the political viewpoints, shadings in the relationship between the two main characters]. Redford glared at me the whole time. I thought the reason was because I was not building his part up. He behaved badly, but that goes with the territory. You can't expect decent behavior from a movie star or anyone else in the industry who stays and lives in Hollywood. They're too insecure. They're afraid. You have to make the first move. You're not saying, "Hello," I'm not saying, "Hello." '

The *We* of the title are two Cornell University classmates, impassioned radical Katie Morosky, a Jewish activist with the Young Communist League from New York, and a Wasp jock from Virginia, Hubbell Gardiner, who is a writer – two people ill-mated but sexually drawn to each other, Katie more than he. She is attracted to the fairy-tale prince in Hubbell, he is mesmerised by her energy, moral conviction and drive. They marry and Katie pushes Hubbell, who has shown a natural talent for the written word, to become a great writer with a social message. They move to Hollywood when he signs a contract to adapt a novel he has written for the screen. Once in glitterland, by Katie's standards he sells out, writing commercial trash, while she becomes more deeply involved in left-wing politics. Disillusioned, Katie returns to New York with their infant daughter, divorces him and eventually remarries a nice, Jewish accountant and works for liberal causes while Hubbell goes on to become a successful television writer. They meet one more time and realise that they cannot return to the past.

Close comparison could be made between the love relationship of Katie and Hubbell and Fanny and Nicky Arnstein; the man being more attractive than the woman, who is the brighter of the two.

Extremely selective in his acting roles, the bronzed, square-jawed, sky-eyed Redford was Hollywood's current top heart throb.[3] When first approached by Pollack, Redford adamantly refused the part. The character, he claimed quite correctly, was a man lacking conviction or purpose. The film belonged to Katie, and Redford was concerned about this.

'He didn't like the script, he didn't like the character, he didn't like the concept of the film, he didn't think the politics and love story would mix,' Sydney Pollack says. 'There was nothing about it he liked and in fact, he kept saying to me, "Pollack, you're crazy! What are you doing this for?"' But Redford's trust of Pollack's instincts was strong. 'Maybe he sees something I don't see,' Redford told his wife Lola.

'It had to be those two together [Redford and Streisand],' Pollack continues. 'Barbra understood that. They were so prototypical of what the story was about.'

Pollack had badgered Redford for six months to play Hubbell. He agreed to revise the script to strengthen Hubbell and his role so that it was as germane as Katie's to the picture. Ray Stark, realising the marquee value of Streisand *and* Redford, offered Redford a salary that exceeded Streisand's (the first and only time a co-star would receive more than she did) and a profit percentage of the film. Redford still waffled. Stark finally gave Pollack an ultimatum: If Redford did not agree by midnight 10 June 1972, he was making a deal the following day with Ryan O'Neal, actually Streisand's first choice for the role and for whom she briefly rekindled her affections. A half-hour before that deadline Pollack was on the telephone with Stark to tell him that Redford had agreed to play opposite Streisand.

---

[3] Redford had recently co-starred with Paul Newman in *Butch Cassidy and the Sundance Kid* (1969), and had starred in *Downhill Racer* (1969), *Tell Them Willie Boy is Here* (1969), *Little Fauss and Big Halsey* (1970). He was soon to make *The Candidate* (1972) and would be nominated in 1974 for his performance in *The Sting*, in which he also co-starred with Newman.

At the end of August, Streisand flew to New York, Jason in tow, and then drove up to the film's first location, Union College in Schenectady, New York, where they would remain for a month. By the time principal photography began on 18 September, mother and son were settled in a large, comfortably furnished Victorian house near the campus. Redford and Pollack had suites at the local Holiday Inn. Although there was no friction between the stars, Redford is rather laid-back as a personality and was often unnerved by Streisand's inability just to relax and *do it*. They had opposite acting styles. She liked to talk about a scene, rehearse it several times before the cameras rolled. Redford, an instinctive actor, prefers to create the scene on camera. Her relationship with O'Neal once again cold, she formed a crush on Redford. He was America the Beautiful and she carried that inner glow with her on to the set and before the camera. But Redford was a dedicated family man, his attitude towards her was reserved. This gave an edge to their performances that resulted in a highly charged sexual chemistry between them.

'I think with any small encouragement from Redford, Barbra would have had an affair with him in those early weeks of shooting in Schenectady,' a close member of the crew said. 'When we left Schenectady and set up in New York for the exteriors we shot there, she seemed edgy. Maybe it was her attraction to Redford, maybe just her concern with the progress of the picture. She is a compulsive worrier. By the time the company landed in L.A. for the West Coast and interior scenes, they [Redford and Streisand] seemed more ... connected, I guess. Which didn't seem to alleviate Barbra's constant agitation about the rightness or wrongness of a scene that they had just played or were about to play together.'

'She was in awe of Redford,' Laurents said. 'She was simply mesmerised because she found him so beautiful, and he was ever so pleasant because he thought he was stealing the movie away from her.'

This never did happen. Streisand held her ground, memorably in the early scene when Katie, naked, crawls into bed next to a drunk and almost comatose Hubbell, slowly inching near him until she is in his arms. He has sex with her as if on automatic. Then after he climaxes falls back asleep. 'It's me, Katie,' she says in an agonised whisper to the snoring, inert beautiful man whom she adores. The scene has great erotic power. Here is the insecure, unglamorous girl who seduces the golden man of her dreams and then realises he may never know he has made love to her.

Katie's character had a sympathetic vulnerability, the feminine part of her nature always betraying her need to stand by her man, the masculine to march with the drummer. This duality of temperament in the character she was playing carried over into Streisand's own attitude on the set. She was more unsure than usual, calling Pollack late at night in an apprehensive state to discuss the day's footage: did she play a particular scene right? Should they reshoot it the next morning? The angle of a close-up was too unflattering. How could Hubbell love such an unattractive woman? At the end of the picture she gave Pollack a gold watch engraved: 'For all those 11 o'clock phone calls'.

Pollack admired her insatiable need to understand the character she was playing. Originally intending to become an actor, he had studied with the New York theatre coach, Sandy Meisner, and in the 1950s appeared in several plays and television dramas. His first directorial work had been on television where in five years he directed eighty shows. Then in 1965 he directed *The Silver Thread*, a feature film starring Anne Bancroft. A traditionalist of sorts, his movies were mostly conventional in form, but not necessarily in point of view. He calls himself a romantic and certainly *The Way We Were* reflects it. His major film career took off with *They Shoot Horses, Don't They?* (1970) starring Jane Fonda in the role Streisand had not wanted to play – that of a failed actress driven by financial need into a dance marathon and who eventually commits suicide. The picture firmly established Pollack into the front ranks of American directors, but his early acting experience – from time to time he still appears in his own films, most memorably as Dustin Hoffman's agent in *Tootsie* – gave him a special knack for eliciting great performances from his actors. Streisand felt comfortable with him and respected his opinion, although it did not stop her from harassing him.

Pollack had retained much of the political debating that went on between Katie and Hubbell in Laurents's script. Then at the sneak preview at the Northpoint Theatre in San Francisco, Ray Stark decided the audience was bored during a six-minute scene that Laurents calls 'the entire motivation for Katie's leaving Hubbell', and told Pollack to cut it.

'I didn't even have the negative with me. I just made the cut with a razor blade on the positive print before previewing it the next night,' he said. The second preview was more successful. 'You could just feel it. The chunk that came out was never missed and the audience remained alert,' Pollack insists.

Laurents disagrees. 'It was all wrong. The climax of the picture is absolutely missing. It was cut. What you see now is Streisand and Redford at the beach house [in Malibu] and she has some line about how willy-nilly circumstances make one come to a decision, in her case to get a divorce. The audience seemed to have bought it. But originally there was a scene that preceded it where Hubbell came home from the studio and says, "The studio says they are going to fire me because I have a subversive wife. So unless you inform I'm out of work." And Katie answers, "Well, what if we get a divorce and you don't have a subversive wife." That's the whole point. He had never been involved with politics as she had and he was willing to ask her to be an informer – to destroy the lives of many innocent people – in order to hang on to his Hollywood career and the money that came with it. Katie was too principled for that. She could never betray her friends or her beliefs. Of course, she would leave him after he makes such an unconscionable request of her. They took it out, and nobody noticed. Nobody cared.'

Cast as a character modelled after extreme right-wing gossip columnist, Hedda Hopper, was former child star Marcia Mae Jones (*These Three, Heidi, The Adventures of Tom Sawyer, The Little Princess*), now in her fifties and considering a comeback. When she came on the set everyone, including Pollack, was kind to her. 'It was curious,' she recalled, 'at first I felt like I was home again. It was great. I was wearing this marvellous hat in the scene. Hopper was famous for her outrageous hats. She was also bitchy, dangerously so. It was a good bit, nothing more – although I received sixth billing even *after* being cut from the film. Streisand never came over to speak to me – the usual courtesy when an older performer is in a film. Nor did she ever speak to me. Very cold. The set had a chilling feeling. I had never experienced anything quite like it. I was relieved when it was over.'

Sometimes the set was like that, usually not when Redford was on hand. Streisand was serious about her work and did not waste time with niceties. As Redford said, 'Working with Barbra was just that – *work*.' Pollack added, 'Barbra wanted precision; Redford, spontaneity. Barbra likes lengthy rehearsals and multiple takes, Redford is better in his early takes. After that, he just gets bored,' Pollack added.

The film is filled with illogical plot devices, a confusing chronology and blatant tear-jerking emotion. Yet it not only works, it has a life of its own, not unlike *Casablanca*, where the chemistry that exists between two charismatic stars sustains a familiar story. Not only does *The Way We Were* have a memorable, lushly romantic title song by Marvin Hamlisch, it is a three-handkerchief love story. Sentimental tales, such as *An Affair to Remember, Seventh Heaven, A Star Is Born*, are never highly regarded by the critics, although they are the movies that often survive as classics.

*The Way We Were* would become one of Streisand's most memorable films. Something about it reaches out and touches you. 'It flows like velvet,' Rex Reed, one of a minority of critics who liked the movie, wrote. 'That's why the movie is so likeable. We lost a lot of innocence in the dark movie palace of our youth. *The Way We Were* reclaims it for us. Years from now, in some futuristic movie museum, it just might be one of the movies we'll be looking at and remembering with fondness.' He turned out to be prophetic.

Although there was every reason for the film – 'a torpedoed ship full of gaping holes' – to be a disaster, the chemistry between the two stars, so seemingly mismatched, kept it mystically afloat. 'Redford's the best leading man she's ever had,' Marilyn Bergman recalled, 'and she knew it. Alan [Bergman, her husband and co-lyric writer] and I sat with her when she first saw the movie. She kept nudging me and saying how great *he* was.'

A tremendous bonding had occurred between Streisand and the Bergmans during the work on *The Way We Were*. Thirteen years Streisand's senior, Marilyn Bergman had become the older sister she had never had. Calm, intelligent, her soft voice persuasive, sure, Bergman was a woman of uncommon good sense, supremely talented, able smoothly to handle her creative partnership with her husband, motherhood (the Bergmans were the parents of a teenage daughter), political activism and friendship with even-handed intensity. Streisand admired her talent, her opinions and felt easy in her company.

In 1968 the Bergmans had won the Oscar for their lyrics to 'The Windmills of Your Mind' from the Steve McQueen–Faye Dunaway film, *The Thomas Crown Affair*. They were now contracted to collaborate with Hamlisch on the title song for *The Way We Were*. Hamlisch, who scored the background music as well, had employed the melody as a love theme throughout the film, musical advice that had contributed much to the picture's mood and cohesion. The first concept of the song was written in the minor mode. Hamlisch quickly shifted it into the major. 'If I'd left it in the minor mode, it might have told you too much in advance that Streisand and Redford were never going to get together,' he said. 'So I wrote a melody that was sad, but also had a great deal of hope in it.' The song was originally to be sung by Streisand over the last scene where Hubbell and Katie run into each other in front of the Plaza Hotel in New York and realise that they have no future only the past. Believing the lyrics would dilute the impact, it was not recorded over the scene and titles.

This songless version was shown at the first sneak preview and when Hamlisch looked around and saw how unmoved the audience was when the lights came up, he begged Columbia to let him rescore the ending with Streisand singing the Bergmans' lyrics. The cost of a rerecording session was prohibitive as it involved fifty-five musicians and Columbia was now in a situation where they were approaching insolvency – their stock, due to failed films, high costs and impropriety in management having fallen two-thirds in value since the start of principal photography on *The Way We Were*. Finally, after much discussion, they relented. Then he had to convince Streisand, who thought the song was too sentimental. 'So is "My Funny Valentine",' he told her. 'I hate "My Funny Valentine",' she snapped back.

Hamlisch and the Bergmans wrote a second, more complicated and less romantic number. Streisand made tracks of both songs which were separately scored over the last scene and the final titles. Both versions were shown to Stark, Pollack and the Columbia executives, and a vote was taken. Streisand was the only one who voted against 'The Way We Were', one of the few times that her musical judgment was wrong. The song, with its rueful lyrics, longing to replay the past, coupled with Hamlisch's moving melody, makes a memorably, poignant ending to the film. It is the long moment when Hubbell rushes across the street to hold Katie, seemingly for ever – oblivious to his fiancée waiting nearby – breaking our hearts as his own is so obviously shattered. Katie's we know has been broken long ago. And although we feel each of these two lovers goes on with their lives, it is the way they were that they – and we – will remember.

*The Way We Were* placed Streisand in her own romantic time warp. Elliott was now married to Jenny. His finances shaky, he had moved back to the small Village apartment on Morton Street and Jason now had a half-brother. Pierre and Margaret Trudeau were the parents of two children. Streisand was that loathsome cliché – the great star who came home to an empty bed. She turned her concentration, as she always did, to work. Five years had passed since her last television special, and in the spring of 1972, CBS insisted she honour her final commitment to them. Ken and Mitzie Welch, who had been responsible for her classic rendition of 'Happy Days Are Here Again', contributed the concept of the show – *Barbra Streisand . . . and Other Musical Instruments* – and would supply the special material and musical arrangements. The original design had been to team Streisand with some of the world's greatest musicians – Pablo Casals, Isaac Stern, James Galway. CBS rejected this idea but agreed to a format that would include musicians and music from various countries. The network also demanded that Streisand have either one guest from what they submitted as List A, or two from List B, or three from List C – 'Like a Chinese menu', Mitzie Welch quipped. Streisand and the Welches quickly agreed on Ray Charles, so there was no need to go any further.

Streisand first rehearsed some of her solos in the living room of the Carol-wood Drive house. Mitzie Welch remembered 'an antiques dealer who kept calling her and coming over and showing her things. Right in the middle of a phrase she would jump up and go look at things and come right back to the exact place where she had left off. It was amazing. When you work with Barbra you work with a true artist. She has ears like nobody else has. She seems to hear sounds more acutely. Nothing slips past her.

'One day she came down to the beach [where the Welches had a home]. Jason was friends with our daughter. Barbra had a bathing suit on and I stood and watched her as she ran across the sand. She moved in almost a poetic rhythm, not of this world, unbelievably sexual, not like other people. Her physical presence was tremendous. I said to Ken, "She's really beautiful," and he agreed.'

They recorded and scored a few numbers in Los Angeles before going to London where the show was to be televised. 'We hired all kinds of ethnic musicians – Ghanaian, Indian, Irish bagpipers, Turks and an eleven-year-old British pianist [Dominic Savage]. It was really wild,' Ken remembered. 'Some of them didn't speak English but it was wonderful how we managed to communicate. The two numbers that stand out in my memory was "I Got

Rhythm" with the Irish bagpipers – their beats are not the same. It's not 4/4 time! and a symphony of household appliances – washing machines, sewing machines, orange juicers, vacuum cleaners and Barbra with an electric tooth-brush. Very hard. You had to dial a note and if you had it once you might never get it again. We went an inch at a time. Barbra, dressed as a Turkish belly dancer, sang "People" with a group of Turkish musicians playing their national instruments. Ray Charles did a magnificent job of "Look What They've Done to My Song" and he and Barbra sang "Cryin' Time Again" together. Larry Gelbart, Mitzie and I wrote the continuity.'

The show took eleven gruelling weeks to film. Midway through Streisand entered into an intense affair with a wealthy American, married and the father of two children, who was in Britain promoting his business interests there. They had met through one of her financial advisors. Vital, Jewish, about fifteen years older than Streisand, he had no connection with the entertainment industry. He visited the television set several times but the press were kept from knowing his name and their liaison was conducted in an otherwise secret fashion.

One of Streisand's English friends recalls that she was so in love 'she glowed with it. I think he was very important to her. He was a strong personality, a take-charge sort of man, extremely intelligent. He owned a chain of stores, masses of real estate, sat on the boards of several large companies – very impressive. He had a painful family situation that made divorce uncon-scionable – at least for him. I think Barbra admired that trait in him although it was not easy for her to accept. She spent almost all of her free time with him while she was shooting in London and I know they rendezvoused often when she first returned to the States. I understood her attraction. He was a charismatic personality, very, *very* sexy. But she was really in love and that could only have been self-destructive because he had no wish to leave his family and it seemed sheer madness for Barbra to be in a relationship where she could not even be seen in public with the man she loved.

'We were quite friendly at that time, went shopping together – things like that. She was truly in love. But as the time came for both of them to leave Britain, she was – well – troubled. She was afraid that once they were back in the States where his wife and children lived and where her celebrity would be more inhibiting than abroad, it would be difficult for them to continue their affair. I felt great sympathy for her. At times, she possesses this great vulnerability. There's something – *wistful* – about her, and you think here is one of the most famous, richest women in the world and underneath there is such sadness. Through the years she has renewed this affair but nothing changed – he remains married and Barbra – her fame has never diminished.'

Work was the answer to a broken heart and what better than to be engaged in a comedy? She began filming *For Pete's Sake* shortly after her return to Los

Angeles. The film, written by Stanley Shapiro and Maurice Richlin was produced by Shapiro and Marty Erlichman for Ray Stark and Columbia, and directed by Englishman Peter Yates (*Bullitt*, 1968; *Murphy's War*, 1971; *The Hot Rock*, 1972[4]; *The Friends of Eddie Coyle*, 1973). Streisand's role was that of a hard-up Brooklyn housewife who falls into the clutches of a loan shark and finds herself involved with a call-girl racket, the Mafia, and urban cattle rustling, all enacted with farcical humour: outrageous disguises, pratfalls, wisecracks and corny, old-time comedic set-ups (hiding a man in a closet when a husband returns home unexpectedly). Since *What's Up, Doc?* was proving to be one of Streisand's top money-makers, Columbia and Erlichman believed another madcap comedy was in order. However, *For Pete's Sake* turned out not to have the same winning elements of humour.

For her role as Henry (short for Henrietta), Streisand wanted a short, gamine hairdo that would also be comfortable under the many wigs she had to wear. Just before the picture went before the camera, she attended a games party at the Welches, who both loved puzzles, charades and word play. 'Julie Andrews, Blake Edwards, Carol Burnett, Tony Perkins – all good games players were there,' Mitzie recalled. 'I would have had Stephen Sondheim if he was in town! And there was Harvey Corman [not related to Cis] and his wife Donna. Well, before the party I had had my hair done at a chic beauty salon in Beverly Hills owned and run by Jon Peters. So had Donna Corman. When Jon did my hair he said, "I know you work with Barbra. I have to meet her. I want to know where her head's at." I laughed at that and he said, "I mean it. Fix me up. Let me do her hair or something."

'I told him I didn't have anything to do with her personal life. So a few days later she comes to our house for the party and she sees Donna with this very short wonderful haircut and she said, "Who did that?" to me. Barbra some-times speaks in staccato sentences not explaining a lot. I said, "Did what?"

' "That haircut. That's what I want for *For Pete's Sake*." Actually, it then had the awful title *July Pork Bellies*. "I want that kind of hair." "Oh well, the guy that did that wants to meet you," I told her. And I gave her his number. The next thing I know they call us from Mexico – "Hi. We're here together." I said, "I guess you liked the haircut!" She laughed. The next time I saw her she looked marvellous, hair cropped short, very gamine – and she was head-over-heels in love.'

---

[4] In the UK called *How To Steal a Diamond In Four Easy Lessons*.

# 23

S HE HAD NEVER met anyone quite like Jon Peters. Forget any stereotypic ideas of a hairdresser. Peters, with his wolfish smile, sharp eyes concealed behind dark shades and a stallion's mane of thick, black hair, looked more like a young mafioso. He drove through the imposing front gates of her Carolwood Drive house in a flashy red Ferrari. The car was well known in the high-priced hills above Sunset Boulevard. His fee for a haircut and styling ran into the hundreds, but he seldom made a house call to a first-time client. Streisand was different. She was important to him. He could have more women than he wanted. He was rich enough – worth several million dollars with his three salons and the beauty products that bore his name. What he wanted was class A entry into the film industry. Once he had that, he planned to make important pictures. He saw his future as a contemporary Darryl Zanuck – a movie-maker with power and pzzazz. He never doubted his ability to take the precarious jump from hair impresario to movie mogul. All he needed was the right connection.

He left the car on the curved driveway just below the front doorway of Streisand's house and slung a Gucci bag with his equipment over his shoulder. He wore tight designer jeans which left little doubt about his attributes. When she joined him in the living room twenty minutes later, he was about to leave. She apologised for being late. 'Don't ever do it again,' he grinned and removed his sunglasses. She noted that his dark, quick eyes took full inventory of the measurements of her body. 'You know you're a cute little thing with a very foxy body and a great ass,' he said as she turned to lead him to her dressing room where he was to cut her hair.

He was testing. She could throw him out. She did not.

Five years younger than Streisand, Peters had dropped the *h* in John as she had cut the middle *a* in Barbara. He was smart, quick and charismatic. Women were drawn to him and he used his hormonal appeal on them to his advantage. In and out of trouble in his youth, he was streetwise and at the same time possessed an arrogant charm. Born twenty-six years earlier in Van Nuys, California to a Cherokee Indian father, a short-order cook who died when he was a child, and an Italian mother, a hairdresser whose family owned Pagano's, a well-known Beverly Hills beauty salon, Peters did time in a reform school for petty larceny before he was twelve, the youngest juvenile in his group. During the day he had done road work – dug ditches, helped lay pipes, cleared out fallen branches and trees – under armed supervision. At night he was shackled to his bed. None of his youthful trials had broken his spirit, instead they had powered his drive to show the world he was someone to be reckoned with. Upon his release, his uncles gave him a job in their beauty salon, washing hair and sweeping up the cuttings. 'I'd come in and see all these women,' he recalled, 'and I thought, "Wow! this is it"' A year later, in 1961, at fourteen, he borrowed $120 from his mother, dropped out of school and made his way by Greyhound bus across the country to New York.

His macho manner and dark, good looks made him appear older. With some fast talking (his special talent) he got a job in a sleazy all-night hair salon where his speciality became dyeing the hair of whores to match their poodles. He learned quickly how important hair is to a woman, how intimate and reliant her relationship can be to a person who can make her look better than even she thought possible. He studied styling, paying for his lessons by boxing quasi-professionally, married 'an older woman' of fifteen and then began salon climbing from good to 'in' to tony to top.

On returning to the Coast, he had his marriage annulled, went to work as a stylist for Gene Shacove (the model for Warren Beatty's hairdressing lothario in *Shampoo*), and wooed a client, actress Lesley Anne Warren who had appeared with Elliott Gould in *Drat the Cat!* and was the lead in the Rodgers and Hammerstein 1965 television production of *Cinderella*. Slim, dark, perky with a pleasant singing voice and manner, Warren had dreams of becoming a film star, which Peters encouraged. They were married in 1967 shortly after she was cast in a supporting role in the Disney musical *The Happiest Millionaire*, which starred Fred MacMurray, Greer Garson and Tommy Steele. Peters became her manager, promoter and agent. He believed he could make her into another Judy Garland, overlooking the obvious – that her voice was not memorable – and forgetting that Garland *was* a star when she married Sid Luft, who went on to promote her later career. Warren gave birth to their son Christopher in 1967 and her career, despite Peters' constant promoting, merely ambled along. It was clear that though she had talent and was likeable, she did not have star quality.[1]

In 1970 the decade of the hairdresser entered in full swing. Peters became an entrepreneur. Los Angeles and Valley salons were fairly stodgy, not like the newer ones in Manhattan with their sophisticated black and white decor,

---

[1] Lesley Anne Warren made a stunning 'comeback' in *Victor/Victoria* (1982) in the comedic role of James Garner's Chicago showgirl mistress, for which she was nominated for an Academy Award as Best Supporting Actress.

where stylists, *sans* drab uniforms, wielded blow-dryers with the speed and grace of fencing experts. He managed to raise $100,000, opened two sleekly modern salons in upper-middle-class San Fernando Valley sections, a thirty-minute drive over the canyons from Beverly Hills, introduced the blow-dryer, hired only attractive young operators and stylists and became the American Vidal Sassoon, 'cutting, cutting, *cutting*,' which he claimed, 'reached in me a creative side that had never been explored'.

'Jon is smart, fucking smart, big-time smart,' a friend elaborates. 'He's a fucking genius with money. He knows just how to parlay a small investment into a gold mine, how to raise money without putting a dime up himself. He was a college-of-one, self-taught. His mind is always working, never placed on hold.'

It did not take him long to see where the blow-dry action would pay the most. He opened the Jon Peters Salon on glamorous Rodeo Drive, one of the most famous high-priced streets in the world. His clientèle were the young, the beautiful, the rich, the famous, the idle divorcees and the neglected wives of Hollywood CEOs. *Have blow-dryer, will travel*, was how he was described by many of his friends and peers. He became known in the short span of a year for his sexual prowess as much as for his chutzpah and business ability. Rumour mongers barked at his heels like hungry dogs (most of them clients he had not romanced), saying he was 'having it off' with many of the alluring actresses, models and Hollywood wives he attended. With three salons, a wig factory and two beauty supply companies he was, at twenty-five, the head of a $10 million empire with 300 employees, and estranged from a less-than-patient Lesley Anne Warren.

An old friend of Peters claims, 'He comes out of the Hugh Hefner paradigm. Girls are sort of like, "I can have all this, so why not?"'

Walter Yetnikoff, who was head of CBS Records, put it more crudely. 'We're both equally crazy, but Jon is a better penis lapper than me – or so the reputation goes.'

Streisand took to Peters right away but she was wary. 'Stop coming after me,' she told him shortly after their first encounter. 'You're not my type.' When he asked to see her the following Sunday she told him she was playing tennis. He had never played the game before but showed up with a racquet and, not even knowing how to score, beat her. 'Then I told him I liked more distinguished men,' she later recalled. 'Men who smoked pipes. So he comes over wearing a velvet jacket over a T-shirt and jeans, glasses and a pipe. He even traded in his Ferrari for a Jag. Jon never lets up.' And constantly he told her how great she looked; why didn't she show her body more in the movies? He dug her body, thought she had a great ass, terrific legs. No one had told her that before.

Their sexual draw was powerful, her need to feel young and desirable –

strong. She did, indeed, like the haircut he gave her and asked him to design the wigs she had to wear in *For Pete's Sake*, agreeing he would have screen credit.

'How about Mexican food?' he asked after making a dinner date.

'Swell. Love it,' she replied.

'Be ready at five.'

'I usually don't eat that early,' she responded.

'You usually don't have to fly to Mexico first,' he countered.

It was a bold move, very theatrical and she accepted. They flew down in a private plane that he had chartered to a picturesque beach resort near Acapulco. That was when she called Mitzie and Ken Welch.

With amazing swiftness their relationship moved from fling, to affair, to live-together lovers. Streisand was besotted. Sex played a major role, but there was more. She was ready for an affair that did not have to be hidden from the world. In the beginning she was rebelling against the restrictions of her recent relationship with a married man. After all, why should she – Barbra Streisand independent woman and star – align herself with a man who could never be fully hers? The survivor in her fought for better and won. Peters was one of the few men who was her emotional, if not her intellectual, equal. And even though she knew she could never dominate him, that they were certain to wage a power war if they were to become a couple, she sensed that under the bravado, the prima donna theatrics, the hustler's moves and the streetwise patter, lay insecurity and that was something with which she could closely identify.

'I came from the street, from jail and all that,' he once said. 'I'd go into the salon and see ladies with diamonds, sophisticated people from good families ... I used to throw up before work every morning because I was so frightened.' He'd been that way in the boxing ring, and still fought a tough fight winning most of his bouts. Outsiders did not see him as insecure, any more than they saw Streisand in that light. Like her, he was the ultimate survivor, armour-plating his vulnerability with brassy self-promotion.

They spent whatever free time she had while making *For Pete's Sake* on his ten-acre Paradise Cove ranch near Malibu, a hybrid mixture of frontier crudeness and Bel Air chic. Expensive country fabrics covered the large custom-made couches. There was a state-of-the-art sound system and hand-rubbed pegged-wood floors. A Jacuzzi whirlpool bath was constructed from an old wine vat. There were two corrals and a large riding paddock for jumping horses. Streisand, an urban creature who had hated camp and outdoor life as a child, learned to ride Cupid, the lively horse Peters gave her as a present. Spending less and less time in her Holmby Hills home, she worked in the garden he set aside for her at the ranch growing orchids, wore T-shirts and dungarees, helped to feed his pet lion which he kept in a cage but took for walks around the ranch on a chain lead, did her own laundry, baked bread and went on day trips to the public beach in Malibu with Jason, now seven, and Peters's son, Christopher, who was five.

'He makes me happy,' she told close friends when asked *Why, Peters?* and who perceived him as a master con man, albeit one with certain appeal and quick intelligence. Some observers, who believed they detected an undercurrent of violence in his character, were fearful for Streisand. But there was no denying how much more relaxed, natural and content she appeared. She seemed transformed by an inner shine. 'Jon is a very macho man,' she proudly declared. 'He's got scars all over his hands from fighting.' His seeming lack of fear and brazen disregard for social decorum filled her with admiration. He once carried her out of a party that he wished to leave, propped on his shoulders, refusing to let go of his hold on her despite her laughing but insistent protest.

He accompanied her on location to New York where *For Pete's Sake* began shooting in September 1973, taking a suite at the Plaza Hotel while she officially occupied the Central Park West penthouse. Although separated, legally he and Lesley Anne Warren were still married. Professionally, he was responsible for Streisand's wigs and hairstyles. Privately, he took charge of her appearance, choosing younger, sexier clothes for her, advising her on projects, playing new music, new sounds for her to consider to record. They conferred a great deal on and off the set and the gossip columnists picked it up. By the time they returned to Hollywood their affair was an open secret and they gave a press interview where they admitted they were in love and were to be regarded as a couple. Streisand was glowing, happy, and let him do most of the talking.

Having successfully taken over her private life, Peters moved in to pilot her professional endeavours. Unlike her relationship with Elliott, she relied on Peters's business and creative judgment. It would not be long before he would sell out his hairdressing empire at a good price and engage his talents for hustling and promotion in the film business under Streisand's aegis. He warned her from the outset of *For Pete's Sake*'s poor potential. The story was ridiculous. In the early rushes, which he attended with her, it was obvious that there was no on-screen chemistry between Streisand and Michael Sarrazin, her leading man. She had turned down the strong leads in *Klute* and *Cabaret* that had won respectively both Jane Fonda and Liza Minnelli Academy Awards. Clearly, Peters suggested, she needed guidance that she was not getting from Marty Erlichman, her agents, Freddie Fields and Sue Mengers or Cis Corman. The reviews when the film was released the following June proved his instinct about *For Pete's Sake* was sound.

'Streisand looks like Jerry Lewis with cleavage as she runs through the kind of silly plot that Lewis thrives on. But Lewis *is* a genuine crazy,' Paul Zimmerman of *Newsweek* wrote. 'Streisand, saddled with a script beneath burning, comes out an abrasive wise-mouth who cannot plead comic insanity.'

With Peters at her shoulder, Streisand had been striving to navigate her career into forward action since the previous December. He had sat in on the recording sessions for her solo *The Way We Were* single and the album with the same title,[2] helping her decide which tracks were best, offering suggestions which she respected and incorporated. Released in November 1973, the single reached Number One in the charts by mid-February 1974 and remained in the top ten hits for five months. By March 1974, the album was also Number One. The single won Streisand *Billboard*'s award as the top single of the year. The song was also given a Grammy as Song of the Year, and in April earned Marvin Hamlisch an Academy Award for Best Film Song.[3]

On Valentine's Day, 1974, Streisand and Peters bought in addition to the ranch, a rustic eight-acre property in adjacent Ramirex Canyon, a gorge in the Santa Monica Mountains which rises out of the Pacific at Malibu. 'It had aluminum sliding doors and it was white stucco. In other words, it was really crummy,' is how she described the original house. The place did have beautiful views and seemed to offer them privacy which was impossible at the house on Carolwood Drive where fans peered over the gates trying to catch a glimpse of her. In a major renovation campaign to improve, enlarge and personalise the new dual-owned property, Peters hired a professional group of toy makers from Mill Valley, near San Francisco, to work on the inside construction because of their wood-carving talents. They lived in the guest house (which would later also be restructured) as they worked, panelling the walls in old, scorched and oiled wood, adding clear and stained leaded-glass panels to many of the windows and building in beds, cupboards and cabinets. In a short time, the house took on the appeal of Geppetto's workshop.

'The kids' rooms were all built in, which was so great,' Streisand recalled. 'Both boys had ladders to climb, one to a loft, one to a bunk bed. Each room was different. My son's was in red velvet with the wood. And Christopher's was done in an Aztec print.'

She was in a deeply romantic mode. At night she lit the house with dozens of candles and she and Peters curled up on an upholstered mattress that

---

[2] This album was later retitled *Barbra Streisand Featuring 'The Way We Were' and 'All in Love Is Fair'*, when Rastar Productions, producers of the Columbia film, filed suit against Columbia Records charging breach of contract as it was in direct competition with the soundtrack album, and maintained that record buyers would be misled into buying Streisand's solo album under a false premise. The suit was settled out of court and the album title changed.

[3] Hamlisch was the first individual ever to win three Oscars in one night – Best Song and Best Original Score – *The Way We Were*; Best Score Adaptation – *The Sting*, arranged from music by Scott Joplin.

occupied the space opposite the twelve-foot stone fireplace wall in the living room. Lush bouquets of fresh garden flowers scented all the main rooms in the house. They made love, talked endlessly, fought fierce battles, Streisand almost always ending up in tears and with apologies the following day, scenes witnessed by friends surprised to see her be the one to give in. She listened to Peters's advice, trusted his opinions on film scripts that were submitted to her, discussed the possibility that he produce her next record and that they both become involved in the production of her second film for First Artists. Jon Peters was now in the Barbra Streisand business.

A small theatre production of *Yentl* in Brooklyn which she read about renewed her interest in the project, but no studio was yet ready to back an ethnic period picture with transvestite undertones, even with Streisand in it. She still owed one more film to Ray Stark, who sent her over a sequel to *Funny Girl* titled *Funny Lady*, written by Jay Presson Allen who had won an Academy Award for her adaptation of *Cabaret*. 'He'll have to drag me to court before I do this,' she declared, refusing at first to read the script. Finally, when she did, and Peters had as well, she agreed to appear in the film. 'This is better than *Funny Girl*,' she said, reversing her decision. Unlike the earlier rejected version, Presson's screenplay depicted an independent woman valiantly struggling in a man's world, a theme with which she identified.

Principal photography would begin in the spring of 1974 just when she was settling into the remodelled house, now called the Barn. For the first time she felt resentment at having to be a mother and 'wife' with a career.

Moving into the Barn with Peters and the two boys gave her a seductive taste at what really being 'Sadie, Sadie, Married Lady' could be like. At heart she was an extremely private person, not much of a party-goer, terrified of crowds. Strangely, although it might seem that she had one of the most recognisable faces in the world, usually when she took the boys shopping or to the public beach, people did not know her. 'They think I'm too small or too short, or what would I be doing on a public beach?' she said. 'If I were Barbra Streisand would I be on a public beach? So they look at me kind of funny, or they say, "Boy, you look a lot like her." They don't even ask me if I *am* her. And I say, "Yeah, yeah, I've been told that before." Sometimes I do these elaborate lies: "No, I'm not her. What would I be doing here if I were her? I wish I had her money. Ha, ha, ha." Sometimes it's easier to just tell the truth. "Yes, I am her." But it *is* a pain in the ass to have to sign things.'

She had a small clique of close friends – Marilyn and Alan Bergman, Cis Corman and her husband, Marty Erlichman and his wife, Shirley MacLaine. They drove out to the Barn and she helped cook for them with her 'beloved Grace' – the housekeeper who had lived in her household since Jason was an infant and whose laughter and good nature filled her home with a sense of well-being. There was a Steinway in the large open living-room area but she never sang when people were there, it embarrassed her. 'I feel them listening so hard. I feel my power, and it frightens me,' she explained. 'Somehow in a big place, when the lights are on you and it's total blackness out there, you're singing alone, it seems like it's the place to do it, to do the thing I do. But I no more could sing a song in a room with my friends than jump off a bridge.'

Seaside picnics and domestic dawdling ended in April when *Funny Lady* went before the cameras. Once again, as with her first three film musicals, this was to be a big-budget movie and as the star and major asset, the studio's investment would be on her shoulders. Where once marquees had glittered names such as Garbo, Hepburn, Dietrich, Hayworth, Turner and Crawford, in 1974 Streisand stood alone. Liza Minnelli, despite her Academy Award for *Cabaret*, had not proven reliable at the box office and Jane Fonda, with her anti-war protesting was politically incorrect and currently off the screen.

'Blame it on Vietnam,' *Funny Lady* scenarist Jay Presson Allen theorised. 'Any time there's a war, society concentrates on its masculine qualities. For the past few years female audiences have been lost because there've been no stars they could identify with in a positive way – except Streisand.'

With Peters, now always at her side, at the wheel of the car on 1 April 1974 she drove through the gates of Columbia for the first day of production on *Funny Lady*. Budgeted at $7.5 million, there would be a fourteen-week production schedule with locations in Atlantic City, Philadelphia and New York. Musical rehearsals had begun several weeks earlier. Herbert Ross, who was functioning as dramatic and musical director with his wife, Nora Kaye, former prima ballerina, as his assistant, had devised a drastic budget-cutting system. Fourteen musical numbers were filmed by multiple cameras in sixteen days.[4] Columbia was still undergoing such financial difficulties that they were on the brink of bankruptcy and David Begelman, Streisand's former agent, and Alan Hirschfield were brought in to reorganise the company. Four years later Begelman would be forced to leave in the wake of an embezzlement scandal that rocked the industry. For now, Streisand believed in him and in the theory that having once looked after her interests he would protect them in his new position. Time proved otherwise.

James Caan, who had shot to near-stardom with *The Godfather*, was cast opposite her as songwriter, producer, entrepreneur Billy Rose. Omar Sharif returned as Nick Arnstein. The team of John Kander and Fred Ebb, composers of *Cabaret*, wrote the new songs in the score and Peter Matz was back on board

---

[4] The major songs recorded were 'So Long, Honey Lamb', 'Blind Date', 'I Found a Million Dollar Baby', 'Clap Hands, Here Comes Charlie', 'Am I Blue?', 'How Lucky Can You Get?' and the 'Crazy Quilt' sequence (the last a series of show scenes where the sets deconstruct as Streisand and the chorus perform).

as both arranger and conductor.[5] Veteran cinematographer James Wong Howe, winner of two Academy Awards, came out of five years' retirement to photograph the picture. And Streisand's personal designer choice, Bob Mackie and Ray Aghayan, did her costumes. The story steamrolls through the years when Fanny divorces Nick, moves on to romance, marriage and divorce to supershowman Billy Rose, and finally to her hit as radio's 'Baby Snooks'.

Streisand and Stark fought constantly, mostly over her interpretation of Brice. Stark, still struggling to protect the image of his late mother-in-law, wanted her played more sympathetically. Streisand saw Brice rather as 'a tough lady who hid her inner softness under a carapace of flinty wisecracks and never aimed to be lovable at the cost of her own personality. I'm not playing me any more,' she added. 'I'm completely relaxed.' Peters was standing nearby to smile his agreement.

She also fought with her opinionated leading man. 'I'd yell at her,' Caan recalled, 'put her down and call her a spoiled rotten thing, and she would call me this or that and we'd carry on ... I remember for some reason, it was very important to Herb Ross to get a shot where we both got covered in talcum powder. Barbra [was wearing] this beautiful green-spangled dress and made up just right. She said, "I don't think that Jimmy should hit me in the face with this powder. That powder is toxic, you know, and I'll get it in my lungs." ' Caan, sensing that a big argument was brewing, took matters in his hands. 'Barbra, I think you're right,' he said. ' "Maybe I shouldn't hit you with the thing. Maybe you'll hit me and then I'll pick it up and I'll go to hit you with it and then I won't." She said, "Oh, that's terrific. That'll be great!" I said, "Now, mind you – if you blink or back off when I start to raise my hand, I'm gonna whack you with it ... 'cause it's only the idea that you're ready to accept it that'll stop me." She said, "OK. I won't blink."

'So we set the scene up and did it. She hit me in the face with the powder. I picked it up and drew my hand back and she just stood there. She did not blink. I hit her square in the face with it. I'm telling you I went to the floor laughing, I couldn't stop, and she looked at me ... I mean, I really felt bad ... She called me names. She said, "You lied to me!" ' Caan couldn't stop laughing and finally Streisand saw the humour in it and laughed with him. 'He had his fingers crossed so God shouldn't strike him dead, and then he let me have it,' Streisand added good-naturedly.

Ross, of course, had worked with Streisand before and he found her quite a different person than previously. 'Her commitment was not 100 per cent to the film. *Funny Lady* was virtually a movie that was made without her – she

[5] Marvin Hamlisch also contributed a couple of 'thematic' musical cues linking *Funny Girl* with *Funny Lady*. However, Jule Styne and Bob Merrill, whose music had been incorporated, were not given screen credit, although Hamlisch was.

simply wasn't there in terms of commitment.' Her main concern was always Peters, where he was, what he thought of what she was doing. The crew was often kept waiting while she located him by telephone. There is no doubt that her relationship with Peters was more important to her than the film she was making. It was as simple as that, but she never gave less than was required of her.

Peters, watching from the sidelines, felt that Streisand should 'be playing hotter, sexier, younger roles'. And, of course, she was making the movie because of her old contract with Stark and for far less than she would be paid elsewhere. Streisand was torn. She had truly liked the script, had even enjoyed being able to play in scenes with Sharif and show him how little their affair now meant to her. Her mind, however, was on Peters and a project that they had decided they would do together for First Artists with Jon producing – a modern version of *A Star is Born*. One day Peters arrived on the set of *Funny Lady* with a jewellery box containing a diamond and sapphire butterfly. A week later it was announced in the press that, as well, he would produce her next album, *Butterfly*.

Columbia Records balked. There was no way they were going to allow her lover, who had no musical experience, to produce an album. Streisand persisted. 'Do they think I would let Jon produce a record if I wasn't absolutely sure he could do it?' she defended. 'I believe in imagination. I believe in taste. These are the important ingredients, and they're all things he has.' Despite Columbia's displeasure, Peters began work on the *Butterfly* album before shooting ended on *Funny Lady* and Streisand did double time, recording for *Butterfly* the contemporary sounds he had chosen for her and performing for the cameras the old-time tunes of *Funny Lady*.

The executives from Columbia Records were unhappy from the first playback session. Peters had chosen the title *Butterfly* to reflect the many moods Streisand could effect in her music. He had wanted her to sing 'God Bless the Child', the Billie Holiday standard and a medley of 'A Quiet Thing' from the Kander and Ebb score of *Flora, The Red Menace* and a song dropped from Stephen Sondheim's *Anyone Can Whistle* – 'There Won't Be Trumpets' ('Recording that medley is what first got me thinking about doing a Broadway album,' Streisand later claimed.) The record company did not think they were contemporary enough and they were cut, not without a fight on Streisand's part.

Most of the songs that Peters had chosen and she had approved presented her in a different aspect. This was going to be a whole new Barbra. Gone was the romance, the nostalgia of *The Way We Were*. Gone was the funny girl, the funny lady. She was into woman – not just woman but *avant-garde* woman, always liberated (well, *almost*) and with very little sense of morality and absolutely no remorse for blatant promiscuity. The songs were delivered in a gospel-rock, either with a back-up group or with Streisand over-dubbing herself, two selections, 'Love in the Afternoon' and 'Guava Jelly' (which would eventually be released as a single as well) with fairly explicit sexual lyrics. 'Love in the Afternoon' is prescient of *The Bridges of Madison County* in that the lyrics tell the story of a country woman, bedded once so memorably by a man just passing through – oral sex is implied – that she never forgets him.

The effect of 'Guava Jelly' is even more startling. The lyric concerns a woman's desire to have 'it' rubbed on her belly. The comparison is to guava jelly, and the metaphor pulls no punches as Streisand, over and over, more and more breathlessly, pleads, 'rub it, rub it'. Tom Scott, who had worked with Joni Mitchell, arranged and conducted. Columbia Records insisted on some more staple cuts. The finished album is eclectic in a way that none of her albums had been before. Side one reflects more of what Peters and Streisand were trying to accomplish. At one point in 'Jubilation' she achieves a true revival-meeting style that equals Mahalia Jackson in full gospel voice. Side two presents some of the old Barbra with 'I Won't Last a Day Without You', which qualifies as one of those 'doormat' songs – women who can only be strong with and through their men – that she has always professed to hate. Then, with 'Let the Good Times Roll', she winds up back where she began – raunchy – no longer talking about good times but gratifying, orgasmic sex.

Before the album's release the press warned that it was going to be a disaster and that Peters was the culprit. 'This is possibly the best singing I've ever done,' she replied. 'For the first time in my life ... my work [referring to recording] has become fun for me, and it used to be a drag. My attitude has changed towards people. I'm less afraid. That's Jon. It kills me to have him put down more than to have me put down.'

The album sleeve was a photo collage of Streisand and Peters, she looking at him worshipfully, playful shots of them touching, clowning, embracing. His dark, piercing eyes and black beard gave rise to sinister press descriptions of him as 'Streisand's Svengali' and 'Film Empress' Rasputin'. The lovers, now turned musical partners, waited anxiously for the critics to speak. To their own jubilation the *New York Times* review was a rave. 'Beyond the fashionable cracks at Peters' profession [as a hair-stylist] – and there have been many these past months – his role as record producer certainly has enhanced this album. *Butterfly* is one of Streisand's finest albums in years.' Not all the critics agreed, but most thought it *was* her most daring and Columbia was not displeased when *Butterfly* hit the charts at a lucky thirteen and remained in the top twenty for the next five months.

The final weeks of shooting on *Funny Lady* in early August was a time when everyone on the set, along with the rest of the nation, was gripped by the Watergate break-in, the impeachment articles, and Nixon's resignation on 9 August. Streisand sat in her dressing room between takes watching as the House Judiciary Committee solemnly and cautiously went about the business of trying to remove a President from office. 'Expletive deleted' became a joke on the set as committee members kept everyone in suspense about the infamous eighteen-minute gap in Nixon's White House tapes.

Her gift to Stark when filming ended was an antique mirror upon which she had scrawled 'Paid in Full' in blood-red lipstick. A few days later she sent him a plaque engraved with the words, 'Even though I sometimes forget to say it, thank you, Ray. Love, Barbra.'

However unhappy she might have been working for Stark or displeased Peters was that she was playing an older woman out of touch with the *now* generation, *Funny Lady* was warm and funny and gorgeous. She looked sexy, sang at her top form and brought a mature freshness to the role of Fanny Brice. Her reviews were raves, the picture a huge success, but she was less interested in *Funny Lady*'s triumph at the box office than she was with the projects she was working on with Peters. Her ambitions for him were sky-high. Instinctively she understood his gnawing hunger for fame and riches. He talked about becoming one of Hollywood's top producers. He could see himself quite clearly as the head of a great studio. She took him seriously, believed in his visions, became furious when members of the press referred to him in a derogatory manner as 'a hairdresser'. 'He's not using me,' she defended him to friends. 'He gives much more than he takes.' Her drive for his success was as strong as for her own – maybe at this moment – even more, for the lady was in love and she wanted the world to know how wisely she had chosen.

# 24

ON CHRISTMAS MORNING 1974, Streisand rose at dawn and made bagels and hot chocolate in the kitchen of the Barn for Jason and Christopher to eat when they came down to the living room to open their gifts, stacked under a towering nine-foot tree decorated with pine cones and candy canes. It was the first time she had ever celebrated the Christian holiday. The bagels were her bid for inter-denomination. She viewed this as a time for family. She and Peters were now on such good terms with Lesley Anne Warren that the three of them attended Gestalt therapy sessions together in which the analyst encouraged them to release their emotions, and to recognise them in response to each other. To those close to her, Streisand appeared less tense, more open. She laughed more easily, luxuriated in her maternal role and domestic responsibilities.

The boys became friends, collaborating on monster movies with an 8mm camera that was a present to Jason from Elliott. Streisand was supremely happy. She oversaw the selection of every flowering bush, tree, and stone for the path that led to the stable, which was being converted into a multi-level villa eventually to contain guest quarters, a gym and a projection room. With time to indulge her passion for collecting, the Barn was quickly filling with newly found pieces. As a couple, Peters with his platform saddle shoes and hip-hugging corduroys worn without underwear – Streisand in tight jeans tucked into high boots, her hair bleached blonde and worn straight and loose – looked cool, sexy, *with it*.

He made her feel young, she made him a movie producer. He had gone from no status as 'a kid with dirty underwear going to beauty school' to millionaire Emperor of Hair to the producer of Barbra Streisand's next movie, a $5 million musical, the fourth version of *A Star Is Born*.[1] And in January 1975, with

---

[1] The original story upon which all four versions of *A Star Is Born* were based was written by Adela Rogers St John. *What Price Hollywood?* (1932), directed by George Cukor, starred Lowell Sherman as an alcoholic movie director who helps waitress Constance Bennett achieve film stardom while he sinks into drunken ruin. *A Star Is Born* (1938), directed by William Wellman, has Fredric March as an alcoholic actor and Janet Gaynor as the movie hopeful he grooms into stardom as he self-destructs. *A Star Is Born* (1954),

*Butterfly* still in the charts, Streisand and Peters were trying to convince Warner Brothers, who were putting up the money for First Artists, to hand him the directorial reins of the movie as well.

The original concept, conceived by husband and wife novelists John Gregory Dunne (Dominic Dunne's brother) and Joan Didion in the fall of 1973, had only a fleeting connection with the earlier versions of *A Star Is Born*. It was a love story about two rock singers, one on the way up, one on the way down. The background was the contemporary, rat-packed world of groupies, rock concerts and tours, drugs and psychedelic flip-outs – far from the artificial, un-hip glory of Hollywood in its golden years. Still, the up and down professional careers of the two lead characters bore enough similarity to the much-reprised Warner's classic that Dunne and Didion went to their ex-agent, Dick Shepherd, now head of Warner Brothers Studios to see if they could do it under the studio's aegis. Shepherd liked the idea and agreed to their writing a con-temporary rock version of the film, the rights of all three previous films being owned by his studio. Dunne and Didion were not *aficionados* of the *A Star Is Born* movies, but they were avid rock enthusiasts and had just returned from travelling around with rock stars Jethro Tull and Uriah Heep. They were also highly respected literary authors of the contemporary scene. By the following spring a script was completed and submitted to director Peter Bogdanovich for consideration. Bogdanovich thought it was awful.

The script passed next to actor/director Mark Rydell, who loved the screen-play, which he called 'a savage look at the rock world'. Refusing to pay Rydell anything near the price he was asking for his services, Warner instead agreed to let him develop the project without payment and gave him three months to work with Didion and Dunne on the script, line up two stars, 'and get some of those spectacular concert scenes off the drawing board'. If he succeeded, Warner would then sign a lucrative contract for him to direct the film. At the end of this time the heavy-handed screenplay – glaringly raw-boned and with two characters who were not sympathetic – was in deep trouble. Liza Minnelli, Elvis Presley, Carly Simon, James Taylor, Cher and Diana Ross all turned down one or the other of the two leading roles. Rydell went to Kris Kristofferson, a top Country and Western star who had become an increasingly popular film personality after playing Billy in *Pat Garrett and Billy the Kid*, following it as the romantic star of *The Sailor Who Fell from Grace with the Sea*, a sleeper movie that became a cult film. Kristofferson possessed a commanding presence – tall, lean, crusty, wary-eyed, a macho-man who could become surprisingly tender and vulnerable. He liked the script and committed himself to the project, but without a female star Warner would not bank it. When Rydell's three-month

with George Cukor back at the helm, presented Judy Garland and James Mason in a musical version of the same story.

free period elapsed, Warner took him off the project and handed it to director Jerry Schatzberg. In June 1974, Sue Mengers received the script as a submission for Streisand. First Peters read it.

'I discovered this project,' he later insisted. 'I was the one who found it for Barbra, and convinced her to do it.' He neglected to add that he let her know how much he wanted to produce it. Later he was to say, 'The character in *my* movie is a guy who's fighting all the time and hitting all the time. And he can't relate. It's the macho guy, which is very much like me.'

He saw the story from a personal angle and offered changes before Warner, Schatzberg, Dunne or Didion even realised he was to be involved if Streisand accepted the female role. 'Two people fall in love,' he explained. 'She becomes a super superstar by realising what the most important thing to both of them is: communicating. Wanting to have children. Not the thousands of agents and press agents and all that stuff that control their life. He's a guy who spent the first thirty years of his life fighting – very aggressive – and then met this woman and fell very much in love and realised that this was his chance to live. But he accidentally dies. For us [he and Streisand] the understanding of it – through film – was a very heavy thing. Do you know what I mean? That's why the script had to be perfect. Because it has to be right for us.'

The press treated Peters's bid through Streisand to produce as a joke. She was devastated by their jibes and sarcasm – 'Hair today and gone tomorrow!'

'Anyone who wonders how a first-time producer can make a $5 million film with the top female star in the country just has to take a look at the way I produced Barbra's album. Or how I run my beauty salons. I employ three hundred people. I'm a businessman, man, that's all,' Peters defended.

As a First Artists film,[2] Streisand had creative control. She was unhappy at this stage with Kristofferson, with whom she had once had a brief affair ('one of her flings' as she called them). This had been after her divorce and the end of her romance with Trudeau. After a few dates, Kristofferson had essentially dropped her. She was too demanding, too needy for where he was at that time in his life. Except for her respect for his musicianship Streisand had not given him much thought since then, but when she was told he had been cast as the declining rock star in the film she agreed he was a good choice. No innuendo was meant. Kristofferson was at the height of his popularity.

In the one truly farcical time before Kristofferson signed on, Streisand called Schatzberg and suggested that Peters play opposite her. The director dismissed it as a gag but quickly found out she was serious. 'Can you sing?' Schatzberg

---

[2] Warner would now get the distribution rights, reimbursing First Artists for two-thirds of the film's negative cost upon delivery of a finished film. Streisand would receive 25 per cent of the gross returns.

asked Peters sensibly. After all, the male lead as written was a famous rock singer. 'No,' Peters told him, 'but you can shoot around me and dub.' Schatzberg refused to cast him. Dunne and Didion were off the script after finalising a deal that gave them 10 per cent of the film, and Jonathan Axelrod, a bright, young scenarist was rewriting. By this time Dick Shepherd had been replaced at Warner by John Calley.

'I'd never met Peters before,' Calley recalled. 'He came in and said that in his and Barbra's view, the screenplay was moving away from being suitable for Barbra. I agreed with them. Forget about whether the screenplay was good or not, the issue was "Is it right for Barbra?" Peters said, in effect, "It's very simple, either we get to take over the screenplay and make it work for Barbra or we take a walk. It's entirely up to you. Do whatever you like."' Calley had no alternative. Warner did not want to lose a Streisand musical. Axelrod became a casualty and Schatzberg soon followed.

Peters, flying in the face of his detractors, was determined that he was going to direct. 'Why not?' he shouted at one reporter who ignited his temper. 'Directing is a thing I've done my whole life! It's getting people to do what I want them to do!' He was showing the press around his Malibu ranch, kicking rocks out of his path as he went with the hard-stub toe of his expensive boots. 'When I started this place it was all dirt. Look at it now,' he said with a sweep of his hand that indicated his domain.

The week before Christmas 1974 Peters gave a party for the employees of his hairdressing empire to tell them that Jon Peters, Inc. would soon be in other hands. His interest was now fully focused on the movie he was about to produce. He walked out of his offices without a second glance. That part of his life was over. For the next month he and Streisand spent their evenings in front of the fireplace at the Barn tearing the script apart. 'We're going to make this a love story,' he told Marie Brenner of the *New Times*. 'They're the most beautiful people and the love they have for each other is the same feeling as Barbra and I have for each other ... we're going to make it much closer to the 1936 version, the one with Janet Gaynor. That was magic. That's what we want to achieve.'

Streisand agreed. They were a team, but it appeared that Peters had taken the lead. 'She was ecstatic, really,' one friend said. 'Very proud of him, strongly believing in his ability, gaining a new kind of strength, more womanly, through his.' Brenner was prescient in observing that 'What Jon Peters appreciates very well is that he is living with a large entertainment corporation and that the merger looks permanent ... [but] that kind of power is rarely benign. It is not enough for Jon Peters to mastermind the career of his private conglomerate. He is not satisfied with a minor role as Barbra's shield, giving her the privacy she says she now wants. Yes, he sees himself as the take-charge guy in her business life ... but even more, he sees himself as the lead in their larger-than-life real life movie. He believes he is on the way up, all the way up. The only question now is the quality of ascent.'

Streisand, Newman, Poitier and McQueen had come into First Artists giving the impression to outsiders and the press that they were all big buddies and were going to work together and do these great projects. This was not the reality. Streisand harboured resentment that her partners would be participating in the profits from her film. 'That became sort of the attitude,' recalled Ed Holly, who had joined the company as Senior Vice-President in Charge of Finance, and would in two years become President. 'When Barbra and Jon were preparing the picture, the company was at the poorhouse steps. All the partners were behind in their pictures.[3] Barbra had delivered only one, *Up the Sandbox*, which was not a commercial movie but it showed the kind of thing she wanted to do. It expressed a new spirit, a new thinking. Warner literally forced her not to drag her feet on *A Star Is Born* as they were at the court-house steps [with First Artists]. They agreed to an expanded budget of $6 million. It created problems. This was a higher budget than the other partners could expect and would also lower profits or raise losses, whichever was the case. The stars just could not be in bed together. The egos were too big. Even those nice, easy to deal with people – Sidney and Paul – could not work with Barbra.

'Jon came on the Board of Directors of First Artists. From a business standpoint the execs of the company did not deal directly with the stars. We dealt with whomever they put on the board and in Barbra's case it was Jon. We had some pretty hard fights along the way. Jon could only see things from Barbra's standpoint so we were in conflict in that what might be best for Barbra might not necessarily be best for the company and the stockholders. So immediately we had a fight on our hands. He was a tough fighter, a hard negotiator, and not always fair. But that's Jon. Barbra used him as a buffer and a go-between. She did not like to deal with people except on a creative basis.'

The script remained a difficult problem and Streisand called Arthur Laurents and asked his help. She had four different scripts and sent them to him. 'After I read them,' he recalled, 'I told her she should play the other part [the role of

---

[3] As it was organised, each of First Artists founders agreed to make three films for the company. In 1971 Steve McQueen had joined the company. A year later Dustin Hoffman agreed to produce films independently through First Artists but never exercised his option to buy stock and had been feuding with them from that time (although he was later to make *Agatha* and *Straight Time* under their aegis). Paul Newman produced and starred in *The Life and Times of Judge Roy Bean*, *Pocket Money* and *The Drowning Pool* which were not successful at the box office. Sidney Poitier made low-key and limited interest ghetto movies with all-black casts (First Artists had expected him to replicate highly commercial movies like *In the Heat of the Night*). Streisand's *Up the Sandbox* had lost money. First Artists' only successful film at this time was Steve McQueen's *The Getaway*.

the star on the way down], which was much more interesting, and that only one of the scripts was really good. "Which?" she wanted to know. The one written by Joan Didion and John Dunne. And I added, "But you're not going to do that one." And she asked, "Why not?" and I said, "Because it's tough." Barbra wanted, what I guess all insecure women want – to be romantic princesses.'

By the summer of 1975, with Streisand and Peters still working on the screenplay, Warner issued an ultimatum that *A Star Is Born* would have to go before the cameras by 2 January 1976. They had at this point, due to conflicting commitments, lost Kristofferson and Warner had refused to go along with Peters replacing him. 'What about Brando?' Streisand proposed during one meeting. 'I always wanted to play with Brando. Why does it have to be a musical?'

Peters leaped up from his chair exclaiming that they had recently talked to Brando at the studio. 'The son of a bitch, he wanted to fuck Barbra! I was ready to kill him! I take him off, and I kiss him! He's beautiful! I love him, the bastard! They'd make a great pair. Imagine. Streisand and Brando!'

Eventually, Kristofferson – upon winning a co-above-the-title credit shared with Streisand – came back on the project. What was now needed was a deft writer who could take the forty pounds of script and revisions and turn it into a workable screenplay with a believable, strong role for Streisand. 'It would be nice if the picture was good,' one Warner executive said when Frank Pierson was asked to work on yet another revision, 'but the bottom line is to get her to the studio. Shoot her singing six numbers, and we'll make $60 million.'[4]

Pierson had written the screenplays for *Cat Ballou*, *The Anderson Tapes* and *Dog Day Afternoon* and directed one film, John le Carré's *The Looking Glass War* (1969). He was keen on directing and played his cards carefully. He presented Streisand and Peters with a fresh approach to the story which they both liked. But he did not wish to rewrite the script unless he was also hired as director. Peters nodded his agreement. He had decided he would not direct after all, he told Pierson. 'Why?' Pierson asked.

'How could I direct Barbra and keep our relationship? I had to decide which was more important, our love or the movie.' One sensed this had been an issue that they had chewed over for a long time. Streisand had, in fact, grown fearful that if Peters were to direct the stress would be too much for her. What if they fought bitterly? 'You and Barbra make the picture,' he told Pierson. 'I'm here [as producer] to expedite. You need somethin', I'll kick ass to get it.'

---

[4] No less than thirteen writers, including Streisand and Peters, had worked on the screenplay leading up to Pierson's involvement. They were Joan Didion, John Dunne, Jonathan Axelrod, Bob and Laura Dillon, Jay Presson Allen, Buck Henry, Arthur Laurents, Renée Taylor, Joseph Bologna and Alvin Sargent.

Pierson, a benevolent-looking bespectacled man, prematurely grey (he was thirty-eight), his broad chin hidden by a neatly clipped beard, planned to keep the basic story line: the man going steadily downhill and self-destructing as the woman keeps ascending. The real change that he envisioned was in the relationship between the lead characters. In earlier film versions of *A Star Is Born* and in the Dunne–Didion progenitor, her success and his failure were seen in terms of a competition which he lost, because she won. Pierson dropped that approach on the basis that in the 1970s working women contributed a large share of the family income and husbands no longer found this humiliating. In Pierson's screenplay the tragedy was that the woman's deep love was not enough to keep alive an artist whose career – which was the measure of his manhood – comes crashing down around him.

Next came the issue of the ending. 'I hate him if he kills himself and leaves her all alone, this little girl,' Peters told Pierson, who reminded him that Garbo threw herself under a railroad car in *Anna Karenina*, Ronald Colman had his head lopped off in *A Tale of Two Cities* and Ali MacGraw died of a sudden illness in *Love Story* – all phenomenally successful pictures. None the less, Pierson compromised, revising the script to have the man die in an auto accident – although, as he is drinking beer while driving at over 140 miles an hour in blinding sunlight, his death still evokes suicide.

Weekly conferences were held with Pierson as Streisand and Peters contributed to the creation of the characters. More and more Pierson realised how autobiographical the fictional lovers were becoming. 'People are curious,' Streisand told him, 'they want to know about us. But I don't want you to use too much. I don't know if I should tell you this or not, because someday they'll want to do my life story, and I don't want to use it up.' She then shared some of her Brooklyn childhood memories with him along with stories of the passion and growing violence in their relationship. She was confident that no two people had ever loved as ardently as they had. Theirs was an historic affair. They were each contributing a greatness to the other's development. There had been no other show-business couple to compare with them. Maybe, Elizabeth Taylor and Mike Todd if he had lived. They were unique and their experiences were profound.

Peters was anxious to incorporate details of their life together, 'how we make love, fight and love again. A fight can be an intimate thing between two lovers, can really strip them naked, lead to an ultimate sexual experience. Hate and love are the two most passionate emotions we feel. Put them together and – *wham!*' The scene where the rock star, now named John Norman Howard, and Esther Hoffman meet, ended with the line 'You've got a great ass,' one of the first things Peters said to Streisand. And Esther snaps at the press who dog her trail, 'When is it ever enough, goddamn it!' – words she shouted at reporters who would not leave them alone.

'It's not our life,' Streisand interjected. 'You don't want to make it too real.' However, a love scene in a bathtub encircled with burning candles, the only light in the room, was taken from their personal experience, as was the romp in the open field on the fictional anti-hero's ranchland. And when it was time to create the sets, Streisand had the fictitious Esther's apartment decorated as though it were hers, bringing furniture, fabrics, carloads of things from her attic and cellar storerooms (many of these items from the walk-up over the fish restaurant that she and Elliott had once shared) to make the set feel as though it was once someplace where she had lived.

While Pierson was working on the script Streisand was supervising the Barn's transformation from its rustic past into an *Architectural Digest* vision of country life. The mattress that doubled as the living-room couch was now covered in fur and antique Victorian pillows, the bathtub in the master bedroom was rebuilt from natural stones cemented together. The house was all earth tones, and the wood artfully aged. Every wall, nook and cranny was overflowing with objects – art deco statuary, collections of startling variety, antique throws and shawls, Tiffany lamps, mammoth tropical plants, *objets d'art* of every description and 'in such profusion only an impression of magnificence is generated ... It is like a magical attic, in which every trunk and old discarded hat rack or moose head has a sentimental history, printed on a card.' Hats and boas were draped on hangers for display on the backs of doors. Period shoes with marcasite buckles and satin bows were lined up on open shelves.

Outside you could barely walk without tripping over building materials as a natural rock swimming pool – a large version of the bathtub – was in the throes of construction, a double tennis court under way, and two houses on adjoining property, which they had just bought as additional guest houses were being rebuilt and redecorated, one in art deco style, the other in art nouveau for her to furnish and decorate as authentically as possible. Streisand was relishing her time away from the cameras *potchkehing*, as she called it. Peters had gained ten pounds and strutted around 'like Nixon eyeing improvements at San Clamente'. With revisions still being made on the script of *A Star Is Born*, he joined forces with Marty Erlichman to produce a film for Barwood, Streisand's company, based on the life of Bruce Lee, the diminutive Chinese-American martial arts expert who had died a sudden and mysterious death two years earlier.

Streisand was learning to play the guitar for a scene in the film and 'drove everybody crazy playing it morning, noon and night'. She also wanted to write a song and plucked away on the melody trying to get the right chords. She cried in the bathroom after a guitar lesson because her teacher wrote songs and she thought she could not. Peters followed her into the john. 'You can do it,' he insisted, 'you can do anything you set your mind to. *Try* to write a song! Go on try!' One day when Paul Williams, who with Kenny Asher (also the musical conductor) had been signed to write the score for the film,[5] drove up to the Barn for a conference, Streisand played the melody she had been working on. Williams was knocked over. It was 'wonderful' he said. 'She was like a little girl ... kind of shy. She had been taking guitar lessons, and she was watching her fingers to make sure that she got the chords right.'

Williams jubilantly told her that she had composed the love theme and promised shortly to have words for the song. To her irritation, these were the last lyrics he wrote before they went into the pre-recording sessions, but she felt newly confident when she played and sang the song, now titled 'Evergreen', for Marty Erlichman, who was certain it would be a big hit – as big as 'The Way We Were'.

Despite Streisand's optimism, all did not go well on the scoring stage the day they recorded 'Evergreen'. Ed Holly recalled that when Phil Feldman, who preceded him as President of First Artists, 'a very strong, hard-hitting man whose main function at the time was as a trouble shooter', got the word mid-morning that the conductor was quitting, they both hurried down there. 'Barbra was yelling and screaming – really out of control – but she couldn't define anything. We decided to send everyone out for a long lunch break. An hour later she returned and spoke to Howard Klein, the Vice-President in Charge of Production. By three o'clock, when I return to the scoring stage, she ordered, "I want this many violins, etcetera". She had figured out in her head during lunch what was wrong. So immediately the call went out to get the additional musicians that she wanted. At three o'clock she was back – highly energised – additional musicians on board and within an hour they were recording. The difference from the morning session was dramatic. She had whipped the musicians into a frenzy and the final effect had been good. The orchestra had not been full. She is such a perfectionist. She can't stand things not coming out exactly right and not being terribly articulate, it frustrates her. She hears things that no one else hears, has terrible fights with everyone she works with. She doesn't seem able to discuss and reason. She is a yeller – and it grates on people with whom she is working. Perfect usually means doing things *her* way.'

After legally extending the start date by one month, *A Star Is Born* went before the cameras on 2 February 1976. Peters was getting his feet wet in the picture business and loving every bit of exposure to it. 'He was just like a feisty sponge,' Holly says. 'He could absorb anything that was going on and was a

[5] In the end Paul Williams wrote the lyrics for 'Evergreen' (music Streisand), 'With One More Look at You', 'Watch Closely Now' and 'Spanish Eyes' (music Kenny Asher), and 'Everything' (music Rupert Holmes). Additional songs were 'Queen Bee' (words and music Rupert Holmes), 'Crippled Crow' (words and music Donna Weiss), 'I Believe in Love' (Alan and Marilyn Bergman) and 'Lost Inside of You' (words and music Barbra Streisand and Leon Russell).

quick study, but his attention span for anything other than the picture was zilch. None of us knew how to handle him other than to just accept the fact that he and Barbra were a couple, and that he was there and if you accepted Barbra, you had to accept Jon and we formed ways of working with him. He was sort of adopted by Howard Klein who really taught him what picture making is all about. Jon's ambition exceeded even Barbra's.

'I know I'm not an easy person to work with,' Peters admitted. 'I know what I want and I'm going to get it. I was terrified, but I couldn't show them that, could I? I had to get things done. I was the producer . . . so I walked through people. I had to.'

Seldom did a day go by without reports appearing in the press on their affair and the problems on *A Star Is Born*. The Streisand–Peters merger was the Jackie Kennedy–Onassis love story of that time – everyone seemed tuned in, espousing opinions, predicting the outcome (mostly negative, the affair would end with shooting on *A Star Is Born*). The media, fans and the just plain curious had made their way up the narrow mountain road, overhung with great oaks and eucalyptus, to the gates that led to the front gardens of the Barn. Streisand and Peters hired private guards and bought two attack dogs.

The scenes with fans and press in the picture took on a greater sense of reality, emulating her own experiences as flashbulbs exploded in her face as she drove out of her own driveway, the way people grabbed at her, tore at her clothes, tugged at her hair as she tried to pass them to go into a restaurant or attend a public affair. All of them wanted a piece of her, believed they were entitled to it and grew angry if she yelled obscenities at them. Her affair with Peters had tossed her into an arena of pit bulls. She could no longer go to the beach with the boys and count on not being recognised, even though she now employed wigs and disguises – big glasses, Garbo hats that shaded her face. She was the *now* woman newly found by the young twenty-somethings. She hated it all and when she was not at the studio, she remained cloistered behind the gates at the Barn with her gun-toting guards and attack animals.

Frank Pierson was finding his task as director fraught with dangers. He was a man caught in the middle between the producers of the film and the studio whose money he was over-spending.

'I don't feel you want to love me,' Streisand told him one day when shooting was not going well. 'All my directors have wanted to make me beautiful. But I feel you hold something back; there's something you don't tell me. You never talk to me.' Pierson apologised and added that he was just not the demonstrative type.

'You fight like hell with Jon, you fight like hell with everyone you lean on,' he told her.

'I know,' she answered. 'But Jon is so strong! I never had a father; I was always in charge of myself. I came and went as I pleased. I can't stand for someone to tell me what to do.' Then, her voice grew strident with sudden venom. 'Ray Stark always used to bully me, the son of a bitch. You'll pay for every lousy thing Ray Stark ever did to me!'

One of the most important locations in the film – the retreat in the desert that John Norman Howard, the fictional rock star builds – became a bitter struggle between the director and his star. Streisand did not want to spend so much time in such bleak, unfriendly open spaces. She had convinced Peters that they should use the Barn as a location – the rock star's fatal accident could occur on the Pacific Coast Highway. Finally, she gave in and an area near Tucson, Arizona was chosen and, as they waited to move the crew and cast there, Peters flew with her to New York for a TV telecast of a Muhammad Ali fight in Madison Square Gardens. As they came down the aisle of the packed arena to take their front-row seats, a man broke through their protective entourage and reached out to grab Streisand by the arm. Peters took a swing and connected.

This was the reality of her life, the cost of fame. She was viewed by some as a public possession to be grabbed at and touched at will, an invasion of her privacy that infuriated and disgusted her. Why *her*? Other celebrities were not subject to such bruising attention. Top singers were almost always singled out – Garland, Sinatra, the Beatles. Music made a connection, incited people where straight drama did not. The incident with the over-enthusiastic fan brought the role of Esther Hoffman closer into focus.

'Pow! I let him have it!' Peters told Pierson on their return. 'He made a motion like he's gonna touch, maybe he's gonna hit Barbra: He's gonna hit my woman! I go crazy! Bam! Pow! They're pullin' me off him. The cops come take him away. You can't go anywhere with her! That's the meaning of "star"! We gotta get that in the picture!'

Peters had a streak of inner violence that while it could be used to protect her, could also be turned against her. Ugly fights between Paul Williams and Peters, where the two men came close to blows, caused Williams to walk out on a live recording session. Tensions did not ease as the picture got under way. Pierson reported a fierce fight between Streisand and Peters over a scene she had just played to his disapproval. When Pierson went for his car, Barbra darted out of the hedges where he was parked, 'For God's sake, take me home!' he claimed she cried, jumping inside and huddling in a dark corner of the vehicle. 'He gets so furious. I don't know what to do!' She sat huddled up and silent as they drove out to Malibu. When they arrived at the Barn, Peters was already there, lights illuminating the entire property. He stood hulking in the doorway as she got out of the car. There were an awkward few minutes in which neither moved towards the other. Then Peters went inside and Streisand followed. Pierson remained parked there for a short time. Hearing nothing, he left.

The two stars worked in different ways. Kristofferson had a more direct approach to acting. To play drunk, he *got* drunk. When he was to be high in a scene he got stoned. She hated that. He was also slower than she was in getting a scene down, and required more time to rehearse. However, one time, when the script called for them both to cry, Kristofferson was able to do so, while Streisand needed menthol blown in her eyes to cause them to water.

'Jesus, Barbra,' Kristofferson apologised, 'I wish I could do something to help you. It's my fault, I'm not giving you what you need.'

Streisand fumed as she walked away and drew Pierson to one side. 'Did you hear what he said – the *ego*? He thinks what he does controls what I do!' she sneered.

Kristofferson, realising he was in an undeclared sparring match with Streisand, tried to duck the wild blows. (Later he was to say that making the film was 'an experience worse than boot camp!') A man of great personal strength and sexual appeal, there was about him the legendary aura of the lonely, wandering American, rootless, searching. He had that hungry, sensitive look that had made Gary Cooper a star, and in his music and lyrics the particularity and intellect that had brought Bob Dylan to the front. The son of an army general, he was born in Brownsville, Texas, a border town where Mexican-American feelings were rife. It was a tough background and he wanted to be able to write about the injustices he had witnessed. He majored in creative writing at Pomona College, then went to Oxford as a Rhodes scholar. To please his father he joined the army, went through officer's training, served in Germany and ended as a major teaching English at West Point. All the while, he wrote songs and sang them to his own guitar accompaniment, bursting on to the music scene in the late 1960s to become a top Country and Western concert and recording star – singing his own message-filled lyrics, which he also did in several early films.

The enigma of *A Star Is Born* is that Kristofferson was playing a singer-composer, which he was, and yet someone else was writing his music. This became a grating matter, one over which he was at odds with Peters. There was also concern that his performance as a music star on his way down might seem too realistic to the public, a fear that was not without substance.

The bathtub love scene between Kristofferson and Streisand became another cause of dispute. Kristofferson came on the set nude under his bathrobe. Peters insisted he wear flesh-coloured shorts. 'What the hell are they afraid of?' Kristofferson shouted, but he acquiesced and when they rehearsed the intimate scene, the doors to the rehearsal room were kept open, by Peters's orders, so that Kristofferson would not be alone with Streisand. Peters ran around the set screaming obscenities, yelling that that 'fucking bastard is going to pee all over Barbra!' Pierson tried to calm him down as Streisand kept shouting, 'It's

OK! It's OK!' Finally the scene was shot and Peters dashed over to the tub and helped Barbra out.

All their differences became news events reported in *Time, People* and the tabloid press. A massive live concert with 55,000 people was a major scene in the movie. It was shot at Sun Devil Stadium in Tempe, Arizona and even though the concert was being used for the company's purpose, the audience had to purchase tickets at $3.50 a piece. The crowd waited for over two hours in blazing 90-degree heat as the cameras and stars got ready. Shouts and jeers became insistent and Streisand, in the outfit she wears in the filmed sequence, a crocheted hat and coat over some tight pants, took over the microphone, working to calm the audience, amazingly getting them to laugh, telling them what was going to happen when the cameras began to roll, singing a song from the movie to appease them as the technicians worked madly behind the cameras preparing for the shot.

'Look at her directing the crowd!' Peters told *Village Voice* reporter Arthur Bell as they stood on the sidelines. 'Seventy thousand people [somewhat of an exaggeration], they'd do anything she'd say. It's like Brooklyn, you know what I mean? She's got balls. She's telling that crowd what she wants. I give to you, you give to me. See her working that crowd? See that?'

'If this film goes down the drain,' Streisand told Pierson later when they watched the rushes which she felt had missed what she wanted captured, 'it's all over for Jon and me. We'll never work again.'

Her love for him was obvious to all. The big question was whether they would get married when the film was completed. 'Perhaps,' she told one interviewer. 'I hope so – but marriage is not the most vital issue in our lives right now. He talks about it. I talk about it, but not at the same time. I'm all for women's liberation: do it because you feel it. All women should call their own shots, not in a militant manner but with the conviction that they've got a helluva lot to offer other than looking pretty and passive.'

None the less, looking sexy for Peters was one of her high priorities. On screen and privately she had never dressed more provocatively, tight pants showing her well-rounded buttocks, clinging fabrics and deep cleavage revealing her shapeliness. And for the first time in her life someone else's success meant as much to her as her own. Their fights and vehement disagreements contributed to the power of their mutual attraction. Streisand firmly believed Peters's promise to make her the greatest star in the world.

But Peters also kept his keen, brown eyes set on his own future and a time when his star might eventually outshine hers. His hunger for power in the industry was insatiable, equal to Streisand's. Maybe, after all, he was the one, the *poifect* match she had sought for years to find, the man to be the masculine to her feminine.

# 25

S HE WAS AT Frank Pierson's shoulder every inch of the way. No decision was made without her. She made sure of that. There was hell to pay if she was not consulted. She was executive producer and Peters the producer, a step below. They could not be ignored. No matter what she, as an actress, contributed to her films, the end result was a reflection of the director, his or her vision and ability to see it through. That is where the ultimate control is – for film is a director's medium. That was what she wanted – to direct her own films. She could taste the power, the ability to fulfil her personal visions, the scenes she saw so clearly in her head. But studios were resistant to give women the opportunity to direct, another example of Hollywood's 'boys' room' mentality, and she was going to need ammunition.

'You lay it out and it's shit,' she told Pierson as they were setting up a scene towards the last week of production on *A Star Is Born*.

He led her away from members of the crew with whom they had been working. 'You're rude,' he told her. 'There's no reason to talk that way to me, so don't do it any more. You're in a rage. What's that about?'

'Because I should have co-director credit,' she replied. 'I've directed at least half of this movie. I think I should have the credit for it, don't you?'

'Well, I'll tell you,' Pierson answered, after fielding his surprise, 'I've contributed a lot to your performance. So it's a deal. I'll split my director's credit with you and you can share co-starring credits with me.'

She stared at him with cold appraisal.

'Why didn't you fight to direct it from the start?' he asked.

'I wanted someone to be a buffer between Jon and me.' Her ice-blue eyes scrutinised his face for a reaction. 'What about the credit?' she persisted. 'I don't think I can insist on it. People criticise me enough as it is; they're always waiting to attack. I think it's something you have to give of your own free will.'

This was mid-April. That week Pierson won the Oscar for his screenplay of *Dog Day Afternoon*. Neither Streisand nor Peters congratulated him. About midnight, Peters came to his hotel room. 'You don't listen,' he shouted at Pierson and went over a long list of things he (and presumably Streisand) saw as infractions. Pierson went into the bathroom to urinate. Peters kept yelling at him. Pierson suspected that Peters wanted him to resign but he never came to the point and suddenly he blurted out: 'I'm not afraid of your Oscar!' and departed.

Their battle with Pierson continued straight through to the end of production. As soon as Streisand received the tape copy of his cut of the film, she set up a $500,000 editing room in the pool house at the ranch where the editor, Peter Zimmer, and a group of assistants worked under her constant and critical eye as she had them cut Kristofferson's footage. 'Primarily, she felt that her character needed more time on screen,' Zimmer recalled. 'She felt that some of the sequences were too heavy with Kristofferson. I would say that she made major changes, not so much with the story line, but as far as the characters were concerned. Her character became much more pertinent.'

No scenes were to be left of Kristofferson's character before his decline when his great strengths as a performer, his emotionality, the sensitivity, the intimacy he created with an audience explained his stardom and Esther's respect for him. This remains a major flaw in the movie, one Streisand refused to recognise in her determination to focus the story on Esther, to make it a Streisand film despite Kristofferson's co-star billing.

Fourteen-hour days, seven-day weeks, she sat on a hard, high stool labouring with complete concentration as she studied the strips of film on the small eight-inch wide Moviola screen. She had learned how to operate the KEM editing equipment which allowed her to fast-forward, reverse and freeze-frame the footage. She was alone at last with her image, able to inject her vision on Pierson's cut, not an easy task, for as director Sidney Lumet insists, 'no movie editor ever put anything up on the screen that hadn't been shot'. During the scoring process she fiddled incessantly with an electronic control board, bringing the drums up, the guitars down, her voice out. She would stop the film and have it run backward. She would hear things no one else could, finding fault with a certain beat, a missed stress. She remained after all the engineers had left and worked until exhaustion overtook her. With Cis Corman, Sue Mengers and Marilyn Bergman and some other close friends as advisors, she supervised the editing for five months on a final cut 'like a crazy person', one of her staff said.

Streisand was too involved with her career and the fate of *A Star Is Born* to devote much time to her role as mother. Plans had been made for Jason to join Elliott, Jenny and their three young children for the summer in Holland where Elliott was filming. But for the time she had Jason, nine, and Christopher, seven, both in her care and was finding the responsibility of two active boys difficult. Television producer Bob Shanks, the man who had given her the chance early in her life to appear on national television with Orson Bean, and his wife Ann, vividly recall the day they spent at the Malibu complex filming an interview between Streisand and Barbara Walters. They arrived early in the morning with Cis Corman, Walters and the crew. Streisand told Jason and Christopher to play outside. About 2 p.m. in the afternoon, Peters asked Streisand, 'Where are the boys?' She shrugged her shoulders. 'Did they have lunch?' he prodded. She said she hadn't seen them since morning. 'That's fucking great!' Peters exclaimed and went out in search of the boys.

'By that time,' Ann Shanks reconstructed, 'we thought we had about two-thirds of the interview done. Barbra has a propensity for drawing people into what seems at the time to be minor decisions. She picks someone outside her closest circle. On this day it was me.' Shanks, a former actress, talented photographer and theatre producer, has a distinct style – chic Bohemia, you might call it. She is outgoing, very, *very* funny, a natural comic and an irrepressible mimic. Streisand immediately appeared to bond with her.

'Barbra had chosen a pink sweater for the interview. "Whaddaya think?" she asked me. "Good, good," I said. "Pink is good."

' "For me?"

' "Yeah. Especially for you." '

Sue Mengers had joined the group earlier and she turned to her. 'See, Ann says pink is good for me.' (Apparently, Mengers had not approved of the choice.)

'So she wore the pink sweater in the interview section Bob and the crew had already finished. Now, suddenly, she wanted to look at what had been shot. "Ya *still* think pink is good for me?" she asked in this kinda half-quetchie, half-coy voice. "Yes, I still do," I replied.

' "Naaaw," she drawled. "I don't think so." ' She changed the sweater and there was nothing that could be done but scrap four hours of work and reshoot. Walters was not too happy, but gamely went through the interview a second time.

One section, shot late in the day, included Peters. When that was shown to her, Streisand became quite upset. 'I hate it!' she protested. 'I look awful.'

'You may *think* you look awful, but I know *I* look great,' Peters shot back. There was some sharp bickering between them. Streisand made the crew rerun the film that had been shot. 'See – stop it! Right there! That's a bad angle for me.' It was agreed that the offending shot could be edited out without any problem and she was satisfied.

The discussion now led to the editing of *A Star Is Born*.

'I just saw the end credits,' Mengers announced. 'I couldn't believe that you had taken both an editing and a wardrobe credit.' Mengers is a woman with a strong personality and a strident voice and her tone made it perfectly clear that she was soundly disapproving.

'Why shouldn't I have those credits?' Streisand snapped. 'I picked out all my clothes. It's my taste that you see reflected on screen. And I have worked hard on the editing of the picture. I deserve the credits and I'm taking both of them.'

'You can't do a thing like that in Hollywood,' Mengers reprimanded. 'There are unions. You'll have an ugly fight on your hands *and* you'll be the laughing stock of the town!'

'Well, I did the work and I want the credit!' Streisand shouted.

Mengers stormed out. The argument was not settled until shortly before the film was released. Streisand did not receive film credit for either of these categories.[1]

Peters finally invited Pierson to view Streisand's cut of the film. Pierson wrote later, 'All night the film ran over in my head. Kris's character often seems an unpleasant drunken dangerous bore; she seems silly – why would she love him? I see she has speeded up the film by cutting his establishing scene, moments of boyishness, of feeling the pain of his existence, that makes us feel for him and with him; she has cut his reactions ... the sadness, the wonderful wasted quality Kris brought the part, the exhaustion and the playfulness with which he courts her ... is diminished or gone.'

Streisand had been successful in centring the story entirely on her character. The other players are plastic. Kristofferson's songs are tuneless, his voice and delivery show no sign of once having been of the calibre to make him a rock idol. One wonders what Esther ever saw in him. She is, in fact, irritated by him from their first encounter, and only after that candlelit bath together, now sexually involved with him, does she change in her attitude. Also, there is an inherent age problem: Streisand – though dressed young appears to have outgrown her clothes and her role.

Then there is the score. Kristofferson's songs (not of his composition) are painful to the ears and although Streisand is supposed to become a rock star of the magnitude of a Janis Joplin, the songs that make an impression are closer to the old Streisand mould – 'Evergreen', 'The Woman in the Moon', and 'Lost Inside of You'. The most puzzling question is how she allowed herself the self-indulgence to sing for nearly eight minutes, as in concert, at the end of the film – completely obfuscating the impact of the climactic scene that follows Kristofferson's death and the Grammy Awards Ceremony where she is announced as Esther Hoffman Howard, taking on her husband's name professionally for the first time. In the medley that follows, one assumes the segue from the poignancy of 'With One More Look at You' to the hard-rock up-tempo of 'Watch Closely Now' is to telegraph the message that Esther is on her own and going to be all right. However, she is just dandy before Kristofferson is killed in the car crash and the audience has no doubt that,

---

[1] The final credit for film editor was Peter Zimmer, ACE; for wardrobe: Shirley Strahm, Seth Banks.

after a proper period of mourning, she will be just dandy again, for she has displayed great inner strength and determination for the major portion of the picture.

None the less, Streisand's performance is commanding. The camera work is extremely good and there are times when the story tugs at your heart. Still, Streisand's *A Star Is Born* is not just a flawed film, it is a travesty, turning legend into pulp fiction.

None of these criticisms are meant to diminish Streisand's elephantine efforts to make what she believed would be a great film. She knew by instinct what was missing from the previous versions of *A Star Is Born*, both in their statements about female suffering and in their emotional architecture. She did not want to make herself a victim in the same way that Gaynor and Garland had been in their renderings and in that she succeeded. But there are deep flaws in the story structure and character development and weak dialogue that undermine the picture.

'You have to understand the way she saw it,' John Gregory Dunne explained. 'It was her life on the line. If the picture went down, she went down with it. She just had to do what she thought was right.'

'*A Star Is Born* was the beginning of Barbra's examining her own power,' Peters added. 'It was a discovery period for her. And she started to realise that she could do it, she could take control of her life. I was the tool, in a way. The halfback. I was the one who ran interference for her – because there were a lot of changes she wanted to make, but she couldn't always articulate it.'

So consumed was she with getting everything right as she saw it that even when the finished picture was shipped for exhibition, it was accompanied by the following note: 'In setting your usual level of sound please make sure that Reel 1 and Reel 2 are allowed to play *as loud as possible*. The color is also at its best at 14½-foot candlepower ... Barbra Streisand.'

Premièred on 18 December 1976 at the Village Theatre in West Los Angeles, the first reviews from the Hollywood trades were laudatory. Streisand and Peters basked in glowing optimism, certain *A Star Is Born* would validate her dedication to the project and diminish any effect from the bad publicity that ran rampant during the making and cutting of the movie, none of which had wounded her so much as a lengthy vitriolic article written by Frank Pierson and published in *New West* and *New York* magazines disclosing personal conversations between them.[2] Pierson did not attend the preview but did comment that he liked what Streisand had done to the final cut. One thing has to be said regarding Pierson's position as director: he knew from the outset that Streisand and Peters had the definitive word on all decisions and on the final cut. This was bound to create problems unless he accepted the weakened

---

[2] Some conversations are quoted in this chapter.

circumstance in which this placed him. So ardently had he wished to have the credit that he made his pact with the devil and then refused to abide by that compromise.

When the largely negative critical response appeared nationwide in the press, Streisand and Peters were unprepared. '*A Star Is Born: dead on arrival*', bannered *Rolling Stone*, which summed up its critique by saying, 'If only the music had been better, if only Streisand and Kris Kristofferson were rock singers, if only his role had been developed. If only ... it might have been good.'

'*A Star Is Still-Born*,' Rex Reed wrote, adding: 'They haven't remade *A Star Is Born* they have buried it six feet under.' *A Star Is Shorn*,' jibed the *New Times*.

Streisand was in shock. People she knew who had seen the movie had called it brilliant. Both she and Peters believed the reviews were personal attacks. She felt bitter, and although *A Star Is Born* was an immediate box-office success, grossing $9.5 million in the first nine days of its release, eventually to earn over $140 million, Streisand's greatest money-making picture, she never forgot any of the words written by the critics castigating the film. Even the huge five million album sales did not mitigate her resentment. What did please her was having her song 'Evergreen' become such a huge commercial hit.

With the success of *A Star Is Born*, Peters's career as a producer was now guaranteed. '[Most of my life] I've fought for what I believe in and was not above using violence. Now, though, I've found different ways to communicate emotionally,' he commented. 'Since being with Barbra, I have gotten it together. She has shown me things can be different. I've evolved as a person. My desires and passions are the same but I don't feel as threatened,' he paused and added: 'You know, James Dean lived my kind of frantic life.'

They were working on another project about a clown – Streisand was wild about clowns. They did not actually have a story and they brought Arthur Laurents out to the Coast to see if he could offer some help. The project never took off, but they spent a lot of time together and their early closeness was somewhat recaptured. 'Peters taught her to have fun,' Laurents says.

One day as Peters walked with Laurents on the grounds of the ranch, he turned to him and asked, 'Would you speak to your friend for me?'

'About what?' Laurents inquired.

'The kid's gay. She should face it now.'

'Jason was only twelve,' Laurents recalls, 'and I said, "How do you know?" And he said, "He's interested in antiques." ' It was crazy. There is no connection, but he had an instinct and he wanted to save 'his woman', as he often called her, any pain that might be waiting for her, oblivious to his own possible contribution to that pain.

Peters was set to produce a second film, *The Eyes of Laura Mars*, a thriller with voyeurism as its theme, on a one-picture deal for Columbia, which hoped that Streisand would agree to play the lead, a photographer specialising in sex-and-violence compositions. Despite the fact that Irvin Kershner, who had directed *Up the Sandbox*, would direct, and that she would be working with Peters, Streisand refused to accept the role of the psychic Laura Mars, who could 'see' the future murders of some of her friends as well as her own. It was not a role she wanted to play and the trials of *A Star Is Born* had exhausted her. She needed time to recharge, time to be with Jason, and to have some space for a spell without Peters whom she alternately battled with and passionately loved. To Columbia's disappointment, Peters did not pressure her to join him in his project for them.

'The truth was, Jon wanted to make it this time on his own and felt he was perfectly able to do it,' a friend recalled. 'I don't doubt that he led Columbia into believing Barbra would come on board. It helped him close the deal. But *Star* was a big winner, he had brought it in on budget and Hirschfeld and Begelman [at Columbia] knew he was a helluva lot smarter than the public had been led to believe. Begelman – this was before the shit hit the fan and he was caught up in those embezzlement charges – stood behind him, and he was a strong power at the studio those days. They did insist that he come up with a big star.'

Blonde, cool, green-eyed Faye Dunaway, who had just won the Academy Award for Best Actress in *Network*, was cast as Laura Mars. Dunaway was one of the most sought-after female stars, having also been nominated for Best Actress twice before, in *Bonnie and Clyde* and *Chinatown*. Peters was determined to make a stylish thriller. *Laura Mars* was shot almost entirely on location in New York 'to capture that disturbing New York contrast between *haute couture* chic and dangerous street decay that Laura's photography reflects', he said.

After the script was completed and pre-production set, Streisand remained in Malibu while Peters went off to New York. She threw herself into the work of designing and decorating the three additional separate houses, making a total of five dwellings (the smallest 3,500 square feet), each self-contained on two acres of land, that were now part of their Malibu complex. They had fought fiercely when the first guest house was under construction. In terms of decorating taste they were decades apart and stylistically at odds. Peters leaned towards either a *now* or a ranch look; Streisand – to art deco, art nouveau, Victorian and American Primitive. Sometimes their fights ended with them sleeping in different houses for a night. 'I hate that lamp! Jon bought it,' she told a reporter, adding: 'And the glass doors in the dining room, too. I kept threatening to tear them out. They should be stained glass.'

'They were very competitive with each other,' a staff member recalled. 'At times it seemed that they enjoyed in a strange way yelling at each other and the drama that went along with this type of behaviour.'

Peters was not a man whom she could control and although that appeared to be what she wanted, it was also most often the reason that they fought. He would not be governed by a woman and she was unable to do anything else. Compromise was simply not a part of her character. 'Well, I guess you'd say she was hooked on him,' a close observer noted. 'I'd say they were obsessed with each other. Jon was turned on by the fights they had. He liked an element of danger, of risk. They were like teenagers sometimes, teasing, daring.'

Peters now had his own team working for him although Streisand was never far in the background. After her experience with Pierson and the publication of his article on the shooting of *Star* with its vivid uncompromising descriptions of Peters and herself, Streisand became adamant that anyone who worked for them either on their domestic or business staff sign a document vowing never to talk to anyone publicly or otherwise about them. This created a row between Streisand and Peters, who refused to have anyone working for him sign such a paper. Michael Meltzer, a young man and former CPA hired as a general assistant to Peters, recalled that one day, when they were driving to the studio in his employer's specially built black Mercedes convertible, Peters said to him, 'Michael, one day soon I'm going to own a studio.'

Meanwhile, Streisand always got what she wanted. Once it was a garage near their offices at the studio which was leased and occupied. Within an hour of her request, it was emptied and the lease turned over to her. 'You had to handle Barbra and Jon with kid gloves,' Meltzer recalled, 'because you couldn't tell when something would explode in your face. Working for them was a tough environment. Both of their lives were dedicated to work. They argued a lot. His ego was as healthy as hers. The staff knew how to get out of their way when they were on a tirade. Barbra was suspicious, insecure. She worried that Peters was unfaithful. One night she called me at 2 a.m. Jon was to have arrived on a flight earlier that evening from New York and he had not. She wanted to know if I knew where he had gone. She called back in a half an hour to say he had arrived home bearing gifts.'

Although ostensibly Meltzer was working for Peters, it was his job to renegotiate prices for things Streisand wanted to buy. There was one store in Los Angeles where she bought many of her art deco pieces. After she picked them out, Meltzer was sent down to haggle over the price with the owner. 'No matter what price I got she wasn't satisfied. I had to try another time to get it cheaper. She had this fetish about money. She was generous in terms of large amounts – big charities, things like that – but absolutely mean and niggardly about the salaries of the working people she hired. I recall once that Jon had hired some young Mexican workers who had no green cards and paid them $3.50 an hour (scale at the time) but the work wasn't getting done fast enough. Barbra wanted them to work overtime. They asked for an additional 25 cents an hour overtime. She told me to fire them and have them replaced. It killed me, but I did it. Another time I had to fire an older domestic couple who had been with her since she first came to Hollywood. They seemed to have outlasted their usefulness. She gave me orders that the couple had to be out by Saturday of that same week and she and Peters would be away and return then. With Barbra, when she's done with you, she's done with you. When your employment was over so was the relationship. It didn't matter that you were working for Jon. Barbra had to be in control. You had to absorb her passions and lose your own initiative. At the end of the tunnel where does it leave you?

'I quit after eighteen months. When one works for Barbra you become sucked up into her life, you have no life of your own. I was on call twenty-four hours a day. Because both Barbra and Jon were terribly demanding, the slightest error could result in severe verbal tirades. I found this to be very difficult. One always had to be thinking about the consequences of every act, for you never knew when you could get tripped up. Yet, whatever her failings, I was in awe of Barbra, blown away by being in her presence. Being with both of them was like being in the centre of a high-energy field.'

A *Star Is Born* received four Academy Award nominations: cinematography, sound, original sound score and its adaptation, and original song – 'Evergreen', which Streisand sang to thunderous applause at the Awards ceremony on 28 March 1977. After all five nominated songs had been presented, Neil Diamond opened the winning envelope and jubilantly called out, 'The winner is ... "Evergreen".' Paul Williams, the song's lyricist, accompanied Streisand on stage, whereupon she said teary-eyed into the microphone: 'In my wildest dreams I never thought I would win an Oscar for writing a song.'

'I was going to make a comment about, "Isn't it nice they gave *me* one too," ' Williams candidly recalled, 'but I kept my mouth shut about that. What I *did* say was, "I'd like to thank all the little people," then I remembered I *am* the little people [he is on the short side]. I was far from sober.' At the Grammys a few weeks later when they won for Best Song of the Year, he thanked 'Barbra for writing a beautiful melody, and Dr Jack Wallstader for the valium that got me through the whole experience'. Her relationship with Williams had been difficult from the offset, but, as he fully admitted later, he was heavily on drugs and alcohol at the time and not easy to work with.

Since the release of *A Star Is Born* and the incredible success of the soundtrack recording, the 'Evergreen' single and an album, *Streisand Superman*, that went platinum, more fans than ever made their way up the narrow road leading to the complex. Streisand reached a point of near-paranoia. The property was now encased by an eight-foot metal fence with concealed television scanners and electronic gates. There were three guards who rotated eight-hour shifts. Signs posted on the fence and gates declared: 'Danger. Beware. Guard Dogs Trained to Attack.' Twice one of the three Dobermans thus trained bit guests, and one person sued (the case was settled out of court). In attempting to protect herself, to keep the prying and the uninvited out, Streisand had merely placed restraints upon herself. She was, in effect, locked in. She also found herself to be bored and lonely with Peters away, and with Jason flew to New York to join him. Loneliness was not her only impetus. Rumours that Peters and Dunaway were having an affair had filtered back to her.

Jason was enrolled at Dalton, a private day school on the East Side, Peters moved into the Central Park West penthouse in the Ardsley with them as he worked on the film and the Dunaway threat was dispelled. Then she was faced with another problem. First Artists, saved by the financial success of *A Star Is Born*, was pressing Streisand to honour her contract and make the third film owing to them very soon so that the momentum would not be lost.

'There was a script that was originally meant for Steve McQueen and Ali MacGraw,' Blossom Kahn, who was director of new projects recalled. 'Neither one of them wanted to do it and I was sent to New York with the express purpose of convincing Barbra to do the film. It was set in the midwest and was about a young farm gal who lived near a small town and – and this city man comes through and sweeps her off her feet (an early *Madison County*). Straight romantic drama. I thought it was not right for her. I was there doing something I did not believe in, but I was determined to give it a good try.

'For about two weeks I was at her apartment day and night. Jon was there almost every evening. They were at each other all the time. Terrible fighting. Love-hate. It embarrassed me but it didn't seem to bother them that I was there. I'd take a scotch and sit it out until things cooled or they were suddenly lovers again. She was terribly worried about the possibility of someone kidnapping Jason. She didn't want the car to take him through Central Park when he was driven to and from school. She was afraid of everything. Neurotic to the enth degree. One day she asked me to accompany her to the doctor for a tooth extraction. She had an abscess that had kept her up all night. When we got to the dentist's office she kept insisting that I come inside with her while the deed was being done. Thank God, the dentist and nurse finally cajoled her into letting me stay in the reception room.

'Phil Feldman, then the President of First Artists, called me every day – "How're you doing?" he'd ask. I'd repeat: "I'm not getting anywhere." Then towards the end of the second week she told me, "There's no use in your wasting your time here, Blossom. I'm not going to do it." I liked Barbra but was intimidated by her. She has a tremendous presence. It's an attitude, but there's also something mesmerising about her eyes – so blue, and when she talks to you, often unblinking. Jon was *shrewd*. He wanted to be Svengali. And [with her] there is that little girl who wants to come out and be loved, who uses her vulnerability. I'll never forget the scene in the dentist's office. She was so childlike, terrified. You felt you wanted to hold her hand to keep her from being scared.'

Capitalising on First Artists' eagerness for her to make a film, Streisand pressured them into advancing $200,000 for story costs to develop *Yentl*. 'We all were doing everything we could to get Barbra to work and *Yentl* was all she wanted to do,' Ed Holly said. 'We did not feel the project would be commercial. Even the Jewish community would be upset [because of *Yentl*'s cross-dressing and wedding night scenes].'

At about this time Sue Mengers received a script entitled *The Main Event*, written by two TV-comedy writers, Gail Parent and Andrew Smith, to be submitted to her client, Ryan O'Neal. He liked the battle-of-the-sexes 1940s-style story – about a perfume executive who loses all her money to an embezzler, but left with the contract of a washed-up fighter is determined to turn him into a money-making champion. The real battle is a sexual one between the woman manager and the male fighter, reminiscent of old Tracy–Hepburn movies.

Ryan suggested Mengers send the treatment to Diana Ross, who was Ryan's Malibu beachfront neighbour and lover. 'Ryan used to jog in the nude,' Ross recalled. 'He wasn't easy to ignore.' Mengers decided it would be better to reunite the team that had made *What's Up, Doc?* so successful at the box office, and she sent the script to Streisand. Peters read it first and with his background in boxing he decided it would be a good picture for him to produce with Streisand as the star. She was reluctant. *Yentl* remained her top priority and *The Main Event* did not immediately appeal to her, so she wavered for several weeks.

'Why am I not working?' she rhetorically asked Sydney Pollack, who remained a good friend. 'What am I saving myself for? This is stupid. I should be out there, Sydney. So, every picture won't be great. I mean, I haven't done a picture in so long [just over a year]. I sit here and wait and wait and wait – for what? For Chekhov to come along? For Shakespeare to come along? I'm getting older, and there are a million things I want to do,' she rationalised. '*What* am I saving myself for? And yet I say to myself, why would I want to go and do something that I'm not really stimulated by? And then I argue with myself. I talked to Truffaut once, who said, "You do your work and at the end you have a body of work. Some of it is good and some of it is not good, but the stuff that's good will override what isn't good – that's what a body of work is. You can't just sit and wait for the perfect script." '

Although it was a superficial project, she did have enormous trust in Peters's instinct that *The Main Event* would be a commercial success and it would also fulfil her contract with First Artists. And so her sabbatical was ended and after numerous rewrites on the script, on 2 October 1978, the film went into production at the Main Street Gym in downtown Los Angeles under the direction of Howard Zieff, who had recently had a box-office hit with the Walter Matthau–Glenda Jackson comedy *House Calls*. Zieff signed on with much the same restrictions as Pierson had in his contract. Streisand was to have the final word. Once again, a director would be cast as middle man between her and Peters.

One time Peters and Zieff were watching the Muhammad Ali–Leon Spinks fight on television. Around the fifth round, Streisand suddenly jumped up and began to do vigorous exercises dancing back and forth in front of the screen. Peters demanded she sit down. 'I just can't sit and watch Muhammad Ali, who's always been a winner, lose,' she said.

'Then leave the room,' Peters ordered. She did after the next disastrous round for Ali, who after fifteen rounds lost his champion heavyweight title to Spinks. For Streisand, losing was never an option for herself or for those whom she considered winners.

Seven years had passed since Ryan and Streisand had worked together and been lovers. They had remained friends. 'You like the fights?' she asked him one afternoon at the Barn reflecting on the recent match, adding mistily, 'My stepfather liked the fights. I always wanted his approval. He never liked me. He used to sit in his undershirt, drinking beer and watching the fights on television. And, you know, one time I crawled underneath the TV picture when I went by so I wouldn't interfere with his view. He never even noticed. He would *never* see me. He just stared at the fights.

'When he went off, I thought it was my fault and so did my mother,' she continued, Ryan recalled that her glance was somewhere off in the distance. 'Then one day, when I was in *Funny Girl* on Broadway, I scratched the cornea of my eye and my understudy [Lainie Kazan but not the same incident that had caused her to be fired] was getting ready to go on in my place. Everyone was telling me not to go on because I might hurt my eye. Then I got this card and a little dish of candy from my stepfather – he was out in front, in the audience. So I said, "I'm going on." The doctor anaesthetised my eye so it wouldn't tear. I never did a show like that. It was the best performance I ever gave. After the show, I waited in my dressing room for him but he never came back.' She was silent for a moment. 'I still have the candy dish. I've never been able to part with it,' she added quietly, suddenly giving a new insight into her relationship to the man she always claimed she hated but whom she wanted desperately to love her and whom she appears to have been more willing to forgive than she has ever admitted.

'Am I cool about Barbra and Ryan playing love scenes? Hell, no!' Peters admitted to a *Los Angeles Times* reporter. The two men had gone three rounds in the ring together, presumably for publicity and fun, but Peters was seen as the better boxer and twice let go a couple of hard punches that caught Ryan unprepared and sent him reeling.

As she had done with *A Star Is Born*, at the end of principal photography, Streisand took over the editing of Zieff's final version and 'cut the film to her own purpose'. She had worked out fastidiously for all the road work and exercise scenes and there is an over-abundance of close-ups of her body parts, particularly her rear, that smack of self-indulgence, but the movie scoots merrily along, the jokes are funny and Streisand and Ryan – although they are *not* Katharine Hepburn and Spencer Tracy or Rosalind Russell and Cary Grant – *are* engaging. Made on a comfortable $7 million budget and with an extra-ordinary $8 million advertising budget,[3] *The Main Event* would gross over $80 million of which Streisand would receive $1 million as her fee and 10 per cent of the gross – a whopping additional $8 million (she would make upwards of $15 million on *A Star Is Born*).

The most surprising thing about Streisand's association with *The Main Event* was the compromise the script made to her avowed principles. The character she played was a woman of stubborn independence and liberated individuality. Yet, in the end, she surrenders her fighter/lover's championship and the money that will save her from financial collapse in order to get her man. This was not the message of a woman who spoke so high-mindedly about women's need to be treated as equals and to be given the same opportunities as men. Peters was later to say, '*The Main Event* was my fault. I pushed Barbra into that. It was time to do a movie and I wanted her to do a comedy. But it was material she really didn't like.' It appeared that passion had won over conviction.

She recorded the title song as part of her *The Main Event – A Glove Story* album, and it hit the charts within two weeks of release in June 1979. Shortly thereafter she became embroiled in the problems at First Artists. She had no more pictures to deliver under the terms of her contract, but she owned a large number of stock shares in the company. The foundation upon which First Artists had been formed had been shaky from the start. None of the stars had worked to make the whole as good as the parts or even the parts as good as they should have been. And by the time Streisand had completed her last commitment to the company, so had the other partners and it was obvious that none of them cared to continue their involvement.

Ed Holly had replaced Phil Feldman as President and it was his thankless job to try to work out a sale of the company's assets.[4] When this was completed,

---

[3] Advertising budgets for films are usually set at no more than 20 per cent of the total production cost.

[4] 'An Australian firm got interested and offered a full price for the company and there was general agreement that this would be a reasonable price and everybody at that point sort of wanted to get their money and run,' Ed Holly remembered. 'The Australians, sensing that they had a good chance of getting 40 per cent of the stock just with stars' shares went to them individually and got agreements with three of them, Barbra being one, to sell their stock. Newman would not sell. I decided to fight the Australians, who – if they owned 100 per cent of the company was fine – they could do what they wanted, but I wasn't going to let three of the star stockholders sell control of the company. I simply was not going to let this happen when there would be 2,000 small public stockholders who would then be out on their investment.

Streisand was suddenly free to make whatever film she chose as long as she could get backing and distribution. There was no doubt in her mind that the film she *must* do was *Yentl* and that now no one would stop her from directing it even if she had to finance the project entirely with her own money. She began work on the script, seen then as a straight dramatic film. The story took possession of her. The relationship of Yentl and her father filled her with envy, his death brought her renewed pain over the loss of her own father.

On a trip to New York in the fall of 1979, she accompanied Shelley to their father's grave in a Jewish cemetery in Queens. She had been seven the last time she had been there. Upon her father's tombstone were written the words 'Beloved Teacher and Scholar'. Shelley took a photograph of her standing beside it. When it was developed the following day she was surprised to observe that the name ANSHEL was carved on the tombstone of the grave adjoining the grave of Manny Streisand. 'I couldn't believe it,' she said. 'That's a very unusual name. Not like Irving. And right there next to my father's grave was a man named Anshel, who was Yentl's dead brother whose name she takes when she disguises herself as a boy. To me it was a sign, you know, a sign from my father that I should make this movie.'

This discovery had such an impact that she asked Shelley to go with her to visit a medium, 'a nice, ordinary-looking Jewish lady', Streisand recalled. 'We sat around a table with all the lights on and put our hands on it. And then it began. The table began to spell out letters with its legs. Pounding away. Bang, bang, bang! Very fast, counting out letters. Spelling M-A-N-N-Y, my father's name, and then B-A-R-B-A-R-A. I got so frightened I ran away. Because I could feel the presence of my father in that room. I ran into the bathroom and locked the door. When I finally came out, the medium asked, "What message do you have?" and the table spelled out S-O-R-R-Y. Then the medium asked, "What else do you want to tell her?" And it spelled S-I-N-G and P-R-O-U-D. It sounds crazy, but I knew it was my father who was telling me to be brave, to have the courage of my convictions to sing proud! And for that word S-O-R-R-Y to come out ... I mean, God! It was his answer to all that deep anger I had felt about his dying ... And I thought ... life is going by so fast. I have to stand up for what I believe in. I can't be frightened any more. I don't want to be some old lady saying, "I shoulda made that movie *Yentl*." '

She and Peters had bought back the rights from First Artists just before the

'So I filed lawsuits in both federal and state courts against the Australian company under the loophole law and the three star stockholders – Barbra, Sidney Poitier and the estate of Steve McQueen who had just recently died. This forced the hand of the Australians, who came back and bought the whole company and that was how it was resolved. But it is a strong indication of how little First Artists meant to the stars themselves. They were willing to sacrifice their autonomy – their ideal – for financial gain.'

company was sold. Her plan was to direct and star in the film while he produced it. Peters tried all means possible to talk her out of going forward, especially since every major studio in Hollywood had turned it down. Not only was he certain that if filmed, *Yentl* would be a dismal failure at the box office, he was not convinced that she could be persuasive as a young boy. One night he was greeted as he entered their home by a slim young man. 'She came out dressed as a *yeshivah* boy with a pipe and a hat and I thought it was a guy robbing the house,' he said. 'I was going to punch him in the mouth.'

Directly following *The Main Event* and the dissolution of First Artists, Peters had formed PolyGram Pictures with Peter Guber, who had been the head of worldwide production for Columbia and they were preparing *An American Werewolf in London* for production. Peters, now flying on his own and seeing his star rising, did not have the time to devote to Streisand or her projects that she would have liked.

They fought bitterly. She was determined to go forward with *Yentl*. 'It was a time in my life when I needed to be really independent, both personally and professionally,' she said. 'I thought to myself: I have to make this picture, and I have to also be the producer.'

It was a scary time for Streisand. She was nearing her fortieth birthday. Peters was away a good deal of the time, surrounded by some of the most beautiful young women in the business. She drew her small circle of close friends more tightly to her and joined in efforts to raise funds through celebrity galas to help re-elect President Carter and defeat Ronald Reagan. She was back in therapy, but prime in her mind was *Yentl*.

After many weeks of trying to discourage her, Peters reluctantly placed an announcement in *Daily Variety* that Streisand would direct *Yentl* for his company. Rusty Lemorande, Peters's executive in charge of creative development, was sent to Eastern Europe to photograph authentic locations in Hungary, Austria, Czechoslovakia, Romania, Poland and Yugoslavia. When he returned, Peters had another change of heart.

'You're not going to do it!' he recalled telling her. '"We're going to do something else together." I was a little domineering, I guess, and I remember her looking at me and saying, "Just because you said that, I'm going to do the movie *no matter what*." '

Whether Peters was involved or not was no longer important to her. She was determined to make *Yentl*, and when she left the room, eyes brimming with angry tears and determination, she knew the end of their affair was imminent. There could be no room in her life for a lover who, despite the passion she still felt for him, did not support her 100 per cent.

# 26

A MINK COAT HELD closed over a plaid wool shirt tucked into belted designer jeans, her head down, Streisand slipped out of her building on Central Park West and into the waiting limousine before the two reporters stationed outside her door reached her side. The day was grey, one of damp, penetrating cold and intermittent spells of freezing rain. Her hair was frizzy, falling in corkscrew ringlets on her forehead. She looked preoccupied, perhaps in pain. She was meeting Jon for lunch. It was over. Had been for a month, since New Year's Eve – the turn of the decade, 1980 – the first in seven years that they had not spent together. She was going to try to be civil about it, but it was no less painful than her divorce from Elliott and just as complicated, for they had mutual business interests and owned property together. Peters still had a stake in *Yentl*. They did not see eye to eye about its future and although he had been persuaded to go on with the project, he was fighting hard to have the film shot on location in the New York/Lake Placid area and not in London and Czechoslovakia where costs could accelerate without his supervision. Streisand wanted all rights, which meant she would have to find other financing.

They were lunching at Café des Artistes, little more than a mile's drive from the Ardsley straight down Central Park West. The energy of the city was mightier on such cold, windswept days. People walked faster, the upper half of their body breaking through the layers of cold. Even the skyscrapers that faced the park seemed to be in violent motion as the wind whipped around their pyramidical, ziggurat towers. It was two o'clock, an hour chosen because they expected the chic West Side restaurant would be emptying out. She had thought their meeting place had been kept a secret, but photographers accosted her the moment the driver helped her out of the car.

'Go to hell!' she shouted at *New York Post* photographer, Martha Cooper, who was snapping away close to her face as she headed for the front door, which swung open the moment she approached and then closed immediately after she was inside, two employees now barring the press from entering. Peters stood to greet her from a table off to one side, standing beneath one of the restaurant's famous, colourful art nouveau murals. Once her fur coat was removed, the contrast between them was glaring: Peters – post-Beatle haircut and rabbinical beard impeccably groomed, recently custom-made Savile Row suit, white shirt and Sulka tie with a perfect Windsor knot; Streisand, hair flying, California casual.

They talked for about an hour. Neither ate very much. When they rose to leave, Peters had a wistful look in his unusually dense dark eyes. Both of them wanted to make their parting as amicable as possible. Neither was actually sure why it was ending. For Streisand, it had been the most consuming relationship of her life, for Peters certainly the most important. Their impact on each other had been immense. They had had – as Stephen Sondheim wrote in a lyric – *a good thing going*. Sure, it had been a bumpy ride, but never dull and both of them had moved forward, grown. She looked at him now and she was proud. He had made it into the big time, the *very* big time. 'Look at you,' her expression said. 'You're a *mensch*, a *real mensch*!' They reached the front door and made a decision to get into her car and dismiss his. She dropped him at his New York offices and rode back home alone. She had succeeded without much struggle in reclaiming the rights to *Yentl*. She would now be on her own producing, directing and starring in the film if she could raise the required capital, which she estimated at this stage as $13 million. And she would not have Peters to help her.

A power conflict had overwhelmed the great passion they had shared. They were terribly competitive and she seemed to fear that Peters's rise to power in the industry diminished her own. Peters had evolved from film apprentice to studio mogul. He no longer needed Streisand to lead him down the corridors of power, nor did he want her presence to lessen his own accomplishment. He also could not resist the attention of a beautiful woman and Streisand was too proud, too liberated, too much her own woman to deal with a lover's adultery, especially one who was no longer under her thumb.

This last year, 1979, she had taken an emotional journey back to her roots. Never a fully practising Jew, she none the less strongly felt her Jewishness. To understand more thoroughly the culture and motivations in *Yentl*, she had painstakingly researched the period, the history of the Eastern European Jews and the laws and social structure that formed their world in the late nineteenth and early twentieth centuries. She sought out specialists in the field, rabbis from the three factions of the faith – Orthodox, Conservative and Reform.[1] At the same time, Jason was to celebrate his thirteenth birthday in December and

[1] Streisand did much of her research at the Hillel Center at UCLA, where she later bestowed funds for a Jewish performing arts centre. The Pacific Jewish Center, where Jason Gould was bar mitzvahed, had been co-founded by TV critic and writer Michael Medved. In April 1981, following a significant contribution by Streisand, the Center's grade school in Santa Monica was renamed and rededicated the Emanuel Streisand School.

was studying for his bar mitzvah. The ceremony, held in a synagogue or temple, is not a sacrament, nor a sacramental ritual. It simply signals the arrival of a Jewish boy at the age when, presumably, adult reason and responsibility commence. It is usually held on the Saturday closest to the boy's birthday, in Jason's case 5 January 1980.

Both Streisand and Elliott, who was separated from Jenny at the time, had met Rabbi Daniel Lapin of the Pacific Jewish Center. 'I explained to her,' the Rabbi recalled, 'that in order for the bar mitzvah to have any meaning, in a deeper sense, for her son, he would have to know and see that it meant something to her, too.' Rabbi Lapin recommended that she study Judaism along with Jason. This coincided beautifully with her research for *Yentl*. Once a week she would meet the Rabbi and discuss what she had learned and pose tough theological questions.

The intense study of their faith and heritage brought her close to Jason, who had developed into an intelligent young man with a sense of humour and curiosity about many things. He liked to write and his school essays showed that he had a flair. He seemed pleased to be sharing more private times with his mother, engaging in a project with her. During her seven years with Peters they had not been able to manage as much time together as either one of them would have wanted.

The impending bar mitzvah also brought her into closer contact with Elliott, although not in a romantic sense. That had been over for many years, but there was a strong feeling of family as Elliott and his father, as was the custom, stood on the *bima* with Jason, and she, in her front-row seat in the small synagogue, watched the passing of ancient tradition from father to son as Elliott and the ageing Bernard Gould read with Jason from the *Torah*. The bar mitzvah is a ceremony of joyous celebration, and therefore a party following the ritual is appropriate. Three tents were erected at the Malibu compound. Kosher and Chinese caterers were hired. Streisand danced with Jason and a nimble Bernard and managed a turn around the floor with Elliott, who also danced with Diana. Later her mother got up on the bandstand and sang 'One Kiss'. There was exultant Jewish, Russian and popular music, the last so that Jason and his friends could dance, although most of the young people were too shy.

With Jason's bar mitzvah behind her, and her business arrangements with Peters settled, she began the ignominious task of pitching *Yentl* yet again, this time along with film taken of the location sites in Czechoslovakia that she wanted to use and a screenplay by Ted Allen. Warner Brothers and Columbia Pictures passed. She went to United Artists, the budget at this point up to $14.5 million. They said they *might* consider the project if she was to sing in the film. Ted Allen claims he had suggested this from the outset and, as Streisand did not want to do a 'Ray Stark–Herbert Ross musical', that *Yentl* sing her thoughts. Streisand saw this as a viable compromise. *Yentl* could be 'a realistic fantasy ... a film with music'. Late evenings were spent in her living room with Michel Legrand at the piano, Streisand jumping up from her cross-legged position on the floor and going over to the piano as a thought came to her, and the Bergmans nearby scratching out words to proposed songs by Legrand.

She was now working on the screenplay with help from the venerable author Isaac Bashevis Singer. Ted Allen mused that the script he wrote and she discarded 'gave indications of the anti-Semitism in Eastern Europe that drove the Jews to America and I don't think that Barbra liked that. She had another concept.' What she had always seen in the story was Yentl's burning need to study the *Talmud*,[2] and perhaps become a *talmid chachem*, a learned scholar, an expert on *Talmud*. The *talmid chachem* is the most honoured figure in the life and culture of traditional Jewry, but women were denied access to the *Talmud* and its learning. Yentl did what she did because she believed women should be equal to men and that equality could only be achieved through education. It was also a story of unrequited love, of a young woman who loses her father, the one kindred spirit she has in life, and how she must come to terms with this terrible loss.

As soon as Legrand and the Bergmans had a number of the songs that would express Yentl's feelings, Streisand recorded them on tape and made another attempt to interest the studios. This time around, United Artists came forward. A film with Streisand singing was quite another matter, but they fought to get a deal that would protect them if Streisand the director should fail. What they wanted her to do was to give them the right to approve the final cut. Streisand struggled to retain her power.

While these negotiations were in progress, Sue Mengers brought her a lucrative proposition. Mengers was married to Belgian director Jean-Claude Tramont who, four weeks into production on the film *All Night Long* for MCA/Universal, had fired Gene Hackman's co-star, Lisa Eichhorn, an intelligent American-born actress who had attended London's Royal Academy of Dramatic Arts. The role of Cheryl Gibbons, the neglected wife who finds her sexuality with the night-manager of an Ultra-Save Drugstore, an establishment with a particularly weird clientèle, called for an earthiness that Eichhorn did not exhibit in the rushes. Production was halted and Mengers asked Streisand to replace the fired actress.

[2] The *Talmud* is a massive and monumental compendium of sixty-three books: the learned debates, dialogues, conclusions, commentaries, commentaries upon commentaries, commentaries upon commentaries *upon* commentaries, of the scholars who for over a thousand years interpreted the *Torah* (the first five books in the Bible, also known as the Five Books of Moses) and applied its teachings to problems of law, ethics, ceremony and traditions.

The film was really about Hackman's character, the frustrated George Dopler, who hates his job, is in an unhappy marriage, and finds himself in love with a married woman (Gibbons) who is having an affair with his son, whose ambition is to write Country and Western songs. Cheryl Gibbons originally had only five or six scenes, but the chance to stretch herself and play a Marilyn Monroe, waiflike blonde temptress appealed to Streisand. An added inducement was the $4 million fee *plus* 15 per cent of the gross that she was offered. For this stipend – the highest Hollywood had ever paid to a performer at this time – she would only have to take six weeks from her work on the screenplay of *Yentl*, and the money would help her finance the film.

After a four-week hiatus while her role was being developed, production on *All Night Long* was restarted on 9 June 1980 and remained on location in and round Los Angeles for the next six weeks in a heatwave that brought temperatures over 100 degrees and in the last week, a major strike by the Screen Actors Guild involving residuals on video, cable and pay television. Streisand had only one more scene to shoot in which she was to slide down a fire pole (her husband in the film was a fireman). It was not until late October, the strike settled, that she returned to do the remaining shot. 'Uh-uh,' she said, terrified as she stood on the edge of the second-floor perch where she was to grab the pole for her descent, 'I don't think I can do it. I have a weak stomach.' After several of the crew and Hackman himself slid down it to prove to her that she would be all right, she did the slide in one take.

*All Night Long* was not a film that Streisand fans would shout about. She played her blowsy, sexually awakened housewife exactly on key, in character, without any razzle-dazzle or Streisand mannerisms and she *supported* Hackman in several of his strongest scenes. Although not for everyone, the gritty American working-class world it portrays (as seen by Tramont's unique foreign eye) is gripping, Hackman gives an indelible, moving performance and Streisand proves how good an actress she really is. But all her energies were now turned to *Yentl*.

'I constantly had to give up everything,' Streisand recalled of her dealings on *Yentl* with United Artists. 'I didn't get paid for writing, I got paid Directors' Guild scale for directing, which I think is something like $80,000, and I got paid much less [$1 million] as an actress than I did in *All Night Long*. And then I had to give back half my salary if we went over budget [now $16.5 million]. But it didn't matter to me. Nothing mattered to me except getting this movie made.'

There had, by this time, been numerous rewrites of the screenplay, including Singer's, one by Elaine May and several by Streisand. Finally, English television writer Jack Rosenthal, author of *The Bar-Mitzvah Boy* which Jule Styne had transformed into an unsuccessful musical, was hired. Streisand and Rosenthal worked together. Unaware that the financing of the film largely depended on her soundtrack album, Rosenthal kept trying to cut Streisand's numerous songs, mostly ballads which seemed to stop the flow of the story. They had 'great rows' over this and Streisand always won out in the end.

*Yentl* took her on a long journey and during this odyssey she had been forced to face many of the demons in her life – her sense of desertion, of being a woman in a man's world, of perceiving herself as ugly, guilt at not being the daughter she believed would have pleased Diana. 'I've lived so many years feeling guilty,' she said. 'Jewish guilt. And I'm finding out about life, talking to people, hearing what they feel and think. They've got the same *mishigas* as I do ... People are afraid of their own feelings. Their own sexuality. The other day while I was driving to my [group therapy session], I was having an anxiety attack. Couldn't breathe. I was in a rage, feeling miserable, upset, like I was going insane. Like maybe I *am* insane, I'm such a terrible person and maybe I really am these awful things you read about and how do I deal with that and live with myself?

'But when I got to the session the therapist said, "Look, you're all mad, and so am I; there's only one difference: I respect my madness." He stripped half of my anxiety away. Because it was OK to be crazy, we're all crazy, and if you can respect your own madness – far out.'

Her 'craziness' manifested itself in her intensity about things that mattered to her. She was in a state of constant tumult. She wore people down, desperate to endow them with her sense of urgency, and *Yentl* had become her *raison d'être*. Although finally forced by United Artists to surrender control over the final cut, she was rigid in her determination to maintain control over all the major elements of the film.

She had won her battle to film *Yentl* in Czechoslovakia and at Lee International Studios just outside London, where she arrived in February 1982, two months before the start of principal photography. One major issue with United Artists remained unresolved. Her original contract had not included an agreement that she supply a completion bond, a form of Hollywood insurance in which a private company agrees to pay an amount over the budget that the producer spends on the film.

'The day before we were going to start shooting,' she recalled, 'United Artists said they would close down the production if I didn't give in and take on the completion bond. It was ridiculous, because they paid the company $700,000 which I needed in making the movie [which meant she would have to supply the deficit out of private funds or raise it elsewhere]. They didn't trust me. Not in that way, I suppose.

'The night before the first scene was shot, I prayed to my father. "Tell me what to do." I didn't know what to do. I felt as though I had too much power. You want it desperately for so long and then you want to give it away.' Actually she did not retain the control she wanted. There had been the last word on the final cut that she had been forced to forfeit, and she had desperately wanted to hire the brilliant Italian cinematographer Vittorio Storaro (*Reds*), and could not because his $250,000 fee was beyond the budget allowed by United Artists.

'I had to tell Storaro that I couldn't afford him, and three days later I woke up in my insanity ... *My* insanity. I had just given away a half a million dollars to set up a chair in my father's name for cardiovascular research at UCLA. I thought to myself, "I just gave away $500,000 but I didn't treat myself to a $250,000 gift of Storaro?" It taught me a lesson about my own lack of love for myself. And *Yentl* is really about that, too. Yentl finally learns to appreciate herself, too.'

On 14 April 1982, just ten days short of her fortieth birthday, Streisand walked terrified on to the sound stage where she would shoot *Yentl*'s opening shot. Cast and crew applauded and she was presented with a director's chair, her name printed on it. She made the rounds, shook hands with everyone. A prop man was embarrassed by his sweaty palms. 'Believe me, there's no one more nervous than me. We're all going to make mistakes, especially me. I will make most of them. So I need you,' she assured him.

Not long before filming began, her old friend William Wyler died. His wife Tally sent her a note – 'You never got a chance to talk to Willie about *Yentl*. But I know there were things he would have liked to have told you. So when you're on the set and there's a moment when you don't know what to do – just be very quiet and maybe you'll hear Willie whisper in your ear.' Often Streisand would go off to one side and seem as though she was silently communing with either Willie or her father.

Her need to get things right led her to expect the cast and crew to research their respective areas. Just prior to production she had given Mandy Patinkin, who was playing Avigdor the man Yentl loves but to whom she can't reveal her true identity, a seven-volume set of books entitled *The Legends of the Jews*; and to Amy Irving, cast as Hadass, the young woman Avigdor loves but who marries Yentl disguised as a boy, several books on keeping a kosher kitchen.

'To get the feel of the music, movement and crowds, and also because of the wedding scene in the film, Barbra would try to attend as many Hassidic weddings as she could possibly find,' Jeanette Kupferman, the film's historical consultant, remembered. ' "Can you find me a wedding?" became a familiar request ... Needless to say, Barbra was a great hit with all the gorgeously attired Hassidic matrons, who were greatly flattered by her interest in them ... "Is that really a sheitel?" she would inquire, sticking one finger under the elastic of a magnificent upswept coiffure. "You must give me your wig-maker's name," or "Say, could you tell me about Havdala candles?" '

She claimed she was sick every day on her way to work because it was all so overwhelming. 'I kept remembering that a friend of mine, Irvin Kershner, said,

"One day at a time." I don't know how I survived it but I'm proud I did. I didn't think I would at times.'

At one point the English tabloid papers claimed she was having trouble with her cast and crew, who resented her arrogant and autocratic style of direction. To quash these allegations the crew sent a letter with the signatures of all involved to the newspapers calling the accusations lies. 'She has captivated us all with her dedicated professionalism,' the letter stated.

'She'd fix my hair ribbons, brush an eyelash off my cheek, paint my lips to match the colour of the fruit on the table. I was like her little doll that she could dress up,' asserted Amy Irving, barely five foot four, her physical delicacy accentuated by the gauntness of her face and the startling contrast of her pale skin and of her vivid blue eyes and dark hair. 'For the scenes where I had to laugh,' Irving added, 'she'd stand behind the camera pulling the strings of an imaginary Hadass doll, making it burp and cry until I'd completely crack up.'

The most difficult scene in the film – the kiss by Hadass in her seduction of Anshel/Yentl – was done in one take. 'I had asked Amy to be very maidenly before that scene,' Streisand explained, 'and she did it beautifully. But then in the bedroom, where she comes on erotically, I asked her to let all her sexiness out, and wow! did she let it out.'

*Yentl's* cast and crew, led by Streisand, left London in early July for Prague, where they would then travel to the small village of Roztyly, a two-and-a-half hour journey, to begin shooting on the first exterior scenes in Czechoslovakia. Heavy rains had deluged the small village, turning all the roads into rivers of mud. Despite the unexpected weather conditions, Roy Walker, the production designer, with the help of the Czech crew who had joined the company, managed to create Yentl's village of Yanev out of a section that had formerly been a few wooden houses and a pig farm. The smell of sewerage and urine pervaded the area and there were flies the size of beetles.

The Soviet-dominated country, once celebrated for its experimental theatre work and its many fine films, had been in a period of heavy-booted repression since the democratically inclined Alexander Dubček was replaced as party leader in 1970. Now, twelve years later, conditions had worsened. Efforts were continually made to stamp out dissent, including mass arrests, union purges, and religious persecution. However, Czechoslovakia's economy was in serious jeopardy and the Czechs had been wooing Western film companies who needed old-world locations for their projects, offering lower production costs and the use of the film studio in Prague.

Diana was half-crazy over the idea of her daughter making a movie in an unstable country behind the Iron Curtain where people were being murdered or just disappeared. Then there were the lack of healthy food, the distance from home – or even from a Western hospital should something happen. 'She was a typical mother crying on the phone,' Streisand told Canadian talk show host Brian Linehan, a strong sense of pride in her voice as she added: 'She didn't want me to go; she was scared.' That Diana cared that she might be in jeopardy mattered a great deal to her. However much she had felt cheated by the loss of her father's love, her need to be reassured of her mother's love was even stronger.

She flew in vegetables and fruit, two items in severe shortage, to make sure her company remained in good health. Not until she arrived in Roztyly could she have known what faced her. Across from an unlovely square was a small hotel, which she took over to provide rooms for the cast and key people in the company. Czech members boarded with local families. Her room was unprepossessing: a bed up against the wall, in the middle a small table with one chair, next to the bed a table with a mirror, and a cracked washbasin. Threadbare curtains covered the windows which looked out on to some grubby buildings, but in the distance there were gardens filled with flowers and giant poplars, firs, woods, a river with a bridge that was built during Yentl's time.

Never before had she made a film outside the embracing paternalism of a studio, a controlled environment in which she knew everything would be weighted to her best advantage. She dug in, nails cut stubby-short, a great sacrifice on her part, and was never heard to complain about the conditions. The scenes that were the most difficult for her to shoot were those in which she was both actress and director. She had to learn how to get the best out of her fellow players and whether the camera was placed right, to splinter her concentration without losing it so that she was aware of what was happening around her.

'I had to make all the decisions,' she said, a residue of awe in her voice at her own accomplishments. 'I had a co-producer who handled the day-to-day budget stuff, but I had to make all the other decisions – where we shoot, how long we remain in one place.' Her intention was to make *Yentl* a *realistic fantasy*. 'Just by having the music you make it a fantasy,' she explained. 'Music is not real. People don't stop to sing ... *Yentl* was beautiful pictures, fairy-tale images. I wanted it to be a romantic film.

'I trusted my instincts a lot. I had to constantly remember that I was wearing four hats [Director, Producer, Writer and Star]. I found the experience very humbling. I was very moved by it. That power is very humbling. And I found myself being very soft-spoken, feeling even more feminine than I have ever felt. More motherly, more nurturing, more loving. I had patience I never dreamed I would have. I never wanted people to feel that I was so powerful ... I wanted people to be able to come up to me and give me a suggestion. Because if they can make it better, then I'm gonna use anything they can offer me.'

'She was an American woman directing her first film in a European and Eastern European film culture, yet she was able to react as the situation required,' her co-producer, Rusty Lemorande commented. 'My respect for her grew enormously.'

Jon Peters showed up in Roztyly just before the company was to move on to its next location, the old Jewish quarter of Zatec, in Bohemia – the north-east section of Czechoslovakia. Peters still had some business matters with Streisand that needed settling, papers that they had to agree on to sign, but this could have been done through lawyers and the mail. The truth was, he still cared deeply about her and wanted to make sure that she was all right.

'She treated him like any good friend and as such expected him to realise that she was working under stress and did not have time to do much *schmoozing*,' a crew member recalled. 'In Europe shooting ends at 7 p.m. and Barbra had a buffet table loaded with fresh vegetables and other things not easy to obtain in Roztyly. All the townspeople would gather and take things, but they were very polite, careful not to take too much. Jon was terribly impressed with the way Barbra was handling the whole scene, but he didn't have the stomach for a place like that – the smells, the bugs, the mud roads. He left the next day. I remember seeing her walk with him to the car that was to take him to the nearest railroad station. Her hair was cut in a boy's bob and she looked gamine, truly young, no more than the sixteen years old she was supposed to be in the film. It was a miracle how young she looked. Jon couldn't take his eyes off of her. They had a long clinch, bear-hug style. She turned away the moment he was seated in the car and started calling out orders to a member of the crew who was nearest to her. I caught her looking back once – just as his car slipped out of sight around a bend in the road.'

The exteriors for Bashev, the village where Avigdor and Yentl/Anshel study, were shot in Zatec before the company moved back to Prague. In that ancient city she filmed a scene on the famous Charles Bridge, which had been closed so that the film company could replicate a time when only carts and horses crossed its giant span.

She preferred to film in long, continuous takes rather than short, choppy scenes that could be put together in the editing room. The camera movements were graceful, rhythmic, inspired by the music. 'I had only nine days to do the musical rehearsals for this film,' she recalled. 'In *Funny Girl* I had six months. But I had done a lot of my work on tape. And I couldn't have somebody like Herb Ross stage the musical numbers. I didn't want *Yentl* to be that kind of musical.' She even choreographed the dancing.

Once back in London, the film almost complete, her problems began. By the time she had dubbed the sound track, both dialogue and music, she had gone $1 million over budget. Completion Bond, the company who had insured the film, gave her an ultimatum. Either she finished dubbing *Yentl* in six weeks or they would take the movie away from her and hire another film-maker to complete it. 'I need ten weeks and I'll put up $1.7 million of my own money,' she told the United Artists' representatives, who had flown to London. They insisted that it be handled through their offices for tax purposes.

'It was all about money,' Streisand said. 'I kept saying, "Please, we're going to ruin the movie. I'm going to die from the pressure. This is supposed to be a joyous experience." I did anything to get it done so that they could never take it away from me. And in the end UA didn't touch my movie. Not a frame.'

She likened her directing approach to her natural talent in singing. 'It is very rare when a moment of inspiration hits you. It's when things come from your unconscious. They pass through your cerebral state, coming from your guts, your soul, the place that's in the very core of you. You can't think about it too much – if you do, it's gone.'

Making *Yentl*, and the sixteen years that she had devoted to its development, had had a tremendous impact on her life. She was not a 'born-again Jew', but she had gone deeply into her Jewishness. 'I talked to all the rabbis I could talk to, searching for different points of view from the Reform, Conservative and Orthodox rabbis. It's a complex thing. It's men through the centuries who have found a way to use Jewish law to enslave women. That was a fascinating thing for me to find out. Part of me, my whole life, I've always been very desperately curious about knowledge ... I love knowledge ... What Yentl learns by the end of the film is that if you really care about yourself, then you don't settle. You go on to find more of what your dreams are about, what you want out of life.'

Jon Peters returned to Hollywood with a new attitude towards *Yentl*. He had never felt *Yentl* was a property Streisand should film. Now, he got behind her 100 per cent. She welcomed his support but it changed little between them. '*Yentl* was Barbra's way of saying *kaddish* for her own father,' he said. 'She created him on film so she could love him and say goodbye to him. She buried her father in the movie and dedicated it to him. I cried when I saw the movie. I sobbed, actually. I wish I had produced it,' he confessed later.

That would have been a great mistake. *Yentl* is uniquely Streisand's movie, and until the last half-hour of the film, it is a personal triumph. The musical soliloquies work beautifully, her performance is impeccable. The picture has a lyrical glow to it. She *is* sixteen in this movie, where she never seemed young in *A Star Is Born*. She achieved what she set out to do – make a romantic fantasy. It is also a film about human freedom, male as well as female. It fails in the last section – Yentl/Anshel's marriage to Hadass *after* the blundering wedding night simply does not ring true, and the last song – when Yentl is on board ship for the United States, breaks the spell that has so marvellously been cast, for suddenly the viewer is faced with exactly the kind of musical number Streisand said she wanted to avoid.

*Yentl* was premièred on 16 November 1983, at the Cinerama Dome in Hollywood. 'I ran out and bought all the chocolate-covered marzipan and walnut cookies I could carry and sat there and stuffed myself,' she admitted. 'That's how scared I was.' She was desperate for her child to be accepted and the early trade reviews assured her this was the case.

'To put it succinctly and at once, Barbra Streisand's *Yentl* is a triumph – a personal one for Streisand as producer, director, co-author and star, but also a triumphant piece of filmmaking,' the *Hollywood Reporter* lauded. 'At long last ... she has realized her dream. Magnificently.'

It had cost her a lot and, unlike the lyric from the old Fanny Brice song, there was one thing she *hadn't* got, and that was her man. Jon Peters had entered into a new relationship. Jason was almost seventeen and about to leave home for New York where he would be attending New York University Film School which he had chosen over the equally fine film school at the University of Southern California. Sure that he wanted to be involved in some aspect of films – acting, writing, directing – he also had a need to go out on his own, to be his own person and perhaps to place some distance between himself and his mother. She had sacrificed precious time at his expense to make *Yentl*. There was no new man in her life, at least no one who mattered, and no new project that had excited her into action.

She went to the Bergmans' for Thanksgiving and came home alone to the house on Carolwood Drive. She spent very little time at the Barn any more. 'She denies her unhappiness,' Elliott said. 'But she is *so* unhappy. She doesn't have a life – not a *real* life – and it remains to be seen whether she will ever be capable of love.'

Vehemently she denied it, but most of her life she had loved a phantom father. And what chance had Elliott or Jon or any man had against one created to perfection by a grieving daughter's dreams? Like Yentl, wasn't she now free? She remained hopeful that the right man would enter her life. She had picked up the threads of her relationship with the married man whom she had been seeing before she met Jon, but his situation had not changed. She would concentrate on finding another story that grabbed her by the heart. Meanwhile, she would go back, once again, into therapy.

She met Richard Baskin, the Baskin-Robbins ice-cream heir, at a small social gathering at Christmas time and they were mutually attracted. A bear-like man over six feet four inches tall, his imposing size, his Samson-like dark curly hair and his protective manner brought out the deeply feminine woman inside her, and her vulnerability was answered by a soft spot in him. He had seen *Yentl* and told her how good it was, that its ethnic roots had touched him. He played the guitar, wrote songs and had been the musical director on a low-key film, *Honeysuckle Rose*, about a Country music star that featured Willie Nelson. Like Barry Dennen's, his had been a privileged childhood and youth. A decade younger than Streisand, a self-contained, cerebral man, proud to become her lover – which he soon was – he moved into the Carolwood Drive house in February. A Streisand whim, friends said. It wouldn't last. Where were the crashing cymbals, the explosive scenes that so marked her serious love affairs? She would soon get bored with *compatibility* and trade it in for a more stimulating *combative* relationship. Two years later they were still together.

# 27

'SHE SHOULD ONLY live and be happy,' Diana said to one of her neighbours who commented harshly on Streisand's live-in relationship with the much-younger Baskin. The old wounds would not heal but Diana seemed to have mellowed, become less critical. Roslyn, who had moved out of her mother's apartment but still lived in Los Angeles, was not having much luck in her career. Although she had a pleasant voice and was attractive, she did not have Streisand's drive or her exceptional talent. The half-sisters had a delicate relationship, their hostilities, resentments and jealousies not yet resolved. Roslyn had thought Streisand would help her in her quest for a career in movies. What she got were non-speaking extra parts in two of her sister's films – in *A Star Is Born* she sat at Streisand's table during the Grammy Awards scene, and in *The Main Event* she is one of the women working out in the aerobics class with Streisand at the beginning of the picture. Streisand was at a loss at what else she could or should do for Roslyn. But the guilts lingered.

'Everyone wants a small piece of me,' she complained to an intimate. 'I *have* to be protective.' She worried about Jason. He seemed to be having a difficult time finding himself and they did not communicate well. Telephone conversations were unsatisfactory and when he came home for holidays she seemed always to be involved in a consuming work project. Baskin remained in residence, but friends noted a difference in their relationship. Where once there had been harmony, there was evidence of backbiting, of a crumbling romance. 'All the men in my life have said, "Can't you stop working at seven o'clock?" I never understood what they meant,' she told an interviewer.

Work filled her life and she was once again following in her earlier footsteps – bringing the man in her romantic life into her work, placing him in a position of power but having to deal with her as the ultimate authority, setting a standard that he felt he must live up to or his masculinity would be compromised. Baskin understood music and recording techniques and so she teamed up with him in that area of her career.

In the late summer of 1985, no movie on the horizon, she decided to return to her roots to do an album of Broadway songs. 'It's time I did something worthwhile,' she told Stephen Holden, music critic for the *New York Times*.

She felt she had to stop recording songs 'that any number of other people' could sing as well if not better than she could. She yearned to do something she truly believed in. 'Broadway music is the music I love, it is where I come from, it is my roots,' she stressed. Although she had recorded dozens of songs using rock rhythm sections, she felt out of her 'element singing music with a strong, regular backbeat ... Because I am a singer who believes in the moment. I do each take of a song differently. You can't do that with rock and roll because everyone says that you have to sing on the beat, and that's very hard for me.'

She joined forces once again with Marty Erlichman from whom she had split during the Jon Peters years as Peters had, in effect, acted as her manager. Erlichman went to Columbia Records with her wish to do a Broadway album. 'Barbra's contract with them says she has to deliver X albums,' he explained, 'but they have to be approved albums – meaning most of them have to be contemporary. Columbia would not approve this album. It was not considered to be a pop album. Therefore, she didn't get the advance she was entitled to and it wasn't going to count as an approved album contract, except if it sold 2.5 million copies, at which point it would automatically become an approved album, whether they okayed it in advance or not.'

She went ahead with her plans even though she did not think Broadway songs were mainstream any longer. Originally she had wanted to make a double record, and agreed to a single slip LP under pressure from the record company. Never too proud to eat crow, she called Peter Matz, with whom she also had not worked in a long while, and asked him if he would agree to co-produce, arrange and conduct the orchestra. Matz, who had done the orchestrations for most of her early albums and certainly was at least partially responsible for their success, agreed. They would produce the majority of the songs. Baskin, with David Foster, would handle the production on the other cuts.[1] The four of them (Streisand immediately and totally immersed) began 'marathon listening sessions to find a blend of obscure songs and standards'.

After weeks of listening to show scores by Kern, Hammerstein, Rodgers and Hart, Bernstein, Berlin, the Gershwins and other legendary Broadway tunesmiths, she centred on the one composer she had all but completely ignored throughout her early recording and concert career – Stephen Sondheim. 'It's like growing into a part like *Medea* or *Hedda Gabler*,' she remarked. 'It's not good when you're twenty. You need to be older.' For an unreleased cut in 1974 from the *Butterfly* album, she had recorded Sondheim's 'There Won't Be Trumpets' from *Anyone Can Whistle* and then changed her mind as

---

[1] Richard Baskin ended up producing two of the cuts, 'Not While I'm Around' and 'Something's Coming'.

Columbia had wanted her to do more contemporary songs with simpler lyrics. Now she appreciated their complexity and was drawn to Sondheim's sophistication and intellectualism.

The song that particularly attracted her was 'Putting It Together' from Sondheim's then current show, the 1985 Pulitzer Prize-winning *Sunday in the Park with George*. She called him at his home in New York although they hardly knew one another. 'I told him of my conversation with my record company ... that I wanted to do an album of Broadway songs. And they were very resistant and unhappy, and they said, "Barbra, you can't do a record like this. It's not commercial. This is like your old records. Nobody's going to buy it." Every word they said only encouraged me. I wanted to put all their comments into this song. And I thought, "What a great way to open this album." '

The actual lyrics of the song related to the art world, as the French painter George Seurat was the main character in the show. 'She wanted to make [the song] relevant to the music business,' Sondheim remembered, 'so she asked me if she could fix one word to replace "lasers", and I said, "Why not use 'vinyl' instead?" and she leaped at it and thought that was wonderful. And I said, "Let me look at the rest of the lyric, if you want to personalize it. I'm sure I can make it more record-oriented and less art-related," which is what it was in the context of the show. Once you get into it, then it becomes fun to do, and that's why I did it.'

'I would talk to him for hours,' Streisand added. 'I felt I couldn't ignore the truth ... you don't hide it; you use it. So I told him, "Here I am, a very successful recording star and yet I have to fight for everything I believe in. I'm still auditioning after twenty-three years." I asked him if he could encompass that thought and he wrote, "Even though you get the recognition/Everything you do you still audition." You see what I mean?'

Sondheim had never been known to custom tailor a song for a singer. 'Barbra Streisand has one of the two or three best voices in the world for singing songs,' he explained. 'It's not just her voice but her intensity, her passion and control. She has the meticulous attention to detail that makes a good artist ... Although every moment has been thought out, you don't see all the sweat and decisions that went into the work. It is as though she just stepped out of the shower and began singing at you.'

'He believes as I do,' Streisand says about Sondheim, 'that art is a living process, that it's not set in stone, that it breathes and it grows and it changes. It blew my mind when I said things to him like "I never understood 'Send in the Clowns'. What would you think about writing a second bridge that would kind of tell us more about this relationship?" And no problem. I've asked him to make a lot of changes like that, and at first we'll be on the phone and he'll say, "Wait a minute. You can't do that." And then he says, "Let me call you back" and in two hours he calls me back and it's done. I don't know quite how he does these things. He's very, very organized.'

*The Broadway Album* became a predominantly Streisand-sings-Sondheim album as she added to 'Putting It Together', 'Send in the Clowns' (*A Little Night Music*), 'Somewhere' and 'Something's Coming' (*West Side Story*, music by Bernstein), 'Not While I'm Around' and 'Pretty Woman' (*Sweeney Todd*), and 'The Ladies Who Lunch' and 'Being Alive' (*Company*).

Working with Sondheim was, she asserts, 'one of the most exciting collaborations I've ever had, because we both talk fast, we think fast; so it was like shorthand half the time ... we practically didn't have to finish sentences. It was so exhilarating, there were moments I was screaming with joy over the phone.'

Sondheim came out to the Coast and worked along with her in the recording sessions. Here were two of the truly towering talents in the music world, both intense personalities, both perfectionists. Sondheim in sweatshirt and sneakers, sitting on one chair, his feet up on another, would pull at his close-cropped pepper and salt beard as he laboured over each word he scratched out on a pad of music paper. Streisand, comfortably dressed in a jogging suit hovered nervously nearby. Much in awe of Sondheim, she considered him one of the twentieth century's greatest theatre composers. His mind was as quick as hers, and there was an instinctive knowledge of how to adapt his lyrics and music for her needs.

'Everyone in the studio knew that they were part of something important,' claimed Alan Bergman, who with Marilyn attended most of the three-week session. 'The musicians, rather than escaping to the halls, stayed in their chairs and listened to the playbacks. Every take was different – a fresh meaning to a phrase, a new bend to a note.'

The album was released in early November 1985, and shot right up to Number One on the *Billboard* chart (there had been an amazing 800,000 advance sale). Streisand had always believed in it but she had not expected it to be such a big hit, and it renewed her faith in the public's taste for good music. She had the conviction that if she followed her intuition on what was best for her that she *would* succeed and she had proved, once again, this was right.

'The Broadway Album soars with full-bodie, tender bel canto renditions of ballads by Stephen Sondheim, Rodgers and Hammerstein, and a *Porgy and Bess* medley that stand among the most thrilling performances of [Streisand's] 23-year career,' Stephen Holden wrote in the *New York Times*.

This same instinct for doing what she believed in with a passion pressed her to take on a film adaptation of Tom Topor's play, *Nuts*, about a high-class prostitute who kills one of her clients, in self-defence. Deeper than that, it asked the question, 'What is normal?' Numerous writers attempted to write a script that would please her and failed. Finally, she recalled two of them, Darryl Ponicsan and Alvin Sargent, who were now working on a screenplay. While she was waiting for the results of their collaboration, she saw Richard Dreyfuss in the Los Angeles Company's production of Larry Kramer's *The Normal Heart*, certain that she had grasped a new vision to her. The supporting character of the wheelchair-bound Dr Brookner (a part she would develop and enlarge) grabbed at both her intellect and her emotions, and was one she was sure she could play, not just well but with real understanding.

She believed the play to be about everyone having the right to love, something that she felt had universal appeal. It was also about the shocking lack of government assistance in researching a cure for AIDS and she wanted to do something positive to get the world to wake up to the appalling devastation of the disease. The two weeks she had spent with Kramer in their tense, emotional, volatile story conferences in the study of the Carolwood Drive house, had convinced her that *The Normal Heart* could be one of the most important films she would ever make.

They had talked hours on end about homosexuality, mothers and sons, about AIDS, and how the story could be told more from the view of Dr Brookner the AIDS specialist. They concentrated on her frustration, her fight for more research money, and the bond that exists between her and Ned, actually the central character in the play, a gay activist very much like Kramer.

'I felt great warmth toward her,' Kramer says, his keen brown eyes focused on a past memory. 'I went away believing we were in agreement.' He assumed that he was to be responsible for the final screenplay of *The Normal Heart*, which was semi-autobiographical and a raw piece of his life. When he returned to New York his lawyer greeted him with the news that Streisand was demanding the right to employ another writer on the script if she felt it was required. She was adamant on this point. She had to have control of the final script. Kramer, who had an impressive history in films having had his own production company and produced and adapted for the screen D.H. Lawrence's *Women in Love* (1969) for which he had been nominated for an Academy Award, refused to bow to this demand and the deal collapsed.

Streisand was crushed. Losing the rights was a great disappointment and yet, somehow, she refused to let go of her belief that she would one day make *The Normal Heart*, a credo strengthened by the fast multiplying deaths from AIDS of many of her former close associates, Liberace among them. She knew that she could never relinquish what she saw as her *vision*, the only thing she truly trusted, and she could not produce and direct a film where she did not have control of the script. Some might interpret that as a need for power. It went deeper. Making a movie where she was so completely involved meant her mortality was at stake, her ability to create an art that would last. 'It's like the lyric of Steve Sondheim's "Finishing the Hat",' she has said. 'Look, I made a hat where there never was a hat.'

Once again she was deeply involved in her first love – making movies – and it was a world to which Richard Baskin was an outsider, as he had suddenly seemed to have become in her home. She had surrounded herself with a female staff, feeling more comfortable and better able to relate to women. With her secretary Kim Skalecki living in the guest house, a team of women assistants working on the premises every day, she was seldom alone, and work carried over into the evening hours. She also had to make time for the running of her vast business enterprises, the overseeing of the Barbra Streisand Foundation – which distributed over $1 million yearly to various causes that ranged from AIDS to abused children, battered women, university medical chairs (in her father's name), environmental and civil rights groups to supplying musical instruments to lower grade schools so that the young students could play in a band – and, added to all this was her pre-production work on *Nuts*. Her relationship with Baskin, although not explosive in the way that she and Peters had been (and not as passionate either), was under tremendous stress. Then along came the catastrophic explosion of the nuclear power plant at Chernobyl to thrust her actively back into two more rings of activity – live concerts and politics – that she had shied away from for over a decade.

'It was April 26, 1986,' Marilyn Bergman recalled. '[Barbra and I] were talking about the disaster at Chernobyl. She called me that morning, and she was absolutely horrified at what happened. The question was, "What can be done about this?" And the answer was, "The only thing that I know to do about it is to take back the Senate for the Democrats."'

Bergman was a founding member of the Hollywood Women's Political Committee, formed two years earlier, spawned from strong anti-Reagan presidential sentiment. HWPC aimed to influence the vote by raising large sums of campaign money for the candidates of their choice through gala dinners and balls, and operated 'on the explicit conviction that politicians could learn from listening to their Hollywood donors'. The movie industry had proven to be a vital campaign aid. At the time of the Chernobyl disaster, there were six Democratic senatorial candidates in close races.

Streisand was not a member of HWPC, although she would soon join. Bergman was suggesting she do a concert to help raise funds so that the Democratic anti-nuclear candidates would be elected. Streisand was reluctant. 'I'm still not comfortable singing in public in front of a large audience,' she countered.

'It became a discussion of what is more frightening: performing in front of an audience, or nuclear annihilation,' Bergman explained.

The months that followed might be called 'the political awakening of Barbra Streisand'. A few days after Bergman's conversation with Streisand, Bergman had lunch with Stanley Sheinbaum, an ardent liberal activist, and told him that her friend wanted to learn more about nuclear issues. Sheinbaum accepted the challenge. Dinners were arranged at his home and at Carolwood Drive where she could meet policy experts who would brief her on the subject. Leading scientists such as Marvin L. Goldberger, then President of the California Institute of Technology, and Sidney Drell, from Stanford, were drafted as tutors.

Sheinbaum provided Streisand with literature, books and articles on the Reagan administration's nuclear politics. She was an avid student. 'She started with very little knowledge,' Goldberger recalled, 'and a great deal of suddenly awakened concern ... I had two roles: one was that of someone who knows a great deal about nuclear power, nuclear reactors, and has also spent an awful lot of time worrying about strategic weapons and international security. So in a sense I was a resource person that tried, when necessary, to separate for her fact from fiction. Secondly, both I and my wife tried to think about what was the appropriate vehicle for her to make the maximum contribution in this area about which she was greatly concerned.'

Marilyn Bergman took over from there. 'Marilyn realised the way Barbra Streisand could help win back the Senate [for the Democrats] was to raise money,' HWPC's treasurer, attorney Bonnie Reiss, said, 'and the way she could do that was to sing.'

Streisand was not easily convinced. The many years she had absented herself from concert work had increased her trepidation. Finally, in mid-summer, with the election only three months away, she agreed to do a concert but the event would have to be limited to invited guests and presented in the safe and comfortable setting of her secluded, well-protected Malibu ranch. Tents were to be raised over tables set for formal outdoor dining. To transform the grounds of the ranch to a professional outdoor auditorium necessitated the logistical task of carving out an amphitheatre from a stretch of flat lawn and wiring it for sound and lights in three weeks' time. None the less everyone at the HWPC was enthusiastic, for not only would Streisand be performing live for the first time in many years, she would be doing so in her own home, a great enticement to potential ticket buyers who were being asked to pay $5,000 to see the concert.

No one was more excited about the event than Streisand. 'After all of my insistence that I didn't want to sing in public any more, I sang,' she said. 'Chernobyl had erupted in lethal radiation. The arms race was bankrupting the nation and the world. And I wanted to add my one voice to demands for action.' The dinner-concert was called One Voice, which had a double-edged meaning: a solo concert (although Barry Gibb sang two songs with her) and the message that each person could make a difference in the fight against the proliferation of nuclear energy. Baskin joined forces with her as musical producer, Randy Kerber was the musical director, Streisand and Marty Erlichman, executive producers and Gary Smith and Dwight Hennion, who had presented most of her television shows, were to produce the live concert for Home Box Office with those proceeds going to the Barbra Streisand Foundation to distribute.

Despite the pressing demands of her work on *Nuts*, which was moving closer to the start of production, Streisand oversaw the transformation of her property into a professional outdoor arena, wrote the script with Marilyn and Alan Bergman, prepared and rehearsed seventeen songs, and recorded on audio cassette hundreds of individual, personalised invitations, 'which,' one observer wrote, 'landed on the decks of Hollywood's most powerful men and women like a summons'. Within a few days, over 300 people, the capacity audience, sent in their cheques.[2]

The night of the concert, 6 September 1986 – a warm evening tempered by a soft Pacific breeze – Streisand was flushed with nervous excitement as she waited for her entrance music in the newly constructed, temporary dressing-room area behind the stage. Robin Williams, seemingly awed by the star-studded audience, opened the concert with some humorous patter. Seated on impeccable white chairs set up in semi-circular rows on the grass skirt facing the stage were some of Hollywood's greatest stars (and liberal Democrats): Shirley MacLaine, Warren Beatty, Sally Field, Bette Midler, Jane Fonda, Goldie Hawn, Walter Matthau, Jack Nicholson and Chevy Chase among others, and in a grand show of solidarity, ex-husband Elliott Gould, ex-lover Jon Peters and Jason. Streisand would be judged by her peers but they were also her friends, people who held the same political views as she did. They were here to support a cause they all believed in so she was guaranteed a receptive audience, not that she would ever give anything but her very best.

Her entrance in a flattering white, beaded, turtleneck sweater, white evening skirt slit to the knee, was met with thunderous applause. 'You're nice. You're all friends. Thank you for being here,' she smiled and waved and threw kisses. The sheltering sky was star lit. A soft breeze made wisps of her frizzy blonde hair, worn loose and to her shoulders. Rather than the usual thirty-five man orchestra she was accustomed to in the past, she had engaged a versatile group of mostly synthesiser instrumentalists – 'Eight guys and some big electric bill!'

---

[2] In Washington, Marilyn Bergman met Senator George J. Mitchell, chairman of the Democratic Senatorial Campaign Committee, who proposed that all the proceeds from the ticket sales be turned over to the DSCC. Bergman was insistent that HWPC control the profits to ensure that none of the money went to Democrats whose views her organisation did not approve. A middle road was chosen. The funds would be split among its own political action committee and the DSCC to be dispersed to California Democratic Senator Alan Cranston, who faced a tough re-election, four liberal Democratic challengers, and one incumbent, Senator Patrick J. Leahy of Vermont.

she told her audience. Randy Kerber conducted from his position at the keyboards.

Her songs were geared to the theme of the evening – helping to save and protect the environment, our love for others, our pride in our country – which gave the concert a soft, often sentimental edge, although there were some satirical jabs at the Republicans in specially written lyrics by the Bergmans. She made a beautiful segue from a short speech about non-proliferation of nuclear energy into 'People', sung with more wisdom than passion, and imparting new meaning to the lyrics. 'Over the Rainbow', which she proclaimed 'the greatest movie song ever written', was dedicated to Judy Garland who was so identified with it. Streisand sang it against an exquisite piano backing by Kerber as a song of great hope. The bridge was especially youthful and carefree. She could easily have been Dorothy on the road to Oz, a young girl touched with wonder, her dreams still intact. Garland's underlying plea for love and protection, the vulnerable voice and misty eyes that had mirrored severe human suffering, were stifled. Streisand had made the song her own and it was a *tour de force*. She even improved Yip Harburg's somewhat saccharine coda by changing 'if happy little bluebirds fly' to the more universal 'if all those little bluebirds fly'.

The two duets with Barry Gibb, 'Highway to the Sky' and 'Who's Sorry Now?' were the least successful of the evening's programme. Then came an especially moving rendition of 'Papa Can you Hear Me?' from the score of *Yentl*, sung as the darkness of night encroached, in the flickering light of a single candle: 'in memory of all those great father figures – Abraham Lincoln, John F. Kennedy, Gandhi, Sadat'. This was followed by 'The Way We Were' which had a much more contemporary sound than any previous arrangement along with numerous mellismatic sections. For an encore she ended the evening with a stirring interpretation of 'America the Beautiful', beginning *a cappella*, and eventually asking the audience to join in. As they did, they clasped hands and swayed as though moved by the night wind.

Streisand was visibly affected by the emotion generated by her audience. Tears filled her eyes as she left the stage after her final bow. Much as she had grown to fear public appearances, she had missed the instant gratification and the outpouring of love she received from a live audience.

The dinner-concert raise $1.5, an amount that exceeded by $500,000 the proceeds from a Republican fund-raising dinner for President Reagan the following night, a fact that caused much jubilation among HWPC members and a certain pride to Streisand. There was no doubt that the large sum garnered from Streisand's concert helped the Democrats regain the Senate, for five of the six senators who received funds for their campaigns from the event won their seats.

With the concert, Streisand had crossed over into becoming an active member of HWPC, which was composed mainly of women 'rising steadily through the Hollywood power structure, to establish themselves as forces within the industry'. Her political consciousness had been fully awakened (her social consciousness had always been apparent), and there would be no back-stepping. From this point she would be frank and forthright in speaking out for what she believed in and supported, so much so that there would often be unfounded rumours that she planned to run for the Senate.

On 1 October Streisand was rudely awakened at 7:42 a.m. by a violent earthquake that struck California and that measured 6.1 on the Richter scale. It took six lives and sent upward of 100 injured people to hospital. Houses were severely damaged, cars crushed beneath fallen concrete. It had hit with enormous force. Shaken but unharmed, she rang Diana right away to make sure she was all right and then, once that was ascertained, checked the house for damage, which turned out to be minor. But she was left fearing for the time when the 'big one' would hit. Apart from that, the earthquake seemed symbolic of the sudden shifting changes in her life.

Her affair with Richard Baskin ended and he moved out of the Carolwood Drive house. 'One day he was there, the next he was gone,' a friend said. 'I was surprised. She really like him a lot.' His departure should have been more traumatic, perhaps, than it was considering they had lived together for three years. The key reason might well have been that during most of that time she had been off the screen. Making movies, the thing she loved most to do, had always created heavy scenes between her and the important men in her life. As soon as she became mired in the all-consuming work on the filming of *Nuts*, trouble had brewed between her and Baskin, who was not involved in the production and found himself an outsider in her life as she devoted herself day and night to the filming process.

*Nuts* was premièred on 20 November 1987 to mostly favourable, although not wildly enthusiastic reviews. She had given one of the finest performances of her career, one that should have lifted her prestige as an actress into the same category as Meryl Streep, but it never happened and despite her bravado acting, *Nuts* did not do well at the box office. Audiences appeared to be sending Streisand the message that they did not want to see her in non-musical movies, especially one with such a heavy subject. Depressed by the public's verdict on *Nuts*, and with Jason in New York and planning to remain there for the holidays, she went off to Aspen, Colorado for Christmas and New Year with the Bergmans. And it was there that she picked up her brief acquaintance, a former superficial meeting at that year's Grammy Awards, with *Miami Vice* star Don Johnson, who wasted no time reeling her into a fast-paced courtship. In less than a week it became a passionate affair.

'If I want to meet people, I have to talk to them first because so many are intimidated by me,' she said. 'So if a guy does make the first move [as had Jon Peters and Johnson], he is already a step ahead.'

He had grabbed hold of her arm at a party shortly after her arrival, pulled her off into a private corner and then left early with her. Seven years her junior, he had lived his life fast and claimed he had no regrets. 'I have done everything I've ever taken a fancy to. The only things I haven't done are things I haven't thought of.'

Johnson could be called tough but, as friends and co-workers avouch, 'he could have charmed Hitler'. He was the natural fantasy man for any Jewish woman with Streisand's background – the blond, bronzed, macho gentile man with the physique of a beach lifeguard and a smile that could light up a funeral. By New Year they were a pair, by February a couple.

'I'm happy, very happy,' Streisand declared to the press. 'And I have never been very happy, so it's something I'm learning. It's as if I were a child again.' She had expressed similar sentiments in the early days of her affair with Peters. In truth, the two men could stand comparison. Both were younger, cocky, streetwise, had spent time in juvenile reformatories, and were aggressive both in business and sex. Johnson was also a good athlete, bordering on the professional in golf, tennis, skiing and powerboat racing. There was another side, however, to his swaggering, macho, womanising reputation. He was intelligent, sensitive and – having suffered a great sense of loss with his parents' divorce when he was a youngster – wanted to settle into a close family situation so that his son, with his former lover, Patti D'Arbanville, would have a real home with him. Although Streisand enthusiastically helped to decorate his recently purchased million-dollar ranch house in Aspen and spent all her free time with him, they did not actually take up double occupancy of any of their individual residences. In fact, Elliott, separated from Jenny, and having a particularly tough patch at this time, was living at Streisand's Malibu ranch, a gesture Streisand made to help him out, for she would always have a protective and close feeling for the man who was the father to her son.

Named the 'Female Star of the Decade', at the ShoWest Convention in Las Vegas on 25 February 1988, she arrived late to acknowledge the tribute accompanied by Johnson. Jon Peters was seated on the dais and he leaped up from his chair and embraced both of them as they were being seated.

Never able to cut connections with the former men in her life, she let Peters host a party for her forty-sixth birthday on 24 April while Johnson was on location in Calgary making *Dead-Bang*, an action film. Shortly after this celebration, lonely and seemingly head-over-heels in love again, she flew to Ireland to be with him. She believed she had at last found a man with whom she could be happy ever after. They were photographed arms entwined, gazing with hungry eyes at each other.

In mid-September, she and Johnson recorded a single, 'Till I Loved You', together. It turned out to be their farewell song. Ten weeks later, Johnson and Melanie Griffith (one of his four ex-wives) announced, to Streisand's shocked disbelief, that they were going to be remarried. Griffith had spent several months in a rehabilitation centre for alcoholism after completing her acclaimed performance in *Working Girl*. Streisand knew that Johnson had been seeing Griffith but solemnly believed it was out of concern for Griffith's health and her struggle against her addiction, a situation with which she was in great sympathy. The world suddenly came crashing down on her.

She had somehow failed once again to sustain a meaningful relationship. This time she was the spurned woman and she was furious at Johnson for ending their affair in such a brutal, public manner. For weeks she brooded about him and the cruel press coverage that made her out to look a fool.

Media interest in Johnson's defection finally waned and she was able to press all her energy into a new project, a film adaptation of Pat Conroy's *The Prince of Tides*. It would be another monumental undertaking as she would produce, direct and star in the movie. More than that, *The Prince of Tides* was about family and forgiveness and she was at a place in her life where she thought she could forgive her mother for what she called in her first interviews on the prospective project – 'emotional abuse'. It would bring Jon Peters back into her life as a protector, the one who would, when every studio turned her down on the project, talk Columbia into financing it for her. It would also create a new deeper relationship between her and Jason, whom she would cast in the picture as her son, and with it, the realisation and acceptance of the fact that Jason was homosexual.

# 28

A S JASON'S PARENTS, Elliott and Streisand now had something they had to face together. In 1989, when Jason was twenty-three, neither he nor they had discussed the matter of his homosexuality in public or, it seems, in private. Elliott has admitted having had a total block on the subject and it was not until five years later, after Jason himself went public, that his father told English journalist Corinna Honan, 'Yes, [Jason] is gay. That's his preference, his business. It's something that's new to me and it's an acutely delicate subject. But I'm more than just empathetic. Whether it has been a problem for Barbra, I don't know. It's really important not to be prejudiced and both of us are devoted to him.

'I just want Jason to be comfortable with himself and happy and find his way of expressing love. He could be a polar bear for all I'm concerned; he's as precious to me as anyone can be. I told Jason a couple of years ago that I feel fortunate and grateful that we have one another. I told him I love him. He said, "I didn't always know that. I know that now." '

During the time Streisand was readying *The Prince of Tides* for the cameras, she and Elliott were privately and understandably concerned. AIDS was spreading wildly, cases doubling, then tripling each year. His parents suffered guilt, *Was I to blame*? 'I think Jason's being gay is deeply psychological,' Elliott responded. 'It's a result of conditioning, I think ... [I blame myself] for not being a more visible father. Barbra won custody when we were divorced. I wasn't fair to him. I left him in that environment without me. I think he was affected by not having love at a vital stage of his life, though the affection and love developed later. Barbra was consumed with her business and career and I just wasn't there.

'I can't fault Barbra for being something she can't be. I can only fault me. I know my intentions were positive, but it has been a great trial for Jason to overcome this lack of love. He's a very worthy, decent guy. I think he and Barbra have a bit more of an adult relationship now. She loves her son and he's as loyal to his mother as he can be.'

One thing that brought Streisand and Jason closer was his seemingly dedicated wish to become an actor which had surfaced in the past few years. She had seen him in several local non-professional productions and thought that he possessed a true gift. He had also played bit parts in three unreleased movies that year. When Streisand first read *The Prince of Tides* about the Wingos, a South Carolina family whose children grow up repressing nightmarish traumas, she recalled thinking: 'Jesus, I'm perfect for this part [as the middle-aged Jewish psychiatrist, Dr Susan Lowenstein, who falls in love with her suicidal patient's brother, Tom Wingo]. I identify with the woman completely, even to the line in the book that says she is in the middle of ageing extra-ordinarily well.' She also saw part of herself in the traumatised Wingo children and in the relationship between Dr Lowenstein and her sullen, teenage son, Bernard. When she started to cast, Jason was living away from home in a small West Hollywood apartment, pursuing his acting career.

'Jason has never asked me for anything. He has never been ambitious,' she later said. 'He doesn't have a desire to be famous or anything like that, because, you know, it's complicated being my son and Elliott's son, problems of competition and all that. But here my kid calls up one day and he says, "Mom, about that role, I hear you're getting ready to cast someone else. I thought you thought I'd be good for it."'

Streisand had decided upon a young actor, Chris O'Donnell (later to make a name for himself in *Scent of a Woman* with Al Pacino), who was a star quarterback of his high-school football team. 'Barbra showed me this kid that she had cast for the role of her son,' Pat Conroy, author of *The Prince of Tides*, remembers, 'a very handsome blond kid. Of course everyone looks wonderful in Hollywood, but I said, "That ain't the kid," so she said, "I already hired him." I still said, "That still ain't him. This kid Bernard is not a good athlete, that's the point." So she sort of flipped through other kids she'd auditioned. She finally came to this one kid. I didn't know it was her son. But he showed a snarling, wonderful teenage quality [and looked like Streisand, which had to have some bearing on the casting]. I said, "*That's* the kid, right there."' Streisand recalls this happened when Conroy saw a picture of Jason on the piano in her living room. Memory is like that, often elusive, finding its place in other than original surroundings. Whoever is correct, the main point is that Conroy saw Jason as Bernard before Streisand and when she was resisting what to others seemed both logical and right. Even when Jason was finally signed to play the role, the news was kept from the media and not announced until months later when the film was already in production and on location. 'I thought, deep down, "Well, it's dangerous. We could both get attacked for this,"' she confessed.

'Every film she directs involves a working out of a part of her own life,' Marilyn Bergman added.

'I think she read *The Prince of Tides* seven times,' says Cis Corman who was to be executive producer on the film. 'She knew the book so well she would tell Pat what he had written on page 376. I mean after *Yentl*, she could have become a rabbi. Look, it's a painful process for her but with moments of joy.'

Making a film with Streisand meant feeding her insecurities. 'You have to keep saying "You're beautiful, you're wonderful,"' Corman admits. None the less, most of the actors who have worked under her direction will tell you how sensitive she is to their problems, perhaps because she is so conscious of her own.

Streisand said at the time, 'A lot of this movie is very meaningful to me because it's about not blaming your parents. We've all come from some type of painful childhood. But if you blame your parents, it keeps you the victim. The mother in me makes me possibly a better director. Women can bring a certain kind of nurturing quality to a film,' a point Amy Irving had affirmed about Streisand as a director during the making of *Yentl*.

Three weeks before leaving for South Carolina, where the film was to begin shooting and only days before 24 April 1990, Streisand's forty-eighth birthday, Diana, now eight-two, was rushed to the hospital with severe chest pains and underwent by-pass heart surgery. Streisand was in a panic. Work was put aside as she stayed with Roslyn by her mother's side. 'It changed my whole perspective of the importance of the film,' Streisand confessed. 'The film became non-important. The relationships with people I love began to matter more than the movie.'

Diana was now an elderly woman. She had been much maligned publicly by her elder daughter and had never had any means of refuting or ameliorating Streisand's constant barbed statements about the emotional abuse she had suffered at her mother's hands. She had not been a demonstrative or, at times, a supportive parent, but she had done what she thought was best. She was not equipped to handle either the situation she found herself in after her husband's death or to nurture a daughter's 'fancies'. But neither had Diana ever turned her back on her daughter no matter how bitter and cutting Streisand's statements were about her to a press eager to exploit celebrity-revealing comments to sell their publications. Diana had inherited her own pain, an unsympathetic mother, the fear that she could not make it on her own. She had been born into a time when women had much less chance of achievement unless they were beautiful, which she was not, and she had lost the husband she loved and been humiliated by the man she believed would make a home for her children and herself. She was a victim of her era and her inadequacies.

Streisand had been fighting her mother all of her life. Underneath there was an unseverable cord. She loved Diana, always had. She had clung to her, slept in her bed for years after Manny's death, had wanted to make things good for her from the time of her first success, needed affirmation of Diana's approval and love more than any one other person in her life. She had a lot to think about now and was determined to make sure Diana knew she loved her before it was too late.

With Diana on the road to recovery Streisand took Jason and about 100 members of the cast and crew on location to the small town of Beaufort, South Carolina. Beaufort was where Pat Conroy had spent his teenage years, and where he would later teach English and coach football at his high school like his alter ego Tom Wingo. In the book the town was named Colleton, but Conroy had described it unmistakably. Beaufort was in the Low Country where warm white sands meet the south Atlantic. The town boasts a beautiful natural harbour. Offshore there are dozens of inlets and waterways where small fishing boats troll for sweet gulf shrimp. High bluffs, densely wooded with subtropical growth, rise to the north of town, and some of the surviving older houses are made of crushed oyster shells. Others, built high for coolness, have wide front porches and old-fashioned gardens where jessamine, oleanders, and wisteria mingle with oak trees bearded with Spanish moss. From above came the sound of sea birds, the drone of heat-drawn bugs and in the evening cool, what Streisand called, 'a quiet, mystical quality'.

It took time building the required sets and so it was not until 18 June that the film went before the cameras. The first scene to be shot would be one of the last in the picture, with Tom Wingo reunited with his wife and three daughters after his affair in New York with Dr Lowenstein, walking with them on the beach, although fifteen endings would be shot before that one was chosen.

Nick Nolte had been cast as Tom Wingo, deeply Southern, a man of great outer strength and inner turmoil, born into a dysfunctional family. His twin sister, Savannah, is a famous, gifted, troubled poet, and a suicidal patient of Dr Lowenstein. Caught up in her own difficult family situation – a philandering husband and a difficult teenage son – the middle-aged Lowenstein persuades Wingo to come to New York and help her to fill in the missing information that she hopes will unlock the mystery to Savannah's deep depression. During these voluntary, non-paying sessions, he reveals the hidden secrets of the Wingo family, which include an abusive father, murder and rape. Dr Lowenstein and Wingo fall in love and enter into a relationship which helps each of them to resolve their personal situations.

Both Warren Beatty and Robert Redford were previously discussed as possibly playing Tom Wingo, but neither was right for the character, who required a strong macho appearance, sensitivity and the ability to 'unleash torrents of raw emotion'. Nolte, at six feet one inch, 210 pounds, had a brawny, bruising physique. He was rugged, blond and raspy-voiced and his background had been rough and tumble. Raised in Omaha, Nebraska he had gone to Arizona State College on a football scholarship and transferred to three other schools due to poor grades and a low tolerance for alcohol. He turned to acting, supporting himself in the beginning as an iron worker. Fourteen years later he was still in touring companies, taking college courses whenever he had the time to obtain the credits he lacked for his diploma, and joining in the anti-war demonstrations that proliferated during the Nixon years. He was arrested and placed on five years' probation for counterfeiting draft cards with false information and married and divorced twice before, in 1976 at the age of forty-two, he made his first breakthrough as the co-star of the Irwin Shaw television mini-series, *Rich Man Poor Man*. He quickly became a popular Hollywood star known as 'a tough guy with soul and natural acting ability'.

Nolte had not fared well in his relationships with women and was at this time caught in a hostile divorce with his third wife. Streisand seriously had to consider if he might have difficulty taking direction from a woman. She decided to chance the risk as Nolte projected just the right blend of grit and tenderness required for the role. 'In the movie, Wingo would have to come to trust a female therapist, while in real life he was going to have to trust me, a female director,' Streisand later said. This did not become the problem she anticipated. Nolte had a great respect for her.

'Barbra likes to explore,' he said. 'We shot some key scenes in several different ways. We also had long discussions about male-female relationships. It was the first time I had worked with a woman director. In working with male directors I've found that the male actor and director have a kind of collusive attitude about the emotional points of scenes. With Barbra, there is a lot of continued exploration.'

Their love scenes ignited sparks. 'I don't find it that easy to bare my soul, to do intimate things in front of a camera,' she admits. 'I'd rather do it in private. I had to yell, "Cut!" when things got too hot [with Nolte]. His make-up was all over my hair. You couldn't see my blonde streaks.' She had even more difficulty with appearing nude. She wears a scant nightdress in one scene after a great deal of discussion about it with Nolte and Cis Corman. 'I just find it rather sexier to wear sheer clothes in bed,' she defends. The love scenes she found most satisfying in the film were those that dealt with deep, mutual affection, Lowenstein cradled in Wingo's arms in a chair. 'The woman goes back to the safety of childhood again, being held by the father or someone who loves you,' she explained.

The act of touching someone's face, their hand, or being held, comforted by someone and being in their arms, had great meaning for her. In her direction of the scene where Wingo has his final catharsis she recreated her own visual memory of the time the touch of her therapist's hand on hers had caused her to open the flood gates of her emotions and weep. In a two-hour documentary laser disk on the making of *The Prince of Tides*, which she narrates, she illustrated what she wanted Nolte to experience when Lowenstein takes Wingo in her arms, his head on her breast, as he wept after revealing the hidden secrets in his family. 'Oh, this is interesting, this is what it feels like to be held by your mother.'

The documentary is all about her directional approach to the making of the film and, while fascinating and insightful as to the reasons behind many of her choices, it also reveals the strikingly egotistical manner in which she thinks of her work, the way she takes total possession of its creative process. 'I did this to the script,' 'I wrote that scene in my mind over and over,' 'I rewrote,' 'I improvised,' are used throughout. One could easily surmise that she was the sole author of the screenplay. Never once does she say that she is working from a script adapted by Becky Johnston and Pat Conroy from his novel.

Despite their differences on *Yentl*, she had brought Jack Rosenthal to Beaufort from London to 'humanise the dialogue'. One evening when they were working over dinner in a Chinese restaurant, he bit down on the thighbone of a roasted duck, smashing his molar to fragments inside his gums. It was, he says, the least painful part of the three weeks he spent 'working with Barbra on the script'.

She refused to let things go and would spend hours on the smallest detail, driving her co-workers as hard and as long as herself. Yet, difficult as she is in any work situation as a director Streisand is unquestionably sensitive to mood, to frame, to moment, and she has caught some extraordinary images in the film which she points out in the documentary – the Wingo house rising in morning mist from the marshes, the grace of the land, the view from Lowenstein's skyscraper terrace looking down on night-time New York City – but Stephen Goldblatt, the picture's cinematographer is never mentioned.

Then there is the music by James Newton Howard. Streisand once mentions 'Jim' in relation to the music, but clarifies no further of whom she is speaking. She had a brief affair with Howard during the time he was scoring the movie. They had been working closely together. Howard was a sensitive, attractive man and there was a musical union of ideas, a time – placed in musical context – when they were 'breathing' together. It is something that an accompanist and a singer can have. With the work done on the scoring, the affair ended simply, no seeming resentments on either side. Howard delivered a lovely score that fully captures the mood of the picture and often helps to define the action – the atonal reverse of a theme to indicate a character's alienation, the balletic section that takes Wingo and Bernard through their football sessions.

Film is undeniably a director's medium. 'I like to see my visions come to life,' Streisand says. If a director does not have a vision, he or she should not be one, but without all the glorious technical, artistic and creative talents that contribute to the final film, a director would be paralysed, unable to bring that vision to life, a world of its own. Streisand's inability to share or give credit to her co-workers has to do with her complete absorption in the movie she is making and her inability to think of it as anyone else's but her own.

She does, however, give full credit to the great violinist Pinchas Zuckerman, heard dubbing the solos for Dr Lowenstein's virtuoso husband, Jeroen Krabbe (who brilliantly managed the difficult fingering). Jason had one scene in which he also had to be seen playing Fritz Kreisler's difficult violin piece, 'Präludium und Allegro', and doing so in a manner that would show a tremendous gift. ('If I could play the violin like that, I'd never touch a football,' Wingo tells him.) He had three months to accomplish the fingering and body movements. After three lessons he played 'Twinkle, Twinkle, Little Star' on the instrument. 'I couldn't stop laughing,' Streisand confessed. 'I know I hurt him and I hate that, but he was so awful. However,' she added proudly, 'by the time he had to play it in the scene, he was able to do it like a young prodigy. His hands were so stiff from practising he had to soak them every evening. I *knew* my son could master it.'

Directing her son presented some problems. Jason was always prepared, always professional and almost always good-natured. 'There's not a bad bone in his body,' Streisand says. But he is his mother's son and has strong opinions. They clashed more than once. Streisand had him playing one scene over and over to his irritation. 'You've told me what you want, now tell me what you don't like!' he snapped at her. She attempted to do so and finally he did the scene as she envisioned it. In the last scene he has with Wingo, set in Grand Central Station, the script called for him to walk off briskly to catch his train, sadly leaving behind the man who was a father figure to him and had helped him become an acceptable athlete. After several takes, Streisand shouted at him, 'Walk like a man! Walk like a *man!*' meaning this was the moment in the film when he would become an adult, but it sounded like a put-down to members of the company.

While they were in Beaufort, mother and son came to a deeper understanding and appreciation of each other. Jason acquitted himself well in the part of Bernard, giving a real and sympathetic performance. He is always right on, believable. He bears a close resemblance to his mother although like Elliott, his eyes are dark, his hair brown and curly, but his prominent nose and full mouth mark his Streisand lineage. Slim at the time, fairly small of stature, possessing a winning boyish smile, he never appears to be too old for the role.

Jon Peters visited Beaufort during the location shooting. He had recently remarried and he and his glamorous blond wife, Christine, an interior decorator, had adopted a little blonde girl they named Caleigh. Streisand was asked to be the child's godmother and accepted. Marriage and adopting a child herself – preferably a girl, she asserted, seemed a feasible idea to her, although there was no man of any importance in her life. *The Prince of Tides*, however, had numerous children in the cast and she enjoyed working with them by her own admission more than any of the other actors. Tom Wingo had three young daughters, played by talented children with whom she spent much time. There were also the flashback scenes of the young Tom Wingo, his sister and brother. The three child actors cast in the parts went on to California with the company to shoot in an indoor tank the beautifully choreographed underwater swimming scene that has such a magical look in the picture. Streisand spends over half-an-hour on her documentary on the auditions and screen tests of these children, as proud of their natural acting ability and their attractiveness as she would be if they were her own.

'[I've been] thinking about how I want to spend the rest of my life,' she said at the time. 'I want to work with children. I feel a lack of children in my life. My son is very grown up. I was thinking of adopting a child, but I'm not too sure I want to do that as a single parent. It wasn't too hot for me, and I don't particularly want to do that to another child.'

It was clear in viewing the rushes of the film that she was getting a spectacular performance out of Nolte and the other performers. It is Dr Lowenstein who does not thoroughly satisfy. There is a strained seriousness to Streisand's performance that often interferes with believability. She is stiff, mannered, and in many two-shot or group scenes lit too importantly, almost hammering in the point that she is in the shot. This is particularly true of the scene where Nolte sees her across the room at an art exhibition and she appears to be standing in an aureole glow, making it impossible for anyone to miss her presence. 'I don't think about acting much,' she says defensively. 'It is easier if the part is very much you. And this character I understood very well.' The dual role of director and actor was a challenge which she had been extremely successful in handling with *Yentl*, but much less so on *The Prince of Tides*.

'It's Barbra's talent for performing that works against her abilities as an actress,' Nolte contends. 'It's really a lonely job to be a singer, a totally different mentality. As an entertainer, it's all about *me*. The lights have to be right for *me*. [Entertainers] come on the set, and they don't know how to share. They don't want to stick around for off-camera work. They have not grown up with a sense of teamsmanship. It makes it very hard for them to be taken seriously in the acting community. Barbra's much more tolerant as a director. You really don't have time to focus on yourself, and in that position she works real fine.'

Streisand acknowledges the difficulty of directing herself. 'When I direct, I become very patient, very compromising, for a perfectionist,' she says. 'There is a certain kind of acceptance of things you cannot change that would be very helpful in life. I live my life when I'm directing the way I would like to live my life when I'm not directing.'

Photography was completed on *The Prince of Tides* in late September. Now she spent long hours in the dubbing room and on the editing, like an artist working on a canvas – 'Finishing a Hat', 'Putting Things Together', as Sondheim had written. It would be fifteen months before it was released, her work done and judgment made. She always said she liked the times between projects to *potchkee* around, shop, redo her houses, read, read and *read* and plan her next adventure in movie making. She was redecorating both the Carolwood Drive house and the New York apartment with Frank Lloyd Wright and Gustav Stickley furniture. New paintings by Gustav Klimt and Egon Schiele hung on the walls. She was restless.

She saw Caleigh whenever she could in California, keeping her overnight. The little girl with her sunny smile and golden hair had fully won her affection. Caleigh was in some way the winning child she would have liked to have been and the daughter she would have wanted to have. Caleigh was so pretty, so feminine, so receptive to and giving of love. She cared deeply for this outgoing youngster and was concerned for her happiness because Peters and Christine were already having serious difficulties in their marriage. Her instinct was to protect Caleigh from the insecurities a child of divorce might suffer. She wanted to be there for her, remembering that she herself had had no such support. Thus, on the days and nights, usually once or twice a week, that Caleigh was with her, she made sure that her calendar was clear of other appointments. In the evening she would read to Caleigh and stay with her until it was time for the child to go to sleep.

Her relationship with Caleigh was curious. After all, the child was the adopted daughter of her ex-lover. But through Caleigh a solid link with Peters, who was a caring father, was maintained. Also, Jason's homosexuality left little hope that she would ever have a grandchild. 'I don't know,' one of her close friends offered, 'I think Barbra feels somehow she can relive her life through Caleigh – that is, the life she would have liked to have had. She's become with Caleigh a part of a fairy tale. Caleigh's world is all pink and beautiful – or at least Barbra is trying to make it so. You know she is always reliving the so-called pain of her childhood. And yet, that is exactly what has made her strong. Pain does that for people. Cuts the chaff from the wheat. Separates the people with guts from those who are weak. Barbra *had* to make it – and she did. And one thing – she has never been ashamed that she was once poor and has always been proud of her heritage.'

Streisand has always strongly felt the connection between herself and her Jewish roots. Her work on *Yentl* further strengthened them, along with her pride in the heritage of the Jewish people. Perhaps the only Hollywood star in its history who has been so publicly proud of being a Jew, she has never been given enough respect for her decision to portray Jewish women who could be admired – Fanny Brice, Katie Morosky, Yentl, all seminal roles, and soon in *The Prince of Tides*, Dr Susan Lowenstein. Culturally, it has meant that whatever the public does not accept about Streisand, it has had no problem with her Jewishness and implicit in that acceptance is respect for her ethnic pride. It is a great part of what has made her the enormous icon that she is. The other quality that endears her to the public is her vulnerability. She can make all the tough statements in the world, but she fools nobody. Beneath the sometimes rigorous façade is a soft-hearted, emotional woman.

Elliott has said, 'She uses her vulnerability and insecurities as a seduction, like a laser beam. It's very attractive, and that's part of her art. [However] her vulnerability is like one of those snowstorms in a globe that you shake; it's behind glass. She plays vulnerability and has always played it really masterfully.' But then Elliott himself also exudes a pervading aura of vulnerability and since his breakdown, shortly after their divorce, of someone who has suffered a damaged life.

While she waited for the 11 December 1991 première of *The Prince of Tides* she put together a four-disc autobiographical album *Just for the Record ...*, a compilation of previously recorded released and unreleased songs that allowed her briefly to tell her life story in the liner notes, giving her reasons for their inclusion and explanations about how they came to be made. The design divided her career into three decades: the sixties ('dedicated to the memory of Peter Daniels, who became my first accompanist'), the seventies ('to my beloved Gracie [Davison, her late dedicated housekeeper who had been with her since the time Jason was a youngster] whose laughter I still miss and to Howard Jeffries (sic), who would have liked this record),[1] and the eighties ('to my mother who is 82 years old and still has a beautiful voice. And to Cis Corman who's been my best friend through the 60s, 70s and 80s').

Putting together this album was a highly emotional experience. It begins with that first private recording she made of 'You'll Never Know' at the age of thirteen and includes numerous previously unreleased recordings of songs that she felt best told the story of her career as a singer. During the process of making it she had Marty Erlichman contact Barry Dennen to see if he would give her the tapes over which they had fought so bitterly thirty years earlier. Dennen remained reluctant, but might have capitulated had Erlichman not come back to say that Streisand had changed her mind about including them.

*Just for the Record ...* has been deemed by several critics as an egotistical trip down Streisand's memory lane. It is, in fact, a remarkable album giving the listener a rare chance to listen to the development, changes, maturing and tastes of one of the world's greatest contemporary song stylists. It also allowed – via the lengthy written notes interlarded with over 150 pictures from her own

---

[1] Howard Jeffrey became a 'working buddy' of Streisand's during the filming of *Funny Girl* when he was assistant choreographer to Herbert Ross. They became friends. He also worked with her on most of her subsequent musical films. He died of AIDS in 1988. His name is misspelled in the dedication.

private collection – Streisand to tell things from her point of view.

'She throws a lot of stories around,' reporter Hilary de Vries wrote of an interview with her shortly before the première of *The Prince of Tides*. '[Most of them] designed to portray Streisand as the victim triumphant, one who creates art in the face of a deprived childhood, dictatorial directors and an anti-woman industry. The effect, however, is of someone anthologizing her life as she lives it, studying herself from a slight remove, with the lighting just so.'

'I'm just interested in the truth,' she told de Vries, who was interviewing her for the *Los Angeles Times*. It is, of course, a question about whose truth. Streisand's? Elliott's? Diana's? Jason's? Peters's? The men and women who worked with her during her long career, who shared her early years? She has told the same stories frequently to the media – fictionalising, embellishing, replaying the memories over and over in her mind to react anew, analyse, free herself of guilt or in some cases learn to take it. Then, the truth has often been obfuscated, distorted or dramatised, not an unusual occurrence for the creative, self-involved or for those people who simply want to charm, impress or shock to gain attention. If you tell a story enough times it begins to have its own truth and that is how it was with Streisand. By constantly repeating stories about her deprived childhood, her unhappiness as a child became a solid foundation on which she, and the public, could understand where she came from, why she did some of the things she has done. It also allowed her audiences their own vision of the woman they were watching, which added another dimension to her performance, as it had done with two of her vocal predecessors, Billie Holiday and Judy Garland.

She has the habit of telling stories when she does not want to talk or answer questions. 'The other day I went to the theater to see the trailer of *The Prince of Tides*. And when I'm in New York, I, like, take a cab,' she began the de Vries interview. 'I don't have a 24-hour-a-day-limousine. I grew up in a poor family, and you don't think of hiring cars, but [I suddenly found myself terribly late]. And in a sweat suit – schlocky – the way I'm dressed most of the time, to tell you the truth. Well, not schlocky ... So I started to run, and could *not* get a cab. And it reminded me of when I first started on Broadway and the nights when I couldn't get a cab to my own show [*Funny Girl*], and I would plead with people on Central Park West – tears running down my face – to take me to Broadway ...' Always with such stories there were references to the past and never to the amazing highs in her astounding life – always to the pathos, the defenceless experiences that were a part of her history.

*The Prince of Tides* met with good reviews upon its general release on Christmas Day, almost all the critics extolled her talent as a director able to draw superb performances from her cast. Her own performance was consistently panned, a great disappointment to her. She had, perhaps, taken on too much. *The Prince of Tides* would have been even better had she directed another woman in the role of Dr Lowenstein.

Her fiftieth birthday on 24 April 1992 found her impatient with herself. The redecorating was completed and there was no one special man in her life. She was beginning to feel her age although she still looked a decade younger. And the men she was attracted to grew younger as she aged. 'Poor baby is miserable,' Elliott said. 'She makes herself occupied with so many things because she's so afraid to fail. So afraid of the truth.'

One of her closest old friends sighs deeply as he adds, 'It's the mirror that she has to face each morning, unadorned, make-up free, no flattering pink spots, no chance to cut and edit. That's at the core of Barbra's great sadness. She can only be what she wants to be – that Hollywood image of glamour – by artificial means. She is not a great beauty. I don't think she is able, or ever will be able, to accept that. She sees the homely Jewish girl from Brooklyn, *crazy Barbara, the girl with the big beak*, looking back at her. She does not, and cannot see what *we* see – the rare beauty that is under her public disguise. She's an original species, a one-and-only, and she has no way to judge. Barbra's greatest tragedy and her greatest blessing – is that she was not born beautiful. That is something with which she may never come to terms.'

# 29

**P**EOPLE WERE TALKING. Streisand was smitten with a young man, a 22-year-old tennis star, several years younger than Jason, and twenty-eight years her junior. Even blasé Hollywood was in a fit about the news. His name was André Agassi, styled the 'King of Grunge' and that same year, 1992, he would earn $11 million. On the courts, his dark ponytail falling below the back of a black cap, wearing scruffy clothes, black socks scrunched down over his tennis shoes, gold hoop dangling from his ears, a Ché Guevara beard framing his striking face with its sharp features, bushy brows and quick-shifting eyes, he looked and was a shaggy anti-hero to the young people who came to see his showman style and killer skill. Adult tennis buffs often greeted him with sneers, treating him like a bad Las Vegas lounge act. He had broken the 'Mr Clean', all-white tennis dress code. He was a maverick and a valuable commodity in a sport where adult participation and viewership were on the decline. 'Agassi is tennis's marketing tool for its next generation of fans,' Harvey Araton of the *New York Times* wrote. 'He comes MTV-ready, and if he turns the stomachs of a few parents, he also induces their kids to ask, "Can we get tickets for the Agassi match?"'

'He's very intelligent,' Streisand said in his defence (or perhaps her own), 'very, very sensitive, very evolved – more than his linear years. And he's an extraordinary human being. He plays like a Zen master. It's very in the moment.'

Agassi was *today, tomorrow* – and that is where she wanted to be. She was fifty, middle-aged, but she thought of Agassi as being older than his given age and herself as being younger. That narrowed the gap. He was vital, strong, moved like a gale wind, talked up a storm, was cocky, self-assured and utterly irrepressible.

They had met briefly at Aspen during the Christmas holidays, shortly after the release of *The Prince of Tides*, and began seriously dating in the spring of 1992. 'I've been learning about the sweet mysteries of life and this is one of them,' Agassi confessed to Maureen Dowd of the *New York Times* when asked about his relationship with Streisand. 'I'm not sure I can fully explain. Maybe she can't either. But it doesn't matter. We came from completely different worlds, and we collided, and we knew we wanted to be in each other's company right then.'

Streisand appeared happy, animated. Her close friends respected her right to live her life as she chose. Jason was supportive. She was accustomed to Diana's disapproval and she cared little for what Hollywood thought. The relationship was not as all-consuming as her more serious affairs in the past had been and while Agassi was off on the tennis circuit she involved herself intently in 'minding the store'.

The Prince of Tides was doing exceptionally well at the box office, already having made back triple its cost, and promised to be one of her biggest money-making movies yet. Although it was one of the five films nominated for Best Picture, she felt she was personally snubbed at the 64th Annual Academy Awards, her successful directorial efforts not included as one of the five nominated directors in that category.[1] She complained that it was because she was who she was, that she was a woman, that Hollywood would never open their minds to her.

Her rejection by the industry raised a good deal of controversy. 'Barbra was the first woman to really wield power,' said Lynda Obst, producer of The Fisher King which was nominated for five Academy Awards (it received one – Best Supporting Actress, Mercedes Ruehl). 'Barbra raised too much confusion in the beginning of her career. She threw her weight around. People are grudging in their admiration. There's so much commercial respect for her, but they also withhold a certain kind of embrace.'

Considering that the film was nominated for Best Picture and seven other nominations (including Nolte's performance and that of Kate Nelligan as his mother but not Streisand's portrayal of Dr Lowenstein), it is surprising that she was entirely overlooked. But there are just five directors nominated and as one Academy voter ventured, 'she was sixth good'. None the less, she took it as a personal rejection and went public with her feelings. The final five directors chosen were all men, a point that she stressed. They were also worthy nominees. The Prince of Tides, though beautifully photographed and well acted was a flawed film, Streisand's directorial hand is sure in all scenes in which she did not appear but, as her role was major, she was in a good percentage of the picture.

The awards and the controversy over Streisand not being nominated bolstered the box-office receipts on The Prince of Tides. She remained bitter even when in June, just two months after the Academy Awards, Sony (who now

---

[1] Nominated for Best Picture were The Silence of the Lambs (winner), Beauty and the Beast, Bugsy, J.F.K., and The Prince of Tides. Nominated for Best Director were Jonathan Demme, The Silence of the Lambs (the winner), Oliver Stone, J.F.K., Barry Levinson, Bugsy, John Singleton, Boyz N the Hood, and Ridley Scott for Thelma and Louise.

owned Columbia Pictures), finalised a $60 million multimedia entertainment contract with her, one of the largest deals yet to be made in the industry. Recent record contracts, with equally high figures, were made by Michael Jackson and Madonna with Time Warner, but Streisand's involved both records and movies and included gross percentages, which greatly increased the base amount.[2] Sony was also to continue to maintain distribution rights to her lucrative thirty-seven-album catalogue, which had accounted for more than sixty million album sales since 1964, the largest number for any recording artist during that period.

'An artist like Barbra Streisand comes along once in a generation, so you hold on to her,' said Al Teller, former president of CBS Records (now Sony Records). Mega entertainment attorney Peter Dekom added, 'Few artists have a proven track record that they can sing, act, write, direct and produce. Barbra is a multiple threat in every category.' And Irving Azoff, then chairman of Time Warner's record business, chimed in, 'There are few entertainers who ever create an audience demand across both the music and film entertainment spectrum the way that Barbra does. She typifies taste and elegance, not only commercial success.'

The industry believed that she was being recognised and acknowledged for her achievements. Streisand did not see it that way. She would never forgive the Academy and she remembered too well how hard she had to fight for stories she believed in, how record executives always made her feel like she was auditioning the songs she wanted to include in her albums. Power was complete autonomy and it was doubtful that she would ever be able to command that. She had been the most powerful *woman* in Hollywood for years, but the industry remained an exclusive men's club. It was a barrier she was unable to break.

'Language gives us an insight into the way women are viewed in a male dominated society,' she said on 12 June when she accepted the Dorothy Arzner Award, named after the mould-breaking director/film-maker. She went on to illustrate:

---

[2] Under the contract components of Sony's deal with Streisand, she was guaranteed $5 million advance per album for six albums plus an unprecedented 42 per cent royalty rate on the wholesale price of each unit sold (approx. $2.90 on each album sold at 1992 prices). She also was granted what is referred to as a 'favorite nations' clause, which guaranteed her a royalty rate that exceeded any other artist on the company's roster. On the film end of the contract, which did not require her to deliver a specific number of pictures, she was to receive a $4 million advance against 10 per cent of gross revenues for every movie in which she appeared, $3 million for her services as director and Sony was to commit $2 million a year over an estimated ten years for development funds and operating expenses to Streisand's Barwood Production Company to hire writers and executives to create film properties that she would either direct, act in or produce.

'A man is commanding – a woman demanding.

'A man is forceful – a woman is pushy.

'A man is uncompromising – a woman a ball-breaker.

'A man is a perfectionist – a woman's a pain in the ass.

'He's assertive – she's aggressive.

'He strategises – she manipulates.

'He shows leadership – she's controlling.

'He's committed – she's obsessed . . .

'If he acts, produces and directs, he's called a multi-talented hyphenate. She's called vain and egotistical.

'It's been said that a man's reach should exceed his grasp. Why can't the same be said for a woman?'

She ended by telling the group of professional women in film, 'We are a remarkable breed. We are the girls in the hood – sisterhood, that is . . . Nature designed us to be creators – to give life . . . Let's create images that show life, not only as it is, but how it could be. Let's use our collective female energy to make films that reflect our nurturing instincts and put that out into the world. Because the world surely needs it.'

Never a company- or a studio-owned artist, her independent behaviour, her seeming feminist activism, made her a continual target for criticism by the Hollywood 'boys' club'. She was accused by the establishment of being a perfectionist in a business that necessitates compromise. She hated such accusations. 'Perfection is . . . a child when it's born,' she once snapped back. 'Perfect is too small a word for it, it's a miracle. It's God. It's mind-blowing. It's more than perfect. And yet it shits and pisses. There's no such thing as perfection, because everything seems to fall apart sooner or later.' What she wanted was to be allowed to follow her own convictions, to do the best job she was capable of performing, of turning out a movie in which she had pride. In order to accomplish that it had to be done *her way*. Hollywood had a company mentality. It was loath to invest in something not yet proven to succeed at the box office. If it could have done so it would have made her into an ethnic Doris Day, appearing in the same formulaic musical until time forced her to retire. Streisand had refused to let herself be packaged, frozen and sold like an ice-cream bar by a studio and she certainly would not allow the films she chose to direct, or produce, or both, be devoured by the system.

Headstrong and as unstoppable now as she had been as a child, she pressed on choosing subjects as future projects that were controversial and could only create difficulty for her in obtaining full studio backing to augment the development funds given to her by Sony. She purchased with Robert De Niro's Tribeca Films rights for the book, *To a Violent Grave: An Oral Biography of Jackson Pollock* by Jeff Potter, published in 1985, about the tumultuous relationship between the famed abstract artist and his wife/manager, Lee Krasner. De Niro's late father was a painter and the project had two strong co-starring roles for him and Streisand. She optioned a story about Lieutenant-Colonel Margarethe Cammermeyer, who was forced to resign from the Washington National Guard when she acknowledged that she was a lesbian. She was given a screenplay, *The Mirror Has Two Faces*, written by Richard LaGravenese, who had been responsible for the script of *The Fisher King*, and became immediately involved.

A Tri-Star project, *The Mirror Has Two Faces*, was very loosely based on a 1959 French film starring Michelle Morgan about a plain, unattractive woman who starts life over again after plastic surgery. LaGravenese had given the story a deeper interpretation. In his script a plain woman with low self-esteem is transmogrified when she finds her own inner beauty – the theme thus having become: self-love physically changes people's looks. The story-line and characters still required much work, but it was a project that brought into focus some of her own experience.

Her wish to make *The Normal Heart* remained strong. She saw the Kramer play (and the story of Colonel Cammermeyer) as being about people's right to love whomever they choose – of tolerance, of acceptance of other people's lifestyles, and of not being penalised for being who and what they are.

Within the activist gay community there were rumblings that she, as one of Hollywood's biggest stars, had not done enough for AIDS. Elizabeth Taylor had already stepped forward and become the AIDS spokesperson for liberal Hollywood. Where was Streisand, they asked? They complained that she had given *only* $350,000 in 1991 for AIDS research and treatment and most of that delegated for children afflicted with the disease. But this is an unjustified and uncharitable criticism. Streisand had endowed academic chairs in women's studies at the University of California, cardiovascular research at UCLA, and another at the Environmental Defense Fund. Her Streisand Foundation continues to grant over $1 million a year to civil liberties, environmental causes and AIDS. And she often was moved to add large sums for other causes and catastrophes like the Valdez oil spill as they came along. She believed she could accomplish more as an advocate for the gay community by being able to make a commercial film that would reach a large audience and show them as being like everyone else in their need for and their right to love. She also had personal motivations. Jason's homosexuality, of course, but Stan Kamen, a close friend and her agent at William Morris, since she and Sue Mengers had parted, had recently died from AIDS and she had been intensely upset by his death, and the frustration of knowing there was no medical cure for the plague and that resources for research were limited.

This was several years before the film *Philadelphia*, starring Tom Hanks in an Academy Award performance, broke the Hollywood stand-off on stories about AIDS patients. *Philadelphia*, however, focused on an AIDS patient's right to continue a career in the workplace rather than the character's right to love.

Hollywood was not yet ready to explore this theme. Streisand would continue to walk in the face of gale winds with *The Normal Heart*. Renegotiations with Kramer for the rights were set in motion in the spring of 1990. Things went much more smoothly this time. Both gave in a bit, a compromise was reached. Kramer would write the script, but she would still retain the last word. Once again he flew to California for story conferences at her house. Both had changed. 'She was a softer person, also more conscious of how hard she had been on herself in the past,' Kramer reflected, 'She talked a lot about it, about not trying to be the perfectionist all the time. She had been in the kind of therapy where you get in touch with the inner child. She was more considerate, somehow gentler.

'I had known for two years that I was HIV Positive and I thought I was shortly going to die. Literally the first week I started work with her I got an emergency call from my doctor in New York. How he got Barbra's number I've never known. But my blood work had just come in and he called to tell me that he had to put me on AZT right away and wanted the name of a pharmacy in Los Angeles so that I could start immediately. I was very upset and Barbra was marvellous, comforting and organisational at the same time. I'll never forget it – or her. She put her arms around me, she contacted the pharmacy, and we talked.

'I was violently anti-AZT. There were different schools of thought about whether it was good or not and until we had more medical details I was reluctant to take it. So this was a big emotional thing. Also, AZT can have scary side-effects on your body and I thought, "Holy shit!" I was afraid that I would have these skin lesions and not be able to work so well and this was what I had been wanting for years – for Barbra to come back on the project.'

Kramer recalls that when his doctor rang from New York Streisand sensed it was something serious. 'She said if you want to talk privately to take it in the bathroom which adjoined her study. When I came out I was shaken and she said, "What's the matter?" And I told her. Then she put her arms around me and hugged me close to her, very maternal. I was terribly moved. I couldn't hold back my tears.

'From then on it was, "How are you feeling? How's it going? Are you having any side-effects?" There was great warmth. Much different than in 1985 when I felt more like a hired hand. Fortunately, the medication did help and I did not have any side-effects, so I carried on working.

'Barbra writes in the old-fashioned way, in which every shot and every angle is described. She wants a sense of what the camera is doing, what you start to focus on, where does it move, what's the action so that she can follow. She is a person who questions everything. If you had a comma there yesterday, and you don't have one today, why has it been removed? And she knows and she remembers that there was a comma there. She has a low file cabinet, really an open drawer, that has every scene of every version of the script that I have written, she has written and anyone else has written. It is broken down by scenes and she will remember which one had what and constantly compare them. Then she will record on tape exactly the sequence she wants so that there will not be any chance of a slip-up. I would then bring it into her the next day sort of polished.

'We'd work from three-thirty in the afternoon often until eight or nine in the evening. The rest of the house had undergone redecoration. There was new art, a great deal of mission furniture, but the study remained basically the same. She always looked lovely. She has such beautiful skin – unbelievable skin, her eyes are such a clear blue and her hair always seems right even when it's just hanging. She wore the same kind of clothes to work in – designer-type jogging outfits.

'There is something about her that is very touching. She is very vulnerable. You can feel it and whether she is opening it up to you or not you are in the presence of it. Maybe that is what the great singers have. They can sing these songs about how the world has touched them, or love has touched them, and you want to say, "It's all right." And she remembers all the bad things the press ever said about her. I asked her why she held on to things for so long, why didn't she let it go, and she replied, "I can't seem to help it. How do you do it? You've been criticised so much. Why doesn't it bite the shit out of you?"

' "Well, it used to," I told her, "but you cannot take a strong opinion about something and not know that you are going to offend somebody, somewhere. Let it go, let it go," I kept telling her. She's trying so hard to be everything. To be the most perfect person, the most admirable person. People talk about her lust for power, her need for control. Control is a very harsh word for the way people use it against her. She wants to run her company her way, she has that right. A case in point. "There are things you write that I can't put on the screen," she told me. "Give me an example," I asked.

' "Well, the scene where the two men make love believing they have engaged in safe sex and there is a spot of semen on one of the guy's chest, and they don't know whose it is and one of them indicates that it could be poisonous."

' "That is what I wanted to show. That a slip like that could kill you. I think it's very moving." And she replied, simply, with finality, "You can't show semen on somebody's chest." '

Her affair with Agassi came to a sudden end. She had gone to Wimbledon to watch him play Pete Sampras in the quarterfinals in June and cheered him on wildly to no avail. Agassi lost the match. By September, he was dating a younger woman and soon after would pair up with the actress Brook Shields, who was closer to his own age. At this point there was no other man in Streisand's life. Jason was in New York attending film classes at New York University where he had made a short movie, in which his father and his grandmother, Diana, appeared, that was highly praised. He was now concentrating, not on acting but on a career as a writer and director. Streisand remained for a while in Manhattan. She was lonely, 'very lonely', close friends say. Jason suffered from a fear of heights, a phobia that had been a fairly recent development and could not take the elevator up to the penthouse apartment. This meant they met at more impersonal locales, restaurants, other people's homes.

'I think, strangely enough, that Barbra wants to make *The Normal Heart* for Jason,' Kramer said. 'I believe it's her way in fighting for his acceptance and his right to love who he wants and be proud of who and what he is. It's the ultimate gift, the utmost. If she's nervous about anything, that's where the nervousness comes. It is not easy to do a film about homosexuality when your son is involved in it. Also, I suspect that when the movie is finally made it will come out more about Jason because he wants to work on it. He has exceedingly good taste and I think Barbra, and Cis Corman, too, respect his ability.'

Jon Peters and his wife Christine were in the process of a divorce. Streisand's concern was Caleigh, only three years old at the time. She identified closely with the child, felt her bewilderment at being the victim of a broken home. Her friendship with Peters remained solid. Both he and Christine saw Streisand's involvement with Caleigh as a stabilising factor in the little girl's life. Streisand decorated a bedroom in the Carolwood Drive house for her; a story-book room in pink and white with crisp organdy curtains and shelves filled with books and dolls. The child was closely attached to Streisand and was visibly happy to be with her. Peters had the responsibility of her care but Christine also shared custody. Caleigh was still too young to know how she would be affected by Streisand's involvement in her welfare and rearing. Affectionate by nature, Caleigh and Streisand hugged and kissed a lot. Caleigh called her 'Baba' and Streisand doted on her. 'I want only the best for her, the most love and affection that it is possible to give her,' she told close friends, who noted the happiness Caleigh brought to Streisand. 'She sees Caleigh as her own. It's amazing how much she loves that child,' one commented.

She had always been a champion of children's problems in a world where they have so little control over their lives. Caleigh brought this issue closer to home.

'One night when I was putting [Caleigh] to sleep,' she recalled, 'I started to sing her a lullaby. "Rock-a-bye-baby on the tree top. When the wind blows, the cradle will rock. When the bough brakes, the cradle will fall ..." "The cradle will fall???" she exclaimed. What was I supposed to tell her? I mean really that's a frightening thought [to tell a child.]'

She created garden space for a proper play area with a sand box and slide and a playhouse where Caleigh could have lemonade and cookies with a friend in the afternoon. She made sure Caleigh had playmates, inviting children from her pre-school to the house, took her to the beach where they built sand castles together, went shopping with her for clothes allowing the child's taste to guide her purchases, and accompanied her to the paediatrician for her regular check-up, holding her hand so she would not be frightened. One could read many things into her close attachment to the winning blonde child whose blue eyes and wide smile were so appealing. She was the child she would have wish to have been, the girl she always wanted, the tie that would keep her bound to Peters, the granddaughter she might never have. But, perhaps, the most obvious explanation was that Caleigh satisfied a need in Streisand for a continuing bonding with another person.

Streisand re-entered the political arena when Bill Clinton won the Democratic nomination in the summer of 1992. She had not been energised by Michael Dukakis in the previous election. Now, along with the Bergmans, she joined whole-heartedly in working for his election, as impressed with Hillary Rodham Clinton as with her husband. Finally there was an especially intelligent potential First Lady, reminiscent of one of her longtime idols, Eleanor Roosevelt. Mrs Clinton seemed to understand the domestic issues at stake – AIDS research, health care, a woman's right to abort, the state of the environment – and would not be hesitant to raise her voice to bring them to the attention of the country.

She met the Clintons the night of 16 September at a HWPC fundraiser held on the expansive lawns of the $39 million, 49-acre Beverly Hills estate of reclusive film producer Ted Fields, one of the five top national Democratic donors. It was the first time in six years that she sang in public, this time not as a solo performer but on a programme crowded with Hollywood's Democratic supporters who either spoke or performed – among them Warren Beatty, Annette Bening, Goldie Hawn, Whoopi Goldberg, Stephen Spielberg, Candice Bergen (wearing glasses), Jack Nicholson (in shades), Michelle Pfeiffer, Dustin Hoffman, Richard Dreyfuss, Danny DeVito, Rhea Perlman, Dionne Warwick and Mike Nichols and Elaine May, who did a rare stand-up comedy routine. Beatty introduced Clinton, who appeared somewhat overwhelmed by the stellar gathering and their eloquent outpouring of support.

'Warren Beatty said he hadn't known me a long time,' he said during his speech, 'but I was sitting there thinking I have known many of you a long time. I have seen your movies or sung your songs and just imagined that life could be as it seems to be in the lyrics or up on the screen.' And he added, 'I have always aspired to be in the cultural elite that others condemn.'

Streisand, simply dressed in a black scoop-necked, long-sleeved Donna Karan gown, her hair casually brushed loose to frame her face, commanded a huge ovation as she stepped up to the microphone. 'Six years ago,' she told the Hollywoodites who had raised over $1 million that evening, 'I was motivated by the disaster at Chernobyl. Now I'm motivated by the possibility of another disaster: the re-election of George Bush and Dan Quayle.' The crowd roared, and she sang 'On A Clear Day You Can See Forever', followed by 'Happy Days Are Here Again'.

Maybe they were. A dedicated Democrat, it seemed that for the first time in sixteen years someone she could identify with had a good chance of making it into the White House. She liked the man a lot. He had the kind of charisma that she admired and he *listened* to his wife, to *women*, to what just plain people had to say. He was the kind of man to whom she could easily have become attracted. They spoke for a while later that evening. He told her his father had died before he was born and he understood she had lost her father at a young age. 'It has a way of affecting your whole life,' he said.

'Yes,' she replied. 'It's a tough thing to overcome. I'm not sure you really ever do. It hurts to think mine never got to know I became famous, that I achieved some good things. But that you are on your way to becoming President, that's a tough one not to share.'

Clinton smiled down at her from his great height and nodded his head, then they were joined by several others who wanted to shake the hand of the man they hoped would soon be President of the United States.

# 30

'HOW COME NOBODY attacked the Republican White House for their involvement with Arnold Schwarzenegger, Charlton Heston and Bruce Willis?' Streisand shot back at a reporter who asked her views on the media accusations that the supposed Hollywood–Clinton connection was a threat to 'the very fabric of this Republic'. Her man had won and this time she was a part of the pre-inauguration and post-inaugural celebrations as well having a front-row seat when he took the oath of office. A huge Hollywood contingent had come to Washington to the final gala of Clinton's inaugural week, attended by 19,000 guests at the cavernous Capital Center. The gigantic celebration was nastily referred to in the press as a 'Hollywood–Washington production'. Streisand sang 'Evergreen' as the President and the First Lady held hands. Then, an enthusiastic audience thundering their approval, she gave her all to 'On a Clear Day You Can See Forever' and 'Happy Days Are Here Again', the latter to five ovations that did not stop until she introduced the President-elect, at which point the vast crowd stood up, all at once, all whistling, all hurrahs and clapping.

Streisand handed the microphone over to Clinton who stood on stage under a white spotlight, a black stool used in her act behind him. 'Thank you for sharing with me my last night as a private citizen,' he told them, and turned to Streisand who was still standing on the podium and gave her a warm, tight, bear hug.

One staff member, who had also worked on the Reagan and Bush pre-inaugural galas, found the Democrats 'much more fun, much more casual. Everybody is in a party mood. No prima donnas. No ozone layer of spray over everything. Four years ago all the gowns seemed to be red, white or blue. This year – solid sequins – the brighter and funkier the better.' Streisand wore, in contrast to the glittery evening dresses chosen by Goldie Hawn and others, a striking three-piece pin-striped Donna Karan suit, the floor-length skirt slit to the thigh, referred to in the *Washington Post* as 'the peek-a-boo power suit'.

The highly successful Karan, America's leading woman designer, and now one of Streisand's closest friends, had created a new, daring, sophisticated look for her. The two women not only shared a love of fashion, they had many of the same views and social commitments. They were part of 'the sisterhood' – those women who, like Streisand, competed in a man's world. Karan, tall, dark-haired, comfortably built – trim, but not model-thin – was handsome, middle-aged and ran a spectacularly high-profile fashion house. But the financial backing for her enterprise came from businessmen who were interested more in the profit column than the designer's need to express herself creatively, a situation that Streisand also dealt with in making movies.

Once again Streisand was under attack from the *Washington Post*, which was particularly vituperative in its assault on what it called 'Clinton's wooing of entertainment royalty', adding that film stars were 'incapable of serious involvement with the politics industry of Washington'. Streisand was singled out as a prime target and referred to demeaningly as *La* Streisand'.

'When I directed a movie,' she replied to a *Los Angeles Times* journalist, 'it was as if I was being told how dare I attempt to infiltrate a man's domain. Now, it's: How dare I be interested in politics. Forgive my tone if I sound angry but I am!'[1]

The extraordinary meanness of the press did not stop Streisand from enjoying the thrill and excitement of the historic occasion. She stayed at the Stouffer Mayflower Hotel, instantly renamed in the press as 'the power hotel of the week' as other guests included President Clinton's mother, Virginia Kelley, her husband Dick, Clinton's brother Roger, Mrs Clinton's two brothers, Tony and Hugh Rodham, Vice-President Al Gore and his family, political guru James Carville, Barbara Walters and a long list of top film, concert and television performers. Streisand was also being called, 'the woman fast becoming the top celebrity'.

The following day, 20 January, she sat teary-eyed at the stirring inauguration ceremony, the weather crisp and cool, a winter sun lighting the podium as Bill Clinton, his broad, usually smiling face sombre on this occasion, was sworn into office. The new President seemed enveloped in an aura of youth; he was, after all, only forty-seven, a year older than John F. Kennedy had been when he was assassinated. This was truly what Streisand had come to Washington to witness, the central simple reality. A man she believed in was taking the oath of office as President of the United States. It was a moment that signalled the turning of a great page. She had soaring hopes for the future of the country. She who complained so much, who suffered such heavy Jewish guilt, nurtured a negative approach, saw the black side rather than the white, the half-empty glass to the half-full, who claimed to feel threatened and

---

[1] Jack Valenti, President of the Motion Picture Association of America Inc. immediately wrote a letter to the editor of the *Washington Post* in Streisand's defence. 'Barbra Streisand has read deeper and absorbed more about what ails this society than most of the bureaucrats who inhabit the higher reaches of our government,' he stressed.

frightened so much of the time, felt optimistic. The Clinton administration was one with which she could personally identify. She felt an insider, like somehow she belonged.

This was to usher in a new phase of her life in which she would speak up and out, become an activist. 'We [Hollywood executives and stars] have the right to be taken as seriously as automobile executives,' she told an interviewer after one of the media sneeringly addressed her as 'the princess of tides'. 'No one would question the president of G[eneral] M[otors] talking to people in Washington.'

Streisand carried away many memorable moments throughout the day: 'a cheerful thumbs up and wink from out-going President Bush through a limousine window as the car pulled away from the White House; Mrs Clinton and Mrs Bush chatting amicably as they raced through Capitol corridors towards the West Front; Clinton stooping to pet Millie [the Bushes' dog] when the Clintons arrived at the White House; young First-Daughter, Chelsea, unable to suppress a yawn even during the very peppy singing of the national anthem by Marilyn Horne.' She was mesmerised by these personal recollections and in awe of the history that she saw at every turn. She had become in these few days a part of that history. The thought thrilled her, whipped up a deep sense of patriotism that was equal to her pride in her sex and her heritage.

And she had a handsome escort to the various activities, ABC TV anchorman, Peter Jennings, a distinguished-looking news reporter with a self-assured air and great popular appeal, who had recently separated from his wife. Streisand perhaps saw in him some of the same attraction that once had drawn her to Pierre Trudeau, the intelligence, political and worldwide grasp of issues mixed with good looks and considerable charm. There were eleven official inauguration balls. Streisand, in a grey jersey Karan gown ('cut down to here and slashed to there'), briefly attended the most high-profiled one, the Arkansas Ball at the Washington Convention Center, with Jennings, departing shortly after the Clintons moved on.

Streisand held court, according to the *Washington Post*, at what was called *the* after-the-ball Inauguration Day party at the chic Jockey Club. Jennings had to report back to work and she came with Donna Karan. The only persons missing were the President and First Lady. Jack Nicholson could be heard laughing his diabolical laugh. Warren Beatty and Annette Bening passed around a picture of their new baby daughter, Lauren Bacall cha-cha-ed, Jack Lemmon, Kathleen Turner, Chevy Chase, Shirley MacLaine, Robert De Niro and Richard Dreyfuss were there along with a host of Kennedys and well-known politicians. At 1.30 a.m. Streisand, 'wearing a long black hooded cape which made her look like Marie Antoinette fleeing revolutionary Paris', made a getaway through the kitchen, the bar and out the front door with Karan close at her heels.

Streisand's relationship with Jennings would remain on the basis of 'just good friends' although she relied on him for inside information on many of the topics that interested her. They spoke often and met whenever she was on the East Coast. Her obvious and ongoing public comment on issues caused the media once again to proclaim that she was about to declare for political office. She made it as clear as she could that she was not interested in running for anything, she was merely an involved citizen. A lot of press was given to the supposition that she had the ear of the President, which she hotly denied. In mid-May 1993, she was invited to the White House Washington Correspondents' Dinner and then 'granted 5 minutes with Clinton. I talked with him about what was being done for AIDS research,' she averred. 'The month before, some of us from the entertainment industry were invited to the health-care meeting. We didn't even have dinner with Clinton. We saw him afterwards. We had dinner with his mother – whom I adore because she's this resilient, optimistic woman.

'There was all this criticism that Hollywood people were getting into areas that they are not expert on but we were asked to come to the White House for communication ideas – we were called there for them to tap into our communication skills – how to get a message across to the American people. We've been called "air-heads" and "nitwits". This is so unfair. And it's smearing the main industry in our community. It's saying there isn't a brain around. Did the entertainment industry create the national debt?

'The media are in a Hollywood-bashing mode these days. They reported contemptuously that Janet Reno and I had dinner and "hashed out issues". Why two prominent, hard-working women, isolated by their position, should not want to talk to each other is beyond me. Why such venomous response toward people from Hollywood? Why are we so threatening to the media? We have the right as an industry, as people, as professionals, to be taken as seriously as automobile executives – an industry that is having trouble selling its products abroad. On the other hand, we make something that the whole world wants to buy, it improves our balance of payments, creates jobs and pays a lot in taxes.'

She wandered the Capitol on this trip as a tourist, visiting the Smithsonian and Monticello. 'The most moving moments were being at the National Archives,' she confessed, 'and holding the Emancipation Proclamation and Louisiana Purchase and seeing the film at the Holocaust Museum about the survivors who were reaffirming the preciousness of life, struggling to maintain their dignity, helping one another to gather strength to survive. They didn't surrender to cynicism – which is killing our country and preventing our pulling together.'

Nothing was going to stop her from speaking her mind. She was, and always had been, pro-choice, for the equality of women, for the protection of the environment, a dedicated liberal. 'That's why I have a foundation to fortify my beliefs,' she told Robert Scheer of the *Los Angeles Times*. 'That's how I give back. That's how I raise my voice. And whether the right-wing conservatives like it or not, I will keep on raising it.'

In the early days of January 1994, she got Sammy, a fluffy white bichon frise with dark button eyes and an affectionate nature. She had been without a dog for many years. Sadie, whom she had adored and she did not think she would ever replace had died before she made *A Star Is Born*. Sammy followed at her heels wherever she went in the house.

On the morning of 17 January, the devastating earthquake she had always feared would come to Los Angeles, seemed to have arrived. She awoke in the house on Carolwood Drive to a sudden shifting of the bed beneath her, the sounds of breaking glass, wood creaking, the house groaning and shaking. The first thing she did was get out of bed, carefully avoiding the glass from a nearby broken window, and go in search of the young puppy, frantically calling his name. When she found him sitting under her dressing table 'he was so calm he calmed me', she said. She then called her mother, who was frightened but not harmed. Thankfully, no one in the household had been injured but it was a terrifying experiencing and she had lost many of her treasured pieces of pottery and glass.

She had recently finished work on a new album, *Back to Broadway*, that included many of the songs she had not been able to record for the first Broadway album. Sondheim theatre music was well represented with 'Everybody Says Don't' (*Anyone Can Whistle*), 'Children Will Listen' (from *Into the Woods*, and perhaps Sondheim's most important song), 'Move On' (*Sunday in the Park with George*), 'I Have a Love' and 'One Hand, One Heart' (*West Side Story*, lyrics only – a duet with Johnny Mathis). But this time Sondheim did not have as great an influence over the recording sessions. She included two songs, exquisitely rendered, from Andrew Lloyd Webber's yet-to-be seen *Sunset Boulevard*, 'As If We Never Said Goodbye' and 'With One Look'.

*Sunset Boulevard* was in rehearsals for its West Coast première, and Don Black and Christopher Hampton, the English writers who shared credit for the lyrics, were in Los Angeles. She wanted some small changes to be made to adapt the lyrics of 'With One Look' and 'As If We Never Said Goodbye' to her needs (as Sondheim had done with 'Putting It Together' on the earlier album) and she asked Black and Hampton to meet her at the Carolwood Drive house to discuss it.

'It was the highlight of my professional career,' Black, who also collaborated with Lloyd Webber on *Song and Dance* and *Aspects of Love* and wrote the lyrics for 'Born Free' and many other hit songs, stressed. 'She is a great story teller with phenomenal instinct into the proper phrasing and interpretation of a lyric. It was what every songwriter dreams of – to have a song sung by Barbra Streisand.

'Christopher, myself and David Caddick, who is Andrew's musical director and was also on *Sunset*, went together. Christopher couldn't stay long as he had another engagement but he wanted to meet her. The three of us went to her house. It looked a very modest house as we drew up to the gates. It wasn't that long driveway that you have in your fantasy as the approach to a home belonging to a star of her calibre. Inside it was another matter, marvellous taste, but again not what you would expect. What would that be? Shangri La, I suspect.

'She was late. There was a problem that had suddenly developed with a tooth and she had gone to the dentist. This was mid-morning, an especially bright autumn day. Her secretary greeted us and made us comfortable in the living room where a piano occupied one corner. We waited about a half an hour. Christopher was about to leave when she came in, her attitude sisterly. "Hi, hello everybody," she greeted, very family-like. I was struck with how ordinary she looked. Nothing starry about her – casual clothes, almost no make-up, tennis shoes. "How are you guys for tea, coffee?" she asked. There was no feeling at all that you were in the presence of such a famous woman. It was quite amazing. After about five or ten minutes of chit-chat, Christopher left and there was just me and David Caddick seated at the piano. He said nothing for hours on end – he wasn't asked to.

'She sat down opposite me and kept offering snacks – little potato latkes, olives, nuts. She'd push a dish closer to me on the table between us. Meanwhile, she dissected the lyrics with forensic precision. Her main concern was "With One Look".

'"Will people know what I'm talking about?" she asked. "As written it's about a silent movie star. People are going to hear it on the radio or by record and if they haven't seen the show they won't know what I'm talking about."

'She wanted to put a few words of explanation in the verse. I didn't agree with that. "Songs from musicals are specific," I told her. We talked about it for a long while. There was nothing argumentative about it or dictatorial or demanding. She was flexible but we went over every comma and crotchet of the song. At the end I did say, "Well, let me think of something." Her secretary then interrupted with some papers she had to sign and sandwiches were brought in and I took the time to write some lines for the front of the song. I think they were something like – "They don't want me any more, they all say I'm through, but it's time they knew – With one look" and so on.' My intention was to set up right away that this was a star past her prime but still defiant.

'There is a line – "One tear from my eye," and she wanted "one tear *in* my eye makes the whole world cry". I admired her intense involvement. She cared so much about every detail. There was a comfortable collaborative feel to the session. Very affable. This went on for hours with David still at the piano, very respectable, just poised there. Finally she said, "Well, maybe we should try it."

'She was now seated next to me on the couch having a cup of tea and she puts the cup down and without rising and without the piano sings the opening lines of "With One Look". This remarkable voice came out. After the first few bars David found her key and backed her and it was just unbelievable. Here was this most ordinary-looking woman having a cup of tea and singing liquid diamond in my ear. I ran out of goose bumps.

' "Well, what do you think?" she asked. "Is it OK? I haven't sung for years. You know I haven't done a concert in so long. You really think it's OK?"

She was so insecure, very uncertain about it and really it was just wonderful. There was no pretending. I had the highest respect for her. Then when we stopped the session she played some of the tracks she had already recorded for the album and she told me how Sondheim rewrote everything for her. I could understand why he did it. She gives a lyric new meaning, fresh interpretation. She is simply the greatest singer of our time. Still, as she played the tracks she would ask, "Does it sound like it's mixed right here? Could you hear the breath?" – more like a singer just starting her career. There was no doubt in my mind why she has stayed at the top. Because she doesn't release a record – she *unveils* it.

'Andrew had agreed that I should work with Barbra, but I was still apprehensive and showed him what I had done. You're dealing with two icons. How many people are there in their strata? It would have been terrible if Andrew hated it but Barbra loved it. It would be a nightmare that doesn't bear thinking about. But Andrew thought the lyrics were right for her purpose. In the end he produced the songs and worked on the arrangements for the recording.'

Black was also with her when she recorded the two songs from *Sunset Boulevard*. He was ecstatic with the first take, more so with the second. She went on to do about twenty more. 'I thought, "Oh my god! Don't keep singing because this voice can't last!" but it did. Then she has the engineer play back the same line from each of her takes. She has a sheet and ticks off which phrase or word she likes the best of each. Then she has them put together. It's a miraculous job of stitching, a surgical skill. "I like the breath on take twenty-two," I heard her say. And you're sitting there and it's simply mind-boggling.

'She wanted various musical phrases and she would sing them to the trombonist or the trumpeter and say, "You know it would be very nice if you could play something like –" then she would *la-la* a few notes that took on an instrument sound. She is unique.'

*Back to Broadway* went into the charts almost immediately upon its release and its great success sparked Streisand and Marty Erlichman to the idea that the time was right for her to return to the concert stage. Her past appearances before a live audience had always put her through 'great misery ... every night I was terrified'. Then, as she explains it, on 24 April 1993, 'Donna Karan gave me a wonderful birthday party and Liza Minnelli got up to sing and I am sitting there thinking, "How does she do this? How does anyone get up in front of people and sing?" I could never get myself to sing at parties ... with people looking at me. I can sing on stage because it is a black curtain out there. I can just see a few people and even that disturbs me. So I was fascinated just watching her and it became a challenge. I didn't like accepting that fright. I am frightened about a lot of things, but what I hope is good about me is that I go through the fear.

' "Why can't I do this?" I thought. Besides, so many fans wanted me to sing live. People were saying, "You owe it to them." It was starting to get to me.'

'I had returned to London,' Don Black remembers, 'and Alan Bergman rang me up and said Barbra wanted to open with "As If We Never Said Goodbye" and would I make some changes [that had not been made for the record], make it more relevant to a singer who was coming back after being away from the concert stage for a long time. "I don't know why I'm frightened. I know my way around here. The cardboard trees, the painted sea ..." that's Norma Desmond. I changed it to "the band, the lights, familiar sights..." and various little bits throughout and then I faxed it to Alan and he faxed back Barbra's suggestions. There were six or seven phone calls as well. Again, the minutest details.'

The song had personal meaning for Streisand, who had begun her career in live venues – cabaret and the stage – and had grown steadily fearful of maintaining these appearances. That fear had not disappeared but a concert tour would greatly enhance her recording potential. A record album and a pay-per-view TV special (later scrapped in favour of a Home Box Office special) would be the natural spin-offs and should generate tremendous revenues.

Money was much in her mind. She was rich, but not rich enough to do all the things she wanted to do without concern for her future. There were the films she wanted to make that did not appear to be commercial and there were her foundation and the various deeply felt causes to which her financial support, even in a small way, could make a difference. And on a more personal note, she was refurnishing her New York apartment, with priceless American eighteenth-century antiques and paintings, this time responding to a private tour of the White House which remained vivid in her mind.

As far back as December 1991, she had told Tom Shales of the *Washington Post* that she was considering doing a tour for financial reasons. 'I actually am running out of money, because I don't work very often,' she told him. 'I've bought all this land [California beachfront property] and I can't sell my other land [the Malibu ranch], so I might have to go out and sing just to pay for my house.' The ranch was proving to be a tremendous drain on her resources. The taxes were exorbitant and the maintenance, with the vast grounds and the five houses on them, was enormous. Also, the estate had served its purpose in her life. The decoration of the houses had each been like making a movie. Once finished, she wanted to go to the next project. Art deco and art nouveau were no longer her passion. She wanted money to buy primitive and Early American art as well as furniture of the arts and craft period. Negotiations were begun with Christie's auction house for a public sale of some of the contents of the ranch's houses.

In August 1993 Kirk Kerkorian, the owner of the new $1 billion, 5,000-room MGM Grand in Las Vegas, unaware that Streisand was even considering a return to the concert stage, called Erlichman and, thinking he might lure her with the offer, proposed to donate $3 million to her favourite charities if she would make a one-time appearance – New Year's Eve – at his hotel less than two weeks after the opening of the world's largest hotel-casino project. The offer came at a propitious time. Her movie projects were at a temporary standstill, 'plus', as she says, 'the show was to be on New Year's Eve. I hate New Year's Eve. It is a very lonely night for me ... never a happy time. There is such an obligation to be happy. So, I thought: What a great way to escape New Year's Eve ... doing a show.'

Kerkorian's offer was the perfect opportunity for Streisand to initiate a live concert performance. She did not, however, intend to appear without private compensation. Erlichman offered Kerkorian a deal whereby she would perform at the MGM Grand for two nights, 31 December and 1 January, which could earn Streisand close to $10 million for each performance;[2] additionally, the shows would be filmed (the best performance of each song being used) for television. Kerkorian, who knew that Streisand's appearance could well be the entertainment coup of the decade, swiftly agreed to the new terms. Other name acts such as Paul McCartney or Michael Jackson might well draw the crowds, but their appearance – since they had toured widely in recent years and had been seen on cable television – would not be as newsworthy.

Everything else in Streisand's life was put on hold as she began work with the Bergmans on the concept for her appearance. Her idea was to make the concert an autobiographical trip through her life and career using music and film clips as the milestones. Not only would she write most of the script, she would also direct, but she wanted to be surrounded by people whose judgment she could trust – Erlichman, Cis Corman, the Bergmans, Dwight Henion, who had produced so many of her television specials.

---

[2] The $20 million estimate included the expense and payroll of producing the concerts, which would be deducted from that amount as well as the $3 million Streisand still planned to turn over to her foundation for charitable distribution. Kirk Kerkorian rightly gambled on the fact that she had rarely performed in public for more than twenty years and that the two concerts would be quickly sold out.

She approached Marvin Hamlisch, who twenty-one years earlier had worked with her on *The Way We Were*, to take on the job of conductor. Since they had made *The Way We Were*, for which he had won two Oscars, Hamlisch had received a third Academy Award for his adaptation of Scott Joplin's music for *The Sting*, won four Grammys, a Tony, three Golden Globes and had composed the music for the Pulitzer Prize-winning show *A Chorus Line*, as well as of *They're Playing Our Song* and *The Goodbye Girl*.

'I didn't need the job,' he says, 'but I would never have said no to it. I thought it was the right thing to do. I also thought it would be a very historic kind of event for her to come back to the stage after twenty-seven years and I wanted to be part of it. I just thought I was made to do this. When I was asked to think over the situation – conducting for Barbra – to me that was a privilege. We are talking about a great voice . . . a great lady.'

Tickets went on sale for two New Year's concerts at the MGM Grand in early October. Erlichman claims that the telephone company did not want the Las Vegas tickets to be on sale during the week – they were afraid incoming calls would overload the system. Over a million requests were clocked in the first Sunday they chose, only the earliest callers being able to purchase tickets. Streisand was overwhelmed with the response. An idea brewed now that Las Vegas could be the launch for an international tour, although she was petrified of the enormity of such an undertaking, of the possibility that she would suffer terrible stage-fright, of forgetting her lines and lyrics.

For years she had been accustomed to scripted dialogue filmed in short pieces and of knowing that if she mis-spoke it could be reshot or edited later. Finally, she agreed that if she was superbly prepared and if she could use some kind of tele-prompter system large enough for her to see from the stage that would help, but the musicians, technicians and venues had to be the very best. Erlichman went off on a lengthy trip to view the arenas and concert halls in some of the major cities that he thought would prove the most viable for her and she went into rehearsals on the largest soundstage at Columbia Pictures, the same one on which she had recorded the songs for *Funny Girl* and *Funny Lady*.

Her first ambition was to have the sound for her live performances controlled as perfectly as it was when she was in a recording studio. For this task she hired one of the top acoustical technicians in the country, Bruce Jackson, who had worked for six years with Elvis Presley and ten with Bruce Springsteen. 'I had heard that she was impossible to work with,' Jackson said. 'She definitely kept everyone on their toes. If you disagreed you had to stand your ground. She would listen and try to rattle you. If you showed you were rattled and gave up ground, you were dead. She *was* demanding, but I found if you give her what she wants, she is in fact a great pleasure, very stimulating.'

'She knew what she wanted, but she didn't know how to get there,' said

Tom Gallagher of Aura Systems, the company which was manufacturing a special speaker system for the concerts. 'It was our job to keep experimenting until we got it right.'

Streisand wanted an intimate, controlled sound and in the size of the arenas where she would be singing, this would not be easy to achieve. After many ideas had failed, Jackson finally came to her with the suggestion that carpet be laid on the floor and heavy drapes hung on the walls of the concert venues. 'I knew this would be hugely expensive, but when I mentioned it to Barbra and Marty, they both said: "Yes, do it."'

She was to be backed by a 64-piece orchestra. Donna Karan was designing the two gowns she would wear in the two sections of the concert so that she would not only look marvellous but would be able to move largely unrestricted by them. To keep herself as calm as possible she listened to meditation tapes when she was not needed. The entire effort was as concentrated and as carefully choreographed as a Broadway show. The rehearsals at Columbia were her out-of-town try-outs. Nothing was left to chance. Every comment she was to make on stage was drilled over and over to achieve near perfection.

'Barbra would tell me these stories [about her life],' Hamlisch recalls, 'and I would say, "Put it in the show." She has a wonderful way of putting the truth out there almost with a little bit of whimsy, and that way you realise she is one of us. She is this person who has this great talent, but she is talking to us like she really cares. A very important thing about the concert was to have her fans see her as she is.'

The last few days before the first show, Friday night, New Year's Eve, 1993, were mayhem. The immense MGM Grand Hotel's Grand Garden arena seated over 13,000. All the doors except one leading into the arena were sealed for security reasons, but this meant that 13,000 people would have to line up single-file, airport-style and pass through metal detectors (specified VIPs were ushered through a rear door). Tickets were astronomically priced from $50 to $1,000, with 4,000 of the seats at the top level, the average price per person being more than $500, and some fans had paid brokers three and four times face value for choice seats. Would they now be in a rage at having to stand in line for up to an hour to take their seats? And would this create a disgruntled audience who would be difficult to woo in the first few songs of her programme? Streisand weighed all sides of the question and decided that she could not appear unless she felt secure and therefore would take the risk.

Wild expectation spread through the crowds as they waited to pass through the security check and enter the arena on New Year's Eve. The performance had been scheduled for 8 p.m. Around half-past eight numerous white stretch limousines drew up to the kerb. As each celebrity stepped out cheers went up from the crowds. There were Liza Minnelli, the President's mother (an inveterate gambling and Las Vegas enthusiast), Coretta Scott King, the widow of slain civil rights leader Martin Luther King Jr, Prince, Quincy Jones, Michael Crawford, Alec Baldwin, Kim Basinger, along with Streisand's former directors Peter Bogdanovich and Sydney Pollack. No one appeared disgruntled that the luminaries did not have to wait in line. 'Never in my life did I think I would see her live,' one woman who had paid $500 for her ticket and had been waiting since 6 p.m. said. Another agreed. 'I had to be here. What if she doesn't feel comfortable on stage and decides to never do another concert?'

As soon as she stepped out on the stage at the MGM Grand she would hear the thunderous roar of the crowd and know that making movies might be her passion but the stage was the only means she had of getting immediate gratification. And she was to come face to face with the reality of her life. There was no one in the entertainment world to equal her, not Frank Sinatra, Michael Jackson or Madonna. She was no longer just a superstar. She was a living icon.

# 31

S HE STOOD OUTSIDE her dressing room, distanced from the backstage mayhem that existed in the last few minutes before her show was to begin. Her black gown with its deep-cut neckline gracefully framed her slim, curvaceous figure. Around her neck was a glittering display of diamonds. Her shoulder-length light brown hair, streaked blonde, was loose and softly styled. With a small wave of her left hand she motioned the three members of her staff who hovered close by, still tending to her hair, make-up and gown, to move away. The gesture was regal, immediately obeyed. For a brief moment she stood poised, alone, the famous chalky white undulating hands – lithe fingers like those of a Shiva goddess, elongated nails blushed with lacquer – were clasped tightly before her, the only outward sign of her nervousness.

The stage manager, a tall, broad-shouldered young man in a business suit and a dark-haired pony tail, moved to her side. He carried a walkie-talkie, held close to his mouth. 'Give the houselights a flash,' he said into it, a signal that the star was ready to appear. People would now be rushing to their seats. A minute later the house lights were ordered dimmed.

'Two minutes,' he told Streisand.

She stepped forward. The young man at her elbow handed her a lighted cigarette and she took a quick puff as he guided her cautiously across the cable-strewn area to the bottom of the backstage staircase that she would have to ascend to enter the unusual balcony set. Several members of the staff were clustered at the foot of the steps, one held out a paper cup filled with cold tea as she approached. She leaned in close and sipped from it with a straw. The overture was nearing the end. The 64-piece orchestra, conducted by Marvin Hamlisch, was situated on her right where it could be seen by her and the audience, although a curtain concealed the area where she stood. Hamlisch looked over to her and she nodded that she was ready. The music swelled.

This was the moment she had feared. She took a deep breath, closed her eyes, lifted her chin as though struggling for air.

'To one side, please,' Streisand's pony-tailed escort called to the crew as he helped her up on to the rather steep flight of stairs that led to the upper level of the set. 'We're on our way to the stage,' he said in his walkie-talkie.

Out front the audience was wild with enthusiasm. Applause filled the air. The orchestra was playing the opening bars of Streisand's great standard, 'Happy Days Are Here Again'. She paused for a moment and then continued up as the assistant helped to straighten the skirt of her long gown behind her so that she did not take a mis-step as she ascended to the top.

'Ready?' he asked as she stood poised to enter.

'OK,' she called over her shoulder. 'Happy Days Are Here Again' came to a rousing finish. The curtain was drawn aside and Streisand, head back, a wide smile on her luminous face concealing her inner fear, stepped out to a thunderous ovation.

She stood on the balcony area to stage left of the giant proscenium, the orchestra visible behind her through tall, mock windows of the palatial, columned, two-storey living-room set. A fireplace flanked one end, the balcony the other. Chairs, tables, sofas – in the French style – and magnificent sprays of white flowers decorated the stage. She seemed pinned in the brilliance of the aureole spotlight. Someone in the audience yelled, 'Come on, Barbra!' and, still smiling, she stepped closer to the balcony rail. The vastness of the Grand Garden arena was awesome. People were still applauding and calling out to her. She remained poised, gracefully composed as she looked out to the sea of blurred faces. Hamlisch raised his baton and as the soft opening bars of 'As If I Never Said Goodbye', were heard, silence cloaked the arena. All eyes were focused on her as she stood bathed in light, her nervousness evident, a hesitation in her manner. The entire audience seemed to lean forward as though to let her know that they were reaching out to her.

'I don't know why I'm frightened,' she sang in clear, pure tones, Don Black's rewritten lyrics seeming to express her own thoughts.

> 'I know my way around here,
> The band, the lights, familiar sights,
> The sound here.
> Yes, a world to rediscover,
> But to stop my heart from pounding
> I may need a moment.

She grasped the microphone tightly and breathed into it.

> Why, everything's as if I never said goodbye.'

Cheers rose from the audience at these last words but she did not allow them to intrude on her pacing of the song.

> 'I've spent so many evenings
> Just trying to resist you.
> I'm trembling now

> Just thinking how I missed you –
> Missed the fairy-tale adventures
> In this ever-spinning playground.
> We were young together.'

With infinite grace, she slowly started down the steps to the main area of the stage. The emotional response of the audience to the words she sang was almost tangible. People were caught up in thought, remembering. For some, Barbra Streisand had been a presence almost all their lives; others recalled the thirty years that had passed since she had burst like a meteor on to the public scene. They had been through a lot with this off-beat, original, feisty Jewish lady both in her life, the country's and their own. It is difficult to believe that once she had been perceived as homely. She was beautiful in most of their eyes. Her talent made her glow.

She had reached the bottom of the staircase and walked to centre stage.

> 'I've been in the wings too long,
> All that's in the past
> Now I'm standing centre stage
> I've come home at last.'

An amazing thing happened then. Tremendous, tumultuous cheers greeted this declaration and the audience shot to its feet. Shouts of 'We love you, Barbra!' rang through the great arena. Streisand was visibly moved. She took a short breath and grasped the microphone tighter as she waited for about thirty seconds for the cries to subside. When they did not, she raised her hands and motioned for the audience to sit down – and as they obeyed, as if royally commanded, she continued her voice clear and strong, filled with passion.

> 'And this time will be bigger
> And brighter than we knew it.
> So watch me fly,
> You know I'll try and do it...
> Yes, everything's as if we never said goodbye!'

Her voice swept up to a thrilling end note. There was a moment of stunned silence and then frenzied applause, bellowing cheers, a standing ovation. She looked out at the ocean of faces and tangle of arms outstretched towards her. Her nervousness had begun to evaporate. The roar of the crowd washed over her. The careers of other stars who were her contemporaries had come and gone and come and gone again. She, alone, had sustained her popularity. At this moment of such tremendous adulation she could not help but know that this was true. A smile skimmed her face.

'Aren't you nice. What a wonderful audience,' she said in a slow, deliberate voice, so well-milked that her words were distinct to the people at the farthest reaches of the cavernous arena where the cheering continued. The Donna Karan dress she wore was split to the knee on one side and as she walked across the stage, a shapely leg was exposed. She glanced down over the footlights to the front row and introduced the President's mother, Virginia Clinton Kelley, and Coretta Scott King. Then she continued on with her performance, in essence a one-woman Broadway show, using autobiographical material – her childhood dreams, relationships, family ties and social positions.

The concert format employed the off-stage voices of various fictional analysts, male and female, allowing her to travel back in memory to her childhood in Brooklyn, her love affair with movies – and with Marlon Brando. On a giant screen his image was projected in a scene from *Guys and Dolls* looking young, vital, *gorgeous*. Utilising film special effects technique, Streisand aged eleven replaced his leading lady, the enchanting Jean Simmons, in the clip and sang with him the engaging Frank Loesser song 'I'll Know'.

Jason and Elliott and Caleigh, on Jon Peters's lap, were seated near to the stage. An entire page of photographs of herself with the little girl was featured in the programme and she spoke directly to her from the stage about the bedtime stories they read together and then dedicated 'Caleigh's favourite song, "Someday My Prince Will Come", to her, pictures of the two of them together projected on the giant screen behind her. This was followed by a moving rendition of Sondheim's song of loving protection, 'Not While I'm Around' from *Sweeney Todd*, sung to Jason, and also accompanied by images from their past. At the end she blew him a kiss and said, 'I love you.'

'I love you, too,' he called back. She nodded her head and her eyes misted. Never before had she so publicly revealed her innermost feelings towards her son and both Jason, seated beside Elliott, and the audience reacted to this. From this moment on, there was the rare sense that the performer and the audience had touched each other, shared private time together. Their cheers and their silence were personal gestures of their love for her. She sipped tea between songs, fidgeted with her hair, brushed it back from her face. But every word she spoke and sang was being projected on huge closed-circuit video screens placed strategically and visible from almost any angle to the members of the audience as well as to herself. At one point, a startled look gripped her face as she realised she had mixed up the lyrics to 'Evergreen'. She had been mis-cued. Momentarily she froze while Hamlisch and the orchestra vamped behind her. Then she smiled sheepishly and joked, 'And it's my own song!' She continued on, the orchestra making a seamless continuum under Hamlisch's baton.

After intermission she appeared in another Donna Karan ensemble – a white tuxedo jacket worn over a floor-length skirt, split hip high on one side. It was modelled after the pin-striped outfit she had worn at the pre-inaugural gala and which had caused one woman critic to write snidely that 'even a strong, successful woman has to play the *femme fatale* role'.

As soon as she told this anecdote, Mike Myers, a comedian from the popular satirical television show *Saturday Night Live* came running up on stage cross-dressed hilariously as his 'wickedly funny alter ego', a Long Island housewife with a Streisand obsession, and shouted in a deep, affected, feminine New York-eese accent, 'Barbra, don't listen to *that* woman!' The act was well-rehearsed and Streisand laughed naturally and mocked Myers as he described her skin as being like 'buttah' and her nose as 'something to die for'.

In the closing segment, she was highly successful with the optimistic philo-sophies in the final three songs, 'Happy Days Are Here Again', sung while historic clips were shown on the screen, 'On a Clear Day You Can See Forever', with its affirmation of a positive and bright future, and the poignant Bernstein–Sondheim classic, 'There's a Place for Us'. Streisand had made the programme feel as if it were custom-made, as though the lyrics had been written for her. This was true, of course, in the case of 'As If We Never Said Goodbye' and in Sondheim's 'I'm Still Here' ('sometimes a kick in the rear, but I'm here ... One day you're hailed for blazing trails, next day you're nailed for fingernails ... Producing, who does she think she is – a man? ... I kept my toes and kept my space, I kept my nose to spite my face ...').

One could carp at the interpretation of some of the songs. She seemed unable to project the deeper meaning of the 'doormat' or 'victim' songs. 'Can't Help Lovin' Dat Man' fell a bit short of total sacrifice and 'Lover Man' missed a young girl's yearning. And even 'The Man that Got Away', which was superbly sung, eclipsing Garland's notorious mis-accents, seemed none the less to slip through her grasp. She had greater success with 'My Man'. The audience went wild when she finally left the stage after many bows. Once she was gone, the huge amphitheatre previously filled with the vibrancy of her voice and the power of her personality, seemed suddenly silent despite the sounds of the milling crowds as they departed.

They called her 'divine', claimed there was 'not one wrong note' in her performance; in fact, she had hit a flat top note in 'The Man Who Got Away'. There was something historic about being one of those present at this first concert in Las Vegas. People had flown in from all over the world. 'You came all the way from Sydney just for this concert?' one woman was asked. 'Yes,' she replied. 'She hasn't sung in public in – what is it? – twenty-four or twenty-seven years? What if this is *it* and she never appears again? She is the greatest singer born in my lifetime. There's no one to equal her and never has been.'

Seldom before had she interacted with her audience with such immediacy. Pauline Kael had once written in the *New Yorker*, 'When Streisand sings, her command of the audience is in her regal stillness; she distills her own emotions.

You feel that she doesn't need the audience – that she could close her eyes and sing with the same magnetic power. Streisand's voice is her own instrument.' This was true. Yet this one time she had exposed herself to an audience while at the same time keeping her distance, an ability that great politicians like Roosevelt and Churchill possessed but is not apparent in many entertainers.

After the show, she bombarded Erlichman, Hamlisch, Henion, the Bergmans and Cis Corman with questions about the sound system, the tele-prompter, the visuals, the lighting – all the technical angles that she feared might have been flawed. But to a close friend who came backstage, she asked: 'Was the neckline of my dress too revealing? My mother will have a conniption.'

The next night, she looked radiant. For this performance the audience included such celebrities as Michael Jackson, Steven Spielberg, Gregory Peck, Mel Gibson and television host, Jay Leno. If anything, the audience response was even more zealous than the previous evening. 'Tonight was the way I hoped it would be,' she said later at a reception she gave in her massive hotel suite. 'Everything felt right.'

The high she received from the concerts was apparent in her attitude. The financial rewards were awesome. The two shows had grossed over $12 million, topping her expectations, and more than twice the gross of any previous pop or rock concerts which sometimes attracted up to 90,000 fans. Of course, no star had ever charged such ticket prices. Then there had been the concert souvenir merchandise, ranging from $100-bottles of Streisand-signature champagne to $25 T-shirts which had already generated more than $1.5 million.

Having dealt head-on with her stage fright and found a viable way to secure herself financially so that she *could*, without too much concern for the future, proceed with the projects close to her, both commercial and charitable, she told Erlichman she was ready to go out on the road. He was to solidify plans for the proposed tour which would kick off at the Wembley Arena in London that coming April, 1994, and travel to Washington DC, Detroit, two appearances in California – Anaheim and San Jose – and end at Madison Square Garden in New York City. She would be on the road for several exacting months and there would still be many anxieties, pressures and demands outside of, and because of, the tour to be confronted – the films she wanted to make, her recording contracts and her private concerns for her mother who was nearly crippled from arthritis, Jason, Caleigh, and 'the age thing'. She was in her fifties and had become that show business cliché – the great star without a man in her life who could not bring her cheering audiences home with her at night.

She wanted to simplify her life, to 'move on'. 'I like the idea of evolution and change,' she explained. Between ever-escalating costs and devastating bush and forest fires in the Malibu region she had decided to rid herself of the responsibility of the ranch and before leaving for Las Vegas negotiations were instigated for her to donate it in its entirety to the Santa Monica Mountains Conservancy for a conservation institute. This would benefit her tax status as well as relieving her of the burden the ranch now represented. Next, she decided to sell off most of the contents of the five-ranch houses. The time before leaving for England allowed her to select what she wanted to put up for sale at Christie's in Manhattan. The choices were often difficult. She was attached by memory to many of the pieces. 'Sometimes when it's been hard to relate to people, I could relate to inanimate objects,' she said about her vast collection. 'They didn't give me an argument, they didn't think I was crazy. And therefore we had a good relationship. I also love to be surrounded by beautiful things. But I'm at a more whole place now. I can relate to people, have relationships, and have objects. Now they are less precious to me. It has to do with one's growth psychologically and a shifting of priorities.

'I feel like letting go of things. I don't want to have things in storage. I don't want to have them in boxes and in the basement. I want other people to enjoy them if I don't have room for them any more. It's a good feeling to use these things for a while and pass them on during your own lifetime,' she added.

But Streisand's relentless need to create environments for herself was symptomatic of her entire personality. Everything had to be a perfect setting. She saw things as a complete vision.

'I don't put a black vase in a gray-and-burgundy room,' she said. She chose monochromatic rooms, did not wear prints. She liked 'black and white movies, and the family photographs on the living room piano are black and white – colour photos would disturb the harmony.' Even the wrappers on the candy in her candy dishes had to be colour-coordinated.

The two-day Christie's sale was set for 3 and 4 March, 535 lots, some containing several items. Every piece had to be appraised and the lowest acceptable bid agreed upon. Streisand had kept careful records on what each item had cost. If withdrawn or unsold, Christie's would still charge her a fee which had to be taken into consideration. On the other hand, it was a star auction for the company, a coup worth a fortune in publicity, and they traded this off to Streisand's advantage when working out the cost details of the sale. Celebrity sales always brought higher prices for certain objects due to the nature of their provenance.

She gained widely circulated, free publicity in an unprecedented arrangement with *Architectural Digest*, whose usual policy was not to feature a photo article on houses or furnishings up for sale. On this occasion they agreed to show the part of the ranch collection that was to be auctioned, and at Streisand's insistence, what she considered her prize piece in the sale, the magnificent Tamara De Lempicka painting, *Adam et Eve*, was highlighted with her on the cover. The magazine photographers descended on the property directly following her return from Las Vegas and spent nearly a week on the shoot from early in the morning until nightfall. Shortly after they were dispatched, Christie's packers arrived. Both operations were closely monitored by Streisand.

Included in the sale with the De Lempicka (estimated sale price $800,000–$1 million), were her cherished 'Peony' ($300,000–$400,000) and 'Cobweb' ($800,000–1 million) leaded glass Tiffany lamps that she had bought and paid for on the lay-away plan when she was first appearing on Broadway, the two antique cars ($50,000–$65,000), an exquisite diamond and jade Cartier clock ($100,000–$150,000), an amazing assortment of art nouveau glass and furniture, art deco bronzes, silver and furniture, along with a host of memorabilia and less important items.

She remained in Los Angeles during the sale, which received international coverage. When notified of the amount her collection had brought – nearly $6 million – she was stunned. The more valuable pieces went for near what they had been appraised at, but the items in the second day of the sale – the memorabilia whose worth depended upon how much the public was willing to pay for something that belonged to Streisand – sold in some lots for ten to fifteen times what was expected.

With this good news, she left for London and the first leg of her tour. Before she even arrived, the English press ran banner headlines about 'The selling of Barbra Streisand'. Never had there been a concert appearance with as much pre-performance publicity, most of it centred around the astronomical ticket sales for the four shows she was to do (the 12,000-seat arena was already sold out for all performances) and the fact that a week before the first concert many had changed hands at ten times their face value.[1] Selfridges, the Oxford Street department store, constructed a Barbra Streisand Boutique with everything from a £10 coffee mug to a £300 wool-and-leather embroidered jacket; in between there were watches, mugs, posters, scarves, purses, totes, T-shirts, polo shirts, baseball caps – almost all with her picture and the concert logo which she helped to design with graphic arts representatives from Sony Music, her merchandising agent. To add to these obvious money-makers, stores stocked reissues of most of her albums. Wembley Arena would also have several boutiques with the same merchandise and the programme for the concert, composed with her help, would cost £13 ($20), of which she received a 45 per cent royalty.

Marty Erlichman, Cis Corman (Marvin Hamlisch had arrived earlier to rehearse the orchestra) and several members of her staff – secretary, hair-stylist, make-up artist, dresser and a bodyguard, accompanied her to London on Concorde, arriving late Sunday evening, 17 April 1994, a momentous date for her as she had never before appeared in concert in Great Britain. Dressed comfortably but in less-than-elegant fashion in a brown-leather jacket, baggy

---

[1] London tickets were £48.50, £105, and £208.

pants, wedgee scuffs and a wool beret, she emerged sleepy-eyed behind her tinted glasses and was met by an entourage of police, senior airport officials, airline VIP representatives and concert promoters, as well as over fifty members of the press and a host of fans. With her hefty guard in front of her, Erlichman at her side, she munched an apple as they made their way through the crowds to a waiting Daimler limousine that would take them to the Dorchester Hotel, where she had a £1,000 a day suite filled with the white and yellow flowers she so loved (especially tulips) and pre-stocked with the Queen's and her own favourite bottled water, Malvern, boxes of Reese's Peanut Butter Cup chocolates and Hershey mint bars.

On early morning television the following day she told her interviewer, 'I don't like to be famous. I don't like the press to follow me. I don't like to talk about myself and I want to be remembered for the work I do, not the articles about me or what people think about me. It's just not a thing I get off on – the applause, the roaring applause of the crowd. It doesn't affect my being. I want to please people, I want to give them what they want, but I feel I'm doing that now through the movies and the albums I make.' She had, however, been greatly affected by her reception in Las Vegas, which had left her on a high for several days thereafter.

Nothing, even her previous stays in London, had prepared her for the British media. It was not so much the considerable numbers of them that stalked her every move – she was used to that – but their derisive, scornful attitude. She was front-page news in almost all the many daily papers except the *Financial Times*, and the articles featured every possible negative – she was pampered, difficult, money-hungry, 'the most steely woman on earth', dressed 'decidedly down-market', and had the Wembley Arena fully carpeted because she thought it would be 'too draughty' (no member of the press having thought to ask the real reason for the last 'idiosyncrasy'). She took it as good-naturedly as she could.

'You have got to get this right,' she admonished one journalist gently. 'The British always say Strei-*sunned*. My name is pronounced with a soft "s", like the stuff on the beach. *Stry-sand*.' On Tuesday afternoon, between rehearsals at Wembley, she took time out to appear in the car park for a charity event, to hand over the keys to one of fifty Variety Club Sunshine coaches (her personal donation) to be used to transport disabled children to holidays and events they otherwise could not afford to attend. She accepted flowers from a lovely dark-eyed child. 'Flowers, oh, flowers,' she exclaimed with tears in her eyes. She would, in fact, contribute $10.2 million from her tour revenues to charity.[2]

---

[2] In the United States Streisand's charitable contributions from the tour included $25,000 each for musical education – instruments, equipment and teaching staff – to schools across the country, including her old high school, Erasmus Hall. Sony Music matched each school donation.

She was too busy rehearsing, making sure there were no glitches in the first concert, Wednesday night, April 20, just twenty-four hours away, to nurse her usual pre-show jitters. Whenever she did have a moment free she would meditate alone. She feared the British critics would be hard on her, that there was some kind of general group response to her American brashness, her feminist positions and her money. They would come to hear her, bringing their 'attitude' with them. She could not change, nor did she care to do so. She was who she was and what she was and that was that. Take it or leave it. But she could do everything at top form – sing, perform, look her best. She rehearsed until the orchestra was too exhausted to go on. Relentless activity kept her from thinking about the moment she would step out on stage for the first concert. Stage fright once again assailed her. She listened to meditation tapes, trying, as she said, 'to have a positive attitude because I easily get sidetracked into this abyss of fear and I have to get myself out of it'. The scathing pre-concert articles in the press had greatly upset her.

What she perhaps did not realise was that the more vilified by the media – both American and British – the more her grip on the public strengthened. 'She is not just a singer,' a fan who had bought tickets for all four Wembley concerts insisted. 'She is a role model – the living proof that if you believe in yourself, you can do anything you want. She had a terrible childhood, but she was determined to succeed. She is an inspiration to us all.' Another added, 'Her mother told her she was ugly and couldn't sing. The press always criticise, but she is a born survivor.'

She represented a woman's triumph over adversity and her constant tales of her unhappy childhood, her perception of being homely, her unstable love affairs, the media abuse, made her seem vulnerable and reduced the distance between her and her fans. 'She is living proof that you can do anything,' one said of her. 'She would have been a secretary if she had listened to her mother,' Giles Coren of *The Times* concurred. 'That early rejection is of great importance to English fans and [Wembley] will be as much a show of solidarity as an entertainment. They will come in their droves to show Barbra's mother just how wrong she was.'

The day of the concert Streisand took precious minutes out to call Diana. 'She said she hoped I'd be able to see the show when it comes to Los Angeles,' Diana told reporters. 'I said I hoped so, too.' These were not the words her daughter sought to hear. Her drive to succeed, her insatiable ambition, her need to be famous, recognised as *somebody* had always gone hand in hand with her hunger for her mother's applause, a show of maternal hubris. She would never feel she had succeeded until she received it. The irony was that Diana's apathy had driven her to become a star of the greatest magnitude and it was why she was never satisfied with what she achieved and always feared that with one mis-step everything she had accomplished would vanish.

# 32

**B**EFORE SHE SANG a single note she was given a standing ovation that lasted for five minutes. In a rare public display of emotion, she brushed tears from her cheeks with the back of her hand. Finally, the audience sat down again and she sang her opening number. The show was almost identical to the Las Vegas concerts, although she inserted some chit-chat about England and the English, not spontaneous – every word projected in clear view of the audience on the autocue.

As she said, 'This is a very special night, very special to me,' the words rolled across the prompt screens. 'People ask me why I'm on the road for the first time in twenty-seven years,' she began. 'Hey if you came from California with the earthquakes, mudslides and the fires, *you* would hit the road too.' She took a sip of the herbal tea she preferred. 'I love England, especially cucumber sandwiches with the crusts cut off,' she exclaimed to a few titters. Some video footage was shown of Princess Margaret at the opening twenty-eight years earlier of *Funny Girl* as well as additional clips of Prince Charles greeting her backstage, all of them looking incredibly young. 'Who knows, if I had been nicer to him I might have been the first real Jewish princess ... Princess Babs,' she joked. 'I can imagine what the newspaper headlines might have been. "Blintzes Princess Plays the Palace" and "Barbra Digs Nails into Prince of Wales!"' This time, there was the sound of genuine laughter.

An ardent, spirited audience, they seemed not to mind the autocue as she told them at every performance, 'I could never be here otherwise. I have a fear of forgetting the words, which I once did in front of 135,000 people [the Central Park concert in 1968], and it's a fear.'

She was welcomed back to London with great emotion. The audience kept rooting her on. 'Thank you, thank you,' she repeated over and over. At the close of her last song, a curiously chosen anti-climactic interpretation of 'For All We Know', they watched her go off-stage and jumped to their feet applauding for her to return. When she did, they grew silent, expecting her to sing an encore. With disarming hesitancy, she said, 'I didn't think you'd get all my jokes and stuff,' bowed and to audible gasps of disappointment, did not return.

None the less, as people filed out, the general feeling was that this had been an experience of a lifetime and worth every penny.

A stellar list of British celebrities had attended – Elton John, Michael Caine and Shirley Bassey among them. Don Black was there at her special invitation. 'What did you *really* think?' she asked.

'You were wonderful,' he replied. 'But all that psychiatrist thing doesn't work. Over here we don't go to psychiatrists so much. What we do is sit down and have a nice cup of tea and a chat with somebody and we sort ourselves out that way.' After the concert she entertained her personal guests at the small, exclusive Blake's hotel. Streisand appeared almost giddy at the lively celebration which did not end until 4 a.m. The reviews the next morning were mixed, many of the critics still deploring the price of the tickets, the psycho-babble of the script, the autocue, even the cost of a bottle of champagne during the interval, £28 (which had not seemed to bother the general audience). None the less, there were only glowing accolades for the greatness of her voice.

'She is the supreme communicator,' wrote Tony Parsons in the *Daily Tele-graph*. 'Streisand has an ability to talk directly to an audience's heart that is surpassed only by Sinatra. When [she] takes flight, she makes music that is full of memories and a sense of loss ... she is unquestionably the last of the great romantics.'

London hailed her as 'the ultimate pop diva'. It was difficult to turn on a radio music station that was not playing her records. Almost every newspaper edition carried some story about her; Elton John was giving her a £200,000 party (a figure much inflated, but it did cost almost half that) on Sunday, 24 April, her fifty-second birthday at his country estate; she had refused to attend the 'celebrity-packed' publicity party Sony had planned (and cancelled) for the previous night, to her record company's chagrin, because she was not given control of the guest list which would have allowed her to exclude much of the media. Prince Charles was attending the concert on Monday, the 24th; Diana gave an interview from California; a full-page colour layout of Streisand and Caleigh appeared in one daily, and there were a constant barrage of stories with similar banners to 'Barbra Streisand strikes up the band's anger', (*Daily Mail*, 22 April), an example of the English penchant for using a play on words. Hamlisch had only brought twelve of his key musicians with him to London. The remainder of the orchestra were local and were furious when they were asked to sign, the day before the first concert, an agreement of confidentiality binding them not to discuss anything having to do with Streisand's appearance to the press. In fact, such letters were distributed to the employees of the Wembley Arena, as they were to those at the MGM Grand, and would be at every place that she would appear.

The stage crew was barred from watching rehearsals. One person said, 'I was told by my boss that I must look away if I see Streisand because she doesn't like people staring.' A member of the orchestra complained, 'It's the principle I object to – the assumption that we are going to leak material about her. I have played for some of the finest opera singers in the world but I have never come across anything so reminiscent of a prima donna.'

Still, no one in the orchestra refused to sign the agreement, which bore a great similarity to the ones the Queen's staff were required to sign. Had they not signed, they were warned that they would be replaced. This was all part of Streisand's driving need for both privacy and control, most difficult to obtain when she placed herself so prominently in the public eye. She hated not being in control of what was written about her, certain the truth would not make its way into print. She wanted it *all* – the power, the glory, the fame *and* the privacy accorded non-public figures. Times had changed since her early years as a star, the media was in command. Gone were the days when studios and publicity representatives fed the press at their will. The press were voracious for stories about the famous and for a time Streisand became a competitor to Princess Diana, pictures and stories about her, however insignificant, in overwhelming demand. It was as though the media thought she was just too talented, too famous, too rich, too outspoken not to take her down for it.

But there is something in her demand of employees to sign papers binding them to silence, to threaten the loss of their jobs if they discuss their work with her, that is at extreme odds with all her professed liberalism. There is nothing unconstitutional about such tactics, but they are a gagging order, an infringement on the right of the free speech of others, while she enjoys a platform for all her comments, ideas and positions on various issues. The double standard here is both shocking and disappointing. One expects more of a woman like Streisand who is always out there fighting for her own personal rights.

Monday night's concert was also a fund-raiser, a percentage of the revenues estimated at £150,000, to be donated to the Prince's Trust. Streisand had last seen Charles in 1974 during his visit to Hollywood. He had arrived at the studio where she was filming *Funny Lady* as she was recording the song 'So Long, Honey Lamb'. During the twenty minutes they chatted, Streisand had shared her mug of tea with him.

Charles is a great fan of hers and he seemed truly taken with her as a person. Members of the recording orchestra remembered observing the intense eye-contact between the two. 'Sparks flew,' one musician (who did not want his name revealed) observed. They met again at a champagne reception before the concert and she warmly clasped his hand in hers twice during their five minutes of conversation, neither seeming inhibited by the others present (Marvin Hamlisch, Marty Erlichman, Charles's equerries, members of the management staff of Wembley Arena, and several photographers). During her performance Charles, dressed conservatively in a dark-blue suit, sat rapt with attention in a reserved balcony area thirty yards from the stage with celebrities including Joan Collins and Priscilla Presley. In the section of the programme where Streisand usually showed video filmage of Caleigh and herself and then sang 'Some Day My Prince Will Come' for the child, she introduced the Disney song and remarked on her fondness for songs featuring imaginary princes. 'What makes this song extra special is that there's a real one in the audience tonight,' she announced.

When she had finished singing, Charles rose to his feet with the rest of the audience and joined in a two-minute ovation which ended with the crowd stamping their feet and demanding more. She returned to sing 'Somewhere'. Charles jumped to his feet again and applauded vigorously when she was done. Smiling broadly, Streisand waved at him and made a gesture of a bow.

The sound of applause did not appease her great sense of loneliness at being away from Caleigh. 'I am devoted to my goddaughter,' she told anyone who asked about the inclusion of Caleigh's photographs in the printed programme. She called California often to speak to her. Although only on the first engagement of her tour, Streisand was already missing the child, and after the fourth and last show in London (each separated by several days as she did not like to give concerts back to back) she returned to Los Angeles expressly to see her. Then, after a joyful but short reunion, she and Erlichman rejoined Hamlisch, the orchestra and her technicians in Washington DC, where the President and the First Lady attended her first-night concert there. She was fighting the beginnings of a cold, but after her Washington concerts continued on to Detroit for two concerts at the Palace of Auburn Hills arena. 'In Detroit,' she says, 'I thought, I *don't know how I'm going to get through the next fifteen shows.* It's very exhausting physically. It's a lot of breathing; you have to be in pretty good shape. And I don't work out vocally. I don't practise. It's the most boring thing you can imagine, doing scales. So I just said, "Fuck it, I can't [do scales]. I'm too tired the day after a concert." '

Her next venue was to be the Arrowhead Pond in Anaheim, the home of the Mighty Ducks hockey team and with 19,200 capacity the largest of all the arenas in which she had performed. By the time she arrived in Los Angeles her cold had worsened. She was suffering from viral tracheolaryngitis, placed on antibiotics and told by her doctor that she must rest her voice.

Originally scheduled for Wednesday, 25 May the first of the six Southern California concerts was postponed to Thursday, 2 June to give her a chance to recover sufficiently. The show was also scheduled to go to San Jose in northern California. A glittering array of celebrities (Michael Jackson, Warren Beatty, Goldie Hawn, Walter Matthau among them) attended opening night along with some of the most important people in her life – Elliott and Jason, Jon Peters and Caleigh, André Agassi, Don Johnson, Ray and Fran Stark, and in the front row Diana and Roslyn. As she ended her first number and came down the steps from the balcony set and walked across the front rim of the stage, she glanced down over the footlights to the front row. Diana, eighty-five and severely arthritic was on her feet applauding with the rest of the delirious crowd. Streisand leaned forward.

'Mom, you stood up. Take it easy, Mom. Sit down. I'm glad you're here. I love you,' she said, straightened, stood still for a moment and then motioned with her hands for the audience to be seated.

There was no sign of laryngitis as she launched into her programme, which now included a ten-minute *Yentl* sequence – 'a masterly staged affair that proved to be the most crowd-pleasing sequence of the show'. She received even greater acclamation at the finish. 'One sensed it was for more than the music,' Robert Hilburn of the *Los Angeles Times* wrote, 'It was also in admiration of the independence and determination Streisand has shown over the years in such pursuits as film directing.'

Since London she had also changed the ending of the concert, which had been the melancholy song 'For All We Know' about the possibility of two people never meeting again, to the brighter more uplifting 'Somewhere', from *West Side Story*.

'If there's such a thing as a concert ticket that's worth the money, this might be the one,' *Daily Variety* declared. She played the second concert on 4 June, but – her throat still giving her problems – the last four shows were cancelled. As the Arrowhead Pond was booked ahead for several weeks, it was decided she would return to Anaheim after San Jose and New York to end the tour with concerts there, on 10, 18, 22 and 24 July.

Her throat problems were cured by the time she opened at Madison Square Garden on Monday night, June 20 for the first of five concerts. The majority of theatres are dark on Monday and almost all Broadway's current performers turned out to welcome her home. She was, after all, a Brooklyn girl, one of their own. Attending her triumphant return were Liza Minnelli, Chita Rivera and the casts from almost every show along the Great White Way. She seemed relaxed, looked marvellous (she had fresh copies of her two gowns made for each city on the tour) and was in magnificent voice. She had returned to the New York concert stage the same week that the city played host to the Gay Games. 'One of the best things about the games', she told her enthusiastic audience, 'is that I can walk down the street and not be recognised because there are so many impersonators.'

After singing 'The Man Who Got Away', she told Liza over the microphone, 'Your mom sang that great.' Rex Reed commented that it was the ultimate in *chutzpah*, but Liza laughed and did not appear to take the remark as an affront.

Reed was not completely won over as the cheering, stamping aggregation in the Gardens indicated they all were. 'There's no denying her talent,' he says, 'but it's always the voice that gets to you, not the interpretation. Every inflection, every modulation, every supersonic high note seems canned on vinyl. You could be home listening to records. She doesn't have the vulnerability of Garland or Piaf, or the kind of moment-to-moment self-discovery that breeds the art of spontaneity. She's such a perfectionist . . . she's not about to open the doors and let you in.'

Reed was in the minority. It is almost impossible to compare Streisand with Garland and Piaf. They are cut from a different cloth: both victims, exposing their bruised, fragile selves to their audiences who listened to them in quite a different way than Streisand's audiences listen to her. Streisand's fans are not sharing her pain, they are celebrating her strength to overcome all the obstacles that they perceive she has overcome – turning homely into beautiful, ethnic into mainstream, daring to cross over into a man's world as director, producer and business executive. She is a dignified feminist, a liberal proud of the word and never afraid to voice her opinion. And she has maintained uninterrupted stardom and popularity for more years than any other entertainment figure except perhaps Sinatra. She is far more intelligent than either Garland or Piaf and approaches her work in a more intellectual way. They were unique, most certainly, and they could move you to chills and tears, make you want to run up on stage and hold them in your arms, to save them. And especially in Garland's case, forgive anything and everything – even when she could not hit the notes or remember the lyrics. Much more is expected of Streisand and she makes sure that, to the best of her ability, she will live up to her own, high expectations.

The tour, coupled with her multimedia projects, had given her more star power than anyone, rock star or opera diva, on the concert circuit. And by the time she completed all the performances, with two shows added to her Madison Square Gardens appearances, it would be the biggest money-making turn in entertainment history. The previous December, before appearing in Las Vegas, she had told Barbara Walters, 'Let me say this, I have a long way to go. I have a lot to learn. I'm still sensitive to criticism. I go through periods when I can just laugh at it, you know? And periods when I think it's just plain mean. You have to accept life for what it is. The pain and the joy; the hate, the love. My musical director [Hamlisch] came to see me and he gave me a book called *Life Is the Message*, about changing the world. Well, we cannot change the world. It's such an overwhelming feat, but yet by changing ourselves each of us in a very small way *can* change the world.'

The tour had helped her battle with her fear of appearing before a live audience, although the demons remained, if less active, but had she changed the world even a little by doing it? Hardly, although throughout her long career she had changed public tastes, their view of beauty, the idea that without a formal education you could not walk as an equal with intellectuals, the concept that women were not emotionally equipped to stand toe to toe with male power brokers. The tour, including Las Vegas, had grossed over $64 million by doing things *her way*.[1] All the final decisions were hers – from music to script to performance, set, sound, merchandising and road arrangements. There was a totality in her efforts, the only way she knew how to work. She dealt always from strength to strength. This had not been a 'comeback' tour as so many of Garland's had been. Streisand was a great star for having been unavailable to the public for so many years.

'She's God's bell,' says exercise guru Richard Simmons, one of her most steadfast admirers. 'In the eighth grade I was two hundred pounds. And I saw her emerge from not the most beautiful girl in the world to the most beautiful woman that I've ever seen in my entire life. She helped my self-image.'

Her own self-image was another matter. Nothing was ever enough. She had to prove herself over and over and *over* again. It was an obsession. Something ate at her from the inside, drove her on. No one who worked with her could ever match her pace. In mid-July 1994, she returned to Los Angeles to complete the four concerts at Arrowhead Pond. Rumours had preceded her that she might cancel. The weather was unduly hot and humid. She was once more having some trouble with her throat. She did, indeed, appear to the overwhelming enthusiasm of her audiences. On the final night Hollywood turned out in force, a great many of those who had already attended the Las Vegas, New York or earlier California concerts, returning to hear her again. She received standing ovations from the time she stepped out on to the stage. After the final number she asked the audience if they cared to remain while she performed for the television cameras. There was a scramble as the majority raced back to their seats.

While the taping ensued friends and VIP guests had been escorted backstage to an airless, white-walled room to wait for Streisand and pay her homage. They sat restlessly as they watched her on the large monitor, hearing again 'that crystalline voice rising, rising – and then, at the break where almost every other singer goes reedy, blazing higher so that you feel [as Marvin Hamlisch puts it] that she's *pulled you through*'. Warren Beatty placed his arm around an exhausted, very pregnant Annette Bening. Elliott and Jason were there with Diana, seated in a wheelchair, and Shirley MacLaine squatted, Indian style, as she talked to her. (It is rare that Beatty and MacLaine, though brother and sister, ever attend anything together.) Caleigh stood patiently beside her father despite the lateness of the hour. Finally, the screen went blank. The filming session was over and it was very late. A chosen few of those waiting were

---

[1] That figure does not include the money earned from concert merchandise, the HBO special, and the royalties from the concert album. However, the expenses of the tour were high – $20 million on the road and $4 million in Las Vegas, Streisand claims.

escorted into Streisand's adjoining white carpeted, heavily mirrored dressing room where silver-framed photographs of Jason and Caleigh were displayed.

'You did good,' Diana said grudgingly. 'I'm proud of you.'

Still looking glamorous and appearing fresh, Streisand replied 'Thanks, mom,' her words spoken so softly she could barely be heard.

The next morning she was at Sony Studios by ten o'clock, editing footage for the television special and mixing tracks for a projected album of the concert (actually an accretion of several of the concerts). Home Box Office expected that the televised concert would, like the tour, break viewer records. She swore she would never do a tour again. 'You have to put make-up on, comb your hair. You have to wear high heels. My feet get cramps!' she complained.


As soon as she came off the road Streisand immersed herself in work once more on *The Magarethe Cammermeyer Story*, now planned as a made-for-television movie, under the title *Serving in Silence*. She had begun *Serving in Silence* in the fall of 1992 after reading a newspaper article about Lieutenant-Colonel Cammermeyer, a highly decorated Army nurse for twenty-six years who had been discharged for revealing in a security-clearance interview that she was a lesbian. The highest-ranking military official ever discharged for homosexuality, she had become a leader in the fight to overturn the military's ban on homosexuals.

'Barbra had a passion about wanting to do this project,' Cis Corman said. 'It was such a blatant case of discrimination and prejudice.' Convincing the Colonel to have a film made of her story was not easy, not even for Streisand. Finally, she conceded, and Streisand pressed forward with Craig Zadan (a former close associate of Stephen Sondheim) and Neil Meron, who had produced the Emmy-nominated *Gypsy* with Bette Midler, as producers, while she remained the executive producer. What the project needed was a star to play the Colonel. In the spring of 1994, Glenn Close had just left the Los Angeles cast of *Sunset Boulevard* and had time in her schedule before preparing for the November opening in New York. Streisand was about to depart for England. She believed that Close would be superb in the role, bringing both the strength and the feminine qualities of Cammermeyer to it. Close, one of the screen's finest actresses, thought so too, and agreed to become part of the project, both as star and as co-executive producer with Streisand. The two women had immediate rapport and a writer was hired and the enterprise set in motion.

Presenting a major story about lesbians on the small screen seemed on the face of it to be insurmountable. Advertisers were reluctant to buy time, there was concern at a possible viewer boycott. But the potency of the involvement of Streisand and Close was enough for Lindy DeKoven, NBC's senior vice-president of mini-series and motion pictures for television, to accept the project.

'What the network ordered and what it got were two different things,' Craig Zadan recalled. 'The network assumed it would be predominantly courtroom scenes. But what evolved in the writing was a love story. Glenn told us, "Under no circumstances are you to take out any of this love story. Otherwise, as an actress I'll have nothing to play." ' The script was not as graphic as what was suggested for *The Normal Heart*, but it did contain impassioned scenes of two lesbians embracing and kissing.

The movie was being shot on location in Vancouver, Canada when Streisand ended the tour. A group in New York called the Family Defense Council had already raised the spectre of an advertiser boycott unless the lesbian kiss was cut. Close's co-star, Judy Davis, was threatening to quit, fearing her role would be sacrificed to satisfy the hostile group.

Not only was Streisand working on the controversial *Serving in Silence*, she was engaged once again in rewrites with Larry Kramer on *The Normal Heart* and with Richard LaGravenese on *The Mirror Has Two Faces*. The last seemed to be developing more into a commercial property, one that would not present as many problems as the Kramer vehicle did. Dedicated though she was to *The Normal Heart* she desperately wanted to be able to show a studio that she could make a simple commercial film and bring it in on budget and on time. But time was the very thing Kramer did not have. If *Mirror* should go into production first he would be difficult to deal with. She did not want this to happen, nor to lose *The Normal Heart*. She was going to have a juggle the two in such a way that Kramer could be appeased. But it appeared that Streisand had walked right into the eye of a hurricane.

# 33

'I'M A SHY person,' she told an interviewer for the *Los Angeles Times* who asked if she had plans for another tour, 'and I don't *have* to go out on the road again. I lost weight and sleep. I thought I would disappoint people, that I wasn't good enough. It all worked out. It was right for me to gain this confidence to feel absolutely at ease onstage, to feel I belonged there and deserved to be there, that I could give and receive the love of those audiences. I really *am* grateful to those people. For too many years I didn't appreciate my own singing ... But it's not my love; my love is making movies.'

The process of film-making, the idea that she could create people, lives, realise *her* visions, had intrigued her since the very first days when she worked with Willie Wyler on *Funny Girl*. As an actress she had been able to become Fanny Brice, but the vision had been Wyler's. Being able to function as both her own producer and director, as she had in *Yentl* and *The Prince of Tides*, had given her additional power over the script, budget and production. She made the major decisions, chose material that personally involved her, could make a statement or live out a fantasy, but she had to be strongly motivated, the story and characters absolutely clear to her. She was not alone in the category of actor-director. Clint Eastwood, Mel Gibson, Kenneth Branagh and Jodie Foster also starred in major films under their own direction and none of them had faced strong resistance from the critics as had Streisand. Recognition and acceptance was of major importance to her, rejection, criticism cut deeply.

Columbia was pleased that she had chosen to work on a commercial project such as *The Mirror Has Two Faces*. The character she was to play bore some similarity to Katie Morosky in *The Way We Were*, the intelligent woman, plain to look at but with inner beauty who after a struggle wins the love of the handsome hero. For years she had been pressing Arthur Laurents, without success, to come up with a story line for a sequel. For a time Robert Redford held the rights and had been equally enthusiastic and had also approached Laurents to no avail. Now she had a project on a similar theme and one with the same chance for commercial success. 'I think I'm always drawn to films about the mystery of appearances,' she told the press. '*The Mirror Has Two*

*Faces* is a really charming love story. But it has serious overtones about vanity and beauty, the external versus the internal.'

LaGravenese had sent her his first revised draft while she was on tour. She thought it took a wrong turn and asked him to rewrite. When she received this version she decided she liked the first one better, although it required more work. After several weeks of unsatisfactory story meetings with La-Gravenese she called in Carrie Fisher, who had successfully adapted for the screen her novel *Postcards from the Edge*, believing Fisher might give her character sharper focus. Fisher's fee for the work was higher than the budget allowed and Streisand went back to LaGravenese with more detailed suggestions and he began work on what would become the final shooting script.

*The Normal Heart* was once again placed on a back burner and she was caught between Kramer's wrath and her own guilt. Not only did she love the project, she had great sympathy for Kramer's physical situation, his fear of dying before the film was made. Kramer was also a close friend of Jason's, and as one of the country's leading gay activists almost always got press coverage when he chose to speak out on any related topic. She knew he would be furious that she was, yet again, delaying the project and would not be silent in his protest. She anticipated trouble and it came just as soon as it was announced that *The Mirror Has Two Faces* was to be her next film.

'Why are you doing this piece of shit?' Kramer, unable to contain his anger, yelled at her when she told him her plans.

'It's not a piece of shit!'

'It is a piece of shit. Everyone I know says it's a piece of shit.'

'Who said it's a piece of shit?'

'Well, Jason said it's a piece of shit.'

'Jason says it's a piece of shit?'

'Yes. He did.'

'She seemed suddenly reflective and I pressed my point,' Kramer recalled. ' "This is the peak of your life. You don't have two years to waste your time and your energy and your intelligence making a piece of shit," I continued. "That's not how you create a great body of work." She was troubled and I hated having to hurt her.

' "I've already created a great body of work!" she defended. "I've tried so hard not to be so hard on myself. Why are you doing this to me? I want to try to make a movie without going through so much *sturm und drang*. I want to do it as an exercise to show I can go in, make a movie fast, not drive everyone nuts including myself and get out and on with the next one. Anyway, everyone is pressuring me to do it."

' "No one has more power than you."

' "That's what you think. It's not easy. I've said I'd do it – and Jeff Bridges will kill me [the actor who was to play opposite her]."

' "Why don't you send him the script of *The Normal Heart?"*
' "Oh, he'd be wonderful, but I couldn't do that!"
'In Hollywood, they don't live in the real world,' Kramer commented after telling this story. 'And so, she scheduled *The Mirror Has Two Faces* first and *The Normal Heart* was to be delayed until after it was finished.'

Meanwhile, *Serving in Silence* was being prepared for television release and she was directly involved in the final work. Ironically, in view of her expressed feeling at a previous time that there were great differences between heterosexuals and homosexuals, she now offered an altered opinion to the press, 'I would like people to identify with the people in the story [the Colonel and her lesbian lover]. We're basically more similar than different.' She worked extremely well with Glenn Close, whom she greatly admired for her 'dignity and integrity'. The show was not to be aired for ten weeks, but the press was already publishing caustic articles about the project proclaiming that the network took it on only because of Streisand's and Close's involvement and because they would then get the right to re-air Streisand's HBO concert special.

'Why is it,' Colonel Cammermeyer inquired, 'that every time I see something written about her [Streisand], it's never without some negative connotation. What *is* it about the fact that she's talented, enriching, caring, gives of herself emotionally and financially to the things she believes in – what is it about that that is so offensive to people?' A parallel, Cammermeyer believed, existed between her 'own experience as a lesbian in the military; both worlds are ruled by boys' clubs that close ranks against women who don't toe the line'.

*Serving in Silence* was aired on NBC on 6 February 1995 to generally good reviews and high ratings and was nominated for Emmys in several categories including Best Original Film Made for Television and Best Actress in this classification, but did not receive an award. Streisand was always disappointed and bitter when her work with film was overlooked for awards. But by this time her energy and enthusiasm had been channelled into the development of *Mirror*, although she continued working with Kramer on *The Normal Heart*, and attempting to find financing and a star to play opposite her so that she could schedule the film to follow *Mirror*. For the time being Kramer, whom she genuinely respected and cared for, was appeased.

In November 1994, she was occupied with fund raising in support of California Democrats running for state or national office, no concerts but luncheons and galas at which she was, along with numerous others, a celebrity guest. She took time out from her political activities to attend a gala in his honour when Prince Charles arrived in Los Angeles, his first visit in twenty years. They had only a brief opportunity to talk, but a close observer once again noted their 'terrific eye contact. It was like POW!' Charles was staying at the elegant and secluded Bel Air Hotel situated in Stone Canyon which weaves through the mountains above Sunset Boulevard in West Los Angeles. With its enchanted gardens, eleven acres of private parkland, ancient trees, and its graceful artificial lake – home to a bevy of swans – the hotel resembled a French country château and the stunning accommodation mirrored this theme. A few days after Charles and Streisand spoke at the gala, he arranged a private meeting in his luxurious suite of rooms, where they spent an hour alone together.

By this time a few pressmen, having picked up word of her visit, had gathered at the front gates. Hair flying in the cold November wind, head down, huge dark glasses hiding her face and wearing a belted coat and high boots, Streisand hurried into a waiting car which whizzed her away. The idea of Streisand and Charles ever being romantically involved seemed bizarre enough somehow to make sense. Charles is a fan, that is true, and they had got on well when they had seen one another, however briefly, in London during her tour. But there was more than a breath of romance in the secrecy and the lack of other participants attending the encounter to arouse the interest of the media.

As Christmas 1994 approached there was still no one special man in her life. She remained in close contact with Peter Jennings and sought out his advice on political matters that concerned her, items she read about in the newspapers and wanted to hear about in greater depth. Jennings had charm, warmth, a fine intelligence and his own sphere of fame. But he was also dating a younger, very attractive television producer – Katherine Freed.

Why was she not able to find a soulmate, a man who would love her deeply and to whom she could return the depth of that love? She was no longer the fame-hungry girl who had married and divorced Elliott, or the besotted woman who had given herself so completely to Peters and then allowed the making of a movie to break them apart. She had met, worked with, and had affairs with some of the most powerful, vital, intelligent and sexy men in the world. Whatever man she was drawn to had to measure up to the best of those gentlemen and, so far, none had. The man she wanted could not be intimidated by her immense fame, her iron-hard dedication to everything she attempted. He must share her enthusiasms, her convictions, her expectations as well as having a career of merit on his own. In addition he had to be sensitive and understanding when necessary, strong and protective when required. He could not be married or have 'a roving eye'. Such a man was not easy to find. But she never abandoned the possibility that he was out there.

Streisand had agreed to give a lecture on 3 February 1995 at the John F. Kennedy School of Government at Harvard on 'The Artist as Citizen' and was jotting down notes all the time on what she wanted to say – which mainly was a defence of the right of Hollywood celebrities to speak out on politics. Having experienced the prejudice of the media towards the politically active members of the film colony during the presidential election, the subject was one that she had been agitating over for many months. The week before the speech was to be presented, she flew to New York to consult Jennings. Her fear was not so much the speech itself, but the question-and-answer period that would follow where she might be called upon to respond on subjects or matters on which she was not sufficiently knowledgeable. Jennings acted as a consultant, but did not do any rewriting on her speech.

Ivied academia was in a frenzy of excitement at the prospect of her forthcoming appearance at Harvard, much more attention being paid to her than a recent visit to the school by Secretary of State Warren Christopher. The school's Institute of Politics had to hold a lottery so great was the demand for tickets in the 700-seat auditorium. Arrangements were made for a camera news pool to be set up to cover her televised appearance. Special machines were installed to check for counterfeit tickets and Cambridge police were stationed at every door and stairwell. Streisand remained terrified of an attack or a shooting by some crazy person, even though no incident of suspected violence had occurred during her concert tour.

She arrived by private jet in Boston with her secretary Kim Skalecki two days before her talk, and was driven to the Charles Hotel, where she was given the presidential suite. That night she holed up in her rooms rewriting her speech yet one more time. The following day she had a 'wonderful lunch' with John F. Kennedy Jr and twenty-five intense, serious, idealistic students, at which she discussed issues from welfare to defence spending. She grew misty-eyed when the youthfully handsome Kennedy had met her earlier and accompanied her on a tour of Harvard. Thirty-one years had passed since her treasured meeting with his father. Later she audited a class on constitutional law, for which she even did the homework after a run-through on her speech in the deserted auditorium.

Her nerves increased as the time for her to speak approached. After the audience was seated, she stood in the wings waiting for a lengthy laudatory introduction by Harvard University's interim president, Albert Carnesale, to end. When she finally stepped out on the stage that had previously played host to the likes of Mikhail S. Gorbachev, Newt Gingrich, Al Gore and a plethora of presidential hopefuls and administration officials, she was '*really* nervous'. Wearing a conservative charcoal-grey pin-striped, severely tailored Donna Karan dress, a single strand of pearls, her nails 'seriously sculptured', she had clasped and unclasped her hands, hugged her knees, rocked backwards and forwards and clenched the arms of her chair as Carnesale went on about her accomplishments.

'You heard of *shpilkes*?' she asked in a Brooklyn accent, to a chorus of laughter and vigorous applause when she finally stepped up to the microphone. Standing in front of a large wall hanging with *Harvard University – John F, Kennedy School of Government* and the school's emblem emblazoned on it – she sounded much like the impassioned Katie Morosky in *The Way We Were* as she told the students, 'I must admit I'm confused by [Speaker of the House, Newt Gingrich's] thinking. He proposes taking children away from poor mothers and placing them in orphanages. If that's an example of mainstream culture, let me say I'm happy to be a member of the counter-culture. I am also proud to be a liberal. Why is that so terrible these days? The liberals were liberators – they fought slavery, fought for women to have the right to vote, fought against Hitler, Stalin, fought to end segregation, fought to end apartheid. Liberals put an end to child labour and they gave us the five-day work week! What's to be ashamed of?' With a shrug of her shoulders, she spread her hands palm up in a gesture that indicated *you know what I mean?*

Defending the right of a celebrity to be involved in politics, she asked, 'What is the sin? Is it caring about your country? Why should the actor give up his role as citizen just because he's in show business? For his role in the movie *Philadelphia*, Tom Hanks had to learn quite a bit about being a gay man with AIDS. Should he have remained silent on this issue? For thirty years Paul Newman has been an outspoken defender of civil liberties and a major philanthropist. Would it be better if he just made money and played golf? Or, is Robert Redford a bubblehead because he knows more about the environment than most members of Congress? ... Most artists turn up on the humanist, compassionate side of public debate because ... we have to walk in other people's shoes and live in other people's skins. This does tend to make us more sympathetic to politics that are more tolerant,' she proudly acknowledged.

Eyes glancing down to check her notes from time to time, she went on to castigate the far right for 'waging a war for the soul of America by making art a partisan issue'. She suggested that the arts programme were minimal – 'the Public Broadcasting System costs each taxpayer less than one dollar a year – they hardly could be under attack for the money's sake. Maybe it's about shutting the minds and mouths of artists who might have something thought-provoking to say.' She reminisced about her childhood with stories about how her father had walked home from his teaching job to put the money he saved in the *pushke*, the charity box that many Jews had in their homes. She pointed to her own experience as a member of the Choral Club at Erasmus High School, stressing how important it was for children anywhere to 'find solace in an instrument to play or a canvas to paint on', a plea that the government should not cut such necessary funds.

During the fifty-minute speech she appeared ardent and edgy in turn. She gestured a lot, brushed her shoulder-length, blonde-streaked hair back from her face, wet her lips, drank water when she paused. After her closing remarks, she was given a standing ovation. Carnesale came forward and announced that there would be a short recess and then their guest would answer questions. Backstage, Streisand appeared excruciatingly anxious and had to be calmed. The feared question period was next.

A round of applause greeted her return to the podium.

A Harvard senior, Christopher Garcia, asked the first question. 'Why are you being so defensive?' adding that it sounded like the artistic community was 'out of touch with society'.

He was barraged with hisses and Streisand raised her hands in a gesture that seemed to mean: *I'll answer that.* 'Why are you a Republican?' she countered.

Her discomfort in this section of the programme only grew as the questions became more technical than philosophical. Several times she fended these with an honest 'I don't know enough about that to give you an answer.' When asked if she had plans in politics, she replied, 'Political ambition and political fervour are two different things.' Finally, with only one more question allowed, a young woman praised her as articulate, wealthy and intelligent. Streisand gave her a crooked Fanny Brice smile. 'You've got a guy for me?' she asked.

She had put herself on the front line. She was always setting tough goals for herself, a higher mountain to climb, a new set of obstacles to overcome, critics to win over. The press were generally positive to her appearance and her speech, but arch-conservative author Arianna Huffington wrote a stinging rebuttal in the *Washington Post*. 'Barbra, how could anyone hear anything over the din of such high-pitched melodrama?' she charged. 'Why do you insist on characterizing conservatives' wish to curtail tax-payer subsidies for the arts as motivated by "disrespect" for art and artists? Is your wish to cut the defence budget motivated by "disrespect" for our military and its servicemen?' Her suggestion was that the private sector raise the $167 million yearly budget necessary to sustain the arts.

Holding scant regard for Huffington's opinion, Streisand was not upset by her diatribe. She had spoken out on issues that were meaningful to her and believed she had a right to public address.

By the end of summer her attention was consumed by pre-production pressures for *Mirror* which would go before the cameras in and around New York in late October. Casting had been a relatively simple matter. With Jeff Bridges now definitely signed to co-star, Pierce Brosnan, the suave, handsome Irishman, fresh from his role as James Bond in the most recent 007 movie, was cast as the devilishly attractive other man (in this case Streisand's movie brother-in-law), Dudley Moore as Bridges's drinking buddy and Lauren Bacall as Streisand's glamorous mother.

'Everyone was optimistic on the first day of shooting,' a member of the crew recalled. 'I've worked with Barbra on several other filmed projects and she seemed calmer, more assured. Having known her for thirty years or more I've watched as she has changed. All of us do over such a span of time, of course. But with Barbra the change has been as dramatic as everything else in her life. She's lost touch with the real world, sees things only from her point of view. She has always been self-involved, demanding, a workaholic. But she once had a marvellous zest for life, wanted to eat up the whole world. That's not there any more. What I feel she's lost is her sense of humour, the ability to laugh at herself. She's so damned serious these days.

'She's always been like that little girl with a curl in the middle of her forehead – one day she's very good, the next day she's horrid. She can be your best friend and sympathetic supporter. Then the wind changes and she can cut you off in the most appallingly cold, cruel manner. In recent years I've seen it happen with scary frequency. On the set of *Mirror* it became a common occurrence. I was terrified that what I was watching was the total unwinding of someone I had loved and admired very much. The filming process itself was like a bad movie. I began to wonder – "Where is all this going and what is it all about?" She became paranoid. There was no contradicting what she said. She was the only person in the world. It was megalomania to the nth. One night I came back to the apartment I was using while we were in New York and I cried. It was as though I had lost someone very near and dear to me.'

She had gone into this project believing that it would be far less complicated or emotional than *The Normal Heart*. It was going to be the movie that would show the studios she could make a non-musical, commercial film on budget, prove that she was a reliable, bankable director. One week into the filming she knew she had made a mistake in casting Dudley Moore in his role. He was too comedic, too much the drunk from *Arthur*, which changed the focus of the scene he was in.

'It was hard to tell if he was playing an inebriated character or if he *was* one,' a member of the crew commented. 'One thing was sure – Barbra and Moore were incompatible and *she* was the producer, star and director.'

Moore was quickly replaced by George Segal, whom Streisand had worked with so well years before in *The Owl and the Pussycat*. Then right before Christmas the director of photography Dante Spinotti and his eight-man crew were replaced by Andrzej Bartkowiak, who had worked with her on *Nuts*, and new technicians. This was a major change. The director of photography sets the tone of the picture. Streisand was not happy with the way she looked in the daily rushes or with the shots that Spinotti had filmed. 'She had been complaining about the camera work almost from the beginning of the production,' one person on the set said. 'There were too many gauzes around the lens. Her eyes – one of her best features – got very soft.'

Two days later she dismissed Alan Heim, an Oscar-winning film editor and replaced him with Jeff Werner, who had also worked with her before. The winter months were brutal. Exterior shots had to be postponed, interior sets constructed in overtime hours. A movie that had originally been budgeted at $35 million dollars quickly escalated by many millions, to the shouts and fury of the studio executives. Streisand was on edge and the set was bristling with palpable tension. Cis Corman, who was co-producer, was more diplomatic than Streisand and did her best to smooth relations between the major cast and crew members and Streisand. Even Jeff Bridges, who has a reputation as being easy going, found her difficult. '[She] can piss you off, but if I get pissed off, I can't work. So I don't allow myself to get there,' he said at the time.

The set was closed, no outsiders allowed. When they were on location, shooting a scene in a store or a restaurant, the area was blocked off and guards patrolled with walkie-talkies. 'The whole team [cast, director of photography, crew, security] is a walking thermometer for You Know Who,' one observer reported. 'The word would pass – she's feeling OK ... she's getting make-up ... she's left the trailer ... she's due momentarily ... she's coming.'

On a rare morning in January, *New York Post* entertainment reporter Cindy Adams was permitted on the set, an indoor antiques and collectable bazaar with 100 booths on 25th Street, which was transformed into an 'Annual Antique Spring Market' for the scene being shot. (Streisand had cased it earlier and bought numerous pieces for the penthouse.) This meant that in the midst of New York's winter freeze – the coldest, snowiest January in fifty years – the cast had to wear light spring clothes. The crew arrived at 5 a.m. to set lights, camera angles, dress the walls with early American quilts. Streisand entered at 9 a.m. 'in a little pink cardigan and promptly rearranged the lights, camera angles plus whatever else could be rearranged. Renata, her handsome assistant with the long blonde hair, at her side,' Adams related.

The scene to be shot had Streisand studying an early American patchwork quilt in a wall showcase as a short distance away Segal asks Bridges about his sex life with his mousey wife, 'So, did you do it already?'

The scene had not yet met with Streisand's approval by the time lunch was called. At 9 p.m. that evening, having munched on a sandwich for dinner, she was watching the dailies and making notes for the following day's work, deeply involved with the movie she was making, struggling to bring it to realisation as she envisioned it. *Mirror* now belonged to her, possessively. She was totally immersed. She returned to her apartment about 11 p.m., studied her lines for her next day's scenes, fell asleep exhausted and was up and working on them again by 7 a.m. in the morning.

So consumed was she with the production of *Mirror* that she had allowed to slip from her attention the fact that her option on *The Normal Heart*, which she had never given up believing in, had expired on 2 January. When Kramer's representative pressed for a decision on her part to either renew her contract or allow Kramer to take it elsewhere, she made no reply. Finally, as April approached, *Mirror* still shooting and overages mounting, Streisand insisted she would make *The Normal Heart* once her present commitment was complete and she had been able to sign a male star and a director, having decided she would not direct herself. Jason called Kramer and suggested that he (Jason) would be up for director if Kramer could convince his mother that he could do it. Kramer was hoping for a more experienced director and thought this might not be a good idea.

Then, on 8 April, Kramer, who had still had no further word on whether Streisand would pick up her option, was interviewed by *Variety* in an article that was reprinted and excerpted widely: 'This woman has had this play since 1986, She doesn't own it any more and my health is deteriorating and I would very much like to see the movie made while I'm alive. She was all set to make *The Normal Heart* about a worldwide plague, and at the last minute she switches to a film about a woman who gets a face-lift. I didn't think that was decent of her to do to me, her gay fans and the people with AIDS she talks so movingly about.' And he added, 'My ten-year journey of futility with Barbra to make *The Normal Heart* has been almost as long as my fight as an AIDS activist to end this plague.'

Streisand then issued a public statement: 'I am painfully aware of the ticking clock. Therefore, I am now stepping aside and will no longer be involved with the project. I wish Larry only success in getting *The Normal Heart* made.[1] I personally have a strong commitment to projects that reflect and further the needs of the gay community.'

'Barbra was deeply hurt by Larry's attitude and the harsh coverage she received in the press over the now abandoned property,' a close friend confided. 'I think *The Normal Heart* was almost as important to her as *Yentl* had once been. And Larry had made a great impression on her, brought her a special awareness of both the plague and the gay community. But once he went public, she went ice cold on him. She felt she had put in almost as much in the project as he did, that he should have understood how much she cared, what it meant to her. She took it as a personal stab.'

On 15 April she sent Kramer a fax accusing him of being self-destructive, of having acted unreasonably, of demanding too much for himself when she had not received compensation for the many years she had worked on the movie. 'I love this project – and I was trying to get it made ... for your sake as well as mine ... I have to finish *Mirror* as you would have wanted me to finish *Heart*.' And then she asked him to stop making statements that *Mirror* was a movie about a woman with a face-lift, requesting that he read the script before making unjust judgments.

Things grew worse on the set of *Mirror* after the fracas over *The Normal Heart* and anonymous interviews were given to the press by at least two members of the crew about the difficulties on the film and Streisand's frenetic behaviour, tantrums and all-round ill-humour. Ultimatums were levied. No one was to

---

[1] *The Normal Heart* was optioned by director John Schlesinger within a week of this statement.

speak to any member of the press or their jobs would be on the line. 'This is my first major film,' one associate told me. 'I'm scared shitless. She has the power to make it difficult, if not impossible, for me to do another film with TriStar, and with the manic way she has been acting I have little doubt she would do so if she knew I was talking to you. Every day I walk out on the set and I can't believe what I am seeing and hearing. There is a dark cloud of fear, of apprehension, of wanting the filming to end. But now, just when we all thought that was about to happen, she has decided she must reshoot a major sequence. That's another five to seven days' work, not to mention the reconstruction of a set. I know I'm going to turn off my phones and my pager and sleep for four days when the last shoot is in the can. Barbra? She has a summer of supervising the editing ahead of her, then the advertising and publicity campaign, working out the release and distribution. And she is not going to let go of this film until she drives everyone and herself working on post-production crazy.'

In her defence, Richard LaGravenese says, 'I love Barbra. She is terribly maligned, misunderstood.'

'Be careful of the wishes you make, they may come true,' Stephen Sondheim has written. Streisand has always wished for more than what she has – be it career, money, achievement, love. Streisand wished to be a great star and it happened, but not without her constant attention to what she was doing and how she could achieve her goal. With Elizabeth Taylor, she is one of only two behemoth Hollywood survivors, albeit the only one of the two who is still in the business of making movies. Unlike Taylor she has not had to fight drugs, weight problems, multiple divorces, tragedy and severe and frequent illness. She does not move her fans to tears or her friends into becoming protective shields. And her greatest triumphs are not in the distant past. Without Taylor's natural, spectacular beauty, a mother to goad her, or anyone to guide her, she was forced to invent herself, make herself over, sell the world on what and who she was and she is still in there selling, pushing.

'You just push, push, push and never let up,' Barbara Walters once said to her.

'If I push, it's because I want things to be better,' she replied.

Pushy, hungry, grasping, brilliant, possessor of one of the greatest popular voices in her lifetime, dazzling in her accomplishments, infuriating in her absolute refusal to alter her personality or beliefs to please anyone other than herself, Streisand is, none the less, a living kaleidoscope of the last half of the twentieth century. She represents so many touchstones in our lives. Recall the young Streisand as the homely Fanny Brice as she looked into the mirror and with spunky confidence sang, 'I'm the Greatest Star'. Recall, too, how she stood next to the exquisite Ingrid Bergman at the Academy Awards, dressed in a shocking, see-through dress, holding Oscar tightly in her grasp, as she shouted, 'Hullo, Gorgeous!' Think back to that marvellous cinematic moment when in a radiant close-up in *The Way We Were*, the handsomest man in Hollywood, Robert Redford, had taken her in his arms and how the tears ran down her cheeks. She was the homely girl who could become beautiful, and she remains the dreamer, the wonderer, the believer in most of us that anything can be won, against the worst odds, if you have the guts and the vision to see it through.

Chutzpah, guts, strength – call it what you will, Streisand defines it. She has also dared – off and on screen – to hazard beyond ordinariness into the adventurous extreme. She made ethnicity a great advantage, turned style around so that it mimicked her own, and she has a voice that has never grown reedy or dropped into tobacco or alcoholic huskiness. It is a voice that takes us with it as it soars. It comes from somewhere deep inside her, given to her by her special god, perhaps to make up for the things she did not have – a father, beauty, inner peace; a voice that can only happen once.

# Discography

The Recording Industry Association of America sets the standard for gold and platinum discs. From 1958 to 1974 the basis for a gold record or album was $1 million in *wholesale* revenues. In 1975 this was changed to designate 500,000 units sold *and* $1 million wholesale revenues. The platinum standard was created in 1976 and certifies one million units sold *and* $2 million in revenues. UK and foreign album sales are not included in these computations.

All albums with the exception of those* are available on compact disc.

### I Can Get It For You Wholesale
Cast Album, Columbia, April 1962

Produced by Goddard Leiberson
Music and lyrics by Harold Rome
Musical direction and vocal
  arrangements, Lehman Engel
Orchestrations, Sid Ramin
Streisand sings one solo: 'Miss
  Marmelstein'
She is also heard on 'I'm Not a Well
  Man', 'Ballad of the Garment Trade',
  and 'What Are They Doing to Us
  Now?'

....................................................

### Pins and Needles
25th Anniversary Edition
Columbia May 1962

Produced by Elizabeth Lauer and
  Charles Burr
Under the supervision of Harold Rome
Music and lyrics by Harold Rome
Musical direction, Stan Freeman

Vocal arrangements, Elise Bretton
Singers: Barbra Streisand, Jack Carroll,
  Rose Marie Jun, Alan Sokoloff and
  Harold Rome with Stan Freeman at
  the piano
Streisand sings five solos: 'Doing the
  Reactionary', 'Nobody Makes a Pass
  at Me', 'Not Cricket to Picket', 'What
  Good is Love?', 'Sitting on Your
  Status Quo.'
She can also be heard with Harold
  Rome, Jack Carroll and Alan Sokoloff
  on 'Four Little Angels of Peace'

....................................................

### Streisand Live 1963
Bel Cano 5001

An in-performance album recorded at
the Hungary i that was sold and
circulated heavily until Streisand placed
a restraining order on it

Songs: 'Anyplace I Hang My Hat is
  Home', 'Keepin' Out of Mischief

Now', 'Cry Me a River', 'Lover, Come Back to Me', 'Have I Stayed too Long at the Fair', 'My Honey's Loving Arms', 'Soon It's Going to Rain', 'When the Sun Comes Out', 'Much More', 'Like a Straw in the Wind', 'Right as the Rain', 'Down with Love', 'Bewitched', 'Happy Days Are Here Again'

..................................................

### The Barbra Streisand Album
Columbia, February 1963

Produced by Mike Berniker
Music arranged and conducted by Peter Matz

Songs: 'Cry Me a River', 'My Honey's Loving Arms', 'I'll Tell the Man on The Street', 'A Taste of Honey', 'Who's Afraid of the Big Bad Wolf?', 'Soon it's Gonna Rain', 'Happy Days Are Here Again', 'Keepin' Out of Mischief Now', 'Much More', 'Come to the Supermarket (in old Peking)', 'A Sleepin' Bee'

Streisand's first album in the top ten of the charts. Made Gold.
Grammy Awards: Album of the Year, Best Female Vocal Performance

..................................................

### The Second Barbra Streisand Album
Columbia, August 1963

Produced by Mike Berniker
Arranged and conducted by Peter Matz
Additional material by Peter Daniels

Songs: 'Any Place I Hang My Hat Is Home', 'Right as the Rain', 'Down with Love', 'Who Will Buy?', 'When the Sun Comes Out', 'Gotta Move', 'My Coloring Book', 'I Don't Care

Much', 'Lover, Come Back to Me', 'Have I Stayed Too Long at the Fair', 'Like a Straw in the Wind'

In the top ten of the charts. Made Gold.
Grammy Awards: none

..................................................

### Barbra Streisand/The Third Album
Columbia, February 1964

Produced by Mike Berniker

Songs: 'My Melancholy Baby', 'Taking a Chance on Love', 'As Time Goes By', 'It Had to Be You' (arranged and conducted by Ray Ellis), 'Just In Time', 'Draw Me a Circle', 'I Had Myself a True Love' (orchestrated and conducted by Sid Ramin) 'Bewitched (Bothered and Bewildered)' (arranged by Peter Daniels), 'Never Will I Marry'/'Make Believe' (arranged and conducted by Peter Matz)

In the top ten in the charts. Made Gold.

..................................................

### Funny Girl (Cast Recording)
Capitol, April 1964

Produced by Dick Jones
Music by Jule Styne, lyrics by Robert Merrill
Musical Director, Milton Rosenstock
Orchestrations, Ralph Burns
Vocal arrangements, Buster Davis
Featuring Barbra Streisand, Sydney Chaplin, Kay Medford, Danny Meehan and Jean Stapleton

Songs sung by Streisand: 'I'm the Greatest Star', 'His Love Makes Me Beautiful', duet with Chaplin: 'I Want To Be Seen With You'; 'People', duet with Chaplin: 'You Are Woman, I Am

Man'; 'Don't Rain on My Parade', 'Sadie, Sadie', 'Rat Tat-Tat-Tat', 'Coronet Man', 'Who Are You Now?', 'The Music that Makes Me Dance'. Other Songs: 'If a Girl Isn't Pretty', 'Who Taught Her Everything', 'Henry Street', 'Find Yourself a Man'

In the top ten in the charts. Made Gold.

......................................................

## People
Columbia, May 1965

Produced by Robert Mersey
Piano accompaniment, Peter Daniels
Arranged and conducted by Peter Matz and Ray Ellis*

Songs: 'Absent Minded Me', 'When in Rome (I Do as the Romans Do)', 'How Does the Wine Taste?', 'My Lord and Master', 'Love Is a Bore', 'Don't Like Goodbyes', 'People', 'Fine and Dandy',* 'Supper Time',* 'Will He Like Me',* 'I'm All Smiles',* 'Autumn'*

Number One in the charts. Made Gold.

Grammy Award: Best Female Vocal Performance

......................................................

## My Name is Barbra
Columbia, 1965

Produced by Robert Mersey
Orchestrations and arrangements by Peter Matz

Songs: 'My Name Is Barbra', 'A Kid Again/I'm Five', 'Jenny Rebecca', 'My Pa', 'Sweet Zoo', 'Where Is the Wonder?', 'I Can See It', 'Someone to Watch Over Me', 'I've Got No Strings', 'If You Were the Only Boy in the World', 'Why Did I Choose You?', 'My Man'

In the top ten of the charts. Made gold.

Grammy Award: Best Female Vocal Performance

......................................................

## My Name is Barbra Two
Columbia, October 1965

Produced by Robert Mersey
Conducted and arranged by Peter Matz

Songs: 'He Touched Me', 'The Shadow of Your Smile', 'Quiet Night', 'I Got Plenty of Nothin'', 'How Much of the Dream Comes True?', 'Second Hand Rose', 'The Kind of Man a Woman Needs', 'All that I Want', 'Where's the Rainbow?', 'No More Songs for Me', 'Give Me the Simple Life', 'Brother Can You Spare a Dime?', 'Nobody Knows You When You're Down and Out', 'The Best Things in Life Are Free'

In the top ten of the charts. Made Platinum.

......................................................

## Color Me Barbra
Columbia, March 1966

Produced by Robert Mersey
Conducted and arranged by Peter Matz

Songs: 'Yesterday', 'One Kiss', 'The Minute Waltz', 'Gotta Move', 'Non C'est Rien', 'Where or When', medley: 'Animal Crackers in My Soup', 'Funny Face', 'That Face', 'They Didn't Believe Me', 'Where Thine that Special Face', 'I've Grown Accustomed to Her Face', 'Let's Face the Music and Dance'; 'Sam You Made the Pants Too Long', 'What's New Pussycat?', 'Small World', 'I Love You', 'I Have Stayed too Long at the Fair', 'Look at That Face', 'C'est Si

Bon', 'Where Am I Going?', 'Starting Here, Starting Now'

In the top ten of the charts. Made Gold.
........................................................

### Harold Sings Arlen (with friend)
Columbia, March 1966

Produced by Thomas Z. Shepard
Arranged and conducted by Peter Matz
Music by Harold Arlen

Streisand sings: duet with Arlen: 'Ding-Dong! The Witch Is Dead'; solo: 'House of Flowers'
........................................................

### Je M'appelle Barbra
Columbia, October 1966

Produced by Ettore Stratta

Songs: 'Free Again', 'Autumn Leaves', 'What's Now My Love', 'Ma Première Chanson (the first song of Streisand's own composition to be recorded)', 'Clopin-Clopant', 'Le Mur', 'I Wish You Love', 'Speak to Me of Love', 'Love and Learn', 'Once Upon a Summertime', 'Martina', 'I've Been Here'

In the top ten of the charts. Made Gold.
........................................................

### Simply Streisand
Columbia, October 1967

Produced by Jack Gold and Howard A. Roberts
Arranged by Ray Ellis
Conducted by David Shire

Songs: 'My Funny Valentine', 'The Nearness of You', 'When Sunny Gets Blue', 'Make the Man Love Me', 'Lover

Man', 'I'll Know', 'More than You Know', 'All the Things You Are', 'The Boy Next Door', 'Stout-Hearted Men'

Hit Number Twelve in the charts. Made Gold. (Richard Rodgers wrote on the back of the album one of Streisand's most treasured accolades: 'Nobody is talented enough to get laughs, to bring tears, to sing with the depth of a fine cello or the lift of a climbing bird. Nobody, that is, except Barbra. She makes our musical world a much happier place than it was before. Sincerely, Richard Rodgers.')
........................................................

### A Christmas Album
Columbia, October 1967

Produced by Jack Gold
Numerous arrangers

Songs: 'Jingle Bells', 'Have Yourself a Merry Little Christmas', 'The Christmas Song', 'White Christmas', 'My Favorite Things', 'The Best Gift', 'Sleep in Heavenly Peace (Silent Night)', Gounod's 'Ave Maria', 'O Little Town of Bethlehem', 'I Wonder as I Wander', 'The Lord's Prayer'

One of Streisand's largest selling albums, it hit Number One in the charts. Made Triple Platinum.
........................................................

### Funny Girl
Columbia, July 1968

Motion-picture sound track
Produced by Jack Gold
Arranged and conducted by Milton Rosenstock
With Omar Sharif, Kay Medford

Songs sung by Streisand: 'I'm the

Greatest Star', 'I'd Rather Be Blue', 'His Love Makes Me Beautiful', 'People', 'You Are Woman, I Am Man', 'Don't Rain on My Parade', 'Sadie, Sadie', 'The Swan', 'Funny Girl', 'My Man'
Sung by others: 'If a Girl Isn't Pretty', 'Roller Skate Rag'.

Hit Number Twelve in the charts. Made Platinum.

......................................

### A Happening in Central Park
Columbia, September 1968

Produced by Jack Gold
Arranged by Peter Matz
Conducted by Mort Lindsey

Songs: 'I Can See It', 'Love Is Like a New Born Child', 'Value', 'Cry Me a River', 'People', 'He Touched Me', 'Marty the Martian', 'Natural Sounds', 'Second Hand Rose', 'Sleep in Heavenly Peace, (Silent Night)', 'Happy Days Are Here Again'

A number of songs from the live concert were not included on the record. Although it only rose to Number Thirty in the charts, it made Gold.

......................................

### What About Today?
Columbia, 1969

Produced by Wally Gold

Songs: arranged and conducted by Peter Matz: 'Ask Yourself Why', 'Honey Pie', 'Punky's Dilemma', 'That's a Fine Kind o' Freedom', 'Little Tin Soldier', and 'Goodnight'; arranged and conducted by Don Costa: 'What about Today', 'The Morning After'; arranged and conducted by Michel

Legrand: 'Until It's Time for You to Go', 'With a Little Help from My Friends', 'Alfie'

This album only went up to Number Thirty-One in the charts.

......................................

### Hello, Dolly!
Twentieth Century-Fox Records, December 1969
Motion-picture sound track

Produced by Lennie Hayton and Lionel Newman
Arranged and conducted by Lennie Hayton and Lionel Newman
Music by Jerry Herman

Others on record: Michael Crawford, Danny Lockin, Marianne McAndrew, Walter Matthau and Louis Armstrong

Songs sung by Streisand: 'Just Leave Everything to Me', 'Put on Your Sunday Clothes', 'Before the Parade Passes By', 'Love Is Only Love', 'Hello, Dolly!' (sung with Louis Armstrong), 'So Long, Dearie', (entire cast).
Other songs: 'Ribbons Down My Back', sung by Marianne McAndrew; 'Elegance', 'It Takes a Woman', 'It Only Takes a Moment'

Rose only to Number Thirty-Two in the charts. Remained in the charts for forty-six weeks. Made Double Platinum.

......................................

### Barbra Streisand's Greatest Hits
Columbia, December 1969

Composed of song tracks extracted from previous records, both albums and singles and includes: 'People', 'Second Hand Rose', 'Why Did I

Choose You?', 'He Touched Me', 'Free Again', 'Don't Rain on My Parade', 'My Coloring Book', 'Sam, You Made the Pants Too Long', 'My Man', 'Gotta Move', 'Happy Days Are Here Again'

Hit Number Thirty-Two in the charts. Remained in charts forty-three weeks. Made Double Platinum.

.......................................................

### On a Clear Day You Can See Forever
Columbia, July 1970
Motion-picture sound track

Produced by Wally Gold
Arranged and conducted by Nelson Riddle
Music by Burton Lane, lyrics by Alan Jay Lerner
Other artist: Yves Montand

Songs sung by Streisand: 'Hurry, It's Lovely Up Here', 'On a Clear Day You Can See Forever', 'Love With All the Trimmings', 'She Isn't You', 'What Did I Have that I Don't Have?', 'Go to Sleep'
Songs sung by Montand: 'Melinda', 'Come Back to Me', 'On a Clear Day You Can See Forever'

The album did not make it into the charts.

.......................................................

### The Owl and the Pussycat*
Columbia, December 1970

Produced by Thomas Z. Shepard
Performed by Blood, Sweat and Tears

Streisand does not sing on the record, which does include dialogue (both Streisand and her co-star George Segal are heard) and incidental music from the picture.

.......................................................

### Stoney End
Columbia, February 1971

Produced by Richard Perry

Songs: 'I Don't Know Where I Stand', 'Hands Off the Man', 'If You Could Read My Mind', 'Just a Little Lovin'', 'Let Me Go', 'Stoney End', 'No Easy Way Down', 'Time and Love', 'Maybe', 'Free the People', 'I'll Be Home'

Hit Number Ten in the charts. Made Platinum.

.......................................................

### Barbra Joan Streisand
Columbia, August 1971

Produced by Richard Perry

Songs: 'Beautiful', 'Love' (arranged by Nick de Caro); 'Where You Lead', 'Space Captain' (arranged by Fanny); 'I Never Meant to Hurt You', 'The Summer Knows' (arranged and conducted by Dick Hazard); medley: 'One Less Bell to Answer', 'A House Is Not a Home' (arranged by Ken Welch, orchestrated by Peter Matz); 'Mother', 'Since I Fell for You' (arranged and conducted by Gene Page); 'I Mean to Shine', 'You've Got a Friend' (arranged by Head).

Hit Number Eleven in the charts. Made Gold.

.......................................................

### Live Concert at the Forum
Columbia, October 1972

Produced by Richard Perry

Songs: 'Sing/Make Your Own Kind of Music', 'Sweet Inspiration', 'Where You Lead', 'Sing/Happy Days Are Here Again' (arranged by Don Hannah); 'Don't Rain on My Parade', 'On a Clear Day', 'My Man', 'People' (arranged by Peter Matz); 'Starting Here, Starting Now' (arranged by Don Costa); 'Didn't We' (arranged by Claus Ogerman); 'Stoney End' (arranged by Gene Page).

Hit Number Nineteen in the charts. Made Platinum.

.................................................

### Barbra Streisand ... and Other Musical Instruments
Columbia, October 1973

Produced by Martin Erlichman
Arranged by Ken Welch

Songs: 'Piano Practicing', 'I Got Rhythm', 'Johnny One Note', 'One Note Samba', 'Glad to Be Unhappy', medley: 'People'/Second Hand Rose', 'Don't Rain on My Parade'; 'Don't Ever Leave Me', monologue: 'By Myself', 'Come Back to Me', 'I Never Has Seen Snow', 'Auf dem Wasser zu Singen', 'The World Is a Concerto', 'Make Your Own Kind of Music', 'The Sweetest Sounds'

.................................................

### Barbra Streisand featuring 'The Way We Were' and 'All in Love Is Fair'
Columbia, January 1974

Produced by Tommy LiPuma
Arranged by Marvin Hamlisch

Songs: 'Being at War with Each Other', 'Something So Right', 'The Best Thing You've Ever Done', 'The Way We Were', 'All in Love Is Fair', 'What Are You Doing the Rest of Your Life?', 'Summer Me, Winter Me', 'Pieces of Dreams', 'I've Never Been a Woman Before'; medley: 'My Buddy'/'How About Me?'

Hit Number One in the charts. Made Platinum.

Grammy Award: Song of the Year ('The Way We Were', music – Marvin Hamlisch; lyrics – Marilyn and Alan Bergman)

.................................................

### The Way We Were
Columbia, January 1974

Produced by Fred Salem
Arranged by Marvin Hamlisch

Motion-picture sound track. It includes the one song from the movie – 'The Way We Were' – sung and reprised by Barbra Streisand

It hit Number Twenty in the charts. Made Gold.

Grammy Awards: Song of the Year (Hamlisch/the Bergmans); Best Original Motion Picture Score (Hamlisch)

.................................................

### Butterfly
Columbia, October 1974

Produced by Jon Peters

Songs: 'Love in the Afternoon', 'Guava Jelly', 'Grandmother's Hands', 'I Won't Last a Day Without You', 'Jubilation', 'Simple Man', 'Life on Mars', 'Since I Don't Have You', 'Crying Time', 'Let the Good Times Roll'

Hit the charts at Number Thirteen. Made Gold.

................................................

### Funny Lady
Columbia, March 1975
Motion-picture sound track

Produced by Peter Matz
Arranged and conducted by Peter Matz

Songs: 'How Lucky Can You Get', 'So Long, Honey Lamb', 'I Found a Million Dollar Baby in a Five and Ten Cent Store', 'Isn't This Better?', 'Me and My Shadow', 'If I Love Again', 'I Got a Code in My Doze', 'Great Day', 'Blind Date', 'Am I Blue'; duet with James Caan: 'It's Only a Paper Moon'/'I Like Him'/'Her'; 'More Than You Know', 'Let's Hear It For Me.'
Sung by Ben Vereen: 'Clap Hands, Here Comes Charley'

Hit Number Six in the charts. Made Gold.

................................................

### Lazy Afternoon
Columbia, October 1975

Produced by Rupert Holmes and Jeffrey Lesser

Songs: 'Lazy Afternoon', 'My Father's Song', 'By the Way', 'Shake Me, Wake Me', 'I Never Had It So Good', 'Letters that Cross in the Mail', 'You and I', 'Moanin' Low', 'A Child Is Born', 'Widescreen'

Hit Number Twelve in the charts. Made Gold.

................................................

### Classical Barbra
Columbia, February 1976

Produced by Claus Ogerman

Songs: 'Beau Soir', 'Brezairola', 'Verschwiegene Liebe', 'Pavane', 'Apres un Rêve', 'In Trutina', 'Lascia c'io pianga', 'Nondnacht', 'Dank sie Die, Herr', 'I Loved You'

It is worthy of note that Streisand received a Grammy nomination for this album: 'Best Classical Vocal Soloist Performance'.

................................................

### A Star is Born
Columbia, February 1976
Motion-picture sound track

Produced by Barbra Streisand and Phil Ramone
Arranged and conducted by Kenny Ascher

Songs: 'Watch Closely Now', 'Queen Bee', 'Everything', 'Lost Inside of You' (arranged by Pat Williams), 'Hellacious Acres', 'Evergreen' (arranged by Ian Freebairn-Smith), 'Woman in the Moon', 'I Believe in Love', 'Crippled Crow', 'With One More Look at You'/'Watch Closely Now', 'Evergreen' (reprise)

Hit Number One in the charts. Made quadruple Platinum.

Grammy Awards: Best Female Pop Vocal, Song of the Year – 'Evergreen', Streisand/Paul Williams

................................................

### Streisand Superman
Columbia, June 1977

Produced by Gary Klein

Songs: 'Superman', 'Don't Believe What You Read', 'Baby Me, Baby', 'I Found You Love', 'Answer Me', 'My Heart

Belongs to Me', 'Cabin Fever', 'Love
Comes from Unexpected Places',
'New York State of Mind', 'Lullaby for
Myself'

Hit Number Three in the charts. Made
Platinum.
......................................

### Songbird
Columbia, May 1978

Produced by Gary Klein

Songs: 'Tomorrow', 'A Man I Loved', 'I
Don't Break Easily', 'Love
Breakdown', 'You Don't Bring Me
Flowers', 'Honey Can I Put on Your
Clothes', 'One More Night', 'Stay
Away', 'Deep in the Night',
'Songbird'

Hit Number Twelve in the charts. Made
Platinum.
......................................

### Eyes of Laura Mars*
Columbia, July 1978
Motion-picture sound track

Numerous producers
Songs: Streisand sings only one song –
'Prisoner'
......................................

### Barbra Streisand's Greatest Hits, Volume 2
(Volume 1, December 1969)
Columbia, November 1978

Numerous producers and arrangers

Songs: 'Evergreen', 'Prisoner', 'My Heart
Belongs to Me', 'Songbird', 'You
Don't Bring Me Flowers' (duet with
Neil Diamond), 'The Way We Were',
'Sweet Inspiration'/'Where You Lead',

'All in Love Is Fair', 'Superman',
'Stoney End'

Hit Number One in the charts. Made
quadruple Platinum.
......................................

### The Main Event
Columbia, June 1979

Numerous producers

Songs: Streisand sings the title song and
reprises it. The rest of the album
includes vocal and instrumental work
by various artists.

Hit Number Twenty in the charts. Made
Gold.
......................................

### Wet
Columbia, October 1979

Produced by Gary Klein
Numerous arrangers

Songs: 'Wet', 'Come Rain or Come
Shine', 'Splish Splash', 'On Rainy
Afternoons', 'After the Rain', 'No
More Tears (Enough is Enough)' (duet
with Donna Summer), 'Niagara', 'I
Ain't Gonna Cry Tonight', 'Kiss Me
in the Rain'

Hit Number Seven in the charts. Made
Platinum.
......................................

### Guilty
Columbia, September 1980

Executive producer, Charles
Koppleman
Produced by Barry Gibb, Albhy Galuten
and Karl Richardson
Arranged by Barry Gibb, Albhy Galuten
and Peter Graves

Songs: 'Guilty' (duet with Barry Gibb), 'Woman in Love', 'Run Wild', 'Promises', 'The Love Inside', 'What Kind of Fool' (duet with Barry Gibb), 'Life Story', 'Never Give Up', 'Make It Like a Memory'

Hit Number One in the charts. Made quintuple Platinum.

Grammy Award: Best Top Vocal by Duo or Group (with Barry Gibb)

..................................................

### Memories
Columbia, November 1981

Includes songs recorded on earlier albums.

Songs: 'Memory', 'You Don't Bring Me Flowers' (duet with Neil Diamond), 'My Heart Belongs to Me', 'New York State of Mind', 'No More Tears (Enough Is Enough)' (duet with Donna Summer), 'Comin' In and Out of Your Life', 'Evergreen', 'Lost Inside of You', 'The Love Inside', 'The Way We Were'

Hit Number Six in the charts. Made quadruple Platinum.

..................................................

### Yentl
Columbia, November 1983
Motion-picture sound track

Produced by Barbra Streisand, Marilyn Bergman and Alan Bergman
Arranged by Michel Legrand

Songs: 'Where Is It Written', 'Papa, Can You Hear Me?', 'This Is One of Those Moments', 'No Wonder', 'The Way He Makes Me Feel', 'No Wonder' (reprise), 'Tomorrow Night', 'Will

Someone Ever Look at Me that Way?', 'No Matter What Happens', 'No Wonder' (reprise), 'A Piece of Sky', 'The Way He Makes Me Feel' (a second version recorded separately), 'No Matter What Happens' (a second version recorded separately)

Hit Number Nine in the charts. Made Platinum.

..................................................

### The Legend of Barbra Streisand: a two-disc LP
The woman and the music in her own words
A one-hour interview programme
This is a demonstration-only recording, released for radio play as publicity for the movie, Yentl
Columbia A2S 1779
Produced by Westwood One for Columbia Records
Written and produced by Bert Kleinman
Hosted by Phil Hendrie
Interview by Mary Turner
Executive producer, Norman Pattiz

Songs: segment one: none (introduction); segment two: 'People', 'Minute Waltz', 'Where Am I Going?'; segment three: 'Second Hand Rose', 'My Man', 'He Touched Me'; segment four: 'Free Again', 'Sam, You Made the Pants Too Long'; segment five: 'The Way We Were', 'All in Love Is Fair', 'Evergreen'; segment six: 'My Heart Belongs to Me', 'You Don't Bring Me Flowers', 'Songbird'; segment seven: 'No More Tears (Enough Is Enough)', 'Woman in Love', 'Guilty'; segment eight: 'Papa, Can You Hear Me?', 'The Way He Makes Me Feel' (studio version);

segment nine: 'Where Is It Written?',
'A Piece of Sky'

..............................................

### Emotion
Columbia, October 1984

Executive producer, Charles
Koppelman
Produced by Barbra Streisand, Richard
Perry, Maurice White, Jim Steinman,
Albhy Galuten and Richard Baskin
Numerous arrangers

Songs: 'Emotion', 'He's Mine' (duet
with Kim Carnes), 'Time Machine',
'Best I Could', 'Left in the Dark',
'Heart Don't Change My Mind',
'When I Dream', 'You're a Step in the
Right Direction' (music by J.
Mellencamp, lyrics by Barbra
Streisand), 'Clear Sailing', 'Here We
Are at Last' (music by Barbra
Streisand, lyrics by Richard Baskin)

Hit Number Nineteen in the charts.
Made Platinum.

..............................................

### The Broadway Album
Columbia, November 1985

Produced by Barbra Streisand, Peter
Matz, David Foster and Richard
Baskin
Arranged by Peter Matz and David
Foster

Songs: 'Putting It Together', 'If I Loved
You', 'Something's Coming', 'Not
While I'm Around', 'Being Alive'; 'I
Have Dreamed', 'We Kiss in the
Shadow', 'Something Wonderful',
'Adelaide's Lament', 'Send in the
Clowns', 'Pretty Women'/'The Ladies
Who Lunch', 'Can't Help Lovin' that
Man', 'I Loves You Porgy'/'Bess You Is
My Woman', 'Somewhere'.

Hit Number One in the charts. Made
triple Platinum.

Grammy Awards: Best Female Pop
Vocal, Best Arrangement
Accompanying Vocal ('Putting It
Together', Peter Matz)

..............................................

### One Voice
Columbia, April 1987
Life performance

Produced by Richard Baskin

Songs: 'Somewhere', 'Evergreen',
'Something's Coming', 'People',
'Send in the Clowns', 'Over the
Rainbow', 'Guilty' (duet with Barry
Gibb), 'What Kind of Fool' (duet with
Barry Gibb), 'Papa, Can You Hear
Me?', 'The Way We Were', 'It's a New
World', 'Happy Days Are Here Again',
'America the Beautiful'

Hit Number Nine in the charts. Made
Platinum.

..............................................

### Till I Loved You
Columbia, November 1988

Songs: 'The Places You Find Love', 'On
My Way to You', 'Till I Loved You'
(duet with Don Johnson), 'Love
Light', 'All I Ask of You', 'You and Me
For Always', 'Why Let It Go?', 'Two
People', 'What Were We Thinking
Of?', 'Some Good Things Never Last',
'One More Time Around'

Hit Number Ten in the charts. Made
Platinum.

..............................................

### A Collection ... Greatest Hits and More
Columbia, October 1989
Many of these tracks first appeared in other albums.

Songs: 'We're not Making Love Anymore', 'Woman in Love', 'All I Ask of You', 'Comin' In and Out of Your Life', 'What Kind of Fool' (duet with Barry Gibb), 'The Main Event'/'Fight', 'Someone that I Used to Love', 'By the Way', 'Guilty' (duet with Barry Gibb), 'Memory', 'The Way He Makes Me Feel', 'Somewhere'

Hit Number Twenty-Six in the charts. Made Platinum.

........................................................

### Just for the Record
Columbia, September 1991

A four-disc boxed set which includes seventy-seven tracks culled from released and unreleased recordings made by Barbra Streisand over the thirty-one years of her then recording career, along with some material from her private archives, and early television and night-club appearances. The set also came with a booklet of her own album notes and photographs.

Produced by Barbra Streisand and Martin Erlichman
Co-produced by John Arrias
Project co-ordinator: Karen Svenson

Songs from disc 1: 'You'll Never Know' (recorded by Streisand December 1955 at the age of thirteen), 'A Sleepin' Bee' (April 1961), 'Moon River' (January 1962), 'Miss Marmelstein' (December 1962), 'Happy Days Are Here Again' (May 1962); selections from Live at the Bon Soir) previously unreleased material, recorded November 1962, which was to have been Streisand's first album): 'Keepin' Out of Mischief Now', 'I Hate Music', 'Nobody's Heart (Belongs to Me)', 'Value', 'Cry Me a River', 'Who's Afraid of the Big Bad Wolf', ('I Had Myself a) True Love', 'Lover Come Back to Me', 'Spring Can Really Hang You Up the Most' (February 1963), 'My Honey's Lovin' Arms' (February 1963), 'Any Place I Hang My Hat Is Home' (August 1963), 'When the Sun Comes Out' (June 1963); from *The Judy Garland Show* (October 1963): 'Be My Guest' (with Judy Garland and Ethel Merman), medleys with Garland: 'Hooray for Love'/'After You've Gone'/'By Myself'/''s Wonderful'/('I Like New York in June) How About You?'/'Lover Come Back to Me'/'You and the Night and the Music'/'It All Depends on You'/'Get Happy'/'Happy Days Are Here Again'

Songs from disc 2: 'I'm the Greatest Star' (March 1964); closing night of *Funny Girl*, Winter Garden Theatre, 26 December 1965: 'My Man'/'Auld Lang Syne'; 'People' (September 1964), 'Second Hand Rose' (sung by Diana Streisand Kind, a home recording made April 1965), 'Second Hand Rose' (as part of Act II medley of TV show, *My Name is Barbra*, April 1965), 'He Touched Me' (October 1965), 'You Wanna Bet' (December 1965), 'House of Flowers'/'Ding, Dong the Witch Is Dead' (April 1966); ('Have I Stayed) Too Long at the Fair'/'Look At that Face'/'Starting Here, Starting Now' (from TV show, *Color Me Barbra*, March 1966), 'A Good Man Is Hard to Find'/'Some of These Days'/'I'm Always Chasing

Rainbows' (from TV show, *The Belle of Fourteenth Street*, October 1967); 'Sleep in Heavenly Peace (Holy Night)' (from TV show, *A Happening in Central Park*, September 1968); 'Don't Rain on My Parade'/'Funny Girl' (October 1968); 'Hello, Dolly!' (July 1969); 'On a Clear Day (You Can See Forever)' (August 1969); 'When You Gotta Go'/'In the Wee Small Hours of the Morning' (recorded and previously unreleased at the International Hotel, Las Vegas, July 1969).

Songs from disc 3: (previously unreleased from aborted album, March 1970) 'The Singer'/'I Can Do It', 'Stoney End'; '(They Long to Be) Close to You' (*The Burt Bacharach Special*, March 1971); 'We've Only Just Begun' (previously unreleased, April 1971); 'Since I Fell for You' (August 1971); 'You're the Top' (with Ryan O'Neal, March 1972); 'What Are You Doing the Rest of Your Life?' (home recording, summer 1972, previously unreleased); 'If I Close My Eyes' (December 1972); 'Between Yesterday and Tomorrow'/'Can You Tell the Moment?' (previously unreleased, April 1973); 'The Way We Were' (soundtrack version); 'Cryin' Time' (November 1973); 'God Bless the Child'/'A Quiet Thing'/'There Won't Be Trumpets' (unreleased tracks, March 1974); 'Lost Inside of You' (spring 1976); 'Evergreen' (November 1977); 'Hatikvah' (May 1978).

Songs from disc 4: 'You Don't Bring Me Flowers' (with Neil Diamond, February 1980); 'The Way We Weren't'/'The Way We Were' (June 1980); 'Guilty' (October 1980); 'Papa, Can You Hear Me?' 'The Moon and

I'/'A Piece of Sky' (audition tape, spring 1981, for *Yentl*); 'A Piece of Sky' (November 1983); 'I Know Him So Well' (previously unreleased, August 1985); 'If I Loved You'/'Putting It Together' (November 1985); 'Over the Rainbow' (September 1986); theme from *Nuts* (composed by Barbra Streisand, released December 1987); 'Here We Are at Last' (music by Barbra Streisand, lyrics by Richard Baskin, June 1984); 'Warm All Over' (April 1988); 'You'll Never Know' (April 1988).

Hit Number Thirty-Eight in the charts. Made Platinum.

........................................

### The Prince of Tides
Columbia, December 1991
Motion-picture sound track

Produced by Barbra Streisand and James Newton Howard
Arranged by James Newton Howard

Songs: 'For All We Know', 'Places that Belong to You' (the rest of the album is instrumental music).

........................................

### Back to Broadway
Columbia, July 1993

Produced by Barbra Streisand, David Foster, Andrew Lloyd Webber and Nigel Wright

Songs: 'Some Enchanted Evening' (arranged by Johnny Mandel and David Foster), 'Everybody Says Don't' (arranged by Barbra Streisand and Bill Ross), 'The Music of the Night' (duet with Michael Crawford, arranged and conducted by Andrew Pryce Jackman for the London Symphony

Orchestra), 'Speak Low' (arranged by Johnny Mandel and David Foster), 'As If We Never Said Goodbye' (arranged by Andrew Lloyd Webber, John Cameron and David Cullen), 'Children Will Listen' (arranged and conducted by Jonathan Tunick), 'I Have a Love'/'One Hand, One Heart' (arranged by David Foster and Bill Ross), 'I've Never Been in Love Before' (arranged and conducted by Jeremy Lubbock), 'Luck Be a Lady' (arranged and conducted by Jeremy Lubbock), 'With One Look' (arranged by Andrew Lloyd Webber and David Cullen), 'The Man I Love' (arranged by Johnny Mandel), 'Move On' (arranged and conducted by Michael Starobin)

Hit Number One in the charts. Made double Platinum.

...................................................

### Duets
Capital, October 1993

Executive producers, Charles Koppelman, Eliot Weisman and Don Rubin
Produced by Phil Ramone
Co-produced by Hank Cattaneo

This is a Frank Sinatra album in which he sings duets with other singers. Streisand paired with him on 'I've Got a Crush on You'.

...................................................

### Barbra: The Concert
Columbia, September 1994
Two discs

Produced by Barbra Streisand and Jay Landers
Numerous arrangers
Conducted by Martin Hamlisch

Songs on disc 1: 'As If We Never Said Goodbye', 'I'm Still Here'/'Everybody Says Don't'/'Don't Rain on My Parade', 'Can't Help Lovin' that Man', 'I'll Know', 'People', 'Lover Man', 'Will He Like Me?', 'He Touched Me', 'Evergreen', 'The Man that Got Away', 'On a Clear Day'

Songs on disc 2: 'The Way We Were', 'You Don't Bring Me Flowers', 'Lazy Afternoon'; medley: 'Once Upon a Dream'/'When You Wish Upon a Star'/'Someday My Prince Will Come'; 'Not While I'm Around', 'Ordinary Miracles', medley: 'Where Is It Written?'/'Papa, Can You Hear Me?'/'Will Someone Ever Look At Me That Way?'/'A Piece of Sky'; 'Happy Days Are Here Again', 'For All We Know', 'Somewhere'

Hit Number Ten in the charts. Made double Platinum.

Special Grammy Award: Lifetime Achievement Award

...................................................

### The Garland Duets
Paragon 1001

A collection of duets from the Judy Garland television show includes the Garland–Streisand 'Be My Guest', 'Get Happy/Happy Days are Here Again', and 'Hooray for Love'

This material minus the 'Be My Guest' duet but containing the segment with Ethel Merman is available on the home video release, Judy Garland and Friends.

Streisand has also recorded numerous singles some of which, including a deleted stage version of Funny Girl, have never been otherwise released.

# Theatre

## Another Evening with Harry Stoones

Gramercy Arts Theater ........... Opened
21/10/61
Produced by ...................... Jeff Harris
Directed by ............... G. Adam Jordan
Music ............................. Jeff Harris
Music Director ................ Abba Bogin

*Cast*

Susan Belink (later known as Susan
Belling), Dom de Luise, Barbra
Streisand, Sheila Copelan, Virgil Curry,
Diana Sands, Kenny Adams and Ben
Keller.

Songs: 'Jersey' and 'Value'

Closed 21/10/61

..................................................

## I Can Get It for You Wholesale

Shubert Theater ......... Opened 22/3/62
Produced by ............... David Merrick
Directed by ............... Arthur Laurents
Book (based on his novel) ........ Jerome
Weidman
Music and lyrics ............. Harold Rome
Orchestrations ................... Sid Ramin
Musical direction ......... Lehman Engel
Choreographer .................. Herb Ross
Dance arrangements ...... Peter Howard
Costumes ................. Theoni Aldredge
Sets and lighting ......... Will Stevenson
Armstrong
Production supervisor ...... Neil Hartley

*Cast*

Harry Bogen .................. Elliott Gould
Mr Pulvermacher .......... Jack Kurschen
Mrs Bogen (Momma) ........ Lillian Roth
Martha Mills ................. Sheree North
Ruthie Rivkin ........... Marilyn Cooper
Teddy Asch ................... Harold Lang
Miss Marmelstein ....... Barbra Streisand
Blanche Maltz ................. Bambi Linn
Tootsie Maltz ............. James Hickman
Meyer Bushkin ................ Ken LeRoy
Sheldon Maltz ................ Steve Curry

Songs: 'I'm Not a Well Man', 'The Way
Things Are', 'When Gemini Meets
Capricorn', 'Momma, Momma,
Momma', 'The Sound of Money', 'Too
Soon', 'The Family Way', 'Who
Knows?', 'Ballad of the Garment Trade',
'Have I Told You Lately?', 'A Gift Today',
'Miss Marmelstein', 'A Funny Thing
Happened', 'What's in It for Me?', 'Eat
a Little Something', 'What Are They
Doing to Us?'

Songs: 'Miss Marmelstein'

Closed 8/12/62 – 300 performances

..................................................

## Funny Girl

Winter Garden ........... Opened 26/3/64
Producer ......... Ray Stark in association
with Seven Arts
Production Director ....... Garson Kanin

Book.......................... Isobel Lennart
Story......................... Isobel Lennart
Music.............................Jule Styne
Lyrics............................ Bob Merrill
Choreography ................Carol Haney
Musical director ..... Milton Rosenstock
Orchestrations................ Ralph Burns
Dance orchestrations ...............Luther
                                        Henderson
Scenery and lighting..Robert Randolph
Costumes...................... Irene Sharaff
Vocal arrangements .........Buster Davis
Production supervisor .... David Pardoll
Associate director ....... Lawrence Kasha

*Cast*

Fanny Brice...............Barbra Streisand
Nick Arnstein ............Sydney Chaplin
Rose Brice ..................... Kay Medford
Eddie Ryan.................Danny Meehan
Mrs Strakosh ...............Jean Stapleton
Florenz Ziegfeld, Jr......Roger De Koven
Tom Keeney .............Joseph Macaulay
Heckie........................Victor R. Helou
Mrs Meeker............Lydia S. Fredericks
Mrs O'Malley..................Joyce O'Neil
Zeigfeld tenor..............John Lankston
Vera (also understudy)..... Lainie Kazan
With: Buzz Miller, George Reeder, Royce
Wallace, Robert Howard, Buzz Miller,

Alan Weeks, Dick Perry, Joan Cory, Rose
Randolf

Songs: 'Sadie, Sadie',* 'Find Yourself a
Man', 'If a Girl Isn't Pretty', 'I'm the
Greatest Star',* 'Coronet Man',* 'Who
Taught Her Everything',* 'His Love
Makes Me Beautiful', 'I Want to Be Seen
with You',* 'Henry Street', 'People',*
'You Are Woman',* 'Don't Rain on My
Parade',* 'Rat-Tat-Tat-Tat',* 'Who Are
You Now?',* 'The Music that Makes Me
Dance'*

*Song by Streisand

Closed 1/7/67

1,348 performances

..................................................

### Funny Girl (London Production)
St James's Theatre.......Opened 13/4/66
Production directed by Lawrence Kasha
Fanny Brice...............Barbra Streisand
Nick Arnstein ...............Michael Craig
Rose Brice ..................... Kay Medford

Songs: as above

Closed 15/7/66

# Film Cast and Credits

## Funny Girl

Columbia Pictures ..................... 1968
Producer............................ Ray Stark
Director...................... William Wyler
Screenplay .................. Isobel Lennart
Musical sequences director-
    choreographer .............Herbert Ross
Photography .............. Harry Stradling
Production designer.... Robert Luthardt
Set decoration .......... William Kiernan
Songs........... Jule Styne/Robert Merrill
Music director ..............Walter Scharf
Sound ....................... Charles J. Rice
Film editor............. Maury Winetrobe,
                              William Sands
Costumes..................... Irene Sharaff

### Cast

Fanny Brice...............Barbra Streisand
Nick Arnstein ................. Omar Sharif
Florenz Ziegfeld .......... Walter Pidgeon
Rose Brice ..................... Kay Medford
Eddie Ryan......................... Lee Allen
Georgia James................ Anne Francis

Academy Award: Best Actress, Barbra
Streisand (shared with Katharine
Hepburn)
Academy Award Nomination: Best
Picture, Harry Stradling, Best
Supporting Actress, Kay Medford
Best Title Song, Jule Styne and Robert
Merrill

.................................................

## Hello, Dolly!

Twentieth Century-Fox .............. 1969
Producer.................... Ernest Lehman
Associate Producer........... Roger Edens
Director........................... Gene Kelly
Screenplay ................. Ernest Lehman
Book (musical).......... Michael Stewart
Play (*The Matchmaker*) Thornton Wilder
Photography .............. Harry Stradling
Production designer........ John de Cuir
Set decoration.......... George Hopkins,
          Wallace Scott, Raphael Britton
Art direction......... John Martin Smith,
                   Herman Roseberg
Music direction...........Lennie Hayton,
                     Lionel Newman
Costumes..................... Irene Sharaff
Songs......................... Jerry Herman
Choreographer ..............Michael Kidd
Dance arrangements ....... Marvin Laird
Sound ....................... Jack Solomon,
     Douglas Williams, Murray Spivak,
                     Vincent Vernon
Film editor.............. William Reynolds

### Cast

Dolly Levi ................. Barbra Streisand
Horace Vandergelder... Walter Matthau
Cornelius Hackl ...... Michael Crawford
Barnaby Tucker............ Danny Lockin
Irene Molloy ...... Marianne McAndrew
Minnie Fay........................ E.J. Peaker

Academy Awards: Music Direction, Art
Direction, Set Decoration

Academy Award Nomination: Best
Picture, Photography

.......................................................

### On a Clear Day You Can See Forever
Koch/Lerner-Paramount ............. 1970
Producer..................Howard W. Koch
Director................. Vincente Minnelli
Screenplay ................. Alan Jay Lerner
Photography .............. Harry Stradling
Production designer........ John de Cuir
Set decoration .......... George Hopkins,
Raphael Bretton
Songs: Burton Lane, Alan Jay lerner
Music supervisor-
arranger-conductor.....Nelson Riddle
Choreography ............ Howard Jeffrey
Sound Benjamin Wingler, Elden Ruberg
Film editor.............. David Bretherton

### Cast

Daisy Gamble/
Melinda Tentrees.....Barbra Streisand
Dr Marc Chabot........... Yves Montand
Warren Pratt.................. Larry Blyden
Dr Mason Hume ............ Bob Newhart
Ted Pringle................. Jack Nicholson
Robert Tentrees.........John Richardson
With: Simon Oakland, Pamela Brown,
Irene Handl, Mabel Albertson, Leon
Ames

.......................................................

### The Owl and the Pussycat
Columbia/Rastar ....................... 1970
Producer........................... Ray Stark
Director.........................Herbert Ross
Screenplay ......................Buck Henry
From the play by............ Bill Manhoff
Photography ............. Harry Stradling,
Andrew Laszlo
Music.....................William Saracino
Music director .......... Richard Halligan
Production designer.John Robert Lloyd
Art direction......... Robert Wrightman,
Philip Rosenberg

Set decoration ............Leif Pedderson
Sound .................. Arthur Piontodosi,
Dennis Maitland
Film editor................. John F. Burnett

### Cast

Doris........................Barbra Streisand
Felix Sherman............... George Segal
Barney ..........................Robert Klein
Eleanor............................. Roz Kelly
Landlord .....................Allen Garfield

.......................................................

### What's Up, Doc?
Warner/Saticoy ......................... 1972
Producer.............. Peter Bogdanovich
Director............... Peter Bogdanovich
Screenplay ..................... Buck Henry,
David Newman, Robert Benton
Photography ................ Laszlo Kovacs
Production designer...........Polly Pratt
Art director .........Herman Blumenthal
Set decoration ................John Aichen
Music director ................. Artie Butler
Music supervisor ...............Ray Phelps

### Cast

Judy Maxwell ............Barbra Streisand
Howard Bannister...........Ryan O'Neal
Eunice.......................Madeline Kahn
Frederick Larrabee .... Austin Pendleton
Hugh Simons...............Kenneth Mars
Mrs Van Hoskins....... Mabel Anderson

.......................................................

### Up the Sandbox
Barwood/First Artists.................. 1972
Producers.................Robert Chartoff,
Irwin Winkler
Associate producer.....Marty Erlichman
Director.....................Irvin Kirshner
Screenplay ..................... Paul Zindel
Novel.......... Anne Richardson Riophe
Photography ...............Gordon Willis,
Andy Morton

Art director ................. Harry Horner
Music director .......... Billy Goldenberg
Set director ............... Robert de Vestel
Sound ........................ Keith Stafford
Film editor ............... Robert Lawrence
Casting director ............. Cis Corman
Costumes.................... Albert Wolsky

## Cast

Margaret Reynolds...... Barbra Streisand
Dr Beineke ................... Paul Benedict
With: David Selby, Ariane Heller, Jane
Hoffman, John C. Becker, Jacabo
Morales, Barbara Rhoades, Stockard
Channing, Isobel Sanford, Conrad
Bain, Paul Dooley, Anne Ramsey

...................................................

## The Way We Were
Columbia/Rastar ...................... 1973
Producer........................... Ray Stark
Director.................... Sydney Pollack
Screenplay ............... Arthur Laurents
Novel...................... Arthur Laurents
Photography .......... Harry Stradling Jr.
Music director ......... Marvin Hamlisch
Title song.............. Marvin Hamlisch,
                Alan and Marilyn Bergman
Production designer.... Stephen Grimes
Set decoration.......... William Kiernan
Sound ........................ Jack Solomon
Film editor ............... Margaret Booth
Costumes................. Dorothy Jenkins,
                               Moss Maybry

## Cast

Katie Morosky ........... Barbra Streisand
Hubbell Gardiner ........ Robert Redford
Carol Ann....................... Lois Chiles
George Bissinger .......... Patrick O'Neal
J.J. ............................ Brad Dillman
Paula Reisner.............. Viveca Lindfors
Hedda Hopper ......... Marcia Mae Jones
Rhea Edwards ........ Allyn Ann McLerie
Bill Verso ................... Herb Edelman

Brooks Carpenter ..... Murray Hamilton
With: Sally Kirkland, Diana Ewing, Eric
Boles, Don Keefer, Dan Seymour,
George Gaynes

Academy Award: Best Title Song,
Marvin Hamlisch (music), Alan and
Marilyn Bergman (lyrics)
Academy Award Nominations: Best
Actress, Barbra Streisand, photography,
Harry Stradling, Jr

...................................................

## For Pete's Sake
Columbia/Raystar/Persky-Bright-
Barclay .................................... 1974
Executive producer ......... Phil Feldman
Producers............... Martin Erlichman,
                             Stanley Shapiro
Director.......................... Peter Yates
Screenplay ............... Stanley Shapiro,
                             Maurice Richlin
Photography ................ Laszlo Kovacs
Music director ................. Artie Butler
Title song.... Artie Butler, Mark Lindsay
Film editor ................. Frank P. Keller
Sound ........................... Don Parker
Costumes............... Frank Thompson
Hairstyles......................... Jon Peters

## Cast

Henrietta Robbins ...... Barbra Streisand
Pete Robbins ............ Michael Sarrazin
Mrs Robbins ............... Estelle Parsons
Fred ....................... William Redfield
Mrs Cherry ................... Molly Picon
Nick............................ Louis Zorich
Loretta ..................... Vivian Bonnell
Bernie ....................... Richard Ward
Judge Hiller........ Heywood Hale Broun

...................................................

## Funny Lady
Columbia/Rastar/
    Persky-Bright/Vista ................. 1975
Producer........................... Ray Stark

Director..........................Herbert Ross
Screenplay ..............Jay Presson Allen,
Arnold Schulman
Story......................Arnold Schulman
Photography .........James Wong Howe
Music director .................. Peter Matz
Original songs .. John Kander, Fred Ebb
Production design ....... George Jenkins
Costumes.....Ray Aghayan, Bob Mackie
Film editor.............. Marion Rothman
Sound ........................Jack Solomon

*Cast*

Fanny Brice...............Barbra Streisand
Billy Rose........................James Caan
Nick Arnstein ................. Omar Sharif
With: Ben Vereen, Roddy McDowall,
Carole Wells, Larry Gates, Heidi
O'Rourke, Samantha Huffaker, Matt
Emery, Joshua Shelley, Corey Fischer

Academy Award Nomination:
Photography, James Wong Howe, Peter
Matz, Song: 'How Lucky Can You Get'
(John Kander, Fred Ebb)

..................................................

### A Star Is Born

Warner Bros/First Artists ............. 1976
A Barwood/Jon Peters Production
Executive Producer .....Barbra Streisand
Producer..........................Jon Peters
Director...................... Frank Pierson
Screenplay ........ John Gregory Dunne,
Joan Didion, Frank Pierson
Story. William Wellman, Robert Carson
Photography .............. Robert Surtees
Film editor......................Paul Zinner
Production designer...........Polly Platt
Musical concepts........Barbra Streisand
Music producer.............. Phil Ramone
Music underscore ........ Roger Kellaway
Music supervision ......... Paul Williams
Music conductor ..........Kenny Ascher
Set decorator .................. Ruby Levitt
Art director ................William Hiney

Choreography ............. David Winters
Sound .....Robert Knudson, Dan Wallis,
Robert Glass and Tom Overton

*Cast*

Esther Hoffman .........Barbra Streisand
John Norman Howard......................
........................... Kris Kristofferson
Bobby Ritchie.................. Gary Busey
Gary Danzinger ............. Oliver Clark
The Oreos.. Vanetta Fields, Clydie King
Quentin ...................... Marta Heflin
Bebe Jesus........................ M.G. Kelly
With: Sally Kirkland, Joanne Linville,
Paul Mazursky

Academy Award: Original Song,
'Evergreen' music by Barbra Streisand
(music), Paul Williams (lyrics)
Academy Award Nomination:
Photography, Robert Surtees, Original
Song Score, Roger Kellaway, Sound

..................................................

### The Main Event

Warner Bros/First Artist/Barwood . 1979
Producers...Barbra Streisand, Jon Peters
Director........................Howard Zieff
Screenplay . Gail Parent, Andrew Smith
Photography .................... Mario Tosi
Production designer...... Charles Rosen
Music....................Michael Melvoin,
Paul Jabara, Bruce Roberts
Music supervisor ............. Gary Le Mel
Music editor.............William Saracino
Film editor............ Edward Warschlika
Set designer...................James Payne
Original songs performed by Barbra
Streisand: 'The Main Event' by Paul
Jabara and Bruce Robert, 'Fight' by Paul
Jabara and Bob Esty

*Cast*

Hillary Kramer...........Barbra Streisand
Eddie Scanlon
(Kid Natural) ...............Ryan O'Neal

David............................ Paul Sand
Percy........................ Whitman Mayo
Donna Rochester......Patti D'Arbanville
Leo Gough..................James Gregory
With: Chu Chu Malave, Richard
Altman, Joe Amaler, Seth Banks,
Lindsay Bloom, Eal Bowen, Roger
Bowen, Sue Casey

### All Night Long
Universal................................1981
Producers.............. Leonard Goldberg,
Jerry Weintraub
Director.............Jean-Claude Tramont
Screenplay .................... W.D. Richter
Photography ............... Philip Lathrop
Production designer....... Peter Jamison
Music directors ..............Ira Newborn,
Richard Hazard

*Cast*

George Dopler ............Gene Hackman
Cheryl Gibbons .........Barbra Streisand
Freddie........................Dennis Quaid
Bobby Gibbons............ Kevin Dobson
Helen Dopler................... Diane Ladd
With: Ann Doran, William Daniels

### Yentl
MGM/UA ...............................1983
Executive producer.......Larry De Waay
Producers................Barbra Streisand,
Rusty Lemorande
Director....................Barbra Streisand
Screenplay .................Jack Rosenthal,
Barbra Streisand
Story..................Isaac Bashevis Singer
Photography ...............David Watkin
Production designer.......... Ray Walker
Film editor..................Terry Rawlings
Art direction...............Leslie Tomkins
Set director ...................'. Tessa Davies
Music director ........... Michel Legrand
Music......................Michel Legrand,
lyrics by Marilyn and Alan Bergman

Costumes...................Judy Moorcroft
Casting director .............. Cis Corman
Musical sequences staged by Barbra
Streisand

*Cast*

Yentl........................Barbra Streisand
Avigdor ....................Mandy Patinkin
Hadass .......................... Amy Irving
Papa .....................Nehemiah Persoff
Reb Alter Vishkower ..........Steven Hill
Shimmele .................. Alan Corduner

Academy Award: Best Score
Academy Award Nominations: Music
direction, Best Song ('Papa, Can You
Hear Me?'), Art Direction, Best
Supporting Actress (Amy Irving)

### Nuts
Warner Bros ............................1987
Producer...................Barbra Streisand
Director..........................Martin Ritt
Screenplay ...................... Tom Toper,
Darryl Ponicsan, Alvin Sargent
Play ............................... Tom Toper
Photography ........ Andrzej Bartkowiak
Art director ..................... Eric Orbom
Set director ................. Ann McCully
Film editors...... Rick Spare, Jeff Werner
Sound editors ............ Julia Evershade,
Virginia Cook-McGowan
Music arranger and
conductor ............. Jeremy Lubbock
Music......................Barbra Streisand

*Cast*

Claudia Draper ..........Barbra Streisand
Aaron Levinsky.........Richard Dreyfuss
Arthur Kirk .................... Karl Malden
Rose Kirk .............. Maureen Stapleton
Judge Murdoch .........James Whitmore
Dr Herbert Morrison ......... Eli Wallach

With: Leslie Neilson, William Prince,
Dakin Matthews, Robert Webber,
Hayley Taylor Block

..................................................

### The Prince of Tides
Columbia Pictures .....................1991
Producers................ Barbra Streisand,
Andrew Karsh
Director....................Barbra Streisand
Screenplay Pat Conroy, Becky Johnston
Novel............................ Pat Conroy
Photography .......... Stephen Goldblatt
Production designer..........Paul Sylbert
Music director... James Newton Howard

*Cast*

Tom Wingo...................... Nick Nolte
Dr Susan Lowenstein ..Barbra Streisand
Lila Wingo ................... Kate Nelligan
Sallie Wingo................Blythe Danner
Bernard Woodruff ...........Jason Gould
Herbert Woodruff..........Jeroen Krabbe
Savannah Wingo......... Melinda Dillon
Eddie Detreville ............George Carlin
Henry Wingo ................Brad Sullivan

Academy Award Nominations: Best
Picture, Best Actor, Nick Nolte, Best
Supporting Actress, Kate Nelligan,
Music, Photography, Sound

..................................................

### The Mirror Has Two Faces
TriStar Pictures/Columbia ...........1996
Executive Producer.......... Cis Corman
Producers.................Arnon Milchon,
Barbra Streisand
Screenplay ...........Robert LaGravenese
Director....................Barbra Streisand
Photography ..............Dante Spinotti,
Andrzej Bartkowiak
Production designer............ Tom John
Film editors..... Alan Heim, Jeff Werner
Costumes................. Theoni Aldredge
Sound .......................... Tom Nelson

*Cast*

Rose.........................Barbra Streisand
Craig..............................Jeff Bridges
With: Pierce Brosnan, George Segal,
Mimi Rogers, Brenda Vaccaro, Ell
Macpherson, Lauren Bacall

# Television Credits

**The Jack Paar Show**
NBC/TV, New York City, 5 April 1961

Host: Orson Bean

Streisand sang 'A Sleepin' Bee'
.............................................

**PM East**
Group W Television, New York City
Streisand did thirteen shows from
October 1961 to January 1962.

Host: Mike Wallace
.............................................

**The Joe Franklin Show**
Channel 11, New York City

Host: Joe Franklin

Streisand did three late-night talk
shows in the autumn of 1961.
.............................................

**The Gary Moore Show**
CBS-TV, Los Angeles, 29 May 1961

Host: Gary Moore

Streisand sang 'Happy Days Are Here
Again'
.............................................

**The Tonight Show**
NBC/TV, New York City, November
1962–February, 1963.

Host: Johnny Carson

Streisand made four appearances.

The shows were live and very few of the
early shows were taped. On one taped
show she sang 'Spring Can Really Hang
You Up the Most'.
.............................................

**The Ed Sullivan Show**
CBS/TV, New York City, 9 June 1963

Host: Ed Sullivan

Streisand sang, 'When the Sun Comes
Out'. On other Sullivan shows
Streisand sang 'Lover Come Back to
Me', 'My Coloring Book', 'Cry Me a
River'.
.............................................

**The Bob Hope Show**
CBS/TV, 1962

Streisand did a hillbilly routine with
Hope and 'Miss Marmelstein'.
.............................................

**The Judy Garland Show**
CBS/TV, Los Angeles, 6 October 1963
Musical director, Mel Tormé

Host: Judy Garland

Guests: Barbra Streisand, the Smother Brothers, Ethel Merman

Streisand sang: a duet with Garland ('Be My Guest'). Medley with Garland: 'Hooray For Love'/'Lover Come Back to Me'/'After You've Gone'/'By Myself'/'How About You'/'You and the Night and the Music'/'It All Depends on You'. Duet with Garland: 'Get Happy'/'Happy Days are Here Again'. Trio with Garland and Ethel Merman: 'There's No Business Like Show Business'. Solo: 'Down with Love', 'Bewitched, Bothered and Bewildered'.

(There is also a video release *Judy (Garland) and Friend* containing the complete Streisand appearance with the exclusion of the 'Be My Guest' duet.)

.................................................

### My Name Is Barbra
CBS/TV, New York City, 28 April 1965
Black and white

Host: Barbra Streisand
Executive producer Martin Erlichman
Produced by Dwight Hemion
Directed by Joe Layton
Arranged and conducted by Peter Matz
Set designs Tom John

Songs, Act One: 'My Name Is Barbra', 'Much More', 'I'm Late', 'Make Believe', 'How Does the Wine Taste?', 'A Kid Again', 'I'm Five', 'Jenny Rebecca', 'My Pa', 'Sweet Zoo', 'Where Is the Wonder?', ''People'.
Songs, Act Two: 'Second Hand Rose'. Medley: 'Give Me the Simple Life'/'I Got Plenty of Nothin''/'Brother Can You Spare a Dime?'/'Nobody Knows You When You're Down and Out'/'The Best Things in Life Are Free'.
Songs, Act Three: 'When the Sun Comes Out', 'Why Did I Choose You?', 'Lover Come Back to Me', 'You Are Woman', 'Don't Rain on My Parade', 'The Music that Makes Me Dance', 'My Man', 'Happy Days Are Here Again.'

.................................................

### Color Me Barbra
CBS/TV, New York City and Philadelphia, 30 March 1966
Colour

Host: Barbra Streisand
Executive producer Martin Erlichman
Produced by Dwight Hemion
Directed by Joe Layton
Arranged and conducted by Peter Matz
Set designs Tom John

Songs, Act One: 'Draw Me a Circle', 'Yesterday', 'One Kiss', 'The Minute Waltz', 'Gotta Move', 'Non C'est Rien', 'Where or When?'
Songs, Act Two: Medley: 'Animal Crackers in My Soup'/'Funny Face'/'That Face'/'They Didn't Believe Me'/'Where Thine That Special Face'/'I've Grown Accustomed to Her Face'/'Let's Face the Music and Dance', 'Sam You Made the Pants Too Long', 'What's New Pussycat?', 'Who's Afraid of the Big Bad Wolf?', 'Small World', 'Try to Remember', 'Spring Again', 'Have I Stayed too Long at the Fair?', 'Look at that Face'.
Songs, Act Three: 'Any Place I Hang My Hat Is Home', 'It Had To Be You', 'C'est Si Bon', 'Where Am I Going?', 'Starting Here, Starting Now'.

.................................................

### The Belle of 14th Street
CBS/TV, New York City, 11 October 1967
Colour

Host: Barbra Streisand
Co-Stars: Jason Robards, Jr, John

Bubbles, Lee Allen and the Beef Trust Line
Executive producer Martin Erlichman
Produced by Dwight Hemion
Directed by Joe Layton
Arranged and conducted by Peter Matz
Art direction Tom John

Songs: 'I Don't Care', 'Sweet Little Alice Blue Gown'. With Robards and Allen: 'We're Two (Three, Four, Five) Americans'; 'Liebestraum', 'Mother MacCree', 'Hark! I Hear Them' (adapted from Shakespeare's *The Tempest*), 'My Melancholy Baby', 'Everybody Loves My Baby (But My Baby Don't Love Nobody But Me)/A Good Man Is Hard to Find', 'Some of These Days', 'How About Me?', 'I'm Always Chasing Rainbows', 'My Buddy', 'Put Your Arms Around Me, Honey.'
Sung by others: 'You're the Apple of My Eye', 'I'm Going South'.

......................................................

## A Happening in Central Park
CBS/TV, filmed live on 17 June 1967 in New York City
Released 16 September 1968
Colour

Executive producer Martin Erlichman
Produced by Robert Shereer
Associate producer James S. Stanley
Music director Mort Lindsey
Art director Tom John
Costumes by Irene Sharraff

Songs: 'The Nearness of You', 'Down with Love', 'Love Is Like a New Born Child', 'Cry Me a River', 'I Can See It', 'Love Is a Bore', 'He Touched Me', 'I'm All Smiles', 'Value', 'Marty the Martian', 'Natural Sounds', 'Second Hand Rose', 'People', '(Sleep in Heavenly Peace) Silent Night', 'Happy Days Are Here Again'.

......................................................

## The Burt Bacharach Special
CBS/TV, Los Angeles, 14 March 1971
Colour

Host: Burt Bacharach
Special guest: Barbra Streisand

Arranged and conducted by Burt Bacharach

Songs: Streisand sang: 'One Less Bell to Answer'/'A House Is Not a Home' in duet with herself. With Bacharach at piano and in duet '(They Long to Be) Close to You', and 'Somewhere in this World'.

......................................................

## Barbra Streisand ... and Other Musical Instruments
CBS/TV, London, 2 November 1973
Colour

Executive producer Martin Erlichman
Concept Ken and Mitzie Welch

Guest stars: Ray Charles, Dominic Savage

Songs: 'Piano Practicing', 'I've Got Rhythm', 'Johnny One Note'/'One Note Samba', 'Glad To Be Unhappy'. Medley: 'People'/'Second Hand Rose'/'Don't Rain on My Parade'. 'Don't Ever Leave Me', 'By Myself', 'Come Back to Me', 'I Never Has Seen Snow', 'Auf dem Wasser zu Singen', 'The World Is a Concerto', 'Make Your Own Kind of Music', 'The Sweetest Sounds'.

......................................................

## Dick Cavett Special
CBS/TV, 1975

Host: Dick Cavett
Guest Stars: Barbra Streisand, James Caan

Songs: 'The Way We Were', 'Don't Rain on My Parade', 'My Man', 'The Man I Love'. Duet with Caan from *Funny Lady*, 'It's Only a Paper Moon', 'I Like Him (Her)'; 'How Lucky Can You Get'.

....................................................

### The Stars Salute Israel at 30
ABC/TV, Los Angeles, 8 May 1978
Colour

Host: Barbra Streisand
Special Guest: Prime Minister Golda Meir (interviewed by Streisand via telephone and satellite)

Song: 'Hatikvah'.

....................................................

### 22nd Grammy Awards
CBS/TV, 27 February 1980
Colour

Streisand sang a duet with Neil Diamond: 'You Don't Bring Me Flowers'.

....................................................

### Putting It Together – The Making of the Broadway Album
HBO – CBS Fox Video, April 1986
Filmed 29 October–12 November 1985
A Barwood Film

Executive Producer Barbra Streisand
Produced by Joni Rosen
CBS Co-ordinator Jeanne Mattuissi
Edited by Tom McQuade
Conductor-arranger Peter Matz

Interviewer: William Friedkin
Guest artists for 'Putting It Together': Sidney Pollack, David Geffen, Ken Sylk
'Somewhere' musical video directed by William Friedkin

Songs included: 'Putting It Together',
'Pretty Woman', 'Send in the Clowns', 'Something's Coming', 'If I Loved You', 'Can't Help Lovin' that Man', 'Somewhere'.

....................................................

### One Voice
HBO, originally filmed 6 September 1986

Executive producer Marilyn Bergman
Produced by Martin Erlichman and Barbra Streisand
Co-producer Ellen Krass
Directed by Dwight Hemion
Written by Barbra Streisand and Marilyn and Alan Bergman
Musical producer Richard Baskin
Musical director and conductor Randy Kerber
Producer designer René Lagler

Guest stars: Robin Williams and Barry Gibb

Songs: 'Somewhere', 'Evergreen', 'Something's Coming', 'People', 'Send in the Clowns', 'Over the Rainbow', 'Guilty' (duet with Barry Gibb), 'What Kind of Fool' (duet with Barry Gibb), 'Papa, Can You Hear Me?', 'The Way We Were', 'It's a New World', 'Happy Days Are Here Again', 'America the Beautiful'.

....................................................

### Barbra: The Concert
HBO, April 1995
Repeated on NBC, September 1995
Colour

Production conceived and directed by Barbra Streisand
Executive producer Martin Erlichman
Written by Alan and Marilyn Bergman
Musical direction and arrangements by Marvin Hamlisch

Production designers Marc Brickman and David George
Sound designer Bruce Jackson
Clothes by BSDK (Barbra Streisand/Donna Karan)
Editor Tom McQuade
Special appearance: Mike Meyer
Voice-overs: Steven Susskind, Judith Gordin, Phil Austin

Songs: 'As If We Never Said Goodbye', 'I'm Still Here'/'Everybody Says Don't'/'Don't Rain on My Parade', 'Can't Help Lovin' That Man', 'I'll Know', 'People', 'Lover Man', 'Will He Like Me?', 'He Touched Me', 'Evergreen', 'The Man that Got Away', 'On a Clear Day', 'The Way We Were', 'You Don't Bring Me Flowers', 'Lazy Afternoon'. Disney medley: 'Once Upon a Dream'/'When You Wish Upon a Star'/'Someday My Prince Will Come', 'Not While I'm Around', 'Ordinary Miracles'. Medley: 'Where Is It Written?'/'Papa, Can You Hear Me?'/'Will Someone Ever Look at Me that Way?'/'A Piece of Sky', 'Happy Days Are Here Again', 'For All We Know', 'Somewhere', 'What Are You Doing the Rest of Your Life'*

*There were two recorded versions of the concert: the video release was *Barbra: The Concert Live at the Arrowhead Pond*, Anahem, July 1994 (the laser disc of which includes a bonus track 'What Are You Doing the Rest of Your Life', but excludes the Disney medley. The audio version on Columbia CD, and minicassette, includes the Disney medley and was recorded at Madison Square Garden. The network telecast of the concert included the Disney medley along with other additional material.

Streisand has also given extensive interviews on television programmes that include: *Dick Cavett, Barbara Walters, Sixty Minutes with Mike Wallace, Larry King Live, C-Span* and the *Today Show*. There is also a laser disc narrated by Streisand on the making of *Prince of Tides*.

**As producer:**

..................................................

***Serving in Silence***
The Margarethe Cammermeyer Story
NBC, 6 February 1995

A production of Barwood Films Ltd, Storyline Productions, Inc and Trillium productions Inc. in association with Tristar Television

Executive producers Barbra Streisand, Glenn Close, Craig Zadan, Neil Meron, Cis Corman
Produced by Richard Heus
Screenplay by Alison Cross
Directed by Jeff Bleckner
Music by David Shire
Production consultant Margarethe Cammermeyer

*Cast*

| | |
|---|---|
| Colonel Margarethe Cammermeyer | Glenn Close |
| Diane | Judy Davis |
| Far | Jan Rubes |
| Mary Newcombe | Wendy Makkena |
| Captain Bonnie Kern | Susan Barnes |
| Agent Coleman | William Converse-Roberts |

# Notes

## 1

*This chapter was greatly helped by interviews with Larry Kramer, Maureen Stapleton and others.*

**p. 3** 'Listen, I cried ...', interview, Kramer.

**p. 5** 'I didn't grow up ...', *Los Angeles Times*, 8 December 1991.

**p. 6** 'with the mosaics changing colors ...', Christie's, *Catalogue*, 3 March 1994.

**p. 7** 'I have exciting news ...', Kramer.

**p. 7** 'I was so impressed ...', ibid.

**p. 8** 'I'm at a place in my life ...', interview, Gene Shalit, November 1987.

**p. 9** 'What I found difficult ... control over the story', Kramer.

**p. 9** 'My mother is a perfectionist ...', *New York Times*, 22 December 1991.

**p. 10** 'I felt totally comfortable ...', interview, Gene Shalit, November 1987.

**p. 10** 'I don't believe any of the women ...', private interview.

**p. 10** 'It is fascinating to me ...', *Los Angeles Times*, 8 December 1994.

**p. 11** 'Marty and Barbra didn't always agree ...', interview, Stapleton.

**p. 12** 'learned my own judgement ...', interview, Gene Shalit, November 1987.

**p. 12** 'How old are you?' *Los Angeles Times*, 7 April 1988.

**p. 12** 'the end title music ...', ibid.

**p. 13** 'I'd like you to meet Don Johnson ...', *US*, 3 October 1988.

...............................................

## 2

*This chapter was benefited from numerous personal interviews including that with Maureen Stapleton.*

**p. 16** 'That character ...', *Los Angeles Times*, 24 August 1995.

**p. 17** 'I have this persona ...', ibid.

**p. 17** 'I don't think Barbra ...', private interview.

**p. 17** 'run into the woman ...', Don Johnson interview, *Playboy*.

**p. 18** 'He has a killer instinct ...', private interview.

**p. 18** 'One day, Don said to me ...', *US*, 3 October 1988.

**p. 18** 'Barbra not only ...', ibid.

**p. 18** 'Don makes me feel ...', ibid.

**p. 19** 'It helps to have ...', ibid.

**p. 20** 'When I first read ...', Streisand, record notes, *Just for the Record*.

**p. 20** 'My mother could never make up ...', ibid.

...............................................

## 3

*Camp Cascade and Fleischmanns was reconstructed through numerous personal interviews with attending campers, instructors and the archival records of the area.*

**p. 26** 'There was something about Manny ...', interview.

**p. 27** 'Many of his students ...', interview, Nathan Clark.

**p. 27** 'He was, I think ...', ibid.

**p. 31** 'It was terrible ...', *Daily Mail*, 23 April 1994.

........................................

*4*

*Much of the material on Streisand's family, Brooklyn and the various schools described was obtained through interviews with neighbours, schoolmates and co-workers of the Rosen-Streisand family; through school, city and state records, the archives of Columbia University, Erasmus Hall High School and George Westinghouse Vocational High School (formerly Brooklyn High School for Specialty Trades), and the Brooklyn Historical Society. Erasmus Hall was recreated with the help of former students, teachers and archival material at the school to which I was given access.*

**p. 32** 'Couches to me ...', *Life*, December 1963.

**p. 36** 'It was so strange ...', *Playboy*, October 1977.

**p. 37** 'I remember their taking ...', ibid.

**p. 37** 'I hated those men ...', ibid.

**p. 38** 'You are *not* leaving ...', ibid.

**p. 38** 'He never talked to me ...', ibid.

**p. 39** 'Why do you take *his* side ...', ibid.

**p. 40** 'Barbra was a very complex child ...', *Daily Mail*, 23 April 1994.

**p. 40** 'I knew that she resented ...', ibid.

**p. 40** 'Ever sleep on a couch ...', *Life*, December 1983.

........................................

*5*

**p. 42** 'He was really mean to Barbra ...', *People*, 12 December 1983.

**p. 43** 'When she came home ...', *Daily Mail*, 23 April 1994.

**p. 44** 'When I was nine years old ...', *Playboy*, October 1977.

**p. 44** 'She was critical of me ...', ibid.

**p. 45** 'I was a character in the movie ...', interview, Barbara Walters, Museum of Broadcasting.

**p. 46** 'Somehow, it made me think ...', ibid.

**p. 46** 'a smart-ass remark ...', interview.

**p. 47** 'In every other high school ...', ibid.

**p. 47** 'I never knew how big ...', Frommer and Katz, *It Happened in Brooklyn*, p. 178.

**p. 47** 'between the kids from the poor part ...', ibid.

**p. 47** 'I was never asked to any of the proms ...', *Playboy*, October 1977.

**p. 48** 'some of the kids ...', interview.

**p. 48** 'She often appeared ...', ibid.

**p. 48** 'Why go out for an amateurish ...', *Playboy*, October 1977.

**p. 49** 'great echo sound ...', ibid.

**p. 49** 'It's only wind and noise ...', ibid.

**p. 50** 'My mother went first ...', *Streisand*, record notes, *Just for the Record*.

**p. 52** 'At first, I was awfully disappointed ...', ibid.

**p. 52** 'It was a thrilling experience ...', *Life*, December 1983.

**p. 52** 'I was so sure Barbra ...', *Daily Mail*, 23 April 1994.

........................................

*6*

*Malden Bridge was recreated from interviews with former members of the company and archival material.*

**p. 53** 'I was this absolute misfit ...', interview, Barbara Walters, Museum of Broadcasting.

**p. 53** 'he would sit there ...', *Playboy*, October 1977.

**p. 54** 'Ma, look, one bedroom ...', ibid.

**p. 54** 'I wouldn't take just stuff ...', ibid.

**p. 55** 'Incidentally ...', interview, John Patrick.

**p. 55** 'Can't you just see me ...', *Seventeen Interviews with Film Stars and Super Stars*, Macmillan, New York, 1965, p. 147.

**p. 56** 'I loved the idea ...', *Playboy*, October 1977.

**p. 57** 'There's *something* about her ...', Reise, Randall – *Her Name is Barbra*, p. 48.

**p. 57** 'It was the single *worst* ...', *ibid.*

**p. 57** 'I never meant to neglect ...', *Daily Mail*, 23 April 1994.

**p. 59** 'She was extraordinary ...', interview.

**p. 59** 'A week or two later ...', Riese, Randall – *Her Name is Barbra*, p. 53.

**p. 60** 'I had never been exposed to literature ...', ibid.

**p. 62** 'I learned a lot in Brooklyn ...', *Los Angeles Times*, 16 March 1965.

**p. 62** 'I would read magazines ...', ibid.

**p. 63** 'When I sing ...', ibid.

**p. 63** 'It's not the best production ...', Rivers, *Enter Talking*, p. 59.

**p. 63** 'The place seemed furnished ...', ibid., p. 61.

**p. 64** 'The actual performance ...', ibid., p. 64.

**p. 64** '*She* was going to be ...', Jordan, *The Greatest Star*, p. 31.

**p. 65** 'She was waiflike ...', interview, Milton Mensch.

**p. 65** 'We lived in total poverty ...', Jordan, *The Greatest Star*, p. 32.

**p. 66** 'I kept telling her ...', Riese, Randall – *Her Name is Barbra* p. 59.

**p. 66** 'He was strumming ...', Jordan, *The Greatest Star*, p. 33.

..................................................

**7**

The author conducted interviews with Bob Schulenberg and Barry Dennen for this chapter. Schulenberg and Dennen were also given copies of their previous interviews with Rene Jordan for his 1975 book The Greatest Star *which they claim contained erroneous statements attributed to them. They corrected and amended all quotes used from the book in this chapter. Interviews were also conducted with several other people who were close to Streisand during this formative time in her career.*

**p. 68** 'swathed in cloaks and veils', Jordan, *The Greatest Star*, p. 33.

**p. 68** 'What part ...', ibid.

**p. 69** 'I feel that singing ...', ibid.

**p. 69** 'I hear high range ...', ibid.

**p. 70** 'The whole production was ...', interview, Dennen.

**p. 71** 'We spent the afternoon ...', ibid.

**p. 71** 'Trying this – trying that ...', ibid.

**p. 74** 'I thought ...', Dustin Hoffman, *All about Barbra*, Archives, Motion Picture Academy of Arts and Sciences.

**p. 76** 'The first time I saw her ...', interview, Schulenberg.

**p. 77** 'She and Barry talked about ...', ibid.

**p. 78** 'It looks good', Jordan, *The Greatest Star*, p. 40.

**p. 78** 'Little girl ...', Streisand, record notes, *Just for the Record*.

**p. 78** 'It's curious ...', ibid.

..................................................

**8**

*I am most grateful to the interviews given to me by Arthur Laurents, Lainie Kazan, Bob Shanks and several other people who were involved in or witness to this period in Barbra Streisand's life, which have helped me to reconstruct the scenes in this chapter.*

**p. 81**  'When she got off the ...', Larry Storch, *All About Barbra*, Archives, Motion Picture Academy of Arts and Sciences.

**p. 82**  'A few days later ...', *Life*, 9 January 1970.

**p. 82**  'At the Bon Soir ...', ibid.

**p. 83**  'What do I do?', interview, Dennen.

**p. 84**  'He really cares about me,' interview, Schulenberg.

**p. 84**  'There was a certain date ...', Jordan, *The Greatest Star*, p. 44.

**p. 85**  'They were very short-sighted ...', Jordan, *The Greatest Star*, p. 48.

**p. 85**  'Well, what have you got lined up?', Riese, Randall – *Her Name is Barbra* p. 86.

**p. 85**  'The tapes ...', interview, Dennen.

**p. 85**  'I made her walk ...', *Time*, 10 April 1964.

**p. 86**  'She was half ...', interview, Schulenberg.

**p. 86**  'I said no to Barbra Streisand ...', interview, Bob Shanks.

**p. 87**  'We went over them ...', ibid.

**p. 87**  'a repentant lover ...', ibid.

**p. 87**  'When I sang that ...', *Life*, 22 May 1964.

**p. 88**  'Usually at the end ...', Gavin, *Intimate Nights*, p. 248.

**p. 88**  'Do something!', *Time*, 10 April 1964.

**p. 89**  'I was pretty hard to reach ...', Streisand, record notes, *Just for the Record*.

**p. 89**  'I can't stand it ...', interview, Schulenberg.

**p. 89**  'I wrote that I was born ...', *Wall Street Journal*, 14 May 1993.

**p. 90**  'I remember ...', Jordan, *The Greatest Star*, p. 54.

**p. 91**  'The part I liked best ...', Streisand, record notes, *Just for the Record*.

**p. 93**  'Do you like it?', Howard Kissel, *David Merrick – The Abominable Showman*, Applause Books, New York, 1993, p. 237.

**p. 93**  'Is this girl sane?', ibid.

**p. 93**  'I had never seen her ...', interview, Laurents.

**p. 94**  'When she sang ...', ibid.

**p. 94**  'How many times ...', Kissel, *David Merrick*, p. 237.

**p. 95**  'When I returned ...', *Life*, 22 May 1964.

**p. 95**  'This strange-looking ...', ibid.

**p. 95**  'A freak ...', ibid.

...............................................

**9**

*This chapter has been enormously helped with interviews with Arthur Laurents, Jack Kruschen, Peter Matz, Garson Kanin, John Patrick, Luther Henderson, Lainie Kazan and numerous members of the companies of* I Can Get It for You Wholesale *and* Funny Girl, *and with Arthur Gelb of the New York Times. The author was also given access to Garson Kanin's private* Funny Girl *archival files.*

**p. 99**  'Bad for Barbra ...', interview, Kruschen.

**p. 100**  'I was tough ...', interview, Laurents.

**p. 100**  'She looked like ...', *Playboy*, November 1970.

**p. 101**  'This child was too good to be true,' ibid.

**p. 101**  'He'll never dance,' ibid.

**p. 102**  'When an entertainer ...', ibid.

**p. 102**  'He was always doing bits ...', ibid.

**p. 103**  'I used to hear her warm up ...', interview, Kruschen.

**p. 103**  'Nobody remembers ...', interview, Laurents.

**p. 104**  'Two singers ...', interview, Arthur Gelb.

**p. 104**  'I couldn't believe ...', *All*

*About Barbra*, Archives, Motion Picture Academy of Arts and Sciences.

p. 105 'mousey-coloured hair . . .', ibid.

p. 105 'We were walking around . . .', *Life*, December 1963.

p. 105 'About 4 a.m.', ibid.

p. 106 'The only window . . .', *Playboy*, November 1970.

p. 106 'Get rid of it . . .', Jordan, *The Greatest Star*, p. 69.

p. 106 'I knew no one . . .', interview, Laurents.

p. 107 'I told her . . .', interview, Laurents.

p. 107 'I have dealt with revolting people . . .', Jerome Weidman.

p. 109 'So she came to me crying . . .', ibid.

p. 109 'Barbra decided . . .', *Daily Mail*, November 1994.

..................................................

**10**

p. 110 'It was my love . . .', *Daily Mail*, November 1994.

p. 110 'I don't think she even . . .', ibid.

p. 112 'It was a difficult thing to do . . .', *All About Barbra*, Archives, Motion Picture Academy of Arts and Sciences.

p. 113 'I was very friendly . . .', interview, Laurents.

p. 114 'They brought in a paid audience . . .', Jordan, *The Greatest Star*, p. 182.

p. 116 'I hear that first album . . .', ibid., p. 84.

..................................................

**11**

p. 119 'Elliott even looked . . .', interview.

p. 119 'I liked Ed . . .', Streisand, record notes, *Just for the Record*.

p. 121 '*I'm* still here,' Home Box Office, The Concert.

p. 122 'I didn't have it to pay', *Playboy*, November 1970.

p. 122 'I hope the Dodgers . . .', ibid.

p. 126 'Merrick was never in favor . . .', Jordan, *The Greatest Star*, p. 98.

p. 127 'I pointed out that Bancroft . . .', interview, Patrick.

p. 127 'A classmate of Ray's . . .', ibid.

p. 127 'Ray thought . . .', ibid.

p. 128 'Mr Robbins . . .', ibid.

p. 128 'Isobel was an excellent . . .', interview, Kanin.

p. 129 'I liked Barbra immediately', ibid.

p. 130 'She was playing Streisand's record . . .', Edwards, *Judy Garland*, p. 209.

..................................................

**12**

For this chapter, interviews were conducted with Garson Kanin, Marian Seldes, John Patrick, Luther Henderson, Lainie Kazan, Peter Matz and various other people. Mr Kanin also kindly allowed the author to go through and use material, including letters, in his files from the stage production of Funny Girl, which he directed.

p. 132 'People like to feel miserable . . .', *New Yorker*, November 1929.

p. 132 'It was scary . . .', *Playboy*, October 1977.

p. 135 'If we could give him an image . . .', Kanin's private papers.

p. 136 'Her voice came off . . .', Jimmy Breslin, *Daily News*, 4 December 1965.

p. 136 'Elegance is making an art of life . . .', Kanin's private papers.

p. 137 'Finally, it penetrated . . .', ibid.

p. 138 'Once in a while . . .', interview, Patrick.

p. 138 'It's a front, Barbra . . .', *Life*, 22 May 1964.

p. 139   'a screaming, four-letter fight
...', ibid.
p. 139   'Elliott was fighting ...',
interview.
p. 140   'an absolute hush ...', Taylor,
*Jule*, p. 244.
p. 141   'I got it now ...', ibid., p. 245.
p. 141   'At that moment ...', ibid.

...........................................

### 13

*Many of the quotes in this chapter came
from the same source interviews and
archival material as in previous chapters.
The author also had access to several of
the scripts in progress used during the out-
of-town try-outs and the final production
of* Funny Girl.

p. 142   'She had a killer instinct ...',
interview.
p. 145   'For some reason ...',
interview, Patrick.
p. 145   'Our curtain went down ...',
Kanin archives.
p. 145   'Isobel felt ignored ...',
interview, Patrick.
p. 146   'Whatever Ray Stark ...',
interview, Kanin.
p. 147   'My own impression ...',
interview, Patrick.
p. 147   'A gardenia is like a free spirit
...', *Time*, 10 April 1964.
p. 147   'She is like a barracuda ...',
ibid.
p. 148   'He looked at her ...',
interview.
p. 148   'I felt like such a failure ...',
*Playboy*, November 1970.
p. 153   'I always knew I wanted to be
famous ...', *Look*, 5 April 1966.

...........................................

### 14

*This chapter owes a great deal to two
members of the Smith-Hemion production*
*team who chose to be anonymous and to*
*Rex Reed.*

p. 155   'Some stories make it sound
...', *New York Herald Tribune*, 6
September 1964.
p. 155   'I can always take down ...',
ibid.
p. 156   'I like listening to Streisand ...',
*New York Herald Tribune*, 1 March
1964.
p. 158   'Ya know, why me?', *Playboy*,
October 1977.
p. 162   'I did it for Ray ...', Streisand,
record notes, *Just for the Record*.
p. 162   'She was so vulnerable ...',
*Daily Mail*, November 1994.
p. 164   'OK, you have twenty minutes
...', *New York Herald Tribune*, 27 March
1966.
p. 165   'She's not dumb ...', ibid.
p. 165   'Hoarse?', ibid.
p. 165   'Somebody else could do this
...', ibid.

...........................................

### 15

*Material in this chapter was gathered from
the author's own involvement in the
adaptation of* Funny Girl *to the screen,
correspondence with Sidney Buchman,
interviews with Arthur Laurents and
members of the London company of*
Funny Girl *and archival material.*

p. 168   'My husband and I ...', *Daily
Telegraph*, 3 March 1966.
p. 168   'I hope you will approve ...',
*New York Times*, 2 February 1966.
p. 168   'Those girls didn't have a thing
...', ibid.
p. 169   'The only thing she has not
learned ...', *Look*, 15 October 1968.
p. 169   'The only way I can account
...', *Life*, 18 March 1966.
p. 169   'To say I love Barbra ...', Gloria
Steinem, *Look*, 5 April 1966.
p. 170   'I can't suddenly get poor ...',
ibid.

p. 170   'She loves from the point of view ...', *Daily Mail*, 9 September 1994.

p. 171   'I don't want your child ...', ibid.

p. 171   'The conversation all revolved around ...', interview, Laurents.

p. 172   'Well, she isn't my ...', *Hollywood Citizen News* (by Sheila Graham – syndicated), 9 April 1966.

p. 177   'I'm not sure it was because I was an actress ...', *New York Herald Tribune*, 7 October 1966.

p. 177   'My God, I'm a mother ...', *Ladies' Home Journal*, August 1966.

p. 178   'I remember two things ...', interview, Laurents.

...............................................

## 16

p. 183   'We were all very unsure ...', Madsen, *William Wyler*, p. 381.

p. 184   'the worst time of my life', Kanin archives.

p. 184   'They were getting ready ...', Sharif, *The Eternal Male*, p. 73.

p. 185   'At point I think ...', Madsen, *William Wyler*, p. 387.

p. 185   'My principal concern ...', ibid., p. 389.

p. 186   'I just don't expect obedience ...', ibid., p. 391.

p. 186   'going everywhere ...', ibid., p. 392.

p. 186   'eleven versions of every scene ...', *Los Angeles Times*, 17 September 1967.

p. 187   'I had good ideas ...', *Playboy*, October 1970.

p. 187   'a certain type of woman ...', Sharif, *The Eternal Male*, p. 77.

p. 188   'Did I love my wife?', ibid.

p. 188   'He made himself ...', interview.

p. 188   'what really got me down ...', *Playboy*, October 1970.

p. 189   'I make women happy ...', Sharif, *The Eternal Male*, p. 78.

p. 189   'If it was Barbra's plan ...', interview.

p. 189   'the self-confidence ...', Sharif, *The Eternal Male*, p. 56.

p. 190   'Every day Barbra would see ...', interview, Anne Francis.

p. 191   'I feel like a boxer ...', *Los Angeles Times*, 17 September 1967.

p. 191   'People were saying ...', interview.

...............................................

## 17

p. 192   'Why in hell ...', *Chicago Tribune Magazine*, 27 August 1967.

p. 192   'Barbra's always been a cheapskate ...', ibid.

p. 193   'It's true I lusted ...', *Los Angeles Times*, 27 October 1968.

p. 193   'I know Elliott thinks it's just ...', ibid.

p. 194   'I don't believe ...', *Playboy*, November 1970.

p. 195   'like a diva soprano ...', *Vogue*, June 1970.

p. 197   'I talked to Elizabeth ...', Hirschorn, *Gene Kelly*, p. 291.

p. 197   'strangely moved ...', *Hello, Dolly!* Archives, Motion Picture Academy of Arts and Sciences.

p. 198   'Like Barbra ...', ibid.

p. 198   'I'd heard ...', Hirschorn, *Gene Kelly*, p. 293.

p. 199   'If only there'd been ...', ibid.

p. 199   'What I needed ...', interview.

p. 200   'painful to adjust ...', Hirschorn, *Gene Kelly*, p. 294.

p. 200   'The trouble with Barbra ...', ibid.

p. 201   'As if contending ...', ibid.

p. 202   'It was not, in retrospect ...', ibid., p. 296.

p. 203   'Betty Hutton once said ...', ibid., p. 295.

...............................................

## 18

*I am much indebted to the archival material at both AMPAS and BFI for all the chapters in this book dealing with the making of a film. Special interviews for this chapter included friends and co-workers of Alan Jay Lerner.*

**p. 206** 'I always wanted to meet ...', *Playboy*, October 1977.

**p. 207** 'a particular desperation ...', *Newsweek*, 5 January 1970.

**p. 207** 'The audience cannot be lied to ...', ibid.

**p. 208** 'Barbra also stands to make ...', *New York Times*, 9 October 1968.

**p. 209** 'a little guy ...', interview.

**p. 210** 'When Alan came to me ...', Citron, *The Wordsmiths*, p. 221.

**p. 210** 'if he was really working hard ...', ibid.

**p. 210** 'We spent a whole day going over ...', Jordan, *The Greatest Star*, p. 181.

**p. 211** 'Sparks flew', interview.

**p. 213** 'It was inspired ...', Vickers, *Cecil Beaton*, p. 529.

**p. 213** 'The most uncongenial atmosphere ...', ibid., p. 533.

**p. 214** 'Barbra is one of two kinds of superstars ...', ibid.

**p. 214** 'I like B.S. ...', ibid., p. 534.

## 19

**p. 217** 'Well, Ma ...', *New York Times*, 23 February 1970.

**p. 217** 'Barbra loves Rozie ...', ibid.

**p. 217** 'Yeah, my voice ...', ibid.

**p. 218** 'There is so much more to learn ...', ibid.

**p. 221** 'He pointed mutely ...', Albert Goldman, *Elvis Presley*, McGraw Hill, New York 1981, p. 436.

**p. 222** 'I always knew ...', *New York Time*, 13 October 1969.

**p. 222** 'something of a paradox ...', *New York Times*, 5 October 1969.

**p. 222** 'We have a very deep personal ...', ibid.

**p. 225** 'heavy Victorian ornaments ...', Trudeau, *Beyond Reason*, p. 47.

**p. 225** 'black sheep ...', ibid.

**p. 225** 'Charm is the power ...', James Lord, *Picasso and Dora*, p. 45.

**p. 225** 'a sort of old-fashioned gallantry', Trudeau, *Beyond Reason*, p. 42.

**p. 226** 'He flew Barbra ...', ibid.

**p. 227** 'Barbra wanted us to get back ...', *Daily Mail*, November 1994.

**p. 227** 'After she *schlepped* ...', interview, Dennen.

## 20

*I am especially indebted in this chapter for the help of Ed Holly and Blossom Kahn (both formerly executives of First Artists), Madeline Gilford, producer of* Broadway for Bella, *Michael Edwards, a key figure in the opposing camp of two of Bella Abzug's later campaigns for the Senate, author and screenwriter, Herman Raucher, and the access Warner Brothers Studios gave me to their archives.*

**p. 230** 'a cool suspicion', interview, Kahn.

**p. 231** 'I would think ...', *Playgirl*, February 1984.

**p. 231** 'Schopenhauer's theory ...', *New Yorker*, 14 November 1970.

**p. 232** 'put in thick white ...', Riese, Randall – *Her Name is Barbra*, p. 310.

**p. 232** 'She only calls me Herbie ...', ibid.

**p. 234** 'They shared a kind of mirror image ...', private interview, Lee.

**p. 234** 'I would much rather ...', *New York Times*, 5 June 1970.

**p. 235** 'everything in stainless steel ...', ibid.

p. 235  'Hey! Now I can see ...', ibid.

p. 237  'I remember the various ...', *Playboy*, October 1977.

p. 237  'I didn't know how dangerous ...', ibid.

p. 237  'wearing his *M*A*S*H* ...', ibid.

p. 238  'skirting insanity ...', ibid.

p. 238  'She made chicken soup ...', interview, Raucher.

p. 239  'It seemed as tough ...', interview, Lee.

p. 239  'The place was jammed ...', ibid.

p. 240  'Barbra Streisand; delicate snarl ...', *New Yorker*, 14 November 1970.

............................................

**21**

p. 243  'Actually, I believe women ...', *Playboy*, October 1977.

p. 243  'Look, this was my first real home ...', *Architectural Digest*, May 1978.

p. 243  'my burgundy era ...', ibid.

p. 245  'Richard was always trying ...', Streisand, record notes, *Just for the Record*.

p. 246  'I can't throw away ...', *Ladies' Home Journal*, August 1966.

p. 246  'the things you read in the papers ...', *New York Post*, 23 May 1976.

p. 246  'never knew what was ...', ibid.

p. 247  'used to live inside films ...', Wakeman (ed.), *World Film Directors*, vol. II, p. 133.

p. 247  'stealing from everything ...', ibid., p. 134.

p. 250  'he made your skull ...', Brownstein, *The Power and the Glitter*, p. 241.

p. 250  'If I would have known ...', concert, Los Angeles, 15 April 1972.

p. 250  'Ya know – to conquer ...', ibid.

p. 252  'I'm very fragile emotionally ...', *Mike Wallace – Sixty Minutes*.

p. 253  'Barbra was baffled ...', Jordan, *The Greatest Star*, p. 218.

............................................

**22**

*Interviews for this chapter were conducted with Arthur Laurents, Marcia Mae Jones and Mitzie and Ken Welch among others.*

p. 254  'Ray was looking ...', interview, Laurents.

p. 256  'They were insecure ...', ibid.

p. 256  'The person who was terrific ...', ibid.

p. 257  'He didn't like the script ...', *Première*, July 1980, p. 11.

p. 258  'I think with any small encouragement ...', interview.

p. 258  'She was in awe of Redford ...', Jordan, *The Greatest Star*, p. 221.

p. 259  'I didn't even have ...', *Première*, July 1980, p. 11.

p. 259  'It was all wrong ...', interview, Laurents.

p. 260  'It was curious ...', interview, Jones.

p. 260  'Working with Barbra ...', Riese, Randall – *Her Name is Barbra*, p. 339.

p. 260  'It flows like velvet ...', *Daily News*, 19 October 1973.

p. 260  'a torpedoed ship ...', *New Yorker*, 15 October 1973.

p. 261  'If I'd left it in the minor mode ...', Gilbert and Theroux, *The Top Ten*, p. 229.

p. 262  'Like a Chinese menu', interview, Mitzie Welch.

p. 262  'an antiques dealer ...', ibid.

p. 262  'We hired all kinds ...', interview, Ken Welch.

p. 264  'Julie Andrews, Blake Edwards ...', interview, Mitzie Welch.

p. 264  'That haircut ...', ibid.

............................................

## 23

**p. 265** 'You know you're a cute little thing ...', *Woman*, 5 November 1978.

**p. 267** 'Jon is smart ...', interview.

**p. 267** 'He comes out of the Hugh Hefner ...', ibid.

**p. 267** 'We're both equally crazy ...', ibid.

**p. 269** 'Jon is a very macho man ...', interview.

**p. 270** 'It had aluminum sliding doors ...', *In Style*, April 1994.

**p. 270** 'The kids' rooms ...', ibid.

**p. 271** 'He'll have to drag me to court ...', Jordan, *The Greatest Star*, p. 234.

**p. 271** 'They think I'm too small ...', *Playboy*, October 1977.

**p. 272** 'I feel them listening so hard ...', ibid.

**p. 272** 'Blame it on Vietnam ...', 'Women in Film Art', *New York Times*, 16 April 1991.

**p. 273** 'I'd yell at her ...', Swenson, *Barbra*, p. 136.

**p. 273** 'Her commitment was not 100 per cent ...', University of Southern California Film Archives.

**p. 274** 'Do they think I'd let Jon produce a record ...', ibid.

...............................................

## 24

This chapter has been greatly helped by material in the Archives of the Performing Arts at the University of Southern California, Special Collections, and the archives at Warner Brothers, the Academy of Motion Picture Arts and Sciences, the British Film Institute and the special film archives at the University of Wisconsin, Madison, Wisconsin. In addition, the author conducted numerous interviews including those with Anthony Newley, Arthur Laurents, and Ed Holly and Blossom Kahn of First Artists.

**p. 277** 'a kid with dirty underwear ...', *Woman*, 5 November 1978.

**p. 278** 'a savage look at the rock world', Marie Brenner, *New Times*, 24 January 1976.

**p. 279** 'I discovered this project ...', ibid.

**p. 279** 'Anyone who wonders ...', ibid.

**p. 279** 'Can you sing ...', interview.

**p. 280** 'We're going to make this ...', *News Times*, 24 January 1976.

**p. 280** 'What Jon Peters appreciates ...', ibid.

**p. 281** 'That became sort of the attitude ...', interview, Holly.

**p. 281** 'Jon came on the board ...', ibid.

**p. 282** 'The son of a bitch ...', Pierson, *New West*, 22 November 1976.

**p. 282** 'How could I direct ...', ibid.

**p. 283** 'I hate him if he kills ...', ibid.

**p. 283** 'People are curious ...', ibid.

**p. 284** 'in such profusion ...', ibid.

**p. 284** 'like Nixon ...', *People*, 26 April 1976.

**p. 285** 'a very strong ...', interview, Holly.

**p. 285** 'He was just like a feisty sponge ...', ibid.

**p. 286** 'I know I'm not an easy ...', ibid.

**p. 286** 'I don't feel you want to love me ...', *New West*, 22 November 1976.

**p. 287** 'Pow! I let him have it!', ibid.

**p. 288** 'Jesus, Barbra ...', *Village Voice*, 26 April 1976.

**p. 288** 'What the hell ...', ibid.

**p. 289** 'Look at her directing ...', ibid.

**p. 289** 'Perhaps ... I hope so ...', *People*, 26 April 1976.

...............................................

## 25

The material in this chapter was gathered from the same sources as the previous *chapter, with the addition of interviews conducted with Ed Holly, Blossom Kahn, Arthur Laurents, Michael Meltzer, Bob Shanks, Ann Shanks and others.*

p. 290   'You lay it out and it's shit ...', *New West*, 22 November 1976.

p. 290   'You don't listen ...', ibid.

p. 291   'Primarily ...', Riese, Randall – *Her Name is Barbra*, p. 380.

p. 291   'No movie editor ...', Sidney Lumet, *Making Movies*, Knopf, New York, 1995, p. 181.

p. 292   'Barbra had chosen ...', interview, Ann Shanks.

p. 292   'I just saw the end credits ...', ibid.

p. 293   'All night ...', Pierson, *New West*, 22 November 1976.

p. 294   'You have to understand ...', Swenson, *Barbra*, p. 186.

p. 294   '*A Star Is Born* was the beginning ...', *Los Angeles Times*, 2 January 1977.

p. 295   'Peters taught her ...', interview, Laurents.

p. 296   'I hate that lamp!', *In Style*, June 1994.

p. 297   'Michael, one day soon ...', interview, Meltzer.

p. 298   'I quit ...', ibid.

p. 299   'There was a script ...', interview, Blossom Kahn.

p. 300   'Ryan used to jog in the nude ...', Taraborrelli, *Call Her Miss Ross*, p. 349.

p. 300   'Why am I not working ...', Swenson, *Barbra*, p. 191.

p. 301   'I just can't sit ...', interview, Meltzer.

p. 301   'When he went off ...', Swenson, *Barbra*, p. 193.

p. 301   'Am I cool ...', *Los Angeles Times*, 2 January 1977.

p. 302   '*The Main Event* was my fault ...', Swenson, *Barbra*, p. 192.

p. 302   'An Australian firm ...', interview, Ed Holly.

p. 304   'It was a time in my life ...', *Playgirl*, February 1984.

p. 304   'You're not going to do it!', ibid.

**26**

p. 309   'I constantly had to give up everything ...', *Playgirl*, February 1984.

p. 310   'I've lived so many years feeling guilty ...', ibid.

p. 310   'The day before we were going to start shooting ...', ibid.

p. 311   'You never got a chance ...', Swenson, *Barbra*, p. 250.

p. 311   'To get the feel of the music ...', ibid., p. 245.

p. 311   'I kept remembering ...', *Los Angeles Times*, 1 November 1983.

p. 312   'She'd fix my hair ribbons ...', Swenson, *Barbra*, p. 248.

p. 313   'I had to make all the decisions ...', *Playgirl*, February 1984.

p. 314   'She treated him like any good friend ...', interview.

p. 314   'I had only nine days ...', *Los Angeles Times*, 1 November 1983.

p. 315   'It was all about money ...', ibid.

p. 315   '*Yentl* was Barbra's way ...', Swenson, *Barbra*, p. 251.

p. 315   'I ran out and bought ...', *Playgirl*, February 1984.

p. 316   'She denies her unhappiness ...', *Daily Mail*, 17 September 1994.

**27**

*This chapter was especially enhanced by interviews with Stephen Citron, Peter Matz and numerous other fine musicians and musicologists.*

p. 318   'All the men in my life ...', *Wall Street Journal*, 14 May 1993.

**p. 319** 'Broadway music . . .', Stephen Holden, *New York Times*, 10 November 1985.

**p. 319** 'Barbra's contract . . .', Swenson, *Barbra*, p. 273.

**p. 319** 'marathon listening . . .', Zadan, *Sondheim & Co.*, p. 289.

**p. 320** 'It's like growing . . .', ibid.

**p. 320** 'I told him . . .', ibid.

**p. 320** 'She wanted to make . . .', ibid.

**p. 320** 'I would talk . . .', ibid.

**p. 320** 'He believes as I do . . .', ibid.

**p. 321** 'Everyone in the studio . . .', cover notes, *The Broadway Album*.

**p. 322** 'I felt great warmth . . .', interview, Kramer.

**p. 323** 'It was April 26, 1986 . . .', *Wall Street Journal*, 14 May 1993.

**p. 324** 'She started with very little knowledge . . .', ibid.

**p. 324** 'After all my insistence . . .', Streisand, record notes, *Just for the Record*.

**p. 325** 'You're nice . . .', 'One Voice' transcript.

**p. 327** 'If I want to meet people . . .', *Cosmopolitan*, September 1995.

**p. 328** 'I have done everything . . .', ibid.

**p. 328** 'I'm happy . . .', ibid.

. . . . . . . . . . . . . . . . . . . . . . . . . . . . . . . . . . . . . . . .

**28**

*The laser disk,* The Making of The Prince of Tides, *was invaluable in the work on this chapter. I was also fortunate to have the co-operation of several of the staff and technicians on the film.*

**p. 330** 'Yes [Jason] is gay . . .', Corinna Honan, *Daily Mail*, London, 17 September 1994.

**p. 330** 'I think Jason's being gay . . .', ibid.

**p. 331** 'Jason has never asked me . . .', Joe Morgenstern, *Cosmopolitan*, October 1991.

**p. 331** 'Barbra showed me this kid . . .', Robert Epstein, *Los Angeles Times*, 26 December 1991.

**p. 331** 'I think she read . . .', Hilary de Vries, *Los Angeles Times Sunday Magazine*, 8 December 1991.

**p. 332** 'A lot of this movie is meaningful . . .', ibid.

**p. 332** 'It changed my whole perspective . . .', Stephen Holden, *New York Times*, 22 December 1991.

**p. 334** 'Barbra likes to explore . . .', ibid.

**p. 334** 'I don't find it that easy . . .', laser disk, *The Making of* The Prince of Tides.

**p. 335** 'The least painful part . . .', *Daily Mail*, July 1995.

**p. 336** 'I couldn't stop laughing . . .', laser disk, *The Making of* The Prince of Tides.

**p. 337** 'I've been thinking about how . . .', Stephen Holden, *New York Times*, 22 December 1991.

**p. 337** 'It's Barbra's talent for . . .', ibid.

**p. 337** 'When I direct . . .', ibid.

**p. 339** 'She uses her vulnerability . . .', *Daily Mail*, 17 September 1994.

**p. 340** 'She throws a lot of stories . . .', *Los Angeles Times Magazine*, 8 December 1991.

**p. 341** 'Poor baby is miserable . . .', *Daily Mail*, 17 September 1994.

. . . . . . . . . . . . . . . . . . . . . . . . . . . . . . . . . . . . . . . .

**29**

**p. 342** 'He's very intelligent . . .', *New York Times*, 4 October 1992.

**p. 345** 'Perfection is . . .', *Playboy*, October 1977.

**p. 347** 'I had known . . .', interview, Kramer.

**p. 347** 'She said if you want to . . .', ibid.

**p. 348** 'There is something about her . . .', ibid.

p. 349  'I think, strangely ...', ibid.

p. 349  'One night when I was putting Caleigh ...', concert programme, London, April 1994.

..................................................

## 30

*This chapter owes a great debt to the perceptive interviews given to me by Larry Kramer, Don Black and various others.*

p. 352  'How come nobody attacked the Republican ...', *Los Angeles Times*, 23 May 1993.

p. 353  'incapable of serious involvement ...', ibid.

p. 353  'When I directed a movie ...', ibid.

p. 354  'We have the right ...', ibid.

p. 354  'wearing a long black-hooded ...', *Washington Post*, 20 January 1993.

p. 355  'granted 5 minutes ...', ibid.

p. 355  'The most moving moments ...', ibid.

p. 356  'It was the highlight ...', interview, Black.

p. 358  'She wanted various musical phrases ...', ibid.

p. 359  'great misery ... every night I was terrified', *Los Angeles Times*, 23 May 1993.

p. 359  'Donna Karan gave me ...', ibid.

p. 359  'I had returned to London ...', interview, Black.

p. 360  'the show was to be ...', *Los Angeles Times*, 23 May 1993.

p. 361  'I didn't need the job ...', *Los Angeles Times*, 21 August 1994.

p. 362  'Barbra would tell me ...', ibid.

..................................................

## 31

*This chapter owes a great deal to several backstage people involved in The Concert,*

*who asked for their names not to be included in my acknowledgments.*

p. 369  'I like the idea ...', Christie's catalogue, Streisand auction.

p. 370  'Sometimes when it's been hard ...', ibid.

p. 370  'I don't put a black vase ...', *Architectural Digest*, December 1993.

p. 372  'You have got to get this right ...', *Daily Mail*, 20 April 1994.

p. 373  'to have a positive attitude ...', ibid.

..................................................

## 32

p. 375  'What did you *really* think?', interview, Black.

p. 375  'I was told by my boss ...', *Daily Mail*, 22 April 1994.

p. 377  'In Detroit ...', *Vanity Fair*, November 1994.

p. 378  'There's no denying her talent ...', Rex Reed, *New York Observer*, 4–11 July 1994.

p. 379  'Let me say this ...', Barbara Walters interview for ABC, 13 December 1994.

p. 380  'She's God's bell ...', *New York Magazine*, 15 April 1994.

p. 381  'You did good ...', *Vanity Fair*, November 1994.

p. 381  'You have to put make-up on ...', ibid.

p. 381  'Barbra had a passion ...', *Wall Street Journal*, 3 February 1995.

p. 382  'What the network ordered ...', ibid.

..................................................

## 33

*This chapter was especially helped by interviews with Larry Kramer, Richard LaGravenese and members of the staff and crew of The Mirror Has Two Faces, as well as Amy Rosefeld and other political science students who attended Streisand's appearance at Harvard.*

p. 383 'I'm a shy person ...', *Vanity Fair*, November 1994.

p. 384 'Why are you doing ...', interview, Kramer.

p. 385 'In Hollywood ...', *Wall Street Journal*, 3 February 1995.

p. 385 'Why is it ...', ibid.

p. 388 'What is the sin ...', archives, Harvard.

p. 389 'Everyone was optimistic ...', interview.

p. 390 'It was hard to tell ...', ibid.

p. 390 'There were too many gauzes ...', ibid.

p. 391 'The whole team ...', ibid.

p. 392 'This woman has had ...', interview, Kramer.

p. 392 'Barbra was deeply hurt ...', interview.

p. 393 'This is my first major film ...', ibid.

# Bibliography

Beaton, Cecil, *Cecil Beaton's Diaries, 1963–1974*, Weidenfeld & Nicolson, London 1978

Bordman, Gerald, *American Musical Revue*, Oxford University Press, New York, 1985.

——, *American Musical Theatre*, Oxford University Press, New York, 1978.

Brady, Frank, *Barbra: An Illustrated Biography*, Grosset & Dunlap, New York, 1979.

Brownstein, Ronald, *The Power and the Glitter*, Pantheon Books, New York, 1990.

Carrick, Patrick, *Barbra Streisand: A Biography*, Robert Hale, London, 1991.

Citron, Stephen, *The Wordsmiths: Oscar Hammerstein and Alan Jay Lerner*, Sinclair-Stevenson, London, 1996.

Conroy, Pat, *The Prince of Tides*, Houghton Mifflin, Boston, 1986.

Considine, Shaun, *Barbra Streisand: The Woman, The Myth, The Music*, Delacorte Press, New York, 1985.

Dunne, John Gregory, *The Studio*, Farrar, Straus, Giroux, New York, 1969.

Edwards, Anne, *Judy Garland: A Biography*, Simon & Schuster, New York, 1975.

Engel, Lehman, *This Bright Day*, Macmillan, New York, 1974.

Friedrich, Otto, *City of Nets*, Harper & Row, New York, 1987.

Frommer, Myrna and Katz, Harvey, *It Happened in Brooklyn*, Harcourt Brace, 1986.

Gavin, James, *Intimate Nights*, Limelight Editions, New York, 1992.

Gilbert, Bob and Theroux, Gary, *The Top Ten – 1956–1981*, Simon & Schuster, New York, 1982.

Harvey, Stephen, *Directed by Vincente Minnelli*, Harper & Row, New York, 1989.

Hirschorn, Clive, *Gene Kelly*, W.H.Allen, London, 1974.

Jordan, René, *The Greatest Star*, Putnam, New York, 1975.

Kael, Pauline, *For Keeps: 30 Years at the Movies*, Dutton, New York, 1994.

Kimbrell, James, *Barbra – An Actress Who Sings*, Branden Publishing Company, Boston, 1989.

——, *Barbra – An Actress Who Sings, vol. II*, Branden Publishing Company, Boston, 1992.

Knepp, Donn, *Las Vegas*, Lane Pb Co, Menlo Park, California, 1987.

Laufe, Abe, *Broadway's Greatest Musicals*, Funk & Wagnalls, New York, 1977.

Laurents, Arthur, *The Way We Were*, Harper & Row, New York, 1972.

Lennart, Isobel, *Funny Girl, Lyrics by Bob Merrill, Music by Jule Styne, A Random House Play*, Random House, New York, 1964.

Lerner, Alan Jay, *The Musical Theatre – A Celebration*, Collins, London, 1986.

——, *The Street Where I Live*, Hodder & Stoughton, London, 1978.

Liberace, *Liberace: An Autobiography*, Putnam, New York, 1973.

Lord, James, *Picasso and Dora*, Farrar, Straus, Giroux, New York, 1993.

McClintick, David, *Indecent Exposure*, Wm Morrow, New York, 1982.

McCullough, David, *Brooklyn ... and How It Got That Way*, The Dial Press, New York, 1983.

Madsen, Axel, *William Wyler*, Thomas J. Crowell Company, New York, 1973.

Miller, Allan, *A Passion for Acting*, Backstage Books, New York, 1992.

Minnelli, Vincente, *I Remember It Well*, Doubleday, New York, 1975.

Monti, Ralph, *I Remember Brooklyn*, Birch Lane Press, New York, 1991.

Morris, Jan, *Manhattan '45*, Oxford University Press, New York, 1987.

Riese, Randall, *Her Name is Barbra*, Birch Lane Press, New York, 1993.

Rivers, Joan, *Enter Talking*, Delacorte, New York, 1986.

Sharif, Omar, with Marie-Thérèse Guinchard, *The Eternal Male*, Doubleday, New York, 1976.

Spada, James, *The First Decade – The Films and Career of Barbra Streisand*, A Citadel Press Book, Carol Publishing Group, New York, 1974.

——, *The Woman and the Legend*, Doubleday, New York, 1981.

Suskin, Steven, *Opening Night on Broadway*, Schirmer Books, New York.

Swenson, Karen, *Barbra: The Second Decade*, A Citadel Press Book, Carol Publishing Group, New York, 1986.

Taraborrelli, J. Randy, *Call Her Miss Ross*, Birch Lane Press, New York, 1989.

Taylor, Theodore, *Jule: The Story of Composer Jule Styne*, Wm Morrow, New York, 1979.

Teti, Frank, and Moline, Karen: *Streisand Through the Lens*, Delilah Press, New York, 1983.

Tormé Mel, *Judy Garland: The Other Side of the Rainbow*, Wm Morrow, New York, 1970.

Trudeau, Margaret, *Beyond Reason*, Paddington Press, London and New York, 1979.

Uslan, Michael and Solomon, Bruce, *Dick Clark's the First 25 Years of Rock & Roll*, Crown Publishers, New York, 1981.

..............................................

## Magazines and Periodicals

*Architectural Digest*, May 1978, December 1993

*Ladies Home Journal*, August 1966, August 1969

*Life*, 22 May 1964, 6 November 1964, 18 March 1966, 9 January 1970, December 1985

*Look*, 18 March, 1966

5 April 1966, 15 October 1968

*Time*, 10 April 1964, 19 August 1966, 7 September 1970

*Vogue*, June 1970

*Playboy*, November 1970, October 1977

*Vanity Fair*, November 1994

*Première*, July 1980

*Showmusic*, Spring 1995

*In Style*, June 1994

*Vanity Fair*, November 1994

*Cosmopolitan*, April 1969

*McCall's*, April 1975

*New Times*, 24 January 1975

*New West*, 15 November 1976

*New York*, 15 November 1976

*TV Guide*, 1 October 1994

*Saturday Evening Post*, 27 July 1963

*Redbook*, July 1965

*Hollywood Reporter*, *Variety* (daily and weekly) over 100 entries

..............................................

## Archives

William Wyler Collection, UCLA
Special Collections Film, USC
Special Collections Film, University of
    Wisconsin
Screen Actors' Guild of America

Directors' Guild of America
Academy of Motion Picture Arts and
    Sciences
British Film Institute
Warner Bros Studio Archives
Museum of Broadcasting
Brooklyn Historical Society

# Index